EARL DAVID OF HUNTINGDON

1152–1219

for Christine

EARL DAVID OF HUNTINGDON

1152–1219

A Study in Anglo-Scottish History

K. J. STRINGER

Edinburgh University Press
1985

© K. J. Stringer 1985
Edinburgh University Press
22 George Square, Edinburgh

Set in Linoterm Plantin by
Speedspools, Edinburgh, and
printed in Great Britain by
Redwood Burn Ltd, Trowbridge

British Library Cataloguing
   in Publication Data
Stringer, Keith John
Earl David of Huntingdon 1152–1219
1. David, *Earl of Huntingdon*
I. Title
942.03'4   DA209.D3
ISBN 0 85224 486 X

CONTENTS

PREFACE

This book could not have been written without the support of the Master and Fellows of Corpus Christi College, Cambridge, who by electing me successively Bridges Research Scholar and a Research Fellow of the College provided the opportunities to venture upon advanced study. Much of the preparatory work on this and other projects was completed during my tenure of these positions. I am also deeply obliged to the College for the warm and generous hospitality with which it has welcomed me back on research visits to Cambridge after my move to Lancaster. *Floreat antiqua domus!*

This study endeavours to bring closer together the historians of England and Scotland in the central Middle Ages. It is therefore fitting that I should also be able to express my sincerest thanks to three scholars and friends who have, in their different ways, contributed greatly to breaking down the barriers created by the traditions of national historiography. The late Professor John Le Patourel encouraged my investigations into the Anglo-Scottish nobility, and they have benefited considerably from the framework provided by his own penetrating insights into the history of the Anglo-Norman baronage. It is naturally a cause of regret to me that he did not live to see the book published. To Professor C. R. Cheney, who solicitously guided my first researches at Cambridge, I am heavily indebted for much constructive criticism and the kindly concern he has continued to show for all my work. I am also especially grateful for the help I have received in manifold ways from Professor G. W. S. Barrow, who has been a constant source of assistance and inspiration since my undergraduate days at Newcastle upon Tyne. It was he who originally suggested that Earl David was a subject worthy of study; he maintained a lively interest in the progress of my researches; and he played a crucial part in the negotiations for the publication of the longer than average book that results. Moreover, a great deal of what I have learned about Scottish history has stemmed from discussions with him and from his own writings and example. Although he will not agree with all the interpretations it contains, in important aspects this book is as much his as mine. Special words of thanks are also due to Dr G. G. Simpson, who with tireless patience introduced me to the medieval archives of the Scottish Record Office, where he was formerly an Assistant Keeper, and whose thesis on Earl Roger de Quincy represents an indispensable point of departure for all students of the Anglo-Scottish baronage. Two friends and colleagues at Lancaster, Dr P. D. King and Dr A. Grant, gave

vii

up valuable time to read and comment on every chapter in typescript. To Dr King, who saw the work in a less finished state, I owe a large debt of gratitude. While I must take sole responsibility for the defects that remain, his perceptiveness has saved me from some dubious arguments and many stylistic infelicities.

It is pleasing to record my experience of unstinted assistance and co-operation from the owners and custodians of muniments. I am indebted to the following private owners for leave to print in the Appendix those of Earl David's charters drawn from their records, some of which are now in public custody: the Earl of Dalhousie, Captain R. Fergusson-Cuninghame of Caprington, the Earl of Rothes, and the trustees of the Earl of Winchilsea. Other *acta* of Earl David appear with the approval of the Dean and Chapter of Lincoln, the Keeper of the Records of Scotland (Scottish Record Office), the Keeper of Western Manuscripts in the Bodleian Library, Oxford, and the authorities of the British Library, the National Library of Scotland and the Public Record Office. The task of collecting the bulk of my unpublished source material has been facilitated by the skill and courtesy of the staffs of the libraries and record offices just mentioned. The late Marquess of Northampton readily gave access to his archives in the Estate Office at Castle Ashby. I acknowledge also the willing aid afforded by the officials of the Archives Départementales de l'Eure, the Essex Record Office, the Lincolnshire Archives Office (whose kindnesses included the loan of a microfilm of the cartulary of Crowland abbey, *penes* the Spalding Gentlemen's Society) and the Northamptonshire Record Office; by the archivists of Balliol College, Oxford, and Emmanuel College, Cambridge; and by the staffs of Cambridge University Library, the Library of the Society of Antiquaries of London and Newcastle University Library.

I gladly record the help and consideration I have received from the Secretary of Edinburgh University Press and his staff, and thank them not least for their whole-hearted willingness to take on this book at a time when it seemed that the constraints of modern publishing would force me to dispense with the texts of Earl David's charters.

In remembering these friends and other parties who have significantly eased my path, I hope I have thanked them adequately. But the greatest debt is to my family and especially to my wife, to whom this book is dedicated. No author could hope for more support, understanding and encouragement than she has given. Books also evoke memories of places: for Christine and me, of Cambridge, Newbury, Hexham and Abbotrule.

K.J.S.   *University of Lancaster, 1983*

AUTHOR'S NOTES

1. Places in Great Britain have been given their counties as existing prior to the Local Government reforms of 1973–5.

2. In a book that deals as much with Scotland as with England, it would seem no more than common courtesy to acknowledge such differences as now exist between the two countries in the rendering of technical terms. As a rule, I have therefore chosen to adopt in a Scottish context modern Scottish words (e.g. feu, infeftment, teind) and their English counterparts (fee, enfeoffment, tithe, etc.) in an English context.

3. Like many other scholars, I have been guided to narrative materials that I might otherwise have missed by A. O. Anderson's translated selections in *Scottish Annals from English Chroniclers 500 to 1286* (London, 1908), and *Early Sources of Scottish History 500 to 1286* (Edinburgh, 1922). I have also consulted to my great benefit *Calendar of Documents relating to Scotland preserved in H. M. Public Record Office, London*, ed. J. Bain (Edinburgh, 1881–8). In the notes to chapters, however, references to chronicles have invariably been given to the standard editions in Latin or Old French, some of which are conveniently extracted in *Annals of the Reigns of Malcolm and William, Kings of Scotland*, ed. A. C. Lawrie (Glasgow, 1910), and references to documents calendared by Bain have been made wherever possible to the printed full texts.

Comes Dauid frater Regis Scocie vniuersis sce matris ecclie filijs p[rese]ntib[us]
⁊ futur[is] [...] futur[...] me caritatis intuitu dedisse ⁊ concessisse ⁊ p[rese]nti
carta confirmasse Deo ⁊ ecclie sce Trinitatis Lond[on] ⁊ Canonicis in eadem
deo seruientib[us] p[ro] salute anime mee ⁊ anime M. vxoris mee ⁊ p[ro] salute a[n]i[m]aru[m] patris
⁊ matris mee ⁊ h[e]redu[m] meo[rum] duos solidat[os] ⁊ sex denarios redd[itus] q[uos] ip[s]i Canonici
m[ihi] reddere co[n]sueuer[un]t de s[e]p[t]em acris t[er]re ar[a]bilis ⁊ duab[us] g[ra]ng[i]etis ⁊ de dimidia acra p[ra]t[e] In villa de Totehã. Sc[ilicet] q[uicq]uid in hoc tenemento ⁊
eis p[er]tinencijs habui siue alia retinemento. Habebu[n]t eti[am] Canonici ujg[...]re
in p[ur]am ⁊ p[er]petuam elemosinam libera[m] ⁊ q[ui]etam ab om[n]i s[e]c[u]lari seruicio ⁊
exactione. Ita u[t] Canonici receperunt me ⁊ M. vxore meam ⁊ I. filiu[m] meu[m] ⁊ h[e]-
rede[m] ⁊ g[ra]ciam mea[m] in b[e]n[e]ficijs d[om]i s[u]e concedentes nos p[ar]ticipes fieri
omniu[m] bonor[um] que fient in ecclia sua tam p[ro] viuis q[uam] p[ro] defunctis in p[er]p[et]uu[m].
Et ut volui hanc donationem ratam ⁊ stabilem h[ab]eri in p[er]petuum. Eam p[re]-
senti carta ⁊ sigilli mei munimine corroboraui. Hijs testib[us] Will[elm]o Diac[ono] Bartholom[eo] capellano. Dauid de Ellebi. Gileb[erto] de Huera. Hug[one] de Harleton Rob[er]-
[er]to fil[io] Rob[erti]. Philipo gronago Will[elm]o de Toleuill. Hug[one] de R[...] R[...] fil[io] Will[elm]i senescall[i].
Henr[ico] de Huera. Gileb[erto] ⁊ Todeha. Galfr[ido] de Siluton Joh[ann]e de Lyelue R[...] ai[...]
Gileb[erto] de Eds[...] Nicol[ao] de Gualle. Hug[one] de Aurno Rob[er]to p[...] Turs ⁊ alijs multis.

ILLUSTRATIONS

PLATES

MAPS

TABLES

CAITHNESS

SUTHERLAND

ROSS

Nairn Forres Elgin   Banff
THE LAICH   BUCHAN
Inverness
                              GARIOCH
ARGYLL
OF   M O R A Y   M A R   Aberdeen
MORAY   BADENOCH
                                        The Mounth
ARGYLL   ATHOLL   MEARNS
OF
SCOTIA   Brechin Montrose
                                        Forfar
                        STRATHEARN   ANGUS Dundee
                              GOWRIE
                        Perth   St. Andrews
                MENTEITH   FIFE   Crail
                        Stirling
                              Dunfermline
                LENNOX
                        Edinburgh   Haddington
        STRATH- Glasgow
        GRYFE CLYDESDALE   L O T H I A N   Berwick
        CUNNING-   Lanark
        HAM   Peebles Melrose
KINTYRE KYLE   Selkirk Roxburgh
        Ayr   Jedburgh

MAR Earldoms and
      important districts
                                  LIDDES-
  •   Major royal castles   DALE
      and other centres   ANNANDALE ESK-
                              DALE
      Land above 800ft
CARRICK GALLOWAY Dumfries

        0   20   40   60   80 km
        0 10 20 30 40 50 miles

Map 1. Scotland *c.* 1200

1

THE SETTING

Earl David, the fifth earl of Huntingdon of the Scottish royal line, was the youngest son of Earl Henry of Northumberland and Countess Ada de Warenne: his grandfather, David I, and his elder brothers, Malcolm IV and William I, were successive kings of Scots from 1124 to 1214. His earliest appearance in surviving record is as a witness, at the age of six, to the great charter for Kelso abbey issued by King Malcolm at Roxburgh during the Easter court of 1159.[1] Roxburgh exhibited the conjunction of administrative, commercial and ecclesiastical elements by this date typical of the chief seats of the Scottish realm. Its castle did duty as a favoured royal residence, the headquarters of a sheriffdom, a state prison, and a major mint. The thriving burgh boasted a recent suburban extension, while Roxburgh's standing as an influential religious focus had been assured since 1128 when the Tironensian community at Selkirk, the first in Scotland, had been transferred to near-by Kelso under an abbot whose alternative style 'of Roxburgh' persisted into the 1150s.[2] As at Dunfermline, Edinburgh, Jedburgh, Perth and Stirling, it almost seems as if castle, burgh and neighbouring monastery had been begun in a single conscious enterprise to exalt royal authority and display the king's power. The witness-list of King Malcolm's charter 'reads like a *Who's Who* of contemporary Scotland, at least of the country south of the Forth'.[3] The ecclesiastical dignitaries included four heads of houses representing the new continental religious orders that were setting the pace of reform in the twelfth-century Scottish Church; the lay following on this especially solemn occasion by no means comprised Norman-Frenchmen alone, but the leaders of this new incoming élite were to the fore.

The scene confronting young David at Roxburgh in 1159 reflects the momentous advances of his grandfather's reign (1124–53), when the traditions of Scots kingship had been brought firmly within the mainstream of European development. Undeniably, the vitality of King David's realm in its institutions of government derived not just from reforms on the Anglo-Norman pattern but also from the ancient Celtic aspects of royal power. In the final resort, however, rulers relied much more upon personal loyalties than administrative technique to enforce their will. Every king who wished to assert his position had thus to attach to himself a strong body of followers through whom he could express and extend his supremacy. Later Norman England appeared to support 'as many lords as it has neighbours',[4] and King Stephen's *dominium* was contested and ineffectual. By contrast the kingdom of Scots seemed like a promised land. David I rapidly established his reputation as a generous patron; he expanded his patrimony through confident leadership in gainful undertakings and brought additional reserves within reach of his adherents. Royal lordship and the king's clientage grew in strength together. Native sources of loyalty formed an essential foundation on which to build. In particular, a lesser ministerial class had already proved its worth to the monarchy and had compensated in some measure for the earlier lack of co-operation between great lords and the crown.[5] But King David's eminence rested above all else upon harnessing to the royal interest the ambitions of the knights and churchmen from England and northern France who were brought into the warmth of his favour. Norman-Frenchmen were the chief agents of the king's will, predominating at court and in the holding of office; they monopolised royal patronage. David I created within the realm a new French-speaking secular vassalage and a virtually new Church whose respective concerns were very closely identified with his own.

The strengthening of the Scots monarchy meant greater freedom from the English crown and fresh assurance in pursuing objectives through war. The superiority of the Norman king-dukes had been conceded in principle by King David's immediate predecessors.[6] Even though Scottish kingship was not exposed to the same risks of disappearance as the tribal kingships of the Welsh, precedents had been set which might be transformed into something more definite and real; and Henry Beauclerk had deliberately intensified his suzerainty, most notably by singling out for preferential treatment the future David I, when still a young Scottish prince, and drawing him into his direct vassalage. For a time resident at King Henry's court and trained there as a knight, in 1107 or thereabouts David had secured with Norman help the appanage he had claimed in southern Scotland as heir presumptive to Alexander I;[7] by 1113 he had been endowed with the earldom and honour of Huntingdon as the husband of Maud de Senlis, thus beginning the association between the Scottish royal house and this great midland fief that was to endure almost continuously until the late thirteenth century. He had served as a royal justice, travelled in France, and acquired rights of lordship in *Basse-Normandie*: 'loaded with gifts David sat at the king's side among the greatest magnates'.[8] It may be that Henry I's activity on all fronts was 'not a continuation of eleventh-century Norman imperialism but a rejection of it'.[9] Yet policies of consolidation were not necessarily compatible with the rights and dignity of the Scots crown. In establishing prince David as one of his most celebrated 'creations' Henry was preparing, potentially at any rate, for a more detailed involvement in Scottish affairs than his own preoccupations elsewhere would for the most part allow.

But David I, though bound to the Anglo-Frankish world by upbringing, marriage and tenurial ties, proved to be no cat's-paw of Norman policy. From 1124 he gloried in the honour of his kingly office, stressing his sovereign rights on the Norman or Capetian model. He refused to share his authority with any lay superior and was concerned to avoid humbling himself, once enthroned, by giving homage even for his English lands alone.[10] It was his responsibility to govern; and in opening his kingdom to foreign influences he ensured that this policy would as far as possible subserve his own designs. Anglo-continental colonisation in King David's realm thus has peculiar interest and importance. In England and Wales the allocation of lands and other privileges to immigrant Norman-Frenchmen had enabled the king-dukes to achieve mastery where their control had formerly been spasmodic or non-existent, overturning native ruling dynasties or reducing them to humiliating submission. In Scotland, King David reigned and ruled.

Although vast wealth continued to be controlled by old-established families often only nominally subject to the king, lay incomers, in the main *Bas-Normands*, were fashioned into a nobility of service within the framework provided by feudal practices. Occasionally initiative doubtless came from below; but evidence shows that King David methodically drew on his contacts with the Norman world to recruit men by personal invitation, some before he became king.[11] There was an orderly distribution of land, with reassurances for loyal native lords; and whatever the circumstances in which these newcomers seized their opportunities, their material standing rested very largely upon King David's sole decision. While some were the kinsfolk of important Anglo-Norman magnates, it is true of nearly all of them that they were by origin small under-tenants or even landless knights, precisely the sort of men most likely to appreciate advancement and be steadfast in his service. Scottish historians have been slow to recognise that this following was therefore as much a *parvenu* vassalage as that raised up alongside lords of acknowledged status by the chief potential competitor for its devotion, King Henry I, and the element of political calculation was surely as pronounced. Robert de Brus of Cleveland, alone of David I's powerful friends in England, was endowed by him in Scotland; and he could not retain his loyalty.[12] The spectacular gains went to a small cohort of highly regarded adherents. Few may have been migrants in the strict sense, pulling up their roots and liquidating whatever assets they might possess in their homelands. Nevertheless, with one noteworthy exception, these newcomers were firmly attached to King David personally, and for the time being the problems of dual allegiance were largely circumvented. Because he and not the Norman kings had made them, they were in spirit, as on parchment, his *probi homines*.

That the creation of a new nobility and the bringing of the Scottish Church into conformity with the standards of Latin Christendom were merged as a single political achievement also lacks due recognition. There is no doubt of the genuine piety sustaining David I's patronage of religion, or of the continuity underlying all the changes. But the new Church itself owed almost everything to his stimulus and favour. He was therefore secure in his

3

supremacy over it; and the development from Celtic Christian traditions to stricter orderliness and hierarchy added an extra dimension to the mobilisation of effective royal rule. Though their spiritual functions mattered greatly, the communities of monks and canons regular from England or France and the newly founded or reconstituted dioceses, usually reserved for bishops with Norman names, also gave territorial expression to the king's authority by confirming his hold on areas already subject to him, or by enforcing royal claims in exposed regions of uncertain allegiance. Further, King David resolutely defended the new ecclesiastical polity in its rights and powers against domination by the English Church. He co-ordinated 'the great attack on the Canterbury primacy from Scotland, Wales and Ireland',[13] successfully defied the metropolitan claims of York, and pressed for an independent church province with St Andrews as the primatial see. Constitutional links existed between Scottish monasteries and parent communities in northern France, but no continental house within the immediate jurisdiction of the Norman king-dukes was permitted to establish a daughter in Scotland;[14] he restricted wherever possible the governmental powers of mother houses in England, at the same time increasing the degree of dependence upon himself.[15] The Augustinian plantations swiftly took on the character of royal *Eigenklöster*; and although the Cistercian colonisations brought in a spiritual élite which, rejecting lay proprietorship, retained intimate ties with the European-wide order to which it belonged, close relations between individual abbeys and the king were accepted as natural and desirable. Moreover, Melrose began to supervise a Scottish family which, excepting Dundrennan, was attached to Rievaulx only through her. At precisely the moment when the new orders were failing to attract crown support in England,[16] church organisation and the Scots king's authority advanced together. Rather than diminishing the resources of the kingdom,[17] in the circumstances of the day King David's support for a revitalised Church was inseparably bound up with the expansion of royal power.

David I maintained his pre-eminence, and his authority prevailed, because impetus and direction lay securely with the king. The centralisation of royal control in southern Scotland and the annexation of lowland Moray were among his outstanding triumphs; and by adapting the strengths of the Anglo-Norman *regnum* he was able to profit splendidly from disunity within it. He enjoyed the substance of power while Stephen struggled for the shadow. Norman overlordship, in whatever guise, was confidently repudiated; 'le roi n'est pas un seigneur comme tous les autres'.[18] In the north of England King David pushed back the frontier of the Norman king's direct rule by exploiting on his own account the mixture of military force, diplomacy and patronage that had created it, effectively as recently as the reigns of William Rufus and Henry I. From 1141 these lands passed out of the homage of the English crown, and for all practical purposes the Tweed-Solway boundary ceased to exist. 'It was men who mattered, not lines on a map.'[19]

King David's accomplishments were indeed remarkable; yet at his death in 1153 they were far from ensuring that uniform control was imposed upon the lands he had claimed to rule. Royal lordship had different connotations in different districts, ranging from full power to a vague *superioritas*, for the kingdom still lacked firm territorial and political definition. Nor could it have been known for certain what shape it would ultimately assume. Under David I's grandsons, Malcolm IV and William I, the true picture is of a government strengthening itself on the foundation of his achievement and continuing to strive through military pressure and the securing of loyalty to convert wider claims into actual control, with the extent of its power fluctuating through advances in one area or reverses in the next. By 1153 or a little later 'the whole of southern Scotland (save only for Galloway) seems . . . to have been brought within a single administrative system based on well-established sheriffdoms and large feudal lordships'.[20] But the great Celtic earldoms of *Scotia* remained in the hands of native dignitaries whose support for the king was reluctant or restrained: with few exceptions the relationship was at best formal and ceremonial. 'Thus', in Bloch's phrase, 'did the idea of the public office yield to the undisguised realities of power.'[21] It was still possible for the royal will to be opposed by regional lords who cultivated and were accorded kingly status,[22] although occasionally it pleased them to offer tribute or military aid as a token of the 'high' king's suzerainty. Galloway, remote from the main centres of royal strength in Lothian, was barely absorbed within the kingdom; the Western Isles (formally subject to Norway), Kintyre and Argyll remained virtually autonomous. Up to their final defeat in 1230 the MacWilliams resisted the king from bases in highland Moray and Ross; the rulers of Caithness were quick to ally with his enemies, undermining his overlordship and disputing his government. There was yet another disputed frontier. In 1157 Malcolm IV recognised the greater strength of Henry II of England by surrendering the northern shires, but this cession of war gains, albeit a major reverse and in the end definitive, was by no means regarded on the Scottish side as an acceptable readjustment of territories. Malcolm and William therefore contested several marchlands where their influence was feeble or resented; but that influence always had the potential to be enlarged.

They acted by strengthening royal power in all spheres, reinforcing their lordship in Lothian, Fife and Angus, and assuming positions for further advance. They took a pronounced interest in the affairs of the north and the south-west, drawing these regions away from their local particularist associations and gradually integrating them more closely with the remainder of the kingdom. As the system of government was extended into peripheral areas by means of new castle-burghs and sheriffdoms, so they continued to build up a secular nobility and a reformed Church whose territorial strength augmented their own. The realm remained a land of opportunity for lay settlers from England, Normandy and Flanders, one celebrated as such in French romance,[23] although the infeftments of King David's successors seldom duplicated the rich allocations of the first colonial phase. New knights' feus proliferated, however, in Clydesdale, Galloway and Nithsdale. By 1214 incoming fief-holders were strongly entrenched in Fife, Gowrie, Angus and Mearns; north of the Mounth large lordships were assigned in Aberdeenshire and eastern Moray, while military operations opened up areas for settlement beyond the Great Glen. The regenerated Church continued to associate itself with the expanding powers of the crown, at once benefiting from and contributing to the extension of effective government and control. Strengthened by further grants, the foundation of new monasteries, and improvements in diocesan administration, it retained its close connections with court patronage; and in Galloway, Argyll and the mainland of the far north it exercised its privileges and responsibilities on the very extremities of royal influence.[24]

The administration also turned more systematically to extending royal supremacy through collaboration with native magnates hitherto accustomed to greater independence of action. Royal favour tended to be divided between ancient dynasties, offered the opportunity of maintaining their ascendancy under the crown, and rising families whose wealth flowed directly from support for the king. Individual potentates received land in return for express knight-service commitments; and individual earldoms or provinces became more subordinate to the claims of royal lordship. Increasingly the king surrounded himself with an aristocracy in which Norman-Frenchmen shared place with native-born lords. He needed the support of the latter for a firm basis of government, but the advance of his powers also made them more subservient to his will. They assimilated Anglo-Norman conventions; distinctions of race began to be broken down by marriage alliances which bound native families to Anglo-continental houses and some to the royal line itself. Mighty representatives of the old territorial nobility were gradually merged with the new into a more strongly based aristocratic community at the king's command.

At the same time, the interaction between political consolidation and relations between the Scottish and English kingdoms entered a different phase. Henry II's gathering up of his inheritance in Britain embraced the recovery of lost possessions and the reassertion of Beauclerk's overlordships, but also their enhancement wherever possible. The initiative could not be maintained by the Scottish crown. Restoring and sustaining direct rule over northern England, King Henry steadily hardened his relationship with the Scots king until an explicit recognition of his suzerainty was substituted for weaker forms of dependence; and although in 1189 Scotland was released by charter from all subjection, King John dealt with William I in 1209–12 as *de facto* lord superior. The Angevin rights and claims of overlordship were primarily exploited for the purpose of ensuring stability in the north, but Scottish concern to rule an independent kingdom and recover the Border shires was directly at odds with this policy. Much rested on the play of political fortune. Scottish demands for the northern counties were prosecuted by war in 1173–4 and again in 1215–17. On the other hand, in relations between secular powers generally, homages were acquiring a stricter meaning;[25] and the ancient English claims to hegemony, formulated in more exacting terms, from time to time resulted in a genuine undermining of the dignity and actual power of Scots kingship.

It would be wrong, however, to imagine that the history of Anglo-Scottish relations in the twelfth and thirteenth centuries is merely a matter of the claims and counter-claims of the respective ruling houses. No doubt it is understandable that in the past most attention has been paid by scholars to dealings between the two governments. That historians should have been particularly attracted to the causes and consequences of contention is perhaps equally understandable; and this, together with the undeniably turbulent course of Anglo-Scottish politics during the later Middle Ages, has tended to give the impression that conflict was the natural order of the day. Yet the fact remains that for a period of very nearly eighty years up to the outbreak of the so-called wars of independence in 1296, the English and Scottish crowns experienced continuous peace and often friendly contact. Earlier, from Henry II to John, peaceful co-existence was punctuated by attempts by one side or the other to re-define the relationship to its own advantage. Success lay with the Angevins rather than the king of Scots, and containment of Scottish ambitions preceded *détente*. But from the mid-twelfth century many influences were combining to bring the kingdoms closer together in spite of the periodic discord that disrupted relations between them. The effective expansion of the Scots king's control north of the Tweed required the utmost vigilance and peace with England; the early Angevins were diverted by continental entanglements even more completely than the Norman kings, a condition stimulating but, paradoxically, also limiting their interest in Scotland. Each government had a good deal to gain from alliance with the other, and as they gradually modified their positions to avoid damaging clashes of principle, a further consideration came ever more prominently upon the scene. Far from the Scottish gains of King David's Norman vassals being 'in many cases . . . incidental but useful additions to their established English estates',[26] the reality is that their total landed interest south of the Tweed was comparatively modest. Moreover, as long as northern England continued to be under occupation almost the whole of this would remain either lost through forfeiture or absorbed within the Scots king's personal sphere of influence. But from the second half of the twelfth century the concerns of important men ceased to be so firmly limited to the area of Scottish royal power; more than ever before, not just dynastic ties but also ties of property gave them interests beyond its confines. Thus the king consulted with the barons and claimed their service, but increasingly his leading nobles, whether of Anglo-Norman or native ancestry, had to take account of bonds with England and the English crown. In turn, a growing number of knightly houses and religious corporations accumulated possessions in both realms, often through the operation of magnate patronage.

7

There is a strong case for believing that study of 'cross-Border' proprietorship can offer further insight into the concord between kings and peoples, which would persist unchecked for the greater part of the thirteenth century and about which a significant amount is already known, but chiefly from the standpoint of the two governments themselves. The range of interests enjoyed by the great lords and their connections had its origins in King David's policy of opening up his kingdom to incomers from England and northern France. He had raised up 'new' men by preference, and his successors, emulating his style of kingship, brought in 'new' men of their own. Yet whatever the royal anxieties, it proved impossible, especially as magnates married and inherited, to curb the assembling of estates straddling the Border line and to maintain an effective division between the landholding societies of the two kingdoms. Not until the years of endemic warfare from 1296 would the Tweed-Solway frontier become a firm obstruction to the successful pursuit of individual concerns and ambitions. If a direct association can be established between David I's 'Normanising' policies and the development of a stronger government upon which his successors could profitably build – as well as substantial, though ultimately temporary, gains in northern England – in the long run they appear also to have contributed positively to a *modus vivendi* between the crowns, which was destroyed only when events moved unexpectedly in England's favour upon the failure of the Scots royal dynasty in the direct line of descent.

Against the manifest problems and limitations of medieval biography must be weighed the advantages of studying an important figure 'as a mirror of his age'.[27] The life and interests of Earl David of Huntingdon bring into view politics and society within two kingdoms at different stages of development from the position of an especially privileged magnate who, between 1185 and his death in 1219, was a prominent landholder in each country. The aims of this inquiry have been facilitated by the growing concern of Scottish historians with respect to the medieval baronage. Most fundamental of all are the specialised papers of G. W. S. Barrow, which have recently been taken a good deal further in his indispensable Ford Lectures.[28] In England a stronger tradition of feudal studies has shifted attention more decisively from kingship and institutional history towards the role of the secular aristocracy in medieval society, but has produced only a handful of monographs on individual contemporary or near-contemporary barons.[29] Furthermore, these men have been written about mainly to illustrate their eminence at the centre as leading actors on the constitutional stage, and this serves to encourage a one-sided view of the magnate class.

By focusing upon a single man, the present book seeks to treat together issues which can easily be ignored or are prone to be discussed separately. Politically, the interest stems most obviously from Earl David's vigorous part in Anglo-Scottish warfare and diplomacy. In order to give a balanced picture of his career no less attention is paid to his stature in society in terms

8

of land, tenants and affinity, for which the earl's surviving written acts, brought together and edited in the Appendix, form the principal corpus of information.[30] A major theme to be developed from the charters is the connection between crown patronage and the expansion of Scots royal power. One of the main distinguishing features of aristocratic society in early medieval Scotland by contrast with England is the extent to which territorial influence was monopolised by a modest number of large landlords; and perhaps one of the issues to emerge most clearly from modern scholarship is the growth of Scottish royal administrative strength. Yet although the sum total of truly great barons was small, concern with monarchical institutions must not be allowed to obscure the degree to which the Scots king relied upon his higher nobility in order to rule successfully. England was developing a much more advanced royal bureaucracy than Scotland, where in a far greater measure the power of the crown is to be explained in terms of the ability to make effective use of local landowners, and especially the magnates, as a means of securing stability and control in the provinces. Earl David demonstrated how essential such support could be and reminds us that in this rising kingdom the granting of substantial endowments was always a more deliberate and calculated business than simply rewarding loyalty with riches and honour. Another leading theme involves the nature of a magnate's personal wealth and standing in the more centralised English realm during a vital period of change and readjustment after Stenton's 'first century of English feudalism', when due partly to the actions of the stronger Angevin monarchy important limitations were imposed on the development of aristocratic power. Just as from 1185 Earl David's life lay firmly in both Scotland and England, so we must attend to his concerns on each side of the Border by dividing our time between them, the earl's activity in one country offering a comparative standpoint for insights into the exercise of his lordship in the other. In this way we can hope to illuminate the main differences, and the resemblances, between the governments, societies and economies of the neighbouring realms.

Above all, however, this book has a twofold purpose. As a conspicuous representative of a powerful but neglected body which was not fully integrated into either kingdom, Earl David introduces us directly to that world in which numerous barons, knights and churchmen were closely connected across the Tweed-Solway boundary by tenurial bonds stemming from marriage and inheritance, or colonisation and patronage. On the one hand, David's chief importance depends upon defining his role as a major force in promoting Anglo-Scottish contacts. On the other hand, his attitudes and actions naturally invite a broader approach. This study will therefore conclude by concentrating upon the whole complex of Anglo-Scottish property ties arising out of the Norman interest in Scotland and the significance of these connections for the social and political history of the kingdoms which they bound together – and which enjoyed unbroken peace between governments from 1217 to 1296.

2

EARLY LIFE

At the time of Earl David's birth in 1152[1] the Scottish royal house had an attachment to the French way of life that went far beyond the self-conscious imitation of an attractive foreign culture and the operation of patronage. The third son of Earl Henry of Northumberland by Ada de Warenne and grandson of King David I and Maud de Senlis, David was born into the highest rank of Norman-French society. Queen Maud, granddaughter of Lambert, count of Lens, was a great-niece of the Conqueror; Countess Ada, 'whose illustrious ancestry cannot be impugned',[2] was a daughter of William, second earl of Warenne – himself a kinsman of the Conqueror – a granddaughter of Count Hugh of Vermandois, and a great-granddaughter of King Henry I of France. Descended from the dukes of Normandy and the Capetians, David and his elder brothers Malcolm and William were in fact very nearly as rich in French blood as Henry II of England, the grandson of Henry Beauclerk and their own great-aunt Maud, daughter of Malcolm Canmore and St Margaret. Contemporary observers knew this full well, and that matrimonial stratagems had so drawn together the two royal dynasties that they belonged to the same intimate family circle.[3] To say that in later life David, of the grandsons of King David I, 'was most completely absorbed into the dominant Anglo-Frankish *milieu*'[4] is thus a trifle misleading. The house of Canmore, although conscious of the ancient traditions of its kingship, was already a true part of that social order whose conventions it so admired.

A posthumous son, David knew his father only by reputation, and of the relationship with his mother little can be recovered. For almost half a century Countess Ada was an active patron of the diffusion of Anglo-Norman influences in the northern kingdom. In her wake came knights to settle in southern Scotland from the Warenne estates in England and Normandy, as well as from the neighbourhood of her dower lands in Northumberland.[5] Her pious offerings were well distributed amongst the new religious communities assured of a prosperous future north of the Tweed, although her special interest was the Cistercian nunnery with which she graced her burgh of Haddington. In England she was a supporter of Nuneaton priory, Warden abbey and the Augustinian canons at Hexham.[6] With her long experience as first lady of the Scottish court since her marriage in 1139, Ada enjoyed deserved prominence in the counsels of Malcolm IV, who succeeded David I as a boy in 1153.[7] In attesting King Malcolm's *acta*, David is always associated with his brother William.

Normally they are in their mother's company, and David also witnessed two of Ada's personal charters possibly given at court.[8] We may assume that in early childhood he resided with William in King Malcolm's household, perhaps permanently but at least from time to time, and that Ada was concerned to keep a close mother's eye on the upbringing of her sons.

Soon after the Scots throne had devolved upon William in 1165, illness and advancing years forced Ada to retire from court and abandon public life. David had been removed from her influence in July 1163, assigned as a hostage for the Woodstock agreement between Malcolm IV and Henry II in resolution of differences arisen since their accommodation at Chester in 1157. The dispatch of Scots princes to the royal court in England was almost routine, so that David's father and grandfather had each served as a hostage for good faith between the realms, in fact if not in name.[9] Yet the terms under which David was detained marked a significant new departure. An authoritative source reports how he was handed over with other sureties as a pledge for peace and 'for King Malcolm's castles which King Henry wished to have'.[10] Henry II knew the value of castles as weapons of political control: the repossession of a castle was his right as lord superior and its surrender the vassal's obligation.[11] But this demand was for Scottish castles and as such provides an invaluable insight into Henry's attitude towards Scotland over a decade before William the Lion, in circumstances of abject personal submission, relinquished Berwick, Roxburgh and Edinburgh into Angevin custody.

If it is right to suggest that in 1163 Malcolm IV, who was already King Henry's vassal as earl of Huntingdon, paid homage only to Henry II's heir, the young Henry, and in respect of the Huntingdon honour alone,[12] this fell far short of Angevin aims. After Malcolm's cession of Northumberland, Cumberland and Westmorland, King Henry's first care had been to re-occupy and strengthen the principal strongholds beyond the Ribble and the Tees in a systematic programme for reasserting his *dominium* over northern England.[13] The threat to seize castles in Scotland shows his concern, in a manner complementary, to reinforce the Scottish alliance with material guarantees. For Henry II no less than for the Conqueror, 'the protection of his northern frontier beyond Yorkshire could never be dissociated from the hostility that was manifest in France'.[14] Malcolm IV could afford to surrender his youngest brother more readily than his castles. Yet by pressing for Scottish castles as if they were the appurtenances of a subject fief, Henry II showed how alarming the historic claims of overlordship were when stated in feudal terms. Already he was giving notice of his intention to define a relationship that was prejudicial to the rights and dignities of the Scots realm, and providing an indication of what might be expected if the balance of forces shifted more heavily in his favour. It is also significant that David's public career began in these circumstances, for the problems raised by relations between the two kingdoms were to dominate so many aspects of his future activity.

David was back in Scotland soon after Malcolm IV had died in December 1165, his release from Angevin hands being an appropriate gesture of
peace upon King William's accession. [15] Sent to England as the younger of
two brothers of the king of Scots, he returned as next in line to the throne,
and effectively occupied this position until William, who for long remained
unmarried, secured a legitimate son in 1198. David's improvement in
personal fortune prompted one contemporary, presumably well aware that
David I had survived six elder brothers to succeed as king in 1124, to dub
him David 'of good hope'. [16] Young David's activity begins to leave important traces in Scottish record. His high status distinct from the status of
other laymen was invariably recognised by the precedence he was accorded
in the witness-clauses of royal *acta*, the use of the style *frater regis* or *frater
meus* proclaiming his special closeness to the throne. In the first decade of
King William's reign, his itinerary places him at the main bases of government in Lothian and the central Lowlands, but also at royal centres as
remote as Elgin in Moray. [17] In regular attendance upon the king during this
period, he was also respected as an influential figure by powerful new
incoming families and participated in their written business. [18] As 'Dominus
Dauid frater regis', he was named surety in 1170 for King William, who had
agreed to maintain the arrangement between Robert de Quincy and Newbattle abbey over a lease of land at Prestonpans in East Lothian. [19]

But to be the king's only surviving brother meant more than this.
Royal charters have been found which express the notion that David had
consented to King William's dispositions, as when temporalities were
confirmed to the bishopric of Glasgow 'Dauid fratre meo idem ex parte sua
plenarie concedente et hoc coram me confitente'. [20] Such examples, however, are rare and the use of David's name in this way lacked the consistency
of official policy. For William, secure in his hereditary title, to have con-
tinually emphasised David's right to the throne would have been premature
and impolitic when he could anticipate children of his own. Thus David was
never designated to succeed as King David had designated his successor by
1144 and in 1152. Accordingly, too much should not be read into the
respectful title *dominus*: it was occasionally applied to David, but only as a
courtesy in non-royal sources. [21] Yet William had pressing obligations to his
brother that could not be unduly postponed. Family duty and political
expediency determined that David be supported in the dignified manner
fitting to his high estate. He was permitted to draw an annual allowance
from the crown's judicial profits, though we know of this pension only
incidentally and it is uncertain how valuable a perquisite it was or for how
long it was paid. [22] David was also entitled to an establishment in land. Real
estate was the essential concomitant of wealth and standing, and the creation of appanages for the younger sons and brothers of a king of Scots a
recognised procedure.

Upon first glance, the generous provision of endowments for royal
cadets may seem perversely at odds with the policies of centralisation and

expansion pursued by the twelfth-century royal government. The territorial kingdom was naturally regarded as in some sense family property, subject to conventions similar to those of baronial inheritances, and kings were expected to provide for cadets just as other lords catered for theirs. But far from weakening the crown, this could be a way of promoting harmony in the royal family, of buttressing royal lordship in areas beyond the effective reach of the king's administration, and even of preparing for the full integration of important districts into the *terra regis*. No twelfth-century king of Scots fathered a surviving younger son. Of the younger brothers known to have gained appanages, three inherited the kingdom, although this cannot have been anticipated at the moment of their endowment; and Alexander I's reluctance to install the future King David in Cumbria, Teviotdale and Lothian south of Lammermuir had undoubtedly been reinforced by fears of a permanent loss of resources that were vital to the crown. But David I administered these lands by employing many of the procedures he would later adopt as king, and when his appanage reverted to the royal domain, it came back as the chief support of a government aware of its burgeoning strength.[23] Before his own accession King Alexander had acquired the earldom of Gowrie and may himself have controlled much of southern Scotland; his brother Ethelred was earl of Fife, while a more remote kinsman, Matad, held Atholl.[24] Attention turned again to territories south of the Forth-Clyde line when in 1152 William took possession of the earldom of Northumberland, an interest subsequently reduced to the lordship of Tynedale.[25] At one time or another David personally was King William's man for the earldom of Lennox (an acquisition rather than ancient royal domain) and large holdings in north-eastern Scotland, besides the honour of Huntingdon. These lavish endowments, in an age when many of the great fiefs of the medieval kingdom had already been shared out, underlined the high prestige of his birth; but this was more than a matter of finding an honourable establishment for a prince of the blood. Within the realm the direct involvement of a royal cadet in the affairs of *Scotia*, or Scotland proper, was reasserted. It announced King William's ambition to further his control over the northern mainland, and as the agent of his brother's lordship David was of first importance in consolidating and advancing royal power beyond the Forth-Clyde isthmus. In his hands the appanage was a major source of strength to the king in the government of the realm.

David's endowment was a protracted procedure rather than a single event. Of the Scottish lands Lennox, apparently the first substantial grant, was not a permanent gain and it is appropriate to deal with it separately from his other possessions in Scotland. Our starting-point is King William's charter, issued between 1178 and 1182, establishing David's written title to the *comitatus* and additional lands in eastern Scotland for ten knights' service.[26] Lennox was an enormous compact territory, embracing almost the whole of modern Dunbartonshire and a large tract of western Stirlingshire. Bounded by Loch Long on the west, it sprawled eastwards beyond Loch Lomond and the Ben Lomond massif to the Kilsyth Hills. The southern boundary ran along the north bank of the Firth of Clyde from Baron's Point to Old Kilpatrick, six miles up-river from Dumbarton. It then passed by Baldernock to Kilsyth, closely following the line of the Antonine Wall. The northern march came down from the Britons' Stone (*Clach nam Breatann*) in Glen Falloch on a course largely determined by the head waters of the Forth and the Carron. The area contained by these bounds was some four hundred square miles.[27]

In spite of the attentions of Sir William Fraser and William Forbes Skene, the early history of Lennox remains pitifully obscure. Documentary record says practically nothing about the province prior to the thirteenth century, in marked contrast with neighbouring Clydesdale and the sheriff-dom of Stirling. None of the charters copied into the recently rediscovered earldom of Lennox cartulary belongs before c. 1200, and though this source has some uses for reconstructing earlier conditions, it casts little light, if any, upon David's administration.[28] There is no established chronology for his acquisition of the earldom but much confusion.[29] For clarification, first reference must be made not to a Scottish source but to Jordan Fantosme. His lively account of the Anglo-Scottish hostilities of 1173–4 is more than a memorable piece of contemporary war-reporting, for he knew enough to place his narrative against the wider background of Scottish policies and diplomacy. When he writes about King William and David, he is entitled to careful consideration.

Fantosme's statement that David gained Lennox in April or May 1174[30] appears to be corroborated by the only extant written act given by David for the province, concerning his grant of the churches of Antermony and Campsie to Kelso abbey. At first sight, the *terminus ante quem* of this charter is supplied by the chief witness to King William's confirmation, Richard de Moreville, who was most probably dead by late 1189.[31] On closer inspection, however, the latest date of issue was presumably much earlier than this. It is not enough to say that in the confirmation charter King William's title lacks the distinctive phrase *Dei gratia* which, in imitation of Angevin practice, was systematically adopted by royal chancery scribes in late 1173 or in 1174. The text of the confirmation is known only from the fourteenth-century Kelso abbey cartulary and the possibility of a copyist's omission cannot be discounted; alternatively, the original document may have been an 'external' production, drafted and penned by a scribe unfamiliar with the king's new style. But David's charter was dated at Roxburgh, and Roxburgh castle, and effectively the burgh also, were commandeered by Henry II under the treaty of Falaise of autumn 1174. David himself was detained in Normandy until the castle had actually been surrendered, probably by February 1175; it was garrisoned by Angevin troops until December 1189; and it seems hardly possible that David at any time during the fifteen years of Angevin occupation was issuing charters at this forfeited centre beyond his brother's jurisdiction. The most likely date for David's Lennox charter is thus no later than 1174, and this squares well with Fantosme's report. Nor are the date-limits of King William's charter to David (1178 × 1182) an obstacle to this argument. True, it was given in terms appropriate to new gifts. But the composite charter which brings together and verifies individual conveyances spread over a number of years is a recognised type.[32] The public and oral act of giving, rather than the act of providing written testimony, was after all the essential deed; and this royal 'grant' records an advanced stage in the lengthy process of endowing the king's brother.

Lennox, a land-division of long standing, was one of the largest ancient Scottish earldoms or provinces. Although it was historically the northern rump of the old British kingdom of Strathclyde, whose chief stronghold was at Dumbarton (*Dùn Breatann*), the Dalriadic settlements had enabled Gaelic-speakers to establish dominance in Lennox, and in its society and culture the area had in consequence developed a greater affinity with Argyll, Kintyre and Gaelic Ireland than with those regions farther to the south and east where the Scots royal power was strongest. It is a land of striking physical contrasts. The Highland Boundary Fault, bisecting Lennox from near Aberfoyle to Helensburgh, sharply distinguishes between the continuation of the Argyllshire Highlands, a bleak inhospitable landscape, and the low country from Glen Fruin to the Campsie Fells. Notably in the Vale of Leven and in the wide valley of the Endrick Water there were already rich farmlands to supplement the food-rents in cattle and cheeses from upland graziers. Though Lennox has always had a largely pastoral aspect, it was in this productive lowland zone that David's immediate successors resided by preference and from it that they drew a sizeable share of the wealth supporting them as leading magnates of the realm.[33]

Materially Lennox was a princely endowment. Strategically, its importance was outstanding. David's apparent predecessor was Alwyn mac Muiredach, earl or mormaer of Lennox, whom the contemporary Gaelic poet Muiredach Albanach eulogised as the head of a distinguished ruling house for long connected with the province.[34] Since Lennox lay outside the ancient crown domain, King William was not reducing his own traditional reserves, and he was hoping to augment his powers greatly. Hitherto the Scots kings had maintained an imperfect superiority over this intensely Celtic district: though Anglo-continental settlers had begun to colonise the middle and lower Clyde region by about the mid-twelfth century, they had been installed south and west of the cathedral burgh of Glasgow, and direct royal influence in Lennox remained at best occasional.[35] Yet potentially Lennox was a formidable bastion between the king's chief bases in the central Lowlands and the warlike, fiercely independent population of the Western Isles and seaboard. Major highland passes affording access to southern Scotland lay inside or close to its boundaries; but since this was a region where long-distance travel was easier by water than by land, it was the position of Lennox in relation to the sea-lanes of the Clyde basin that was especially vital. Whoever was lord of Lennox was *ipso facto* lord of Loch Long. His territory also dominated the Clyde estuary along the right bank from Loch Long to Glasgow; it embraced the whole of Loch Lomond; and it commanded access to this great freshwater route-way by the porterage (*tairbeart*) between Arrochar, at the head of Loch Long, and Tarbet.[36]

Fear of Hebridean raids and incursions from Argyll was real enough. The unruly Isles lay in theory under Norwegian sovereignty; and although King David had claimed tribute payments and jurisdiction as the overlord of Argyll and Kintyre, the loose bonds associating this area with the wider kingdom had been shaken off at his death. Recurrent disturbances in the 1150s had been all the more serious because of their co-ordination with risings in 'Argyll of Moray' and Galloway. In 1164 Somerled, the ruler of Argyll and *Innse Gall*, had brought his fleet up the Clyde unopposed to make landfall near Renfrew. This foray had ended with Somerled's death in battle and the rout of his forces, but the possibility of future, more testing inroads remained. Awareness of the dangers is reflected in the grouping of large regional fiefs already held by the Steward and the Constable in the south-west whose distribution, following one line of argument, 'suggests very strongly a deliberate and well worked-out policy of defending a vulnerable coastline and doorway to Scotland against attacks from the Isles and Galloway'.[37] In point of fact, however, this valuable observation does not tell the whole story. These great lordships were not designed simply to seal off troubled areas so that the king could concentrate on regions where his grasp was secure; they served at once as the actual means of establishing and consolidating important advances into territory where royal power was formerly weak or uncertain and as a vital preliminary to further expansion. The northernmost fief was the Steward's great lordship of Strathgryfe, including (by *c.* 1200) Bute at the mouth of the Firth of Clyde.[38] By placing a strong royal representative opposite Strathgryfe, King William was complementing existing arrangements for the security of the kingdom but was also hoping that in time his action would reap the reward of a forward base for intervention in remoter areas, to bring them in turn more effectively under the crown.

It has been argued that 'king William left the west to its own troubles',[39] but David's tenure of Lennox suggests more than token royal attention to this turbulent region. And yet David's interest did not endure. The exact date is uncertain, but he resigned his right no later than the 1190s, when the earldom was resumed by the native mormaer dynasty.[40] Attempting to explain his temporary proprietorship is one of numerous intractable problems concerning the earldoms of early medieval Scotland. From a general standpoint, the growth of royal power saw the gradual intensification of the king's control over these district lordships, thanks partly to steadily increasing scope for intrusion to obtain political advantage. An earldom might be allowed to lapse altogether, and in cases involving heiresses or rival claimants royal intervention could be decisive in determining possession and descent. At the same time, the role of royal cadets ought not to be overlooked. Of the earldoms which between *c.*1100 and 1174 were at one time regarded as appanages, Gowrie (perhaps we should add Moray) was subsequently absorbed as royal domain; Fife descended through a dynasty notable for its support of the crown; and Atholl was brought closer to the king due to the ties of kinship stemming from Matad, the first historical earl. In this light David's association with Lennox was in keeping with a well-established political tradition. On the other hand, the aim was not so much that the native higher aristocracy be destroyed but that royal government be strengthened by emphasising the earls' role as public officers directly dependent on the throne. The inheritance of sons was often assured, where succession was denied the decision might later be reversed, and the stability of great native-born lineages of actual or potential loyalty was a distinctive feature of the twelfth-century kingdom.[41]

The inherent flexibility of royal policy towards the earldoms provides a context for David's short-lived dealings with Lennox. The suggestion that he was formally granted Lennox in custody during a minority is unconvincing.[42] So far as they go, the available sources support the assumption made here, that the earldom was allocated not in wardship but in inheritance, to the exclusion of all other claims. King William is found confirming the *comitatus* by 1182 as a normal infeftment (*in feudo et hereditate*); and in imposing a service quota of ten knights, a remarkably light burden by English but not by Scottish standards, no distinction was made between Lennox and David's holdings in eastern Scotland. Of all the other earldoms of the kingdom only Fife, arguably, was brought under the crown as a fief by knight-service. On the face of it, therefore, this was a purposeful attempt by the king to establish a strict and durable relationship on the basis of dependent tenure.[43] It must be acknowledged that King William's 'Lennox' charter, the original text of which has been lost, is notable for its linking of a series of individual grants with a single holding clause and, not least, for its laconic brevity. The charter is, nevertheless, undeniably authentic as it survives; its tenor is echoed in Jordan Fantosme; and David, who in disposing of churches in Lennox to Kelso abbey acted *sicut dominus*, plainly regarded himself as more than a mere custodian. In addition, although it was obviously not the normal practice, he may have been accorded comital style in right of the earldom.[44]

Was there a pronouncement of forfeiture against an old-established dynasty that was later rescinded? While no evidence can be adduced to explain why the native family should have suffered deprivation, it is just possible that it had flouted royal authority in the 1150s or 1164 and had then been obliged to pay the price of rebellion. Whatever the reason, when Lennox reverted to Alwyn mac Muiredach's line there is no sign that David was aggrieved by its loss or felt that adequate efforts had not been made to defend his position. We could understand this more readily if – the question of wardship aside – his resignation coincided, as is possible, with King William's second grant to him of the earldom and honour of Huntingdon in 1185 as a *quid pro quo*.[45]

What is undeniable is that David left behind him in Lennox more than a passing impression of his power. To be sure, the mottes discovered by fieldwork in this area, as yet unexcavated, cannot be related to David with any confidence,[46] and so far as is known he did not attempt to secure his influence by infefting trusted supporters. The infiltration of Anglo-Norman social influences, while not radically transforming the province's Celtic character, was primarily sponsored by the thirteenth-century native earls. Their patronage brought in the Crocs, Flemings, Grahams, Lindseys and other new men.[47] The acquisition of large endowments by Paisley abbey in Lennox (and in Argyll and Kintyre) must likewise be dated after 1200. Nonetheless, royal authority had been represented by David's lordship, and that lordship was not easily forgotten. He enforced the king's right to levy an aid (*auxilium*) from Lennox; and jurors empanelled before papal judges-delegate at Ayr in 1233 could still recall how he had tried against ecclesiastical prohibition to include church lands in the assessment.[48]

Although Lennox was not annexed as a recognised possession of the royal house, the memory of David lived on. More to the point perhaps, by first denying the rights of the native line and then acknowledging them, the crown was displaying its sovereignty to advantage; and after David's intervention the native earls could only be secure in their lands by accepting a tighter alliance with the king than had previously been the case. Royal agents were active in Lennox collecting the king's forinsec dues in the 1190s; the bishop of Glasgow began to bring the rudiments of diocesan organisation to the province; and the bishop's burgesses won their share of trade.[49] By the fourth decade of the thirteenth century the crown had secured an important advanced base when a sheriffdom, centred on the new royal castle-burgh of Dumbarton, had been founded in collaboration with the earldom family. Steadily Lennox became more closely integrated in the normal government of the realm.[50] In 1238 King Alexander II, reserving Dumbarton for the crown, confirmed Earl Maeldomhnaich in his earldom 'sicut aliqui comites nostri comitatus suos liberius et quietius de nobis tenent et possident'.[51] There was no knight-service commitment, but by replacing feeble ties with a stricter dependence the king had imposed his political will. Indeed, Lennox had shed something of its character as an exposed frontier lordship and now provided a base for the forceful expansion of royal power into the north and west.[52] David's tenure of the province remains one of the most ill-recorded aspects of his activity. But the deficiencies of the available evidence must not be allowed to hide the fact that his intervention helped to prepare the way for the gradual inclusion of the western Highlands and Isles within the wider administrative framework of the *regnum Scotie*.

David's identification with the expanding power of the king's government in northern Scotland will be seen to reassert itself for his landholdings in the north-east Lowlands. But from the outset of his career David was also intimately involved in the broader range of royal preoccupations. Soon after 1165 he made his earliest known visits to King William's English possessions by crossing the Cheviots to the hunting-lodges at Donkley Haugh in upper Tynedale and by accompanying the royal court to Huntingdon.[53] The Liberty of Tynedale had been restored to William shortly after the yielding up of the northern counties in 1157; and William had presumably given homage for the honour of Huntingdon as King Malcolm's successor when in attendance upon Henry II in Normandy in 1166.[54] The allocation of English lands to members of the Scottish royal house as a means of fortifying ties of peace and dependence was a well-tried technique of management in the political cupboard of the English crown.[55] Such was the value of the midland honour in this regard that King Henry, anticipating his agreement with King Malcolm in 1157, had summarily deprived Simon de Senlis III, the rival claimant to the estate in the senior line of descent, although King Stephen had allowed Simon to inherit from his father in 1153.[56] Homage owed for lands outside Scotland gave Henry II no authority over the realm itself. Yet with the restoration of the Huntingdon honour in 1157 the Scots were obliged to concede a formal dependence upon England that had lapsed during Stephen's reign; and Malcolm IV was apparently the first of his line to undertake explicit vassal ceremonies for lands in England after elevation as king.[57] It was an early triumph for Henry II's policy, not only to recreate a dependent relationship but to intensify it. The impairment of prestige and dignity inherent in acknowledging claims to secular overlordship, however expressed, was a blow to any king who cherished the pre-eminence of monarchy.[58]

But this was only one aspect of the relationship between the governments. On the Scottish side, Tynedale and the Huntingdon honour were not acceptable compensation for the major loss of lands in northern England, and the object of recovering the Border shires was arguably the single most important consideration governing the formulation of King William's policy throughout his reign. From the Angevin point of view, the danger was not just that in 1168 William was already contemplating an alliance with King Louis VII.[59] Possession of property in England placed at his disposal power and influence that might well be exploited towards ends incompatible with Angevin interests. Tynedale was but a day's ride from Roxburgh, and its extensive franchises enabled King William to assume an especially privileged position in this lordship, almost as if it were an extension of his kingdom.[60] The honour of Huntingdon could not be held in safety save in faith and allegiance to the English crown. By 1165, however, the estate had been in Scottish hands for more than thirty years in all. A source of knights as well as revenue, it served as a recruiting-ground of vassals, some of whom were raised to prominence in Scotland, and the strongholds it supported dominated the major routes between London and the north.[61] Its use as a military base against King Stephen had been averted by the transfer of the fief to Earl Simon de Senlis II in 1141. But in 1157 the honour had returned under Scottish control; relations between the kingdoms remained precarious; and in 1174 David would be operating from the estate as his brother's ally in advance of renewed Scottish campaigning in the north.

For the moment, however, Henry II dictated events. In 1170 King William and David were summoned to his Easter court at Windsor. Henry's intention, on his return to England after four years' absence, was to secure their recognition of his eldest son as his crowned successor; and on 15 June, the day after the young Henry's coronation in Westminster abbey, they commended themselves to the *rex novus*, expressly reserving their faith to Henry II.[62] The chronicle sources are not precise enough to define closely the exact import of this ceremony, though both men were associated in their undertakings with 'all the earls, barons and free tenants of King Henry's realm'. It seems probable that pledges of general allegiance were exacted rather than oaths of homage, and William was quite properly acknowledging the young king in his capacity as an English earl.[63] David's circumstances were less straightforward, since he had no responsibilities as a fief-holder subject to Angevin lordship. Nevertheless, we must presume that he offered fealty as a *fidèle du roi* in full and solemn form. Fealty was a purely personal contract and therefore less compromising than the specific obligations of tenure; but it was a bond notwithstanding. While in 1163 the Scots king's homage had been strengthened by securing David as a hostage, in 1170 dependence was reinforced by drawing David, the apparent heir, into the formal sovereign allegiance of the English monarchy. On 31 May King Henry had bestowed upon him the belt of knighthood.[64] Henry II was not so much 'moderating his attitude to the king of Scots'[65] as seeking by these arrangements to consolidate his position.

David's next appearance in England marks his most publicised entry into the political arena. He returned about Easter 1174 not as a loyal ally of Henry II but in support of the young King Henry's rebellion, begun the year before. On paper the forces arrayed against Henry II constituted a formidable opposition, but when David joined the struggle the young Henry's party had made few concrete gains after months of hard campaigning that had carried the torch of revolt throughout the Angevin dominions. The rebel effort was ill-organised, with the individual protagonists more intent upon the pursuit of their disparate objectives than upon collaborative exertion, and this had enabled King Henry and his captains to defeat or contain their adversaries with remarkable ease. The war had gone particularly well for Henry II in England. King William's summer invasion of 1173 had been a challenge more serious in intention than in execution. When he had received intelligence of the approach of Richard de Lucy's army he had withdrawn in disarray, pursued by the barons of Northumberland who had burned Berwick and harried the Merse in a retaliatory action, forcing a truce which was to hold until the end of March 1174. The Justiciar had retired south, collected reinforcements *en route*, and crushed Earl Robert of Leicester and his Flemish stipendiaries near Bury St Edmunds in October. Leicester's confederate Earl Hugh Bigod had fallen back upon Framlingham, declining further action.

The rebellion was in danger of collapsing through lack of momentum, and in late 1173 Henry II may well have thought his victory assured. But the war in England continued for another year and gained new vigour when David took the field. The importance of his alliance had been recognised on the eve of hostilities. Henry II had made the first moves to enlist Scottish support, provided a bargain could be struck without dangerous concessions; and while rejecting King William's offer of assistance in return for Northumberland, he had (Fantosme reports) promised David a patrimony in land 'as will satisfy all his demands'.[66] But King Henry's rebuff had immediately driven William into close negotiations with the young Henry, who had countered his father by readily agreeing to convey the northern counties into William's charge. The Scots king, 'hoping to make good old losses by a new conflict', had joined the rebellion on these terms, though his main advisers had not been unanimously in favour of the alliance.[67] While not wishing to break with his brother, David himself had perhaps nursed reservations about William's political judgement and, not least, its effect upon his personal interests: there is certainly no evidence that he had been a leader of the Scottish invasion forces in 1173;[68] and William's grant to him of the Huntingdon honour – although it would prove to be a major landmark in his career – cannot in fact have decisively strengthened his commitment to the war. David's title had been ratified by the young King Henry, who had confirmed the conveyance with the new seal cut for him on the orders of Louis VII. In augmentation, he had given the whole of Cambridgeshire, a county traditionally associated with lordship of the honour.[69] Yet neither principal could guarantee David's seisin of the estate, which so far as Henry II was concerned had been forfeited when King William had violated his peace; and since it must have appeared increasingly improbable that the rebels would triumph, a speculative grant can hardly have seemed an adequate incentive for entering the struggle to a prince once flattered by inducements of substantial reward in Henry II's service. Significantly, Jordan Fantosme explains that by Easter 1174 William had taken David's homage for the earldom of Lennox 'observed by all his barons'. The king's brother required a suitable appanage. But, as Fantosme indeed implies, in choosing this moment to endow David with Lennox it is likely that William had also sought to allay his misgivings and ensure his whole-hearted participation in the rising.[70]

Whatever his personal qualms, once identified with the insurrection David threw himself into the conflict with a zeal and determination compelling the respect of friends and enemies alike. At the expiry of the winter truce King William launched fresh assaults in the north while David was dispatched to carry the war to the Midlands. His presence was urgently needed to boost the flagging morale of the midland rebels and to impede the mobilisation of an expeditionary force strong enough to oblige William to retire from the field as in 1173. David and his escort left Scotland in April or May.[71] They probably travelled through Northumberland, by-passing the principal loyal castles at Wark, Prudhoe and Newcastle, and across the Vale of York. Their passage was unopposed. King William had recently negotiated a neutrality pact with the bishop of Durham;[72] Roger de Mowbray and Earl William de Ferrers were new recruits to the rebel camp, perhaps encouraged in their stand by David's intervention, and could help to guarantee his safe conduct farther south.[73]

David's presence in the Midlands provided a vital rallying point. Leicester castle, the chief rebel base, had undergone close investment in July 1173, and although the siege had been raised when Richard de Lucy had rushed his levies north against King William, the earl of Leicester had failed to reinforce his garrison with fresh reserves.[74] Captured at the battle of Fornham, Earl Robert was imprisoned at Falaise along with Hugh, earl of Chester. Earl Hugh's supporters continued to hold out in England but had been forced on to the defensive by a strong cordon of loyalist garrisons between Bolsover and Shrawardine. The earl of Derby, operating from Tutbury and Duffield, was placed to aid the Leicester rebels, but he had remained at peace with Henry II throughout 1173 and his military ability was suspect.[75] Hugh Bigod's activity was restricted to East Anglia. Consequently the Leicester garrison and their local sympathisers had been thrown back on their own resources, lacking a leader and a lord until they were able to place themselves under David's command 'that they might act with greater confidence through having a prince of great name'.[76] Leicester, supported by outposts at Mountsorrel and Groby, bestrode Fosse Way, the main road from the West Country to Lincoln. Huntingdon castle, strengthened by David with men and supplies,[77] stood by Ermine Street. Another major highway to the north ran from London to Northampton and through Leicester to Nottingham. The rebel castles in the Midlands did not 'virtually cut the realm in two'[78] as they were easily turned; but Leicester and Huntingdon were excellent centres from which flying columns could harass the principal lines of communication between King Henry's chief bases in the south and north.

A continuator of the chronicle of Ralph Niger gives a brief but graphic description of David's intervention: 'Coming from Huntingdon to Leicester, he allied the townsfolk to himself and ravaged the whole province with fire and sword.'[79] His castles held out until the very end of the rebellion in England, and at least for a while David was able to wrest the initiative from the loyal garrisons at Nottingham and Northampton, from which the siege of Leicester had been supported in 1173.[80] Huntingdon castle may have been quickly neutralised. One account says that a siege army took up position in early May and that the garrison was 'for a very long time contained'.[81] In any event, Leicester became the main operational base, as perhaps had been David's intention all along. His advisers certainly seem to have regarded Leicester as the key to effective offensive action.[82] He moved against Northampton and engaged the borough militia defending the town under Bertram de Verdun. The burgesses suffered heavy losses and David returned triumphantly to Leicester with considerable booty and many prisoners.[83] Other loyal power bases in this area were few. A sortie by the Leicester knights on Castle Donington, commanding the Trent valley near the confluence with the Derwent, may have been mounted on David's orders.[84] He claimed tribute payments to ensure protection from his troops, just as King William bolstered his war-chest by levying protection money from north-country landowners.[85] A military historian has recently opined that the young King Henry's rebellion 'was the end of castle warfare – the last civil war fought on the old defensive principles'.[86] David's campaign, however, emphasises the duties of the castle at its most effective: in defence it was the lord's last refuge; in strength, a castle asserted his influence and control over the surrounding countryside. For two months or so, until Henry II's troops were able to march in force against him, David seems to have enjoyed a wide military superiority in this theatre of the war.

There is some evidence that he endeavoured to widen the basis of support by collaborating with other rebel commanders. He had an arrangement with the earl of Derby, who led a contingent from Leicester in a sally against Nottingham and gutted the town.[87] In May one of Roger de Mowbray's sons was apprehended by *rustici* in Lincolnshire as he made his way towards Leicester to raise reinforcements.[88] But this was essentially a war of opportunity with local objectives and no concerted programme of rebellion. For David himself the first priority was unmistakably command of the Huntingdon honour; and if the success of David's policy depended upon his military strength, this in turn substantially depended upon the contribution made to it by the honour's resources.

Leicester was an excellent strongpoint from which to dominate the *territorium* of the estate; and David's interest in Huntingdon was not purely military. This place was the *caput honoris*.[89] David's main preoccupation is more obviously revealed by four of his written acts, all issued for the honour in 1174.[90] The great value of these charters is that they elucidate aspects of David's campaigning on which the chronicles are lamentably sketchy. The earliest in the series, addressed to the bishop of Lincoln and the clergy and laity of the whole *comitatus* of Huntingdon, confirmed King Malcolm IV's grant of the church of Great Paxton (Hunts) to Holyrood abbey. It was given at Haddington in East Lothian, apparently just before David's expedition to the Midlands,[91] and although he could not yet warrant possessions in the honour, the Holyrood charter served to broadcast his intentions. The remaining *acta* can be assigned to the actual campaign in England. Two are for religious houses of which the lord of the honour was 'founder and patron'. The Cistercians at Sawtry received a confirmation of lands and mills in Great Paxton; a charter for St Andrew's priory at Northampton, directed to David's steward and all his barons and *probi homines* of the honour, ratified gifts in Paxton and Earls Barton (Northants) by Earl Simon de Senlis I.

While it is not surprising that Holyrood had sought an immediate confirmation of its Huntingdonshire benefice before David had left Scotland, that two English monasteries also petitioned for title-deeds provides some evidence of his strong position in the honour. It was the natural impulse of religious communities to obtain as many written sanctions as they could, and the charters added to monastic archives in wartime are not necessarily a reliable guide to the prevailing military or political realities. But those failing to recognise David's lordship or gain his protection undoubtedly suffered for lack of favour. Immediately after the war, the canons of St Frideswide's at Oxford complained to Rome that David, 'qui honorem de Huntindon' tenuit', had unjustly excluded them from their manor of Piddington (Oxon).[92] This property, moreover, was on the very periphery of the honour, isolated from the main concentrations in Northamptonshire and Huntingdonshire where his position appears to have been more firmly based.

But it is the fourth charter in this Huntingdon series which preserves the most telling evidence both that David was determined to exercise *dominium* over the fief and that for a while his local influence was strongly entrenched. This act confirmed a judicial settlement in David's *curia* between William de Audri and Stephen of Ecton and his son concerning land at Draughton (Northants) – 'que est de feudo regis Scocie fratris mei et meo'. In accordance with their agreement, William de Audri had taken the Ectons' homage for Draughton – 'coram me et in curia mea' – and William himself issued two supplementary charters at the same time as David's confirmation or very shortly afterwards, which state that compromise had been achieved 'coram Dauid fratre regis Scot', domino meo, in curia sua'.[93] The court concerned was unquestionably the court of the honour. Military pressure was only the first stage in a deliberate effort to impose effective lordship over the lands David claimed. As far as wartime conditions allowed, he was actively engaged in the running of the estate: charters were passed under his seal; his influence could extend to one of the honour's remotest establishments; and he observed the lord's traditional duty of ensuring that justice was done between his men.

The paucity of evidence is such that before the thirteenth century it is very rarely possible to learn a great deal about the military resources raised by baronial leaders in opposition to the English crown.[94] But by exceptional good fortune we are also able to look in some detail at the following David relied upon to do the fighting or otherwise to assert his power. Flemish mercenaries were stationed at Leicester; a detachment of stipendiary troops may also have been deployed at Huntingdon; and the large debts which

David ran up with Aaron of Lincoln (d. 1186) are perhaps an indication of the extent to which he relied upon those who fought for hire.[95] But David could also count upon men with whom his relationship was not purely financial. Many military tenants of the Leicester earldom had followed their lord into rebellion in 1173 and continued to provide valuable manpower when they entered David's service *pro tempore*.[96] Their fusion into David's personal clientage was facilitated not only by the familial bonds between the Beaumont earls and the Scottish royal house (Earl Robert was David's cousin), but also by the territorial intermingling of the Leicester and Huntingdon honours. The records name other short-term followers: a substantial Northamptonshire landowner, Ralph de Waterville, joined the Huntingdon garrison;[97] one Clerfai from Lincolnshire, who served at Leicester, was possibly related through the Clerfais of Hampole (Yorks, WR) to the lords of Hownam in Teviotdale.[98] These were in essence casual alliances, forged by accidents of war and independent of the obligations of tenurial service.

Further light is shed by the Huntingdon *acta* given in David's name during the campaign and the two contemporary charters by William de Audri. A total of thirty-one individuals occurs in the witness-lists besides David himself, of which fifteen demonstrably represent families holding by knight-service of the Huntingdon fief: William of Ashby, Walter and William of Bassingham (brothers), William and Hugh Burdet (father and son, also associated with the honour of Leicester), Hugh, Walter and William Giffard (brothers), Walter of Lindsey, Hugh and Ralph Ridel, William of Rushton, Roger of Sudbury, Robert of Wilby and William son of Emma (*alias* William de Vieuxpont). Most can be identified as knights with a modest stake in the honour, holding one or two fees or less.[99] William de Audri and Stephen of Ecton also fall into this category, and their compact in David's *curia* was one in which many of these witnesses participated as suitors and judges. Though he held in lay tenure, Ecton had formerly had employment as a clerk of Malcolm IV.[100] William Burdet and Hugh Ridel had served as stewards of the honour for the Scots king, and Ridel was acting as David's principal administrative officer in 1174.[101] Ties of tenure were strengthened by ties of ministerial service. Few were distracted by 'competing tenurial attractions',[102] but of this whole group only Lindsey, Vieuxpont, the Giffards and the Ridels were committed to Scotland through family landholdings in the northern realm. Fief-holding across the Tweed-Solway frontier thus helps to account for part of the tenurial following, but by no means all.[103]

David had claimed their service as lord in the name of King William and the young King Henry; but it is scarcely conceivable that he ever expected unanimous support from the Huntingdon tenantry. In Henry II's reign the notion hardened that no lord should stand between his vassal and the crown in the matter of allegiance: the knight's first duty, exclusive of all other obligations, was loyalty to the lord superior. This doctrine no doubt had little meaning for the discontented, yet it was but one of many influences combining to weaken the bonds between lord and man within the great estates of Angevin England. Magnate authority was being progressively devalued as the vassal's independence was growing.[104] Nonetheless the knights who witnessed David's *acta* and recognised his court were acknowledging his claims of lordship; and government sources explicitly confirm that some were deeply implicated with the rebellion. It may be coincidental that a large proportion was fined *pro foresta*, some heavily, during the punitive forest eyre of 1175.[105] But Hugh Giffard and Hugh Ridel were pledged to surrender hostages by the treaty of Falaise.[106] Hugh and Walter Giffard, and William de Vieuxpont, had in fact attended David shortly before his departure from Scotland and had evidently formed part of the 'warlike company' which, Fantosme tells us, had escorted him on his march through England.[107] Stephen of Ecton was a known dissident with a record of misdemeanours since as early as 1165; William of Ashby was to proffer £200 'pro habenda benivolentia regis'.[108]

Information on most of the remaining sixteen witnesses is very limited. Peter Petitgraunt, amerced in 1175 for consorting with the king's enemies, had Northamptonshire connections.[109] A much weightier figure, Robert de Musters, whose lands were mainly in Yorkshire, was an influential tenant of the honour of Richmond; but he also held lordship at Eltisley (Cambs), near Huntingdon, while his late lord, Duke Conan of Brittany, was David's brother-in-law.[110] Margaret of Scotland, Conan's widow, had declared herself for the rebels and was in Henry II's custody as a prisoner of state.[111] William de Richespaud is found as a tenant of the honour of Wahull (Odell) in Bedfordshire. His lord Walter de Wahull, an ally of the earl of Leicester, had been captured by loyalist forces in Norfolk in 1173. It is possible, but not certain, that William was also a Huntingdon vassal.[112] Richespaud aside, the other identifiable witnesses take us back to the Huntingdon honour. Six laymen were named after Northamptonshire villages entered by the estate and may have occupied a modest position in the tenurial scale: Henry of Farndon, Geoffrey of Holcot, Alcmund and Henry of Oxendon, Walter of Quinton and Philip of Thorpe. Generally they are so undistinguished that it is difficult to know their circumstances.[113] Thomas *clericus* of (Earls) Barton, one of the Northamptonshire demesne manors, was named with his brother Robert and had earlier appeared in Senlis service; Master Thomas de Paraviso, rector of Potton (Beds), had been employed as a clerk of King William; and Alan son of Hugh may already have acquired his Huntingdon fee at Great Paxton.[114] Lastly, Simon Vitor of Gumley (Leics), though not a witness to the charters, was possibly involved in David's attack upon Northampton;[115] other Huntingdon tenants, well-connected in Scotland, gave their service in King William's invasion forces.[116]

The war of 1173–4, it has been stressed, was 'fought in the first place by mercenaries'.[117] But such evidence as exists shows that backing for David's cause was broadly based. He called upon all available reserves and thus no single principle can account for the composition of his command. Even so, tenurial loyalty seems to have been remarkably effective despite the divisive strains of war. Overall the sources identify twenty-nine rebels demonstrably associated with the Huntingdon honour and a further eight 'possibles', of whom the vast majority served under David. His standard attracted no tenants of consequence in England, men who held multiple tenures of other lords and even baronies in chief. He may have expected succour from his second cousin Saer de Quincy II: Saer's son rebelled in Normandy while his younger brother Robert, justiciar of Lothian and a substantial proprietor in Fife, was firmly committed to the Scottish camp; Ralph de Waterville, not landed in the honour but an important recruit to David's party, was Saer's step-son; and in 1175 Abbot William of Peterborough, Ralph's brother, was deposed because, among other delinquencies, he had given fraternal comfort to this 'inimicus regis'.[118] But Saer's personal interests in land and office ranged far wider than the honour itself, and he remained resolutely loyal to Henry II in whose administration he hoped for further advancement.[119] By dividing on partisan lines, perhaps deliberately, his family was certain of sharing in the victor's triumph. Yet though we cannot suppose that David was supported by a full levy of military vassals recruited according to the rules of tenurial obligation, in no small measure his offensive capacity was founded upon the loyalty he and his house, from the days of King David and Earl Henry, had inspired among the gentry of the midland honour. Individuals may have feared to stand aloof in an area where David was asserting his military strength; many wartime supporters or their kinsmen were, however, intimates of his circle in later life.[120] Such evidence gives some prominence to the persisting force of tenurial bonds, although seemingly only when mesne tenants were tied by their main holdings to the lord claiming their service.

For all this, it was merely a matter of time before David's position became untenable. While he was establishing his dominance in the Midlands, few gains were made by the insurgents elsewhere in England; and with King William's discomfiture at Alnwick on 13 July the war moved rapidly towards an Angevin victory. The fighting in the north was over. Loyal troops converged upon Huntingdon castle where besieging forces had prepared an elaborate counter-work (*novum castrum*) to contain the garrison.[121] The castle continued to resist with spirit but surrendered at the end of July on the arrival of Henry II from London.[122]

The rebellion in England had effectively collapsed. With his brother a prisoner and his other allies defeated, David had no choice but capitulation. There are conflicting reports of his movements: he either escaped to Scotland or immediately came to terms, possibly when King Henry received the Scots king's personal submission at Northampton.[123] He was certainly confined in Normandy with William during autumn 1174, participating as a principal party to the treaty of Falaise.[124] Henry II saw no reason to mitigate his demands upon a humbled enemy, and in dictating conditions he was content with nothing less than the categoric subjection of Scotland as a fief of the English crown. The appropriation of the chief castles of Lothian underlined William's status as a vassal-king and imposed restraints upon his power. As and when required, the churchmen of Scotland had to transfer their liege fealty to King Henry, the 'dominus rex'; the leading lay vassals of the kingdom were to acknowledge him as suzerain and sovereign against all men, and expressly against King William should he default. Reaching beyond William to his subjects, Henry deliberately sought to undermine the relationship between the Scots king and his 'natural' supporters.[125] The strength of the Angevin position was demonstrated at another level. By the formal agreements between the realms in 1136, 1139 and 1157, when the claims of suzerainty had been kept in the background, the English crown had hoped for a lasting understanding through territorial concessions, in 1136 and 1139 going well beyond the mere re-establishment of the *status quo ante bellum*. But in 1174, while Tynedale was not withheld, William and David forfeited the Huntingdon honour, this being the one major confiscation of the young king's war. In fact the current Senlis claimant, Earl Simon III, had been recognised by Henry II as lord of the honour in the closing stages of the conflict, 'si illum adipisci posset', and entrusted with the reduction of Huntingdon castle.[126] The chronicle accounts are confirmed by the fact that Simon regarded his title as running from the date of his arrival at the siege; and by the end of 1174 he was holding his honour court at Fotheringhay.[127]

Setting aside the loss of the Huntingdon fief, the immediate effect of the settlement upon David was essentially limited. First of all, probably at Falaise, he did homage and swore allegiance to King Henry and to the young king, saving his fealty to Henry II as liege lord. Here he was renewing his oath of fealty of 1170 and strengthening it with homage. But the liege homage he gave did not entail regular vassalic services and consequently was less rigorous than the direct tenurial bond. Although above all other ties, this was the restricted form of homage owed by rear-vassals exclusively to the English crown, in Glanvill's phrase, 'for mere lordship'.[128] His subordination therefore retained a basically theoretical aspect; and it is possible that David regarded his formal submission in 1174 as little more emphatic than that of 1170. Secondly, David was made hostage until the Scottish castles stipulated for Angevin occupation had been surrendered, when he would be released along with his brother. Again he found himself in familiar circumstances, and although the terms of the treaty were undeniably harsh, it was not a momentous event in David's life. Yet in other ways the year 1174 signalled the beginning of a new stage in his career. He was the only rebel commander not discredited for his part in the rising and its ignominious result, and he had emerged with his reputation untarnished, indeed enhanced. Fantosme, who provides the sole contemporary assessment of David's character and personality, was in no doubt that the war had made his name. His verse-chronicle belongs to a genre of chivalric romance needing epic heroes to give it vitality. But Fantosme, a self-confessed partisan of Henry II, is elsewhere by no means uncritical of the Scots, and his fulsome praise of David's personal bravery and military leadership, even king-worthiness, transcends mere literary artifice.[129] We know as a matter of fact that David's qualities had attracted a strong following about him and that the loyalty he had evoked as a resourceful and enterprising lord survived the war. Moreover, the grant of Lennox had confirmed his pre-eminence among the aristocracy of Scotland and placed him in a key position for the definition and expansion of his brother's administration. King William's imprudence had involved David in an insurrection that had showed few signs of ever having prospects of success. But David was established as a leading public figure whose role in the politics and society of the two kingdoms had brought him to general prominence and renown. Aged twenty-two in 1174, he was on the threshold of a long and distinguished career.

3

LORD OF GARIOCH
AND EARL OF HUNTINGDON

In the cathedral church of York on 10 August 1175 King William and David confirmed the treaty of Falaise with their seals and, together with the chief men of Scotland, publicly acknowledged Henry II as lord superior.[1] Military defeat had entailed drastic concessions. In practice, of course, the exercise of King Henry's sovereign authority over Scotland was to be neither purely nominal nor blatantly oppressive. After he had defined his claims as legal rights, the Angevin's guiding aim was still to guarantee the Scots king's good behaviour; political control which pressed too heavily would only have been counter-productive. Thus the fifteen years of Angevin overlordship, although indisputably humiliating and resented, were the more supportable because for the most part suzerainty was tempered with restraint and was not seriously at odds with continuing political centralisation within the northern realm.[2] These were important years for David. During the decade 1175–85 he remained in regular attendance upon King William, retaining prominence among those from whom his brother sought counsel.[3] His peculiar proximity to the throne was emphasised when he assisted the king in the settlement of disputes and put his seal to important private agreements for their greater security.[4] Above all, David's significance in government was heightened by new endowments firmly related to the advance of royal power in the far north, unmistakably the major domestic concern of King William's administration.

The main outlines of this establishment are recorded in King William's charter of between 1178 and 1182.[5] Morton by Edinburgh was an isolated gain; and while an influential grouping of tenures centred upon Dundee, already a fast-growing commercial port, the bulk of the land lay in mid-Aberdeenshire. This was David's great lordship of Garioch, a solid expanse of property covering about one hundred square miles, which after the loss of Lennox constituted the principal source of his territorial strength in Scotland. Occupying a dominant position between the Celtic earldoms of Mar and Buchan, it ranged from Strathbogie to the parish of Fintray, six miles west of Aberdeen, and from the river Don to the Foudland Hills.

The evidence for Lennox warns against supposing that David entered all these possessions by a single royal decision datable 1178 × 1182. Grounds will be given for suggesting that Garioch was secured within this period; but the interest at Longforgan beside Dundee was first mentioned in 1172,[6] and Morton, no doubt intended as a convenient base for Edinburgh, was probably acquired before Angevin castellans commandeered the castle-burgh in 1175. On the other hand, the royal charter affirmed David's title only to the chief gains, for the formation of this rich eastern fief continued at least until the 1190s. It did not embrace Strathbogie, as claimed by Walter Bower, a late though occasionally authoritative source.[7] But the Inch of Perth had passed to David by 1199; new assets were provided in the Mearns at Ecclesgreig (St Cyrus) and Inverbervie; and he very likely took the main secular interest at Brechin in Angus.[8] Altogether these accumulations gave David a commanding position as the most valued of the king's magnate supporters in the north-east Lowlands. It is noteworthy, however, that whereas in Fife, Angus, Perthshire and Mearns his concerns conformed to the pattern of small, scattered infeftments characteristic of these areas, farther to the north, where close royal control was more tenuous and intermittent, the lands were granted as one large concentrated block.

David's role as lord of Garioch is particularly important for demonstrating the growth of a great estate outside the earldoms as a concomitant of the growth of Scots royal rule. The sources for the north-eastern properties as a whole, all permanent accessions, reveal a much more active personal lordship than was exercised in Lennox. Again, whereas Lennox was only fully exploited as a base for the ongoing expansion of royal influence after David's resignation, from the start his tenure of Garioch was bound up with the aggressive assertion of the king's will over more distant areas. The main issues involve the general strategic or political requirements of the crown, the degree of royal planning in the structuring of David's resources, and the actual impact of his proprietorship. The first point may be addressed forthwith; the others require separate treatment.

The closest parallels to Garioch among the fiefs of the twelfth-century kingdom lay south of the Forth-Clyde isthmus, where a great network of provincial lordships had been bestowed upon a Norman-French élite by the 1160s. Among these, the most important were Renfrew, Mearns, Strathgryfe and North Kyle (Stewart), Cunningham and Lauderdale (Moreville), Annandale (Brus), upper Eskdale with Ewesdale (Avenel), and Liddesdale (Sules). Not every command occupied districts where traditions of loyalty to the king were dangerously weak; regional estates might conform neatly to ancient administrative divisions and did not invariably result from elaborate 'tenurial engineering'.[9] The view taken here, however, is that the crown, conscious of the advantages in placing trustworthy clients in possession of big tracts of territory, did have a deliberate policy of drawing great lords towards peripheral areas where direct royal government was spasmodic, and of concentrating their lands as powerful instruments of control.[10] Avenel, Brus, Moreville, Stewart and Sules – these potentates, the equals of the native earls in all but rank, were often privileged through their tenure of high office as well as by their dominating influence on the social and political life of whole regions; and by the mid-thirteenth century provincial fiefs held by incoming royal appointees were also a distinctive feature of the north-east and far north. For lack of adequate evidence it is difficult to ascertain every stage in the emergence of these northern enclaves. Nevertheless, Garioch represented the first decisive step. Strathbogie may only have passed to a younger son of the earl of Fife as late as 1226; Badenoch evidently came to Walter Comyn no earlier than c.1230.[11] Rather older established than those two were the Freskin lordship in Sutherland and, amongst others on a smaller scale, Cromarty (Mowat), the Aird (Bisset), Abertarff (Thirlestane), Stratha'an (earl of Fife) and Rothes (Pollok); but most of these were probably founded about the end of King William's reign, and there is no positive proof that any had been granted out by the 1170s or '80s.[12] Royal consolidation through controlling the descent of the northern earldoms was another stratagem, although one of limited effectiveness until they had been fully opened up to female inheritance after David's lifetime. 'From Menteith to Buchan this was the land of earls.'[13] But the sole major success for William I was apparently the transfer of Buchan to William Comyn in c.1212; the formation of Thomas Durward's great power base between the Dee and the Don, carved out of the earldom of Mar, may not have been achieved earlier than the 1220s.[14] David's infeftment in Garioch therefore signalled a forceful new departure in the political history of Scotland north of the Tay, and as such engages special attention.

This was a decisive delegation of regional power, for in endowing David King William was securing vital needs of the crown. In the 1170s the northernmost focus of royal rule lay in advance of Garioch in the Laich of Moray, originally annexed to the *terra regis* by King David I. But the Moray Firth coastlands remained an isolated outpost, remote from the principal seats of government in the south and exposed to attack. Farther north, effective control as yet escaped the royal grasp. The bishop of Caithness rarely resided in his see, and while theoretically the Norse earl of Orkney exercised jurisdiction over Caithness and eastern Sutherland as the Scots king's dependant, he was accustomed to behaving as an independent power. Problems of law and order were chronic. In Ross and western Moray, a wild debatable land knowing little peace, leadership devolved upon the MacWilliams, who nursed claims even to the Scottish throne itself and were quick to pursue their objectives by violence. Commanding wide support, they posed a more immediate threat to lowland Moray and the onward advance of royal power.

Such is part of the context for Garioch. Indeed, David had first-hand experience of this turbulent marchland. He accompanied King William to Ross on a holding operation in 1179 – 'with a great army' according to the Melrose Chronicle.[15] Undeterred by this display of force, Donald MacWilliam harried the north until ambushed and killed by troops operating from Inverness in 1187. The success of this punitive action, followed up by retaliatory expeditions to Caithness in 1196–7, was a major turning-point. Confident efforts were made to bring this border area more firmly under royal control through further administrative innovation, ecclesiastical reform and infeftment of incoming families. A castle-burgh was added at Nairn, the nucleus of a sheriffdom by 1204;[16] the organisation of the Moray diocese proceeded in earnest, the new cathedral at Spynie taking its constitutions from Lincoln;[17] lay immigrants secured the western flank; and Hugh Freskin was granted wide lands beyond the Dornoch Firth to remove them from Norse influence. In *c.*1215 the earldom of Ross was revived, and by 1222 Hugh Freskin's son claimed to hold the whole of Sutherland.[18] Though the full realisation of King William's expansionist policy ultimately depended upon the vigilance of his successors, the theme here is that of consolidating, then of pushing forward, the frontier of effective control; and when these measures needed reinforcement, military pressure was swiftly brought to bear, the local levies being strengthened by field armies rushed up from the south.

But royal ambitions in the far north were always firmly related to the condition of the Lowlands between the Mounth (eastern Grampians) and the Spey. The political history of this area had followed a rather different course from that of districts directly to the south. By *c.*1180 the major centres were Aberdeen and Banff, both possibly – though by no means certainly – the headquarters of sheriffdoms.[19] There were already, or soon to be established, royal castle-burghs at Kintore and Cullen, and a royal castle at Fyvie.[20] But the king rarely spent time in this region, while his government as upheld by reliable agents remained more thinly spread than was wise or necessary. Anglo-French colonisation had yet to sweep far beyond the Carse of Gowrie,[21] and the lack of an integrated shrieval system by comparison with the administration of central Scotland and the south-east ensured that the native lords avoided regular supervision and retained wide powers. Local influence was so concentrated that King William was heavily reliant upon the goodwill of the earls of Mar and Buchan, and the bonds linking them to the crown were weakly tied: their attendance was difficult to secure at court and they could not always be trusted to put royal interests higher than their own.[22] David's infeftment might be connected with possible intrusion in the descent of Mar; but the claims of this district as a 'northern bastion of royal power'[23] belong far more to the thirteenth century than to the twelfth.

At this juncture the key importance of Garioch can be properly discerned. Partly David's endowment was a calculated stroke of policy designed to broaden the king's basis of support where it lacked the vitality of the more intensively governed areas of the realm between the Grampians and the Tweed. The problems were scarcely those of a hostile or newly conquered territory; and the military element was less obviously to the fore than in the fiefs of Scottish Cumbria flanking Galloway.[24] Nevertheless, the value of a strong royal vassal underpinning the king's position in central Aberdeenshire was undoubtedly enhanced since in the circumstances of the time there could be no guarantee that overt opposition would be entirely confined beyond the Moray Lowlands. The sack of Aberdeen by Norwegian levies in 1153 had shown how easily strongpoints could be outflanked by a determined sea-borne enemy, and without adequate control of the Highland fastnesses the possibility of land attack inevitably aroused serious concern. A late tradition that the bishops of Aberdeen feared for their remoter assets finds some confirmation in the fact that as late as 1226 the bishop of Moray, when leasing out property in the Laich, had to agree to preferential terms in the event of devastation 'per guerram'.[25] As if to underline the dangers, in November 1186 a raiding party reached Coupar Angus abbey in Strathmore.[26]

Any strategic interpretation which stressed the duties of defence would, however, remain one-sided. Supported by less remote estates, the lord of Garioch was able not only to strengthen positions already won, enforcing his lordship and preparing for possible trouble even if it never actually materialised, but also to participate directly in the success of the offensive drives beyond the Spey. Reinforcement of the king's rule went hand in hand with its advancement farther to the north. Garioch was, to borrow a phrase of Georges Duby, a vital 'seigneurie routière'.[27] When large-scale expeditions were launched against the MacWilliams or other enemies, as in 1179, 1187, 1196–7, 1201–2, 1211–12 and 1214–15, all hopes of victory in the field turned upon the safe movement of troops and supply trains operating far from royal centres in the south. Garioch dominated the Aberdeenshire plain from the Banffshire mountains almost to the sea, so that David was in a position to make himself master of the main roads north to Moray, all of which crossed Garioch or passed close by it. These included the highway from Aberdeen to Elgin *via* Huntly, directly controlled by David over a twenty-mile stretch between Fintray and Culsalmond. An alternative route followed the vale of Garioch, staying within his boundaries until Kennethmont, some thirty miles west of Fintray. It then entered Strathbogie, a great strategic corridor upon which converged the chief thoroughfares north through western Mar. Parties could turn for Huntly or reach Elgin by the hill road to Cabrach and on through the Glen of Rothes.

Now, the need to protect his extended lines of communication would have been forcibly brought home to King William during his first major campaign in Moray and Ross. Perhaps it was in this year, 1179, or the next that David was installed in Garioch to assist in the crucial twin purposes of local consolidation and further advance.[28] Finally, David's contribution took on a certain added significance when his more southerly tenures were augmented with Inverbervie and, apparently, Brechin. Inverbervie dominated the road between Montrose and Aberdeen, and Brechin was important for the passes through the Mounth, the main natural obstacle to travellers between Tayside and Garioch. Although David may not have been responsible, both places were fortified with castles, first mentioned by 1237 and 1267 respectively.[29]

Further comment is necessarily reserved for later. David's estate centres, land management and patronage – these are matters which must be

pursued within the fief at large. It will also be suggested that the compactness of Garioch was no accident of tenurial geography, but resulted from a
conscious act of royal policy to transfer a lordship of regional significance
into single hands.[30] Yet it was in the day-to-day running of their property
that tenants-in-chief acted most effectively on the king's behalf. As will
become clear, David could not devote his full attention to Scottish concerns. But this is very far from saying that he did not exercise a personal
lordship or build up an organisation capable of maintaining continuity of
control during his absences; and David's activity in bringing Garioch and
supporting interests more firmly into line with the predominant social and
political order of the kingdom reveals in abundant measure the close
interconnection between the rise of a new provincial aristocracy and the
expanding powers of the crown.

Even as David was establishing himself north of the Forth his career
continued to unfold under the influence of relations between Scotland and
the English crown. He had a foretaste of the diplomatic activity in which he
would gain prominence in later years when he helped to reconcile Roland of
Galloway and Henry II at Carlisle in August 1186. King Henry's intervention in Gallovidian affairs was one consequence of the subjection imposed upon King William in 1174. Earlier, in the spring of 1181, he had
called King William and David to Normandy for discussions on the disputed election to the bishopric of St Andrews.[31] When the Scots king
attended the overlord's court on the business of his kingdom, the heir
presumptive would normally be summoned with him; but King Henry
increasingly looked upon David more as a valuable supporter than as a
vanquished foe, and aimed to win the alliance of this influential figure in
Scottish society and cement his political dependence upon the Angevin
monarchy. On one visit to France David fought in the *équipe* of the young
King Henry, then temporarily reconciled with his father, in a tournament at
Lagny-sur-Marne in Champagne.[32] There were similar social occasions: in
1182, for example, he was entertained at Chinon. He was also received in
every circumstance of friendship when King Henry kept Christmas at
Windsor in 1184.[33]
    David's rise in Angevin favour reflects a general improvement in
relationships between the governments. On the Angevin side, the reasons
for moderation were especially compelling. The question of the northern
English shires remained unresolved at a time when King Henry faced
mounting difficulties on the Continent. Too oppressive a stance, encouraging the Scots king to capitalise upon these distractions, might bring another
enemy into the field when Henry's resources were dangerously over-
stretched. King William himself was therefore more valued as an ally than
as a discontented client; but while conciliation was the more attractive
policy, only Henry II's tactics had changed, not the strategy of striving to
increase his hold over the king of Scots. The marriage arranged in 1186

between King William and Ermengarde, the daughter of Richard, *vicomte* of Beaumont-sur-Sarthe and lord of Le Lude in Maine, epitomised Angevin policy. To say that 'the new queen was of insignificant family' seems a little unfair to this great-granddaughter of Henry Beauclerk;[34] and any feeling of disparagement was the more easily forgotten when Edinburgh, lost in 1175, was returned as her marriage portion. On the other hand, the alliance undoubtedly emphasised William's dependent status. He and David had been summoned to learn Angevin wishes in this matter in late May;[35] the marriage itself was solemnised at Woodstock on 5 September. It was a lavish state occasion. David joined in the celebrations, 'and very many earls and barons of the kingdom of England . . . and several earls and barons of the kingdom of Scotland'.[36]

At Woodstock, and when he returned to spend Christmas with King Henry at Guildford,[37] David could take pride in his membership of both aristocracies. In March 1185 the earldom and honour of Huntingdon had been restored to King William, who had at once allowed David to be endowed with the honour and receive the title of earl.[38] This was a powerful practical reinforcement of the new understanding between the crowns. Simon de Senlis III, the lord of the honour since 1174, was dead by Michaelmas 1184.[39] His son had predeceased him and a younger brother, presumably illegitimate, was disqualified from inheritance;[40] but there were lawful claimants on the Senlis side – among them the Mauduits of Hanslope, prominent in King Henry's circle – and 'many said they were nearer by right and offered the king great and many things to have justice'.[41] Such was the high value of the Scottish alliance that by no means for the first time in the history of the estate political considerations prevailed over strict heredity. For David himself, then aged thirty-two, 1185 must obviously be regarded as the outstanding watershed in his career. Already one of the most powerful magnates of Scotland, as an earl of the English kingdom he was promoted to the forefront of Angevin society, in rank if not in terms of actual landed wealth in England. It was a major transformation of personal fortune and exercised a decisive influence on his activity, henceforth placed resolutely on a level transcending the Border line.

This new stage in his private life was also a fundamental turning-point in his public career. It is not straightforward to decide why King William transferred the Huntingdon honour to him, unless it be assumed that he was fulfilling a pledge made in 1174 or providing an exchange for Lennox. There was no obvious political motive on the Scottish side. In 1136 King David had resigned the estate to Earl Henry, prudently withdrawing his homage from the English crown.[42] But substitution was not the arrangement adopted in 1185. Technically King William retained superior rights: David's lands were described as 'de feudo regis Scotie'; he called the Scots king to warranty over disputed tenancies.[43] In 1185, William presumably saw no point in resurrecting David I's cautious policy since the treaty of Falaise was still in force. In any case, neither Malcolm IV nor William had shirked giving homage as king for English lands, and William may have hoped to retain some claim on the honour's financial resources, with rights of escheat if David's line fell in. King William's lordship was officially recognised when Richard I confirmed the honour to him in December 1189 and by John in 1200. King Alexander II's tenure would be acknowledged by the regency government in 1217 and 1219.[44]

But there remains the probability that the endowment of David was a precondition imposed by Henry II. It would certainly have required his approval, and there was clearly a good deal to be said for the view that the presumptive heir to the Scots throne could be more effectively controlled through broad lands in England than the Scottish king himself. As will be seen, it would be dangerous to exaggerate the personal wealth and influence placed at David's immediate disposal. The successful development of his position as an English magnate depended above all upon the fruits of continued Angevin favour. In this sense, however, the Huntingdon honour was an ideal settlement. David's standing as a rear-vassal for an earldom of the kingdom was distinctly irregular: because King William stood between him and Henry II, he had not been brought into direct vassalage as a fief-holding client of the crown. Yet the real issue was that material concerns now bound him to Angevin interests, and when necessary his dependence was easily emphasised by holding him directly accountable for the honour, irrespective of the peculiarities of his tenurial status.[45] Moreover, later grants to David of English lands in chief identified his homage incontrovertibly with the special conditions of tenure.[46] Though his position as earl of Huntingdon remained ambiguous, the Angevins succeeded in recreating for him the precise vassalic relationship that had existed between Beauclerk and David's grandfather, and between Stephen and David's father, when they had stood next in line to the Scots throne.[47]

The gradual intensification of David's dependence upon England is one leading aspect of his career. Progressing from hostage (1163) to *fidelis* (1170), liegeman (1174), earl and, ultimately, immediate vassal, he was subjected to increasingly binding forms of subordination. It is instructive to examine from David's standpoint the underlying political implications, which also illuminate the practical benefits accruing to the English crown. To 1185 his activities had been mainly, though not exclusively, confined to Scotland, and his talents and energies had found expression in close support of his brother's policies. Thereafter Earl David and his affinity were committed to a life in two countries, and he was obliged to appraise events not merely from the viewpoint of lands and interests in a single realm. When relations between the kingdoms were stable, it was easy to reconcile his two allegiances; but in times of tension it was difficult to retain the trust of both kings simultaneously, while active support of one ruler against the other automatically involved the risk of reprisals and confiscation. Since the earl could not expect to remain neutral during hostilities, his extensive Anglo-Scottish estates therefore gave him every inducement to promote harmony between the crowns, even if this meant using his political weight to restrain the ambitions of a Scots king conscious of his hereditary claims to the northern shires. That invasion had ended in humiliating failure in 1174 no doubt eased the difficulties of the earl's position. His own desire for peace could be interpreted as loyalty to what he regarded as being the best interests of the Scottish kingdom, provided that Angevin notions of over-lordship were not aggressively asserted. Yet King William personally could no longer assume his undivided loyalty. 'He was whole-heartedly in favour of the pact with the Normans and English, for he saw the force of his counsellors' argument that it would be a valuable source of strength for himself and his people.'[48] These sentiments attributed by Orderic Vitalis to Earl Henry upon Stephen's concessions of 1139 could equally well have been written for David. But the irony of the situation was such that if Earl David's position ultimately depended upon a stable alliance with England, his years of greatest personal prosperity after 1185 would be those when the possibility of renewed Scottish aggression was regarded with especial anxiety at the Angevin royal court.

During King Richard's reign Earl David established a record of exemplary service to the Angevin monarchy. He had the privilege of carrying one of the ceremonial swords at the new king's coronation in Westminster abbey on 3 September 1189.[49] Shortly afterwards he was with Richard at Geddington and probably attended him for the council celebrated at Pipewell abbey.[50] David again joined Richard at Canterbury and Dover on the eve of the king's departure from England in early December.[51] Nine months later the earl was married to a sought-after lady in Richard's gift: Maud, grand-daughter of Ranulf de Gernons and sister of Ranulf de Blundeville, earls of Chester. Dealings between the couple's respective families were rooted in territorial controversy and mutual distrust;[52] but a recent bond had been forged when Ranulf de Blundeville had taken in marriage David's niece Constance, duchess of Brittany and countess of Richmond, in 1189.[53] Like many prominent Anglo-Normans, Earl David married into a family with which he was already closely related. It was, nonetheless, a major social and economic compact, one which strengthened his familial ties and underlined his importance as a great Anglo-Scottish magnate. David's brother-in-law, a young man at the time of the marriage, was destined for a long and momentous career, and contacts were maintained between the two men in their later lives.[54] Maud's *maritagium* included lucrative concerns in Essex and Lincolnshire;[55] and however remote any expectations of inheritance may have seemed when she married Earl David in 1190, the succession to the earldom of Chester of the surviving son of their union, upon Earl Ranulf's death without children in 1232, was the long-term result of this most advantageous alliance. Politically, the marriage was a distinctive mark of Angevin patronage, serving to reaffirm David's commitment as a client of the English crown.

There follows a gap of three and a half years in the earl's recorded activity. That his marriage was celebrated on 19 August 1190, almost two weeks after King Richard had sailed from Marseilles, must suggest that he did not leave for the Holy Land as a member of the king's expedition.[56] He had attended the council of Clerkenwell in March 1185, when the question of a crusade had been broached, and he had participated in the council of Geddington in mid-February 1188, when the bishops had preached holy war.[57] These appeals met with a wide response in England, and individual Scottish landowners also honoured undertakings to fight in the East.[58] Earl David himself may have taken the Cross, but whether or not a crusader's vow was ever fulfilled is debatable. His most conspicuous act of piety, the foundation of Lindores abbey, begun about 1190, could have been a means of redeeming such a promise through commutation.[59]

And yet several late sources explicitly refer to the earl's absence on crusade, or have been supposed to do so. Excluding their known continuators, they may be listed as follows. (1) One of the earliest recensions of John of Fordun's *Gesta Annalia*, written in the 1360s or '70s. This contains two passages about David 'versus Sarassenos pugnans, ut historia de ipso compilata ad longum oppulenter approbat' and 'in praeliis contra Saracenos, ut in historia . . . continetur'.[60] (2) A reference by Andrew of Wyntoun (*c.* 1420) to David 'in Sarasynes'.[61] (3) The *Histoire des Trois Nobles Fils de Rois*, a fabulous account of a crusade against the Turks involving the adventures of a Scottish prince named David. This work went through several printed editions at Lyons and Paris in the early sixteenth century. Its authorship has not been established, though the earliest known text, dated 1463, survives in the hand of David Aubert, librarian to Philip the Good, duke of Burgundy.[62] (4) The *Scotorum Historiae* of Hector Boece, first published at Paris in 1527, which provides a graphic account of deeds attributed to David as a crusader from 1190. It was Boece's David who furnished Sir Walter Scott with a figure for *The Talisman*. (5) A Paris manuscript of doubtful value, possibly referring to David ('de Anglia videlicet comes de Norantone') as a participant in the Fourth Crusade.[63]

As far as they go, these sources are worth some consideration. There is every likelihood that Wyntoun was dependent upon Fordun for his information about Earl David.[64] The *Histoire* was no doubt known to Boece who had studied at Paris; his contemporary John Major had access to 'a similar book . . . in our own vernacular tongue' and assumed, as have later historians, that David was its hero.[65] It appears, however, that the *Histoire* properly belongs to that genre of French romance which borrowed directly from later medieval Scotland a range of materials and themes; and we owe to R. L. G. Ritchie the opinion that the historical prototype was King David II (1329–71), whose eventful career and chivalric interests lent themselves to literary extravagances of this type.[66]

The possibility that Earl David went on crusade thus turns upon Fordun and the degree of faith we may place in Boece, who if familiar with the *Histoire* also drew much of his information about the earl from either his own imagination or some unidentified historical source. The Paris manuscript, which mentions the earl 'of Northampton' as a crusader between 1202 and 1204, seems so suspect as to be worthless.[67] But if David joined the Third Crusade his involvement is not referred to by any of the contemporary authorities, including the eye-witness Roger of Howden, generally a first-rate source for his career. Nor is there evidence in the public records that Earl David enjoyed the recognised privileges of a crusader at this time. Boece has been dubbed 'a prince of story tellers', and Bishop Dowden had no hesitation in denouncing his work as 'wholly fictitious' where it comments on David.[68] Particularly tantalising is Fordun's cryptic reference to a certain *historia*. Was this pure invention? Suspicions are not allayed by the fact that Fordun, followed by Wyntoun, assigned the earl's crusading venture to 1165: he made the mistake of calling David King William's elder brother and needed to explain why he failed to succeed to the kingdom upon Malcolm IV's death.[69] The problem could perhaps be resolved by assuming that the *historia* was a version of the *Histoire* circulating in Boece's day. But such an argument would depend on assigning an earlier date to the latter work than its manuscript tradition suggests, and (if Ritchie's view be accepted) on asserting that Fordun missed or suppressed the fact that it was a parody of the career of King David II. Nevertheless, while late medieval commentators were prone to cite spurious authorities to give a greater air of conviction to their works, recent critical study recognises that for the late twelfth and the thirteenth centuries Fordun, for all his faults, carefully used genuine narrative material no longer extant.[70] He had ready access to the archives of Aberdeen cathedral, amongst other collections. Boece, a canon of Aberdeen and the first principal of King's College, also had these records at hand; and if Fordun's *historia* is an authentic text it possibly survives in its fullest form, garbled and freely extended, in the *Scotorum Historiae*. To suppose that the references to Earl David as a crusader have an element of truth may still seem more difficult than to suppose that they are unfounded. The possible date of his alleged departure to the Holy Land is about 1190; but there can be no certain conclusions.

In any event, the earl reappears in Scotland in February 1194.[71] Howden reports that in March he supported Hubert Walter against Count John of Mortain, acting with the earl of Chester to besiege Nottingham as King Richard was preparing to return to England from captivity. Upon Richard's arrival the castle fell and Earl David held a place of honour at the council on 30 March following its submission.[72] He accompanied the king to Winchester, attending him with King William to celebrate his second coronation on 17 April.[73] In July David spent time on Angevin service in Normandy. While King Richard diverted Philip Augustus in Touraine, he shared command of the levies investing the French garrison ensconced at Vaudreuil. The success at Nottingham could not be repeated. Philip returned unexpectedly from the south, routed the besieging forces, and was to control the Eure valley for another year.[74] David revisited Normandy in July 1197 and was named as a witness at Rouen in September when Count John, at Richard's request, bound himself with the count of Flanders in an offensive alliance against the French crown.[75]

Earl David was giving the military aid and general support which King Richard naturally expected from an earl of his realm. But the increased scope of David's activities did not preclude continued close involvement in Scottish affairs. By the 1190s he had demonstrably lost Lennox, but his remaining holdings in Scotland required supervision; and although his commitments as an English landowner meant that they did not receive his undivided attention, David visited them as regularly as he could. Moreover, just as his English properties entailed obligations as well as rights, so did his Scottish possessions; and the new earl of Huntingdon was concerned to retain his accustomed importance at the centre, among the Scots king's familiars.

On 2 February 1194, for example, he was associated with a solemn agreement in the royal court at Edinburgh between the bishop-elect of St Andrews and Durham cathedral priory concerning the liberties of the convent's churches in Lothian.[76] Ecclesiastical matters again occupied attention in the late 1190s when Earl David witnessed, amongst other undertakings, a weighty settlement between the canons regular of St Andrews priory and the *célidé*.[77] His enduring prominence in Scottish politics can be judged from the many royal charters he attested in the last decade or so of the twelfth century.[78] More than half were given beyond the Tay or relate to the north-east, as might be expected for one of the king's principal magnate supporters in that region. He was allowed the customary courtesy as chief witness, ceding precedence only to church dignitaries; patrons of religion continued to specify prayers and masses for the earl's soul as well as King William's.[79] To this period also belongs the marriage of his illegitimate daughter Ada to Malise, younger brother of Earl Gilbert of Strathearn, an alliance which strengthened the relationship between the royal house and a powerful native dynasty north of the Forth.[80] David's visit to Elgin in May 1196 or 1197 suggests that he took part in King William's campaigns against Earl Harold of Orkney in Caithness.[81]

It is notable, too, that from 1185 Earl David participated at the Angevin royal court when Anglo-Scottish affairs constituted the main item of business, normally attending with King William as he had done in the past. The most memorable of these negotiations was concluded during his visit to Canterbury on 5 December 1189 when King Richard formally released William from all subjection and obedience for Scotland, the rich treasure offered in return emphasising the Scots king's anxiety to recover full sovereignty and *de jure* independence.[82] The surrender of the legal basis of overlordship and the restoration of Berwick and Roxburgh served to increase the earl's value as a focus of Angevin attempts to influence Scottish policies. But for the moment a major source of tension between the crowns had been removed, the prospect of war was further diminished, and England's chief priority was secured. What seems at first an inexplicable *volte-face* was in this sense a continuation rather than a reversal of Henry II's policy. And in these circumstances Earl David was able to enjoy the trust of both kings, giving each of them his unequivocal support and avoiding any conflict of personal allegiance.

King William, however, had not forgotten his claims to the northern counties, although policies involving military aggression remained discredited and for the time being diplomacy was thought to offer the best way forward. He contributed generously to Richard's ransom and refused assistance to Count John's rising in 1194. The stage was set for renewed overtures to a monarch who had earlier displayed in his financial need an especial readiness to placate the Scots. At Winchester in April 1194, with Earl David present, King William offered to purchase the earldom of Northumberland, *impasse* being reached only upon Richard's refusal to transfer the castles.[83] Scottish policy towards the Border shires was to concern David far more directly in 1195 when William, as yet denied a legitimate son, planned to marry his eldest daughter Margaret to Richard's nephew and ally the future Emperor Otto IV, with the intention that Margaret should inherit the kingdom. The couple were to be endowed meanwhile with Lothian by William and with Northumberland and Cumberland by Richard; putting the interests of a daughter above those of a brother, these proposals, if successful, would also have excluded Earl David in advance from the succession.[84]

At this point it is appropriate to refer to the plea made in 1291–2 by Count Florence of Holland, fourth in line of descent from David's sister Ada, during the Great Cause.[85] The central argument was that David had renounced all rights of succession in return for Garioch, that is, no later than 1182. But his supposed charter of resignation, known only from a fourteenth-century text in the Dutch comital archives, is unquestionably a forgery,[86] and any suggestion that the earl had relinquished his rights to the kingdom in early life would seem to make a nonsense of Howden's assertion that an influential aristocratic faction resisted King William's proposals of 1195 on the grounds that custom demanded Margaret should not succeed so long as David and his son were alive.[87] Succession of the nearest male collateral was preferable to that of a surviving daughter, albeit the senior claimant by primogenitary law.

King William had seriously underestimated the strength of support for Earl David from the magnates, who doubtless resented the notion of a German consort holding sway over them as much as they were prejudiced against female inheritance of the realm. The project proved abortive,[88] and it is difficult to know how David viewed these machinations. For thirty years effectively next in line of succession, he must have felt that when William had lain dangerously ill at Clackmannan in early 1195, his path to the throne might soon be clear. It was this incapacity that had given special urgency to the succession question, and it would hardly be surprising if relations between the two men cooled once the earl had learned of the intention to disinherit him. But Howden, who knew David and may have visited Scotland in 1195,[89] made no allusion to any rift when he, our sole authority, reported the marriage plans. There are also positive indications that the brothers were not seriously estranged and continued their normal association. Possibly David was prepared willingly to sacrifice his rights in the interests of state policies. Probably, he acquiesced in his brother's schemes because he realised how faint was their chance of success.

However this may be, the birth of King William's son Alexander on 24 August 1198 was indisputably a significant turn of events for Earl David's career.[90] Although Alexander's title as a king's son, born in the purple, may seem impeccable, no doubt succession customs were still sufficiently undecided to give David a strong claim to the kingdom on grounds of nearness in degree. William was the first king of Scots for a century to be in a position to pronounce upon the right of a surviving son (or indeed daughter) in the lifetime of a younger brother, and if the succession of kings from 1097 has the appearance of primogeniture, with no element of tanistry, accidents of birth and mortality had helped to prevent conflicting claims from arising. Moreover, Count John's ascent to the English throne in 1199, a collateral excluding the direct descendant, was a clear breach of the strict hereditary principle. Not for nothing did King William's sympathies apparently rest with his great-nephew Arthur of Brittany, the primogenitary heir.[91] But Alexander lasted, he was politically acceptable, and he followed his father as king in 1214. His birth may have been the occasion for a genuine formal quitclaim by Earl David, saving his future right; he certainly offered Alexander his homage, although it must be noted that he delayed doing so until four years after the general recognition of Alexander as King William's heir in 1201.[92]

In effect, David was no longer, at least in King William's lifetime, one step from the crown. He is recorded as a witness to only a single Scots royal charter between c. 1200 and 1219, and though he remained far more of a force in Scottish society, both at court and in the localities, than this evidence suggests,[93] the basic shift in circumstances cannot be disguised. The earl's personal prospects were diminished, with the result that his status was more firmly tied to his existing Anglo-Scottish concerns; his interests and the fortunes of his own lineage rested even more fundamentally upon peace between the realms.

Throughout King Richard's reign harmony prevailed, and because there was no breakdown in relations it was easy and acceptable for Earl David to hold lands in both kingdoms. King John's reign, during which the Scots king advanced his territorial claims with renewed determination, proved a more testing period. King William remained reluctant to prosecute his demands through war. Major disorders affected the northern periphery of the kingdom in 1201–2, 1211–12 and 1214; dogged by ill health and anxious for Alexander's peaceful accession, he was loath to risk any action that might further endanger the stability of the realm. Even so, while the Anglo-Scottish peace held until 1215 it was at times precariously balanced. The negotiations of Richard's reign had led King William once again to believe in the possibility of recovering the northern shires. But to allow the Scots king his patrimony, even as a tenant-in-chief of the English crown, would involve too great an accretion to Scottish strength. This was an old argument, yet it featured ever more prominently when England's resources were being mobilised on an unparalleled scale to carry the escalating costs of campaigns in France. But besides troops and money King John needed security. Thus relations with Scotland required all his talents of cajolery and constraint to avoid or delay a military confrontation. The Scots, however, would not accept peace without concessions indefinitely, and as John's troubles multiplied at home and overseas a fresh element was introduced into the situation. Increasing restiveness among the 'Northerners' brought John into conflict with powerful magnates of the north of England. In 1173–4 they had generally eschewed alliance with King William, but by the early thirteenth century many more northern landowners held estates in Scotland or had connections with Scottish-based families.[94] These ties, assiduously nurtured by the Scots king, gave an added incentive to attack; while John's refusal to countenance a negotiated settlement, made plain by the substitution of coercion for prevarication in 1209, undoubtedly increased the chances of war when, after a young and vigorous king had succeeded in Scotland, rebellion finally overtook him. Alexander II sided with the rebel barons in 1215–17, and by then Earl David was too elderly and infirm to throw himself into political life. But at the onset of John's reign, as the Angevin established his position and strove to stem the encroaching tide of Capetian conquest, he was conspicuously active in delicate diplomacy between the realms, not so much as the Scots king's spokesman, but as an accredited emissary of the English crown who worked hard for peace.

Recognising Earl David's value to the new regime, Hubert Walter had invited him with other influential figures, including the earl of Chester, to Northampton in April 1199, where he was persuaded to declare in John's favour as king-elect.[95] King William wasted no time in pressing for the Border shires in return for his recognition and support. Assured of David's alliance, Hubert Walter sent him from Northampton to urge William to hold back until John was crowned and could offer the judgement of his court.[96] The earl was again dispatched to Scotland in early 1200, the timing of this mission suggesting that he relayed proposals for a conference at York.[97] He returned to mediate as John's envoy in the autumn, and escorted William both to and from Lincoln in November.[98] At Lincoln, King William persisted in his claims; but protracted discussions resulted only in a truce pending further negotiation, and since by treating with John personally William could no longer withhold his homage for Tynedale and the Huntingdon honour, a valuable bargaining counter was sacrificed. The Scots king had repeatedly demanded his inheritance, an agreement seemed more remote than ever, and relations between the two monarchs were considerably strained. King William had refused to meet John at Northampton in June 1199; he had broken the appointment at York in March 1200 when an interview had been John's main motive for a brief spring visit from Normandy. On both occasions John had been unable to make preliminary proposals to suggest a basis for profitable discussions; exasperated, William had intimated that if he could not gain satisfaction peacefully he would resort to *force majeure*.[99] Yet nothing is heard of belligerent manoeuvrings by the Scots as a result of the rebuff at Lincoln. Rather, in February 1201 John seized the initiative, making an intimidating display of his power in the Border counties and inspecting the fortifications at Newcastle, Bamburgh and Carlisle. The Scots had lost a major advantage: John and Philip Augustus were at peace for two years from May 1200. Though potentially William remained a dangerous enemy, for the moment his bluff was called.

Although Earl David travelled from court to court in an official capacity, his true role and negotiating authority inevitably remain obscure. It would perhaps be easy to exaggerate his importance at this time. He moved freely between the realms, and his interests in the two kingdoms identified him with John's need of peace to concentrate on France. But the confidence he had gained with his brother through long and meritorious service had recently been undermined: he had been quick to recognise John, nearly two years before William eventually paid homage at Lincoln, and the Scots king could not give him unqualified trust when he was co-operating so closely with the Angevin monarch. Furthermore, the diplomatic envoys acting for John at the Scottish court in these years included other well-connected lords besides Earl David. Robert de Ros and Eustace de Vesci exercised a wide personal influence in northern England and were accustomed to acting in concert: each had married an illegitimate daughter of King William, both men were landed in Scotland, and both were employed on Scottish embassies in 1199–1200.[100] Another of David's kinsmen, Saer de Quincy IV, future earl of Winchester, was active in the exchanges. The son of Robert de Quincy, justiciar of Lothian, he held by patrimony modest estates in the English Midlands and a major fief based on Leuchars in Fife.[101] Saer's brother-in-law Bishop Roger of St Andrews, King William's former chancellor, also gained experience as a mediator between the crowns in 1199 and 1200.[102] The significance of these men in John's Scottish negotiations is confirmed by his personal interest in their advancement. Bishop Roger, for example, was being supported with the custody of Peterborough abbey; and in 1200–1 he was the royal candidate for the bishopric of Lincoln, although his bid foundered when the cathedral chapter refused to be swayed by the king.[103] Nevertheless, John clearly recognised the importance of Earl David's mediation and arguably employed him as chief negotiator and peacemaker. More busily engaged than his colleagues, he also had the most to lose materially in the event of hostilities: when he spoke in John's name he would assuredly have been speaking his own mind, although this does not invalidate the suggestion that he regarded peace as being in Scotland's best interests. He still carried weight in Scottish politics, and the earl's lack of support for an aggressive stance towards England may have served to crystallise existing moderate opinion.

These years gave Earl David a new prominence in public affairs, and in between his missions to the Scottish court he demonstrated his loyalty to King John in other spheres. He had taken ship for Normandy on royal service by July 1199, and he accompanied the king at Château Gaillard, Rouen and Lire in August and September. He helped to assert John's authority at Le Mans and Chinon and was still overseas carrying out operations 'in servitio regis' in October.[104] Shortly after King Willam had declined to meet John at York in March 1200, David attended the Angevin court at Fulham with many prominent curialists.[105] That summer he again crossed the Channel on the king's causes; and in August 1202 he was at Le Mans when John returned in triumph from his victory at Mirebeau. He then remained on royal business in Maine and Normandy until early autumn.[106] He also served in the king's last Norman campaign, appearing at Rouen in November 1203 when Philip Augustus was encircling Château Gaillard a few miles up the Seine.[107]

Earl David continued to support John's continental policy after the loss of Normandy. He was not associated with the opposition to the king's plans for a French campaign in 1205, though he must have sympathised privately with those Anglo-Norman magnates who hoped that a firm peace with the French crown would enable them to retain their fiefs on both sides of the Channel.[108] He waited on John at Windsor in April; he was in attendance when the king mustered his forces at Northampton in May; and he followed the *curia regis* to Portsmouth and Bishop's Stoke, where John expected to make his final preparations for embarkation.[109] That David was advanced a loan of £100 by the paymasters of the army suggests he intended to cross to Poitou.[110]

In September and October, after the projected expedition had been cancelled, the earl again presented himself at court.[111] John, free for the moment of continental entanglements but alarmed by reports of disaffection in northern England and the rumours of a French invasion,[112] was now disposed to resume the discussions with King William. Relations had remained uneasy; nor were they improved by intelligence of John's recent approaches to Earl Harold of Orkney and King Reginald of Man, which must have been resented in Scotland.[113] There were other interventions likely to have offended Scottish sensibilities.[114] But talks about the Border shires were tentatively reopened by the bishop of London,[115] and despite John's former intransigence William and his advisers decided to make renewed attempts at a peaceful settlement. On 30 November 1205 letters of safe-conduct were made out for the Scots king. A specially distinguished delegation escorted him in all honour to York the following February, and as a further expression of good intent Earl David was sent north so that he could remain in Scotland while King William was in England. The best interpretation of this arrangement may be that a lengthy conference was anticipated and that David was still regarded with sufficient confidence in the Scottish royal circle to be given the task of protecting the crown's interests during the absence of the king. The evidence is slight and ambiguous; but at least we know that William had personally requested his presence in Scotland.[116]

An agreement was not secured at York, but we have no further details. King William again met John for fruitless talks at York in May 1207; another meeting requested by John that autumn did not occur.[117] Earl David was apparently uninvolved in these deliberations, though diplomacy as well as other business may well have brought him to Scotland in 1208. His itinerary places him at Selkirk on 6 July, where he would have had the opportunity of sounding out the Scottish position before he reported back to John at King's Cliffe some two weeks later.[118] He was officially on Angevin service 'de Scocia' in early 1209 when Scottish affairs again came to the fore.[119] If he conveyed formal proposals they proved sterile, for when the two kings parleyed in April their negotiations were abortive. All hope of reaching agreement appeared to be extinguished and both countries were poised on the brink of war.

The fortification of Tweedmouth opposite Berwick, a sensitive area where a new castle could easily upset the *status quo*, had given offence to the Scots. Continued prevarication over the question of the northern counties was more irritating still; and King William had begun seriously to explore the possibility of a French alliance, an initiative which seemed especially threatening because barons in northern England were also in touch with King Philip.[120] Earl David's stance as a prominent member of William's war council at Stirling on 24 May 1209 can only be guessed at, but in view of his earlier record as an intermediary it is reasonable to count him among the 'friends of either king' who, according to a plausible account, urged the folly of hostilities and eventually persuaded William to disperse his army.[121] The immediate danger passed, however, John was in no mood for generous gestures, and for the Scots the *forma pacis* sealed at Norham on Tweed on 7 August was a mortifying capitulation. 'King John . . . had terrified his adversary, bullied him into giving hostages, extracted a large sum of money from him, and left him subservient but surely bitterly resentful. For the rest of King William's life John had no cause to fear Scotland.'[122] Three years later, at Durham in February 1212, the Angevin once more dictated terms. Whatever the legal theory – demands for a recognition of overlordship were seemingly not made on either occasion – John behaved as though he were suzerain of Scotland: Falaise was remembered while Canterbury was ignored. Earl David's position was inevitably affected. Until 1209 arguments for peace with England could be expressed in terms of the good of the Scots realm, and the earl's concern to safeguard his lands had not clashed seriously with his political loyalties as a Scottish magnate. Even now a realistic appraisal would have shown that John was arguing from strength. In fact the balance of forces had rested firmly in John's favour at least since 1205, when William may have begun to moderate his demands.[123] Nevertheless, whereas King Richard had accepted money for concessions, John's demands were solely a means of coercion, and peace had been preserved not only without true compromise but in a manner derogatory to the dignity of the Scots king and kingdom. Supporters of the view that diplomacy would prove an effective weapon in fully realising Scottish territorial claims were wholly discredited, and in the longer term the risk of war was therefore intensified.

The issues brought to a head in 1209 had yet wider ramifications for Earl David's career. John had set a high value on his allegiance when Scottish military intervention had been genuinely feared, and for as long as that threat had existed his position had been extremely profitable. There were the normal perquisites of royal service whereby the earl's legal actions were adjourned during his absences as John's envoy to Scotland or on the king's affairs in France;[124] welcome respites or quittances were given on debts to the crown.[125] Attentive to David's Scottish interests, in October 1199 John conferred extensive trading privileges upon the burgesses of Dundee;[126] and of utmost significance were the grants of real property which served to augment the earl's personal wealth and permit some much-needed patronage of loyal dependants. Between 1199 and 1202, John solicitously confirmed and enlarged King Richard's dispositions at Nassington, Yarwell (Northants) and Godmanchester (Hunts); he ratified Richard's grant of Tottenham (Middlesex) and freed the manor from the claims of Jews; and he gave the manors of Alconbury and Brampton (Hunts).[127] In 1205 John offered one of David's natural sons the custody of the heiress of Ralph of Cornhill, apparently hoping to forge a marriage between the earl's family and one of the rising administrative dynasties of Angevin governance.[128] About this time, David celebrated the birth of his youngest son and eventual heir by naming him John in honour of the king, his possible godfather. But since the earl's importance to King John stemmed largely from the degree to which Scotland represented a challenge to his security, David's standing would be affected by any transformation of the political situation. As the dangers of Scottish invasion receded, the alliance between king and earl began to weaken and David was gradually removed from the centre of English political life.

The repercussions for Earl David were serious. Though his English honour carried the prestige of comital rank, there was a closer correlation between his social prominence and its territorial and economic basis in Scotland, where he held sway with important regional powers. Since he lacked an undisputed power base in English society, his fortunes were therefore closely tied to steady support from the crown. He could not afford to be eclipsed by rivals, and he must have been deeply concerned when the king concentrated his bounty upon an ever-more exclusive clique from which he was barred. The change in personal fortunes did not occur without a period of transition; but after 1205 his recorded appearances in John's presence are few.[129] He sent his service to Ireland in 1210 and to Wales in 1211;[130] yet once the crown was no longer prepared to shore up his position through fresh grants of land, in common with others who were not the king's intimates he ceased to be sheltered from the growing oppressiveness of the royal administration. Pressure began to be turned against him concerning his franchises in 1206;[131] two years later he was being pursued over *debita Judeorum* of £300. This amount had originally appeared, as debts to Aaron of Lincoln, on the pipe roll account of 1191, and the abrupt demand for settlement, disregarding in fact earlier quittances, was a clear sign that the earl no longer enjoyed the full support of the English crown.[132] He was fined £200 for encroachments as a result of the forest eyre of 1207-9, contrary to the liberties of the Huntingdon honour. In addition, the earl's 'good lordship' was eroded because the merciless weight of the forest administration also fell upon his tenants, unless they had paid the king for individual confirmations of their immunities.[133] In 1211 David's debts to the Exchequer totalled £1,100; this huge commitment was then reduced, but only to £900 and on condition that he settled within three years.[134] (By a belated act of royal grace, the amercement for forest offences was apparently waived.) The threats to his financial well-being and personal power mounted. Burdened with indebtedness and set stringent terms of repayment, he would be compelled in his extremity to sell off one of the richer and more accessible demesne manors of the Huntingdon honour.[135]

Although in the middle years of the reign there were barons who experienced John's displeasure more intensely, Earl David's treatment showed the kind of harassment that a lord lacking the royal goodwill had to endure, and how it could undermine his influence. Relations continued to deteriorate. In summer 1212 the two men were sufficiently estranged for John to suspect David of conspiring with other magnates to contrive his assassination. Within days of the king's learning of the conspiracy on 16 August, a flurry of government letters reminded the earl that his son was a hostage and ordered him to surrender Fotheringhay castle, his principal English residence. If necessary, the sheriff had instructions to mobilise the *posse comitatus* and reduce the castle by force of arms.[136]

Whether or not Earl David was correctly suspected of complicity is impossible to determine with exactness. It has been suggested that the plotters were spurred on by John's authorisation on 1 June of a detailed inquest into tenure and service in order to augment his resources for an overseas campaign;[137] and David clearly had reason to resent this investigation as a further mark of John's arbitrariness and rapacity. Surviving returns show that a full inquiry was conducted into the dependencies of the

Huntingdon honour in Lincolnshire, and nothing was said by the sheriff about the Scots king's superiority.[138] This earnest scrutiny followed hard on the unprecedented demand for scutage from the earl for the whole fief, due according to the Exchequer account of 1211 in respect of the fourth scutage of the reign (1203).[139] The honour was exempt from scutage *per cartam*: David had a confirmation of this exceptional privilege, along with other liberties, dated 24 June 1190.[140] John was seeking to bring the earl, as lord of the Huntingdon honour, unequivocally into a direct relationship of tenure and service to himself by further challenging his franchises and by placing him on the same level as any ordinary tenant-in-chief by knight-service.

David had additional grounds for believing that his position was particularly precarious as the year 1212 unfolded. In May John had summarily recalled Godmanchester, one of the earl's richest establishments. David had allowed several dependants to take shares in part of this manor, but they were also dispossessed 'without lawful judgement', and his personal influence was depleted twofold. Moreover, these men responded by requesting from David lands of equal worth to those they had lost,[141] and at approximately the same time other feoffees were likewise demanding exchanges for the earl's failure to guarantee their titles. Helen de Moreville, supported by her son (and David's son-in-law) Alan, lord of Galloway, had acted to implead the earl over important Huntingdon interests, and judgement was made in her favour about August 1212.[142] Helen's case had been a good one; but this represented yet another serious blow to David, and it would not have escaped notice that Alan of Galloway, a valuable source of mercenary troops, was then enjoying every advantage of King John's benevolence.[143] In the summer of 1212 David nursed sufficient grievances for him to be embittered. Did they impel him to plot John's death?

To have abandoned the moderation which he had shown in negotiations between the crowns would have entailed not only a major change of heart but involvement in a *coup de main* which had signally failed to win Scottish support; and if Wendover's assertion that King William actually warned John of his personal danger can be accepted, it may seem unlikely that Earl David was thoroughly committed to regicide.[144] However much he may have been out of sympathy with William earlier, there is no sign of a continuing rift. In 1208, for instance, David had been named as the guarantor for William's enormous Jewish debts.[145] The following year the Scots king agreed to the marriage of the earl's eldest daughter Margaret to Alan of Galloway; by 1210 his second daughter Isabel was the wife of Robert de Brus IV of Annandale, whose uncle had been allied to an illegitimate daughter of King William in 1183.[146] In September 1209 David was at Perth with the king when inundations destroyed the castle and forced them to retreat hastily by boat. He was also at the king's great council of Stirling in October of that year when debate was renewed on ways of satisfying the indemnity imposed by John at Norham on Tweed.[147] In any event, the retribution John inflicted upon Earl David was mild by contrast with the Angevin's treatment of the acknowledged ringleaders.[148] The intention was not so much to proscribe him as a rebel as to guarantee his subservience and loyalty. Yet John, perhaps distrustful of David's Scottish interests now that he was no longer useful as an agent of reconciliation between the realms, had found an opportunity to enforce political discipline. It underlined the weakness of David's position when the Scots were quiescent, and marked a clear breach between the earl and the small group of familiars upon whom the king had come to rely.

From 1213, however, as John prepared for a new campaign of re-conquest on the Continent, England was moving rapidly towards political crisis. Assured of the continued co-operation of King William but confronted by intensified difficulties internally and abroad, John desperately tried to stabilise his position by widening his circle of supporters, and Earl David was able to regain a measure of political influence. He had already been reinstated in some degree by early autumn 1212, when he had been employed on unspecified business 'in servitio regis'.[149] On 23 August 1213 he was with John at Southampton when many barons had deserted the king's court in opposition to the projected expedition to Poitou. David did not serve in France; nor can he be shown sending knights or contributing to the Poitevin scutage.[150] Nonetheless, the Justiciar wrote instructing the earl to confer with him at London in August 1214 'super negociis domini regis regnique ejus negociis'. Though the letter was peremptory in tone, it indicates that the administration appreciated the value of his collaboration and was confident of receiving it.[151] A royal directive of 5 March 1215, issued on the day after John had assumed the Cross, ordered the sheriff of Cambridgeshire and Huntingdonshire to allow David his customary third penny.[152] Conciliation was throughout associated with firmness, for as the baronial opposition gathered momentum John was also cautious in his approaches to David. Hostages were retained as sureties for his good behaviour, and Fotheringhay castle remained with royal custodians. Reinforced with outworks and mercenaries in April 1215, it was not restored until the general reconciliation at Runnymede in June.[153]

These measures seem to have helped to secure Earl David's political neutrality before England lurched again into civil war in September. That reseisin of Fotheringhay was conditional upon renewal of his homage has encouraged the suggestion that he had been a party to the baronial defiance of 5 May, but this appears unlikely.[154] There are gaps in the evidence; yet none of his lands seems to have been declared forfeit in the weeks before Magna Carta, and no source names him as a supporter of the opposition camp at that time. His apparent lack of involvement in the discussions of baronial grievances at Stamford, Northampton and Brackley, centres adjacent to his English properties, is perhaps a little surprising, if only because it was unwise to remain undecided in areas where the discontented were predominant. A variety of connections also tied him to the leading rebels. Of the twenty-five barons appointed to enforce Magna Carta, three – all Anglo-Scottish landowners – were his nephews by marriage: Earl Henry de Bohun, Robert de Ros and Eustace de Vesci. Indeed, David's relationship with Vesci may have been one reason why John had suspected him of treason in 1212.[155] William de Mowbray, John Fitz Robert and Robert Fitz Walter were his tenants in the Huntingdon honour. Earl Saer de Quincy, another cross-Border lord, was also his vassal, and personal contacts between David and this remote kinsman were close.[156] But however much familial, tenurial or territorial bonds determined the composition of the baronial party, they did not bring David to the fore of the opposition in early 1215. He may have been waiting to see how the young Alexander II would play his hand, but there was a more private consideration. A valuable insight is provided by John of Fordun, drawing on earlier annals now lost, in his account of King William's death and the inauguration of Alexander in December 1214. When David had attended the new king at Scone and followed his brother's remains to Arbroath for burial, he was, says Fordun, 'neither alert in mind nor active in body', a comment which finds telling confirmation in the terms of John's mandate for the restoration of Fotheringhay of 21 June 1215.[157] During these months Earl David, who was then in his sixties, evidently lacked the vigour for political action.

But by autumn 1215 it was impossible to remain uncommitted any longer. With the crushing of disturbances in Moray and the deteriorating situation in England, King Alexander was free and eager to invade. Resort to war represented a rejection of all that the earl had stood for as a patron of peace between the crowns, but John's uncompromising diplomacy and the consequent lack of genuine progress over the Scottish claims to the Border shires ensured that whenever the political position changed in favour of the Scots there was every chance of hostilities. Events moved quickly and arguments urging armed intervention easily prevailed. Three days after attacking Norham on 19 October, Alexander accepted the homage of the rebel barons of Northumbria. Within three weeks, John was assigning lands belonging to Earl David to his own supporters, the first confiscation being authorised on 6 November.[158] In reality, rebellion for David was the action of a man devoid of choice, unless he was to betray his nephew and incur the outright animosity of powerful opposition magnates in the Midlands. By March 1216 the whole Huntingdon honour, saving the fees of those sub-tenants in John's peace, had passed into the custody of the king's mercenary captain Gerard de Sotteghem; subsequently it was transferred to William Marshal *junior*.[159] David was listed in a government memorandum of spring 1216 as a rebel in arms; the well-informed Barnwell chronicler named him amongst those who supported the claim of Prince Louis to the English crown.[160]

Except for these jejune details there is no light on Earl David's activity during the war. Fotheringhay was in John's hands by January 1216;[161] and although there was a strong rebel faction among the knights and freeholders of the Huntingdon fief, David, weakened by advanced years and failing health, apparently made no direct call upon their service. Simon of Brixworth, for example, joined the malcontents in the defence of Rochester; Robert of Bassingham, once the earl's steward, held out with the rebels at Colchester; Ralph Morin surrendered at Belvoir; and William Burdet served at Mountsorrel.[162] David's bastard sons, Henry and Philip, also joined other retinues, and fought in the rebel army at Lincoln.[163]

On 23 September 1217 David, now aged sixty-five, obtained letters of protection from the English crown. It is surely significant that this safe-conduct was dated on the very day that the regency government opened negotiations with King Alexander, who by this time had become isolated from his former allies and was anxious for peace.[164] The earl's position was as inextricably bound up with the problem of Anglo-Scottish relations as it had been so often in the past. On 19 December Alexander II received possession of the Huntingdon honour, 'which Earl David held of him . . . as Alexander has come into King Henry's faith and service'.[165] Fotheringhay, however, remained at the disposal of William Marshal.[166] That David himself did not secure letters of reseisin until 13 March 1218[167] can probably be explained by a prolonged absence in Scotland which prevented him from coming to the Angevin court and giving homage. He may have stayed in self-imposed exile on his Scottish lands for most of the war, an old man keeping at a safe distance from a kingdom torn by civil strife and invasion.

Earl David died at Yardley Hastings (Northants) on 17 June 1219. He succumbed, so Fordun tells us, after a protracted illness, and although his long-standing intention had been to be buried in the abbey church of his foundation at Lindores in Fife, the earl's servants carried his body no farther than Huntingdonshire for burial at Sawtry abbey.[168] John, his son and heir, survived him as a minor. The eighteenth-century antiquary Alexander Nisbet has possibly preserved a garbled account of the arrangements for custody of the Scottish patrimony in commenting that Henry of Brechin, a bastard son, 'was by King Alexander II made Earl [*sic*] of Garrioch'.[169] The principle of prerogative wardship operated in England and the entire English lordship passed to Henry III.[170] On 16 July Countess Maud, who lived until 1233 but did not remarry, received five manors for her maintenance.[171] On 29 October in the same year Alexander II secured for a token sum custody of the Huntingdon honour, 'which Earl David held of him . . . and the said king of Scots ought to hold of King Henry in chief', although he met with obstruction from William Marshal who, reluctant to forsake his war gains, had reoccupied Yardley Hastings and was to withhold Fotheringhay at least until the end of 1220.[172] On 12 March 1221 it was reported that Alexander had transferred the custody to Earl Ranulf of Chester, clearly King Henry's nominee.[173]

Earl David's obituaries were short, for his activity in later years had been obscure and unimpressive. His retirement from the political stage in Scotland was so complete by 1214 that he seems to have had no place in the administration to advise King William's young successor; in England, if he was privy to the conspiracy of 1212, 'this was his last real political fling'.[174] Yet looking back across the years, David's career was important and eventful. It naturally falls into two main phases, although even after 1185 certain aspects of his activity continued as before. Most notably, he for long retained distinction in Scottish government, both at court and in his holding of land in districts remote from the normal centres of political life; and after Alexander's birth the earl could still be brought into the heart of affairs. But from 1185 Earl David's actions were strongly influenced by the desire to retain both his Scottish and English possessions as a single complex of lands and lordship. There were clear disadvantages in being bound in faith and allegiance to two rulers who had yet to establish a lasting *modus vivendi* because of their failure to resolve their outstanding differences. One thirteenth-century commentator described David as 'a man of great power both in England and in Scotland'.[175] He might appropriately have added that David's prominence in the two kingdoms was never completely assured and always prey to the vicissitudes of practical politics.

In other words, there are dangers in stressing Earl David's importance for Anglo-Scottish relations. Inevitably his standing was affected by issues beyond his control, which would either support or harm his position. Most obviously, in 1215 the political situation in England was so attractive to Scottish intervention, and John's intransigence so manifest, that the earl was swept along by events. Earlier, there is no positive proof that he ever had a decisive say in the formulation of policies, but plainly he interpreted it as his duty to work for peace. In this the manoeuvring and expertise required may not in fact have been unduly taxing. Arguably, only in 1199–1200 and 1209 could he have been accused of disloyalty to Scottish interests; yet on neither occasion was the kingdom favourably placed to become embroiled in renewed hostilities with England. Necessity justified restraint; and thus his own desire for *rapprochement* was prevented from turning into enduring difficulties with the Scots king and did not bring his fidelity into serious question. But if the significance of Earl David's impact on exchanges between the crowns must be qualified in these ways, his career nevertheless brought him positions of honour in Scotland and England, and for thirty years before his forfeiture he was generally able to concentrate upon his broad lands as any magnate would wish. Every allowance made, the earl's activity showed how it was possible to win favour at the two royal courts and serve both political masters, giving to each the support which a good vassal owed his lord. Moreover, in his personal lordship, and as an advocate of harmony between the realms, he represented vested interests which were growing stronger as the pattern of cross-Border proprietorship became increasingly elaborate. The following chapters will give greater weight to the many influences which, viewed from the level of baronial landholding, were steadily drawing the two kingdoms closer together and towards the stability of a genuine understanding.

4

THE ESTATES IN SCOTLAND

(I)

Earl David's far-flung landholdings from 1185 confirmed his political and social prominence on both sides of the Anglo-Scottish Border, and to divide them by kingdom for convenience of analysis risks creating a division dangerously at odds with his outlook, ambitions and actions. The English and Scottish properties had laid upon them similar but separate staffs of officials, just as the great cross-Channel estates of the time naturally fell into different administrative groupings.[1] Yet the earl's land agents drew authority from the same source; their lord imposed a real personal unity upon all his lands by frequent travel about them; and men associated with his property in one realm obtained interests in his property in the other, such was the lack of concern for the Border in the private affairs of this powerful magnate.[2] That these estates lay in two kingdoms did not prevent degrees of integration between them; nor were those in Scotland in any sense secondary to the English. The approach adopted here must be followed on the strict understanding that the history of the earl's Scottish or English holdings can be fully comprehended only against the background of the larger scheme of lordship to which they belonged.

Compared with his English tenures, the Scottish properties are very imperfectly documented. In the absence of equivalent records of royal government, our written information derives almost entirely from title-deeds, in particular from the extant charters passed in Earl David's name, the bulk of which are known from the thirteenth-century Lindores abbey cartulary. Only one text survives for the earldom of Lennox, in which his interest was in any case short-lived, and attention must be directed exclusively to the eastern Scottish possessions. The problem of sparse evidence is compounded by other drawbacks, although none is peculiar to these lands. Normally issued on the initiative of beneficiaries, charters are legal instruments which can impart only the restricted information they served to perpetuate. By their nature they present a fragmentary picture of estate organisation, and plausible conjecture is often all that can be offered instead of certain conclusions. Moreover, David's Scottish *acta* were written by scribes trained in Anglo-Norman traditions of diplomatic, and their stylised *formulae* can easily obscure or ignore divergences from English practice.[3] Our main argument will emphasise that Earl David, as a leading representative of the new landowning aristocracy raised up by the Scottish crown in the twelfth-century kingdom, inaugurated a fresh stage in the development of territorial lordship throughout the estates permanently subject to him.

The political and social changes which were involved largely occurred within the pattern provided by feudal conventions. But the fact remains that no alternative category of historical documentation exists to which we can turn in order to consider the vital question of the relationship between the traditional basis of society and the innovations that were superimposed. Although the great fiefs of the early medieval realm are only now beginning to attract serious scholarly attention, it is clear that the available written material generally conspires to conceal much that was ancient and unaltered within them.

This study then is in essence an exercise in charter analysis. Yet limited and inadequate though the sources are, few contemporary Scottish estates in secular ownership have left an equally ample archive, and David's lands thus seem particularly suitable for what is the first detailed investigation to be published in a neglected field. As the discussion proceeds, we may bear in mind other considerations of a general sort. Because feudalism came late to southern Scotland, and even later to the north, the kingdom was being strengthened by feudal practices when elsewhere lord-vassal relations had often lost their original force. In England, furthermore, the great fiefs of the late twelfth century normally lacked vitality as units of government due to geographical fragmentation and the burgeoning judicial and administrative powers of the crown. The Scots king, however, lacked comparable institutional controls and remained to a far larger extent dependent upon the magnates. The principal burden of providing effective local government fell upon this class, accountable to the king but privileged and powerful, mainly of Anglo-continental descent but by no means exclusively so. The functions of magnate estates in Scotland accordingly retained fundamental importance long after the fiefs founded during the Norman settlement of England were losing ground to other types of social and political organisation. The major comparisons that can be drawn between Earl David's English and Scottish estates highlight this contrast. The dispersion of his territorial resources in England ensured that his personal influence over both lands and men was fragmented also, while by 1185 these possessions had already experienced a century of complex pressures inimical to seigneurial authority.[4] Contrariwise, the present concern is a large landed estate in which it was possible to exercise regional powers and whose emergence as a feudal lordship began with the earl.

Finally, although chiefly assembled when systematic colonisation by royal appointees in *Scotia* proper had effectively just started, even in Scottish terms David's fief was a late creation. When it is appreciated that few Scottish private charters belong to the period before 1170, this gives the undertaking an added relevance. We can trace the ordering of an establishment that in southern Scotland (and indeed in England) was often more or less fully developed when the sources begin to survive in any quantity for study of its internal arrangements. What can be observed is a great fief in the making, how rights of lordship were made more secure to benefit the new

57

lord and, ultimately, the Scots king himself.

Antecedents

Earl David's powerful eastern Scottish estate was constructed in stages. The main outlines were fixed by *c.* 1179 and it attained its widest extent about the 1190s.[5] As befitted a prince of the royal house, this was so substantial an appanage that, even deprived of Lennox, David ranked among the wealthiest and strongest noblemen of the kingdom. However much the English lands contributed to his incomes, these interests were therefore always sufficiently large and important for him to be closely concerned for their control and exploitation. Garioch was by far the major property. To the south, ancillary estates were accumulated in the Mearns at Inverbervie and at Ecclesgreig, now in (but formerly equivalent to) the parish of St Cyrus. One of the earl's bastards held land in Brechin: that this holding also formed part of the endowment is probable although not certain.[6] A third group of tenures, again more disjointed and less compact than Garioch, but collectively imposing, straddled the Tay estuary and focused upon Dundee. Little can be said of the only Scottish estate south of the Forth, Morton in Midlothian. This remote accession apparently fulfilled a dual role as a stopping-place on journeys between England and Garioch and a convenient base for attending court and councils at Edinburgh, which 'was already beginning to assume its historic position as the capital of Scotland'.[7]

In its alienations between Fife and the Mounth, the Scots crown was not concerned to deliver large tracts of territory into single hands. Ecclesgreig, for instance, lay separated from Inverbervie by an intricate distribution of feus held by knight-service or serjeanty.[8] Nevertheless, Earl David's more southerly holdings were in essence unitary, individually embracing several square miles and possessing a full range of reserves to support their economies. Although their recorded history normally begins with their grant to the earl, these self-contained enclaves, each comprising hamlets and farms attached by common subordination to a main settlement – the administrative, economic and perhaps religious centre – were founded on an already age-old system of royal lordship and agricultural exploitation. By long usage the fundamental relationship between the chief touns and their appurtenant members was tributary, expressed in the scheme of payments in kind owed by satellite settlements to parent villages. Typically, demesne cultivation was small scale or altogether absent; typically, these groupings were called shires and had been administered for the crown by thanes or local managers, *ministeriales* indispensable to the running of the land but drawn from the peasantry and lacking full seigneurial rights. The shire structure is well seen at Longforgan in the Carse of Gowrie. Today the large rectangular parish reaching back from the Tay into the Sidlaws delineates the approximate bounds of Earl David's *scira*. Longforgan (formerly Foregrund), *caput* of the shire, lay close to freely drained loams, with several units appendant upon it. This organisation has a demonstrably ancient appearance when first documented.[9] It does not display a crop of place-names containing the distinctive P-Celtic prefix *pit*<*pett*, denoting 'portion' or 'piece', similar to that found at Ecclesgreig (Pitbeadlie and the lost Pethergus, Pethannot).[10] Between Dundee and Strathmore the later Gaelic element *baile*, 'homestead', more commonly identifies a shire's principal dependent holdings.[11] But the etymology of Foregrund itself, a compound of *for* and the Brittonic or Pictish *gronn* ('above the bog'),[12] suggests a settlement date before Gaelic took deep root in this area in the ninth century. In their recent independent writings G. W. S. Barrow and G. R. J. Jones have expertly consolidated our knowledge of the form of royal administration upon which Longforgan-*scira* was based.[13] Shires and thanages, lathes and sokes – whatever the different regional names – were common types of federal lordship or multiple-estate organisation of great antiquity. Survival patterns varied from one part of Britain to another; but Earl David's fief affords important evidence that in eastern Scotland north of the Forth these time-honoured political and agrarian arrangements provided the essential territorial framework for the new order of lands held *per servitium militum*, at least at the primary stage of infeftment between king and baron.

With Scone, Coupar Angus and Strathardle, Longforgan was previously one of the four royal shires of Gowrie, producing food renders in wheat.[14] Ecclesgreig, an ancient Celtic centre of Christian worship whose name embodies the Brittonic or P-Celtic word **eglēs*, from Vulgar Latin *eclesiā*, was also a long-standing shire.[15] The same can most probably be claimed for Inverbervie, certainly an anciently settled village. The name was once Aberbervie (Haberberui), incorporating the P-Celtic element *aber* ('confluence', 'river-mouth'), changed to *inbhear* under Gaelic influence.[16] At Dundee, where David controlled several subordinate holdings as well as the burgh itself, he evidently held much of Dundeeshire, first recorded as a defined land unit in the 1170s.[17] Similarly, the king's lands falling to his power at Newtyle in Strathmore and at Lindores in Fife had surely been administered, either as single properties or as dependencies of wider clusters, by thanes responsible for enforcing discipline and collecting the surpluses to which the crown was traditionally entitled.[18]

Recent royal patronage had made inroads into these holdings, involving some dislocation of their structure, before they had passed to Earl David. The Church had been the chief beneficiary. At Ecclesgreig, for example, the ecclesiastical property of the shire had been transferred to St Andrews cathedral priory; the canons also held the church of Longforgan, its glebe at Kingoodie, and the teinds 'de tota syra de Foregrund'.[19] Newtyle church formed part of the foundation endowment of Arbroath abbey, and in Dundeeshire Hadgillin, now lost, had gone to Hugh Giffard by 1178, possibly through royal grant.[20] These dispositions were part of a wider reorganisation of resources between the Mounth and the Tay as the Scots king had responded to the demands of religious and secular patronage. At

Kinnaird in Gowrie, where King William had made a knight's feu for Ralph Ruffus, Pitmiddle had been reserved for Richard *clericus regis* and was subsequently attached to David's adjacent interests at Longforgan.[21]

As the king had exercised his powers of endowment, the links between *appendicia* and central estates had been weakened or broken, yet traditional arrangements were not seriously distorted in consequence. Even allowing for the twelfth-century 'drift away from the demesne' in England,[22] there is an obvious contrast with the English manors retained for the earl's support. Admittedly, in Northamptonshire his hundredal manor (formerly the soke) of Yardley Hastings still bore some traces of a federal system of land management, just as in Middlesex his manor (formerly the shire) of Tottenham contained the fossilised remnants of a like organisation of reserves.[23] In the northern Danelaw his great soke of Greetham displayed rather more pronounced vestiges of an early order of purveyance.[24] The lay honours of midland and southern England accommodated diverse local conditions; but the pressures of manorialism had long ago combined, through the development of seigneurial demesnes, and patronage and leasing, generally to obliterate antecedent forms under a complex patchwork of superimposed subdivisions. In Earl David's Scottish estates south of Aberdeenshire the ancient pattern of lordship had not been superseded. The basic constituent was not the 'typical' manor, drawing its unity from the needs of the home-farm, but a grouping which in England finds its closest contemporary analogy with the shires of Northumbria, where 'thanes had lingered longer, had given way to barons and knights more quietly and gradually than elsewhere'.[25] Moreover, the size of David's shires, small by comparison with the multiple estates reconstructed by historians in certain other contexts, may be not so much the result of fission as a sign of their greater antiquity. They perhaps represent the original nuclei from which discrete estates of much larger dimensions had elsewhere been formed.[26]

But it was the regional lordship of Garioch, approximately one hundred square miles in extent, that constituted Earl David's chief Scottish power base. Although outliers of the Grampian range are the dominating features, physically Garioch belongs more to the lowland zone of Aberdeenshire and has long been considered a prime grain-growing district. Whereas the toponymic evidence is principally Gaelic in origin, a significant number of place-names retain P-Celtic forms, notably the *pit*-names near Oyne (Pitmachie, Petmathen) and Durno (Pitbee, Pitcaple, Pitscurry, Pittodrie). These names are compounds containing a second Gaelic element; Petmathen, for instance, means 'middle share', from Gaelic *meadhon*. But if they must have been coined no earlier than the ninth century, it may seem realistic to suppose that the word *pit* would only have been widely adopted in naming (or renaming) settlements in areas of Gaelic colonisation already supporting a substantial Pictish population; and in this regard it cannot escape notice that the Garioch lowlands are rich in the oldest group of Pictish symbol-stones.[27] It may well be that the decisive phase of rural

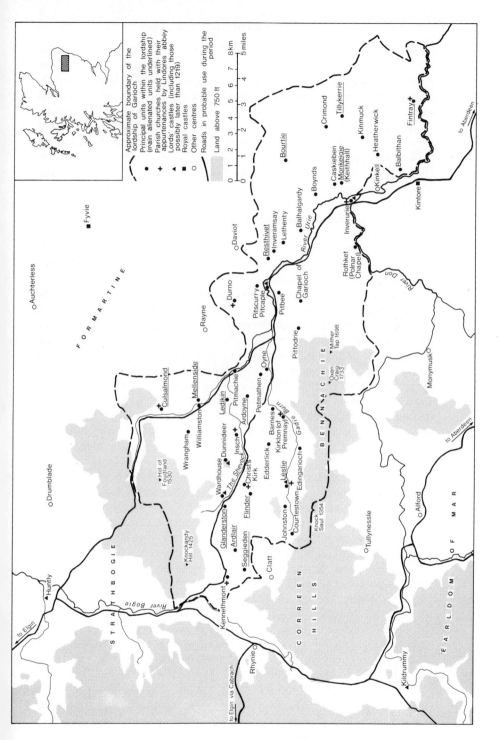

Map 2. Garioch under Earl David

settlement had been achieved in pre-Gaelic times, when the resources of Garioch had possibly been almost as fully exploited as they were in the 1170s. In any event, improvements after the 1170s evidently represent the tail-end of a process of internal colonisation already well advanced. The best farmlands, east of Inverurie and along the valleys of The Shevock and Gadie Burn, had been the chief areas of attraction, and the early modern settlement pattern, showing close correlation of 'the distribution of deep fertile soils with the sites of the farming townships',[28] can already be recognised in the charters. The Garioch Earl David acquired thus boasted a developed agrarian economy, one that had progressed far beyond the tribal pastoralism once regarded as the characteristic basis of the Celtic polity. Though the importance of grazings should be acknowledged, particularly on the slopes of the Correen Hills and Bennachie, also valued as a game reserve, in the earl's grant of rents and taxes from this lordship to endow Lindores abbey the teind of corn and flour took precedence of the teind of butter, cheese and the other proceeds of stock-raising.[29]

Garioch does not appear to have been an exceptionally large integral shire. The *pit*-names flanking Oyne and Durno seem to identify two focal estates to which were attached dependent peasant hamlets. Closer investigation suggests an ancient system of exploitation based overall on a dozen or so districts of villages and farmsteads, whose shape was roughly preserved in the grid of ecclesiastical parishes imposed on Garioch during Earl David's lifetime or shortly before. Individually these composite units present some familiar features. There is no positive proof that they were ever called *scire* and managed by thanes; but there is a strong presumption that this had been the case, perhaps most obviously at Leslie in western Garioch with its principal recorded dependencies, the unidentified Mache and Hachennegort.[30]

A well-established organisation for the management of the king's territorial resources thus formed the point of departure for the development of Earl David's eastern Scottish fief. The bulk of the estate was to be held as the king had best possessed it – 'ita libere et quiete in omnibus sicut ego ipse unquam terras illas tenui et possedi'.[31] This is the stipulation of William the Lion's charter of *c*. 1179, which was sufficiently far removed from the usual jingle, 'sicut alii barones mei . . . feuda sua de me tenent', to provide David's successors in the late Middle Ages with a basis for rights or claims to hold as lords of regality, at any rate in Garioch. It was only in the fourteenth century that the term *regalitas* found its way into Scottish charters as a means of defining a lordship invested with quasi-regal powers. Can Garioch be regarded as a regality in everything but name from *c*. 1179? Unfortunately the evidence is inadequate to establish the true nature of the administrative and judicial privileges acquired and exercised by Earl David personally. The fourteenth-century lords of Garioch who held *regaliter* depended for their title upon royal *acta* conveying the lordship to them in the manner that David had held it, while in 1374 × 1384 Lindores abbey claimed to possess its lands in Garioch, as granted by David, *in liberam regalitatem.*[32] As with the English palatinates, however, we cannot simply assume that the formal immunities actually existed long before they were first recorded. Although Garioch would subsequently be considered to have been granted to David as a regality, the full-blown development of extensive public rights may only have come after his death.[33]

Even so, Earl David undoubtedly began in a position of some strength. Contemporary charters fall far short of being a comprehensive source for peasant liabilities and dues, their classification, origin and relative import- ance. But among the categories of men brought under the earl's power were those called *nativi* (neyfs), who were so completely at their master's disposal as to be treated as his personal possessions.[34] Seigneurial control was evidently reinforced by the ancient justiciary powers of sake, soke, team and infangenthief, not the substance of highest franchise but later the concomitant of tenure *in liberam baroniam.*[35] Judicial authority was the source of coercion and constraint, and these rights of justice, the only ones expressly assigned to Earl David by charter, represented the jurisdiction that chiefly mattered to a lord in ensuring the effective ordering of peasant society. Apart from the emoluments of justice, incomes are described in terms of money rents and issues in kind embracing a wide range of food-stuffs and animal by-products. A lucrative imposition on peasant surpluses was the communal requisitions, customary food liveries in some part sup-planted by money equivalents, which were public in origin and evoke an age when lordship was primarily a personal affair. Thus by delegation David took his cain and the equally archaic but still profitable conveth, exacted from time immemorial in recognition of the king's personal superiority.[36] These were the most basic of common burdens, although possibly they were tending to become territorialised, so that they were mingled with private ground-rents levied on individual holdings. Certainly, authority over the land itself was sufficiently developed for the new lord to demand the latter.[37] Peasant households paid teinds and oblations to parish churches which the earl regarded as rightful appurtenances of his endowment; they were bound to grind their grain at his mills and pay multures; and they kept the mills, a major capital resource, in good repair.[38] Nor does this exhaust the range of dues and obligations that without doubt existed upon David's accession. Profit was to be had from peasant exchanges by charging toll on the sale of livestock and other goods.[39] The subordination of the local community was further emphasised by the duty to render common army service (or com-mutation payments) whenever the king demanded it.[40] On the other hand, there is no explicit evidence that rent had ever been paid in the form of burdensome agricultural works. In the heavily manorialised counties of England, to be a serf was to be liable to regular labour on the lord's home-farm; but the serfdom of twelfth-century Scotland seems to bear closer kinship with, say, the serfdom found by Norman-French settlers in the Welsh March. Labour dues appear generally to have been light and seasonal; as with 'Marcher unfreedom', personal dependence was expressed principally through the delivery of produce payments and cash renders, and 'was not characterized by heavy labour services geared to demesne exploitation'.[41]

These attributes of lordship, so far as they are sketchily revealed in the charters, were seemingly common to all Earl David's lands in eastern Scotland. Though they represent a pre-demesnial system of exploitation, they also testify to an exercise of dominion that had advanced beyond the first stage of lordship over men. But by delegating territory to an incoming magnate the crown expected to gain more power than it had dispersed, for to grant land to a trusted vassal was to fasten a closer control on the countryside and its resources. And the *dominium* of a magnate who ruled over a large, unified district in the king's name would naturally mean far more than the *dominium* of a magnate whose landed base did not include important concentrated holdings. The essential difference between Garioch and David's other east Scottish estates was the quality of compactness over an extensive area, not internal structure. Yet that contrast is fundamental.

The basic question is to determine whether or not this contrast reflects a deliberate royal policy, which recognised that in remoter areas a firm basis of control could be achieved only through a wide delegation of territorial power. There are two recent accounts of the significance of regional fiefs such as Garioch. Dealing with Domesday England, J. Le Patourel has stressed a military or strategic purpose, regarding them as instruments of active penetration, often meticulously shaped by the amalgamation of existing tenancies and royal land in order to discipline broad areas and integrate them more closely in the government of the kingdom.[42] This view has been questioned by G. W. S. Barrow who has argued that the regional infeftments of south-west Scotland (and north-west England) are best explained by supposing that incoming lords assumed administrative divisions whose origins were ancient: 'It is on the cards, though not certain, that they were Celtic.' New fiefs fitted into an old form of district lordship, but one based on 'a thorough-going royal power', by contrast with Anglicised Lothian where single knights' feus, sometimes intricately scattered, were generally the rule; kings did not exercise any close control over the nature of fiefs granted out, but apparently gave what came conveniently to hand – compact blocks, single villages or dispersed holdings.[43] If this thesis is fully subscribed to for Scotland as a whole, it has to be assumed that pre-existing public authority was remarkably effective and, of course, that the actual framework of the feudal settlement was not directly influenced by strategic or political considerations. Such an assumption, however, seems difficult to accept. The extent to which the prestige of the twelfth-century Scots monarchy in peripheral areas was due to inherited Celtic powers will no doubt be a matter for continued debate. But some support for an interpretation stressing royal planning of infeftments on a controlled regional basis has already been offered in the previous chapter, and there is further evidence to be considered which will make it possible to reinforce the argument. While it is clear that provincial fiefs are usually to be found outside the districts where the Scots royal government was strongest, the chief problem is that little has been written in detail about them. More light might be thrown if we were able to decide upon Garioch's origins. Was it a new territorial configuration or anciently established?

It is regrettable that the earlier history of this property is so woefully obscure. Thirteenth-century evidence may help to draw aside the veil. About the 1260s four important divisions formed a half-circle round Garioch: the broad thanage of Formartine with its principal seat at Fyvie, the royal castle-burgh and thanage of Kintore and, on a lesser scale, the thanages of Belhelvie and Aberdeen.[44] These entities represent part of a network of royal rights between the rivers Dee and Spey dating back to Malcolm IV and well before.[45] Other sources direct attention to the rural deanery of Garioch, mentioned by c.1240, which conceivably preserves the rough outline of an ancient civil division.[46] Its core comprised the eleven medieval parishes held contiguously by Earl David: from west to east, Kennethmont, Rathmuriel (Christ's Kirk), Leslie, Insch, Premnay, Culsalmond, Oyne, Durno, Inverurie, Bourtie and Fintray. Also included in the deanery were Clatt and Tullynessle, marching with Kennethmont and Leslie, and Forgue, Auchterless, Rayne and Daviot on the northern flank of the fief. To the south-east, it extended beyond Kintore to embrace the cathedral church of Aberdeen and the parishes of Maryculter and Banchory Devenick, subsequently the nucleus of the deanery of Aberdeen, begun by 1275.[47] Now, before the transfer of the see of Aberdeen from Mortlach (Dufftown, Banffshire) during King David's reign, the chief religious centre between Forgue and Aberdeen was arguably not Monymusk, the site of an old Culdee community and later of an Augustinian priory, but the church of Kinkell across the Don from Kintore. This church has all the characteristics of an ancient mother church or minster that predated the ecclesiastical reforms of the twelfth century: in the 1240s its extensive *parochia* included Kintore and a further five dependent chapels; and when this arrangement first appears in written record it may represent merely the remnant of what had once been a wider jurisdiction. This is at least suggested because though five of Kinkell's pendicles lay within close reach, the chapelry of Drumblade, beside Forgue, was isolated beyond Earl David's lands to the north-west.[48] It might therefore be postulated, albeit very tentatively, that his property was carved out of a swath of royal domain stretching back to Strathbogie, which had once looked towards the *matrix ecclesia* of Kinkell as its ecclesiastical nucleus and possibly to Kintore as the regional administrative *caput*. In this way, perhaps, components of a larger estate, subordinate shires, were withdrawn to found a new subdivision of the whole, while Kintore and Aberdeen were retained as direct centres of royal influence, with Aberdeen rapidly eclipsing Kintore as it continued to consolidate its position.

However this may be, that the fief of Garioch, as opposed to the *decanatus*, was not an ancient integral land-division is virtually certain. As a preliminary point, the twelfth-century kings had been reallocating reserves between Kintore and Strathbogie prior to Earl David's infeftment. The bishopric of Aberdeen had been enriched to support the move from Mortlach; the Anglo-Norman family of Berkeley had acquired Ardoyne (in Oyne); and the Lambertons had taken Bourtie.[49] But alienation had not been heavy, and the creation of David's estate brought a halt to these dispositions in a manner that indicates a distinct change in royal policy, from reasonably small-scale gifts to the grant of an extensive territory *en bloc*. The chief units of his fief were conveyed 'per rectas divisas suas'; presumably their marches were not defined because they were old and unlikely to be disputed. But the district-name Garioch (Gaelic, *Gairbheach*, 'place of roughness') was originally restricted, as the derivation suggests, to the hilly country west of Oyne. This was the usage of King William's charter; the earl's properties on the east were granted under the names of the main settlements.[50] Then by 1195 the term Garioch had begun to take in all these elements, a powerful reason for believing that under David they were first conjoined as a distinct division.[51] In this light we can more readily understand why one of the earl's first cares was to clarify the precise limits of his entire Aberdeenshire lordship by ordering a formal perambulation of its bounds.[52] The component parts were old established; but together they made a new estate, and the express agency of the king would seem clearly discernible.

It is also important that land in the Garioch region had recently been committed to other proprietors, for the effect of Earl David's intrusion upon these parties most plainly reveals the deliberate nature of his fief's compactness. The bishop of Aberdeen remained in undisturbed possession of the probable *scire* of Clatt, Tullynessle, Rayne and Daviot adjoining David's lands on the south-west and north. By contrast, the Lamberton and Berkeley feus were included within the earl's boundaries.[53] This reordering of established interests seems explicable only according to the dictates of political or strategic necessity. Bourtie extended David's lordship north of Inverurie and the castle-burgh he was to found in that place; more significant was the inclusion of Ardoyne, almost midway between the eastern and western extremities of the fief. An additional strand in the argument is that he was also allowed to engross the ancient patrimony of the bishopric of St Andrews in Culsalmond and Monkeigie (Keithhall).[54] Quite simply, had these properties been excluded a solid block of land would not have passed under Earl David's control.

This evidence tends to divert attention from the areas of Norman-French expansion where regional fiefs fitted neatly into established arrangements to those strategic districts in England where the crown had demonstrably intervened to begin great unified commands out of complex configurations, through tenurial readjustments designed either to redraw ancient boundaries or to create separate enclaves where none had existed before.[55] More generally, it appears in fact that current views on the nature of regional fiefs are not totally irreconcilable. The formidable advantages in consigning concentrated territories to trustworthy lords seem plain enough. Their value to expanding governments had indeed long been recognised, especially in marchland zones.[56] Quite apart from special military or strategic needs, strong lordship depended upon a broad territorial base; one that was fragmented dissipated authority and encouraged rivalries between magnates struggling to assert their position. What counted, then, was possession by faithful vassals of whole districts; the Scots king's overall control over the process of endowment was never in any doubt; and in the last resort the preservation of ready-made territorial units, as much as the development of new conglomerations, depended upon a conscious royal decision. Although in Scotland feudal colonisation was usually a more peaceful and ordered affair, there is an obvious parallel with Wales. The ancient cantreds and commotes which Norman lords took over in that land formed an admirable basis for penetration, and 'they preserved or adopted or mangled them as occasion required'.[57]

Too much, therefore, should not be made of an estate's antiquity; by the same token, too much perhaps should not be made of Garioch's 'newness'. But the circumstances of its foundation may help to bring home that crown patronage on such a scale was more than simply a matter of lavish rewards for members of the Scottish royal line or other court favourites.[58] The north-eastern plain may seem more secure to us in retrospect than was realised at the time; fear of disorder was justified by occasional raiding and doubtless fortified by imagined threats of incursions from the Highland expanses. Moreover, it has been argued elsewhere that the stability of this region and safe communications across it were essential to the ultimate success of a prolonged campaign to incorporate the far north in a unified kingdom of Scots.[59] By *c.*1180 a distinctive pattern of small tenancies was already appearing in the former earldom of Gowrie and in Angus, while the Mearns would also be allowed to fragment into individual feus, though not much earlier than the 1190s. Garioch's lord benefited from scattered gifts in his turn. In these districts, where it would have been possible to have made large-scale infeftments, the king's position was the more firmly established and did not need to be secured through sharing out wide territorial powers.[60] But Earl David was also strongly ensconced in advance of the Mounth, and as Scots kings continued to deal with the problem of extending royal control, large blocks of land put into the hands of *immigré* lords would become a pronounced feature of the northern reaches of the realm. The grant of Garioch thus heralded the second main phase in the creation of a powerful regional aristocracy directly under the crown, the first, confined to south-west Scotland, having been all but completed by King David I, long before the emergence of Ayr and Dumfries as major royal bases at the end of the twelfth century.[61] And this onward allocation of huge self-contained commands, whether or not they were adapted to an ancient distribution of territorial lordship and whatever the governmental rights associated with them, looks very much like the continuation of a purposeful policy designed specifically to link outlying areas more closely with the main centres of the kingdom. They served to maintain and advance royal power where, as in northern England, 'the organization of local administration around the sheriff frequently appeared weak and unsatisfactory',[62] as well as in some measure to occupy the gaps between the Celtic earldoms or provinces remaining in native hands until the crown could associate them more firmly with its rule.

Infeftment by royal *fiat*, however, was only the first step, for the success of crown policy ultimately depended upon the innovations effected by the fief-holder in whom the king placed his trust. The importance of regional fiefs can thus be fully appreciated only by studying each in turn; and by assessing the changes introduced in one major estate we can arrive at a clearer understanding of the relationship between the growing strength of the Scots king's government and the rise of the great feudal command. The evidence for reviewing the antecedents of Earl David's holdings is extremely patchy, and we must not overestimate the framework of authority to which the new seigneurial controls would be harnessed. The acquisition of Garioch and less remote lands brought him well-founded judicial and economic rights; but previously lordship had been only to a limited extent interposed between king and peasantry. A good deal would be incorporated into, rather than superseded by, the new structure; but a simpler form of superiority over land and people was converted into firm territorial power by a lord whose ascendancy was defined or enlarged according to immediate needs. This was achieved through administrative consolidation and by patronage; and the remainder of this chapter is principally concerned with the ways in which the machinery of lordship became more institutionalised, at once enhancing Earl David's position as *dominus terre* and bringing the countryside subject to him more steadfastly under the influence of the crown.

Estate Centres and Officials

'Le groupe fédéral . . . était tout premièrement un groupe tributaire.'[63] This quotation seems especially applicable to Earl David's acquisitions. They had been managed to support the king rather than powerful indigenous noble households; and since none had sustained a major royal residence there had been no pressing call for demesne production to supply the variable demands of a peripatetic court. The earl's Scottish shires and his English manors had developed in different ways. One of his charters for Lindores abbey insisted: 'Nolo autem quod predicti monachi aliquem firmariorum meorum uel hominum super terras suas recipiant.' Although apparently unable to jettison all the characteristics of the unfree, the *firmarii* may have included thanes.[64] In any event, we should probably resist the temptation to regard them as peasant rent-payers who, like the *censuarii* of English record, had set their agricultural works to rent. Nor need they indicate, as usually is the case in English sources, a leasing policy involving demesne fields. At the earl's infeftment, the economy which they helped to support was one in which profits were preponderantly drawn from ancient peasant land.

In one important sense, assessment of the impact of Earl David's lordship depends upon whether this system of exploitation persisted practically unaltered, or whether the effect of his administration was sufficiently comprehensive to transform the agricultural routine. The short answer is that there is nothing in our sources to suggest sweeping innovations in the economic organisation of agrarian society. At this level custom would appear to have been king, especially in the deeply conservative region of Garioch. Nonetheless, despite his wide commitments in England from 1185, the earl took his duties as a Scottish landowner far more seriously than a mere absentee solely concerned for the prompt collection of revenue. To say that 'Earl David resided chiefly on his English possessions'[65] gives a dangerously misleading impression of his attitude. He sought quite deliberately to run his lands from above along new lines, and the general stability of local arrangements therefore contrasts sharply with the changes that overlaid them. It was in this context that the administrative consolidation proceeded.

A castle certainly existed at Inverbervie by the second decade following Earl David's death and was probably a creation of his lordship; he may have founded Brechin castle (a possible motte), mentioned by 1267, as an alternative staging-post to facilitate communications between Tayside and his Aberdeenshire properties.[66] These were subsidiary centres of authority. Garioch and the Tayside lands, the main sources of the earl's wealth and power, were made dependent upon two major foci, respectively the castle-burghs of Inverurie and Dundee. In the exercise of strong government it had long been the case that castle and lordship went together, and by *c.* 1200 the Scottish Lowlands had become almost as much a land of castles as England or the March of Wales. But whereas by the reign of King Henry II the rate of baronial foundation of English boroughs had easily outstripped that of new royal creations, and an increasing number of boroughs were not associated with castles,[67] in twelfth-century Scotland the burgh remained to all intents and purposes part of a nucleus of crown influence, which also involved a castle, a sheriff and, more or less closely, a royal abbey or priory. The particular nature of Earl David's principal headquarters thus distinguished his estates from almost every other contemporary fief of the kingdom and placed at his disposal a source of prestige and lordship that very few magnates in Scotland as yet enjoyed.[68] Current research on the early royal burghs suggests that in secure areas some became prosperous centres soon after incorporation; that others were already thriving communities before they actually assumed the legal trappings of burghal status;

and that none of those in either category can be regarded simply as 'an economic counterpart to the new castle'.[69] Such considerations seem relevant to Dundee but not to Inverurie.

The development of Inverurie as the *caput* of Garioch was one of Earl David's first important decisions: the burgh is recorded by 1195; the castle had been established no later than 1199.[70] Although Inverurie was not founded entirely from new, there is no evidence that this place, perhaps a shire dependency but not the central settlement, had enjoyed any special prominence as part of the king's domain. More positively, Inverurie ranked as a chapelry subordinate to Rothket church (Polnar Chapel) until the 1190s when the burgh gained full parochial standing in its stead,[71] a reorganisation which strongly suggests that Inverurie only took on importance at David's command. This departure above all others marked the opening of a new period in Garioch's history. The castle-burgh stood as a visible expression of the seigneurial dominance that now bore down on an outlying Celtic district; lordship had assumed a stronger territorial base.

Of the little burgh, huddled between the castle earthworks and the junction of the rivers Urie and Don,[72] no physical trace remains. The modern town has migrated to higher ground, but the intrusion of a railway embankment, a sewage farm and a cemetery has denied the archaeologist a promising location, while documentary information on the early medieval burgh remains virtually non-existent. This said, however, its trade can scarcely have extended beyond the profits of local exchanges and the limited opportunities they offered for commercial success. Indeed, it seems unlikely that the plantation was originally intended to assume an economic role transcending immediate requirements. Almost everything about this settlement evokes the specially franchised hamlets or 'pseudo-boroughs' of Anglo-Norman Ireland and those French *bourgs* distinct from ordinary villages but still of fundamentally rural aspect.[73] From the earl's point of view, the object was to secure a range of specialist services on the restricted scale appropriate to a tiny market centre in the lee of his castle: supply of the castle's needs in provisions and, in an emergency, in manpower, and a means of redistributing to his advantage such peasant renders paid in produce as were not consumed in his hall. For Norman England itself, it has been recently and cogently argued that magnates often had modest expectations of their burghal creations, as 'the support groups of military and administrative centres'.[74] Earl David's burgh at Inverurie, a simple *burgus castri*, would seem to conform closely to this model.

In describing adjacent estate units, the earl's charters for Garioch adopted indefinite words like *terra, villa* and *territorium*. The davoch (Latin, *davata*), an ancient measure of arable capacity, appears in one text, and it may often be disguised by a form more familiar to south-country clerks, the *carucata*.[75] There is no mention of a home-farm or even of the term *dominicum* in the broader sense of property directly subject to the lord and distinct from parts of the estate given to tenants in feu or to the Church. One scribe, it is true, referred to the *maneria* of Garioch,[76] but this word, though here used territorially, could be so carelessly employed in charters as to make its significance in relation to agrarian practices unclear. What we are allowed sight of is a demesne lordship apparently expressed through direct exploitation by the earl, or by his representatives, of mills, churches, hunting-rights and (at least on Tayside) fisheries, rather than of arable, meadow and pasture.

The argument that under Earl David the economic basis of his estates remained one largely to be explained by other than manorial arrangements compels caution because the available material is so obviously uninformative and one-sided. Title-deeds have greater chances of survival than routine administrative precepts: collections of written *acta* therefore concentrate upon alienated land rather than upon land kept to sustain the lord and will rarely reveal details of estate management. If there were demesne acres in Garioch significant by comparison with peasant holdings, the most likely place to find them is near Inverurie itself, where the earl's lordship impinged most forcibly and where the burgh may have stimulated more immediate forms of exploitation. Land directly identified with the castle probably stretched north to Balhalgardy and possibly as far as Inveramsay, and in the east extensive reserves were still retained to the south of Bourtie after Fintray had passed to Lindores abbey.[77] An attempt was thus made to conserve interests around the *caput*, reserving outer holdings for grants in feu or in alms. Moreover, a bond settlement perhaps burdened with agricultural services lay close by at Boynds.[78] Yet the evidence for Inverurie as a centre of seigneurial demesne remains uncertain and ambiguous. We do know that land between Inverurie and the bridge of Balhalgardy was *ad firmam* to the burgh by 1237. The arrangement may then have been of long-standing; and this involvement in agriculture, albeit presumably with eyes on market opportunities, seems an apt comment on a burgh barely separate economically from the surrounding countryside.[79] In part the burgh's fields may have been worked by the burgesses with their own hands; the bulk of their leasehold no doubt comprised peasant tenements from which, once they had taken their profits, the renders due were channelled to the lord's household.

Nevertheless, even if unaccompanied by radical changes in the traditional agrarian regime, to Earl David personally the castle-burgh represented a broad-based instrument of government, fulfilling as one interdependent unit several roles simultaneously and making his authority felt in an indomitable manner. It was the pivot of economic administration for the castle-area, that is the whole of Garioch, where revenues were received and kept in secure storage or sold. It was the lord's residence and judicial centre. All these functions were different aspects of the lordship it imposed to dominate and exploit the territory subject to its influence. It was also a strong military base, and although the administrative element rapidly subsumed the military, strategic considerations had been uppermost in deter-

Plate 2. Inverurie, looking s w. The motte (now the Bass), trimmed as a result
of alterations in 1849 and 1883, is some 50 ft (15 m) high with a summit area
approximately 60 ft (18 m) in diameter. The tiny bailey (the Little Bass) is
overgrown with trees. The burgh was presumably located E and s of the castle
earthworks, between the rivers Urie (in foreground) and Don. (Courtesy of
the Cambridge University Collection of Air Photographs; British Crown
copyright reserved.)

mining its siting. The low-lying ground to the north-west contains the
richest crop-growing lands of the region: there the well-drained soil series
now distinguished as the Insch Association have 'an inherently high degree
of fertility'.[80] But areas beyond Inveramsay were directly exposed to the
threat of attack from the Highlands, and fear of possible incursions must
have urged the desirability of a safer location. Thus in Garioch proper
alienation proceeded apace and resources were whittled away, leaving an
enclave around Insch probably consisting entirely of peasant land.[81] Closer
to Kintore and Aberdeen, Inverurie benefited from the stability these royal

Plate 3. Fotheringhay, looking ssw. Though the castle was considerably modified from the late fourteenth century, the original motte and bailey, *caput* of the honour of Huntingdon under Earl David and his principal English residence (see p. 113), clearly show. Compared to Inverurie, they have a more 'domesticated' appearance, as is to be expected of a castle at an important centre of demesne farming in midland England. The motte, 23 ft (7 m) high but with a summit 98 ft (30 m) across, is less imposing than the Bass, the bailey much larger than the Little Bass. (Courtesy of the Cambridge University Collection of Air Photographs; British Crown copyright reserved.)

centres afforded and, in turn, contributed to it. The most arresting feature was the castle, and even though held in peace its power was the essential precondition of effective landownership. Built for security as well as display, the motte and bailey furnish one of the best examples of twelfth-century fortification in north-east Scotland, with the massive motte (the Bass of Inverurie) scarped from a high natural mound.[82] The castle was strongly protected; but the immediate requirements of local lordship were not the only considerations. Commanding important crossings of the Don, with the garrison well placed to control the main alternative routes from the south to Moray, Inverurie was also developed as a base from which Earl David could uphold his wider responsibilities as a leading magnate supporter of the crown.

Dundee presents a contrast. The earl's Tayside properties, congregated where there was a stronger tradition of organised royal government, focused upon a prosperous town rather than a garrison burgh. Little is known of Dundee castle, whose recorded history effectively begins in 1291. But Dundee had acquired burghal privileges by 1195, and burgh and castle probably co-existed from the first, founded together by David himself.[83] To the west the intractable water-logged clays of the haughlands of Gowrie posed a daunting challenge to medieval farming; but in Longforgan to the landward, above Monorgan and Kingoodie, lay farmlands naturally conducive to cereal production, while proximity to Dundee and the markets the burgh served may have directly hurried on the development or expansion of demesnial cultivation on a modest scale. It is difficult to prove this from the exiguous charter evidence, but a local administration was emerging at Longforgan that apparently had no further need of a thane.[84] Another possible demesne farm lay at Lindores on the southern littoral of the Tay opposite Dundee, even though much property was hived off to endow Lindores abbey in the 1190s. Here Earl David exercised a strong authority over natural resources, including the quarrying of stone. He arranged for his corn, perhaps his demesne corn, to be ground free of charge at the abbey's mill if his own mill should ever break down; he reserved pasturage on Mugdrum Island for cows and plough-oxen; and he retained a fishery in the Tay.[85] The earl's personal interests in this place appear to have been of a comprehensive order: later, probably in the 1240s, his grandson William of Brechin saw fit to build a castle at Lindores.[86] Further, the ferry routes across the Tay brought Dundee within easy reach for the dispatch of produce to the market or to the lord's table.

In the mobilisation of these concerns on Tayside, manorial lordship may have acquired a relevance unknown in Garioch. But in discussion of the Tayside properties pride of place must inevitably be given to Dundee itself, whose growth, unlike that of Inverurie, was determined not so much by administrative or strategic influences as by a firmly founded and largely independent commercial importance. Medieval Dundee's later claims to seniority over Perth, a royal burgh by 1127, can be treated with the scepticism such manifestations of civic rivalry properly deserve.[87] Yet although the early burgh is sparsely documented, even for a Scottish town, there seems little doubt that the old shire capital of Dundee was already successfully engaged in trade when Earl David acquired it, and provided a sound basis for the more intensive urbanisation that would follow.[88] Scope for systematic archaeological investigation is strictly limited, for the medieval streets below Dundee Law have been swept away by modern redevelopment. But the record evidence, though singularly scanty, does reveal an

active traffic in town houses or tenement plots within a few years of the first
mention of a burgh. Neighbouring religious houses coveted permanent
access to its market; occasionally they were assigned premises there by
David himself.[89] Several of the earl's burgesses can also be identified:
Nicholas of Aberdeen (? *alias* Nicholas son of Agnes), Albert, Richard of
Bedford, Augustine of Dunwich, Walter Lupus, Hugh Parvus and Warin
Purrok (Porrok).[90] Personal names and by-names are so much a matter of
fashion that some of these men could have been native Scots, but English or
Anglo-French immigrants were clearly anxious to win their share of com-
merce. Under David's lordship we have glimpses of the distinguishing
features of genuine urban life, of a rising town as well as a burgh; it is
difficult to imagine that this prominence was achieved at once, but not that
the burgh was superimposed on an already thriving nucleus. In the next
generation Dundee was one of the few places in 'Scocia vltra Marina' that
were sufficiently well known to be represented in the maps of England and
Scotland by Matthew Paris.[91]

There is little information before 1300 with which to reconstruct the
ways in which Dundee built up its coastal and overseas trade. But thanks to
a fine estuary site and harbour, medieval Dundee's prosperity always depended upon sea-borne exchanges, notably wool and hides in return for
grain and wine. Its merchants were dealing in the London market by
1212;[92] and the presence of Augustine of Dunwich among the first burgesses suggests participation in the cereal trade with a leading East Anglian
port. Nicholas of Aberdeen was known in Yarmouth.[93] In all this there is
some danger of overestimating the momentum attributable to seigneurial
direction, in particular the extent of Earl David's personal contribution.
Nevertheless, his concern to promote economic life can be clearly demonstrated. Having secured burgh status for Dundee in a deliberate attempt to
develop the wealth of an expanding community, in 1199 the earl elicited
from King John valuable trading concessions in England and France.[94] He
personally encouraged individual newcomers to put down firm roots, as in
his gift (on beneficial terms) of a toft to Robert Furmage, a probable burgess
of French birth or descent.[95] This eager advancement of a developing town
is easily explained: a prosperous burgh and its proprietor grew rich together. Commercial growth also went hand in hand with diverting cargoes
from Montrose and St Andrews and, more directly, with breaking Perth's
monopoly over the Firth of Tay by preventing merchandise from proceeding upstream; and Perth's attempts to stifle competition through the protec-
tive measures of King William's great charter of 1209 may mark a significant stage in the process whereby Dundee would ultimately outgrow its
upriver rival and become one of the wealthiest towns of medieval Scotland,
with an importance far less than Edinburgh's, but (after the loss of Berwick)
otherwise challenged only by Aberdeen's.[96] At Inverurie Earl David's
burgus was a simple dependency of the castle; but if Dundee was at once an
administrative and a mercantile centre under the earl, the castle there was

always secondary to the town and its flourishing North Sea trade.

It is one thing to indicate the obvious, material changes that enhanced David's lordship over his estates; quite another to say a great deal about the men who ran them. But so far as general oversight and surveillance were concerned, it is a point of prime importance that a new administrative hierarchy was built up and standardised on the Anglo-Norman pattern. The charter sources name a few of the officials involved, none of whom was of native Scottish extraction. Two persons are known to have served as estate stewards. Despite the lack of a surname, Alan son of Hugh can be safely identified as a tenant of the honour of Huntingdon in Great and Little Paxton (Hunts). Closely tied to the earl personally, this man had first proved his worth in David's service during the war of 1173–4, and later made two separate grants to St Neots priory for the good of the earl's soul.[97] Philip the clerk, 'senescallus comitis' towards 1219, held a toft in Dundee, possibly for accommodation on official sojourns. His name suggests an origin outside Scotland, and this is presumably confirmed by his kinship with Robert Furmage.[98] Too little is recorded about these principal administrative officers to say much more about their careers or to comment specifically on their duties, although the appointment of a steward with clerical experience may indicate a drive towards business methods in land management. The two clients who served David as constables were apparently both associated with Scottish castles. Norman son of Malcolm, a prominent knight established at Leslie in Garioch, had clearly acquired the constableship of Inverurie castle by 1199, and although his line's origins remain obscure, his father, the founder of the family fortunes, was a first-generation Anglo-Norman or Flemish settler in Scotland.[99] Saer de Tenes (Tenys) was the earl's other known constable. Like Alan son of Hugh, he had a base in the Huntingdon honour, at Great Doddington (Northants).[100] No doubt this was an acquisition rather than inherited land, for Saer originally appeared in Scotland under the protection of Earl David's mother, Countess Ada de Warenne. It was from her following that he passed into the earl's circle, and his Warenne associations possibly indicate a tie with the family of Tany (Taneyo, Tanie), whose name was probably derived from Tanis by Avranches and whose English possessions were intermingled with outliers of the Warenne honour.[101] In the 1240s a member of this line, Peter de Tany of Eastwick (Herts), was certainly to serve in England as the estate steward of David's daughter Isabel de Brus.[102] Saer is the chief witness as *constabularius* to the earl's charter granting a new knight's feu at Fintry near Dundee: it may follow that he had a professional interest in the transaction as constable of Dundee.[103] Also at Dundee, the burgh grieve or alderman (*prepositus*), conceivably elected by the burgesses rather than David's appointee, was charged with collecting the *firma burgi*.[104]

So far as the evidence takes us, the pattern of this administration was similar in basic respects to that found in the honour of Huntingdon and other contemporary large estates in England.[105] There was a further extension of seigneurial control by deliberate imitation of an Anglo-Norman model. Moreover, it deserves to be stressed that when Earl David imposed this new official body upon his fief, he provided himself with stewards and constables by appointing adherents of English or Anglo-continental origin, in the case of Alan son of Hugh probably by recruiting directly from his own English lands. Administrative consolidation was also a matter of new men.

The limitations of the sources prevent us from advancing far beyond this point. In late twelfth-century England improving landlords began to adjust to a booming economic climate by stabilising or expanding their demesnes wherever practicable and by running them through reeves and bailiffs more intensively than before. In Earl David's Scottish fief, although superintended from above more efficiently and therefore more profitably, moves towards demesne husbandry were apparently unimportant; chief settlements, notably in conservative Garioch, remained more in the nature of collecting points for rents and communal liveries, and thus the immemorial routine of the countryside continued. The only positive evidence for a native officialdom in close association with the earl is provided by the *judex* or judgement-finder and by a solitary reference to Duncan the mair (*marus*).[106] But it should also be recognised as a distinct possibility that, beneath the estate steward, thanes were in places still employed as in the past, either gathering and transmitting all the rents and renders and occupying a position like that of the later *ballivi* of Garioch,[107] or owing a ferme and occupying a position like that of the *firmarii*.[108] After all, Earl David was not a member of a conquering élite which might hope to change the organisation of peasant society through force of arms or redevelopment following upon the devastation of territories; and even under such conditions 'all lordship had to adjust itself to its local context and in good measure to accept it'.[109] The old, Celtic order sustained the new.

The persisting dissimilarities between the earl's Scottish and English estates in fact arose from many causes, and thanks to the commercial importance of Dundee they have a certain paradoxical aspect. Yet there is a danger of assuming that the rural economy of his Scottish lands was hopelessly primitive and backward. To an extent the differences between the two lordships seem more apparent than real, so that even after the advent of English 'high farming' from the 1180s we must be wary of drawing too sharp a contrast. Just as David's English revenues doubtless helped to slow down a more rigorous exploitation of reserves in Scotland, so the security of his Scottish incomes removed some of the impetus towards entrepreneurial endeavour in England.[110] This particular point, a domestic one, must be pursued in a wider sense, however. Though urban development and population growth played upon the contemporary Scottish economy, market demand remained considerably less robust in north-east Scotland than in midland England. Economic pressures were felt, but in smaller ways. Again, while the money supply was increasing, the inflation encouraging – and compelling – large English landowners to adopt commercial farming probably took off more slowly in Scotland.[111] Yet other trends may have retarded a more systematic exploitation of resources: because of a later start and low knight-service quotas, in the Scottish great estate at the end of the twelfth century subinfeudation had not eroded reserves to the same hazardous extent as in the English; and the crown imposed conspicuously fewer demands upon magnate incomes than did the revenue-raising of the early Angevin kings.

For all these reasons the management of Earl David's Scottish lands should not be made to appear seriously out of touch with economic realities. English evidence may further assist interpretation of the Scottish. Estate studies continue to emphasise that south of the Tweed the 'manorial reaction' nevertheless left large areas where demesne lordship remained weak. Especially in the northernmost shires, the south-west and the Welsh March, where Celtic influences were strongest and classical manors few, the profits of demesne farming were always of incidental worth to lords. It may be argued that as *rentiers* they could not seize fully the opportunities that rising food prices and expanding markets offered; not that they were unable to mobilise non-demesnial resources and, albeit possibly after a tentative beginning, defend their financial interests.[112] Even on large estates typical of high-farming enterprise, rents and other exactions were a major item of income, with the contribution of peasant renders tending to increase from c. 1250. Land hunger, sale of villein services, and cheap wage labour helped keep cash returns high; but it is striking that in one recently studied estate, the abbot of Westminster's, the customary land alone could supply almost fifty per cent of the income though in area it was not significantly more substantial than the demesne.[113]

Earl David's position would naturally be clearer if more precise details were available about price movements in Scotland and the composition of his estate revenues. Even so, it is worth saying that a number of circumstances may have told positively in his favour and against any special weakness. One possible argument is that his ability to extract peasant surpluses through disciplinary controls was less limited than that which he enjoyed under a stronger royal authority in England. The ancient communal liveries, political rather than economic in origin, may indeed have so benefited the lord from the first that high returns were guaranteed; groundrents, possibly more open to exploitation, did not necessarily remain unaltered as land values rose.[114] We do not know whether the earl's estates were generally set at ferme to thanes or other local men, as was evidently the case with the Scots king's domain,[115] or whether they were normally accounted for directly; but we may accept that his *firmarii* held for specified periods rather than as feu-fermours in perpetuity.[116] In any event, though renders could be paid in money, the trend towards commutation was undeniably slow,[117] and produce payments gave good protection, however steeply inflation may have climbed. We may well have identified the most persuasive of all the arguments against uncompromising departures from established usages. It seems difficult to believe that receipts would have been decisively increased through heavy demesne production, restricted in any case by traditional procedures, a probably limited potential labour force, and certainly moderate market opportunities. An old order of purveyance remained relevant because it was geared to current realities – and, not least, to current needs.

This is only one lordship, and it is obviously dangerous to pass from particular example to broad hypothesis. In a magisterial and pioneering study, A. A. M. Duncan has written generally upon land exploitation and management in the early medieval kingdom. But, understandably, the evidence he used focuses on Lothian, is biased towards the late thirteenth century, and chiefly concerns monastic estates. His view that ''high farming'' was a less marked feature of the economy of a magnate's estates than careful collection of rents'[118] has still to be tested by the results of fuller studies. Perhaps more controversially, partly because he believes that the gains of commercial farming largely passed the baronage by, Professor Duncan is led to regard aristocratic incomes as unimpressive.[119] Collectively, the higher nobility in England was undoubtedly a bigger and more prosperous group; one or two Scottish regional commands, predominantly pastoral in nature, may not have been worth in economic terms much more than a couple of rich knights' feus in Lothian.[120] But until other fiefs have been looked at in corresponding detail, the present study should at least serve to drive home that there is room for some caution before assuming that by comparison with the economic reserves of individual magnates in twelfth- and thirteenth-century England, Scottish lordships such as Earl David's must inevitably be classed as second-rate. We have no valuations or extents; but if we take our stand on the whole body of evidence under review, we can be reasonably sure that even at the height of his influence as an English landowner, David's interests, financial as well as social, were divided equally between the two realms.

Finally, it is also important to underline that for all the signs of historical continuity Earl David's infeftment involved more than a simple change in the possession of land. The foundation of the castle-burgh of Inverurie and the promotion of Dundee were conspicuous developments in the organisation of the fief, as was the importation of a new estate bureaucracy. These arrangements made for the increased subjection of the earl's territory to his command and underpinned royal controls. An ancient authority over land and people was being absorbed into a pattern of strong aristocratic *dominium*; as far as was possible and desirable, the assertion of power was being taken one stage further to a more direct form of land ownership. And when we turn to Earl David's patronage of lay vassals and the Church, another dimension to the exercise of lordship, themes of change and seigneurial initiative come yet more insistently to the fore.

5

THE ESTATES IN SCOTLAND
(II)

As a patron of laymen Earl David encouraged systematic colonisation of his lands in eastern Scotland by a foreign class, while through his bounty a substantial share of the wealth of the fief was channelled towards representatives of the reformed religious life. Again, research into these aspects of a magnate's activity deals with problems deserving fuller study by Scottish historians.[1] The newcomers will monopolise attention, and their title-deeds give the impression of a far greater control over the distribution of resources, and hence a more active lordship, than in the earl's English estates. Quite apart from extensive perpetual alienations to the Church, in England generations of subinfeudation had ensured that a huge proportion of David's reserves was in the hands of numerous lineages which owed nothing to him personally and were subject to many influences harmful to seigneurial authority. The greatest disadvantage was that a lord's ability to determine seisin and descent, and thus to choose his own vassals, had in essence been lost; and the more fees had passed under the power of their holders, the more the personal element in homage had waned. Moreover, the earl's position could not be significantly restored by the strictly limited assets available for new grants.[2]

The situation confronting David in Scotland was altogether different. The key figures here are the thanes. For all their personal service to the crown, they lacked a true proprietorship and held precariously, the official character of their status outweighing the sense of property right. This at any rate appears to have been the rule north of the Forth, where, through the insecurity of their standing, they were easily displaced by higher authority. What this means is that, because they were denied good title and proper warranty, a lord was under no obligation to accept them: the assumption that in practice they were 'totally supplanted or at best, in a few districts, reduced to a rare minority'[3] may be unduly influenced by the bias of the sources, which focus upon settlements directly affected by subinfeudations. Even so, the reallocation of reserves could proceed without obstruction by a powerful class of native lairds; and the alienations Earl David made had far more behind them than the need to meet his – by English standards – small quota of ten knights' service as a tenant of the crown, or the desire for spiritual salvation. Historians have in general placed too much emphasis upon knight-service and piety and not enough emphasis upon the importance of securing loyalty. Effective control rested in part upon efficient institutions, but most of all the success of Earl David's lordship was founded upon the capacity, free from the encumbrances frustrating him in England, to build up a following settled on the land and yet closely attached to him by personal bonds. Patronage, the essential complement of administrative innovation, thus had a vital role in the reorganisation of the fief. Yet while this forced changes on customary arrangements, it was conditioned in its turn by ancient territories and ancient rights.

Lay Settlement

If we were to proceed by compiling a simple feodary of lay newcomers it would embrace merely a dozen or so names. The sources on free tenants and feus are too slight for a longer roll-call, and information on the relationship between the tenures of this incoming clientage and the holdings retained by freemen of native ancestry is virtually a complete blank. Inevitably, therefore, the strength of particular interpretations of the tenurial structure is often weakened because of the slender basis upon which they must rest. Nevertheless, in following as closely as possible the build-up of the lay tenantry certain facts do seem to emerge with reasonable clarity, and they are offered in the hope that they may contribute to the foundation for further studies.

David's properties had presented few opportunities for advancement to knightly lines when administered as royal domain, and the Anglo-Norman, Breton or Flemish colonisations documented by the early thirteenth century were overwhelmingly the result of the earl's dispositions rather than earlier patronage by the crown. The Lambertons remained at Bourtie in Garioch as mesne lords, although Alexander of Lamberton's marriage to the heiress of Linlathen, Angus, in time compensated for this loss of honour by restoring them to the direct vassalage of the king.[4] The Berkeleys were unable or unwilling to stay on at Ardoyne: King William granted Laurencekirk in Mearns to Walter de Berkeley's coheiress Agatha 'in excambium terre de Arduuen quam ab ea cepi'. David was now free to deal with Ardoyne as he wished, and Agatha's husband secured a convenient extension of his holdings in Kincardineshire.[5]

These transactions underline the careful royal planning involved in the construction of the earl's endowment; his own personal control was expressed through the creation of new interests. He needed to cater for his children according to their rank and station, and the Scottish estates, hitherto spared the cost of providing big family settlements, supported a large share of this responsibility. Admittedly, although Earl David had three sons by Countess Maud, neither Henry nor David lived long enough to require a landed establishment and John, the eventual heir, was only thirteen when the earl died.[6] Moreover, the influence exercised by their four daughters upon patterns of alienation cannot be reconstructed in any detail, although Margaret and Isabel found their respective husbands, Alan of Galloway and Robert de Brus IV, before 1219. But of the known illegitimate offspring, Ada and the two Henrys are reasonably well documented in their father's lifetime.[7] Ada and her spouse Malise, brother of Earl Gilbert of Strathearn, received in *maritagium* part of Newtyle in Strathmore.[8] Both Henrys were born by 1207, and prior to 1219 they adopted the styles Henry of Stirling and Henry of Brechin. The former was ensconced, presumably by his father, at Monorgan in Longforgan; the latter secured, again apparently by paternal gift, the whole secular lordship of Brechin.[9] One claimed an English endowment at Godmanchester (Hunts) in 1215 and thus aspired to some prominence as an Anglo-Scottish landowner through Earl David's favour.[10] It was Henry of Stirling who must have taken Inchmartine in Gowrie and near-by Pitmiddle.[11] Economically, such estates may have offered themselves for disposal from the start. But Brechin was undoubtedly an important concern – probably Henry of Brechin was David's eldest surviving son, with a household of his own to maintain when his father was still alive.

The earl's offspring naturally had first claims upon his generosity. Their known Scottish endowments lay south of the Mounth, and this pattern of grant seems to have been deliberate: Angus and Perthshire were nearer than Garioch to the main centres of government and security. Beyond the immediate family, tenants appearing in written *acta* hailed from various backgrounds, and their origins, so far as they can be recovered, repay investigation. There are merely two identifiable free tenants of Scottish descent, only one of whom clearly reaped the benefit of a new interest. This was the earl of Strathearn, hardly a typical representative of the native community, who gained Kinnaird by Lindores.[12] The other man was Gilbert (Gillebrigde), who in 1172 had received Earl David's charter for Monorgan, feued to him in perpetual hereditary tenure for a nominal rent as a token of his vassalage.[13] This document, expressed in the formal language of an original grant, is a tersely worded statement couched in Anglo-Norman terms of landholding. But it also illuminates how new developments could dovetail into existing arrangements. Gilbert was *nepos* to Bishop Andrew of Caithness, described as a Scot by nation ('nacione Scoctus') in the contemporary tract *De Situ Albanie*, and is no doubt further identifiable as Gilbert Scot, son of Ewen (Eógan) of Monorgan.[14] It is hard to avoid the conclusion that the position of a small native occupier had been regularised by bringing him into a formal relationship of dependency as vassal to the new superior lord.

The subsequent grant of part of Monorgan to Henry of Stirling is difficult to explain. It may have followed upon Gilbert's summary eviction, despite the earl's obligation to warranty, or upon the lack of an heir whom David was willing to accept, at any rate in the whole property.[15] But it cannot be emphasised too strongly that, however numerous the body of resident native freemen who retained their place, there is not a single shred of evidence to prove that such persons secured genuine material advancement as the tenurial structure of this fief was fashioned through fresh allocations of land. All save one of the remaining tenants known from the charters first appear in Scotland as members of Earl David's personal circle, and none was of Scottish extraction. Property was in his gift, yet he preferred to endow men of English or Anglo-continental descent. Patronage as well as higher office would appear to have been closed to local personnel; and the dispensing of rewards saw the rise of an *immigré* lesser nobility of service to replace, or to co-exist with, an ancient ministerial class of thanes, as part of the stronger framework of lordship imposed upon the estate.[16]

Easily the most prominent of those to whom Earl David turned was Hugh Giffard, his beneficiary at Fintry near Dundee. Hugh, whose origins have been traced to Longueville-la-Gifart beside Bellencombre in *Haute-Normandie,* the chief Norman seat of the earls of Warenne, had arrived in Scotland with his brothers Walter and William in the entourage of Countess Ada: he became her tenant at Haddington and William was her clerk.[17] Hugh's fortune had been made by *c.*1166 when he had secured King William's confirmation of Yester in East Lothian, the basis of his family's wealth;[18] and when he began witnessing David's charters in the 1170s he therefore did so as one who had served the earl's mother and found favour at court. He and his brothers campaigned with David in England in 1174, and the grant of Fintry probably acknowledged, or rather compensated for, this support. Giffard was obliged to find a hostage under the treaty of Falaise and suffered the forfeiture of Potton (Beds) in the Huntingdon honour, his only recorded tenancy outside Scotland. Fintry, held in augmentation of another, unspecified feu, gave him a new foothold on Tayside, consolidating his acquisitions from the *terra regis* at Powgavie (in Inchture) and Tealing.[19]

Whereas Giffard's connections enabled him to make his way largely independent of Earl David's support, the remaining incomers, persons of small substance, apparently owed their standing in the realm entirely to his decision. Two cases afford rare glimpses of a magnate introducing men to Scotland directly from his properties south of the Border, in these examples from the Huntingdon honour. Hugh le Bret, associated with Conington (Hunts), secured lands based on Glanderston in western Garioch. The other Huntingdon grantee, who received the whole davoch of Resthivet in Garioch, had the distinctively Norman name of David de Audri, presumably from Audrieu in Calvados (canton Tilly-sur-Seulles, arr. Caen).[20] His father William had witnessed Scottish charters but had not settled in the kingdom.[21] Confined to the honour of Huntingdon, the Audri inheritance was a modest establishment dispersed through several Northamptonshire villages; the Audris of North Cowton (Yorks, NR) in the honour of Richmond were a different branch of the same house.[22] The Huntingdon family's archive is a reasonably rich one, and sheds some valuable light on the mechanics of migration. The patrimony had passed to David de Audri's elder brother Alan, but since this was a declining gentry family, Alan was later obliged to raise capital 'pro urgenti negotio meo' by a series of land sales to local speculators.[23] When he settled seven virgates in Holcot upon David, Alan's slender means must have been stretched to the limit.[24] But for a younger son finding or anticipating little room on the ancestral estate, Scotland might hold out fresh hope; and David de Audri had some reason for believing himself placed to do well there: like Hugh Giffard, his father had supported Earl David in 1174.[25]

The origins of the other vassals are more varied and less easy to track down. Geographically, the earl recruited widely or, put another way, men were attracted from afar by his reputation as a lord and patron. Little can be made of Malcolm son of Bertolf, laird of Leslie in Garioch, who was possibly a Fleming. His charter of infeftment is uniquely addressed to all the earl's *probi homines*, 'French, English, Flemish and Scottish', while there are clear signs of Flemish settlement in the Leslie district at this period – a very modest parallel to the Flemish colonisation of Clydesdale – which are curiously repeated in a fourteenth-century conveyance granting Courtestown (in Leslie) 'vna cum lege Fleminga que dicitur Fleming lauch'.[26]

The antecedents of Henry de Boiville, the recipient of Ardoyne in Garioch, have been obscured in Black's *Surnames of Scotland*, where Boiville is confused with Bos(s)eville. The two surnames are not interchangeable; and the distinction is crucial, for the Bosevilles of Beuzeville-la-Giffard in Upper Normandy had also founded a Scottish branch by *c.* 1200.[27] Bo(i)villes abound in post-Conquest English sources, but the task of running Henry to ground is not entirely hopeless. The Boivilles (= Biéville-sur-Orne, canton Douvres, arr. Caen, dép. Calvados) of Millom in the Cumberland fief of Copeland had well-established associations with the Scottish royal house. Indeed, their range of contacts neatly exemplifies the elaborate network of interconnections which bound together landowning society on both sides of the Border from the early twelfth century. King David I's nephew, William Fitz Duncan, was lord of Copeland, apparently by 1138; and when the Scots king ruled at Carlisle the Millom Boivilles lent their support to the new regime.[28] Scottish lordship in this region also stimulated migration from English Cumbria into Scotland which showed no sign of slackening after 1157.[29] On general grounds, therefore, it would not be surprising to discover that the Millom family was represented in Aberdeenshire under Earl David. More specifically, a junior Boiville branch holding property at Kirksanton in Millom had acquired land in the honour of Mowbray at Newby in Lonsdale. By 1170 their immediate lord was Richard de Moreville, Constable of Scotland, who may have planted in Ayrshire the most distinguished of Boiville offshoots, the line of Boyle of Kelburne, earl of Glasgow.[30] A tenurial tie with the Morevilles, a great Anglo-Scottish dynasty, put the Boivilles directly within Earl David's orbit and, although it is also true that their chief lord, William de Mowbray, was a tenant of the earl in Northamptonshire,[31] that tie may have been decisive. Henry de Boiville of Ardoyne first occurs in David's following between *c.* 1200 and 1202. Earlier, the knight Herbert de Arches of Shadwell (Yorks, WR) had witnessed Malcolm son of Bertolf's charter (1172 × 1185): Herbert held of the senior Boiville line at Bordley in Craven, while he or his son and namesake was to serve as steward in Yorkshire for Alan of Galloway – from 1196 the Moreville heir, from 1209 the husband of Earl David's daughter Margaret.[32] William de Boiville of Kirksanton and Newby (d. *c.*1210) had four younger brothers, one of whom was called Henry. This Henry, endowed at Haverigg beside Kirksanton, could well be our man.[33]

The next case involves Robert and Simon 'de Billyngam' (later, 'de Billighin'), vassals of possible English or Anglo-Scandinavian descent whom Earl David had installed at Durno in Garioch by *c.*1185. There seems little question that their surname derived from Billingham on Teesside rather than Bellingham in Tynedale; and Simon of Billingham is presumably identical with the person of this name who had given property in Hartlepool to Guisborough priory by 1212.[34] If so, the Billinghams, like the Boivilles of Kirksanton, were bound through English interests to an Anglo-Norman house already prominently established north of the Border. Hartlepool was held with Hartness by the Annandale branch of the Brus family, and although it is most probable that the Billinghams had gained Earl David's support long before Robert de Brus IV married his daughter Isabel, we have a further hint on how the common interests of Anglo-Scottish magnates might exert an influence in attracting followers from one lord to another.

Finally, William Wascelin held the larger part of Newtyle in Angus, not through direct infeftment but through his wife Mabel, a lady of uncertain background. Although Wascelin's family was evidently of continental provenance, its actual ancestral home has not been traced. To ascertain the immediate place of origin, we must turn to letters of reseisin issued on William's behalf in November 1217. These letters, drawn up after the baronial rebellion in England, direct us to the northern Danelaw and back to the Mowbray honour. His Yorkshire lands cannot be identified, though Birdsall in the East Riding is a possible location.[35] Lincolnshire provides a more rewarding lead. A William and a Robert Wascelin attested charters in this county in the late twelfth and early thirteenth centuries;[36] both were associated with Redbourne where the third-part of a knight's fee was held in chief by Richard Wascelin in 1212; and by 1194 William Wascelin, mentioning his wife Wimarc, had given eleven acres at Redbourne to Bullington priory.[37] There is nothing to prove that this William secured Newtyle through a second marriage. But it is a strong probability that Wascelin of Newtyle was related to the Wascelins of Redbourne: when the former died his widow took Newtyle to Robert Griffin, identifiable as the steward of Lincoln castle for Nichola de la Haye and as a tenant of the Mowbray honour at Fridaythorpe (Yorks, ER). The Wascelins held in Scawby (Lincs) of the same honour.[38] There can, however, be no simple explanation of the particular circumstances that brought William advancement under Earl David. Neither Redbourne nor Scawby was within the earl's sphere of influence in Lincolnshire. It may be relevant that Hugh Giffard's brother-in-law owned land adjacent to both Redbourne and

Birdsall.[39] We also know that the Mowbrays, allies of the Scots in 1173–4, threw out a noted Scottish branch in the person of Philip, younger brother of William de Mowbray and lord of Dalmeny (West Lothian), Inverkeithing (Fife) and Moncreiffe (Perthshire), whose success inspired other migrants from the Mowbray estates – including no doubt Henry de Boiville of Ardoyne.[40]

This, then, was the body of lay tenants to whom Earl David looked the most expectantly for support in asserting his power. In English record they can be traced, with varying degrees of certainty, to the Huntingdon honour, or to Cumberland and Yorkshire, or to County Durham, or to Yorkshire and Lincolnshire. All, with the possible exception of the Billinghams, belonged to families whose original homes were in northern France. Doubtless we have been unable to identify every incoming vassal and feu for lack of adequate documentation about the process of subinfeudation. Indeed the evidence of place-names may indicate a larger measure of immigration.[41] But if such little mention can be made of native beneficiaries, it is surely not because they preferred to put their faith in oral testimony: as royal vassals, 'native Scots received their charters of land to be held by knight service and serjeanty, along with the new men from Flanders, Normandy, Brittany and England'.[42] The unmistakable conclusion is that favour was monopolised by a distinct settler class, which denied men of local origins access to social betterment in David's service. It might be dangerous to presume that this necessarily serves as a guide to the organisation of other great Scottish fiefs, but such a scheme of settlement is repeated more or less closely in the large southern lordships of the twelfth-century realm.[43] On a narrower front, the information showing recruitment on the earl's English estates is particularly enlightening. Anglo-Scottish magnates thought of their complexes of fiefs as single entities and it was natural for them to create links between their lands in one country and their lands in the other. Yet enlistment of vassals depended not just upon David's possession of an English earldom but also upon his wider connections with Anglo-Norman society. Pre-existing tenurial ties represented only one theme in the pattern of recruitment, for the earl's landed wealth in Scotland enabled him to widen the circle of dependants who looked to him for leadership.

While they were not a large group in terms of known numbers, the plantation of this company on his lands marked a definite departure from the past. At the opposite extreme, the numerous lay tenantry of the Huntingdon honour encompassed a broad spectrum of incomes and social pretensions and, as was the case in general in the Midlands, the bigger fees were dispersed over many different villages.[44] In Scotland, Earl David's feoffees tended to hold equal shares of property, and there was a marked absence of influential vassals, each with a whole series of local interests. Since the Scots crown required modest services, there had been no need to share out the expense and responsibility of raising knights with important 'honorial barons'. The typical place which formed a feudal tenement was a minor estate of less than parochial status – significantly, only two feus, Leslie held by Malcolm son of Bertolf and Newtyle held by William Wascelin, were later described as baronies. But although at Newtyle Wascelin had most of the medieval parish and farmlands 'free of all except minor limitations',[45] he did not control that part known as Balemawe (now lost), which David had given to his daughter Ada upon her marriage. In Garioch, Audri's davoch of Resthivet and the Billingham estate were appurtenances of Durno; Boiville's Ardoyne ('higher part of Oyne') was a dependency of Oyne. Hugh le Bret's Garioch feu 'lay to' Kennethmont, and Giffard's interest at Fintry formed an outlier of Dundeeshire. In these instances vassals had to be content with sub-holdings which were more dispensable than the central estates to which they had been attached. There was only one important exception to this pattern: at Leslie a focal settlement with its *appendicia* was conveyed intact. Though Earl David methodically established outsiders he was able to obtain their support for inconsiderable amounts of land, and accordingly the rewards were too small to create a wealthy group of settler knights. At this time knighthood was beginning to gain acceptance as a mark of genuine nobility; but the normal endowment fell sufficiently short of the landed requirement for the aspiring knight in later twelfth-century England to appear more characteristic of the simple *miles* of the Domesday generation than of 'an élite among the tenants by military service'.[46]

What had persuaded vassals to accept such remote and usually mediocre interests? In one case specific references point to economic stress. Not all lacked land or the expectation of a benefice elsewhere; but Hugh Giffard's large external holdings put him in a class of his own, and his infeftment apparently came about in exceptional circumstances.[47] Unless we are mistaken, patronage largely took the form of settling on the land personal military retainers who had taken service in the earl's household to seek the material backing denied to them in England. David de Audri was a younger son of a poorly-off gentry family, and most of his colleagues appear to have belonged to this disadvantaged class. Surplus children were being obliged to seek honour and fortune away from ancestral patrimonies so that senior lines could protect their position: the lord's need to build up effective power interacted with social pressures from below. Under Earl David's son and successor a new generation of incomers arrived and improved upon their economic status: Robert Griffin from Lincolnshire, Bartholomew the Fleming from the Huntingdon honour, and Simon de Garentuly (= Carantilly, arr. St Lô, dép. Manche).[48] These interlopers formed part of the continuing pressure of the new order upon the Gaelic-speaking population; but again their gains were small. Of course, a stake in a new country always held out the possibility of ultimate social success. Thus Malcolm son of Bertolf, ancestor of the line of Leslie, earl of Rothes, began a Scottish dynasty renowned for its durability and importance. And knightly society always produced adventurers 'in search of glory, profit and female prey'.[49] But in Scotland, perhaps far more than in England, the crown largely reserved to itself the power of truly making men.

It was the evidence of charters that R. L. G. Ritchie had most in mind when he wrote that the newcomer in William the Lion's reign found 'general conditions somewhat as in England'.[50] Yet our charters are almost as uninformative about tenure and vassalage as they are about the persistence of Celtic practices, and therefore afford only limited insight into how far feudal conventions really took root. Three grants for knight-service give precious evidence for the spread of military tenures north of the Tay beneath the tenant-in-chief; several *acta* are abridged as they survive and do not identify the services required. In the full texts as well as in the abstracts, reference to wardship, relief, marriage and aid is lacking; there is no mention of homage and fealty, no emphasis upon the bonds tying a tenant to his lord through counsel and court. English charters of enfeoffment are equally reticent, and our scribes were trained in Anglo-Norman habits. Malcolm son of Bertolf was responsible for the service of one knight. Giffard and Audri acknowledged a half and a tenth of a knight's service respectively. Their limited commitments reflect the size of their benefices. Even the Leslie feu, within about fifty years of its creation, was unable to bear the costs of maintaining a knight without enlargement: by 1232 Caskieben, near Inverurie, had been annexed 'ad incrementum predictarum terrarum' so that the service due could continue to be met.[51] We have no clear means of knowing what these military responsibilities actually entailed. There may have been no expectation of scutage as a substitute for personal service.[52] The resources of fractional feus could have been pooled to find a single knight to serve; alternatively, such a holding's service may have been discharged by an archer or a lightly armed serjeant.[53]

The most revealing insight into the making of a new tenancy is provided by the grant to Hugh le Bret, whose feu was based on lands that three men of Celtic lineage 'have possessed' (*tenuerunt*). It is not certain, however, whether these persons had died, or were evicted, or survived as Hugh's dependants. The incoming may have been associated with the founding of some settlements from scratch, but it was normal for established units to be taken over as going concerns. The best example of such continuity in infeftments is provided at Leslie where it seems that Malcolm son of Bertolf occupied an estate formerly administered by a thane. This well-organised concern possessed a variety of exploitable reserves, which embraced the parish church as 'une simple dépendance du domaine'.[54] Its appurtenances also included the powers of sake and soke, toll and team and infangenthief, traditionally associated with thanes.[55] There was a fusion of immemorial rights and new conditions as an apparently ancient administrative grouping was converted into a knight's feu. Elsewhere, most tenancies seem to have corresponded to age-old sub-units within previously existing estates, thenceforth detached from their centres and run as independent holdings. The more slender, with their possible characteristics of serjeanty service, bear comparison with the tenures of native followers who in northern England

(and eastern Lothian) were styled drengs, ministerial retainers whose estates were 'typically a single ploughgate, or a small township within a shire, or an outlying dependency of a village'.[56] If to continuity of holdings can be added likeness of management, administratively speaking the only major change was infeftment for definite services, and occasionally tenurial distinctions may well have been blurred. Closer than their lord to the soil, vassals were in a better position to undertake direct exploitation, yet there is no evidence of reorganisation for demesne farming as is attested, albeit fortuitously, in the Olifard feu of Arbuthnott in the Mearns.[57] Too often we are denied detailed information of the extent to which change was conditioned by established forms, but we are forced to consider more carefully the impact of these incomers upon an ancient countryside.

The inflexible language of legal documents can disguise degrees of innovation as well as the degree of continuity from the Celtic past, and basic to this is the reality of homage and fealty as a social force. Earl David was not so much recreating in Scotland the kind of loyalty he received in England. English sources show that while close personal ties between a lord and individual vassals still existed, in general many influences had combined by the late twelfth century to thwart attempts to extend seigneurial influence through gifts of land. There are, however, good *prima facie* reasons for believing that vassalic ties had a greater vitality in David's Scottish estates than in the English. His lordship was more comprehensive in several important ways. First and foremost, there was no vassal bound to him whom he had not chosen, for possession rested on personal acceptability rather than earlier title; secondly, since no other beneficiary was in the same social category as Hugh Giffard, vassalic bonds were underpinned by economic dependence; and thirdly, because feudal customs were introduced by this clientage, the problems caused by heritability and trafficking in land were unlikely to set in at so early a date. Moreover, other obvious contrasts suggest that vassalage was more elemental than in midland England. The earl's hold over dependants was strengthened by the feudal geography of the north-east plain, which was favourable to David as the first of the great regional fief-holders north of the Tay. His territorial predominance meant that he was well placed to assert a monopoly of allegiance and prevent vassals from entering into engagements through the patronage of other settler lords in chief. Indeed these lords, generally much smaller proprietors than David, tended to fall under his personal influence also;[58] and as a rule tenants seemingly made only their one contract for service as Scottish landholders. Equally, in a less intensively governed country there were fewer opportunities for vassals to assert their independence and grow rich in crown service. Hugh le Bret probably took employment as a royal falconer;[59] Giffard, of course, was primarily a vassal of the king. But otherwise David's clients had no alternative patron, the closeness of the personal relationship was retained, and through them the earl was confident of entrenching his authority.

Beyond this the sources shed some fitful light. Hugh le Bret acquired his Garioch establishment in exchange for relinquishing his rights, or rather claims, to Conington in the Huntingdon honour. He was thus a locally based vassal, though he undertook to go surety for Earl David in England.[60] But at least four settlers would seem to have had the opportunity, at one stage or another, of holding properties simultaneously in England and Scotland. It was by no means exceptional for small landowners to maintain cross-Border interests, and in William Wascelin's case conclusive proof exists that he did so.[61] It cannot simply be assumed, therefore, that with one or two exceptions this whole body of tenantry formed an inward-looking, local group. Nevertheless, the majority appear most frequently in a Scottish context. This would suggest that David did not draw on them for regular support outside Scotland and that they spent most of their time within the estate, helping to compensate for the earl's inevitable absences in England. They attended on him through local appearances as witnesses to his charters;[62] they occur with him in the witness-clauses of other Scottish acta;[63] and the charter sources also show something of the active social intercourse that bound them together beyond the lord's court.[64] Ties of neighbourhood reinforced ties of tenure. The same material reveals that resident native Scots not only fell outside David's favour but were largely excluded from this milieu. The settler class, whose loyalty was directed chiefly towards Earl David, seems virtually to have formed a community of its own. The principal qualification to be made is that those of David's immediate family to receive Scottish interests from him belonged to its society, as did those Anglo-Normans in his personal following who perambulated with him in Scotland and helped to enforce his authority there, but who did not obtain Scottish feus.[65]

There is little in all this to justify a recent interpretation stressing the frailty of tenurial bonds in the great fiefs of thirteenth-century Scotland.[66] The main problem about such generalisations is that conclusions have had to be made before the local studies that are the necessary preliminary to broader surveys. Though feudalism was being introduced a century after Domesday, it seems clear that this was the feudalism of early Norman rather than of Angevin England. There is an inescapable element of paradox here. Thanes, whose services were linked to quasi-servile obedience rather than feudal obligations, were likely in the longer span to be more submissive to a lord's will.[67] In broad historical terms, dependence began as something quite personal, but once it acquired a tenurial element it was bound ultimately to become less reliable. And yet just as Earl David's lordship over his vassals remained for his purposes firm, so they upheld and extended his powers of command, consolidating the influence brought to bear by his other supporters. It is possible that they were preponderantly a resident rentier group. Their superiority within the fief was obvious, but limited in terms of actual landed wealth. Though some sites may await discovery through fieldwork or aerial exploration, not every tenant can be shown to have built a strongpoint to dominate his surroundings. The inadequacies of the sources aside, for these reasons there is the risk of exaggerating the importance of these vassals; but there is perhaps an even greater danger of underestimating them.

The significance of their contribution is revealed most clearly in Garioch. The settlers in this region, far-distant from the heartland of the kingdom, were the true pioneers. Bound together by common background and common privilege, theirs was a colonial society *par excellence*. Their estates were spread across the vale of Garioch, covering the main lines of advance from the Highlands upon Inverurie; Leslie on the west flank, whose lord enjoyed jurisdiction of life and limb, may have been quickly fortified,[68] just as David de Audri or the Billinghams may have seen to the erection of the motte at Pitcaple (Nat. Grid Ref. NJ 724262). At least by the next generation or so, the main highway through western Garioch to Moray was further protected by a castle, perhaps stone-built, on a fine hill-top site at Dunnideer and by a fortified residence at Wardhouse.[69] Invested with concentrations of local power, vassals at once shared in the earl's lordship and contributed to it; his consent was sought whenever the tenant alienated part of his feu.[70] In between such holdings thanes may still have exercised authority, answerable to David's steward yet struggling to establish a hereditary grasp on the soil. But this network of subtenancies reveals a deliberate distribution in support of the major new stronghold around which the life of Garioch now revolved. The laird of Leslie served as constable of Inverurie castle; and although the burden of castle-guard is not explicitly recorded, the fact that the Billinghams had tofts in the burgh associated with their land in Durno may indicate a regular commitment of this type.[71] The parallels with the royal castle districts or sheriffdoms of southern Scotland and the compact magnate estates or *castellarie* of Domesday England seem very close; and as in the early English castlery the new men settled near Inverurie included those with the character of vavassors or sometime household knights bound in strict subordination to their lord.[72] In size Garioch did not rival great power blocks such as Richmondshire and Pontefract. But as a unit of government it was organised to meet similar needs. Earl David was making his lordship stronger and at the same time contributing directly to the extension of crown influence over the Lowlands of the north.

Ecclesiastical Interests

As is to be expected from the nature of surviving medieval records, most of Earl David's extant Scottish *acta* were written for ecclesiastical bene-ficiaries. These charters illuminate relations between the Church in Scotland and a high-ranking baron at a time when in the Lowlands the Anglo-Norman conception of Christian life and organisation almost completely supplanted the ancient Celtic model. They throw some light on diocesan administration and have particular value for the expansion of the new continental religious orders north of the Forth. As elsewhere in the twelfth-century kingdom, a phase of aristocratic colonisation was married to endowment of the reformed monastic Church. Support of religious communities drawing their inspiration from England and northern France was the essential counterpart of successful penetration by incoming lay lords.

By c. 1180 four major royal monasteries had been founded and provided with property in the north-east: the wealthy Augustinian houses of St Andrews and Scone, the Cistercian abbey at Coupar Angus and, most recently, King William's great Tironensian plantation at Arbroath. Such interests as these communities had acquired by prior title in Earl David's lands were normally too slender to invite molestation, and there was no secularisation of church property on the scale reported in other regions of baronial infeftment in Scotland.[73] The canons of St Andrews, who retained their assets at Ecclesgreig, received a confirmation for possessions in Longforgan after the earl had withdrawn his claims against them; the bishopric, however, lost its ancient patrimony at Culsalmond and Monkeigie in Garioch. When the superiority of the land had passed to Lindores abbey by 1207, only a portion of the cain had been reserved for episcopal use.[74] But we also know that David acknowledged the bishop of Aberdeen's right to teinds and unspecified consuetudines in Garioch. Recognition of a diocesan's entitlement to a share of teinds in one of the remoter reaches of western Christendom was an important gain in an age when laymen might still usurp and distribute teinds at will.[75]

Yet Earl David's attitude towards entrenched ecclesiastical concerns is not a leading theme. Whereas in England contemporary magnates were reluctant to impose new charges on behalf of the Church upon possessions already heavily committed to spiritual uses, rather greater scope existed for pious benefactions in Scotland; and the Scottish monastic establishment, despite heavy dependence upon crown support, continued to benefit from an aristocracy anxious and able to contribute to its vitality. Accordingly, it is David's church patronage that primarily concerns us, for while extensive endowment of the religious was no longer possible in his English estates, this was one of the main ways in which he moulded the organisation of his Scottish fief. At the same time, it will appear that the earl's piety and his desire to ensure his soul's salvation were not divorced from material considerations. For the magnates, as well as the Scots crown, complex attitudes lay behind the support of ecclesiastical reform.

Above all else, Earl David reserved his favour for the monastery he established at Lindores in Fife, which – colonised like Arbroath from Kelso abbey – followed the Benedictine usages of Tiron. The Knights of the Temple in England received a small parcel of land in Perth that brought in 2s. 8d. annually by the late thirteenth century.[76] The grant provides an interesting insight into the cross-Border ecclesiastical ties arising out of the patronage of powerful Anglo-Scottish barons. This, however, is the sole record of David's concern for the Military Orders, though both the Knights

Templars and the Knights Hospitallers had been nobly endowed by David I and Malcolm IV. The gift of a single ploughgate at Kennethmont in western Garioch is the one piece of evidence that David supported Arbroath.[77] Other important *curiales* gave much more. St Andrews priory also gained land at Kennethmont, as well as a toft and a meagre rent-charge at Dundee.[78] But Kennethmont was an upland parish of indifferent agricultural quality; a patron could afford to be magnanimous with a place like this. Kelso is the only beneficiary known to have been offered property by David in Lennox; but his grant, of the churches of Antermony and Campsie, did not take permanent effect.[79] Finally, although the Cistercians won Earl David's attention in England, the Scottish Cistercian community seems to have fallen entirely outside his interest.

These parsimonious contributions serve to give prominence to David's chief act of personal devotion and munificence, and thanks to the survival of the abbey's thirteenth-century cartulary the early history of Lindores can be recovered in some detail. The foundation is traditionally ascribed to 1191, following a note by Walter Bower that the first abbot died in June 1219 after having reigned for almost twenty-eight years. But Bower is a late and inconsistent authority: in another context he assumed that Lindores was founded in the same year as Arbroath (1178).[80] No other chroniclers supply dates of foundation and we are thrown back on the charter evidence.

A significant moment in the foundation history was marked by the quitclaim of submission and obedience, still extant in the original, given by the abbot and convent of Kelso in favour of Guy, abbot-elect of Lindores. It was issued in the Scottish royal court before a large company of notables headed by King William, Earl David himself and Roger, bishop-elect of St Andrews (el. 13 April 1189, cons. 15 February 1198), in whose diocese Lindores was sited. There is no reason to doubt the date, before 1194, proposed for this source by Bishop Dowden, the editor of the Lindores cartulary. Of the twenty-five named witnesses, eighteen also attested the earl's great charter which survives only as copied into the abbey cartulary under the rubric 'Magna carta Comitis Dauid de fundacione monasterij'. Both documents assume that the new convent already existed; and from the duplication of the witnesses it has been supposed, not unnaturally, that they were issued simultaneously.[81] But if Bishop Roger's designation in David's *magna carta* as bishop (1198–1202) rather than bishop-elect is no mere slip of the cartulary scribe, the chronology of these muniments at once takes on a more complex aspect. The *magna carta* may also be compared with two other *acta* included in the cartulary: (1) a charter of King William which confirms the abbey's possessions 'sicut carta eiusdem comitis fratris mei testatur', but which lacks a witness-list as copied; and (2) a letter of Pope Celestine III dated 8 March 1195, the earliest of the letters of grace and *privilegia* bought by Lindores from Rome, which confirms the rights and property of the monks 'sicut carta ipsius comitis protestatur', but which is probably tampered with in its surviving cartulary version.[82] As will appear, however, it is the form of Celestine's letter that presents difficulties, not its date or the ratification of benefactions in the central part of the text.

In content, and therefore in date, the royal and papal *acta* seem to belong together; on the other hand, the *magna carta* displays slight but telling variants. It alone refers to the Inch of Perth, a toft in that burgh and land at Newtyle, although these gains by Lindores are included in Innocent III's privilege of 20 March 1199.[83] Moreover, the king's charter excepts money rents from the teinds of Earl David's property north of the Mounth, whereas the 'great charter' contains no such reservation; Celestine's letter confirms Rothket church and its dependent chapels at Inverurie and Monkeigie, whereas in the *magna carta* Inverurie is described as the parish church. The final contrast is that although the *magna carta*, and the privilege of 1199, refer to the whole of Mugdrum Island, the former saving a single fishery, only the easements of the island and one fishery were confirmed by William and Celestine. (In fact, the royal charter specifically reserved Earl David's rights of proprietorship, and independent evidence indicates that the monks' title to this property goes back no earlier than 1198.)[84] These differences seem sufficient to suggest that the *magna carta*, 'sciatis me fundasse', was a revised, up-dated version of an earlier but now lost foundation charter, presumably contemporary with the Kelso quitclaim, and that it must have been prepared later than March 1195 but probably before Innocent's bull four years later. In drafting this production for sealing, the witness-clause appears to have been retained unaltered, save that it was necessary to change Bishop Roger's style to fit his new status. Thus the *terminus post quem* would be the date of his consecration on 15 February 1198, while support for March 1199 as the latest possible date is provided by the third witness, Bishop Jocelin of Glasgow, who died on 17 March of that year.

In analysing this document there is the disadvantage of dealing with a source at second hand, but there is no good case for doubting its genuineness as a charter passed under the earl's authority.[85] The beginning of a religious house was inevitably a complex business arrangement. Plans for the endowment of Lindores must have been in hand when, possibly by March 1189, Earl David secured a quittance of episcopal dues in Garioch so that assets could be given without legal wrangles to the monks.[86] The *carta* confirmed by King William and Celestine III signals a more advanced point in the proceedings; the 'great charter' must mark a later stage still. In a seminal study V. H. Galbraith demonstrated how the different transactions essential to the founding of a monastery might be recorded in various writings and then, perhaps years later, brought together and perpetuated in a definitive foundation charter, which superseded earlier *acta* and provided a comprehensive record of the protracted process of endowment. Twelfth-century charters had an evidentiary rather than dispositive value, and the *magna carta* conforms exactly to the procedure described by Galbraith.[87]

These remarks are preparatory to further discussion based on the

Lindores archive, in particular of the convent's contribution as a major new force in the structure of Earl David's estates. But on a wider plane, his support of the Tironensian order secures for him a place in 'the richest single chapter in the history of medieval Scottish monasticism'.[88] Though a less fertile plant than Savigny or Cîteaux, the abbey of Tiron had taken a distinguished part in pioneering the monastic revival of early twelfth-century Europe and exercised a broad spiritual appeal. It was no doubt important to King David I when he brought monks from Tiron to Selkirk – he later moved them to Kelso to embellish his great centre at Roxburgh – that unlike Savigny, which never acquired standing in Scotland, Tiron near Chartres lay outside the Norman king's direct political control. In England and Wales Tiron would always be poorly represented, but continued support from the Scots king and his court advanced its senior Scottish representative to assured stature among the new abbeys of the realm; and when Kelso colonised Arbroath and then Lindores, the Tironensians attained the zenith of their influence in the kingdom.

The quitclaim of subjection and obedience given by Abbot Osbert of Kelso to Lindores was unambiguous. Arbroath enjoyed the same independence by letters issued in 1178–9,[89] and in dealing with these colonies Kelso was merely allowing them to assume the position that existed in practice between itself and Tiron. Although Tiron survived the merger of Savigny and Cîteaux as an autonomous congregation and tried to maintain family bonds 'which neither distance nor time should sever',[90] the Tironensians lacked the institutional unity of an order whose head acted as a strong focus of control over remote dependencies. The interchange of personnel between Kelso, or rather Selkirk, and Tiron had swiftly fallen away.[91] In 1176 Tiron had attempted to revive its dwindling authority; but later evidence of a continuing connection is largely confined to the appointment of Kelso in 1267 as Tiron's agent in collecting a rent at Perth.[92] Daughter communities quickly adapted to their own surroundings, and Lindores' independence of Kelso was expressive of the independence Kelso had acquired of Tiron.

The extinction of the rights of the founding monastery was often valued by lay patrons concerned to retain a wide scope for proprietorial intervention. But from the later twelfth century founders of monasteries had in general to bow before the dictates of canon law, and their patronal rights were strictly circumscribed outside the framework of feudal dues and practices. Earl David himself scrupulously enjoined that Lindores was to hold its properties in perpetual alms, 'free of all service and custom, and secular aid and exaction', and that 'none of my successors may presume to claim anything . . . save only prayers for the salvation of the soul'.[93]

Further consideration of the abbey's relations with external authority directs attention to the cartulary copy of Celestine III's bull of 1195, written in a hand of *c*. 1260. According to Bishop Dowden, 'the papal privileges to Lindores follow the usual lines',[94] and he did not dwell on this remarkable text or draw out its significance. As intimated earlier, although the trustworthiness of the source with respect to the monks' possessions can be accepted, unfortunately its form, which combines the characteristics of a solemn privilege with those of a letter of grace, must arouse suspicion. The pope is found declaring that at Earl David's petition he has received Lindores directly into the right and ownership of St Peter, upon payment to the Holy See of two bezants yearly as a token of subjection and obedience. Thus, taking this information at face value, shortly after its foundation the abbey joined the exclusive class of commended monasteries owing an annual census to Rome; and although tribute was also paid by non-exempt houses, Lindores, as is to be expected of a monastery directly subject to the pope, owed census as a mark of full canonical exemption from episcopal discipline ('ad indicium libertatis').[95] The abbey's muniments give no more on exemption until 1290 and are generally unhelpful as regards relations with the bishop of St Andrews. There are, however, indications which point to the exercise of the diocesan's jurisdiction in the later Middle Ages. This does not in itself throw doubt on the earlier existence of exemption; but immediate problems arise because Innocent III's privilege of 20 March 1199 conferred simply papal protection, said nothing about census, and specifically reserved the canonical justice of the ordinary.[96] The reason why the abbey failed to obtain a confirmatory privilege of exemption under papal proprietorship in 1199 seems at first sight irrecoverable, although it may be that Bishop Roger of St Andrews, no longer merely *electus* from 1198, was in a better position to insist upon his ordinary rights. On the other hand, this evidence can be cited as strong support for believing that Celestine's letter is not wholly authentic in its surviving form. For lack of full and reliable information, no satisfactory solution to the problems posed by this difficult text can be reached. Nevertheless, thirteenth-century sources do in fact offer some independent corroboration of the monks' claims and certainly confirm their interest in exemption. The cameral *Liber Censuum*, in its unsystematic record of tribute due from British monasteries, mentions Lindores as owing census by 1228;[97] and in 1290 Celestine's letter, which 'is beginning to disintegrate through excessive age', was exemplified and renewed by Nicholas IV in the terms in which the abbey had allegedly received it, asserting the community's freedom from all spiritual authority save the pope's.[98] Whether this confirmation was later invoked against the diocesan, or whether the monks raised no objection to his powers, is not known. What can be said is that in spite of the special relationship that the Scottish Church enjoyed with Rome, the Vatican Archives name only four other monasteries in Scotland owing census before *c.*1300, and of these Arbroath, Jedburgh and Monymusk were apparently tributary as protected houses.[99] Kelso alone shared with Lindores the claim – in Kelso's case it was an impeccable claim – to be subject to the papacy *nullo medio*.[100]

Lindores therefore possessed or claimed a comprehensive immunity: freedom from parent house, lay patron and diocesan, with the abbey professing commendation into the *tuitio* of the Apostolic See. Yet if Earl David made over his foundation to the pope, the tutelage which Rome acquired was theoretical; whatever David eschewed in formal proprietorship he hoped to gain in personal influence; and the intimacy that inevitably existed between a new monastery and its founder could well have been enhanced. Although committed into papal ownership, Kelso remained in real terms more a monarch's *Eigenkloster* than an abbey commended in a special manner to Rome. And just as Kelso provided King William with a new royal *Eigenkloster* at Arbroath, so the king's brother enjoyed a close and peculiar relationship with the convent of Lindores, whose foundation was naturally designed to advance David's worldly as well as spiritual interests.

Materially, Lindores was capable of pleading poverty when advantageous to do so: in 1414, as a pretext to carry through an appropriation, the monks were to complain that their main resources, 'concentrated far from the monastery, are diminished by the robbers and thieves commonly called "wild Scots"'.[101] But the abbey's later financial worries, real or imaginary, cannot mask its importance as one of the most prominent religious houses in medieval Scotland. At the Reformation the community was ranked tenth for tax purposes of all Scottish monasteries and appreciably less wealthy than only Arbroath, Dunfermline and St Andrews.[102] Moreover, the main basis of its substance in the sixteenth century may be found in Earl David's charters, for the abbey was exceptional in the extent to which its economic fortunes rested upon the foundation endowment.[103]

Contiguous to its site on the southern shore of the Tay, the abbey disposed of a compact establishment, including rich farmlands beneath Ormiston Hill where the monks quickly organised a home grange, now Grange of Lindores. A second estate centre, on the mixed sands and clays running down to the Tay, was created a burgh dependent on the abbey (hence Newburgh) in 1266.[104] The convent's domestic arrangements were facilitated by excellent supplies of water, ready access to building stone in the earl's quarry, and productive fishing stations. Once it had been decided to begin the house outside Garioch in the more settled surroundings of Tayside, the concern was to find a location unburdened by prior claims and one that Earl David could afford to alienate without too great an economic loss. St Andrews priory enjoyed strong influence at Longforgan.[105] Farther north, the old Christian site at Ecclesgreig may have offered itself for consideration, since there was sometimes an inclination to choose a centre of ancient religious associations, as if the sacred traditions of the past would nourish the new plantation. But this property, like Longforgan, had been too heavily depleted as a source of patronage when in crown hands.[106] Newtyle in Strathmore may already have been assigned to lay tenants, and in any event was uncongenial because of its proximity to the Cistercians at Coupar Angus; there were hopes for the commercial development of Dundee that precluded its use as a base. Only Lindores supplied an adequate estate that readily commended itself for the introduction of conventual life. This nucleus was extended by other grants, including Mugdrum Island and the Inch of Perth, with a toft in Perth and another at Dundee. The whole parish (or *scira*) of Fintray in Garioch was held in association with intermediate rights over peasant occupiers at Culsalmond and Monkeigie. But Fintray was the only goodly benefaction in land beyond the abbey's home district. Even at Lindores the monks were not allowed to engross all the earl's property in the immediate neighbourhood.[107]

Overall, Earl David took the necessary steps to ensure that his abbey would flourish and would enhance his reputation as a devoted son of the Church. Nevertheless, the endowment was a carefully controlled outlay, with churches and teinds in fact occupying a more important place than large agricultural establishments. No less than twelve parish churches were bestowed on the monks by David, including all those then in his gift in Scotland. With the churches of Lindores (*alias* Abdie) and Dundee were conveyed eight Garioch benefices, some perhaps of the earl's own foundation, as 'one large ecclesiastical appendage to the Abbey of Lindores'.[108] The churches of Conington (Hunts) and Whissendine (Rutland) in the honour of Huntingdon gave the house a stake in David's English lands and provide another striking illustration of how the church patronage of a great lord in the two kingdoms could create Anglo-Scottish connections reflecting his own. There was a major grant of 'second teinds', namely a tenth of David's personal incomes from Garioch in food liveries, profits and pleas (*lucra et placita*), and 'all other things that can be taxed'. Yet what was the real price of these various offerings to the founder? It could easily be imagined that he was surrendering an unchallenged ownership, for the outright proprietary language of the charters was appropriate to secular interests over which the earl's rights were definite and uncontested. A related gift of a tenth of David's proceeds from the king's judicial profits throughout the whole realm is likely to have involved a substantial net loss of income. But we may learn from the observation that some ostensible grants of teinds 'might simply transfer the tithe from one ecclesiastical institution to another and cost the donor nothing; and tithes were therefore a popular form of gift and endowment for a new house of monks or canons'.[109] Second teinds had indeed been owed from Garioch, on both agricultural and non-agricultural incomes, as part of 'the teind of those things between Dee and Spey' due to the bishop of Aberdeen. Far from David making a grant 'munificent in spirit',[110] in this instance the direct loss to him personally was marginal, no more than the two ploughgates in Kennethmont necessary to buy out a beneficent diocesan's rights.[111]

As for the churches founded and endowed on his Scottish property, Earl David was granting to the abbey more than the patronage alone. They were expressly conveyed with all their assets in chapels, teinds, lands and men. The two English churches were also given as if 'no fundamental difference was recognized . . . between a church and the other profit-yielding appurtenances of an estate'.[112] But in reality these alienations constituted a small sacrifice, for a lay lord could no longer hope to detain parochial revenues without incurring ecclesiastical condemnation. The Church naturally preferred to gather spiritualities into its own hands, and although reformers did not regard cloistered monks or canons as ideal owners of parish churches, monastic *Eigenkirchentum* was less obnoxious than secular proprietorship. English evidence suggests that by *c.* 1160 the influence of successive canonical censures had helped to extend monastic possession to approximately one parish in four. [113] The notion that a church was not a secular property was slower to develop in Scotland, yet if David's conveyance of Scottish churches to Lindores was unusual because in a single conveyance he transferred every benefice at his disposal in the realm, it was but one step in the process whereby the parishes of the medieval kingdom were nearly all appropriated by the monastic Church. [114]

The losses suffered by Earl David in endowing Lindores were consequently less than the total gain by the abbey itself. Although at this time greater resources were available for pious benefactions in Scotland than in England, monastic proprietorship was inevitably shaped by the wish of lay benefactors to secure eternal salvation without serious diminution of their earthly goods. What seems rather less usual about Lindores is that the bulk of its endowment was at a considerable distance from the abbey, for some eighty miles separated the convent from its major interests in Garioch, later described as 'the North Abbacy of Lindores'. [115] The early evidence concerning management policy relates mainly to these remote concerns, which on the basis of such taxation returns as survive, notably for the Holy Land teind of 1274, furnished well over half (about sixty per cent) of its total revenue. [116] Ancient arrangements gave way slowly before new-found rights. Thus, to begin with the monks avoided wholesale commutation of their teinds, not least because proportional liveries tended to be economically more attractive than predetermined renders. Fintray was the base from which to secure and administer their allowances in the north, [117] and the toft they had from Earl David at Inverbervie in the Mearns provided a useful staging-point between Fife and Aberdeenshire. The difficulties posed by the remoteness of Garioch were perhaps further minimised. While we can be sure that the 'home' group of properties on Tayside were exploited for provisioning the abbey, it may be that the more distant assets, although prized for their incomes in kind, were managed largely for ready money: such a form of organisation would have corresponded to the typical Benedictine framework of supply and cash-revenue estates. There was certainly no need to transport perishable food rents cross-country or by sea to Fife if they could be sold for good prices at Inverurie or Aberdeen. [118] Lindores soon found that its second teinds were not always easy to collect. [119] But it was not because they were of small consequence that they were resisted, and the trouble the monks took to enforce their claims, as well as the later attempts by lay lords to readjust the terms of the original endowment, testifies to the burden they represented. In 1252, after protracted litigation over non-payment, the tenant of Crimond and Edingarioch managed to insist that he should pay an annual pension of 8s. instead of the second teinds; but the monks agreed only on condition that he renounced his claims to Tillykerrie in Fintray.[120] Then by a series of covenants in 1260–1 the chief lords of Garioch, or their representatives, attained full relief by exchanging for the *secunde decime* a clutch of valuable local properties and money rents.[121]

As a substantial holder of parish churches, the abbey was concerned to manage the benefices granted by Earl David as a principal source of temporal wealth. Papal permission to appropriate 'ad proprios usus' was given by mandates of Celestine III and Innocent III.[122] The two English churches were too distant for successful exploitation and, as was to have been expected, only limited profits accrued from them.[123] But close to home the annexation of Abdie and Dundee was swiftly effected on terms distinctly favourable to the abbey.[124] Full appropriation of the Garioch churches, two or three of which were richly endowed with glebe, teinds and *altaria*,[125] proved to be a more prolonged and expensive procedure. Almost from the outset the monks' efforts to divert the bulk of parish revenues for their own benefit brought them into contention with the bishop of Aberdeen, who was duty-bound to secure adequate maintenance for the vicars exercising the cure of souls within his diocese. In 1250 Bishop Ramsay remonstrated that the abbey was screwing such high profits from its churches that the vicars did not have a decent living. The incumbents were instructed to pay no more than the old requirements, and the bishop proceeded to press upon Lindores a new ordination that denied it the main fruits and accorded merely fixed annual portions to the convent as corporate rector. The monks immediately appealed to the papal Curia, and the judges-delegate commissioned by Innocent IV's mandate of 20 April 1250 revised Ramsay's allocations to the abbey's benefit, allowing Lindores to recover its profits by taking a sizeable share of parish incomes.[126]

The diocesan had a financial interest in vicarage revenues in the form of synodals and procurations, and perhaps Bishop Ramsay exaggerated the acquisitiveness of the monks. Yet it is a commonplace that under monastic ownership churches tended to be administered primarily for material profit. Indeed, any house whose endowment lay significantly in spiritualities had to ensure that the churches subject to it rendered the maximum financial return. The conflict of interest between the convent and the parishes was difficult to reconcile; and in the 1270s vicars in Garioch, one of whom was withholding the abbey's portion of the lesser teinds, were agitating against Lindores 'concerning an augmentation of their vicarages'.[127]

The initial endowment gave Lindores an excellent start. As the patrimony expanded it was natural that the abbey should have looked mainly north of the Tay for additional sources of wealth. Fife supported one of the densest concentrations of monasteries in Scotland, with the new Cistercian colonies at Culross and Balmerino, founded respectively by 1217 and in *c*.1227, increasing yet further the heavy claims upon the generosity of local lords. But there were also rivals to Lindores' influence in the north, notably Arbroath and Coupar Angus; and Lindores never managed to enlist the broad-based support these establishments enjoyed. Earl David's position at court secured some limited royal favour for the house, and the Scots king maintained his interest after the earl's death. In fact, in the fourteenth century the only proprietorship we hear of is the crown's.[128] Unable, however, to swell its reserves by many important new gifts, the abbey therefore continued to rely chiefly upon David's allocations, supplemented by the grants from his immediate family and tenants. Henry of Brechin, for example, contributed an annuity and selected the house as the burial-place for himself and his wife. A more conspicuous benefactor, David's son-in-law Malise, added the church of Muthill, land at Redgorton north of Perth, and a tenth of his cain and rents from Strathearn and Meikleour.[129] Of David's vassals, Norman son of Malcolm gave Leslie church; William Wascelin and his wife provided an oxgang in Newtyle and stipulated that if they died in Scotland their bodies should be buried at Lindores: 'The support of a particular religious house was frequently the expression of corporate solidarity within a feudal grouping.'[130] More remarkable is the conveyance by William de Camera of all his lordship at Little Hambleton (Rutland) in the Huntingdon honour, with one mark's rent.[131] So far as we know, William was not a landowner in Scotland, and his gift is a striking example of the degree to which a lord's interests might influence the pattern of a follower's patronage.

In the next generation family and tenurial affiliations continued to determine benefactions, and the monks augmented their English holdings with an annual rent-charge in Leicestershire.[132] But as the monks continued to exploit their patrimony, to add to it occasionally, and to reorganise it where necessary, their resources never outgrew appreciably the original endowment. The ruins of the abbey visible today are a poor memorial for a once renowned community, to whose founder its position, as one of the richer monasteries of the medieval kingdom, was very largely due.[133]

The New Beginning

Earl David's eastern Scottish fief found unity in its castles, burghs and new estate officers, through his patronage of the Church and his family, and by the influx of a distinct class of lay dependants closely bound to his allegiance. In all this we can trace the reception of Anglo-Norman influences, yet it is also possible to stress not the contrasts but the underlying resemblances with the past. It is important, however, not 'to mistake persisting forms for persisting realities'.[134] A similar conservatism pervaded the Norman lordships of the March of Wales, where neither conquest nor widespread alien colonisation could obscure the abiding antithesis between Welshry and Englishry, with their firmly drawn differences in law, administration, land tenure and custom.[135] But, as in Earl David's estates, the harnessing of old ways to the new reinforced the lord's status and authority, creating out of the Celtic polity a firmer basis of territorial domination and personal power. For estates were units of government as well as economic complexes, and here the earl's pious benefactions held place alongside the secular re-organisations. When a lord founded a monastery this was not purely an expression of piety and 'the diversion of capital into a non-productive sector'.[136] The activity of Lindores abbey affected many locations within the fief, and not only through its possession of the second teinds. The monks added their own authority to the imposition of lordship through their tenure of churches and lands, and exercised secular jurisdiction through their courts.[137] The returns for David on this investment in *dominium* cannot be measured any more precisely, but they were no less valuable because of that: 'Les abbayes . . . ont été aussi des points d'appui, des centres d'influence; elles ont fourni aux territoires une de leurs pierres angulaires.'[138]

Earl David's estate was assembled over a number of years, but it was not a haphazard creation. The view that his endowment was a deliberate stroke of royal policy designed to advance the king's control finds its most telling support in the grant of Garioch, which gave David the necessary provincial standing to meet some of the pressing requirements of government north of the Forth. The Church fitted neatly into the changes devised to strengthen this remote but strategically vital lordship. Though sited on Tayside, 'Lindores Abbey was as completely the monastery of the Garioch as Deer was the monastery of Buchan and Monymusk that of Mar'.[139] While the administration of this district was primarily ordered in David's interest, he drew it into closer dependence upon the crown through acts of patronage and institutional developments which highlight in miniature the main ways in which the Scots kings were personally extending their powers. To this extent, Garioch presents a mirror-image of the kingdom itself.

Such an analogy would doubtless have seemed particularly appropriate to the fourteenth-century lords of Garioch, who held *in liberam regalitatem* and assumed that regalian powers had always been attached to their land.[140] Arguably, these franchises had only been fully realised and defined in the recent past, in reaction to the increasing strength of the king's administration; but the corollary of this suggestion is that earlier, for as long as the crown remained unable to intervene on a routine, day-to-day basis, formal immunities were superfluous.[141] Lords of regality had a clearly defined place in the organisation of later medieval Scotland: they were entitled to exclude royal officers and, normally, to hear the 'pleas of the crown'. The order and system of their society, however, was far removed from conditions in the twelfth and early thirteenth centuries, when the development of the royal administrative machinery went forward with the rise of feudal lordships, and practice was more often shaped by the pressure of local circumstances. In Earl David's lifetime, the sheriff court and sheriffdom of Aberdeen were at best imperfectly established.[142] His soke courts, with rights of blood justice, afforded important disciplinary powers, their exercise apparently assisted by the king's *judex*[143] but in reality weakly controlled from above. That Bishop Matthew of Aberdeen, who served as a justiciar in *Scotia*, witnessed two of David's charters concerning Garioch may indicate some sort of contact with the emerging justice-ayres. One of these *acta*, also attested by Brocchin the *judex*, records that the bishop had perambulated the (disputed?) marches of a knight's feu.[144] But Scotland was slow to develop the possessory actions which expanded the competence of the justiciary courts in civil causes. By contrast with its contemporary English counterparts, the 'honour' court superimposed for infeft vassals was therefore less easily overridden as a final authority by external rules of law and more in line with the original, 'Stentonian' court, where to tenure and succession the lord 'was relevant at every point'.[145] Though doubts remain about the precise nature of his franchisal powers, Earl David was able to protect his rights as any strong lord would wish, and the more completely since, because of the facts of tenurial geography, disputes between neighbours were likely to arise within the same group of vassals.

Nevertheless, seigneurial government went together with royal lordship. The more we contemplate this fief the more Garioch seems to have occupied a place closely comparable to that of the early vicecomital castlery, with its chief castle-burgh, its court, infeft knights and serjeants, and with the main royal monastery able to augment its resources by drawing a second teind.[146] Chronologically, Garioch stands between the tail-end of the colonising process in southern Scotland and the beginning of widespread feudal settlement in *Scotia* proper. Thus if Earl David deserves to be remembered in the domestic annals of the early medieval kingdom, it is surely because he led the northern advance of royal authority through a technique of government based on provincial fiefs, which had given vital support in the past and would continue to do so in the future. In Angevin England monarchical power expanded as magnate power declined; in twelfth- and thirteenth-century Scotland both grew together in a remarkably tight and mutually profitable alliance.

6

THE ESTATES IN ENGLAND

(I)

Earl David's English landholdings will be examined under similar headings to those adopted for the Scottish fief, but the context is quite distinct. Despite degrees of assimilation between the societies and institutions of the two twelfth-century kingdoms, to pass from north-east Scotland to midland England is to enter a different world. When David succeeded the last Senlis holder of the honour of Huntingdon in 1185, he assumed all the rights and distinction of an earl of the English realm. But while the Scottish earldoms for long remained true administrative dignities,[1] the day had largely passed when the *comitatus*, or the power of an earl, could be a reality of itself in England. During Stephen's reign Earl Simon de Senlis II had undertaken wide duties in provincial government,[2] the weakness of the centre prompting the restoration of important executive tasks to loyal earls; under the Angevin monarchy, what remained to Earl David was his style and the 'third pennies' paid to him more or less regularly, probably as fixed allowances, in remembrance of an age when comital office was not only a matter of social rank and precedence but a thing of might and profit.[3]

Comital standing alone, therefore, made little difference in practice to David's authority in England. The dignity was supported, however, by the territorial base or *honor*, an ensemble of manors and other lands within which he claimed varying powers of lordship. There were also extensive franchisal rights ratified by royal charter on 24 June 1190.[4] The jurisdictional privileges appear unexceptional; but the fiscal liberties embraced, besides release from minor and occasionally obsolete dues, quittance from sheriff's aid, murder fines and, most remarkably, scutage. There were generous and rarely awarded immunities from forest law. Such an aggregate of privilege, intended to cover both the honorial demesne and tenanted land, was a mark of special prestige and could help to offset the earl's lack of local influence in other ways. Yet grants of liberties were not absolute but subject to the king's overriding rights of interpretation. A lord out of favour would find his immunities questioned or ignored by an unsympathetic central administration; and as David's relations with King John deteriorated he was obliged to acquiesce in the undermining of his most prized and valuable prerogatives.[5]

The estate records demonstrate more generally the main ways in which the power of the higher aristocracy in England had been circumscribed by the end of the twelfth century as the crown 'put a hedge around the barons, a hedge of royal controls and royal officials'.[6] By comparison with Scotland,

the estates of most earls and other magnates were effective agents of government and lordly authority only in a limited sense, a consequence also of the
fact that holdings were often more decentralised and of the attenuation of
vassalic ties. They played a part in keeping the peace and dispensing justice,
and they arguably retained rather more importance as focal points of loyalty
based on tenure than some historians have insisted. But their main function
was not so much governmental as social, and less social than economic. And
yet financially also, prevailing forces were threatening to erode magnate
influence still further. In short, the advantages Earl David enjoyed in
developing a strong Scottish power base contrast sharply with the problems
of securing a position of personal pre-eminence in midland England.

For the English lands documentation is limited and haphazard, though
much less so than for the Scottish. There are no contemporary or near-
contemporary manorial accounts, surveys or extents;[7] court rolls are not
available for any manor until the Godmanchester series begins in 1271. Our
concern is the circumstances of one lord and his tenantry in a remoter, less
record-conscious epoch. In one basic sense, however, more important than
the sparsity of material in this period is its bias. Notoriously, the Church
was better able to preserve muniments than were magnate families, and
there are influential books on a number of the greater ecclesiastical, especially monastic, estates.[8] Yet while the lay honours of early medieval England
are more poorly documented and so receive secondary attention, what was
true of one type of estate was not necessarily true of another. Earl David's
lordship corresponds to a critical age of economic change when the development of large English estates was hurried along by rising prices, population
upsurge and booming markets, all of which called for decisive shifts in
traditional attitudes. As well as clarifying other issues, the present analysis
can help to confirm or modify our view of this vital period of transition, a
view hitherto founded on researches predominantly relating to the enterprise of immortal corporations, which benefited from a stability and continuity of landownership that could not be expected of baronial dynasties.[9]

The honour of Huntingdon, the original basis of Earl David's wealth in
England, is the primary concern. Although the material provided by
William Farrer needs to be supplemented and brought up to date, his
factual survey of the honour's fees and their descent remains an essential
and generally reliable point of departure for the subinfeudated portion.[10]
Thus, the geography of the fief and the complexities of its tenurial structure
will not be elaborately treated. Nor is this the place for a connected account
of the passing of the honour between the Senlis earls and the Scots royal
house. But it is a necessary preliminary to the main discussion to establish
how the first century of the estate's development had principally affected
the structure with which David had to work.

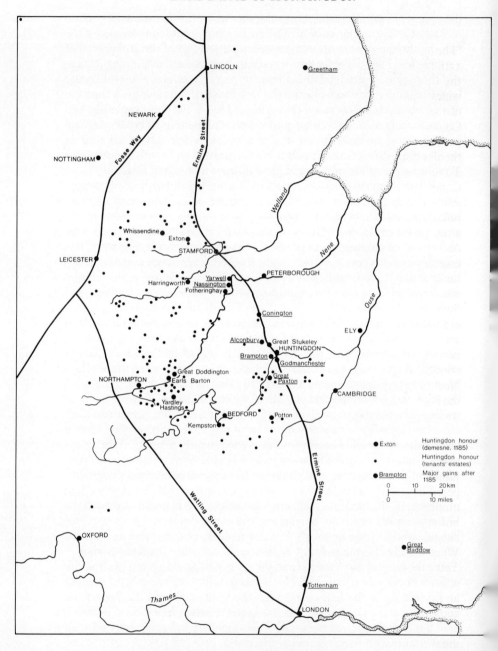

Map 3. Earl David's English estates

Antecedents

'The lands which belonged to the honor of Huntingdon during the 12th and 13th centuries represented almost without exception the vast estates held at the Conquest by Waltheof or Waldeve, son of earl Siward, and by his widow, Judith . . . at the time of the Great Survey.'[11] The received account of the origins of the Huntingdon fief simplifies a complex estate history. Countess Judith's Anglo-Saxon predecessors form a miscellaneous company, and Stenton's claim that some of the more substantial were Earl Waltheof's thegns, though not designated as such, seems insecurely founded.[12] To judge from Domesday values, Waltheof may have had on the eve of the Conquest barely a quarter of the property subsequently in Judith's hands. After 1066 his midland estate had been extended by gains in confiscated holdings, and much of this land fell to Judith, the Conqueror's niece, although by no means all Waltheof's pre-Conquest interests were passed on.[13] The Huntingdon honour as it appears in Domesday Book was in essence a new creation of the Norman feudal settlement. Also, while the honour had assumed its basic shape by 1086, there were important additions and outright losses in the following century. The Northamptonshire Survey records the engrossment of tenures formerly belonging to, among others, the bishop of Coutances and the count of Mortain. These, and new accretions during the Anarchy,[14] compensated for the disappearance of peripheral fees swallowed up in the estates of other lords. And yet few major windfalls in peacetime or war endured. The first two Senlis earls held Northampton, one of the wealthiest provincial towns of the kingdom, and the Scottish earls had rights or claims to Huntingdon; but both centres were resumed by Henry II.[15] All in all, losses tended to wipe out gains.[16]

The honour as it existed in 1185 sprawled through eleven shires, from north of the Trent almost to the Thames and, at the widest point, between the Northamptonshire uplands and the Cambridgeshire fen. In the upper basins of the rivers Welland, Nene and Ouse, where the bulk of its properties lay, the overall picture of dispersion is modified by some local grouping. More than fifty elements were strewn across Northamptonshire, but the majority were bunched in a half-circle east of Northampton. Of this cluster some twenty units were congregated in the adjacent hundreds of Wymersley and Hamfordshoe, both controlled by the lord of the honour.[17] Yet territorially speaking power remained fragmented: even where reasonably concentrated, dependencies were seldom contiguous but intermixed in an intricate pattern with those of other landlords, manor and village rarely coinciding.

Dispersion was a characteristic legacy of the Norman settlement: 'The great estates increased in number, in size and in geographical range.'[18] The total Domesday valuation of Countess Judith's lands had reached just under £600, a figure exceeded by only a handful of contemporary lay fiefs.[19] Although no *carta* was returned for the honour in 1166, Farrer was able to show by working back from the thirteenth-century returns of *servitia* that, as in other midland lordships, the military arrangements were well advanced by 1086. And enfeoffment had been extensive, with some additional land set aside for the Church. Here, as elsewhere, alienation had gone hand in hand with reorganisation of the endowment along more convenient administrative lines.[20] Even so, Domesday shows that a massive proportion of the estate, contributing around thirty-nine per cent of its entire value (£233 out of a total of £595), had already passed into the clutches of free tenants; and this may well be an underestimate.[21] It could indicate a high liability for knight-service, but we have no precise details. There were in any event strong pressures 'to make a baron enfeoff as many knights as his resources would permit'.[22] If the Huntingdon honour was one of the greatest Domesday honours, alienation had cut heavily into the available reserves, and this was to be of profound significance for its future development.

Most obviously, since the Senlis earls coveted Huntingdon as their main patrimony and their Scottish rivals were concerned to exercise direct territorial lordship in the Midlands, the degree to which the demesne had been pruned even by 1086 imposed decisive restraints upon them. Constant demands continued to be placed upon the honour's wealth: clientage, Church and family claimed attention with each change of lord. If, however, the drain on resources could hardly be avoided altogether it was of necessity in some measure restricted and slowed. Incomers 'from Henry I's sphere of influence, the Cotentin, the Avranchin and the eastern borders of Brittany' predominated among those raised to power by King David I as Scottish lords.[23] Less appreciated is the substantial footing achieved by such persons in the Huntingdon honour by the 1130s. They included small men whom David I was willing to enrich in Scotland, but also leading Henrician *curiales*. William of Houghton and Aubrey de Vere, royal chamberlains, Geoffrey Ridel and Richard Basset, king's justices, and William Peverel of Dover – these were aggressive landlords rounding off their estates with Huntingdon interests, although encroachments that were regularised may not be the full explanation.[24] No doubt Beauclerk actively encouraged or connived at these arrangements, so obviously beneficial politically, hoping to exert authority over David I through both lands and rear-vassals. Yet this influx of new mesne tenants was on a scale not to be repeated in the future, while the concerns acquired by one means or another were normally small demesne units, or else established tenancies, more open to appropriation in Henry I's reign than in his grandson's. This renewed pressure upon honorial resources was therefore not entirely uncontrolled – though there were important inroads at Great Doddington (Northants), Sawtry (Hunts), Tottenham (Middlesex) and (possibly some years later) Market Overton (Rutland).[25] In the next two generations families disappeared and others took their place, but the carving out of new fees was sporadic: in 1211 Earl David was forced to acknowledge a liability for scutage on eighty fees *de veteri* but on merely ten fees *de novo*.[26]

The overwhelming commitment of the Scottish earls in their offerings to God's service was to the religious expansion in Scotland: an early interest in the priory of Great Paxton did not prevent the community from failing through lack of endowment; and concern for other houses closely associated with the honour was often token, the chief exceptions being Elstow abbey and St Margaret's hospital, Huntingdon.[27] The Senlis line's patronage of religion was more concentrated, diverting large amounts of honorial property into ecclesiastical hands. Earl Simon I founded St Andrew's priory at Northampton, colonised by Cluniacs from La Charité-sur-Loire and endowed in the honour at large.[28] It was, however, the religious piety of his son, the second Senlis earl, that represented the most serious threat to the economic strength of the twelfth-century estate through lay support for the Church. Nevertheless, although Earl Simon II's investments in his soul's salvation earned him the reputation of a valued benefactor, the main grants of real estate were prudently dispensed. The Knights Templars and St Frideswide's priory, Oxford, were offered manors encumbered by prior claims.[29] Delapré nunnery's original endowment included tenants' fees, some of whose holders had evidently lost favour under Simon's lordship from 1141; the Cistercian house at Sawtry was established upon the patrimony of a leading partisan of King David.[30] A lord dealt in sequestered tenancies where he could, at once consolidating his political influence and protecting the main financial reserves.

In the century after Domesday, property given in enfeoffment or in alms was not distributed with improvident generosity. Alienation had made such early progress that it could scarcely have been otherwise. But the honour had always to sustain more than its lords alone, and while they continued to accommodate lay vassals and to cater for their spiritual welfare this did nothing to enhance their economic position. Nor did the demands upon them end there. Unquestionably, family settlements reduced the patrimony more than any other cause. Although they gained far less than their fair share of the inheritance, Alice, the younger daughter of Earl Waltheof, and her husband Ralph de Tosny II acquired all the Cambridgeshire and Essex demesnes.[31] The successive marriages of Earl Simon I's daughter Maud to Robert Fitz Richard (another of Beauclerk's protégés) and to Saer de Quincy I resulted in further costly and permanent alienations, though a loose form of overlordship was retained.[32] Shortly before Earl David's succession, there was expensive provision for three of Earl Simon III's immediate family: his sister Isabel, wife of William Mauduit, his bastard brother and his widow Countess Alice.[33] On the Scottish side, King William assigned Ryhall (Rutland) and the service of twenty enfeoffed knights to Margaret, countess of Brittany, on her second marriage to Humphrey de Bohun.[34] This grant did not take immediate effect; but in the longer term it was destined to result in a grievous depletion of reserves.[35] Members of the family had to be supported as their rank dictated. Indeed, the Senlis earls were fortunate to have been spared the dissipation of capital assets to which an excess of children would inevitably have led, whereas the Scots earls, with their vastly superior resources, met the recurrent demands of family duty without constantly drawing on the honour's wealth. Yet such responsibilities cut ruthlessly into honorial reserves prior to 1185, and the cumulative effect hit hard.

Reviewed overall, the struggle to maintain incomes in the face of persistent pressures to devolve land thus achieved scant success. In 1129–30 King David had been allowed Danegeld remissions on 125 hides *in dominio*, and if this can be accepted as his full entitlement, it placed him far behind the richest members of the Anglo-Norman baronage.[36] The *acta* of Earl Simon II, the basis of some earlier comment, further emphasise the constraints upon an expansive lordship. He conveyed to St Andrew's, Northampton, land in Ryhall 'donec eis dedero escambium de propria hereditate mea'; the mill of Exton, another Rutland manor, was allocated in return for land given to his clerk 'quousque donem eisdem escambium xl solidorum ad valenciam de hereditate mea in ecclesiis vel in aliis redditibus'. There were other provisional gifts to St Andrew's, one to Harrold priory;[37] and these stop-gap measures cannot be explained simply by the Anarchy. Since most small units had been granted out by 1086, assets readily available for permanent alienation were always in short supply. Important manors had to be divided and occasionally disposed of whole. For a time major grants were confined to the more outlying and expendable estates, but once these had been hived off there was little scope for the kind of discretion in the choice of properties for alienation characteristic of Domesday landlords. Seigneurial control was the more difficult to maintain because of the changing circumstances in which it had to work, while from the mid-twelfth century all magnates were less secure in the authority of their courts and more completely bound by their predecessors' gifts. The fact is that the reserves were so dangerously near extinction by 1185 that they had been shorn of manors providing three-quarters of the Domesday *valet* of the demesnes (£265 out of £352), family claims accounting for no less than fifty-seven per cent of these losses in terms of 1086 values. Attrition in those manors that remained could be so advanced that the manorial structure was tending to decompose. Large ecclesiastical enterprises were generally developing in a different direction and under different influences, with actual incomes capable of climbing far above Domesday levels by *c*.1180.[38] If Huntingdon is in any way representative of the old-established lay honours, and others were being reduced in their turn to 'shadowy collections of feudal superiorities',[39] it is clear which sort of lordship was better prepared to meet the demanding economic conditions of the late twelfth and early thirteenth centuries. By Earl David's accession the erosion of domanial resources had weakened a once great honour almost to the verge of dissolution.

Demesne Manors and Estate Officials

Earl David's wealth in England did not rest solely upon demesne manors, whether on lease or in hand, but this was the case to a considerable extent. Since they were of more or less classical type, there is thus a definite difference in emphasis when the economy of his English lordship is compared to his heavy dependence upon shire renders and burgh rents in Scotland. Additional sources of revenue were derived from franchisal privileges and the enfeoffed properties; yet these were occasional emoluments distinct from regular issues, and by the late twelfth century wider seigneurial rights were sometimes so unprofitable or difficult to maintain that lords could be disconcerted by the amount of income they supplied. In terms of lordly control over the resources of knights' fees, the Huntingdon fief's chequered history surely accentuated the problems.[40] The true substance of the earl's economic strength was based upon his normal manorial receipts.

How much was the honour worth after more than a century of alienations? In an enrolled account for the estate when held *in manu regis* between the death of Earl Simon III and Earl David's succession, the keeper (the honour was probably not at farm) answered for merely £43 1s. 5d. for a three-month term. In the previous Exchequer year, 1183–4, the sheriff had accounted for only £18 11s. 2d. from the lands of the honour in Northamptonshire 'de termino sancti Michaelis',[41] but it was in this county that the remaining demesne was principally concentrated. These figures bear no comparison with such tentative estimates as can be made of the net annual values of the honours of Gloucester (£590) and Arundel (£390), or even of the honours of Long Crendon (£350) and Eye (£340). Closer contemporary parallels are to be found with Cornwall (£210), Lancaster (£210), Peak (£240) and Rayleigh (£250), or even with Berkhamsted (£120), Petworth (£160) and Wallingford (£150).[42] Although comital rank conferred high status, in early Angevin England the financial reserves were not automatically sufficient for the dignity.[43] There were obviously great earls and barons whose position was much less precarious. But at just the moment when earldoms had become in essence honorific, David's estate incomes were perilously low. Further, whereas his predecessor, Earl Simon III, had been able to draw on the revenues of the honour of Gant,[44] David as yet had no other resources available in the kingdom which he could use to defend his standing under the English crown. Almost immediately he was forced to pledge two Huntingdon manors as security for unpaid debts totalling £300 due to Aaron of Lincoln: the discrepancy between social position and economic consequence was complete.[45]

Earl David's predicament would have been serious enough even without any adverse change in the general economic situation in England. But in fact the pressure did not come from one direction only, for new dangers threatened to cut back resources even more alarmingly. The broader frame of reference is well established.[46] Spiralling inflation from *c*. 1180 revealed the grave inadequacy of traditional aristocratic incomes. Coincidentally the crown, also faced with escalating costs, imposed increasingly heavy fiscal burdens upon large proprietors, which could not be simply passed on to their free tenants or minimised by invoking special immunities. Real incomes rapidly fell as expenses mounted. But as inflation accelerated apace, improving landlords took advantage of buoyant prices and an expanding population which widened market demand for foodstuffs. Economic enterprise became at once more necessary and more attractive. Efforts were made to recall manors put on lease for fixed returns, to resume freeholds alienated too generously in the past, to enlarge estates wherever possible, and to run them more intensively as speculative concerns. Only a boosting of receipts held out hope of financial stability; in time, the more assertive attained a new-found prosperity.

How did Earl David, with only limited demesnes laid by, cope with the new economic realities? Two main points should be made at the outset. First, in the high-farming age of the late twelfth and the thirteenth centuries it was naturally by degrees that estate administrations became more professionalised, with the clearest signs showing on ecclesiastical lordships, which were more stable, were often more centralised and, not least, leave fuller archives than lay honours. Secondly, although large landowners were generally anxious to introduce changes and modify their style of life, it seems impossible to maintain that attitudes were entirely dominated by the spirit of making maximum profits. What is feasible is to indicate Earl David's demesne holdings and how successfully they were safeguarded or augmented. Then it will be possible to review some aspects of the domanial economy and the nature of its management.

Though scattered through four shires, the ten demesne manors about 1185 fell into two main divisions. Yardley Hastings, Earls Barton and Great Doddington lay close to Northampton. Kempston (Beds) can also be associated with this cluster, which perhaps suggests concern by the Senlis earls to conserve important assets in the vicinity of the castle-borough before Northampton had reverted to the crown in 1154. The second group, Whissendine, Exton (Rutland), Harringworth, Fotheringhay (Northants), Great Stukeley (Hunts) and Potton (Beds), was strung out over some fifty miles along the axis of Ermine Street, the main highway from London to the north. No centre was more than ten miles from this great thoroughfare; Great Stukeley lay directly in its path; and Potton stood alongside *Brunstrate*, which struck west from Ermine Street at Braughing, swung north through Baldock, and rejoined it at Godmanchester.[47] As staging-posts, these six places admirably suited Earl David's requirements when going to Scotland and returning: on the journey between London and Edinburgh he could spend the first three nights in his own manors without the need for lengthy detours. In this regard, it is tempting to assume a degree of careful planning by the earlier Scots lords of the honour.

Only one of the residences available to the earl as he perambulated from manor to manor, the motte and bailey at Fotheringhay, was fortified as a castle. Future excavations may link him with one or more of the 'moated sites' and 'unclassified mounds' surveyed for the Royal Commission on Historical Monuments in other known centres.[48] That parks were maintained at Exton, Potton and Whissendine certainly indicates the presence of lesser seats in these manors.[49] Charter place-dates show that accommodation was readily available elsewhere,[50] but again it is difficult to relate recorded sites to the residences of the twelfth-century earls.

Fotheringhay, Kempston and Yardley Hastings were the only major holdings. Together they accounted for two-fifths of the Domesday value of all the units retained at Earl David's accession, and alienation in these properties had for long been controlled. A rough idea of the pre-eminence of this triumvirate is also conveyed by inquisitions *post mortem* or extents of the second part of the thirteenth century, which consistently return higher values for these manors than they do for other estates in demesne in 1185.[51] The loss of Huntingdon castle, withheld by the crown and partly dismantled in the aftermath of the young King Henry's rebellion,[52] had recently deprived the honour of its chief administrative focus, and as the running of the fief was organised to meet David's needs it was Fotheringhay, in the heart of the estate, which was developed as his preferred headquarters. The castle may have been erected only in his lifetime, though apparently not by the earl himself. Its prominence over other centres was implicitly acknowledged in 1212 when King John ordered the castle to be taken in hand and probably the manor as well.[53] This, the most serious of several losses due to political reverses at the tail-end of the earl's career, meant the emergence of another main base. In 1219 Kempston was assigned in dower to his widow and only a subordinate centre would have been ventured in this way.[54] Failing Kempston the obvious place was Yardley Hastings. The number of occasions on which David's predecessors had issued charters there reflects the recreation which its great chase afforded for tournaments and hunting; it also enjoyed the influence of an ancient hundredal manor to which the earl's hundreds of Wymersley and Hamfordshoe were appendant.[55] Towards the end of David's life wider administrative duties were added to its existing functions: he died in residence at Yardley, and only after his death in 1219 would Fotheringhay finally come back and resume its role as the *caput honoris*.[56]

Earl David was acutely conscious of the limited nature of his domanial assets, and did his utmost to conserve them, from the moment that they passed into his hands. The paucity of his gifts to the Church provides the most striking evidence of determination to prevent undue retraction of residual resources.[57] Of his fifteen known Huntingdon grants to laymen, eight created fractional fees or conveyed disputed tenancies; three were grants of rent-charges, two of wardships.[58] All these were attempts to dispense patronage without reckless encroachment on demesne acres. To be sure, by the time of David's death the Huntingdon demesne of 1185 had been reduced to probably no more than five manors. It was royal disfavour, however, that took by far the heaviest toll.[59] No doubt as less became available affinities clung all the more tenaciously to the old conventions: a great lord 'doit pouvoir et savoir donner sans trop compter'.[60] But no patron or protector had an inexhaustible supply of land. Limited reserves led to strait-handed patronage.

The earl's policy appears here in a defensive guise. For although the transformation from dispersion to a discerning husbanding of resources should not be too sharply drawn, now more than ever before there was need for austerity and vigilant retrenchment, and accordingly alienation was brought under yet closer regulation and control. It was in David's Scottish lands that the Church and his kinsmen obtained their major gains.[61] More positively, attempts were made to resume past alienations and engross contested properties, for conservation was coupled with an earnest search for resources to offset the expensive losses of an earlier age and to place his fortunes on a sounder footing. Conington manor, on the edge of the Huntingdonshire fenland, had been alienated to a cadet branch of the Senlis line, which evidently controlled it until about 1212 when the family was forced to take out a writ *precipe* against dispossession. This dispute was still reverberating in 1214, but Conington was successfully taken back into demesne.[62] The valuable manor of Great Paxton (Hunts), or the larger part, was recovered from Walter Fitz Robert in unrecorded circumstances.[63] But, not surprisingly, these triumphs were exceptional. Free tenants now enjoyed such protection, thanks to the Angevin legal reforms, that a lord's reserves of demesne could rarely be reconstituted at their expense.[64]

Two lawsuits were especially acrimonious and costly, and both actions ended in Earl David's defeat. The more protracted concerned Whissendine and ancillary holdings formerly held by Richard de Moreville, Constable of Scotland, who had fought on the Scottish side in 1173–4. Although he was subsequently reconciled with the English crown and entitled to reseisin, Whissendine was retained in demesne by Earl Simon III and also by David himself.[65] In 1200 the Morevilles, then represented by Helen de Moreville and Roland, lord of Galloway, took their claims to law. Roland died before the plea could be carried forward, but litigation resumed in 1211 when the case was the more complex because David had recently divided the disputed property into several new fees. That one of those enfeoffed was Helen's son Alan of Galloway indicates an attempt to settle out of court, conceivably on the occasion of Alan's marriage to David's daughter Margaret in 1209. In any event, the earl had effectively relinquished his claims to hold *in proprio dominio*; Alan supported Helen when she petitioned for a recognition two years later and the suit was resolved in her favour in 1212. Earl David's feoffees, including Alan, thereupon demanded suitable exchanges.[66]

It is perhaps some measure of David's depleted resources that the second case again jeopardised his relations with powerful kinsfolk; and it too illuminates the difficulties of making a permanent conquest in the face of persistent family claims. King William's grant to Margaret of Scotland of Ryhall and the lordship of twenty Huntingdon fees was too lavish to stand unchallenged. Having already secured the fees, Margaret is recorded as the lady of Ryhall in 1195;[67] but after Margaret's death her son Henry de Bohun, earl of Hereford, had to claim his right against Earl David, who ultimately recognised the weakness of his defence by failing to appear in the royal courts to answer the suit. In January 1204 he essoined himself *de malo veniendi* and in the following month – from Carham on Tweed, an important Border crossing – *de malo lecti*. A day was set for both parties to be *coram rege* in April: only Earl Henry presented himself and judgement was made for the plaintiff through David's default.[68]

A surer path to land acquisition, though one ultimately undermined by shifting fortunes at court, was found through the traditional processes of aristocratic advancement: a profitable marriage coupled with success in winning further political rewards. The dowry bestowed by Ranulf, earl of Chester, upon Earl David and Countess Maud in 1190 formed the greatest single accretion to his territorial strength in England.[69] Great Baddow (Essex) was a rich windfall, but Greetham in south Lincolnshire, head of 'the largest soke recorded by Domesday between the Humber and the Welland',[70] takes pride of place. Conveyed with Greetham were lands near by at Asterby, Goulceby and Hemingby, and fifteen knights' fees, two of them adapted from Greetham's sokeland. This brought David a major new focus of influence, produced an important expansion in his income, and at the same time provided another convenient halting-place on his travels along the main thoroughfares north. Beyond Rutland there were no demesne manors to serve as points of call if he rode on to York through Newark or Lincoln. But a diversion to Greetham gave direct access to High Street, a well-used ridgeway along the Lincolnshire Wolds linking Horncastle with the chief Humber ferry crossings at Barton and South Ferriby. This route may have become the normal itinerary.[71]

There is little doubt that Earl David's distinctly advantageous marriage stemmed at least as much from Angevin royal favour as from private negotiations between magnates of equal rank. He lacked the ready cash to add new manors by purchase; and it was upon the continued goodwill of the English crown that his other gains in England after 1185 principally rested. Some acquisitions by royal grant were piecemeal.[72] But other gifts were of the first importance to his standing and provide the clearest possible illustration of the maxim that 'a baron's political and economic positions were completely interdependent'.[73] In April 1194, during the king's last visit to England, Richard I confirmed to him on generous terms Godmanchester in Huntingdonshire and property at Nassington and Yarwell in Northamptonshire. This represented land worth 100 marks originally conferred in 1190–1, and the service required was that of a single knight.[74] Richard also restored to the Huntingdon demesne the manor of Tottenham in Middlesex, lately come into the king's hands following dealings by its tenant with the London Jewry.[75] One of King John's first decisions was to ratify these arrangements and assign the residue of crown demesne in Nassington and Yarwell.[76] The final act of royal bounty was dated 1202, when David secured the manors of Alconbury and Brampton (Hunts), substantial interests which were given until he could be found escheated land of equivalent value.[77] An exchange was never made.

This gain of six additional manors in royal service formed the real basis of the earl's economic recovery. With one exception, they did not open up new areas of lordship but constituted natural extensions of the existing demesnes. Nassington and Yarwell formed a contiguous enclave with Fotheringhay in the widest and most favoured part of the Nene valley. Alconbury, held with Alconbury Weston and Lymage, in Great Staughton,[78] was only divorced from Great Stukeley by Ramsey abbey's holdings in Little Stukeley. Brampton lay immediately south of Alconbury and the Stukeleys; Godmanchester, a community of some commercial as well as agricultural importance,[79] marched with Brampton on the east. These acquisitions from the *terra regis* brought invaluable new resources and perhaps new residences as well. Tottenham, although isolated from the demesne blocks being consolidated in Northamptonshire and Huntingdonshire, represented another serviceable addition to the earl's incomes and afforded a congenial resort for attending the royal court at Westminster: his grandfather had long ago acknowledged its advantages as a seat at the heart of English political life when, in establishing a mesne lord there, he had provided for the entertainment of churchmen engaged on business with him.[80] But royal favour was also crucial in another way. Earl David was able to concentrate reserves in areas where he was struggling to achieve local power and leadership, and to extend his personal influence by some limited enfeoffment of trusted followers outside the patrimony.[81] Since he lacked a strong base in the lands of the earldom, crown support was fundamental to his style of 'good lordship'. On the other hand, such dependence upon the monarchy ensured that a lord's position was innately unstable. Any serious withdrawal of the royal goodwill that shored up his status could only lead rapidly to his discomfiture.

The seigneurial reaction to falling real incomes could follow two principal courses. In this estate the first of these, expansion of the amount of land by adding new manors, was a notable feature of Earl David's lordship, but one that rested above all upon the grace he found with the Angevin king. There was also the possibility of increasing returns by a more vigorous policy in the actual use of reserves, that is, by the adoption of progressive management. Yet in husbandry the lord's decision was only one influence amongst others, and not the most important, for the chief determinant of 'the dynamics of the manorial economy'[82] remained the productive capacity of the component parts. In a short account Margaret Moore attempted to throw some light on the economic potential of the Huntingdon honour as a whole.[83] But this study relied heavily upon materials of the late thirteenth and the fourteenth centuries, and since its findings were throughout surprisingly scanty, it does not inspire confidence that much can be discovered about the economy of the English demesnes under Earl David. Contemporary documentation is indeed unsystematic and often jejune. Nevertheless, there is sufficient evidence, mainly concerning the Northamptonshire and Huntingdonshire manors, to turn from the story of properties lost and won and to broaden the scope of inquiry.

First impressions are of the inherent richness of this 'central' group. In part this assessment must be based on inquisitions and extents of the reigns of Henry III and Edward I, sources which, though notoriously treacherous, provide the most complete picture available of the internal structure of the principal demesnes.[84] They reveal a regular manorial order with the home-farms contributing between forty and seventy per cent of the values, for although no manor was quite like another, demesne acres normally constituted the main element of wealth. Here we see something of the profitability of the demesnes under later thirteenth-century conditions, particularly of the arable base. Naturally, the degree to which the economic opportunities were actually realised under Earl David is more difficult to discern.

His agents or local managers were largely spared the limitations of fenland farming and the restrictions of the heavy boulder clays. Five establishments lay in the broad valley of the Nene. High figures for Domesday population and plough-teams offer an early indication of the affluence of this region.[85] The luxuriant cornfields of Fotheringhay, Nassington and Yarwell represented some of the best farming land in the east Midlands, while the quality of the ample meadows on the river gravels at Fotheringhay cannot have been surpassed in more than a handful of Northamptonshire villages. Would that we had the same range of information for any of Earl David's manors as we do for Wellingborough, adjacent to Great Doddington and Earls Barton and in modern times classed together with them as an agricultural subdistrict of central Northamptonshire.[86] Wellingborough was one of the chief supply-manors of Crowland abbey for wheat, barley and sheep, and the manorial accounts from 1258 reveal in unprecedented detail the superior rewards of farming on the alluvial soils and gravel spurs alongside the upper Nene.[87]

The Huntingdonshire manors also occupied good country for grain, cattle and sheep. At Great Stukeley, on the lighter clays and river gravels, St Margaret's hospital, Huntingdon, drew from the demesne four cartloads of hay annually, one strike of wheat every month, and at Christmas one strike of malt, half a strike of grout malt and one ram's carcass.[88] To the south, the multiplicity of mills in the Paxtons reflects the large capital investment in arable farming in the Ouse valley above Huntingdon. Great Paxton's mills were at rent to Sawtry abbey and those at Little Paxton on farm to St Neots priory.[89] Not all these mills, however, were for grinding corn. One was a fulling mill, first mentioned in 1173, which has the distinction of displacing other suggested candidates as the earliest known example in English record. In that year twelve responsible neighbours, including six *molendinarii*, had settled a dispute over the water that could be drawn off from the Ouse for Sawtry's mills without disadvantaging those of St Neots.[90]

Access to demesne pasture and meadows was a valuable privilege and jealously regulated. Elsewhere, Earl David opened part of his hayground at Whissendine to the hospital of Burton Lazars; Aldgate priory had the tithe of the hay from his demesne in Tottenham, the canons receiving their share in haycocks ('per muilones').[91] In Domesday Huntingdonshire, on the banks of the Ouse, Brampton, Godmanchester and Great Paxton were prominent among those villages with 'substantial amounts' of meadowland.[92] As along the Nene, the richness of the meadows lay not only in the attractive nature of the valley gravels but in the occasional floods which encouraged heavier hay crops for winter feed and fertile grazing-grounds. There were water-meadows in the Ouse at Kempston across the Bedfordshire border; at Great Paxton, the 'islands and waters' of Danford.[93] Ever present, however, was the danger that excessive spring or winter flooding would disrupt the manorial routine. At Paxton, the grainlands were set back on higher ground from the meadows occupying the flood-plain of the Ouse (the 'magna aqua'). The same precaution was imperative in the Beauchamp manor of Eaton Socon, upstream from Paxton: here the hay harvest could be disrupted in wet years 'per maximam aquarum inundacionem'.[94] St Neots priory carefully negotiated rights to block up all breaches and gaps if the meadows at Little Paxton were flooded to the detriment of its mills.[95] In Great Paxton Earl David gave Sawtry abbey land beside the river bank to rebuild a mill-pond evidently destroyed by seasonal flooding; the 'ductus de Russlade' had been dug to carry away surface water.[96] While floods increased the yields of hay and grass, they were welcomed only provided the water-level did not rise too high and they did not last too long. Embanking and drainage were necessary measures.

An exceptional document concerning the Hackleton fee beside Yardley Hastings, held by David of Hackleton of the Huntingdon honour, establishes the background for a closer analysis of the manorial economies. This undated text, headed 'Catalla de Hakelinton'', is an assessment for royal taxation, apparently either a unique survival from the returns compiled for the 'thirteenth' of revenues and movables of 1207 or a stray record made for the 'fifteenth' of 1225.[97] Thirty persons are named, including David of Hackleton and his wife, the most heavily assessed taxpayers. The value of grain and legumes plus that of plough animals (£18 12s. 2½d.) is rather more than double the gross value of cows and other livestock (£9 2s. 7½d.). This excess disappears when figures are computed for the tenant-land alone, the respective totals being £7 17s. 2½d. and £8 4s. 4½d. Yet throughout the manor the arable investment must have been more pronounced than at first appears. The recorded capital value of cows, sheep and pigs, compared to that of grain and vegetables, exaggerates their true 'annual' worth several times. Moreover, a large proportion of the freeholders and villeins, though adequately equipped with draught beasts, is not charged for any crops, and the stocks held by the remainder are distributed very unequally, with lord and lady holding the largest amounts. Seemingly, the grain assessed represents surpluses available for cash sale and the assessment was taken in the spring when grain supplies were low.[98] Every allowance made for the obvious drawbacks of taxation returns,[99] Hackleton must be classed as a manor where the farming was decidedly biased towards the arable. Yet in modern times, until the revolution in the land use of Northamptonshire since the Second World War, the Hackleton district, on the heavy claylands, lacked importance for cereal production, and ploughing was firmly subordinate to grazing.[100] In the early thirteenth century land had come under cultivation in this corner of the county which in less expansive periods would remain for pasture.

The evidence for Hackleton, close to the thriving market place of Northampton, focuses attention directly upon the economic pressures of the age. An expanding population placed a premium on arable land: peasants were breaking out ploughlands on the periphery, while lords or their representatives sought to augment revenues through more extensive food production for booming markets. Within Earl David's own manors the available records clearly show the development of resources proceeding in one characteristic way, as remaining reserves of woodland were drawn more closely into the agricultural regime. True, the importance of demesne woods, always more than a marginal resource, lay not simply in the fact that they could be grubbed out to cater for expanding cultivation. David had his great chase at Yardley Hastings and his brushwood at Earls Barton and Great Doddington, 'with hunting and warren'.[101] There were private parklands in other centres, including Exton where the earl disputed woodland boundaries with Henry de Armentiers; and the aristocratic passion for hunting, dependent upon woods and scrub, might easily prevail over concern to increase profits.[102] Woodland also provided rough grazings for livestock, and some stands were worked as coppices to produce underwood and timber for fuel and building. Neighbouring religious houses relied heavily for firewood upon the woods at Yardley, stretching over towards Horton: St Andrew's priory at Northampton was entitled to take two cartloads of dead wood daily; Delapré abbey had one cart gathering wood there each day; and David confirmed to St John's hospital, Northampton, the right to collect thirty cartloads of wood yearly. Yardley ('woodland from which yards or spars are taken') was continuing to live up to its name.[103] St Margaret's, Huntingdon, drew timber from Great Stukeley, while Sawtry was allowed two oaks annually at Great Paxton to maintain its mills in good repair. Clerkenwell priory carried away four trunks each year from Tottenham to replenish its firewood; and the sale of underwood on the London market remained an important item of income at Tottenham well into the fourteenth century.[104]

Skilled woodmanship brought good returns for few expenses. Nevertheless, the remorseless demand for grain ensured that under thirteenth-century conditions colonisation of woodland was far more profitable than conservation, and the balance between the different uses of this reserve shifted far in favour of assarting. Within the Huntingdon honour itself, the right to take green and dry wood 'without view and delivery of royal foresters' was a valued concession; but lord and free tenants could also manage their woods and fields quit of waste of forest, assart, ward and regard.[105] This exceptionally generous franchise was potentially most advantageous, for otherwise the bulk of the honour would have fallen unequivocally under forest law.[106] Like other proprietors, however, Earl David discovered that protection *per libertatem carte regis* was of dubious worth in the face of the malevolent oppressiveness of King John's forest administration. Indeed, such broad immunities as the Huntingdon honour's had already caused concern to the monarchy during Henry II's reign.[107] The stringent forest eyre of 1207–9 led to large numbers of Huntingdon knights and freeholders incurring fines for small assarts. Earl David himself was amerced a total of £200 for purprestures, although this sum may subsequently have been remitted.[108] The regarders made their record and left the claims for exemption to depend on the king's grace and favour. But the detailed lists of waste and assarts of 1207–9[109] provide the best evidence for expansive trends within the earl's chief holdings.

Three of his Northamptonshire manors were demonstrably engaged in woodland clearance. In the Salcey Forest district Huntingdon free tenants took a lead, encroaching in piecemeal fashion mainly from Piddington and Weston Underwood.[110] The earl's demesne at Yardley Hastings was also consolidated by tiny inroads of this kind: in confirming demesne tithes to St Andrew's, Northampton, David felt compelled to specify 'my assarts present and future and my old demesne'.[111] Rockingham Forest offered more substantial opportunities for reclamation. Invasions *sine licentia* 'de dominicis Comitis Dauid' were reported in 1209: at Harringworth there were eight acres of wheat and eighteen acres of oats 'de veteri essarto'; from Fotheringhay the arable was being extended into Southwick and the (now deserted) forest village of Perio.[112] Even if the effect was to add new peasant tenements rather than to develop demesne acreage in the narrow sense, in these places the extent of the colonisation may suggest that the manorial lord was no mere 'consenting party'.[113]

In Huntingdonshire there were no wooded areas on a comparable scale to the forest districts of Northamptonshire. Here and there, however, tree cover was heavy, and two of the largest Domesday concentrations were recorded at Great Paxton and Great Stukeley. In 1185 Paxton was fined for waste and Stukeley for assarts and encroachment, lordly initiative perhaps lying behind what was presented as the vills'.[114] The need to draw new boundaries between Ramsey abbey's property in Little Stukeley and Stukeley *Comitis* earlier in Henry II's reign was most likely the result of recent clearances; and by 1199 sufficient arable had been won from Earl David's woods to make it worth while for St Andrew's to litigate about its rights to the tithes *de essartis*.[115] The name Stukeley itself, first appearing in 1086, denotes an ancient assart ('stump-clearing'):[116] the age-long pressure upon unimproved land mounted from one generation to the next. The records of the forest proceedings at Huntingdon in 1209 are unusually precise.[117] The vill of Great Stukeley had taken in twenty acres of wheat and six acres of oats; separate entries charged the earl with forty-five acres of wheat, oats and fallow. Altogether this represented a sizeable addition to the cultivatable resources, and David vouched to warranty 'libertas sua de Huntedon''. Outside the Huntingdon honour at Alconbury, another colonising manor, communal rather than seigneurial initiative was apparently to the fore. First, Earl David was challenged as if the entrepreneur. It was claimed that he had opened up fifty-three acres of wheat and oats; but the reeve argued, correctly, that the men of the manor had cleared this assart by permission of the king's chief forester, that David had confirmed it to them, and that it was not 'in dominico suo'. Much of this activity, serving to augment the rent-roll, was towards Alconbury Weston, where by the early fourteenth century there was assart land of some three hundred acres.[118]

Within the earl's demesne manors new lands were thus won by the plough. It is sometimes difficult to distinguish in extant records the actions of the lord or his agents, to decide if capitalist endeavour was more dominant than peasant enterprise; and, obviously, more ambitious colonisations were being directed by neighbouring ecclesiastical proprietors, notably the old-established Benedictine abbeys.[119] Yet at least some of the larger additions to the home-farms or rent-paying tenements within David's estate centres may seem to give good evidence of a systematic campaign to boost seigneurial receipts.

But to what extent was Earl David the sole beneficiary of the rising manorial revenues? Central to the 'managerial revolution' is the lord's taking in hand of his demesnes, thus withdrawing them from the *firmarii* to whom it had been customary to commit them for predetermined rents. Otherwise, farmers' profits from expanding settlements and soaring prices tended to escalate as the lord's declined; and there was always the risk that a fixed lease would be transformed into a heritable tenure. The evidence for reclamation on certain manors may appear to indicate that their routine was not developing independently of the earl, even that at all times he stood in an immediate relationship to them, taking all the issues and maximising his returns. Yet land improvements could have been a form of restocking in order to lease out at higher rates and need not imply that direct management was normal; they may have represented only a hesitant move towards true landlord enterprise. Or for lordly initiative should we substitute that of thrusting lessees? At this date analysis of management methods 'must often be tentative, even subjective'.[120] Sufficient information survives, however, to approach this fundamental problem from a different direction by identifying some of the chief estate officials and indicating, albeit imperfectly, their functions within the earl's administration.

The foremost position was, of course, the stewardship of estates. No less than nine persons were called *senescallus* under Earl David in England from 1185 and seem to have been quite distinct from the lesser household stewards.[121] For lack of fuller evidence it is impossible to decide whether there was a high turnover in the office or whether normally more than one steward served simultaneously, each responsible for a different group of manors. Where their backgrounds are known, the stewards were knights of the Huntingdon honour, men of fairly modest standing when they officiated but duty-bound to serve their lord with aid and counsel. Recruitment was plainly bound up with tenurial ties. Yet in important ways these were not typically feudal officials. Whereas earlier Huntingdon stewards, in common with their peers, had ranked 'as leaders of the honorial baronage',[122] now it was not social prominence that was the essential qualification for office, but rather the personal merit that responsible management required. Some certainly belonged to rising ministerial families. For example, Robert of Bassingham's father was Earl David's marshal; a brother Roger was received into the *familia* of Archbishop Hubert Walter and became a canon of Lincoln and Salisbury cathedrals; Richard, perhaps another brother, had a connection with the archbishop's household and deliberated as a royal justice in 1194.[123] Nor was the stewardship hereditary, though this had also been characteristic of large estates when management had appeared straightforward and undemanding. David of Ashby followed his father as steward; but his talents were such that in the 1220s and '30s he moved easily between baronial and royal service in the manner typical of the professional stewards of the later thirteenth century. All that seems to be lacking is non-feudal salaried service, and one steward (albeit a vassal-steward) may in fact have received financial remuneration.[124] At this vital level of management a new expertise was injected into the running of an estate that had perhaps seen little managerial proficiency in the past. As the age of specialist land agents drew closer, the stewardship began to change its nature in response to the challenges of the day.

Only incidental information survives on the steward's general supervisory control. He was his lord's representative over rights of wardship, his surety in financial dealings.[125] To uphold his interests in litigation Earl David occasionally retained accomplished attorneys, notably the local man Reginald de Argentan, sometime royal sheriff and justice.[126] More usually, his legal proxy was the steward. Indeed the steward's activity is seen more clearly in the plea rolls of the central courts than in the ordinary management of the estate.[127] But this hard-worked official, pre-eminent above all other functionaries, was at David's disposal in all matters concerning the fief; and whatever his bureaucratic competence this firmly rested, as the

Seneschaucy later underlined, upon knowledge of the law.[128] Finally, of the local officers, reeves are mentioned for Alconbury and Earls Barton; there were also bailiffs who conducted view of frankpledge in the Huntingdon honour and whose responsibilities may have been agricultural, as well as legal and financial.[129]

Competent administrations were naturally the essential props of lords seeking to augment their estate revenues through immediate economic control; the evidence for the stewards can be placed beside that from the manors; and it is worth noting that when the Huntingdon honour was in royal custody in 1184–5 payments were made in Northamptonshire to officials 'per maneria', which conceivably points to some manors already being directly exploited.[130] But in the last resort, the available information is simply too shaky and fragmented for confidently stating that direct enterprise triumphed over leasing. At the same time, while there are some signs of economic virtue, there are also positive reasons for supposing that in management this fief was experiencing more a period of transition, with old attitudes persisting alongside the new, than of radical transformation.

A general warning can be sounded against exaggerating the speed and uniformity of the departure from traditional techniques. That a recent study has identified merely a dozen lay fiefs in whole or in part under direct management by *c.*1220 reflects the inadequacies of the evidence consulted.[131] But even in the more centralised monastic lordships, arguably better placed to exploit expansive tendencies, the displacement of lessees enjoying varying degrees of security could be a protracted procedure; and some religious houses were demonstrably slow to admit the advantages of one system above the other.[132] Members of the secular aristocracy also responded according to their particular circumstances and requirements. Quite apart from other considerations, involvement in the inconvenience and expenses of direct farming would not have been so attractive, or perhaps even so necessary, for a magnate with far-flung but substantial interests in Scotland which at once claimed an important share of attention and bolstered his incomes. Also to be remembered are the demands of an active public life in the service of two governments. Some reliance upon regular cash revenues rather than production for the market may therefore have been as acceptable to Earl David as it patently was to his son Earl John.[133] Furthermore, what economic success David enjoyed in England stemmed ultimately from circumstances which might actually inhibit a more exacting exploitation of estates. When all is said and done, it was largely through political influence at the Angevin royal court that he achieved the augmentation of his income called for by the initial weakness of his position and escalating costs. It is impossible to show clearly the value of the new manors he accumulated, and some of the lands received were used for retinue service. But from 1202 £120 was allowed against the accounts of the sheriffs of Huntingdonshire and Northamptonshire for his accretions in these counties alone, a figure that greatly underestimated their true

worth.[134] Court favour was not necessarily an alternative to business enterprise since they could go hand in hand. Even so, entrepreneurship was
likely to play a greater part in estates not being enlarged by royal patronage;
to this extent some of the pressure towards progressive land management
was removed.[135]

When Earl David's fortunes at court are fully related to the political
setting to which they belong, a wider perspective can be offered. Whereas
Henry Beauclerk had distributed favour 'as an instrument of social
change',[136] the Angevin monarchs were for many reasons less able and
willing to dispense rewards lavishly. But the higher aristocracy retained
certain expectations. As was their custom, they continued to look for
expressions of the king's goodwill, if only to help compensate for the
recurrent contraction of reserves that family obligations entailed and to
maintain their affinities. The price revolution, coupled with the loss of
continental estates in 1204, placed an even greater premium upon the king's
ability to balance his support for administrative families with a judicious
distribution of bounty to the great dynasties of the realm. Whenever the
plums of government patronage were too obviously monopolised by a small
inner clique, relations between the crown and the magnates were therefore
all the more likely to be hostile; and one feature of John's reign, as of his
successor's, was that too few magnates could identify their interests with the
crown and too many were squeezed out.[137]

Now, Earl David was one who had grown accustomed to basking in the
warmth of Angevin favour; but once King John withdrew his benevolence
the precariousness of the earl's situation was quickly revealed, his well-
being having rested so firmly in royal hands. Of his Exchequer debt of £900
in 1211, £767 was evidently assessed as personal *debita*, including £644
owed to Jews.[138] Great men had to adjust to fluctuating expenses and were
accustomed to living on credit, yet this was no temporary shortage of
liquidity. Pressed to clear his debt, David had settled for £574 by 1214; but
part of this sum could be found only by selling Potton, with its market and
park, for 100 marks.[139] Two years earlier, John had struck at the heart of his
capital assets by resuming Godmanchester and confiscating Fotheringhay;
Whissendine had been lost through an adverse legal judgement. Not all
these lands had stood as demesne in 1212; but feoffees displaced from the
subinfeudated portions had quite rightly demanded compensation from the
earl for loss of seisin.[140] With the king's displeasure, support was denied and
the dangers mounted. Two demesne manors, Exton and Great Paxton,
probably failed to come back after the civil war; Fotheringhay remained in
custody; and other properties had suffered war damage.[141] Lack of royal
favour demonstrated the grave weaknesses of David's position as an English
magnate as surely as royal munificence had previously offset them. His
power base disintegrated, his financial position deteriorated, and his local
prestige dissolved.

But Earl David was unrepresentative of the Anglo-Norman magnate class as a whole in important respects. From 1204, lay landowners who were significant in the kingdom were commonly denied both his range of resources in another country and the benefit of recent successes at court. It is no wonder that their interests clashed directly with those of the crown. The rivalries and tensions of John's reign were kindled in part by a patronage system that channelled the rewards of the king's goodwill to an increasingly restricted group, systematically withholding lands and offices from all save the most privileged magnates, or dispensing them only for exorbitant financial returns. They were intensified by the application of this policy when the higher aristocracy most needed reassurance and relief, and by the vigorous enforcement of unparalleled fiscal demands when they could be afforded least. Although the greatest lords were still considerable proprietors, the magnate class became more and more immersed in debt.[142] The struggle to maintain their station forced the baronage back primarily upon their patrimonial lands and no doubt served to heighten awareness of the opportunities of profits in expanding markets, with private seigneurial enterprise tending to supply the place of favour at court. But Earl David's status in Scotland and his access to the traditional routes of advancement, though not enduring, were perhaps sufficient to slow his own involvement in what others were compelled to regard as the surest way forward, the mobilisation of existing assets through more rational, commercial exploitation.

7

THE ESTATES IN ENGLAND
(II)

In the previous chapter the attention given to Earl David's indispensable gains from Richard I and John shifted some of the emphasis from the honour of Huntingdon. The present discussion of tenurial organisation focuses firmly on this estate, with its huge portion of alienated holdings.[1] As a lord of men in England from 1185, David faced many inconveniences spared him in Scotland. In the northern realm his territorial dominance was reasonably complete, his local prominence and leadership less threatened by neighbouring proprietors. Nor did an articulated system of royal government intervene regularly in his affairs and challenge his position; and the strength of the earl's lordship was underlined through his ability to build up *de novo* a broad-based clientage firmly bound to his interests.

By contrast, his landed influence in England was fragmented, his 'good lordship' contested by many great estate-owners and weakened by the powers of a stronger monarchy. Enfeoffment in the Huntingdon honour was far advanced even by 1086, while during the following century lordly authority had waned as personal ties had been largely superseded by the ties of tenure. Moreover, the Anglo-Scottish war of 1173–4, accompanied by a Senlis restoration, had ensured the expulsion of an influential group of Huntingdon tenants whose families had grown rich in Scots royal service. It was Earl David's first task to create a following to help enforce his personal superiority, and it rapidly became clear that for the most part his position within the honour would be only as effective as the established tenantry desired. He lacked the resources for any general extension of his influence by new land-based relationships, such were the limitations which his predecessors had imposed upon his *dominium*. According to a near-contemporary Crowland abbey source, favourable to the Senlis earls, David 'ejected without summons and judgement all those whom Earl Simon [III] had established as well as many of those established by Simon's father'.[2] The political history of the Huntingdon fief was undeniably productive of dispossession and rival family claims; and independent evidence shows that some revocations did take place from 1185 in order to recover alienated demesne or to restore Scottish partisans to rightful seisin. But many Senlis intimates who in the beginning had no tradition of loyalty to David's house also retained their lands; where *ex parte* attachments were less pronounced, tenurial continuity was considerable. There could have been no question of a new start. The old seigneurial powers of control and resumption were fast disappearing as tenant-right became ever more strongly entrenched. The fee was now the basis of family honour and lineage, at once an alienable and heritable interest. And lordship had been diminished further, most notably by the plural homages which Huntingdon vassals had contracted in their quest for alternative patrons and new endowments; by enfeoffments which had testified to the acquisitiveness of those of recognised power and independence; by the growing responsibilities of the knights in public service; and by the movement of property to religious houses for which Earl David had no special devotion as 'family' monasteries. At his accession David was confronted 'not only with a crisis of revenues, but also with a crisis of control'.[3]

The following account explores several related issues. Chiefly these concern the position of the knights and lesser gentry and, a consideration of particular relevance to this study, the various ties of property linking the honour, on a plane beneath its lord, with the kingdom of Scots. One major theme, however, will be treated more fully in the next chapter. This involves those tenants who in fact can be discussed in direct relation to Earl David because he succeeded in binding them to himself as members of his personal affinity.

Lay Tenants

Between 1185 and 1219 some eighty families possessed mesne fees of the Huntingdon honour by knight-service; a handful held *in libero maritagio*; and at a given moment the normal establishment probably comprised some fifty to sixty different *lignages*. As always, the Huntingdon vassalage lacked social coherence and embraced a wide spectrum of wealth and standing. All Earl David's vassals, of whatever condition, were bound to him, but his lordship was only one tie amongst others, and the majority were men with whom his relationship remained distant and formal. A number of the earl's charters were specifically addressed to the community of the honour, in one instance, 'to all his barons, knights and good men'.[4] First, who were the barons of, or at least in, the honour? Ever since the early twelfth century the estate had accommodated a complement of *curiales* and other important tenants-in-chief of the English realm: by c. 1185 these lords of far more than local distinction included Basset, Hommet, Mauduit, Muscamp, Umfraville and Fitz Robert.[5] Pride of place is reserved for the Dammartins, whose *comté* to the north-east of Paris put them 'parmi les plus puissants seigneurs du centre de la France'.[6] The value of the Dammartin alliance to England largely accounts for the Anglo-Norman interests steadily accumulated by this great family during the course of the twelfth century, its support being even more desirable after Renaud became count of Boulogne in 1192.

The wealth these prominent men enjoyed within the fief was by no means negligible. Walter Fitz Robert maintained Daventry as an important demesne residence and, to judge from later evidence, was the patron of Daventry priory; the Basset and Muscamp fees were assessed at five knights' service apiece; and about 1184 the Dammartin manors had been acceptable security for a loan of £115 from the Lincoln Jewry.[7] These lords of quality, however, were not in the habit of attending Earl David's court or having a voice in his affairs. The remoteness of the ties was emphasised whenever the crown exercised its rights of prerogative wardship and of marriage;[8] and it was further stressed by both the beneficial terms of tenure in frank-marriage (Mauduit, Fitz Robert) and the occasional running down, or outright loss, of assets. In *c.*1190 the Mauduits released their tenant at Othorpe (Leics) from the burden of providing them with hospitality. The Muscamp fee was so given over to sub-tenants that by the early thirteenth century the family had practically ceased to hold in demesne;[9] property reverted to the crown as a result of royal sequestrations. The Dammartin establishment based on Ryhall (Rutland) and Piddington (Oxon), always subject to the vicissitudes of Anglo-French relations, was first forfeited 'per voluntatem regis' in 1194, and the Hommet fee at Mears Ashby (Northants) escheated as *terra Normannorum* in 1205.[10]

All large English honours accommodated rich fief-holders possessing ample external interests. In addition, there were those Huntingdon vassals of good resources who also controlled mesne fees dependent on other midland lordships and occupied an intermediate position between the greater families and ordinary knightly dynasties: for example, Bois, Burdet, Grimbald, Ponton and Sproxton. But what is remarkable in the Huntingdon case are the Anglo-Scottish landholding links that stemmed directly from Scots royal control of the estate. About 1185 five lay tenants maintained far-distant enterprises in Scotland. Displaced *occasione guerre* in 1173–4 but restored under Earl David to their fees in the honour in whole or in part, the lords of this group also included men of especial weight and substance, and all belonged to a larger world than that of many knights. Richard de Moreville, Constable of Scotland and lord of Lauderdale and Cunningham, was of first importance. Walter Olifard I, lord of Bothwell in Clydesdale, was in the second rank of Scottish landowners. The remainder stood lower than he, but still drew significant incomes from Scottish possessions. Hugh Ridel controlled Cranston (Midlothian), although his main support lay at Abbotsley (Hunts) and Wittering (Northants), pertaining respectively to the Huntingdon honour and Peterborough abbey.[11] William de Vieuxpont II of Horndean (Berwickshire) and Carriden (West Lothian) enjoyed property in the honour at Hardingstone by Northampton, as well as more rewarding English gains from the Scots crown in Tynedale. He also held Maulds Meaburn near Appleby (Westmorland) through his first or second wife Maud, sister of Richard de Moreville, and shortly before his death by 1203 he seems to have secured the original family patrimony at Vieuxpont-en-Auge in Calvados.[12] Molesworth (Hunts) was a manor of the Lindseys, their representative being Walter of Lindsey II, lord of Lamberton (Berwickshire) and a vassal of the honour of Chester at Fordington (Lincs).[13]

The number of Huntingdon tenants with Scottish holdings about 1185 would clearly have been larger had it not been for the dependence of their cross-Border concerns upon harmony between the kingdoms. Philip de Colville of Heiton and Oxnam (Roxburghshire) and Hugh Giffard of Yester (East Lothian) cannot be connected with the honour later than 1173–4.[14] Earlier casualties include Ranulf de Sules of Great Doddington, who vanishes from Huntingdon record shortly after he had received Liddesdale from King David I,[15] and – although they did not adopt a consistently pro-Scottish stance – arguably the Brus lords of Annandale, whose tenure of Stretton (Rutland) it is not possible to trace in any connected way.[16] The Scots royal house could retain their midland honour only if they preserved the peace; war as easily divided estates at levels beneath their own. Nevertheless, when Earl David was in a position to offer his protection to the disendowed from 1185, normally intruders were promptly identified and expelled, and fees restored. To pursue a particular case, Walter Olifard had been deprived of Lilford (Northants), a manor which he claimed thanks to the failure of the senior Olifard line in England, and Earl Simon III had bestowed it upon Robert of Haversham. Before this, in the 1140s, Earl Simon II had despoiled Walter's father David of a direct Huntingdon connection by granting Sawtry, his sole English property, to the Cistercians. Obliged to recognise this loss as irretrievable, in 1157 or 1158 David Olifard had formally quitclaimed his hereditary rights to Sawtry in favour of Malcolm IV, the Cistercian order and the monks of Sawtry, in consideration of King Malcolm's grant of the lordship of Bothwell. The Olifards had thereupon fallen apart into two distinct Scottish- and English-based families. But Walter Olifard never relinquished his claims to Lilford – and under Earl David Robert of Haversham was ejected from the manor and the Olifards of Bothwell assumed their inheritance from the senior line. Anglo-Scottish ties, though undermined by periodic misfortune, could be remarkably resilient in the longer term.[17] Where an estate forfeited in 1173–4 had passed to the Church, however, it might be beyond recovery; where it had been treated as demesne land there was a temptation to retain it. Indeed, although Richard de Moreville regained other English interests after 1174, he was unable to resume his principal Huntingdon concerns before he died in 1189. Along with Great Doddington and Potton (Giffard) they were jealously guarded as honorial demesne.[18]

So forfeiture entailed the risk of permanent losses or some years of deprivation. There was to be a further bout of confiscations in 1215–17.[19] Yet the success of families landed in Scotland in retaining a stake in the honour still stands out; and since their cross-Border commitments mirrored his own, they arguably gave Earl David a closer community of interest with his tenantry than might otherwise have been the case.

Brus, Lindsey, Moreville, Ridel, Sules and Vieuxpont can all be associated with the Anglo-Norman nobility of the Davidian settlement.[20] While later twelfth-century Scotland could be a source of considerable wealth to individual newcomers, generally the rewards were sparser and its aristocracy was less of an 'open' class. Nor did Huntingdon families dominate the incoming as before.[21] Nonetheless, if in these respects the special relationship between the honour and the northern realm lay in the past, existing links were appreciably expanded across a range of activity from 1185. Robert de Quincy, a younger son of Saer de Quincy I and Maud de Senlis, had acted as justiciar of Lothian in the 1170s and acquired in marriage a broad lordship administered from Leuchars in Fife. Upon the death of his nephew without issue by 1192 he then inherited the ancestral patrimony in England, including the Huntingdon concern at Eynesbury (Hunts).[22] As with the Olifards, a family might divide into separate English and Scottish branches in one generation only to be reunited in one main stem not later than the next. Robert de Muscamp and Earl Henry de Bohun inherited Huntingdon tenancies and gained Scottish interests besides;[23] the Umfravilles, future earls of Angus, were already nurturing an offshoot in Stirlingshire and East Lothian; Alan, lord of Galloway, gained land at Whissendine and, as heir to the Morevilles, eventually entered into full seisin of their Huntingdon demesne.[24] Furthermore, we have seen how Earl David developed a new administration for his Scottish lands by employing persons who were at some stage Huntingdon tenants, albeit in minor ways, and how he transplanted into Garioch vassals connected with the English honour. Again, certain laymen associated with the honour who secured estates outside the earl's fief in Scotland possibly did so due to his intercession: most notably, a representative of the Carneilles of Great Stukeley, who took control of Guthrie in Angus; a kinsman of the Ashbys of Castle Ashby (Northants), who gained or strengthened a base in Berwickshire; and a cadet of the Luvetots of Hallamshire, who obtained Dalpatrick in Strathearn.[25] As a great Anglo-Scottish landowner Earl David naturally tended to involve others in his own cross-Border world.

Tenurial developments from 1185 thus took place against a background of existing Scottish ties and the creation of new ones. The attitude of the Lindseys towards their assets in the honour was typical of those others in their position. They clung tenaciously to Molesworth and consolidated another Huntingdon interest at near-by Caldecote; they retained the advowson of Molesworth, presenting to the living in 1220 Master John of Berwick, subsequently a canon of Moray.[26] Holdings like these were regarded with much of the earnestness of a local family protecting its inheritance, even when a lord's concerns in Scotland were far more extensive. One powerful justification for such a policy was that English lands might secure access to Angevin royal favour and valuable dynastic alliances. A brilliant marriage had brought Robert de Quincy's son and successor, Saer IV, rich midland fees and the rank of earl of Winchester by 1207; the Lindseys also played the English marriage market, but with less success.[27] Anglo-Scottish bonds, once established, were time and again renewed. Among Earl David's tenants in England there were lords for whom, like the earl himself, the Border presented no insuperable obstacle to the pursuit of private interests and activities. They helped give the honour a character distinctively its own.

But it was of course the ordinary 'knights and good men', vassals of localised and modest estate, who collectively controlled the lion's share of the honour's wealth. So far as the social and economic life of the fief was concerned it was they who chiefly counted, not the important mesne lords whose tenancies were often remote outliers of lands centred elsewhere. Although their horizons were narrower, one honour was not the whole context in which these knights and lesser gentry operated. They were involved in conflicting obligations by the contracts which at this level were also made with other lords. And especially in this countryside of scattered honours, where a magnate's authority was as fragmented as the estates he controlled, the ties of neighbourhood competed strongly with all vassalic ties. By 1173 the Huntingdon tenant in Dry Drayton (Cambs) had reached across the complexities of tenurial geography to undertake 'communi consilio' a new partition of the vill, including those lands 'which previously were disregarded because they . . . had long been waste'.[28] This is a rare glimpse of the collaborative effort so vital when different estates inter-mingled in the open fields of divided villages: legal sources often make medieval landowners seem 'incurably litigious',[29] but court proceedings are better documented than amicable compositions. Matrimony was another obvious force involving knightly tenants in a nexus of social relationships transcending the honour's bounds. One example must stand for many, the alliance between Robert son of Reginald of Oakley, Earl David's steward, and a daughter of Simon Basset. Simon did not hold of the honour, but he was the Oakleys' social equal and, since his Northamptonshire property entered Rushton beside Great Oakley, he was also their neighbour. Bonds of vicinity were strengthened by bonds of marriage, while Basset provided for the couple in Scalford and Ab Kettleby (Leics).[30]

As vassalic ties weakened, other associations inevitably grew stronger. Honour was giving place to county, feudal loyalty to local sentiment and the ties of community. For many Huntingdon knights, the importance of the formal meetings of the county probably overshadowed that of the honour court, which in any case had lost much of its proprietary jurisdiction to the royal courts. Earl David's tenant Alan de Audri conferred his Huntingdon fee at Draughton (Northants) on Roger de Bluckerville 'coram comitatu Norh't'; Robert of Braybrooke was supported by other knights *de honore* when he sealed a quittance in favour of Pipewell abbey at Northampton 'in die comitatus'.[31] Simon de Senlis and Jocelin of Stukeley were among the leaders of the shire gentry at the county court of Huntingdon when Thomas of Arden, king's justice, conducted the array of arms and exacted oaths of fealty.[32]

Just as the lesser vassals were tied to the shire community by neighbourhood, so the Angevin reforms in government and justice bound them by royal service, whether as members of *ad hoc* commissions to investigate the king's rights or as jurors of the Grand Assize, a charge that frequently fell upon those of dependable quality. Knighthood 'had become a qualification for public duties lying far outside the sphere of feudal obligation'.[33] Some fee-holders attained local pre-eminence as permanent officials of the crown, and in 1206–7 three Huntingdon vassals enjoyed a near-monopoly of shrieval office in the east Midlands: Robert of Braybrooke in Bedfordshire and Buckinghamshire, Jocelin of Stukeley in Cambridgeshire and Huntingdonshire, and Walter of Preston in Northamptonshire. These tenants, among others, had been recruited into a tight-knit ministerial élite. When Ralph Morin quitclaimed to Thorney abbey the advowson of Twywell (Northants), in the Huntingdon honour, he secured confraternity for himself and for Thomas Fitz Bernard, whose distinguished career in government employment (master forester, sheriff and justice) was about to end as Ralph's was beginning.[34] Service in the shires tended to supplant service in the lord's court and following; and the crown, by identifying the knights with the bureaucracy of county administration, was reinforcing the principle that obedience to the king overrode all other commitments. In August 1212 King John ordered Walter of Preston to take the necessary steps if Earl David refused to surrender Fotheringhay castle, with apparently every confidence where Walter's first loyalty lay.[35]

Much has been made in recent surveys of the general debasement of lord-man relationships in England by the late twelfth and the thirteenth centuries. This was certainly a feature of the Huntingdon fief; but the evidence does in fact have another side. The lower we descend in the social scale, the less homage was drained of meaning. Knightly tenants joined with Earl David to petition for a confirmation of their liberties in 1190, and although the chief franchisal rights which served to increase the earl's standing with his men were later undermined, the knights acted together in seeking to maintain them.[36] More privileged by charter than other small proprietors, many continued to hold their principal estates of the earl, were sometimes named after them, and normally resided upon them: for instance, Ashby of Castle Ashby, Cogenhoe, Houghton of Great Houghton, Oakley of Great Oakley, Rushton, Wilby and Wollaston. Above all, it was to the knightly vassals in this category, often the representatives of old-established Huntingdon families, that David resorted in order to exert his influence. He set out to win or consolidate their allegiance; and the number prepared to support him through retinue service or in other ways was significant. In some cases they had adhered to his cause in 1174. For those regularly attesting his charters and acting as his estate officials the bonds of lordship remained relevant. Primarily they were loyal to him as their liege lord under the crown; they identified their interests with his and through them he enforced his authority.[37] Countervailing ties were growing stronger, but although no longer in any sense 'a feudal state in miniature',[38] the honour of Huntingdon did retain some of the trappings of a truly feudal community.

The social hierarchy and allocation of wealth within the honour were not profoundly altered between 1185 and Earl David's death. Yet not all the lay tenants at his succession, or their families, enjoyed the same overall economic power more than thirty years later. Vassals ascended the social scale along the conventional avenues of advancement: although among the higher aristocracy in England, as in Scotland, attitudes were hardening against the *parvenu*, 'there were no barriers, only differences and grades of wealth, between the village squire and the baron'.[39] On the other hand, failure to secure a generous patron or success in marriage might lead to social displacement; there were permanent reversals in circumstances due to extinctions in the male line or political imprudence. Does the stability or upward movement of individual fortunes appear to have been more notable than the instances of decline?

This question has particular significance for those of the middling or lesser sort. Postan's well-known argument is that the booming economy from the late twelfth century benefited great lords far more than their social inferiors. As living costs escalated the gentry were grievously depressed as a class; the basis of knighthood changed to one of social distinction beyond the reach of many families because they were unable to defend their position; and thirteenth-century sources 'bear witness to the accretions to the estates of lay magnates and of nearly all the great abbeys: accretions which were almost invariably made at the expense of smaller landowners'.[40] Though some recent criticisms of this thesis have been noted in general surveys and amplified in specialist papers,[41] it is one upon which detailed studies of certain ecclesiastical corporations and secular entrepreneurs appear to confer authority. To develop arguments further, more local studies are the chief priority, and since there have been no complementary investigations based upon selected large lay honours it seems desirable that an analysis be offered here.

Attention must naturally focus mainly, though not exclusively, upon the period 1185–1219. In these years, corresponding to the first and heaviest phase of inflationary pressure,[42] it is possible to identify four families experiencing acute financial hardship: Rushton, Foxton, Foliot and Leidet. To understand their difficulties something must be said on their respective backgrounds before indebtedness overwhelmed them. In this regard they form a contrasting group. One was of strictly local importance, another controlled a large mesne fief, and two held in chief by barony. But all were falling and in each case the decline is largely described in the Braybrooke family cartulary.[43] One of the foremost Christian speculators of his day, Robert of Braybrooke rose from obscurity as a sub-tenant of the Foxtons through active capital investment either in simple land purchases or in the redemption of estates indebted to Jews. Whereas every gentry house was forced to adjust to the changing economic climate, some families undoubtedly responded more effectively than others. Braybrooke, though never a great magnate, provides a model instance of social aggrandisement to set beside the evidence for adversity.

The Rushtons, holding barely three hides at Rushton in the Northamptonshire Survey, would never expand significantly beyond this village.[44] Responsible for one knight's service, they had always to be careful with their resources, but it was perhaps the family's main misfortune not to avoid the penalty of encumbering a small estate with a too numerous progeny. Andrew of Rushton, living in 1163, had three sons; William, his oldest son and heir, fathered two surviving sons and three daughters. They may already have been struggling in Andrew's lifetime when he sold land to Pipewell abbey 'ad grangiam ibidem construendam'. The foundation of East Grange marked a major stage in the growth of Pipewell's endowment in villages near by the abbey, and the monks made other gains from the Rushtons in following years. William alienated more of the patrimony, including meadowland within the abbey precincts 'ad construendum refectorium suum'. The depletion of reserves accelerated in the next generation as financial pressure forced the family to part with land on a larger scale. By 1202 William's heir Robert *miles* had given Pipewell his wood called *Coleshawe* for 24 marks 'ad liberandum me de Judaismo'; he also surrendered part of his assart of *Stortch* to be free from Jewish creditors. A sister made over her dowry in Rushton for six marks 'ad negotium meum maximum expediendum', and the monks bought woodland from his cousins. Alienations had been made to St James's abbey at Northampton. Then Robert of Braybrooke entered the market to take advantage of a family on the very brink of bankruptcy. By 1211 he had purchased such interests from Robert and his nephew that the Rushtons must have been virtually bought out: ruined by debts, they had ceased to be knightly in anything more than name, while Robert's brother was being hounded as a fugitive from justice. Shortly afterwards the family expired in the male line, the remnants of the estate passing through a niece to Hugh of Goldingham.

The Foxtons, whose original base has been described as 'a typical fief of a great honorial baron',[45] were initially better endowed. Yet note the heavy contractual expenses: seven knights' service is the recorded requirement. An unusually well-defined nucleus centred on the family seat at Foxton (Leics) and its immediate satellites in Gumley, Little Bowden and Lubenham. The first evidence of reorganisation derives from monastic archives: Daventry priory acquired all the demesne churches and their valuable endowments; St Andrew's, Northampton, took one carucate and a mill at Scalford (Leics), as well as ten virgates by purchase. Subsequently the family augmented the glebe of Scalford church by half a virgate.[46] Here, at Scalford, the Foxtons were running down their assets in an outlying, expendable estate where effective control was difficult to sustain. But under Earl David's tenant, Richard of Foxton, dangerous inroads were made upon the core of this fee. Even before his time much of the demesne at Little Bowden and Lubenham, and in Braybrooke (Northants) and Othorpe in

Slawston (Leics), had passed to lay tenants – by *c.*1190 Robert of Bray-brooke was the principal of these, a family settlement having secured for him one knight's fee in Bowden, Braybrooke and Lubenham in exchange for property in Normandy.[47] Nevertheless, Richard endowed Daventry with parcels of land in Foxton; one bovate went to St Andrew's. There were gains in this manor by Sulby abbey and St James's, Northampton; Richard's father had added a half-virgate to the endowment of Foxton church.[48] This spate of alienations was not demonstrably caused by financial need. The Foxtons had some reserves to spare and were concerned to make their mark as patrons of the Church. But when a family began randomly to split up the estate from which it took its name, the basis of its patrimony, it was hastening towards decline.

The earliest record of economic importunity shows Richard of Foxton in 1179 borrowing £10 from Aaron of Lincoln, who was entitled to recover the principal and interest from Bisbrooke (Rutland). Richard then dis-charged this bond by pledging the land for 50 marks to Samuel of Stamford. On Samuel's death in 1186, Bisbrooke escheated to the crown and was set at farm for 10 marks *per annum*; the farm ran on for longer than was necessary to redeem the capital debt claimed by the Exchequer; and Richard was not restored until 1198, when the property was in Robert of Braybrooke's custody.[49] The year before, Richard had sold to Braybrooke for 60 marks his entire interest at Gumley, save for certain tenanted land. However, Sulby abbey, which had owned a full virgate in the vill, had had to be given an exchange *ad valenciam* in Foxton.[50] Yet these measures fell far short of reviving the family's fortunes; undermined by the heavy charges borne by the estate in the past, its circumstances continued to worsen. In 1202 Richard's son and eventual heir Richard II claimed four virgates in Foxton as the settlement bestowed upon him and his wife, whose father Eustace of Watford had negotiated the marriage in return for his discharging debts to Jews of 100 marks.[51] By 1208 Robert of Braybrooke had bought up or otherwise acquired nine virgates and six tofts in Foxton. A little later, Richard the elder transferred to Henry of Braybrooke, Robert's son, a further four virgates in Foxton, receiving in return a palfrey and a gold ring.[52] Although comfortably off and perhaps taking baronial style in the early twelfth century, the family appears to have acknowledged that by this stage the obligations of knighthood were beyond its grasp: in 1216 Richard the younger occurs as a mere serjeant.[53] The final blow fell in *c.*1220 when Richard II died without surviving male issue and the fee was partitioned between his two daughters and their respective husbands, Alan Basset and Henry de Oiry. Even then the dower of his widow in Foxton was at once the subject of rival claims and encumbered with *debita Judeorum*.[54]

The Foliots and their successors the Leidets[55] had a roughly similar history to that of the Foxtons: both houses, even as tenants by barony of the English crown, were ultimately hard pressed to support the expenses of knighthood. The Foliots' Huntingdon interest in 1185 included the Bedfordshire manor of Sutton and claims to various properties which they disputed with Earl David.[56] Hitherto, the family was distinguished by service as stewards of the honour, kinship with the great churchman Gilbert Foliot, and illicit (but temporary) 'invasions' during the Anarchy.[57] Yet Robert Foliot's marriage by *c.* 1150 to Margery de Reinbuedcurt, the heiress of the barony of (Chipping) Warden, had scarcely elevated the Foliots into the magnate class. The Warden honour had been valued at around only £94 in 1086. It also carried an onerous *servitium debitum*: fifteen knights were owed, and a surplus enfeoffment of two fees *de novo* was reported in 1166.[58] Marriage extended the territorial base and the Foliots rose into the baronage; but to portray Margery as a 'noble prize' and her inheritance as 'a valuable Honour' serves only to exaggerate their true importance.[59]

The Braybrooke cartulary describes an early loss. Margery's father Richard de Reinbuedcurt

> threw dice with King Henry [1] and lost 25 marks. The king wished him to settle before he rose from the game, and since he had no ready money conditions of payment were set so that if he defaulted the king would receive the money from the manor of Burton. Richard cleared the greater part of the debt, but because he did not observe the agreement and also because the king resented his mistreatment of his wife, whom the king had given him from his chamber, he dispossessed Richard of Burton and kept it.[60]

Such royal pettiness seems more typical of John than of Beauclerk; but the story is confirmed by independent evidence in its essential detail, and it represents a setback from which the lords of Warden never seem to have recovered. Robert Foliot sought to regain Burton Latimer (Northants) from Henry II by negotiating new terms of payment. Yet he too failed to satisfy the king, and by 1166 the Dinans held it 'in voluntate domini regis'.[61] Meldreth (Cambs) and Wroxton (Oxon), once important components of Reinbuedcurt demesne, were also wholly alienated at this stage.[62]

Marriage had raised the Foliots up the tenurial scale, but their income never seems to have been adequate for the status to which they were entitled. Richard Foliot had succeeded by 1176 and was dead by 1203. Since his only son had predeceased him, the estate then passed to Wiscard Leidet, husband of Richard's daughter Margery II. So far as is known the Foliots had not been forced into land sales through financial problems, but certainly their patrimony was crippled with debts. Margery Foliot *senior*, Richard and his brother Elias had all run up large outstanding sums with the Northampton Jewry; and while the Leidets had achieved moderate standing in the wake of the Mandeville earls of Essex, Wiscard's marriage, far from confirming his social rise, quickly reduced him to insolvency. The 200 marks he owed for seisin was a high relief for an estate of such limited potential.[63] The burden of inherited debts aside, alienations had seriously encroached upon Warden itself, the Northamptonshire *caput* of the barony: Warden abbey in Bedfordshire had accumulated such interests there through Foliot patronage that a grange had been begun to run them and the village name was changed to West (later Chipping) Warden to distinguish the place from the abbey's site.[64] At Sutton in the Huntingdon honour there had been grants to, amongst others, the abbeys of Sawtry and St Albans.[65] Moreover, Wiscard lost favour at court: in 1205 he owed 100 marks to regain the king's grace and be restored to his lands.

A less than advantageous marriage and political misfortune had saddled Leidet with commitments well beyond his means. Robert of Braybrooke now made a timely intervention, entering into several transactions with Wiscard and his creditors in 1209–11. He gave a total of 700 marks to free Wiscard of his personal debts to Samuel of Northampton and to redeem the bonds carried on the elder Margery and her sons. In this way, Robert secured one of the original Leidet estates, at East and West Langton (Leics), the manor of Sutton and, by implication, control of the marriage of Christiana, the daughter and heiress of Wiscard and Margery II.[66] From Wiscard's standpoint, these were desperate measures to be adopted only as a last resort. He still owed the crown over £90 which he was being pressed to clear; in 1216 £80 remained unpaid and new expenses were piling up. Two years earlier he had been compelled to waive, partly in Henry of Braybrooke's favour, all his claims against Earl David.[67] To complete the Braybrooke takeover, Henry, who had married Christiana, acquired the whole property when Wiscard died in *c.*1222.

Robert of Braybrooke's dealings with Leidet just before his own death in 1211 formed the last and most ambitious venture in a remarkable business career, of which investments in the Huntingdon fief represented only a part. Distinguished public service was the key to Braybrooke's ascendancy. His earliest notable appearance was as the steward of the lord of Belvoir, baronial service paving the way for rapid advancement in royal service.[68] Robert figures in Wendover's list of King John's 'evil advisers', and although this hardly proves that he systematically abused the privileges of office for personal profit, as a sheriff – one whose responsibilities were increased to embrace four midland shires from 1209 – he was ideally placed to go into business for himself and traffic in the debts of others. It is no coincidence that his major purchases were concluded after entering crown service: official status enabled him to gather valuable intelligence, especially about the credit operations of the Northampton Jews, and provided the opportunity for capital accumulation, even if only through the rewards of a grateful king. He farmed the royal manor of Corby (Northants) upon conspicuously favourable terms from 1205 and enjoyed profitable custodies of ecclesiastical temporalities.[69] He used his position to procure elaborate royal confirmations of his purchases and valuable franchises.[70]

In all, Robert's speculations in the land market involved a minimum outlay of 1,600 marks;[71] and the bulk of his gains from Huntingdon tenants has already been described. The overall pattern reveals two areas of particularly concentrated acquisition, each of which was related to his purchases within the honour. By 1208 negotiations with Hugh de Beauchamp of Eaton Socon and his tenantry had resulted in substantial gains along the Ouse valley from Duloe to Chawston in Roxton.[72] Sutton was a convenient extension of these accumulations. To the north-west, between Kettering and the upper reaches of the Welland, Robert's acquisitions from the Foxtons and the Rushtons (and from Leidet in the Langtons) went hand in hand with a complex series of transactions designed to round off and enlarge the original family holding in the Foxton fee. In a cluster of villages on the Northamptonshire side of the Welland, notably Braybrooke, Desborough, Dingley, Glendon, Great Weldon, Kelmarsh, Rothwell and Rushton, free-holds were secured from over twenty other families: in Desborough alone some 80 marks were invested in new property and the buying out of residual family claims. Most of this money passed to Reginald de Bordell who surrendered his interest there for 50 marks 'and one bay horse, a palfrey, a hauberk and a plough-team', which left him with the basic military equipment of a knight but without the landed requirement.[73]

Along this stretch of the Northamptonshire-Leicestershire border a new unit of lordship was being forged across the divisions of earlier enfeoffments. The patrimonial estate in Braybrooke, where Robert had his manor-house with a private chapel,[74] was the centre from which this activity was directed. In the village itself multiple subinfeudation had created a situation of bewildering complexity, and Robert's progress through this tenurial maze is difficult to chart.[75] But a major inroad was made into the fee of Basset of Great Weldon. The abbot of Bury St Edmunds resigned the service of two virgates; from Daventry priory Robert secured three and a half virgates in Braybrooke and Dingley.[76] By purchase or by patronage Pipewell abbey had formerly dominated the land market in this corner of the Midlands.[77] Robert was now engrossing property that the abbey might otherwise have hoped to acquire, and it is clear whom this house regarded as its main rival around 1200: the monks long remembered Robert as 'a hard man and intensely avaricious'.[78]

The cases considered here provide by themselves too narrow a basis for confident conclusions; but set against such evidence as exists for the wider group of Huntingdon gentry they simply seem to indicate the possible extremes of personal fortune rather than any crisis of the whole class. The taking up of knighthood came to suggest a certain social consequence and growing independence of the great lords. It perhaps encouraged some competitive extravagance. But these changes coincided with the need to adjust successfully to inflationary conditions. On the one hand, there were those who fell because they were unable to slow the pressures breaking up their holdings. Hurried along by indebtedness, the disintegration of family properties got out of hand and they failed to survive as going concerns. To the list of casualties could probably be added the estates of Audri, Boughton and Lisures.[79] Yet just as some families declined so others rose. Public employment and its perquisites dramatically boosted Robert of Bray-brooke. Though his story barely impinges on our records, Robert de Vieuxpont passed from modest circumstances to true aristocracy through his court connections,[80] and other knightly lines profited from government service, if less spectacularly. Ralph Morin of Harrold (Beds), for instance, accompanied Prince John to Ireland, obtaining property in Dublin. Ralph's offices in the English shires brought greater rewards 'whether by warden-ship, or lease, or purchase', and 'laid the foundation for a family of mark'.[81] His new-found influence was reflected in the enterprise of his kinsman Robert Morin, who eloped with a daughter of John Mauduit of Easton Mauduit (Northants), married her against the express wishes of John's lord and cousin Robert Mauduit, *camerarius regis*, forcibly usurped her inherit-ance, and was nevertheless recognised as the lawful tenant in 1212. It was a powerful local family that could steal a march on the hereditary royal chamberlains of Hanslope.[82]

But most knightly *lignages* do not in fact occur as either ruinously in debt or vigorously emphasising their social superiority. That their activities are often poorly documented is an indication of their economic stability: declining or rising families generate more records than those quietly holding their ground. Solicitous conservation of the patrimonial estate was more than a matter of family instinct or legal restraints; sustained over the years it could guarantee financial security. A tenant might limit his expenses by checking the claims of piety,[83] scaling down his contractual obligations, or deliberately avoiding the costs of knighthood. The Huntingdon gentry also added to their property by judicious marriages into land, by success in litigation, by taking on beneficial leases as *firmarii*, by assarting, and by small purchases. All these were ways of procuring the extra substance to maintain one generation and support the next without dissipating the main family property.[84] Such activity was often piecemeal; but many coped with inflation without surrendering their principal assets, and some were merely emulating the example of their predecessors who, acting with astuteness from very early on, had steadily created out of estates of scattered resources holdings that were richer and more compact and manageable.[85] In the late twelfth and early thirteenth centuries any family dogged by bad luck, poor judgement or profligate habits would quickly find its income dangerously inadequate. But those who kept their house in order maintained or repaired their economic fortunes and avoided serious trouble; and arguably small landowners 'were most sensitive to the threat of a deteriorating social position'.[86]

Past achievement did not, of course, guarantee future success. John Morin, Ralph Morin's grandson, was described in 1255 as worth over £30 *per annum* but was apparently reluctant to assume the burdens of knight-hood; his sister had married Robert of Ashby, the clerk of their father's kitchen, a *mésalliance* which contrasts sharply with the Morins' earlier successes. Ashby was without doubt a lowly servant, but one who through small-scale purchases in the neighbourhood of Harrold had acquired numerous lands and tenements.[87] He had also bought his way into a family lacking the endowment to keep pace. John Morin died insolvent about 1263. In the previous year he had demanded from his tenants an aid 'for making his first-born son a knight'; but the continuing history of the family is one of unrelieved distress.[88]

Does this example suggest that inflation only made acute financial needs generally felt when those families able to survive the first shock in the period 1180–1220 found their reserves destroyed by continued rising costs?[89] The possibility of a later thirteenth-century crisis receives no support from the records of the honour.[90] The period of Earl David's lordship stands out as the age of greatest economic hardship for the Huntingdon knights and minor gentry. It is also revealing with respect to Postan's thesis that such impoverishment as then existed within the honour was not accompanied by a shift in the share of wealth to great landowners from their social inferiors. Although individual monasteries made gains, no single magnate or corporation dominated the market in real property as did Braybrooke. For Earl David, entry into this field called for the kind of capital he did not possess. Indeed, there is a case for arguing that in his declining years the earl was experiencing a personal economic crisis in England whereas the majority of his knights were reasonably solvent. A more powerful neighbour, Peterborough abbey, was confining its attentions to 'the area where the abbey was strongest', retrieving fees alienated earlier on.[91] Braybrooke invested and expanded after the fashion of the enterprising monastery; but the redistribution of property helped make a 'new' man. And although his main effort was concentrated on small proprietors, outside the honour Robert also acquired interests from the countess of Clare and influential religious communities. It was his son Henry who bought Potton from Earl David.[92]

Yet there is a further consideration that may affect the nature of our conclusions. Earl David's English demesnes were never so large that he could be an open-handed patron; and established tenants were disadvantaged, too, because the majority of his beneficiaries in England did not belong to Huntingdon families. But openings still existed in Scotland, even if his accession heralded the tail-end of the protracted process of building up estates by incomers from the midland fief. The material gains were scant, for Scotland no longer afforded the same opportunities that had attracted Anglo-Norman knights in the earliest, most profitable colonising phase. Nevertheless, the northern realm had once offered major sources of wealth to Huntingdon families of modest origins, important existing links were being consolidated, and lesser ones continued to be forged. It is too much to say that the Scottish interests of their lords enabled numerous gentry houses to augment their patrimonies or to provide for younger sons; but the possibility remains that sufficient were caught up in this movement overall to influence our impression of the economic condition of knightly lines between 1185 and 1219.

There is, however, another perspective. Individuals enjoyed a greater stability than dynasties. The available data on the fifty or so families recorded as holding mesne fees in *c.*1185 provide some instructive statistics. The descent of a dozen lines cannot be followed for lack of evidence. Of the remainder almost half had become extinct in the main branch by 1300 through failure of direct male heirs. Twelve that succumbed had stood as gentry in 1185 and their property normally passed again into knightly hands, sometimes (because of further failures) through several in swift succession.[93] Under-reproduction could be more readily avoided by the prosperous and well-to-do; but such a turnover of families, comparable with others,[94] obviously cannot be explained on economic grounds alone. There is an especially poignant reminder of the natural fluctuations in family fortunes. Henry of Braybrooke (d. 1234) invested in the manner of his father and achieved a new pre-eminence; but after his grandson died in 1256 the patrimony was dismembered through female succession. An estate industriously constructed could be so easily dispersed by chance. Again, Rushton, Foxton, Foliot and Leidet were undeniably hard pressed; but it was lack of male children that most decisively undermined them. Indeed, awareness of impending elimination may have encouraged heavy borrowing as an immediate solution to financial need, even decisions to sell up, when others might have triumphantly struggled through. Although the distribution of wealth by social groupings would remain largely unchanged, indebtedness was scarcely the only, or most potent, force working for the transmission of patrimonies. Given the ever-present hazards to family survival, all other problems look small.

No one analysing the whole body of Huntingdon evidence would be likely to support the concept of a declining thirteenth-century gentry and a rising aristocracy. More families may have come under economic pressure elsewhere, for every great lordship had its own history. But each estate surely belonged to 'a world, first of all, in which the rise and fall of landed families was a thing taken for granted'.[95]

Ecclesiastical Interests

The numerous holdings of the religious created by Earl David's predecessors and their vassals in the Huntingdon honour permit no full treatment here. The Benedictines were represented by Eynsham, Westminster and the great fenland abbeys of Ely, Ramsey and Thorney, although for all their renown these long-established corporations in fact enjoyed limited influence inside the fief. The religious houses most closely associated with it were newer foundations, with the localised attachments characteristic of communities begun since the Conquest. The Cluniacs at Daventry, Delapré and St Andrew's, Northampton, all drew their main revenues from Huntingdon interests; but as the popularity of traditional monasticism had faded lay support had shifted to the reformed orders, and the honorial records reflect their wide appeal. Aldgate, Harrold, Missenden and Owston were the principal Augustinian convents to benefit from the estate's resources; Pipewell, Sawtry and Warden were their chief Cistercian counterparts. By 1185 the fief had given lavishly of its reserves, responding in each generation to the changing aspirations of the English monastic establishment. In addition, the estate archives are enlivened by the names of far-distant plantations: a few Norman houses and, more interesting and significant, several Scottish abbeys whose continuing connections with the honour will be singled out for special concern.

Earl David made no known religious foundation in England, though a late tradition describes him as the founder of St John's hospital, Huntingdon.[96] In the narrow sense of patronage he was received as lord and patron of Delapré, Sawtry and St Andrew's, all begun by the Senlis line, as well as of the Benedictine nunnery of Elstow, founded by Countess Judith. By 1174 King William had provided a new site at Hinchingbrooke for the nuns of Eltisley, and this may have led David to claim patronal rights.[97] Ecclesiastical patronage emphasised a lord's personal consequence and local standing, although in Earl David's case it seems important not to exaggerate what this amounted to in practice when assessing his position as an English landowner. It is by no means evident that he was able to extend his influence by exercising significant proprietary powers, and of the houses concerned Sawtry abbey – his place of burial – would alone have regarded him as in any sense a major benefactor. Even then, the chief grant of eight virgates in Conington was offered only at his death-bed, a circumstance that embarrassed the monks later on.[98] It is again notable that the muniments of St Andrew's priory preserve two of David's charters written in the conventional form of original grants, but which in reality acknowledge earlier benefactions by the Senlis earls. Reluctance to accept Senlis dispositions without new gifts may have been coupled with a desire to appear more generous than he chose actually to be.[99] Finally, although a patron's most basic responsibility was to afford monastic patrimonies effective protection, as will be seen from certain disputes or lawsuits, this duty was not invariably discharged. The patronal relationship was therefore often formal and, at times, strained.

The other religious houses with which Earl David was connected as the lord of the honour usually figure as recipients of ordinary charters of confirmation rather than of grant.[100] That just one of these *acta* ratifies a contemporary mesne tenant's gift underlines the degree to which lordly authority over subinfeudated lands had been eroded and the difficulty of preventing a damaging loss of incidents. In return for David's quittance of a rent-charge, Aldgate priory received earl, countess and heir in confraternity. The priory's founder was his great-aunt Queen Maud of England, while King David I had supported both Aldgate and another London house of Augustinian canonesses favoured by Earl David, Clerkenwell priory. It is more difficult to explain his concern for the Norman priory of La Chaise-

Dieu-du-Theil (arr. Évreux, dép. Eure). This community, dependent upon Fontevrault, had no previous Scottish or Senlis connection. It was thus a new interest, though one with an established reputation among the Anglo-Norman aristocracy, including David's kinsmen the earls of Leicester.[101] His support was also enlisted by the hospital of Burton Lazars; and the principal beneficiary of his piety, Lindores abbey, acquired ancillary interests from him in England.

The recorded benefactions of the earl, as a donor of English property, conformed to the prevailing spiritual tastes of secular society. They were conventional in a further sense. Reviewed overall, apart from Sawtry the only monastery to receive real estate of any consequence was Hinchingbrooke, which secured a meadow and two virgates in Great Stukeley.[102] Other houses gained a few acres but, more usually, commodities or easements less valuable than land. Such parsimony was not untypical of contemporary magnates in England. *Arrivistes* continued to set up convents as an offering to God and a fitting symbol of their social rise, and the new orders found a fertile soil for some further growth. Yet old aristocratic houses, conscious of the pious generosity, even improvidence, of their ancestors, considered their spiritual responsibilities more or less fulfilled.[103] In Scotland, where western monasticism followed a rather different pattern of development, David had the scope to show the generosity of earlier benefactors in England, and his influence grew in proportion. But he assigned very little of his English property to the Church because so much of it was already devoted to religious uses.

At lower levels, too, 'monastic properties had now to be fitted into the interstices of secular properties'.[104] Long-settled Huntingdon families closest to Earl David in social rank followed the same course as their lord. Modest houses had been begun alongside or within the honour at Alvecote (Burdet), Biddlesden (Bois), Harrold (le Fort), Owston (Grimbald) and Worksop (Luvetot); the Grimbald, Preston and Sproxton families had all contributed handsomely in the past to St Andrew's priory, among other corporations. But this phase of charitable gifts was effectively over by 1185. Ordinary knights were being coaxed to augment endowment incomes, or (e.g., Meppershall, Oakley) spontaneously continued a tradition of giving.[105] Those exceptional families on the way up (e.g., Braybrooke, Morin) eventually secured the reputation of generous benefactors.[106] However, for the more representative, restraint was one factor reinforcing their economic stability. Gifts of churches or assarts protected their landed inheritances.[107] Normally resources were spared only to obtain rights of burial, to found chantries, or to inscribe a kinsman's name in an abbey's martyrology; or else there were explicit monetary compensations with which to discharge personal debts, even to obtain freedom from prison.[108] Declining families were less able still to give gratuitously, whereas the business-minded were as likely to attempt the recovery of earlier alienations as to augment them.[109] Recent studies of the patterns of benefaction to monasteries whose activities hardly impinged upon the honour stress that gentry support could not make up for lack of magnate interest.[110] Within midland England as a whole, monks and canons were competing for rapidly diminishing reserves of gifts.

With the flow of endowments dwindling to a trickle, monastic communities depended upon other means of avoiding more or less permanently fixed incomes and generating the larger surpluses now required. Of those houses important in the life of the honour, Harrold, Sawtry and St Andrew's engaged in minor improvements through forest clearance, while Warden continued to assart from its grange at Midloe and to engross the assarts of others.[111] Pipewell was clearing extensively in Rockingham Forest.[112] Some monasteries had the strength to round off endowments through purchase: Aldgate, Pipewell and St Neots priory were all active in the property market.[113] Ecclesiastical records tend to disguise financial transactions. St Andrew's, however, seems to have been rather more interested in land-purchase in the early twelfth century than it ever was later.[114] Indeed, although some of the communities firmly bound to the honour when Earl David was its lord showed a certain enterprise, we must maintain a sense of proportion. If purchasing by monastic bodies about this time appears 'widespread and general',[115] in the east Midlands large-scale operations of this kind were primarily the preserve of the rich, pre-Conquest Benedictine abbeys, just as they dominated in reclamation works. With few exceptions, the newer church foundations in our records were less obtrusive. They lacked wealth and ostentation, were scarcely 'high farmers', and were possibly at times barely able to maintain their numbers. Their activities thus seem unremarkable; but they were the more typical.

Two controversies which continued to reverberate direct attention to the honour's complex political fortunes and the consequences for the stability of ecclesiastical holdings. Both the convents concerned were entitled to regard Earl David as patron and protector, but neither was secure in his support. The first case may be reconstructed principally from a narrative history of Delapré abbey, compiled about 1237. The eastern portion of Hardingstone (Northants) had originally been assigned to Delapré, as part of the foundation endowment, by Earl Simon II; certain Scottish supporters had thereupon been disseised; and subsequently King Malcolm IV, having evicted the nuns, granted the land in lay tenure to William de Vieuxpont I of Horndean in Berwickshire. Anticipating forfeiture for their support of the young King Henry's rebellion, the Vieuxponts mortgaged the fee to a London Jew; but the nuns regained temporary control of the property when Earl Simon III was restored and pledged himself to redeem it. Earl David's accession then enabled the Vieuxponts to recover the holding, which eluded Delapré's grasp until Abbess Cecily (el. 1220) sought redress at law and successfully carried the suit 'par l'ayde nostre seigneur Jesu Christ et sa douce mere'.[116] In this example, the troubles of a monastery would seem to have been inextricably bound up with the erratic history of the Huntingdon fief. In fact, although Delapré remained in possession, the Vieuxpont claim was still a live issue in the 1250s.[117]

The second dispute was even more convoluted. Soon after 1174 Earl Simon III remonstrated that when King William had occupied his patrimony he had bestowed parish churches on whom and as he pleased.[118] One probable intruder, Master Thomas de Paraviso, the king's clerk, had been presented to the church of Potton in apparent contravention of the proprietorship of St Andrew's, Northampton, whose title rested upon King David's grant and a Senlis confirmation. Although Earl Simon made a new gift of the church to the monks, in *c*. 1184 the earl's follower Philip of Kyme gave it in moieties to Kyme priory and Lincoln cathedral.[119] Nevertheless, by 1189 St Andrew's had been put back in possession and had installed as vicar Ralph Foliot, archdeacon of Hereford, at the instance of King Henry II. About the same time the priory was obliged to allow Thomas, now employed as Earl David's clerk, a compromise payment 'for a firm peace between us and Earl David over the church of Potton'.[120] The living then fell vacant, and by 1196 St Andrew's had agreed to confer it on Thomas, in return for an annual payment and David's written confirmation of their rights. But by a further charter David, acting as patron, gave the church to Master Peter of Paxton, another *clericus comitis*.[121] The Northampton monks' failure to establish unchallenged control of Potton church cannot be altogether divorced from the rivalry between the two lines of earls. Yet at the heart of their troubles lay the refusal of two Scottish lords to uphold King David's original gift in their need to secure parochial patronage for household clerks. Grants in mortmain were becoming increasingly difficult to overturn. But the effect of tenurial insecurity at the top was complicated by a tradition of lordship 'reluctant to recognise that gifts to the Church must stand'.[122]

There remains a final theme, one serving to underline the Scottish associations of the Huntingdon honour. Earl David had conveyed the churches of Whissendine and Conington to Lindores abbey by 1195; William de Camera, a Huntingdon tenant, had given all his lordship and one mark's rent in Little Hambleton (Rutland) by 1215.[123] These grants contributed to a scheme of proprietorship that had already involved several religious corporations in Scotland in the tenure of subsidiary concerns within the estate. King David's gifts to Glasgow cathedral, Jedburgh abbey and Kelso abbey had not endured.[124] But Dryburgh abbey still had some right in the church of Bozeat (Northants) from Beatrice de Beauchamp, the wife of Hugh de Moreville, Constable of Scotland and Dryburgh's founder.[125] Jedburgh continued to maintain rights or claims to the churches of Abbotsley and Great Doddington, with which it had been endowed by the Ridels and Ranulf de Sules.[126] Holyrood abbey was confirmed by Earl David in the especially wealthy church of Great Paxton, originally bestowed by Malcolm IV, while Jedburgh laid claim to other benefices in the honour, at Earls Barton and Grendon (Northants), by the same king's bounty.[127]

As is to be expected of an Augustinian community, spiritualities loomed large in Jedburgh's economy; what is remarkable is how many churches the abbey had been offered in the Midlands and elsewhere in England by c.1200.[128] Examples of the acquisition of property in Scotland by English foundations connected with the honour are less readily to hand. Nevertheless, the archives of St Andrew's, Northampton, disclose that during the first years of the thirteenth century the priory added a small estate in Berwickshire to its existing possessions. This property comprised a ploughgate in Newbigging (in Lauder), given by Helen de Moreville shortly before 1217, and an annual rent of five marks from *Grombelau* (unidentified), Redpath (in Earlston) and Glengelt (in Channelkirk), granted by Helen's son Alan of Galloway. In addition, Helen's other son or step-son Earl Thomas of Atholl gave a yearly pension of two marks from 'Newland' (*Nova Terra*) in Eddleston parish in Tweeddale. These gifts were primarily intended as thank-offerings for the honourable burial accorded by the monks to Roland of Galloway, the husband of Helen, when he had died at Northampton in 1200.[129]

The Anglo-Scottish interests of a landowner were naturally reflected in his grants to religion. Yet what did the titles to these far-off parish churches and other windfalls amount to in practice? First, the Scottish houses were inevitably caught up in the contest with the Senlis claimants. Jedburgh, compromised by a rival Senlis disposition to Delapré abbey, had been in difficulty over Earls Barton and Great Doddington from the start and may never have had any real benefit from their revenues.[130] Dryburgh's possession of Bozeat church had been immediately threatened by a Senlis retainer's grant to the canons of St James's at Northampton; and when Earl David conferred Whissendine upon Lindores he ignored an earlier conveyance by Earl Simon III to St Andrew's, as well as the Moreville claim that the patronage pertained to their lay fee.[131] Moreover, whenever rights of one kind or another were upheld, the practical administrative problems were all too apparent. Appropriation of parsonages could not be carried through systematically; and in the majority of the benefices in which the Scottish abbeys retained an interest the most they could expect, apart occasionally from the advowson, was a fixed pension representing a small fraction of the church's total wealth. But notwithstanding these considerations, beneficiaries were fully prepared to take on such concerns, which were often guarded with zeal and were rarely surrendered lightly. By concentrating upon the experience of Dryburgh abbey over its distant rights in Bozeat, a particularly well-documented case, we shall be better able to judge the strength of cross-Border ties at this level of ecclesiastical interest, both under the protection of Earl David's personal lordship and after his death.[132]

The dispute with St James's had been settled by 1177 and Bozeat formally appropriated to the English canons, reserving a compensation payment of two and a half marks to be collected yearly when the Dryburgh

canons 'will send their messenger to the abbey of St James'. Administratively, it was easier for a monastery to collect an agreed pension than to deal
at first hand with the revenues of a single parish many miles away. In 1232
the canons of Holyrood resigned their rights at Great Paxton to the bishop of
Lincoln, for 20 marks payable to their envoy each year by the sacrist of
Lincoln 'nomine perpetui beneficii'.[133] By 1248 Lindores, retaining its
rights of patronage, had reached a similar arrangement with the diocesan
over Whissendine church.[134] Yet even the collection of a fixed annuity from
a far-distant centre was hardly a straightforward undertaking. In the 1280s,
for example, the Holyrood canons remonstrated that it caused them considerable trouble and expense to get their pension from Lincoln, and when
the chapter apparently dismissed a courier empty-handed they protested
that this was done 'for the sole reason, it seems, that through weariness we
may regard the pension as lost'.[135]

Dryburgh took purposeful steps to circumvent such difficulties. Having been 'often inconvenienced by the length of the journey to collect the
pension in person', by *c.* 1190 the convent had commissioned Sulby abbey, a
member like Dryburgh of the Premonstratensian order, as its local agent in
obtaining the monies. By 1275 Lindores would appear to have reached a like
understanding with Sempringham priory over its pensionary rights at
Whissendine.[136] There were, however, better solutions to the inconvenience
of owning revenue in remote parts. One obvious alternative was to exchange
the money in order to strengthen assets closer to home, and since a number
of English houses were endowed in Scotland as Scottish monasteries were in
England, and faced similar administrative problems, the possibility of
attractive bargains existed. Dryburgh moved in this direction in 1193 when
the convent relinquished part of the Bozeat revenue to clear up a dispute
involving Alexander de St Martin's gift of Bangly in Haddington (East
Lothian), made in reconciliation with Richard de Moreville for his brother's
death in a hunting accident. Richard had stipulated that Dryburgh should
pay ten shillings annually from this land to Leicester abbey where his
brother was buried; but the Dryburgh canons had defaulted in their payments, and on 22 February 1193 the matter was resolved in a 'general
chapter' of the Premonstratensians in England. Leicester agreed to renounce its interest in Bangly, subject to a yearly allowance of five shillings
which Dryburgh empowered the abbot of St James's to deliver direct to
Leicester out of the Bozeat pension. Then, fifty years later, the stage was set
for a more ambitious reorganisation involving the residue of Dryburgh's
annuity and the equally inaccessible concerns of St Andrew's, Northampton, in Berwickshire. An understanding was arrived at in 1243, when St
Andrew's disembarrassed itself of its Newbigging property by releasing it to
Dryburgh in perpetuity. In return, the priory was authorised to collect the
entire Bozeat pension from St James's each year, retaining two marks for its
uses and dispatching to Leicester the five shillings' annual rent assigned in
1193. The remaining 20 pence were reserved for Dryburgh's envoy, but

whether the abbey ever bothered to collect this meagre sum is doubtful.[137] Each party had taken an important step towards the reconstruction of its accretions across the Tweed into more manageable units near the centre of its holdings by joining forces with the other to redistribute peripheral gains along more convenient lines.

But what also emerges is the tenacity with which Dryburgh and St Andrew's clung to their distant assets until an acceptable composition could be concluded; and where such bargains were not struck monasteries might hold on for many decades before admitting defeat. Not until 1285 was Holyrood abbey compelled to sell out to the dean and chapter of Lincoln; the canons reasoned 'we would on no account sell a yearly rent of 20 marks in our own district for 200 marks but we have thought it best, because of the dangers of the roads and the distance of the place, to assent [to its sale] for this sum'.[138] Whereas Jedburgh abbey had lost Grendon church by the 1230s, it jealously protected the connection with Abbotsley well into the fourteenth century, long after the outbreak of the wars of independence in 1296 when, undeniably, the Tweed-Solway boundary began to shape into a firm barrier between the realms. Such rights as it enjoyed were obstinately defended through litigation in 1225, in 1256 and in 1272; subsequent forfeiture had been partly overcome by 1328, when Jedburgh recovered a pensionary interest which was not to be surrendered until 1340, upon appropriation of the tithes and glebe to Balliol College, Oxford.[139] Lindores vindicated its claims to the patronage of Whissendine by process of law in 1213 and again in 1289, and it did not abandon them until 1309 when the church was alienated to Sempringham.[140] The rationalisation or loss of such endowments in another country betrayed the donors' original intentions that they should be held perpetually as a sacred trust. But the zeal with which these tiny and isolated assets were retained until they could be exchanged to buttress local interests, or until they could no longer be held in the face of ultimate administrative failure, superior legal claims or protracted warfare, provides some striking testimony of the reality of Anglo-Scottish proprietorship in the twelfth and thirteenth centuries. The Huntingdon honour participated in the developing social, economic and religious life of the southern kingdom in a manner befitting one of the largest estates of its day. But in Earl David's hands and later it was continuing to contribute to the web of social and property ties criss-crossing the Tweed-Solway frontier, as was appropriate to a fief that enjoyed the special character of an English honour held by members of the Scottish royal house.

8

HOUSEHOLD AND FOLLOWING

The Anglo-French nobility among whom Earl David was so completely at home built up their wealth seemingly 'quite indifferent to the matter of territorial conformity'.[1] To help achieve effective proprietorship, a magnate's personal power was extended through local deputies as a normal course. Yet while some residences were prized above others, it was not the habit of the secular aristocracy to remain for long in any one place. Above all, 'a landlord who stayed at home was as little master of his lands as a king of France who never went south of the Loire'.[2] Earl David's movements can only be glimpsed in skeletal detail, with the emphasis on his attendances at court. But the focal points of his perambulations were always his own estates. As earl of Huntingdon from 1185 he thus extended his accustomed itinerary and committed himself to a life of tireless travelling between two kingdoms, concentrating upon the lands from Aberdeenshire to Middlesex that provided his substance and guaranteed the splendours of his hall. Important links were forged between his Scottish and English possessions at levels beneath his own. As the occasional charter suggests, he was still concerned for his estates in one country when absent in the other; he could communicate administrative instructions by written precept.[3] But the main unity possessed by this great Anglo-Scottish fief was founded upon the fact that its lord was able by continuous itineration to impose a single centralised direction upon the component parts.

Like every lord of consequence, Earl David was attended on his peregrinations by a company whose size and magnificence formed the outward display of his *dominium* and social prominence. This personal clientage accommodated household servants, members of his immediate family, and well-wishers – followers who either journeyed with him or joined him at different centres. None of the institutions of lordship was more important to a magnate. The following or entourage in its widest sense met his needs for domestic and spiritual comfort, administrative expertise and judicious counsel, and afforded general support wherever he sought to entrench his influence. Studies stimulated by K. B. McFarlane's seminal researches have confirmed the decisive role played by magnate retinues in the social and political life of England from the fourteenth century.[4] Yet though household officials have received considered attention, no comprehensive examination of a major baron's household and following in the earlier Middle Ages has so far been published by English or Scottish historians, a gap partly explained by the dearth of such evidence as ward-

149

robe accounts. In default of more informative records, the witness-clauses of Earl David's *acta* are basic to the present inquiry.[5] But although the fifty-three witness-lists extant provide a reasonable basis for discussion, inevitably they will give a distorted impression of a person's relationship with David merely because some acts have been preserved and others have been lost. Moreover, if from internal evidence the *acta* in this collection appear fairly well distributed from *c.*1185, they bear no dates of time and few dates of place. Accordingly, while the country of issue can normally be determined, and while the witnesses to a charter were probably as a general rule present with the earl in person,[6] it is not always possible to distinguish those who were firmly within David's orbit from the birds of passage with whom any powerful magnate was surrounded.[7] Nonetheless, Professor C.R.Cheney and Dr Kathleen Major have indicated how much can profitably be achieved from charter sources in their work on the household staffs of two of Earl David's ecclesiastical contemporaries.[8] The findings set out below are offered as a new contribution in an as yet inadequately explored field.

At the core of the earl's entourage was the household, structured on the customary Anglo-Norman pattern and manned by persons known to have been of Anglo-Norman origin or whose names suggest that this was so. As the Scottish crown developed new techniques of central administrative control, modelled on the English *domus regis*,[9] so did Earl David. The secular 'departments', however, leave few useful traces. Earlier in the twelfth century, household and estate duties had both been the concern of the steward. But a great lord did well to have more specialised arrangements,[10] and there is no sign that the stewards of David's lands ('senescalli') also managed his *aula*. Pressure of business laid upon them in the estates at large from 1185, accentuated by the earl's frequent absences from one country or the other, seems to have justified a division of responsibility so that the charge of the itinerant household was delegated to a domestic steward. Aymer of Oakley *senescallus* and Ala *dapifer* witnessed together for David in England in 1198 × 1209: apparently Aymer was responsible for estate management, and Ala, with the lesser title of 'food-bearer', was the household steward.

Though there existed an establishment of household knights,[11] it is also doubtful that the known constables, mentioned only in Scottish sources, can be described as domestic officers. Associated with castles rather than the household, they 'stand apart from the general body of their lord's ministers'.[12] William of Bassingham, a knight of the Huntingdon honour, served as Earl David's marshal,[13] but although the position was evidently not lacking in dignity, nothing is recorded of his official activity. The evidence is so uninformative that there is no certain reference to the chamberlain. William de Camera, a tenant of the earl in Rutland, had been a notable witness for Earl Simon de Senlis III and is perhaps identifiable with one William, 'camerarius meus', whom Simon had enfeoffed at Barton upon Humber (Lincs) in the honour of Gant. There is still no proof that he was David's chamberlain, though his relations with the earl were sufficiently close for him to endow Lindores abbey in his Rutland property, expressly 'pro salute anime domini mei Comitis Dauid et Matilde Comitisse uxoris sue'.[14]

A powerful lord also depended on a host of minions for the basic domestic services to keep him in the style he required and social convention expected. But since menial servants rarely appear in record, only a few of Earl David's minor functionaries can be identified. The charters refer to a butler, who does not appear to have enjoyed any special standing, a falconer and a porter. One Robert, the earl's *alutarius*, occurs unexpectedly as the subject of a miraculous incident in the hagiography for Thomas Becket.[15] This fortuitous reference to a leather-dresser is a striking indication of the elaborate organisation of lay *domestici* which a magnate like David saw fit to maintain. There are also two notices which may or may not relate to the lesser lay agents of the household: in 1202 Osbert, 'serviens Comitis Dauid', and his man Bartholomew were accused of robbery with violence; in c. 1206 William Lupus and other servants of the earl were involved in a fracas at the Sale Fair of Huntingdon.[16]

More is known about the ecclesiastical establishment. At least four *capellani* were employed at various times in the latter part of Earl David's career. Occasionally the principal chaplain was to the fore in the witness-lists, which shows his prominence as the earl's intimate companion and spiritual adviser, and possibly as a higher secretarial official. Although Arnold attested only once, Richard was a leading member of the household, who travelled in England and Scotland from 1185; Walter witnessed three of David's English charters between 1185 and 1196; and William occurs about the 1190s in the witness-clauses of eleven *acta* of English and Scottish provenance. When they appear together it is in twos rather than threes. The Scots king normally employed two household chaplains, and the *capellani* of a contemporary bishop may not have exceeded this number at a given date.[17] It can be imagined that after David became earl of Huntingdon he also perambulated with two chaplains in his suite.

The identifiable clerks are more numerous than the chaplains. The careers of several of these men (Geoffrey, Gilbert, Henry, Richard and Waltheof), like those of the chaplains, are virtually unrecorded, though we do know a little about the background of the others and how their dependence was secured through modest preferment. Benefices in the earl's gift or otherwise under his influence were an acceptable and easily afforded form of remuneration. Robert's service was praiseworthy enough for David to urge William de Mortimer to install him in the church of Aberdour in Fife. But this living was in the ownership of Inchcolm priory, and Robert had to be forcibly invested, assisted by certain clerks of the Scots king, who brawled with the canons as they stood with their cross and relics before the church door. The canons maintained their protest and he was obliged to withdraw.[18] Unlike Robert, Philip *clericus* does not seem to appear outside Scotland, where he held a toft at Dundee (hence his occasional style 'of Dundee'); and while he frequently attested Earl David's charters, notably in the 1190s, he may have been drawn into the household only when David travelled in the northern realm. Even so, Philip's importance in the earl's circle can be judged by his eventual promotion to the stewardship of the Scottish fief. A person of some repute, he was also a regular witness to charters executed for his master's tenants and neighbours on Tayside.[19]

The activity of the majority of the clerks, however, did not centre on the Scots kingdom alone. Robert of (Earls) Barton took his name from a demesne manor in the Huntingdon honour; his brother Thomas, also a clerk, had served Earl Simon III in the 1160s.[20] But both men joined David's following during his English campaign of 1174, and Robert subsequently witnessed for the earl in England and Scotland. Henry de Nuers, a third clerk with Huntingdon connections, attended the earl assiduously in both kingdoms after 1185.[21] The clerks also included *magistri*, men of some academic distinction who were evidently crucial to the smooth running of his administration. Master Thomas de Paraviso, another of David's supporters in 1174, was a former clerk of the Scots king, his duties having apparently been confined to the Huntingdon fief.[22] Master Peter of Paxton, best recorded of all the clerks, invites special attention. He entered the *familia* after service to Earl Simon III and perhaps to Simon's mother.[23] He collected a personal library of law books, including the *Code, Digest* and *Infortiatum* with the *Institutes*; and his early Senlis associations raise the possibility that he had been educated at the schools of Northampton, a centre of some reputation for legal studies. Appointed vice-archdeacon of Huntingdon shortly before his death in *c.*1230, Peter ended a long career in magnate service with a certain local prominence in the administration of the Church.[24]

That these two *magistri* were among the most valued of the clerks is shown both by their witnessing and by the benefices they procured from grateful employers. Master Thomas was generally active on Earl David's affairs during 1174 and after 1185; Master Peter perambulated with the household on each side of the Border, mainly in the 1190s. Thomas had been allocated the church of Potton by King William. Deprived after 1174 when, as a dutiful adherent of the Scottish crown, he had found himself unacceptable to the Senlis party, he seems for a time to have been supported in David's service as the rector of Abdie in Fife. When Abdie was required as part of the foundation endowment of Lindores abbey, however, the earl intervened to reinstate Thomas at Potton. This benefice functioned as a regular perquisite of household *clerici*: a little later, Peter was instituted rector through David's favour.[25] From Earl Simon, Peter had acquired the living of Great Paxton, which – doubtless because David inherited his services – he retained when Holyrood abbey recovered its corporate rights in *c.*1185, upon payment of an annual pension.[26] He also drew on the demesne tithes at Yardley Hastings by concession of the priory of St Andrew at Northampton, David acknowledging the monks' title to this income as a *quid pro quo*.[27] This favoured *magister* may therefore have been the incumbent of a third benefice in the Huntingdon honour, and possibly combined all three livings in plurality.

So much for the clerks. A significant number entered Earl David's ambit through connections with his English honour, continuity of administration being served by those traceable earlier in Senlis or Scottish royal employment. Individual clerks may have attended the household in one realm and not in the other; but it is also plain from particular cases that many of the clerks, as well as some of the chaplains, were expected to move about with the earl, that there was no clear-cut division of staff for the English and Scottish lands. A benefice was as much a surety of continued support as a reward for past services, and the non-resident who left the ministrations of the parish to a stipendiary priest was a familiar figure in the itinerant households of the great.

Although a firm distinction is drawn between the *capellani* and the *clerici* in the witness-lists (these were clearly not interchangeable titles), ecclesiastical functionaries in baronial no less than in royal service were not narrow specialists. Clerks versed in the law upheld Earl David's interests outside the household as attorneys in the central courts;[28] that Philip *clericus* aspired to the stewardship in Scotland shows that a capable clerk might be assigned executive tasks. Further analysis of their duties directs attention to the earl's surviving charters. To what extent were they engaged in drafting and writing *acta*? While it is accepted that by *c.*1200 English bishops had developed well-organised chanceries, this aspect of a baron's administration remains poorly charted territory. Those of David's *acta* extant as full (or almost full) texts total fifty-five, twenty-two being originals. There are a further thirty-six acts now presumed lost of which there is, in most cases, a reliable record. Nearly all these documents were expedited to provide title to land, or rights on land, in perpetuity, and nearly all were issued no earlier than 1185, that is, in the last thirty-four years of Earl David's life.

Too few attempts have been made to collect systematically the surviving acts of other contemporary barons for statistical comparisons. First and foremost, however, it may be said that the use of charters north of the Tweed had progressed to the extent that the earl's bureaucracy and his beneficiaries valued ink and parchment as much in Scotland as in England. Secondly, it is not difficult to prove that no more than a tiny fraction of David's *acta* can have been preserved. Only fourteen full texts are for laymen; the remaining forty-one are almost without exception for ecclesiastical corporations. It would be rash to assume that laymen had less use for written titles. Quite simply, chances of survival have operated against the records of the private individual or family and in favour of the archives of religious institutions, whose position was more stable and secure. This can be confirmed, at least in some measure, by consideration of the 'lost acts':

twelve are concerned with the Church whereas twenty-four relate to lay-men. There are other indications that the losses have been substantial. Though the thirteenth-century Lindores abbey cartulary preserves fourteen full texts, these are only a selection of the earl's charters for the abbey.[29] This is a useful reminder that a mass of documents, not all of them ephemeral, may have been excluded from monastic cartularies. Worse still are those cases where the muniments of a particular monastery have suffered almost total loss. It is a cause of especial regret that the cartulary of Hinchingbrooke priory was destroyed by fire in 1830, for a few stray records make plain David's interest in this house. Finally, mandates were doubtless often written for his officials, and administrative memoranda are likely to have been produced. None of these is extant.[30]

In the absence of more precise indications, it therefore seems safe to assume that behind the surviving charters lies a much greater volume of written business, one which required regular access to trained scribes. A number of *acta* betray signs of 'external' production.[31] This is only to be expected when, even in contemporary royal chanceries, beneficiaries might still present for sealing charters prepared by their own officials.[32] David's writing-office was not mobilised in the same specialised fashion as the semi-royal chancery of John, count of Mortain, the future king.[33] The clerks of the earl's brother-in-law Ranulf, earl of Chester, worked under the direction of a chancellor; they wrote with reference to a formulary as an aid to consistent practice; and they adopted a system of enrolment.[34] None of this can be claimed for David's household. Nor did the clerical staff necessarily give their undivided attention to his business. Able scribes, 'no mere quill-drivers',[35] found their legal knowledge and draftsmanship much in demand. One earlier Huntingdon clerk, Stephen of Ecton, had been simultaneously retained by King Malcolm IV and the countess of Clare, living half in and half out of either household.[36] Nevertheless, some of the men under review, including those of proven experience in royal or baronial service, attest with sufficient frequency to suggest permanent attachment to the core of the *familia* for significant periods, while most of the charters in this collection display instructive degrees of uniformity in *clausulae* and, where the originals survive, in external appearance. This commands interest for the reception into Scotland of private charters in the main course of Anglo-Norman development; in more specific terms, it again presupposes not a fully-fledged chancery but a regular body of household scribes. If Earl David normally had two chaplains in his suite, the clerks also appear to have served in pairs; and though not every chaplain or clerk was automatically competent to write *acta* in his turn, an establishment of two or three scribes was adequate for the routine work of some of the busiest contemporary administrations.[37] By further analogy with different households, the principal chaplain may have had responsibilities extending beyond the celebration of daily masses to oversight of the scribal work.[38] It can be argued with some confidence that the earl's administration contributed in good measure to the record-consciousness that in the Scotland, as in the England, of David's day became firmly enshrined as one of the fundamental principles of effective government and lordship.[39]

A great man's entourage embraced, besides household servants, members of his own family, and an informal group of advisers and expectant followers who, in return for the lord's protection or favour, helped to assert his prestige and power in the community at large. Lordship and kinship were by no means as complementary for Earl David as for the Comyn earls of Buchan and Menteith, whose broad yet unusually close-knit family ties evoke the kin-based society of the ancient Celtic polity.[40] Support was practically restricted to the basic feudal family unit of parents and children, 'the household or two-generation family'.[41] Wider blood ties focused upon the Scots king as head of the lineage and by far its most powerful representative. David's bastards assisted him in financial dealings, took some part in his negotiations with the English crown, and generally collaborated in the management of his affairs. One assumed responsibility for the earl's military obligations in 1210, commanding ten knights on King John's Irish campaign.[42] This is the public activity of children upon whose private contacts with their father the records rarely touch, although Henry of Brechin and Henry of Stirling often attested his charters and may have been frequently in his company. Yet of the three sons-in-law accumulated by the time of David's death, only Malise of Strathearn witnessed the surviving *acta* with any regularity. Robert de Brus IV makes a single appearance and Alan of Galloway does not appear at all. While marriages may have strengthened existing aristocratic alliances, they did not invariably bring firm attachments into being. About 1210, however, David participated in the arrangements for the marriage between a son of Earl Saer de Quincy and a sister of Earl Ranulf of Chester.[43] Another relation by marriage, Earl Duncan of Fife, witnessed four of the extant charters, three of which were also attested by Duncan's son Malcolm.

How do we identify Earl David's affinity other than household functionaries and kinsmen, that is, the wider 'family' or following which was dependent upon him? In spite of reservations already made, our best guide to the strength of an individual's links with the earl's entourage is undoubtedly the number of his attestations to the surviving charters. Legally speaking, the function of the witnesses was to fortify decisions or grants, whether or not they enjoyed any special relationship with David. Thus, having ensured as far as possible that attestations in a particular name belong to the same person, analysis must aim at defining the earl's 'followers' to exclude those whose connections with him were remote. Men appearing three times or less are accordingly regarded as insignificant. To emphasise that the remainder will include associates of varying prominence in the following, they have been divided into two categories. The first group is represented by the twenty persons each figuring in the witness-clauses of

Table 1. Earl David's 'inner circle'

	Attestations	Tenant by patrimony	Beneficiary	Tenant by patrimony or beneficiary	Estate steward
*Robert Basset	22			×	
*Walter Olifard	12	×			
*Walkelin son of Stephen	12				
William Wascelin	12		×		
*William Burdet	11			×	
*Robert son of Robert	11	×			
*Simon de Senlis	11	×	×		×
*Geoffrey de Waterville	11				
*Richard son of William	10		×		×
*Robert of Bassingham	8	×	×		×
*Nicholas de Adles	7				
David of Ashby	7	×			×
William of Ashby	7	×			×
*Ralph de Camoys	7		×		
*Robert de la Carneille	7		×		
Henry, abbot of Arbroath	6		×		
*Richard of Lindsey	6	×	×		
*Constantine de Mortimer	6				
*Bartholomew le Moyne	6				
*Walkelin de Nuers	6				

* denotes appearing with Earl David in England and Scotland

Table 2. Earl David's 'outer circle'

	Attestations	Tenant by patrimony	Beneficiary	Tenant by patrimony or beneficiary	Estate steward
*Alan son of Hugh	5			×	×
*Walter of Bassingham	5				
Gilbert Dolepene	5				
*Hugh Giffard	5	(×)†	×		
David of Lindsey	5				
Hugh de Lisures	5		×		
*William Revel	5				
*Nicholas de Anas	4				
*William de Folville	4	×			
Matthew, bishop of Aberdeen	4				
*Bartholomew de Mortimer	4				
Robert de Mortimer	4		×		
Philip le Moyne	4			×	×
Norman son of Malcolm	4	×			
Reginald of Oakley	4	×			×
Richard del Peak	4	×			
William de St Michael	4				
*William son of Emma (Vieuxpont)	4	×			
John of Wilton	4				

* denotes appearing with Earl David in England and Scotland
† a tenant of the Huntingdon honour by grant of King Malcolm IV

six or more charters. This is called the 'inner circle', and within it we should expect to find mustered the earl's more important supporters, though they may not have been in personal attendance over long periods. The second grouping, the 'outer circle', contains nineteen men each occurring four or five times, but perhaps includes leading followers as well as less prominent connections. Witnesses may have attested charters so closely alike in date as to have been issued simultaneously: ideally, therefore, only attestations to *acta* passed on different occasions should be counted. But, on the one hand, full details are lacking; on the other, the cases where we may reasonably suspect that a number of a man's attestations should be classed as a single appearance are too few and unimportant to affect significantly the nature of the following as defined above. Lastly, some independent information on the relationship between Earl David and individual witnesses has been added to the accompanying tables, as a preliminary to further discussion.[44]

The main limitations of this method of identifying Earl David's affinity must be firmly underlined. In particular, although three of his Anglo-French lay tenants in Scotland appear in the inner or outer circle, there are reasons for supposing that as a group these men, mostly his own feoffees, are under-represented. Thus when we speak of 'followers', the word excludes several vassals who, if not in the habit of accompanying David in England, were highly valued as a source of personal influence north of the Tay.[45] Moreover, the earl's associates include people of some renown but also those whose identity is uncertain, there being one especially tantalising example. The largest number of attestations is in the name of Robert Basset *miles*, someone apparently close to David over a substantial span. The most promising suggestions as to his identity are that he was a tenant of the Huntingdon fief in Toseland (Hunts) and a kinsman of Richard Basset of Great Weldon, the holder of five fees in the honour.[46] He must be distinguished from Robert Basset of Wolvey (Warwicks), who was evidently dead by 1201.[47] But was he identical with his contemporary and namesake of Rushden (Herts)?[48] Is he one and the same person as Robert Basset of Milton Ernest (Beds), or Robert Basset of Rushton (Northants), or Robert Basset of Diseworth (Leics)?[49] As has been well said, family history in this period 'can degenerate into nightmare'.[50] Even when a witness leaves good traces in the sources, information about him will always be in important ways incomplete; but three case studies will serve to indicate the sort of questions that might be asked in analysing the characteristic features of the inner and outer circles as a whole.

The name Walter Olifard, appearing twelve times,[51] introduces a family recently promoted to greatness in Scotland. Two Walter Olifards, father and son, occur in this period, but the possibility that Walter I, hereditary justiciar of Lothian and dead by c.1190, was ever a familiar figure in Earl David's encourage can be discounted. All the attestations belong to the 1190s or later, and it must have been Walter's son and eventual successor who enjoyed some consequence in David's milieu.[52] The Olifards had commanded magnatial standing since Malcolm IV had invested David Olifard with the lordship of Bothwell, and as was typical of the chief settler families in the twelfth-century Scots kingdom, they combined proprietorship with distinguished employment in the royal service. But Walter II, grandson of David Olifard and reputedly 'the greatest of his line',[53] did not owe his appearance in Earl David's circle exclusively to his importance in Scotland. Fief-holding in the Huntingdon honour had provided the Olifards with the opportunity of Scottish advancement. Lilford in Northamptonshire was the original family seat, and Walter *junior* is recorded as the lord of the manor in 1216.[54] Since his father was deceased in *c.*1190 and since Walter himself did not die until 1242, he may in fact have been a minor in the 1190s, living more or less permanently in David's household for his education and training. One of his earliest known acts of lordship, datable *c.*1208, was to convey to Alan of Swinton the land of Colzie, between Abernethy and Strathmiglo. The mature Walter was thus both David's tenant in England and a neighbouring landowner in Fife. He also held property at Arbuthnott, next door to the earl's toun of Inverbervie in the Mearns.[55] When Walter is first mentioned as justiciar of Lothian in *c.*1215, he had already moved out of David's following; yet as a prominent servant of the Scots crown he could look back upon an association with a magnate whose Anglo-Scottish interests, though far more extensive, were similar in kind to his own.

An equally familiar name in the witness-clauses is that of William Burdet, occurring once in a charter relating to the English campaign of 1174 and eleven times between *c.*1185 and 1212. At least three William Burdets were contemporary with Earl David, and it is not always simple to tell them apart. William I, sometime steward of the Huntingdon honour for King Malcolm, controlled two fees in the estate based on Lowesby in Leicestershire; he also held mesne tenancies of the Beauchamps and the Hanselins; and he was an especially influential vassal of the earl of Leicester.[56] These multiple interests were typical of the well-to-do gentry of midland England, and William catered for his soul in a manner becoming his importance by founding the small Benedictine priory at Alvecote in Warwickshire. It was no doubt this same William who campaigned with David in 1174. His son Hugh accompanied him in this adventure and a decade later succeeded to the family estates; Hugh's son William II inherited as a minor and came of age between 1202 and 1215.[57] Few if any of the attestations in the period *c.*1185–1212, however, are considered to be William II's. Most date before *c.*1200 and all, or the majority, are better attributed to his cousin, yet another William Burdet. In 1202 this man vouched to warranty William II, then *infra etatem*, over land held of the honour of Eye at Allington in the Vale of Belvoir.[58] And by 1214 at the latest William Burdet of Allington also controlled a tenement at Potton, possibly thanks to Earl David's grant.[59] Although William Burdet I had visited Scotland in the 1160s,[60] the Burdets were one Anglo-Norman family well connected with the Scots royal house not to secure a northern endowment. Even so, though they forged alliances with many other lords, their ties with the Scottish earls of Huntingdon evidently remained relevant and beneficial to them.

Our third and final case – free of the complexities caused by the duplication of Christian names within particular families – concerns Richard of Lindsey, who attested six times. This witness endowed Greenfield priory with an annual rent at Fordington in Ulceby by Alford, on the southern fringe of the Lincolnshire Wolds. It is hardly a significant transaction; and his marriage, which brought him land at Blyth in Nottinghamshire, was an unremarkable local match.[61] Yet there is no denying Richard's kinship with one of the most celebrated houses to take root in medieval Scotland, a house which in the thirteenth century counted amongst its members royal chamberlains, justiciars of Lothian and sheriffs of Berwick. Even by c.1180 the Lindseys' Scottish possessions, based on Crawford in Clydesdale, Earlston in Lauderdale and Lamberton in the Merse, were wealthy and extensive;[62] and this was another dynasty whose position in the northern kingdom can be directly related to Scots control of the Huntingdon honour. The original patrimony, however, was not its Huntingdon manor at Molesworth but Fordington and Ulceby, which pertained to the honour of Chester. These lands had devolved upon Richard of Lindsey by 1190, when the service of his fee formed part of the dowry transferred to Earl David in marriage with Countess Maud. By c.1209 Richard's connection with David had been cemented through his enfeoffment at Earls Barton.[63] Notices in the unpublished cartulary of Crowland abbey, unknown to the family historians, fix his place in the Lindsey pedigree: he was a grandson of Walter of Lindsey I of Earlston – like William Burdet I, a former steward of the Huntingdon fief – and a younger son of Walter of Lindsey II of Lamberton and Molesworth (d.c.1222), another of Earl David's supporters in 1174.[64] Richard's cousin David of Lindsey, eventual lord of Crawford, attested on five occasions, sufficient to place him in the 'outer circle'.

These case histories indicate how the discussion can best proceed. To what backgrounds did Earl David's followers belong by race and social position? What were their family affiliations and chief properties? How many can be classed as David's tenants? How did they make their way in the world and how far did the advancement of careers depend upon the earl's support? We can profitably pursue these questions for the majority of the persons before us.

The lack of any representation by men known to have been of native Scottish lineage is at once most obvious and striking. To judge from their toponymics, some followers possibly sprang from English or Anglo-Scandinavian families. In a greater number of instances – Camoys, Folville, Lisures, the Mortimers, Nuers, Olifard, Senlis, Waterville and several more – the family antecedents were undoubtedly French. The earl's attachment to the traditions and outlook of Anglo-continental society was so complete that for those who sought a place at his side it was an advantage not to have been born a native Scot. In terms of social standing, individuals prospered between the time of their first recorded attestation and their last. Some were younger sons who had no inherited estates and were building up establishments from new; others were heirs who entered their ancestral patrimonies and then outstripped their forefathers in rank. For present purposes the express object is to identify where possible a person's interests before his first appearance with David rather than to describe the social position ultimately achieved; heirs apparent can be classified according to their fathers' status. There are problems with this approach. A follower's earliest known occurrence in the entourage can rarely have marked the real beginning of the relationship, while there are those whose property gains cannot be closely matched with the dates of their actual appearances as witnesses. Again, there is the difficulty of ascertaining a man's consequence in this period, since contemporaries conceived of no standard correlation between titular status and economic wealth. As has been said of England, 'there were barons who were comparatively poor and insignificant. There were men of simple knightly rank who were wealthy and held sway over the minds of kings.'[65]

Yet with every allowance made, the general picture seems abundantly plain. Though personnel were drawn from different reaches of society, with few exceptions the prior condition of followers was at best moderate and in many instances completely undistinguished. Two prelates had some contact with Earl David, enjoying the social opportunities afforded by the company of a powerful magnate and participating in his transactions to give them greater weight. Of the four *acta* witnessed by Bishop Matthew of Aberdeen, three concern property in his diocese, one being a charter of infeftment which records that the bishop (as a justiciar of *Scotia*?) had assisted at the formal perambulation of marches. Henry, abbot of Arbroath, was also periodically present with the entourage in Scotland, showing an especial interest in dispositions concerning Lindores, his abbey's sister-house. But while of some significance in David's circle, neither churchman can be safely described as the earl's intimate. Among laymen, there were those of good family but not many of assured eminence. None was a tenant-in-chief by barony of the English realm. In Scotland, Walter Olifard II and David of Lindsey belonged to substantial baronial houses beneath the earls and the other great regional magnates. Hugh Giffard, lord of Yester, though hardly a major aristocratic figure by English standards, was already a prominent baron of the Scots crown.[66] William 'filius Emme' was the oldest son of William de Vieuxpont II and Emma de St Hilaire. His father, the tenant of several estates in Berwickshire and the Lothians, as well as of English possessions based mainly on Alston in Tynedale, stood on a level with Giffard or slightly above him.[67] Richard del Peak was another medium-ranking landowner. He held in chief in Lincolnshire, but deployed more impressive reserves, including a number of Huntingdon fees, as a mesne tenant of midland lordships.[68] Robert de Mortimer's sizeable concerns centred on Attleborough (Norfolk) in the honour of Warenne.[69] Hugh de Lisures, whose manors clustered around his castle at Benefield in the Nene valley, was an influential member of the Northamptonshire gentry.[70] Yet these were the only men of genuine note in their own 'countries' when they became Earl David's associates. Furthermore, all save Olifard qualify merely for the outer circle and apparently cannot be regarded as the earl's familiars. They doubtless had too many countervailing commitments to be assiduous in their attendance upon him.

Beneath this small minority stands a miscellaneous body of lesser proprietors and probably landless men, not always well-born. That many of this group were described as knights shows that although knighthood was becoming a mark of respected rank, the indefinite social usage of the past was slow to acquire precision.[71] An ordinary knight shared the tastes of his lord and indulged them as his resources allowed. Nor was the gulf between a poor knight and a powerful baron ever too wide to be crossed, for entry into the magnate class was an increasingly remote but never impossible hope. Yet wealth in land was hardly basic to access into Earl David's connection, least of all for those appearing with some frequency in his company. Indeed, although some bore the names of substantial families, next to nothing can be discovered about the antecedents of roughly a half of the inner circle, by contrast with roughly a quarter of the outer circle.

Setting aside those who remain little more than names, the origins of lay followers can be further defined according to the location of their principal seats or, if yet to become landed, by the estate centres of their lineages. As might be expected of a major cross-Border magnate, Earl David did not draw support from one area alone. Of the inner circle, Walter Olifard had roots in Scotland and in the Huntingdon honour. In the outer circle, six laymen (or their fathers) were landed in Scotland, and of these Giffard and Vieuxpont had rights or claims to fees in the Huntingdon fief.[72] Here David attracted well-wishers whose interests reflected his own. It is also possible to discover, as for Richard of Lindsey, pre-existing connections with landowners in Scotland involving followers neither holding property north of the Border nor having good prospects of inheriting there. Robert de Mortimer of Attleborough – and the elusive Bartholomew and Constantine de Mortimer – were presumably related to William de Mortimer of Aberdour, who first appeared in Scotland in the household of Countess Ada de Warenne and went on to distinguish himself in royal service.[73] William Revel may have been drawn into David's following as a relation of the earl's neighbours on Tayside, the Revels of Coultra (Fife). The best suggestion as to his origins is that he was identical with William son of Richard Revel of Langport and Curry Rivel (Somerset), whose uncle Henry and elder brothers, Richard II of Langport and Adam, were successive lords of Coultra from the 1170s.[74] There are others whose Scottish ties seem more tenuous and remote.[75]

Nevertheless, the number of actual Scottish landowners (counting fathers and sons) is unimpressive, especially since they are well represented only in the outer circle, apparently on the periphery of the following, not at the centre. Identified by their 'home' districts, most supporters fall into one or other of the following categories. Ten men from the inner circle and six men from the outer circle were chiefly associated with the English Midlands, notably Lincolnshire and Northamptonshire. To these can be added a handful of Huntingdonshire landowners who may have established their holdings before they began witnessing Earl David's charters. Further, there were seemingly landless men who appear to have come from families in this region. Of the inner circle, for example, Geoffrey de Waterville no doubt claimed kinship with one or other of the Waterville houses of Northamptonshire and Huntingdonshire. David had been supported by the Watervilles of Marholm in 1174 and another link with the earl is traceable through Robert de Waterville of Orton, his tenant in Godmanchester.[76] These various relationships were not all begun by David's tenure of the Huntingdon honour from 1185; some certainly date from his intervention in the young King Henry's rebellion.[77] It would also be unwise to assume that from 1185 David spent most of his time in England and that his English possessions were more important to him than his Scottish fief. But the predominant part of the following as defined by charter-witnessing served to consolidate the earl's influence in the area where his territorial ascendancy was more incomplete, their presence helping to compensate for his lack of regional power as a midland magnate.

The next stage is more demanding of the sources. Twelfth-century charters of enfeoffment give greater prominence to the rights bestowed than to the duties owed for them; and when the lord-man relationship acquired a territorial aspect, personal ties were progressively debased, not least by heredity and the tenant's desire to limit responsibilities and acquire land from as many lords as possible. Thus while land grants were intended to reinforce vassalic bonds, in the long run they tended to undermine them. But real property remained the basis of obligations, symbolised by doing homage and swearing fealty, and these transcended the normal liability to military service and the customary *auxilia*. The tenant was expected to assist the lord in his affairs, give counsel, and attend him as a suitor and judge in the formal meetings of his court. In return, the lord was bound to proceed by consultation, provide justice and protection, and advance his vassal's interests. There were rights and duties on both sides. Contractual obligations are often at variance with the way social relations actually function. But this at any rate was the theory of things.

Now, at one date or another significantly more than half of the inner circle (thirteen) and fully half of the outer circle (ten), representing very nearly three-fifths of both groups combined, demonstrably held of Earl David by lay tenure. How many were tenants *jure hereditario*? How many owed their place to patronage? Since greater prominence can be accorded to the vitality of tenurial ties when they may of themselves have brought men into a magnate's following than when they were created through his favour in recognition of past assistance, it is important to distinguish between tenements descended by patrimony, or otherwise in hand, and those newly bestowed. Borderline cases are an unavoidable consequence of the patchy source-material: that no *carta* of 1166 exists for the Huntingdon honour is particularly unfortunate. Nonetheless, seven persons from the inner circle and six from the outer circle can be positively classed as tenants, or men with the expectation of inheriting as tenants, when they joined the earl's suite. They are thus distributed almost equally between both groupings and constitute exactly one-third of the whole. As may have been anticipated, the tenurial ties largely centred upon the Huntingdon honour. In addition, a further five men arguably came into the following as Huntingdon tenants, while others were younger sons or cousins of old-established Huntingdon families: Walter of Bassingham,[78] David of Lindsey, Richard of Lindsey (a tenant *suo jure* outside the honour), and possibly William Revel.[79]

The value of this information is not so much that Earl David looked to the Huntingdon fief for regular support: this estate had a traditional role as a source of 'natural' advisers to the Scots royal house. The central issue is that in this age, when the strength of personal ties based on tenurial relationships was undeniably deteriorating, significant succour and aid actually derived from the midland honour. To this degree the witness-clauses testify to the persistence of close relations between lord and tenant, involving obligations that might still be actively upheld. Admittedly, men of true substance are poorly represented. Turn to the *acta* of the first two Senlis earls and they would appear to show that the honorial baronage was once firmly involved in the life of the estate. Earl Simon II's charters refer frequently to his barons; transactions were effected with their consent.[80] In Stenton's words, 'whatever else a baron may have been, he was his lord's counsellor. . . . The knight's opinion was not often asked by his lord unless some military question was at issue.'[81] And yet did a magnate's major vassals ever contribute as fully to the feudal community of an honour as the formalised *clausulae* of earlier charters suggest?

It was not solely the larger tenants who were noted for the remoteness of their ties with Earl David. In fact, the honour's erratic political history had seriously undermined that continuity of possession so vital to a great landowning family intent upon controlling land and men; and throughout the fief homage in many instances had a fiscal aspect only. The Huntingdon estate, therefore, was not immune from the action of general trends incompatible with the claims of personal loyalty. The point requires no further emphasis; indeed, the attenuation of homage has been accorded considerable scholarly attention, to the extent that the proportion of tenant-followers in Earl David's suite may seem surprisingly high. Yet when one movement predominates there is always room for others; and despite the accent of historical writing we should not be misled into supposing that tenurial

attachments had lost all force. David's succession in 1185 heralded the
return to favour of several Huntingdon lineages which had generally taken
the Scottish side because of their lands in Scotland. But it is also clear,
especially among those attesting on a regular basis, that David relied upon
persons holding one or two fees or less, knights such as William of Ashby,
Robert of Bassingham, William de Folville and Reginald of Oakley, with
interests based mainly, though not exclusively, within the estate.[82] Vassals
of this sort made the most reliable dependants, for they were subordinate to
him in a way that richer property-owners were not. That some moved easily
into his ambit after having dutifully served the Senlis earls suggests that
they followed him simply because it seemed natural and proper. Perhaps
the most interesting of these men was Simon de Senlis, an illegitimate
brother of Earl Simon III. He held a number of properties outside the fief,
yet Conington was evidently the chief concern.[83] There were plural contracts between men and lords but multiple homages could be reconciled
with the claims of personal loyalty. The problem was recognised and
attempts were made to cope with it. It was thus acceptable for vassals to hold
of different English honours and still reserve their principal commitment to
the lord of the fee on which they normally resided, regarding him as their
liege lord beneath the king.[84] Recent researches seem to indicate that by
about the mid-thirteenth century even ordinary knightly tenants had almost
entirely disappeared from a magnate's entourage.[85] In Earl David's following there appears to be represented an intermediate stage in the deterior-
ation of tight personal alliances between a lord in the English Midlands and
his group of tenantry.

Earl David's relationship with his supporters has another dimension. Just
as the lord received faithful service, so benefits were anticipated in return,
for a lord deemed worthy of esteem was one who strove to repay loyalty with
friendship and generosity. This age-old principle of reciprocal obligations
was at the very basis of 'good lordship'. Fief-holders of other honours and
landless men might ally themselves with a magnate in the hope of advancement, and such persons were well represented in David's following, for he
welcomed the enlargement of his influence that resulted from their participation in his *dominium*. That established tenants also sought a place at his
side brings into prominence followers who were legally bound to serve him,
but who could see in his goodwill the same potential advantages as non-
tenants; and while on the lord's side the exchange of benefits might be
accomplished in different ways, material expressions of his support –
especially grants of land, the criterion of wealth and power – were understandably the most keenly desired. But natural though it was for tenants to
hope for further advancement, had already-existing tenurial attachments
always to be revitalised by new gifts? Discussion of the patronage bestowed
by Earl David upon his followers, and how it was dispensed among them,
will serve to clarify the connection between service in the following and

enfeoffments, old and new.

To begin, personal association with the earl was no automatic path to economic betterment. The number of known beneficiaries is too small and their gains are generally too modest. In the English Midlands, where followers preferred to consolidate their interests, there was little scope for lordly promotion of knightly lines. Aristocratic resentment at the amount of land held by lay vassals or the Church was no sudden phenomenon; but in a period of mounting inflation, all magnates concerned for their financial standing, perhaps even those with the means to be generous, were less likely than ever to be open-handed in their patronage. Real property was first and foremost an economic asset, not a source of lavish gifts. Yet escalating costs also led followers to place renewed emphasis upon *largesse* as a cardinal aristocratic virtue; and, in a patronage society, the growing conflict between seigneurial retrenchment and knightly expectation introduced a further element of instability into the relationship between lords and men.

Let us first consider the most shadowy members of the entourage – Bartholomew and Constantine de Mortimer, Bartholomew le Moyne, Walkelin de Nuers, Walkelin son of Stephen and Geoffrey de Waterville, among others. For reasons which will appear, some of these men should probably be placed in the household proper rather than in the wider following. A number attest infrequently. But the majority served the earl as regular witnesses on both sides of the Border from *c.*1185. Few are known proprietors, and the suggestion is that some were unenfeoffed household knights. Constantine de Mortimer and Bartholomew le Moyne are both called knights, but neither seems to have held land. Constantine once attests as 'miles domini comitis', a style which evokes the intimate dependence upon a lord of a *miles domesticus*.[86] These two appear to exemplify the time-honoured notion of personal loyalty, and a firm distinction must be drawn between them and those whose service was demonstrably an incident of tenure. Bartholomew de Mortimer, also unrecorded as a landowner but described as a knight, was a veteran of the Third Crusade and served as David's recognised representative on King John's Irish campaign.[87] We may have identified another unbeneficed vassal serving for his maintenance in the household.

Belonging to families unable or reluctant to provide for them adequately, landless or otherwise impoverished younger sons formed a perennial element in knightly society. Attachment to a powerful magnate was the first step towards acquiring the hoped-for territorial substance; the lord's advantage lay in having armed dependants at his instant disposal to do his will.[88] As has been suggested elsewhere, Earl David may have allocated small feus near Inverurie castle to several household knights, thenceforth supported in independence of the *aula,* but ready for immediate deployment in an emergency.[89] Personal service became tied to the land. However, one follower benefiting from David in England, Richard son of William, received in fee and heritage £5 annually out of the earl's third penny of

Cambridge, 'for his homage and service'.[90] This grant marked a preliminary stage in Richard's career, predating his appointment as the earl's English estate steward about 1209. It bears all the hallmarks of a magnate settling a money-fee upon a household knight to keep him in the following as an annuitant, and therefore provides a very rare baronial record of the kind of which B. D. Lyon, in his analysis of English *fiefs-rentes*, was unable to offer a single example.[91] Recruited to the stewardship, Richard later occurs as a landowner, though it is far from certain that he had been invested with real estate by David.[92]

Indeed, however eagerly household knights aspired to a territorial fief, much of our evidence would indicate that alliance with Earl David was not a sure method of land acquisition for landless vassals. Failure to provide real estate was a strong incentive for the disappointed to look elsewhere. William Revel fought in David's *équipe* in a tournament at Lagny-sur-Marne about 1181, here appearing in a characteristic context for a household knight.[93] He witnessed fairly regularly for the earl in the 1190s; but he was obliged to build up his modest landed fortune independently.[94] A better-documented case of a probable household knight moving to advantage from Earl David's service is afforded by Bartholomew de Mortimer, who joined the affinity of William Marshal *junior,* possibly in time to assist him in enforcing his control over the Huntingdon honour, after the earl's forfeiture, from March 1217.[95] From the earliest days of Norman England great lords had had in their trains knights who were landed and knights who served for wages. In David's following, tenurial service and salaried service were complemented as before. And followings remained expectant. But the conventional picture of landless younger sons actually attaining wealth in their lord's fief finds little confirmation in the present study. Demand for *largesse* exceeded supply.

In fact, the lay followers known to have received real property from Earl David were all of prior landed means. Typically their acquisitions consisted of manorial appurtenances held as fractional knights' fees; Robert of Bassingham was endowed with a disputed tenancy and would later be obliged to ask for an exchange.[96] David had a limited amount of patronage at his direct disposal and he was cautious in dispensing what little existed. In addition to a half-fee at Great Stukeley, Simon de Senlis was assigned, like Richard son of William, an income of £5 from the third penny of Cambridge and a separate emolument of six and a half marks from the earl's third penny of Huntingdonshire, each granted for the quarter-part of one knight's service. He also held lordship at Godmanchester through David's favour.[97] This follower took the lion's share; his only near-rival was Robert de Mortimer of Attleborough, who obtained a half-fee at Godmanchester and, most probably, additional interests in Cambridgeshire: a further half-fee made up of lands pertaining to the Huntingdon honour in Cambridge, Newnham and Barnwell, and yet another allowance, in this instance £4, from the *tertius denarius* of Cambridge. These last are known to have been controlled by Robert's son William, who as Earl David's tenant is found granting them, save for a single dwelling-house, to Adam brother of Hervey Dunning, mayor of Cambridge, for thirty-two marks *per annum*.[98] We thus have two examples, one certain and one very probable, involving worthy lords of manors in which the money-fief (albeit heritable) supplemented gifts of land in heritage. This simultaneous use of two types of contract to reinforce loyalties is important. There can be no better illustration of the gradual transition from the tie between lord and man based on land to the 'bastard feudalism' of later medieval England that rested on the salaried service of the indentured retainer. But we must also say that the earl's endowments, though rarely lavish, generally emphasised the traditional association between tenure and vassalic obligation. The seigneurial world was changing, yet lordship over men was still tied up with lordship over land.

In all, seven lay members of the inner circle and two from the outer circle certainly enjoyed the earl's tangible support. The records of his patronage are without doubt incomplete. Robert Basset, William Burdet, Hugh de Lisures, Philip le Moyne and Alan son of Hugh may all have acquired small tenancies. None can be shown to have held his Huntingdon tenement by inheritance or prior grant; two served as estate stewards and would have expected remuneration over and above the local prestige and influence of their office.[99] Even if made in writing, grants of wardships and other occasional allowances, because of their ephemeral nature, are especially unlikely to survive. Yet on the available evidence followers who relied for perpetual freeholds upon Earl David alone had poor prospects indeed; however much they appealed to his generosity, landed knights could normally count on tiny fees only. Also revealing is that the earl's known patronage was unequally distributed between the different categories of landed dependant. The bulk of it benefited those whose initial attachment to him cannot be related to tenurial service, for even including uncertain cases pre-existing bonds of tenure were rarely reinforced (Bassingham, Senlis, Richard of Lindsey).[100] Thus tenants as a rule probably could not expect to profit directly in a permanent economic sense, save perhaps if also active as office-holders (Bassingham, Senlis, *senescalli*). There is no reason *a priori* why the chances of survival should bring landowners with no proven tenurial ties with David into greater prominence than established tenants as recipients of patronage. It seems inescapable that the former's loyalty had more often to be underpinned by supplementary interests. Dependence was sustained by bestowing endowments and rewarding service. Patronage was therefore a characteristic of their association with David – clients became vassals, and support in land was decisive to the relationship. It appears to have been different for the hereditary tenants, who could apparently be held in service without fresh subinfeudations. In other words, a lord's tenant by patrimony might still be 'miles meus et socius'.[101] But to use this evidence as firm testimony to the persisting reality of homage and fealty, the argument requires some further elaboration.

The preferment a client expected from a great lord was coveted not only for himself but also for his own friends and kinsfolk. To take an extreme case, the three brothers and nine sisters of Hugh de Lisures would all have been anxious for the aid and protection a powerful magnate might bestow.[102] At the same time, 'good lordship' could depend upon success in soliciting favours from the king and the central administration to further in various ways the careers of individual followers and those who mattered to them. Ambitiousness for land and office apart, Lisures had every need of allies in Angevin government when his property was sequestered in 1208 for non-payment of debts; likewise Robert de Mortimer when he had temporarily incurred the royal displeasure in 1194.[103] Earl David's supporters enjoyed the particular distinction of serving a lord associated with two great patronage systems. And yet just as the gifts the earl bestowed in person upon his followers were generally insubstantial – and possibly non-existent as far as their own dependants were concerned – so we must not exaggerate the degree to which interests were successfully advanced by his court connections.

The contemporary Scottish *curia regis* has no John of Salisbury or Walter Map to illuminate its operations as a fountain-head of patronage. As in England, however, 'pour tous, la cour offrait une chance de promotion sociale, la difficulté restant, évidemment, de s'y faire introduire'.[104] In this regard, Earl David was exceptionally well placed to procure preferential consideration for his followers and their intimates. The real problem was that the character of Scots royal patronage was transformed during these years, so that Scotland became less of a promised land than it had been for those adventurers who had found favour in the administrations of David I and Malcolm IV. New estates continued to be founded; but the main contours of aristocratic settlement were being drawn, while in their marriage strategies and office-holding the great families of the realm were seeking to consolidate their power by excluding the *parvenu*.[105]

There are only five examples of Scottish advancement to be considered here. All save that of the Ashbys concern the connections, or putative connections, of clients who are not known to us as hereditary tenants of Earl David, a fact which fits well with the earlier argument that his support in land or other tangible benefits tended to be used to secure new adherents rather than to reward the existing nucleus of vassal-followers. It is possible that the Lisures family established a modest offshoot at Gorton (in Lasswade), Midlothian, in the early thirteenth century; and it can at least be suggested that a kinsman of Ralph de Camoys (de Cames, de Cameis, de Camois, etc.) founded the line of Camoys (Chames, Chamois, de Cameis, etc.) of Ednam and Elliston in Roxburghshire.[106] No information survives, however, to make a case for David's intervention in either instance. We may be on firmer ground with Roger de Mortimer, sheriff of Perth, who by 1194 had been endowed by King William at Fowlis Easter in Angus.[107] Thanks to the support of the Scots royal house, the Mortimers of Attleborough, from whom the Mortimers of Scottish record doubtless sprang, added to their reputation on both sides of the Border line; and if it can be accepted that the late twelfth-century romance *Estoire de Waldef* was written for them,[108] their interest in Earl Waltheof of Northumbria, the great-grandfather of Earl David, is perhaps more comprehensible in this light. Their first Scottish representative, William de Mortimer of Aberdour, though not a noteworthy witness of David's *acta*, appears from independent evidence to have been his friend;[109] David can be regarded in a special sense as patron of the main Attleborough stem; and while it cannot be proved that his good standing at the Scottish court was ever used on the Mortimers' behalf, he could only have welcomed the transfer of Fowlis, adjacent to his burgh of Dundee, to one whose family had shown constancy in his own service as well as the Scots crown's.[110]

The next possibility concerns the Carneilles, another *lignage* entering Scotland in David's lifetime. Robert de la Carneille, a Lincolnshire land-owner, first witnessed for David in 1172.[111] Probably by *c.* 1195, Roger de la Carneille had been ensconced by King William at Guthrie, near Forfar; Robert was enfeoffed by David at Great Stukeley.[112] The precise relation-ship between these two men is unknown, but since the family's chief pro-tector prior to Roger's acquisition of Guthrie was apparently David himself, Roger's advancement may well have rested upon the earl's sponsorship. Certainly, by *c.* 1200 a William de la Carneille occurs as vicar of Dundee, a benefice then in the collation of Lindores abbey, and this may provide an instance of the earl using his ecclesiastical interests to advance his clien-tage.[113] More indirectly, it is possible that one well-connected member of the following was encouraged to offer the opportunity of Scottish expansion to a kinsman of other followers: Clarembald of Ashby, whose distinctive Christian name (whence Clarabad in Hutton, Berwickshire) ties him to the Ashbys of Castle Ashby (Northants), represented in the following by Wil-liam of Ashby and his son David, obtained or consolidated a modest base near Berwick upon Tweed due to the patronage of Walter Olifard II.[114]

And yet this fragmentary evidence serves merely to underline that membership of the following did not bring families as a matter of course within reach of the wider reserves of patronage in the Scots king's gift. However active in pursuit of their interests, with hot competition for limited rewards Earl David could not exert great pressure as an inter-mediary on his clients' behalf. The career of a one-time follower David of Lindsey, lord of Crawford and justiciar of Lothian, seems instructive. The family fortunes having been securely established in Scotland, the next major step was Lindsey's promotion to aristocratic rank in England by marriage with a coheiress to the Suffolk barony of Cavendish.[115] Nor is this the only example of how the continuing advance of an Anglo-Norman house long established in Scotland now depended more upon its ties with England than upon government service and landholding north of the Tweed. The Vieuxponts, represented in Earl David's 'outer circle', had hitherto owed almost everything to the king of Scots. But Robert de Vieuxpont, an ambitious and capable younger son, was obliged to fend for himself; and while his connections failed to draw him into Scottish royal service, they did not prevent him from leaving his mark as one of King John's most energetic and highly favoured agents. Lord of Westmorland from 1203, Robert proceeded along a path littered with the rewards of his master's favour.[116] Notable advances were still possible in the Scotland of King David's grandsons; but Earl David's followers or their kinsmen who substantially improved upon their social circumstances did so outside the northern realm.

Yet if David was unable significantly to influence the direction of King William's patronage on his dependants' behalf, there is little likelihood that he personally provided what they expected at the Angevin court. The English crown controlled greater reserves in wardships, marriages and offices, and was less limited in its capacity to endow favoured lords and their clients. But the government came to be increasingly identified with a newly enriched ministerial class which systematically excluded the magnates from influence over the king. For a time the royal goodwill continued to be extended towards Earl David, and it is salutary that without support from Richard I and John he would have had fewer reserves with which to act as a benefactor of dependants. Yet the privileges that royal indulgence brought were expressed in grants to David personally; and with the effective loss of the king's benevolence from *c.*1205 he could not even rely upon the crown for protection of his existing concerns. In fact apart from David of Lindsey, only two followers stand out for their success in adding substantially to their inherited status. The first of these was Ralph de Camoys, the son and heir of Stephen de Camoys of North Denchworth (Berks), who entered David's affinity when the earl proffered for his custody in 1198.[117] Although Ralph was David's beneficiary at Great Stukeley, his main interests were consolidated or extended outside the earl's estates. He had acquired the small Norfolk barony of Flockthorpe by 1213, and in 1216 the landed base lay in half-a-dozen shires. The build-up of his concerns continued, the largest gain coming through his marriage to Asceline, the heiress of William of Torpel (d. 1242). In her right he secured Torpel and Upton (Northants) and a sixth-part of the barony of Bourn (Cambs). Appointed sheriff of Surrey and Sussex in 1242, he died in 1259.[118] Robert of Bassingham's career followed a similar path. He claimed by inheritance one fee in the Huntingdon honour and a small Suffolk interest; service as Earl David's steward apparently added a half-fee at Bozeat or Whissendine. Robert's wife brought him initially a stake in Yorkshire and then, upon the death of her brother John de Wahull, a moiety of the Wahull honour.[119] As a result, by 1217 the Bassingham property entered nine or ten counties.[120] To be sure, David had encouraged both of these men in their careers; and a good marriage was for those able to pay – men on the way up, not the poorly connected. But to say any more than this would be to say too much. Essentially, Camoys and Bassingham prospered as independent agents.[121]

The next step is to suggest how this study may cast general light on the developing feudalism of midland England, where Earl David's followers normally resided and usually obtained what support he had to offer. Accounts of English feudal society as a changing society, with their emphasis upon multiple homage, tenant-right and the community of the shire, have yet to devote adequate attention to contemporary magnate patronage. But notwithstanding the dearth of specialist investigations, it seems reasonably safe to assume that if this great lord in two kingdoms provided only modest *douceurs*, many fellow magnates must have found themselves unable to secure substantial *largesse* for the followings upon which their local strength largely rested. For their dependants, there were no doubt compensatory attractions, perhaps not least the honour and prestige of serving an important feudatory and the mutual support afforded by a group moving in the same circle. On the other hand, many were the difficulties that faced the magnates as leaders of men. These included the declining rewards of royal patronage and the legal restraints barring the recovery of expensive past alienations. Sooner or later the point was reached where followers' demands would remain largely unsatisfied, or would have to be satisfied in other ways.

This evident crisis of traditional good lordship needs to be seen against a broader background. In fourteenth-century England, lords restored their position through 'new forms of retinue organised on the principle of personal contract in place of the out-dated principle of tenurial loyalty'.[122] Yet the use of money as a means of securing allegiance had had a long history when the indentured retainer first contracted to serve his lord for a fixed annual fee. Even Earl David was allocating *fiefs-rentes* not only to an apparent household knight but also to landed supporters. From the late twelfth century land became increasingly scarce as the money supply became increasingly plentiful; magnates were obliged to give less land and, however tentatively at first, to see in its replacement by predetermined emoluments a medium of patronage which could be more easily afforded in an age of climbing rents and prices. Lords were still concerned to secure loyalty; yet the consequences were all the more profound because this movement, perhaps merely defensive in origin, was quickly allied with another. 'After 1180', as Duby has observed in a European context, 'the profit motive steadily undermined the spirit of largess. Nostalgia for this virtue still lingered, yet it adorned none but mythical heroes.'[123] These remarks may need to be toned down for thirteenth-century England: as estate incomes mounted, retinues seemingly grew larger.[124] Nevertheless, so far as the land itself was concerned, financial difficulties and financial opportunities were tending to work to the same end.

Moreover, progressive landlords appreciated investments for what they were worth, and this contributed in turn to changes in relations between lord and man. It was not so much that enfeoffment was inherently unfavourable to lords; in return for a single gift and warranty, knightly families were theoretically committing themselves to innumerable 'counter-gifts'. But inevitably, with the territorialisation of obligations – once a knight became 'meus miles et meus tenens'[125] – lord-man ties were in the long run undermined. Enfeoffments ultimately decreased rather than ex-tended zones of influence; and contracts emanating from 'the more dom-esticated feudalism of southern England'[126] were especially difficult to enforce. Thus as knights – in part because obliged to – grew in self-reliance, further divorcing themselves from their customary allegiances in the shires, lords turned the more systematically to engagements which were less ex-pensive, but more easily terminated, as a means of creating new and stronger clientage networks in alliance with the local gentry. Exceptionally privileged retainers might still be granted lands, though usually for life only. But above all, the magnates preferred contracts which, on the one hand, protected the territorial power base, and, on the other, revitalised the personal relationship because they dissociated service from the tenurial nexus and avoided the complexities which in the past had frustrated the objective of ensuring loyalty.[127]

Therefore the household knight, ancestor of the liveried retainer, and the *fief-rente*, precursor of the retainer's fee,[128] were the two elements in the structure of Earl David's following pointing to the future; personal loyalty founded on land tenure would not endure because of growing knightly independence that was at once a consequence and a cause of changing aristocratic attitudes towards the lordship of men. And yet, in the final analysis, the most interesting aspect of David's discernible following must be the firmness with which its character remained allied to the past rather than its links with later retinue organisation. The binding ties derived not from regional fief-holding, which in the Midlands rarely played any signifi-cant part in cementing feudal bonds. Furthermore, the evidence is wholly lacking that David assisted followers by manipulating the local administra-tion in the manner made familiar by studies of bastard feudalism, so that ultimately 'protection' alone might provide the major unifying force.[129] Thanks to the king's control of the shires, the earl's influence could not prevail as had that of his predecessor, Earl Simon II, in the 1140s, while inability to secure favourable verdicts in the law courts even for himself directly undermined the interests of certain of his dependants.[130] The ties of obligation stemmed from the traditional loyalties of lordship, with land itself retaining prominence as the means of both procuring and rewarding service. Most significant of all is the role of the hereditary tenants. In the last resort they could make do without new grants, and they did not dishonour their undertakings but observed the normal vassalic duty of supporting their lord by deed and counsel. Thus the very fact of Earl David's failure to dispense patronage more widely, though doubtless straining feudal loyalties, serves to drive home the point that in individual cases proprietary bonds could have considerable strength of their own. Although great changes were set in train, old enfeoffments, even in early thirteenth-century England, might have a foremost place in asserting a lord's ascendancy; and because the force of tenurial loyalty was not yet spent, a lord as far as he was able still gave land in perpetuity to bind new associates firmly in his service.

The nature of Earl David's entourage can now be put into final perspective. The household proper was modelled on Anglo-Norman lines and staffed by Anglo-Norman personnel. Kinsmen were poorly represented. But around this central organisation collected a wider group of followers usually of obscure or moderate standing, some of whom had Scottish connections, though none was demonstrably a native Scot. A few clients were probably household knights and can in a special sense be described as the earl's dependants. Many were his tenants, generally in England, and some were his beneficiaries, but normally in small ways. It is often difficult to differentiate between temporary associate and less transient follower, just as it is difficult to give a clear impression of numbers.[131] Even David's closest advisers among the landed knights had other ties of friendship and perhaps of tenure, and would move in and out of the following as their private affairs allowed; some withdrew support once they saw the opportunity of advancement elsewhere and new men appeared to replace them. Nevertheless, although the composition of the larger affinity fluctuated from date to date and from place to place, it seems possible to reconstruct the main stages in its development.

In the early 1170s, at the outset of Earl David's career, William de St Michael, Hugh Giffard and William de Vieuxpont were especially conscientious in his service. Anglo-Normans whose interests gave them particular attachments to Scotland, St Michael was in King William's employment in 1173, negotiating on his behalf at the French royal court;[132] Giffard had enjoyed prominence in Countess Ada's following; and Vieuxpont also had ties with Ada, for his family held land near hers and supported her priory at Haddington.[133] When these men ceased to witness for David around the mid-1170s, he had already won renown in England and bound fresh followers to his person. Giffard and Vieuxpont apart, two members of the inner circle and two from the outer circle had joined David in arms against the English crown in 1174; in later life, he attracted followers who had family connections with his partisans at that time.[134] Finally, the acquisition of the Huntingdon honour in 1185 served to reinforce old associations and to create new ones, both within the honour itself and the shires through which it was dispersed. From 1185 charter witness-lists reveal a body of advisers which customarily itinerated with the household on both sides of the Tweed-Solway frontier. Around this core clustered local supporters, associates rather than companions, who did not perambulate with the earl but periodically appeared when he halted on progress about the estates. Such was John of Wilton, lord of Wilton (Roxburghshire) and a proprietor in Ceres (Fife), who attested only in Scotland and lived on the fringe of the personal following;[135] or Hugh de Lisures of Benefield, who was occasionally drawn into the following in England just as Wilton joined it in Scotland.[136] The composition of the entourage was elastic and changed its character as David moved about.

By contrast Robert Basset, Robert of Bassingham, William Burdet and Simon de Senlis, among others, journeyed frequently in Earl David's company. In regular attendance upon him, they were his leading followers who gave him advice and friendship in good measure, accompanied him at the Scottish *curia regis*,[137] and participated prominently in the full and solemn meetings of his own court. For all their importance as formal advisory, administrative and legal bodies, 'honour' courts are notoriously ill-documented. Their vitality was greater in Scotland.[138] But even in early Angevin England, although the 'Common Law actions . . . turned the process on right in feudal courts inexorably into a relic of the past',[139] they still retained significance in litigation as courts of first instance and occasionally resolved disputes without recourse to royal justice. Despite the shrinkage in their powers of jurisdiction and discipline, they continued to assist in the running of a lord's estates, enforcing tenurial duties and registering sales, exchanges and family settlements. The court of Earl David's immediate Senlis predecessor, 'curia Comitis Simonis', was of fluid membership, its scope of business broad. Accommodating knights of the neighbourhood as well as enfeoffed tenants, it could meet at Fotheringhay, perhaps already the *caput* of the Huntingdon honour, and deal there with property pertaining to the honour of Gant.[140] Earl David's court makes a few explicit appearances in English, though not in Scottish, record.[141] Like a 'central' royal court (and Earl Simon's), it was apparently a peripatetic personal *curia* with no fixed place of business. Tenants of his Scottish lordship were seemingly unlikely to travel with him in England; but in the witness-clauses of Scottish *acta* their names are frequently jumbled together with those of intimate advisers who, if landed, held estates outside Scotland. These men bore witness and gave counsel not, primarily, as individual tenants with interests in a particular fief, though many of them held of the earl in the Midlands. The vassal's duty to ride with the lord had overtaken the early tradition of self-contained honour courts.[142] For in the strict sense there was only one personal following. Its membership might vary, but there was a single group of trusted advisers crossing and re-crossing the Border with the earl as he perambulated to demonstrate his power and lordship.

This personal following, the nucleus around which others could group, is chiefly to be found among the nineteen laymen of the so-called inner circle of attestors. Seven (possibly nine) of these persons were at one time or another tenants of Earl David by inheritance; four (possibly six) of the non-tenants received fees from the earl. These ties were strengthened by links in other contexts. The men of the inner circle supported David as pledges or when he personally bore testimony to charters.[143] Some belonged to families with established connections transcending the Border line, and may have moved about with David to attend to their own private concerns in the two realms as well as interesting themselves in the earl's business. Nine of them followed him into rebellion in 1215–16, though he was then too old to provide his supporters with active military leadership.[144] Finally, no fewer than five of this inner core saw service as his territorial stewards. Though as such preoccupied in the estates, they rejoined the household whenever he returned to their district, as an indispensable link between the centre and the localities; and it is clear from individual examples that commonly these *senescalli* continued to enjoy a special relationship with the earl after they had relinquished office. The ambulatory nature of his court and the presence of these men within it are especially evocative of the English private *concilium*, a distinct corporate body of experienced administrators, legal advisers and *amici*, which ultimately replaced the honour court as the effective instrument of seigneurial authority throughout a lord's estates.[145] But when formally constituted councils began to proliferate, the divorce of personal service from the tenure of land was almost complete; by that time, 'lords were more interested in protecting their incidents than in selecting their tenants'.[146] In Earl David's following lord-man relationships founded on landholding retained significance. Tenants by patrimony or by patronage predominated at the heart of affairs. But although its character may seem outmoded and imperfect by contrast with later developments, we must assume that the earl's following sufficed to meet his needs. Above all, it provided what every lord desired: the loyalty of a clientage.

9

ANGLO-SCOTTISH PROPRIETORSHIP:
A WIDER VIEW

Earl David's royal birth and lineage provide the key to his life and actions. The grandson and brother of three successive kings of Scots receptive of Anglo-continental innovation, he shared their devotion to the reformed monastic Church; he preferred, as they tended to prefer, to be surrounded by dependants of Norman-French or English descent; and he followed the example of his father and grandfather by marrying into an Anglo-Norman dynasty of great renown. Inevitably, Earl David's status also involved him in high politics, which in turn powerfully influenced his activity. King William's consuming ambition to recover the northern shires precipitated his abortive, though not wholly inglorious, campaign of 1174. The acquisition of the Huntingdon honour in 1185, assuredly the chief milestone in his career, reflected Angevin concern for stability in the north; his forfeiture in 1215–18 was likewise inextricably bound up with the problem of defining the relationship between two neighbouring realms. The earl's Scottish appanage was equally a creature of royal policies. It provides a fine example of the way Scots kings used a new landed aristocracy to strengthen the early medieval kingdom; and most notably in Garioch he stood at the forefront of the onward expansion of feudal lordship in Scotland, a process about which 'our knowledge . . . is not so great that we can afford to neglect even the least of its exiguous traces'.[1]

For thirty years from 1185, however, Scotland represented just one portion of Earl David's world, and the unifying theme of this study lies in his role as a major landowner on both sides of the Tweed-Solway frontier. Yet David was not unique, for he was but one of many Anglo-Scottish barons who contributed significantly to the history of England and Scotland in the twelfth and thirteenth centuries. Although mostly lacking estates in northern France, these lords formed an integral part of that larger 'Norman' aristocracy whose ambitions, transcending individual countries, were for long years limited only by the availability of land for accumulation. But while the great cross-Channel feudatories raised to power through the Norman conquest and settlement of England, and the Anglo-Welsh and Anglo-Irish landowners of a later period, are the basis of recent stimulating investigations, so far Anglo-Scottish magnates have scarcely attracted in published work the consideration they deserve.[2] Generally speaking, English historians have no interest in their Scottish lands and Scottish historians little interest in the English, and it has proved all too easy to underestimate the tendency for estates in the two kingdoms to come together.[3] Thus the view that in the earlier Middle Ages the Border was a sharp dividing-line between two territorial aristocracies has not been seriously contested. In Scottish historiography the growth of an independent kingdom occupies pride of place, while concentration by scholars upon political crises between the realms has tended to reinforce the notion that tenurial interconnections were of an essentially ephemeral kind.

Underlying this opinion is a lingering unwillingness to examine magnates' aspirations from the standpoint of the magnates themselves. Earl David's career has proved particularly suitable for study of aristocratic interests from within. In wealth and influence he led the Anglo-Scottish nobility of his day. Moreover, scholarly emphasis upon the periodic confrontations between the kingdoms in his lifetime has especially obscured the existence of more peaceful contacts. Two main conclusions have emerged about his activity as a great cross-Border lord. First, he readily associated others in his Anglo-Scottish concerns as he dispensed his patronage and enhanced his lordship. Family members, knightly supporters and religious corporations were endowed by him with property in the other kingdom; his burgesses of Dundee, some of whom hailed from England or northern France, were encouraged to increase their share of English trade; Anglo-Norman adherents were sent in to administer his Scottish lands; and an inner group of clients accompanied him on both sides of the Border line. These points serve to stress not the separateness of the estates falling to Earl David's power, but that his holdings in England and north-eastern Scotland were being forged into one complex of lordship whose unity did not rest solely upon the fact that he travelled tirelessly to display his personal authority. Secondly: although in certain ways the earl lived in a world that made national boundaries irrelevant, two kings had power over his person and claimed his allegiance. Provided peace prevailed, he could fulfil his recognised obligations as a tenant-in-chief of either ruler and it was politically acceptable to hold lands in both countries. In wartime, it was clearly impossible to serve two mutually hostile monarchs and avoid the misfortunes of forfeiture. Earl David therefore worked for harmony between the crowns, as an advocate of the peace upon which his own cross-Border concerns, and those of his connections, so obviously depended. To undertake a fuller assessment of Anglo-Scottish proprietorship seems desirable in order to place Earl David's career in perspective, although limitations of space and current knowledge ensure that the present analysis can only be regarded as a preliminary to more extensive and deeper study.

The Magnates

By the reign of Alexander III (1249–86) the pattern of Anglo-Scottish proprietorship displayed an elaborate and intricate structure. Most prominent of all was the Scots king himself.[4] Below him came numerous eminent landowners of magnate rank, and many religious institutions and 'gentry' families. Together they had built up a strong and apparently unassailable position. This state of affairs, however, was not to endure after the outbreak of the wars of independence in 1296, when relations between the kingdoms deteriorated so far that contemporaries might date gifts by reference to time of peace.[5] Yet tenures straddling the Border were much longer in the making than in the destroying. Nowhere is this more evident than in the rise of the cross-Border magnate houses.

Allowance made for the difficulty of defining magnate standing,[6] on the morrow of King David I's death in 1153 few important barons controlled territorial interests in both realms. The earl of Dunbar's title to the barony of Beanley in Northumberland derived from Beauclerk's grants to his father. Otherwise, the estates of this select body had grown from the allocation of fiefs during the first phase of Norman-French expansion into Scotland. Since King David, as a patron of lay incomers, had preferred to promote 'new' men, another feature of the group was that almost without exception their wealth was obviously concentrated north rather than south of the Tweed. In their roots and branches the Stewarts, for example, 'flourished simultaneously in Scotland, England, and Brittany', but Walter I son of Alan's personal stake outside Scotland was confined to minuscule properties in Shropshire and Sussex.[7] Yet it is an indication of the importance of English possessions to these barons that they did not renounce their landholding ties with England, however tenuous, while the opening up of Scotland to Anglo-continental settlement ensured that the proliferation of cross-Border proprietorship was only a step away.

After half a century or so of deliberately restricted growth, the class of Anglo-Scottish magnates began to expand rapidly in numbers, influence and strength. Men of Norman-French origin still predominated, but not exclusively. In fact, nothing could be more misleading than to assume that only recently settled families in Scotland enjoyed English land. Individual lieges of native descent enthusiastically accepted Anglo-Norman brides and from time to time took estates for themselves in the south: a Scottish colonisation of England complemented the Norman colonisation of Scotland, albeit on a far less extensive scale. Bertram, Bohun earl of Hereford, Comyn earl of Buchan, Courtenay, Lindsey of Crawford, Lindsey of Lamberton, Lovel, Merlay, Muscamp, Olifard, Quincy earl of Winchester, Ros, Vere earl of Oxford, Vesci, the ancient Scottish houses of Atholl, Fife and Galloway – all these, and others besides, had brought new blood into the scheme of magnate cross-Border proprietorship by Earl David's death.[8] The securing of land in one kingdom by lords of already-existing substance in the other had become far more pronounced. Though younger sons still flocked into Scotland, there is, contrary to a recent opinion,[9] little to indicate that senior Anglo-Norman lines were unduly circumspect about, or hindered in, taking on Scottish lands as opportunity offered. The Anglo-Scottish aristocracy had assumed a more élitist character and was less welcoming of the *parvenu*. What had changed also was the way in which estates had been founded or augmented, for collateral succession, and more

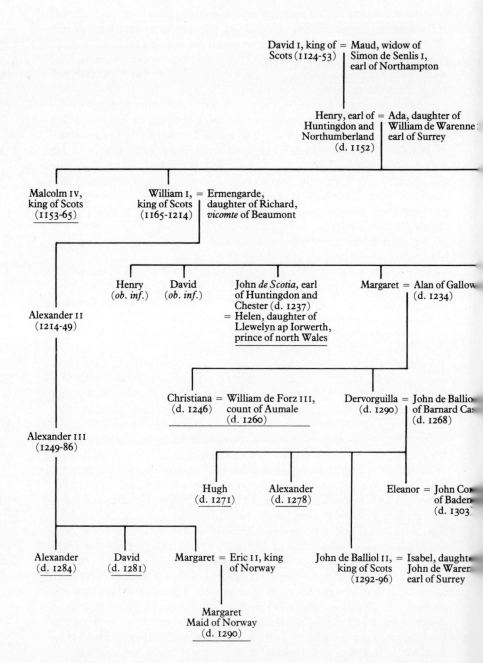

Table 3. Some of the family relationships of Earl David

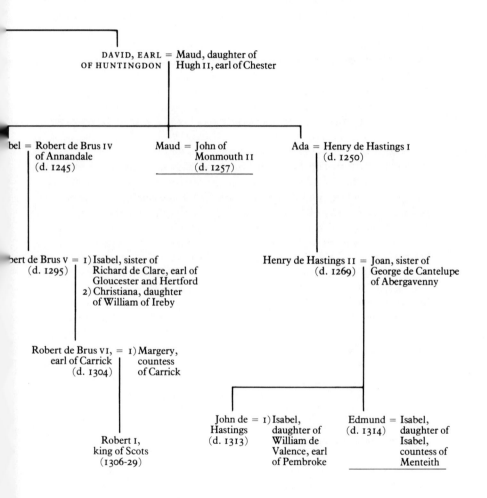

especially marriage, had largely replaced direct royal grants. This again set a pattern for the future. Acknowledged heiresses, a large number of whom were involved in the rise of cross-Border houses, were naturally the most desirable partners; but daughters who had brothers also brought property into marriage, and given the uncertainties of family life every daughter was, of course, potentially an heiress. To cite some early cases, intermarriage with the Morevilles explains the Bertram interest in Berwickshire; Roger de Merlay had acquired Kettle in Fife with a daughter of Earl Duncan; the long-lived Vesci connection with Roxburghshire derived from an illegitimate daughter of William the Lion. An uncle succeeding a nephew had reunited the Quincys in one main Anglo-Scottish branch in c. 1190; by 1207 Saer de Quincy IV had gained through an unexpectedly providential marriage a half-share in the honour of Leicester as first earl of Winchester; and Saer's son Roger, future earl of Winchester and Constable of Scotland, had an equally exalted heiress in prospect. Much had happened by the early thirteenth century to encourage the growth of large cross-Border lordships, in part because their development no longer lay so firmly in the Scots king's hands.

Study of Earl David's family connections will serve to show some of the principal attributes of this aristocracy after his death, and to pave the way for wider discussion of Anglo-Scottish proprietorship and its role in society and politics before the Edwardian wars. When the earl's son and successor John *de Scotia*, earl of Huntingdon and Chester, died without children in 1237, his vast lordships in England and Scotland were reassigned among his four coheiresses and their respective spouses. Ada, wife of Henry de Hastings, and Isabel, wife of Robert de Brus IV, were John's sisters. The third portion of his lands was claimed by Dervorguilla (John de Balliol) and Christiana (William de Forz III), the issue of Earl David's oldest daughter Margaret and Alan of Galloway.[10] Alan himself had died in 1234, leaving no son to maintain the unity of his estates. Balliol and Forz had thus earlier shared in their father-in-law's great cross-Border inheritance with Earl Roger de Quincy, the husband of Helen, Alan's daughter by a previous marriage. Matrimony as an agent of social advance profited them twofold. To begin, we shall concentrate upon Earl John and Alan of Galloway, and the build-up of their chief spheres of influence. Here, too, the heiress was a vital element in landholding astride the Tweed. Brief discussions follow on the antecedents of Hastings, Brus, Balliol and Forz, and on the impact of their new gains upon family fortunes.

In March 1221 John, who was then nearly fifteen years old, passed with his English lands from the wardship of King Alexander II into that of his uncle, Earl Ranulf of Chester. In 1222 he was married to Helen daughter of Llewelyn, prince of north Wales. This was a rich and honourable match. But although Helen was well-born, and although her dowry comprised a financial settlement of 1,000 marks and a territorial endowment of three west midland manors, primarily the alliance was a means of advancing the best political interests of John's new guardian.[11] In 1227 John entered upon his Anglo-Scottish inheritance; then, after a fruitless pursuit of sons, Earl Ranulf left the honour of Chester to be divided into new groupings in 1232. John, *jure matris* the senior coheir, took Cheshire, with wide concerns outside the earldom proper. Family alliances could always bring unforeseen benefits: Earl David's marriage to Maud of Chester in 1190 had proved to be a brilliant success.

The union into single hands of these Huntingdon and Chester interests, ranging from East Anglia and the West Country through to Yorkshire, and from Midlothian to Aberdeenshire, began one of the greatest fiefs ever to stretch across the Border. John was bound to two sovereigns, but since peace prevailed throughout his adult career, dual allegiance did not pose the special problems his father had faced and, although rarely conspicuous on the political stage, he faithfully supported each of the overlords he was obliged to serve. From Henry III he received the routine perquisites of a magnate in the king's favour.[12] He joined the ineffectual *chevauchée* to Brittany in 1230; he welcomed the fall of Hubert de Burgh in 1232; and he held against the earl Marshal in 1233–4.[13]

In his private life from 1232, while there is no reason to dispute the judgement that 'John's uneventful tenure of five years contrasted markedly with his uncle's long and glorious career',[14] the earldom of Chester preoccupied his attention. Chester vassals packed his following and captured his patronage, notably two connections distinguished in Henry III's personal government, William de Cantelupe *junior* and Stephen of Seagrave.[15] He died at Darnhall in Cheshire in June 1237 and, appropriately, he was buried beside Earl Ranulf in the chapter-house of Chester abbey. Yet although it seems rash to claim that he 'was often away in Scotland',[16] John was demonstrably more than *de Scotia* in name alone. On 30 May 1227 he had been knighted by King Alexander at Roxburgh, and it was probably on this occasion that he had paid homage for the Huntingdon honour and his Scottish fief. He evidently remained in Scotland until the following summer, and he returned on other known visits, perambulating his estates and attending the royal court.[17] He showed his devotion to Lindores abbey,[18] and John's care to foster his Scottish interests transcended spiritual responsibilities and the obvious attractions of the rent-roll. The son-in-law of a mighty Welsh prince, John also had the fortune to enjoy, from 1219 to his death, claims as next in line of royal succession to his as yet childless cousin, Alexander II.

Alan of Galloway was a many-sided and more colourful personality. He served as hereditary Constable of Scotland, but under his lordship Galloway 'remained something of a kingdom within a kingdom, knowing its own customs and its own officers'.[19] He was the proud scion of an illustrious Norse-Celtic dynasty, but a dynasty attracted to Anglo-French fashions and accustomed to finding brides from families originating outside Scotland.

Alan himself was more than half-Norman by birth, claimed kinship with the Angevin kings and, in addition to marrying Earl David's daughter Margaret, took wives from each main branch of the powerful house of Lacy.[20] He was by far the greatest magnate in southern Scotland; his lands also entered several English shires; and he laid claim to extensive Irish holdings. While the general trend was of aristocratic aggrandisement from estates in England and northern France, there was no barrier to expansion beyond Scotland by the old-established lords of an ancient Scottish province.

The marriage of Alan's father Roland to the Moreville heiress had made a resounding contribution to the family's status. In 1196, two imposing patrimonies had been merged as one. Galloway was the centre from which the principal accumulations of Lauderdale and Cunningham were controlled, and it remained the chief basis of Alan's strength. His guiding aim was to push out his influence into the western seaboard and create a huge power block on either side of the Irish Sea from territories which colonisation by Gaelic-speakers had already drawn into a single great cultural province. The English crown cultivated his alliance, and that of his brother Earl Thomas of Atholl, partly to win support in subduing Ulster, and partly to embarrass the Scots monarchy by drawing into a special relationship with itself clients capable of exhibiting a remarkable independence in their sympathies and causes. King John's grant to Alan of a vast fief along the northern coast of Ireland as 'lands to be conquered' had been made by 1213, one consequence of this being the encouragement of the Ulster Premonstratensian colony dependent upon Dryburgh abbey.[21]

Yet notwithstanding Alan's wider ambitions, he guarded his English interests with a jealous eye. He may never have taken possession of the late Moreville estate based on Burton in Lonsdale; nor is there evidence of a continuing Galloway connection with Torpenhow in Cumberland, the *maritagium* of his grandmother.[22] But Alan and his mother recovered from Earl David the old Moreville manor of Whissendine, with its park and manorhouse, successfully resuming the action cut short by Roland's death at Northampton in 1200.[23] In another legal battle, he vindicated his claim to Kippax, which had been acquired with other Yorkshire fees through his marriage into the Lacy line of Pontefract; and the bailiff of Kippax was vigilant in Alan's service until, shortly before Alan died, the manor passed to Earl Roger de Quincy.[24] When he settled Whissendine upon his sister and Nicholas de Stuteville, he carefully retained adjacent interests in the Huntingdon honour.[25] Although Alan's English tenures scarcely rivalled those of David or John, he moved in their social orbit and shared the same disregard for the Tweed-Solway frontier. He was among those upon whose advice King John claimed to have granted Magna Carta; but when Alexander II invaded England Alan stood with him and controlled the former Moreville lordship of north Westmorland until the Angevin revival forced him to withdraw.[26] War meant the loss of his more southerly interests and forfeiture in Ireland. Yet when in 1220 Alan returned into the peace of Henry III, the sequestered lands were instantly recovered.[27]

A family's past attainments, however, could not vouchsafe continued prosperity; and great magnate estates were easily dismembered through that most potent cause of dynastic disaster, failure of direct heirs male. William Farrer and R. Stewart-Brown have dealt exhaustively with the reallocation of Earl John's English lands outside Cheshire, and how Henry III bought out with substantial settlements all claims upon the county palatine, annexing the earldom to the crown;[28] the Scottish holdings were divided piecemeal, unit by unit. Far less is known about the partition of the Galloway lands (excluding the Irish block, an acquisition which was not heritable due to the restoration of Hugh de Lacy as earl of Ulster). But when Hastings, Brus, Balliol and Forz gained their respective portions, albeit not without some difficulty and delay, each decisively augmented his patrimonial property in England and either ascended to the upper reaches of the nobility in Scotland or greatly strengthened his existing importance in the northern kingdom. We see at once the inherent dangers threatening the integrity of individual Anglo-Scottish lordships and how, through new dynastic ties, cross-Border links were boosted at their expense.

Little need be said on Henry de Hastings (d. 1250), whose family had attained moderate local standing in England through a tradition of employment in seigneurial and Angevin royal service. When Henry entered on the Hastings inheritance in 1226, this included the hereditary stewardship of the Liberty of the abbey of Bury St Edmunds; the territorial patrimony lay in several English shires, but centred upon the steward's fee of Blunham (Beds) and Lidgate (Suffolk).[29] The economic position of Henry's father William had been precarious: in 1205 he had petitioned King John for relief from Jewish creditors.[30] Blunham lay within Earl David's sphere of influence; Henry's aunt had married the Huntingdon tenant Richard Foliot (d. by 1203); and men with the Hastings surname (not necessarily kinsfolk) had appeared in Scotland by the last quarter of the twelfth century.[31] But Henry's marriage to David's youngest daughter Ada was exceptionally advantageous for a not very affluent gentry *lignage*, which after the death of Earl John was transformed into one of the richer families engaged in Anglo-Scottish landholding, with estates ranging from London to west of Aberdeen.[32]

Here a modest fief was enlarged with acquisitions many times the value of the ancestral inheritance. Robert de Brus IV (d. 1245), the husband of Earl David's second daughter Isabel, was far more secure in his patrimony and lineage. The first Robert of the Annandale line, lavishly rewarded as a supporter of King Henry I, had founded the family fortunes with ample tenures in Yorkshire and County Durham.[33] King David subsequently established this powerful lord in similar strength with the broad valley of the Annan, and Robert found it possible to serve both kings with an equal degree of commitment, his loyalty to David I not being embarrassingly inconsistent with his loyalty to Beauclerk. One of the earliest of the great Anglo-Scottish magnates, Robert began the Augustinian priory at Guisborough, whose canons for long cherished his name and reputation as 'conquistor terrarum Clivelande et de Hertenesse et vallis Anandie'.[34]

The warfare of Stephen's reign inevitably jeopardised the unity of these lucrative accessions. Compelled to choose sides, Robert won distinction as a leader of the Yorkshire forces at the Battle of the Standard; Annandale he settled upon his younger son Robert II. This was a skilful way of minimising the effect of war upon family ambitions, and politics also determined the actual nature of the partition. The ascendancy King David achieved over northern England as far south as the Tees[35] explains why from the first the junior branch held Annandale in conjunction with Hartness, between Dene Mouth and Tees Mouth. Far from content to concentrate their activity upon one country alone, the Annandale lords always regarded Hartness as important, and their possession of this district enabled them to play almost as significant a role in northern England as they did in Scotland. They encouraged the prosperity of Hartlepool as a small town and port; their manor of Edenhall in Cumberland provided a staging-post on the road from Gretna through the Eden valley and over Stainmore.[36] Indeed Robert II expressed his commitment to England by supporting King Henry II in 1173–4, sacrificing Annandale to immediate confiscation.[37] Father and son thus had each had to confront the problem of divided allegiances in wartime. But the partition of c.1138 had not conformed to the line of the Tweed-Solway, and when the Scots had evacuated the north in 1157 there had been no further family settlement to avoid the dangers another war might bring. In any event, after 1174 the patrimony was swiftly reconstituted and the house restored to favour at the Scots royal court: in 1183 King William married an illegitimate daughter to Robert II's older son and namesake, endowing the couple with Haltwhistle in Tynedale. The Anglo-Scottish inheritance had descended to Robert's grandson Robert IV by 1215; and when the latter shared in the Chester lands after 1237 one mighty cross-Border estate, already a century old, was vastly extended in richness and size.

Brus was the only family represented in 1237 of ancient lineage as a landowner in Scotland; its attachment to northern English interests was, however, shared by the celebrated houses of Balliol and Forz. Established at Bywell on Tyne and Barnard Castle, with large appurtenances in upper Teesdale and Cleveland, the Balliols too traced their prominence to the earliest period of Norman-French colonisation in Northumbria.[38] But although John de Balliol's predecessors regarded themselves as primarily among the leaders of northern English society, their commitments were far-flung. Bailleul-en-Vimeu in Lower Picardy was the ancestral home and an abiding interest: as lords of Bailleul, they served the counts of Ponthieu and attended the French king's court.[39] After the Capetian conquests of 1203–4 they had the exceptional good fortune to retain their continental concerns without forfeiting their English lands. Their chief base in mid-land England, the valuable manor of Hitchin (Herts), remained an important demesne holding, despite a mortgage to Jews and alienations to the Church.[40]

John de Balliol, husband of Dervorguilla 'of Galloway' from 1233, therefore belonged to a powerfully connected family with widespread influence. Despite assets in the north country and the Midlands, the lords of Bywell had nevertheless taken no direct part in the twelfth-century incoming to Scotland. Numerous claims have been made to the contrary, but these are wholly without foundation.[41] On the other hand, Enguerrand de Balliol of Dalton in Hartness, *jure uxoris* lord of Urr in southern Kirkcudbrightshire and Inverkeilor in Angus, was a probable younger son of John's great-grandfather Bernard de Balliol II. Enguerrand himself left two sons of some consequence as cross-Border landowners: the younger, Henry (d. 1246), having acquired a Scottish base in marriage, later shared with his wife in the English honour of Valognes; the elder, Eustace, lord of Tours-en-Vimeu, inherited Urr and Inverkeilor, and gained Foston in Leicestershire with a daughter of William de Percy.[42] When John de Balliol succeeded his father in England and France in 1229 the Balliol name was thus already familiar in Anglo-Scottish landholding circles as a result of well-judged marriage pacts. But it was only when John amassed his allocations from the Galloway and Chester estates that the senior branch emerged, as one of the most influential of all the baronial houses to be involved in the life of the two kingdoms.

William de Forz III (d. 1260), titular count of Aumale, represented an even more formidable dynasty, but – for all its territorial greatness – a more recent recruit to the higher nobility. By marrying a rich heiress Forz followed where his grandfather and namesake had led. His grandmother Hawise was sole heiress to Aumale in Normandy (lost in 1204) and the honours of Skipton and Holderness, and her matrimonial career had testified to her singular attractions. Hawise's first and third husbands were William de Mandeville, earl of Essex, and Baldwin de Béthune. Her second consort, William de Forz I, was one of King Richard's Poitevin favourites and a plain military adventurer, but only by him did she leave surviving male issue. Their son William de Forz II inherited Skipton and Holderness, with a host of lesser properties, in 1214 and shortly afterwards succeeded to the honour of Cockermouth upon the death of his great-aunt Alice de Rumilly. The successive gains by William III as one of Balliol's coparceners sufficed in themselves to place him at the forefront of Anglo-Scottish proprietorship; and after the patrimonial lands had fallen to his power in 1241, the Forz estate, from the Home Counties through to Galloway and Garioch, seemed securely founded as surely the grandest baronial complex to come upon the scene of cross-Border landholding in the thirteenth century. In fact, it would not hold place for long; but the notion of what marriage made possible lived on.

Forz's spouse Christiana died childless in 1246, and Balliol took the major share of her inheritance.[43] Christiana's untimely death therefore abruptly displaced the Scottish connections of the Forz line. By contrast, the English and Scottish estates of Balliol, Brus and Hastings, although not immune from the normal hazards of prolonged widowhoods and minorities, descended simultaneously through male heirs until the death-blow of the wars of independence. For John de Balliol personally, greater prestige in English affairs and new interests in Scotland altered the course of his career. As a responsible magnate of both realms, he furnished such administrative support, military service and financial aid as was required by either king. Sometime sheriff of Cumberland, in 1260 he was appointed to the shrievalty of Nottingham and Derby; he served in Gascony, accompanied Henry III to Paris in 1259,[44] and staunchly opposed Simon de Montfort. Between 1251 and 1255 he was a guardian of the young King Alexander III and Queen Margaret. Opening up the horizons of his family through the spoils of two heritages but only one marriage, he moved easily in English and Scottish society alike. Hastings' son Henry II, who inherited in 1256, saw his place primarily in England. But his political prominence as one of the die-hard supporters of the Montfortian cause should not be allowed to obscure entirely his attachment to his Scottish lands, which indeed helped to sustain him in rebellion against the English crown. In 1268, shortly before his death, he may have visited Dundee and assigned property there to Balmerino abbey.[45]

The Brus lords of Annandale stepped even more confidently to the fore of Scottish fief-holding, were active in England as royalist partisans, castellans and sheriffs, and administered their new English manors (notably Great Baddow, Hatfield Broad Oak and Writtle, Essex) as assiduously as the old. They provided confirmation charters for Croxton, Garendon and Warden abbeys, as well as for other midland monasteries; new gifts were offered to Chicksands priory, St Andrew's priory at Northampton and Sawtry abbey.[46] It is impossible, or so it seems, to tell whether their estates in England or in Scotland had greater claims upon their attention. Witness also in this regard the activity of Dervorguilla de Balliol when, during her widowhood, she enjoyed both her heritage and her dower. Admittedly, Dervorguilla's longevity ensured that her sons Hugh and Alexander succeeded to a truncated inheritance in England alone (1268, 1271), while her third son and eventual heir John II entered upon his full patrimony only after twelve years. Yet Dervorguilla divided her time between her main residences at Buittle, near Dalbeattie, Dundee and Fotheringhay, and her good works, like her landholding, brought her distinction in both countries. She established a Dominican friary at Wigtown and, probably, Franciscan convents at Dumfries and Dundee; in 1273 she founded the Cistercian abbey of Sweetheart in Nithsdale, colonised from near-by Dundrennan, a daughter of Rievaulx; and her most celebrated memorial was to begin on a regular collegiate basis the community of Oxford scholars still bearing the family name. Dying at Barnard Castle in 1290 but buried at Sweetheart, Dervorguilla was extolled in the Lanercost Chronicle as 'a woman eminent for her wealth and lands in England and Scotland, but much more for her goodness of heart'.[47] Her interests were truly international, or rather, one should say, non-national.

All three families continued to play the marriage game, adding to their lands and influence in the two realms in a manner characteristic of the Anglo-Scottish aristocracy as a whole. Robert de Brus the Competitor, 'nobilis tam in Anglia quam in Scotia baro',[48] married in 1240 Isabel sister of Richard, earl of Gloucester; his second wife was the heiress to Gamblesby, Glassonby and Ireby in Cumberland. A crusader and a patron of Clairvaux abbey, Robert had his will authorised by the bishops of Glasgow and London and by the *officialis* of Durham.[49] He died at Lochmaben castle in 1295, but was interred 'with his ancestors at Guisborough'.[50] His son, the sixth lord of Annandale, became earl of Carrick *jure uxoris* in 1271. In 1280 John de Balliol II, future king of Scotland, allied himself to a daughter of the earl of Surrey; his sister married John Comyn of Badenoch (d. 1303). The cross-Border commitments of the Hastings family were also strengthened through new marriages. Henry de Hastings II took to wife Joan de Cantelupe, who subsequently (1283) transmitted to his son and heir John the rich Marcher lordship of Abergavenny and other important territories in south Wales and the west Midlands. John's marriage in 1275 to his first wife, a daughter of Earl William de Valence, led ultimately to the Hastings tenure of the great earldom of Pembroke; his brother Edmund acquired rights in the earldom of Menteith through a daughter of Countess Isabel. Marriage and lordship went together. These families were all intent upon developing new areas of influence on both sides of the Tweed; and when the Scottish royal house was extinguished in the direct male and female lines in 1290, the prospects of individuals were dramatically and unexpectedly increased. Claiming their inheritance as lineal descendants of Earl David of Huntingdon, John de Balliol II was inaugurated as king of Scots at Scone on 30 November 1292 and Robert Bruce succeeded to the kingdom on 25 March 1306. Though from 1296 the wars of independence were creating havoc with a family's landholdings, the marriage market in the two kingdoms was played for very high stakes indeed.

On the eve of the Edwardian wars Anglo-Scottish magnates controlled assets in nearly every English shire and Scottish sheriffdom; their power had expanded notably over the past century and had long since ceased to depend on royal bounty in the form of land grants. When considering their position among the total magnate population of both kingdoms we must, of course, keep a sense of proportion. A number of eminent families in Scotland and very many prominent dynasties in England never acquired lands in the other realm to buttress their accustomed revenues. Yet from the reign of King David I onwards an increasingly influential body enjoyed cross-Border fiefs and recognised the benefits of not restricting itself to the opportunities of a single kingdom; and some lords were raised up to the summit of contemporary magnate society. Although impossible to show precisely the amount of property which from time to time it handled, a crude but revealing notion of the importance of the Anglo-Scottish element can be expressed in figures. Eight (out of fifteen) chamberlains of Scotland, twelve (out of seventeen) justiciars of Lothian and five (out of twelve) justiciars of *Scotia* active in the period *c.*1170–1296, many of whom were barons of the first rank, had English tenures.[51] Between 1200 and 1296, no fewer than nine of the thirteen earldoms of Scotland – the exceptions being Caithness, Lennox, Ross and Sutherland – were held at one time or another by cross-Border lords, in part because royal enforcement of female inheritance in Celtic society enabled a growing minority of Anglo-Norman families to acquire comital rank through marriage. Parallel calculations with respect to the English earldoms produce the figure of seven (Chester, Essex, Hereford, Huntingdon, Oxford, Pembroke and Winchester) out of twenty-two; and an analysis of the two hundred baronies identified by I. J. Sanders for thirteenth-century England gives the proportion of one barony (or a purparty) in five.[52] There were other sorts of ties as well: the holding of lands in wardship,[53] and family connections beyond the limits of existing estates, which were remembered if only to sustain claims against a future failure of nearer kinsmen.[54] The Tweed-Solway line was a political frontier, but through the honours, fiefs, offices and dynastic ties maintained in both countries, integration into a single aristocratic society was proceeding apace.

Even the greatest lordships that straddled the Border displayed important divergences in the structure of their wealth. Some magnates controlled estates which were more or less evenly distributed between the realms. In each country they held major castles and broad lands, and numerous knights were dependent upon them; they entered fully into the social and political life of the two kingdoms as they crossed and re-crossed the Border, and achieved prominence in the affairs of either. Had their possessions been confined to a single realm they would have won far less distinction; for some, their membership of the higher aristocracy was founded upon the ability to expand in both lands. Other large establishments were based chiefly in one country with only tiny outliers in the other, and it would be fair to say that their lords were always in the majority among Anglo-Scottish magnates. Nevertheless, peripheral assets over the Border, although generally far-distant and tiresome to administer, were often resolutely defended against molestation and loss, the desire to retain a foothold in another kingdom overriding the awareness of their limited economic worth. Originally cross-Border fiefs had been built up by royal grant, but from the late twelfth century the importance of prudent marriages is revealed at every turn. When Earl Duncan of Fife (d. 1288) married a daughter of the earl of Gloucester, only minor concerns at Carlton (Lincs) and Glapthorn

(Northants) came in;[55] the Suleses' English reserves had received small additions through marriage in Stamfordham and Stocksfield (Northumberland) by 1244.[56] But Henry de Pinkney (d. 1254) of Weedon (Northants) took by marriage the whole lordship of Crawford (Lanarkshire) as well as half of the Suffolk barony of Cavendish; Earl Malise of Strathearn added a third of the Wooler barony *jure uxoris* in 1250; and Earl David of Atholl was baron of Chilham (Kent) by 1266, the barony subsequently passing to his widow's second husband, Alexander de Balliol of Cavers (Roxburghshire), an Anglo-Scottish landowner in his own right. Through a marriage to yet higher advantage, Gilbert de Umfraville (d. 1245), lord of Redesdale, elevated himself to the earldom of Angus. This was not a rich earldom, and possibly Earl Gilbert II, who succeeded after a long minority in 1267, regarded himself as 'chiefly an English baron'. But the title of earl of Angus was proudly and stubbornly retained until the Umfravilles succumbed in the male line in 1381, long after having forfeited the territorial earldom for their loyalty to the English crown.[57] It would be an elementary mistake to assume that just because a lord had important English holdings his Scottish assets were incidental to him. They added to his prestige, and could be crucial to the figure he cut in noble society at large.

How wealthy in fact were the greater cross-Border estates of the thirteenth century? Because of the shortcomings of the evidence, especially on the Scottish side, it is impossible to give a satisfactory answer to this question, or to discern at all clearly the different levels of income. The economic attraction of Anglo-Scottish proprietorship plainly shows in the case of two distinguished magnates, however. The elder John de Balliol's pre-eminence is graphically underlined by his remarkable career as an aristocratic money-lender.[58] In rather more precise terms, his normal revenue before marriage may have been in the region of £500 to £800; after Dervorguilla had died in 1290, it seems that the annual value of her Scottish lands alone was assessed (but no doubt over-assessed) at more than £3,000.[59] The enormous cross-Border holdings of Earl Roger de Quincy (d. 1264) – the product of collateral succession and two particularly important marriages – stretched from Perthshire and Fife, through the Lothians and Berwickshire, to Wigtownshire and Ayrshire, and from Cumberland and Yorkshire, through major groupings in the Midlands, to Wiltshire and Dorset. So far as can be calculated, his Scottish lands, worth about £400 *per annum*, were not significantly less valuable than the English, and together – though not if treated separately – they endowed him with the substance appropriate to a magnate of his high rank.[60] The other main advantages of Anglo-Scottish landholding are even more difficult to quantify. Yet for a magnate to hold part of his property in Scotland in the period before Magna Carta shielded it from the harsh fiscal policies pursued by the early Angevin kings. Conversely, a magnate's role in English landed society gave hopes of access to the larger resources of the Angevin monarchy in offices, lands and pensions, and afforded contact with a wider marriage market. The treatment here needs to be fuller and more systematic, but as the reserves of Scots royal patronage dwindled after the first waves of Anglo-French colonisation, these considerations would have become increasingly important to the nobility in Scotland.

Balliol, Forz, Strathearn and Umfraville were among the major new recruits to the scheme of cross-Border proprietorship by the mid-thirteenth century. But there were many lesser magnate families besides, while Bohun, Brus, Comyn, Quincy, Ros and Sules, among others, had maintained or improved on their position. Indeed, few families kept abreast of the spectacular marriage strategies of the Comyns. By the 1270s a whole series of judicious marriages into property had forged out of a small Anglo-Scottish patrimony two great Comyn estates comprising lands in both countries. The senior line, with its principal bases in Badenoch and Lochaber, was also powerful in central and southern Scotland, holding the earldom of Menteith to 1258. But though Scotland remained the focus of its aspirations, the original English property was not neglected. John Comyn of Badenoch (d. c. 1274), in spite of his vast commitments beyond the Highland line, was an active, indeed grasping, Northumberland landlord; he improved upon this coveted foothold by carrying his influence through marriage into Lincolnshire, and performed valued services to Henry III in the 1260s.[61] Alexander Comyn, earl of Buchan, the exceptionally influential head of the main junior branch from 1233 to 1289, also maintained English ambitions. Through his marriage to Earl Roger de Quincy's coheiress Elizabeth, he made large gains in south-western Scotland, Fife and Lothian; important centres ultimately fell to him in Leicestershire, buttressed by lesser units in a further dozen English counties. The break-up of the Quincy lands, a particularly protracted, complex and litigious procedure, was also to the benefit of the families of Ferrers of Groby and la Zouche, the extinction of one great lineage thus signalling the development of a further three cross-Border estates. The income from the Zouche share in Scotland was set at a minimum of £128 in 1296.[62]

Due to the accidents of family history, more than a few eminent cross-Border houses disappeared; but others survived, some from the twelfth century and many which had come into existence since. The Border defined an administrative boundary between two kingdoms but no barrier between aristocratic communities. Inherent in this situation, however, was the possibility of conflict between royal interests and family landholding. How far was the development of cross-Border ties affected by the decisions of kings?

Although in both countries hereditary rights to fiefs were becoming more secure and standardised when Anglo-Scottish proprietorship began to be a real force, warfare between the realms was one obvious circumstance when kings were obliged to reconsider tenurial patterns. Ties of landholding were bound to suffer: since lords were compelled to choose between two reasonably well-matched opponents, forfeiture in one country or the other was a virtual certainty, and confiscations were especially disruptive when they gave fresh heart to rival seigneurial claims. Even so, we should not be tempted to exaggerate the impact of hostilities upon landed fortunes. Prior to the wars of independence, the trend of relations was favourable to Anglo-Scottish magnates, for as the tenurial ties grew stronger an equally important change was taking place in political exchanges between the two kingdoms. The mounting Scottish desire for *rapprochement* had the same roots as the Angevin, an understanding that effective domestic government depended upon harmonious co-existence; and after Stephen's reign, the wars of 1173–4 and 1215–17 stood out as rare events amid long years of enduring peace. Moreover, disseisin for rebellion rarely led to permanent loss of lands, due partly to the growing reluctance of kings to inflict the full penalty of disinheritance as a political punishment, but also to the tenacity of dynasties in pursuit of lost rights. The Moreville family archive provides a model illustration.[63] Even during the Anarchy this house had endeavoured to exercise lordship over its confiscated Huntingdon fees; and although rebuffed in the short run, the Morevilles were in fact promptly reinstated in 1157. After the young King Henry's war, when the treaty of Falaise specifically provided for restoration to the supporters of William the Lion and Henry II of the lands they had lost in the other realm, Richard de Moreville quickly regained rents in Whissendine; an agreement was concluded with the Knights Templars on the assumption that other losses in the Huntingdon honour would be made good, the prolonged delay in recovering them being due more to Earl David's obstruction than lack of family interest. In Yorkshire, where another private quarrel complicated his position, such was the regard in which Richard held his Lonsdale concerns that he bought them from the hands of William de Stuteville for 300 marks. When strife disturbed the peace between the realms, the unity of Anglo-Scottish estates was often broken. Yet that is not to say that the sporadic outbreaks of war before 1296 seriously disrupted the pattern of cross-Border tenures. Upon the return of peace the connections were usually reconstituted, with minimal delay where rival family claims did not prejudice the case.

When there was no violent breach of normal relations, it is possible to argue that cross-Border landholding was acceptable to the two governments in part because it was not seriously at variance with the immediate political needs of either monarchy. From Henry I to Henry III the English crown set too high a price on peace to fight a war on the issue of the suzerainty of Scotland. But England always desired to influence the Scottish political scene, even if it generally preferred not to jeopardise relations by offending too blatantly the dignity of the Scots king and kingdom. Therefore, cross-Border proprietorship was to a degree welcomed and even encouraged, as seen most clearly – the history of the Huntingdon honour apart – in a number of enfeoffments in chief of individual Scottish feudatories and, relatedly, in the offering of pensions.[64] Exceptionally, there was an obvious reluctance to allow too much honour and power to the Scots king's leading subjects; but the English interests of these magnates and the homages they owed for them provided, at any rate potentially, a strong means of political control. In certain circumstances, they might go so far as to place their Scottish military resources at the Angevin king's disposal.[65] Furthermore, numerically and in terms of wealth the cross-Border aristocracy as a proportion of the magnate community in Scotland – smaller, but in government more powerful, than its counterpart in England – was growing faster. Nor is that all. On the one hand, it was a source of reassurance to the English crown that the fiefs its subjects acquired in Scotland were controlled by a ruler who was himself normally in its homage for English lands. Magnate ambition found an outlet which was not as damaging to the political stability of the Angevin heartlands as the private empire-building that occurred in Wales and Ireland. On the other hand, now and again cross-Border proprietors had recourse to the English king in attempts to protect Scottish tenures through the royal courts or even by securing royal confirmations – although it must be agreed that such instances were not the signs of a general process, while the judicial sovereignty of the English monarchy was vulnerable in its turn.[66]

On the Scottish side, too, there were distinct advantages as well as drawbacks. King William's binding of 'Northerners' to his person as vassals and kinsmen cannot be divorced from his designs upon the Border shires; Anglo-Scottish lords brought useful pressure to bear when the English government's support was desirable or necessary, as during the minority of Alexander III.[67] There are some indications that stricter Scottish notions of sovereignty led to a hardening of attitudes in the 1270s and '80s.[68] Yet then as before, save during the period of Angevin liege lordship (1174–89), the Scots king was free to insist upon rights over his tenants-in-chief identical to those enjoyed by the English crown;[69] and since, when subjects held land in two realms, neither ruler had exclusive claims upon their loyal service, political benefits apparently accrued on both sides.

First and foremost, however, the long years of peace provided the conditions in which Anglo-Scottish estates could grow, not fully independent of kingly power, but increasingly removed from political intervention and manipulation by governments. Inasmuch as the problems likely to arise out of dual homages touched both monarchs, it was a sensible course to work out some kind of mutual understanding and avoid undue provocation. Above all, peace removed the occasions for a true conflict of magnate loyalties. As a result each king could hope to govern successfully through an aristocracy in part tied by allegiance to the other, and politics was less and less at odds with the ways in which cross-Border estates could develop. There was thus a marked contrast with 'the tenurial crisis of the Anglo-Norman period', when the recurrent divisions of England and Normandy between warring rulers from 1087, and the distrust this caused between the English crown and the cross-Channel aristocracy, saw 'politics and patronage intruded into custom and law'.[70] Additionally, growing harmony between the realms went hand in hand with the movement from enfeoff-ment to dynastic alliances and the acquisition of female property; and this was crucial for the rate at which Anglo-Scottish proprietorship advanced. Heiresses especially could transform tenurial geography: that is why the granting of marriages was one of the most jealously guarded prerogatives of kingship. Yet monarchical authority was less complete over the destination of female holdings than over enfeoffments, partly because some female inheritances were not anticipated when marriages occurred but on other counts as well. Although in the last resort neither ruler could be compelled to take the homage of an unacceptable tenant, one king's position was inevitably affected by the other's decision. Briefly stated, the marriages of a ruler's vassals of full age to the daughters and widows of tenants-in-chief landed in the other realm alone were properly subject solely to the second ruler's authority. It was customary for only one king to dispose of a widow when her husband had been ensconced in both countries; if Anglo-Scottish magnates were succeeded by unmarried girls (or, indeed, by male heirs under age), only one monarch could have custody of their individual bodies and hence the power of marriage.[71]

Again, though political considerations could always be invoked, royal rights over marriages did not function exclusively to deny declared enemies or to reward laudable services. Petitioners sought profitable unions as a matter of course and paid for kings to arrange them. Initiative therefore often came from below and interplayed with the king's financial needs: King John was not the only ruler who distributed such bounty 'as if through a market'.[72] Alternatively, in cross-Border proprietorship royal supervision might leave its imprint in fines for permission to marry freely, while the successful transfer of property through marriages apparently contracted without authorisation by either monarch was not unknown. A notorious case occurred in 1288 when William of Douglas, lord of Douglasdale in Lanarkshire and of Fawdon in north Northumberland, abducted the widow of William de Ferrers of Groby.[73] Thus the progressive easing of the poten-tial tensions between politics and property, coupled with the emphasis upon marriage-marketing, allowed cross-Border fiefs to develop more rapidly, because individual magnates were able to give free rein to their ambitions in either realm, and to participate directly in decisions touching their terri-torial wealth. We know that members of Henry III's council once voiced doubts about the advisability of an alliance between the earls of Pembroke and the Scottish royal house. Nevertheless, their arguments did not prevail: Earl Gilbert Marshal married the youngest sister of Alexander II in 1235 and received with her 'a noble dowry in Scotland'.[74]

Once begun or augmented, great Anglo-Scottish fiefs devolved accord-ing to seigneurial practices of tenure and succession, on the whole removed from political meddling save in wartime. In this regard other factors favoured their development. The reception of Anglo-Norman conventions of land-holding into Lowland Scotland ensured that before the legislation of

Edward I closely similar systems of property and family law were observed on both sides of the Border.[75] Anglo-Scottish fief-holding was consequently an uncomplicated legal undertaking. Moreover, prevailing usages favoured the resilience but even more the multiplication of territorial ties. Generally reviewed, family custom witnessed a struggle between dynastic instinct for consolidation and pressure for dispersion. The developing land law from Glanvill onwards accommodated the contradictory pulls between retention and transmission, but tended to lend its weight to those influences favouring distribution. Put another way, lineage-solidarity fostered the strength of already-existing Anglo-Scottish links by husbanding accumulated wealth; the competing pressure towards dispersal, while ruinous to dynastic entrenchment, often ensured their proliferation.

Dynastically, a family's prosperity depended upon an unbroken succession of male heirs who in each generation would unite their parents' lands as one integral cross-Border patrimony, recovering gifts to cadet lines as soon as these ran out. When only one son lived to inherit, the whole estate naturally descended as a single inheritance. But in the event of surviving sons early Anglo-Norman custom had accepted the possibility of a partition of estates, which normally reserved the patrimonial lands for the eldest son and accorded the acquisitions to a younger. In this way a number of cross-Channel estates, though certainly not all of them, had been broken up into separate Norman and English entities. Now, partition between sons did have a place in Anglo-Scottish proprietorship at the magnate level, but by no means as prominent a one as in cross-Channel landholding. This was due in some degree to the fact that the bringing together of fiefs in England and Scotland gathered pace only at a time when Glanvill could assume that in England all land held by military service was subject to descent by primogeniture. But the ready acceptance of this ruling by Anglo-Scottish families in respect of their property in both countries was facilitated by confidence in their ability to resolve such problems of loyalty and distance as confronted them: from the earliest days, indeed, they had set their face against division between senior and junior lines.

If we take the twelfth and thirteenth centuries as a whole, there are merely two important examples of partition between surviving sons, and these each arose in exceptional circumstances rather than from any deep-seated family desire 'to keep English estates distinct from Scottish'.[76] The Brus partition of c.1138 was followed by the division of the Moreville lands: the former had been precipitated by war, the latter was dictated by King Henry II. In the 1140s King David had settled the lordship of north Westmorland upon his Constable, Hugh de Moreville of Lauderdale and Cunningham (d. 1162). But when the northern shires were surrendered in 1157 Henry II recognised the Moreville title only on condition that Hugh stood down in favour of his (oldest?) son and namesake, subsequently a member of Henry II's military household, an Angevin royal justice, and one of the assassins of Thomas Becket.[77] King Henry's concern to reassert systematically his powers in the north country was made fully explicit when Hugh II died on pilgrimage to Jerusalem in *c.*1173. Most of Westmorland proper thereupon escheated to the crown, although Hugh was survived by his brother Richard, successor in 1162 to Lauderdale and Cunningham and the Constableship of Scotland, and by his sister Maud, wife of William de Vieuxpont II. Here the royal will made a rare intervention in succession and descent.[78] But it is also noteworthy that the Anglo-Scottish bond outlasted both partitions, the Brus and the Moreville, because neither estate was divided realm by realm. The lords of Annandale retained Hartness; Richard de Moreville inherited the ancestral fees in the Huntingdon honour – and by 1170 had added important west Yorkshire tenures through marriage.[79] Nor was the Lauderdale line content to accept without question the division of its lands as permanent, this being so much against the family's wishes.[80] Elsewhere, the principle of indivisible male succession was adopted as the best and proper practice. Dynastic sentiment prevailed. Had magnates been reluctant to hold properties in both realms, division into English and Scottish blocks remained a practicable course. In general, however, there was no major force working against their position. Thus, desire to safeguard the lineage was also a desire to build up its status and authority in the one country and in the other.

Some houses, notably the earls of Dunbar, the Brus lords of Annandale and, in spite of a high mortality of sons, the Lovels of Hawick (Roxburghshire) and Castle Cary (Somerset), were remarkably long-lived, and held prominence for generations on each side of the Border line.[81] Furthermore, so long as a family did not die out, the process of accumulating property tended to be sustained. But failure to produce sons, the perennial problem of all nobilities, easily overturned dynastic ambitions. Childless marriages were not unknown. William de Courtenay of Bulwick (Northants) took Hume in Berwickshire with a daughter of the earl of Dunbar: he had died without offspring by 1215, 'and thus ended the short connection of the Courtenays with Scotland'.[82] Earl William of Mar (d. *c.*1280) gained a quarter-share in the Wooler barony with his wife Muriel; but since no children lived to inherit, this interest ultimately devolved upon Nicholas de Graham of Dalkeith and Eskdale, and two Anglo-Scottish estates were reduced to one.[83] There are parallel examples. More commonly, only daughters survived; and yet, as already underlined, there was a direct link between the tendency for property to accumulate around noblewomen and the rise of Anglo-Scottish proprietorship. In this age, before the classical entail (Scots, tailzie) protected patrimonies by at least postponing female succession, the strength of female property rights, and hence of the principle of dispersion, normally guaranteed the inheritance of girls in the absence of sons. A sole heiress brought her husband the entire family fortune with which to forge a larger cross-Border estate (e.g., Lindsey-Pinkney, Moreville-Galloway, Olifard-Moravia); coheiresses necessarily broke it into new groupings. Division obviously created out of one lordship estates of less ample resources.[84] But as a rule the Anglo-Scottish aristocracy was not undermined by unequal marriages: it grew on the basis that 'wealth attracted wealth; land married land'.[85] Moreover, since alliances were often contracted outside the group, the amount of land and political power held by cross-Border lords was not concentrated by marriage into fewer hands but showed a marked inclination to increase. A striking contrast can be drawn between the transience of male lines and the fruitful development of estates.

Other forms of distribution among family members helped to bring new establishments into the pattern of Anglo-Scottish landholding. Where sons carried on the house there were strong social pressures to provide settlements for non-inheriting children. Daughters were entitled to decent dowries (tochers); provision was made for younger sons. Fathers were concerned lest their siblings 'be de-classed';[86] and younger sons especially (as Glanvill complained) might claim a great deal against the first-born. The larger their portion, the greater their prospect of a successful marriage and of founding or reaffirming cross-Border interests of their own.[87] Another form of dismemberment was the widow's entitlement to dower or terce. Her due third and *maritagium* commonly made up a subsidiary cross-Border estate,[88] and the remarriages of widows and the marriages of dowried daughters were also more than alliances of individuals. Indeed, widows who were heiresses rarely remained unmarried, and one or two of these well-endowed ladies, in their lifetime and by curtesy, sometimes enabled several lords to benefit from Anglo-Scottish tenures.[89]

It is true that magnates, wishing to preserve what they had put together, looked forward to the return of satellite family holdings to the central inheritance. The widow's dower (and, when an heiress, perhaps her heritage) came back at her death; collateral branches might not put down firm roots, and heads of houses attempted to secure reversion. But children other than legal heirs naturally demanded full proprietary rights at the earliest opportunity, and they found support in English and, apparently, Scottish law, which from c.1250 ignored the provisional nature of their endowments once issue had been produced. In England, *De Donis* (1285) failed to slow this centrifugal movement. Support for the senior line only went so far: 'The heads of primogenitary dynasties . . . were being deposed and the barring of their reversions meant the erection of those collateral lines into independent families.'[90] Family law and custom worked to the advantage of cross-Border ties throughout, thanks not least to fragmentation among heiresses and the aspirations of junior lines.

Lesser Families and Ecclesiastical Proprietors

The growth of magnate cross-Border estates interacted with the development of other estates reaching from one country into the other, for even as aristocratic property became increasingly conserved for family use, dispersion worked for the strengthening of Anglo-Scottish tenurial bonds in·

additional ways. Several avenues of advancement were open to those out-side the magnate class. Many lesser fief-holders whose interests lay astride the Border had not been promoted as dependants of important Anglo-Scottish barons: for adventurous gentry families, and also for the Church, Scots royal patronage was certainly one route to cross-Border proprietor-ship.[91] But the magnates were like any higher nobility in that they did not part with assets just to support kinsfolk in each generation; and in meeting the expectations of knightly clients and the claims of piety, Earl David displayed a lack of concern for the Border apparently typical of his group. Admittedly, not every Anglo-Scottish magnate enjoyed the same kind of prominence in the two kingdoms. Nevertheless, G. G. Simpson concluded from his detailed study of Earl Roger de Quincy that 'Anglo-Scottish social links existed and flourished under the patronage of this particular great lord'.[92] To take another example, the Morevilles deliberately used their connections outside Scotland to involve others in their own cross-Border concerns. Clapham (Clephane), Haig, Maltalent (Maitland), Néhou, St Clair (Sinclair) – all these lines, and many more, owed their initial Scottish advancement to Moreville support, although few demonstrably retained lands south of the Tweed. The influential family abbey of Dryburgh, colonised from Alnwick in 1152, received with rich Scottish endowments the churches of Great Asby (Westmorland) and Bozeat (Northants). A small interest in East Lothian was secured for Leicester abbey to commem-orate a kinsman buried there following a hunting accident, possibly in the Moreville park at Whissendine, while Helen de Moreville, supported by Alan of Galloway and Earl Thomas of Atholl, provided St Andrew's priory at Northampton with a modest estate in Lauderdale and Tweeddale.[93] It was natural enough for the family to act in this manner, just as great Anglo-Norman barons through their leadership in England and Normandy were able to strengthen the nexus of cross-Channel links by furthering interests and careers. The next step, therefore, is to review in a necessarily tentative fashion the development of cross-Border proprietorship alongside or, as often happened, in the wake of that of the magnates.

The line between magnate and gentry families is, of course, difficult to draw precisely. Again, for lack of evidence many lesser baronial or knightly estates can be studied only when well established: for instance, the Corbet fee based in Glendale and on Yetholm, in the shadow of The Cheviot, which actually embraced the Border line as it struck up towards Windy Gyle; the establishment of the Burradons in Coquetdale and Roxburghshire; or the Derman holdings in Burgh by Sands (Cumberland) and at Auchencrieff and Dargavel (Dumfriesshire).[94] But such connections often occurred because noble patrons in Scotland did not invariably reserve their favours for landless younger sons or for those who had capitalised their resources prior to seeking enrichment in the north, and in some Scottish lordships the incoming of English or Norman-French dependants bore the stamp of a genuine rush. Even in Galloway, to c. 1220 the lords of that often turbulent province were forging landholding links straddling the Border which in smaller ways reflected their own.[95] From time to time connections also developed in the opposite direction, as native Scottish freeholders were assigned interests outside Scotland.[96] At least equally important, though, was the ability of settler families to acquire or expand an English base. Philip de Valognes, chamberlain of William the Lion, secured the Galloway manor of Torpenhow (Cumberland), although it was annexed to the barony of Liddel Strength when his daughter married Robert de Stuteville;[97] by 1211 Adam of Carlisle, an Annandale tenant, held the Brus fee at Edenhall.[98] Lordly favour apart, freeholders in one country opened up or reinforced interests in the other by collateral inheritance, purchase or intrusion. A well-documented instance of intrusion survives from 1202, when an appeal was lodged at Rome, complaining that Ivo of Crosby, 'of the diocese of York', and his son retained land at Ecclefechan in Annandale as security for a loan, although they had allegedly recouped more than the capital debt from its issues.[99] As the opportunities for patronage decreased in the less expansive thirteenth century, gentry families on both sides of the Border, as much as their social superiors, entered into a lively traffic in marriages serving to launch or consolidate Anglo-Scottish concerns. By way of illustration, following the death of Helewise of Levington in 1272 no less than seven minor landowners in Scotland secured interests through marriage in the Cumberland barony of Kirklinton: Nicholas of Auchinleck, Roland of Carrick, Walter of Corrie, William Lockhart, Patrick of Southwick, Patrick de Trump and Walter of Twynholm. Other examples abound.[100] It could be argued that partition between sons found more favour at lower levels than it did with the magnates, and certain families fell apart into English and Scottish branches.[101] Yet, undeniably, there was a stronger current in favour of male primogeniture; and because the successional customs of the great were imitated by their inferiors, gentry families as they rose, or when they fell, generally promoted rather than discouraged the accumulation of Anglo-Scottish tenurial ties.

The evidence for smaller fief-holders naturally tends to focus upon the Border shires. English government sources dating from the outbreak of the Edwardian wars are prolific in additional examples: Blount, Bunkle, Charteris, Cresswell, Jardine, Malton, Paxton, Rule, Somerville, Stanton, Swinburn and Torthorwald, among many other families.[102] In terms of local sentiment and the bonds of community, the Border was always more of a zone than a boundary.[103] But while many influences bound the population of the Border country in one self-contained regional society, the range of interconnections spread far wider than the Borderlands alone. The following roll-call is necessarily selective: Lascelles (Fife, Northumberland, Cumberland, Bucks, Herts, Essex), Montfiquet (Perthshire, Northants), Mowbray (Perthshire, Fife, West Lothian, Cumberland, Yorks), Ridel (Midlothian, Northumberland, Northants, Hunts), Siward (mainly Fife, Dumfriesshire, Northumberland, Northants, Worcs), Wishart (Stirlingshire, Northumberland).[104] Of such lineages, the Vieuxponts showed an exceptional preference for the rights of younger sons, though no preference for the holding of lands in a single realm. By *c.*1200 a sizeable estate had been amassed, almost one of magnate proportions. Important reserves were located in the Lothians and Berwickshire, and there were equally valuable fees in England and Normandy. At this date, however, these widespread interests were dismembered among three sons: Robert, never an Anglo-Scottish landowner, inherited the Norman patrimony and successfully prosecuted the Vieuxpont claim to the entire lordship of north Westmorland; Ivo took most of his father's English property, including Alston in Tynedale, and he was to hold it together with Glengelt in Lauderdale and Sorbie in Galloway, apparently new acquisitions; William received the Scottish estates and land at Hardingstone (Northants), an interest which he staunchly defended against the counter-claims of Delapré abbey.[105] Another settlement at Ivo's death brought one of his sons land at Sorbie, Frolesworth (Leics) and Maulds Meaburn (Westmorland); and when this man was forced to sell out in the 1240s, his whole Anglo-Scottish patrimony passed to John le Franceis, an English royal clerk and Exchequer baron.[106] Instructive in another way is the Valognes family history. Two younger brothers of Robert de Valognes (d.1184), lord of the barony of Bennington in Hertfordshire, had sought their fortunes in Scotland: Philip, *camerarius regis*, of Panmure (Angus) and Roger of East Kilbride (Lanarkshire). Robert was succeeded as sole heiress by his daughter Gunnora, whose husband held the barony of Bennington by curtesy until 1235. In default of surviving children, the English inheritance then passed to the three coheiresses of William de Valognes (d.1219), son and heir of Gunnora's uncle Philip. Collaterals prospered as the main branch fell in. These ladies had married Henry de Balliol, Peter de Maule and David Comyn of West Linton (Peeblesshire), each of whom, having already shared in the Panmure patrimony, received his portion of the honour of Valognes in England. Two inheritances were reassigned to begin three widely scattered Anglo-Scottish estates.[107] For every great cross-Border lord there were many lesser men who made the most of the opportunities for advancement in either realm.

Secular proprietorship across the Border came to have numerous ecclesiastical parallels. Of course, the Church sustained a high level of contacts between the kingdoms in manifold ways, however much the clergy in Scotland desired full constitutional independence of the *Ecclesia Anglicana*. Cistercian houses belonged to an order 'conceived on a supra-national basis, and markedly detached from the structure of the feudal kingdom';[108] all but one of the Scottish Premonstratensian houses were included in the same circary as their counterparts in northern England;[109] and while many Scottish monasteries merged quickly with their local backgrounds, bonds were often maintained with parent houses south of the Border, even if on a purely informal basis.[110] In the making of careers, 'abbots or priors . . . were interchanged between the two countries, almost as naturally as between two counties of England'.[111] Seculars from England (and France) were still able to win high preferment in the thirteenth-century Scottish Church; ambitious clerks domiciled in Scotland who aspired to higher education had all to repair to England or the continent, and the talented moved easily between the kingdoms in lay as well as in ecclesiastical service, none more so than Master Ãdam of Kirkcudbright, a leading light in the Brus *familia*, a servant of the papal Curia, a *medicus* to King Alexander III, and a collector of benefices in both realms.[112]

But that religious corporations were in the habit of acquiring property for their own use across the Border line added a major dimension to the range of ecclesiastical ties; and the brief analysis attempted here could profitably be taken a good deal further on the lines already laid down for England and Normandy.[113] Again, these connections arose often (though in no sense exclusively) out of the interest of the cross-Border magnates. On the one hand, they had a natural desire to distribute part of their wealth in Scotland by bestowing lands, rents and churches for the direct support of houses to which they were especially devoted on account of their role as English landowners. But the grants were not in one direction only, for Scottish foundations were seemingly as likely to acquire possessions in England as English foundations were to in Scotland; and because the movement was a two-way process the build-up of interests extending into both kingdoms proceeded at a faster rate than could otherwise have been achieved. By *c.*1250 the connections, as we might have anticipated, were particularly well developed in the Borderlands. On the East March, Durham cathedral priory's accessions in the Merse, largely owed to Scots royal patronage, clearly dominate; but Melrose abbey, a powerful rival to the black monks of Durham, had – besides other English properties – extensive sheep pastures above Wooler; Coldstream priory maintained smaller Northumberland concerns; Jedburgh abbey claimed property in Tynedale as well as in Cumberland; and Kelso abbey's English interests included assets in Tweedmouth, rights in Glendale from the Corbets, and a tithe of the Umfraville horse stud of Redesdale.[114] Among English houses, the priories of Brinkburn and Holystone drew revenues from Roxburgh and Berwick; Durham's cell on Farne took corn from Oldcambus.[115] On the West March, Holm Cultram abbey, Lanercost priory and St Bees priory had concerns north of the Solway Firth, thanks especially to the attention of the lords of Annandale and Galloway and their tenants.[116] Examples could easily be multiplied; and the interests of benefactors brought some Border houses endowments much farther afield. For instance, Harehope hospital in Northumberland acquired the church of St Giles and other Edinburgh property; Melrose received land at Boston (Lincs), where it erected warehouses for ease of access to the great wool fair; and Kelso had some claim to the church of Whittington (Herefordshire).[117]

Furthermore, there was also a wide range of contacts involving English and Scottish houses sited well outside the Border region. Sources for the

Huntingdon honour identify, besides Dryburgh and Jedburgh, St Andrew's priory at Northampton and the abbeys of Holyrood, Leicester and Lindores.[118] St Peter's hospital at York attracted patronage in southern Scotland from numerous donors, including the lords of Annandale, Galloway and Liddesdale.[119] Of other Yorkshire communities, Kirkham priory had houses in King's Street, Roxburgh; Whitby abbey held land near by at Heiton and Oxnam; and Guisborough priory, richly endowed in Scotland, retained a special claim on the generosity of the lords of Annandale.[120] Lincolnshire is represented by Sempringham priory, Sixhills priory, Crowland abbey (to 1167) and Vaudey abbey (to 1223); Norfolk by Bromholm priory; and Bedfordshire by Warden abbey.[121] The *cultus* of Thomas Becket brought Canterbury cathedral priory a whole succession of rents in Scotland from patrons who included Alan son of Walter (Stewart) and Robert de Brus IV, pilgrims to the shrine.[122] Of Scottish corporations removed from the Border, Dunfermline abbey and Soutra hospital had assets in Cumberland; Arbroath abbey appropriated to its own uses the church of Haltwhistle in Tynedale; St Andrews cathedral priory was entitled to a rent from Ardsley (Yorks, WR).[123] This is by no means a complete list of the cross-Border interests arising out of lay support for the Church, but it is long enough to embrace most of the greater monasteries in Scotland and an impressive array of English houses.

Management

At different levels of proprietorship, therefore, many influences combined during the twelfth and thirteenth centuries to draw England and Scotland close together. Ideally, the development and exploitation of these ties should be examined in depth, family by family, institution by institution. Such an ambitious exercise is beyond our purpose. Yet within the limits of this study, the substance and durability of Anglo-Scottish tenurial connections can be further demonstrated from the standpoint of administration, albeit from sources biased in favour of the Church. Brought together for the most part by the chances of patronage, marriage or inheritance, cross-Border lordships varied considerably in structure. Nevertheless, two main types of estates can be discerned. The nature of the managerial problems differed from the one to the other, although the difficulties encountered were by no means peculiar to Anglo-Scottish proprietors, who also resorted to conventional techniques of regulation. Many lords administered resources based chiefly within a single realm and hence belonged principally to one country. Individual proprietors in this category may never have exercised a personal lordship in the other land, where their status may have been effectively that of absentees. Conversely, certain magnates drew important incomes from each kingdom, clung tenaciously to their dominant position in the two realms, and coped dutifully with the responsibilities of all their estates, even when their main seats were many miles apart. The way in which Earl Roger de Quincy perambulated throughout his lands and employed English hangers-on to supervise his Scottish interests evokes the actions of Earl David a generation before.[124] Religious houses were sometimes well endowed in both realms; gentry owners, figures of local substance in either kingdom, accumulated Anglo-Scottish estates worthy of divided attention. In one revealing transaction, Alan of Clapham, a Moreville tenant and the sheriff of Lauder by 1203, minimised the discomforts of long-distance travel between his lands in Lonsdale and in Lauderdale by negotiating with the monks of Furness abbey the provision each year of one good horse, 'which it is honourable for them to give and for me to receive'.[125]

Naturally monasteries, as immobile corporations, were not geared to continuous perambulation from one centre to another; but for them the practical problem of administering important holdings, even if far-distant, was by no means insuperable. Direct management might be attempted by creating a grange or monastic farm; in especially favourable circumstances it could lead to the foundation of a regular conventual community. Guisborough faced recurrent disputes with the bishop of Glasgow over its six Annandale churches and in 1223 conceded its patronal claims. Nonetheless, these benefices continued to furnish Guisborough with food liveries and money rents *in usus proprios*, and the canons ran a grange at Annan to control the more effectively what they plainly considered to be a major source of wealth.[126] Holm Cultram quickly established a grange to supervise its stock farms at Kirkgunzeon, between Dalbeattie and Dumfries, and steadily expanded from this base through patronage, purchase and assarting. As late as 1294, Holm was glad to take on lease property held by Melrose abbey at Rainpatrick in Gretna.[127] And so one might elaborate. The estate office begun by Durham priory at Coldingham had developed into a fully-fledged religious house by the 1140s, its future assured as Durham's richest cell and one of the wealthier Scottish monasteries.[128]

Yet, paradoxically, the strength of Anglo-Scottish bonds is often best seen when only small and scattered estate units were involved, or when great lords were entrenched primarily in one country alone. Even the remotest parcel in the other realm could hold its attractions and be shielded for as long as possible against loss. Evidence relating to holdings within the Huntingdon honour provides by no means the sole justification for this statement.[129] If prolonged absences were unavoidable, cross-Border lords acted by attorney, in specific examples, to deliver seisin, to receive rents, and to perform 'suit and service';[130] kinsfolk were delegated to rule in their name, occasionally to answer a summons to the host.[131] Where direct management was an unrealistic goal, leasing came into its own. In 1192 the Knights Hospitallers in England leased lands inconveniently situated in Galloway to Holyrood abbey; Melrose farmed to Holm Cultram tenements at Carlisle, reserving rights of lodging for the fair. Earl Patrick of Dunbar leased back into Brus hands his wife's dower in Hartness for a term of eight years from 1218.[132] Leasing reduced a lord's interest in a property to a minimum; yet before the Edwardian wars such a response was prompted not by any desire to be rid of commitments because they were in another country, but by the same administrative considerations that led any lord to allocate outlying, secondary assets to local *firmarii*.[133]

The administrative disadvantages that remained were well understood. In contracting a lease with the bishop of Dunblane in 1266, the hospital of St James and St John at Brackley in Northamptonshire specified elaborate safety precautions. The bishop was to take in hand for an initial term of five years the church of Findo-Gask in Perthshire and all the hospital's lands in Scotland, given to the brethren by Earls Saer and Roger de Quincy, in consideration of 24 marks payable annually at Osney abbey, beside Oxford, to Brackley's courier, who was thus to be spared the burden of travelling each year to Dunblane. Brackley reserved the right of presentation to the vicarage; and stipulated that, *inter alia*, the lessee was to maintain buildings in good repair and assume liability for damages in respect of all arrears. Finally, the bishop of Lincoln was empowered to enforce the agreement by threat of spiritual censures.[134] *Rentier* management did not mean that proprietors were unconcerned to protect subsidiary rights across the Tweed.

Sempringham priory's experience was not, however, untypical. Walter II son of Alan's attempts to found from Sixhills priory a new Gilbertine house at Dalmilling by Ayr had been abandoned in 1238. The foundation endowment was then transferred to Paisley abbey, for 40 marks offered yearly at Dryburgh abbey to envoys from Sempringham for the general use of the Gilbertines, the bishop of Glasgow undertaking to coerce Paisley for default and impose penalty payments.[135] This pension was a source of frequent trouble for Sempringham; to take but one example, in 1246 the priory appealed to Rome because of interrupted deliveries, and was obliged to forgo half of the arrears and its expenses of litigation in return for Paisley's pledge to resume payments.[136] Yet what is surprising about such ties is not that far-flung rents were often difficult to collect, since this was a common drawback for property owners. What impresses is the purposefulness with which both lay and ecclesiastical lords whose concerns were obviously based largely in one country accepted and then hung on to accessions of slight material value in the other. Some outliers were heavily subinfeudated.[137] Grants might fail; contested endowments led to compensation payments effectively extinguishing cross-Border bonds.[138] But there seem to be remarkably few instances of straightforward exchange or resort to selling. Occasionally, insurmountable administrative problems did force lords to reconsider their position and in the end to accept defeat. For example, Dryburgh, Leicester and St Andrew's, Northampton, eventually liquidated English or Scottish gains stemming from Moreville-Galloway patronage through a series of well-documented *excambia*; Wenlock priory preferred to exchange property at Renfrew for less distant assets at Manhood in Sussex; and Vaudey abbey disposed of Carsphairn in Galloway for four marks paid annually by Melrose at Boston fair.[139] But these all appear to be exceptional cases.[140]

Moreover, by their nature our fragmentary sources tend to highlight difficulties rather than the undisturbed enjoyment of normal revenues; the very fact that now and then exchanges took place is in itself revealing of the complexity of the cross-Border tenurial nexus; and it remains clear that among Anglo-Scottish proprietors of every sort there was no general movement towards local consolidation according to the dictates of economic or administrative convenience. Thus, even in the business-like thirteenth century monasteries often clung with obsessive vigilance to haphazard accretions in the other kingdom. Laymen were equally resolute when the problems of management so often urged a more practical approach. For those whose holdings over the Border were small there was, after all, every reason why they should live in hopes of augmenting them. The possibility of progression from a lesser base in one country to prosperity and prominence in both was too real to be discounted. Monasteries could hope to develop endowments on the scale of Durham's in Lothian, Guisborough's in Annandale, or Holm Cultram's in Galloway. The process of gradual expansion from comparatively slender beginnings is indeed particularly well illustrated by the last case. Laymen had before them the example of the grandees whose vast estates enabled them to hold sway among the leaders of aristocratic society in both realms. In fact, in the longer term the dispersal of interests might work directly to a tenant's profit, for even restricted holdings in another country enlarged his influence and afforded more openings for advancement through patronage or good marriages than might otherwise have been possible. There are other aspects to this question, political and economic. [141]

Study of estate management serves, therefore, to underline the marked tendency for proprietors to regard their reserves, however constituted, as integral cross-Border patrimonies. Controlling them through managerial techniques typical of the dispersed tenures of other lords, they generally sought to maintain the accumulations they had put together and lost no opportunity to extend them. The essential unity of estates was further demonstrated whenever produce flowed from a lord's establishments deep in one country to his residences in the other, [142] and by administrative arrangements during minorities. [143] The Border, in short, was largely irrelevant to the scheme of lordship.

The wars of independence put an end to this situation. From 1296 sustained peace punctuated by short wars was replaced by sustained war punctuated by short truces. The Border, once confidently crossed in the name of family or religious institution, was no longer unimportant to the possession of lands and rents. But even as it assumed this character, Anglo-Scottish proprietors were slow to adjust to the new realities, so committed were they to holding interests in both countries. Guisborough complained in c.1318 that 'our churches in Annandale . . . have been utterly wasted on many occasions by the miserable depredations of the Scots'; but these livings were still connected with the priory in 1330. [144] In 1319 the pope authorised the appropriation of Whissendine church by Sempringham since the convent's Scottish pension 'has not by reason of the wars been paid for more than fourteen years'; but it was not until 1368 that the Gilbertines finally resigned their right.[145] Indeed, although long periods of confiscation had to be endured, so far as the religious were concerned the connections might be permanently severed only by the combined impact of recurrent war and the Great Schism. Holm Cultram clung to Kirkgunzeon until the 1360s, and did not abandon the parish church until 1391. In the 1330s Holm had even attempted to develop a new Scottish interest by appropriating the church of Dornock in Annandale.[146] Melrose did not relinquish its Northumberland hill pastures until after 1352; the grange at Colpenhope (now Coldsmouth) in Kilham was back in Kelso's hands in 1370. Durham priory's most exceptional tenacity in this matter is well known.[147] Lay lords, for their part, were also prepared to yield only gradually and reluctantly: notably, the earls of Dunbar, who held or claimed Beanley until it was at last given up in 1335; the Ridels, who prosecuted their claims to Cranston until the 1340s; and the Lovels, who renounced Hawick no earlier than 1347.[148] Nevertheless, instructive as these examples may be, protracted warfare was fatal to the successful tenure of interests in both countries; and cross-Border proprietors, however slowly and grudgingly, were forced to accept the inevitability of having to concentrate their ambitions upon a single realm.

Magnate Allegiances and Anglo-Scottish Politics

Historians of magnate families in the two early medieval kingdoms have often found it easy to ignore the concerns that an increasingly powerful minority held across the Tweed-Solway boundary. We have attempted to remedy this neglect. The emergence and development of the cross-Border aristocracy rested upon three main factors: the interplay of marriage and land acquisition; the desire to retain even minor properties in the other country and to pass on interests intact to eldest sons; the ability of estates to survive the spasmodic warfare of the twelfth and early thirteenth centuries, and then to benefit from a prolonged period of peace between the realms. All these aspects combined to produce a landholding group which, although more strongly entrenched in Scotland, commanded considerable influence in both lands. Some, the earls and the richer barons, clearly belonged to the uppermost stratum of magnate society; many others were evidently of substantial, if lesser, standing; and, prior to Edward I's attempts to subdue Scotland, collectively they controlled a large and ever-growing proportion of the available wealth in land. The territorial links naturally varied in strength from one magnate to another. Yet their outlook as landlords was similar: in it, distance and frontiers occupied no predominant place. Their fiefs in England and Scotland were held for like services and by the same laws of inheritance. Existing rights were clarified and family claims vigorously upheld in the courts of both kingdoms, despite the occasional conflicts of jurisdiction; property could be dealt with by charter 'without the slightest hint that the lands involved were situated in different realms'.[149] In discussing these men it is difficult to think in terms of an English aristocracy and a Scottish aristocracy. What is permissible is to emphasise that, although they were sometimes influential in Ireland, Wales or northern France, England and Scotland formed the main area of their activity; and something has been revealed of the Anglo-Scottish contacts forged in the shadow of the great lords.

Some years ago, J. Le Patourel argued for the existence of 'one, homogeneous, Norman-French baronial society, whose interests extended through the length and breadth of the Norman "empire", into England, into Wales and ultimately into Scotland . . .'.[150] Although he concentrated on a period when the Scottish dimension was not present, or was present in a far lower order, it will be clear how much this account has benefited from Professor Le Patourel's seminal discussions – indeed, that it follows the lines of inquiry which they serve to open up. What must be stressed, however, is that the historical contexts are distinct: while cross-Channel proprietorship generally worked for the political unity of England and Normandy under one ruler,[151] Anglo-Scottish ties developed under two separate superior authorities. Nevertheless, what were the implications of these connections for political relations between Scotland and the English crown?

Let us set out perhaps the most obvious argument, reserving the right to reject it later if it ought to be dismissed as unsatisfactory. It is a commonplace that to make their lordship truly effective all rulers had to inspire affection for themselves among their leading subjects, whose interests they strove to identify with their own. This prerequisite had especial relevance to the Scots king since his great nobles remained peculiarly important in government. But because of the attraction of Anglo-Scottish landholding for almost every major magnate family in Scotland and others normally resident in England, the undivided allegiance of powerful men could not be assumed; and the constitutional historian may feel entitled to suggest that the dual homages they owed for their estates weakened the house of Canmore to a far greater degree than the Angevin monarchs, for cross-Border magnates, as a proportion of a king's aristocracy, occupied a more prominent position in Scotland than they ever did in England. All the while, a sensitive matter of principle between the crowns had not been settled to the satisfaction of both governments. Although the treaty of York (1237), by which Alexander II renounced his claims to the northern shires, made manifest the shift in Scots royal ambitions from aggressive involvement in English affairs to a full commitment to the expansion of the kingdom towards the north and west, the problem of Angevin demands for suzerainty remained. If they became a more central issue, backed up by *force majeure*, which way would the cross-Border magnates turn? At first glance it may seem that the quest for Scottish independence took place against a background of forces threatening sooner or later to cripple successful royal rule;

and that, when the balance of power moved decisively upon the failure of the direct Scottish royal line in 1290, all the advantages benefited Edward I and his imperialist designs.

Beside these initial speculations we must set Professor Barrow's impassioned thesis that Scotland developed in the course of the thirteenth century a distinctive sense of nationhood and nationalist identity.[152] On the one hand, it would be rash to affirm that Scotland was unaffected by the growth of medieval nationalism; this was, after all, a contemporary European phenomenon.[153] There remains, however, the danger of underestimating those pressures which served to counteract Scottish national feeling, or at least to deny it the wider appeal that might have been fostered by the rise of an aristocracy wholly distinct from that of the English realm. And the legal position was not solely that Anglo-Scottish barons were bound for their Scottish lands to one sovereign and for their English lands to another. The desire of Scots kings for their kingdom to be politically independent of England is evident. But by 1157 they had been brought back into the vassalage of the English crown for English possessions, and they continued to render homage and fealty for them, either in person or by proxy, until the last years of the thirteenth century. These kings could scarcely object to their subjects owing allegiance to the ruler who in that sense was their own liege lord any more than the kings of England could protest at their subjects holding property of the ruler who in that same sense was their own liegeman.

It would appear, indeed, that when we seek to understand how cross-Border magnates saw their position, concepts such as patriotic sentiment, or Angevin 'empire-building', tend to obscure the real issues. It can be agreed that these nobles were not necessarily flexible in their allegiance because they had two political masters, although some no doubt valued the greater independence this gave them, as when they appealed to one monarch to uphold their interests against the other.[154] Many were closely tied to Scotland by official service and by the distribution of their main estates. They were thus primarily identified with the northern realm, and there may be little question that generally they did think of themselves as Scotsmen. Even so, they appreciated the ability to move freely in English society as lawful subjects of the English king, and it would be unwise to stress the extent to which they felt themselves to be different from those families in England into which they married and whose estates lay adjacent to their own. There were also great lords whose concerns lay as much in one country as the other. It would not be unjust to say that these potentates were in a minority. But to assert that magnates like John de Balliol the younger and Robert de Brus the Competitor 'were Scots only by reason of the technicality of their homage'[155] is frankly misleading. Rather, their position was more that of feudatories who continued to express their loyalty in personal terms than that of men who were devoted to a particular nation or state. They undertook to assist each ruler with aid and counsel, to maintain his peace, and not to act against his wishes; in general, practice was at one with theory, and it does them no discredit to suggest that in a crisis they may have been genuinely uncertain where their first allegiance lay. Others were primarily vassals of the English crown; yet they accepted that two kings had power over their persons through homages of an equally binding nature. One could go further and say that provided peace prevailed their Scottish homages were less conditional than the English: because the royal bureaucracy was weaker in Scotland, magnates were disposed to co-operate with it rather than engage in struggles for constitutional reforms. Certainly, they might display an interest in Scotland out of proportion to the size of their territorial commitment. The lord of Wooler, 'a man of great repute in the northern parts of England', prepared for his death in 1250 by choosing to be buried in the chapter-house of Melrose; in 1275 the lord of Alnwick, a close supporter of Edward I later to die on campaign in Gascony, was a leader of Alexander III's expeditionary force to the Isle of Man. Both men enjoyed only moderate incomes north of the Border.[156]

Thus Anglo-Scottish magnates exhibited varying degrees of involvement in the kingdoms in which their lands lay. But all accepted that they had obligations as responsible subjects of either king and were mindful of their properties in both realms. In a word, concern to emphasise the 'Scottishness' of the nobility in thirteenth-century Scotland, and indeed the 'Englishness' of the nobility in England after 1204, fails to allow for the views of an important group of lords who may often have been guided less by abstract ideals than by the practical matter of getting and holding land on each side of the Border line. The notion of a *communitas regni* was not merely Scots royal propaganda devoid of spontaneous support from below; yet it had to compete or to interact with a broader range of aspirations than has hitherto been fully recognised.

Given the dearth of specialist studies, further conclusions are of necessity more cautious. It is a paradox, however, that this Anglo-Scottish element was arguably of direct assistance to the rise of a free and independent kingdom of Scots, for reasons quite apart from its contributions within the realm at large. Although family and tenurial bonds existed, it will not do to overestimate the cohesiveness of the group; and important as these men frequently were as royal *familiares* and the holders of high office, it would be easy to exaggerate the extent of their influence over the broad course of politics. Yet concern with peace was one thing on which they could present a more or less united front, for only in peacetime could they be sure of enjoying all the positive advantages that association with the two kingdoms offered. The fact is that England and Scotland were rarely at war between 1154 and 1217 and, notwithstanding periodic bouts of tension, continuously at peace from 1217 to 1296; and while cross-Border magnates were obviously not alone in influencing opinion about peace, it would be wrong simply to discount them and to assume that the *modus vivendi* between the realms depended purely on power politics, that peaceful relations rested on a mere equilibrium of forces. When a Robert de Brus or an earl of Dunbar spoke out against war,[157] or when individual magnates such as Earl David acted as mediators or pledged themselves as sureties for peace,[158] they spoke also for a formidable minority of greater landlords, a group whose views gained added strength from the numerous gentry families and churchmen who had established Anglo-Scottish concerns of their own. Moreover, the role of the magnates as a stabilising force grew in significance since estates developed to a large extent under their own momentum, independent of both kings' motive wills. The contacts thrived and multiplied. Men followed the paths of harmony and due regard had to be paid to their interests by rulers who could hope to guarantee their continued loyalty only for as long as there was no war. In the absence of a conclusive *rapprochement*, they strengthened the basis for co-operation between governments; and the making of the territorial kingdom of Scotland went hand in hand with the stability of an enduring peace.

The inherent weakness of cross-Border proprietorship was that policies of *détente* were always vulnerable to the major unresolved question of the constitutional relationship between Scotland and the English crown, and that the price of concord could never be a humiliating surrender of the powers and liberties of Scottish kingship nourished by the years of peace. The so-called wars of independence severed the extraneous bonds of tenure arising out of the Anglo-Norman interest in Scotland and ensured that loyalty was focused upon a single crown. To that degree the development of Scottish royal lordship entered a new phase. But the final verdict must be that before their estates were irretrievably divided, cross-Border magnates, as patrons of accord and reconciliation, had worked for the dignity of Scots kingship by helping to provide the settled conditions in which kingly authority could prosper and secure a large measure of *de facto* independence upon which future monarchs would build. In the twelfth and thirteenth centuries, the Tweed-Solway boundary lacked importance as an obstacle to landholding bonds, but this fact assisted its emergence as an agreed line of demarcation between governments. The wider world of Anglo-Scottish proprietorship that Earl David of Huntingdon invites us to explore has a major political as well as social significance for the history of the two medieval realms.

APPENDIX.

THE *ACTA* OF EARL DAVID

This Appendix contains, so far as is possible, a complete record of Earl David's extant written *acta*. The acts known to have survived as full texts, including those with missing witness-lists, number fifty-five: twenty-two of these are originals and one is a competent facsimile executed for Sir Christopher Hatton's Book of Seals. In addition, notices are provided of thirty-six 'lost acts'. Here the object has been to include (1) descriptions or abstracts of charters which are too incomplete to justify counting them in with the full texts; (2) incidental references to actual missing *acta*; (3) dispositions which are specifically mentioned and were probably, but not certainly, the subject of individual documentary record. Other acts can be more or less reasonably inferred from the sources, but these have not been listed. Lastly, it was not unusual for a great lord like Earl David to warrant transactions by putting his seal to *acta* issued by persons other than himself. The figures given above are exclusive of such records, which have been omitted from this collection, as have those acts of King William I to which David gave his consent.[1]

The Documents

The full, or almost full, texts record that the earl has granted, confirmed or quitclaimed rights – generally permanent rights – to numerous kinds of property and privileges. Such writ-mandates as may have been directed expressly to his officials have failed to survive. There is no example of the letters patent, *inspeximus* charter or other specialist *acta* that were beginning to be written in the name of contemporary authorities. Only tentative approaches towards the phraseology of these more stereotyped documents may be observed. So far as the means for conveying the earl's will can be studied, the basic writ-charter satisfied all the requirements of the scribes concerned.

It was a multi-purpose instrument. An administrative precept could be included in an otherwise conventional charter granting property and privileges in perpetuity (No.49). Earl David could demonstrate his authority by giving the impression that he himself had bestowed lands and other rights when in fact he was merely confirming his predecessors' gifts (Nos.58, 60, 78). The composite 'foundation charter' of Lindores abbey (No.44) has already been discussed;[2] and it is significant to note, among other instances of flexibility, that a simple grant of tithes could be sanctioned in chirograph form, to strengthen its force by providing both parties with the text of the

212

conveyance (No.4). Of greatest interest among the 'lost acts' is the brief account that survives of Earl David's death-bed gift to Sawtry abbey of eight virgates in Conington (No.80). Although this bequest flouted the principle that freeholds were not devisable, the document which recorded it was witnessed and sealed, and thus conformed in type to the extant *acta* written on the earl's behalf.

The texts display variety in composition and appearance, as is only to be expected of an administration which relied upon clerks working under the supervision of the earl's beneficiaries as well as upon resident household scribes. Nevertheless, the majority of the charters also exhibit telling degrees of uniformity, with the movement towards precise, regular *clausulae* and, in the case of originals, standard physical features tending to triumph over idiosyncracy and diversity. It is a point of first importance in this regard that there are no major differences of form between the earl's English and Scottish *acta*. The Anglo-Norman charter had become familiar and acceptable in Scotland, and the scribe who was skilled in English charter practice was equally competent to give written expression to Earl David's will as a Scottish magnate. To be sure, Anglo-Norman clerks would have naturally fallen back on the formulas of the English charter, which were not developed to suit Scottish conditions. Their inclination was to impose their own phraseology and preoccupations upon the realities of lordship and society in Scotland, and thus to conceal the contrasts between the two countries rather than to highlight them. Yet since charters were formal legal instruments designed to provide proof of title recognised at law, they had of necessity to satisfy legal requirements. This collection therefore reflects the close approximation of English and Scottish law in the late twelfth and early thirteenth centuries, at least at that level revealed by Earl David's dealings with the Church and by his support of lay adherents.

Such detailed comments as follow on the diplomatic of the *acta* are the bare minimum necessary to provide a context for the editing of the charters. A comprehensive analysis has been prepared for publication elsewhere.[3]

Style. Most of David's charters bear the style 'Earl David, brother of the king of Scotland (*or* of Scots)'. With regard to *comes*, this dignity was assumed by David, or attributed to him, with that lack of consistency already noted elsewhere by students of the Anglo-Norman aristocracy.[4] When David had rights or claims to two earldoms before 1185, his personal style did not regularly include the title of earl. There may be one instance of its use by virtue of his claims to the earldom and honour of Huntingdon during the young King Henry's rebellion in 1173–4 (No.27), but it is noteworthy that he is not described as an earl in any of the Huntingdon *acta* which evidently relate to this stage of his career (Nos.23, 34, 58, 75). Nor was it David's usual practice to style himself *comes* after he had acquired the earldom of Lennox in 1174, if indeed he ever adopted comital rank in this respect. He was not accorded the title in his sole surviving Lennox act

(No.35) or in any contemporary royal *acta*, with the exception of a single charter issued between 1175 and 1178. Moreover, this text survives in a cartulary of Glasgow cathedral see and *comes* may be a copyist's interpolation.[5] Stronger evidence for the early use of comital style is provided by the witness-clauses of two original Melrose charters issued by Robert Avenel of Eskdale, who died on 8 March 1185.[6] David's appearances here as an earl might be explained because he attested when he still had control of Lennox, which is possible although not certain. But if, as is arguable, both these *acta* passed on the eve of Avenel's death,[7] it can also be suggested that the title was bestowed proleptically, in anticipation of David's acquisition of the Huntingdon honour at King Henry II's court about a fortnight later.[8]

Be that as it may, it was only from mid-March 1185 that David took *comes* as part of his normal charter style. The territorial designation, though rarely added, was always 'of Huntingdon'. Yet it should be noted further that while his usual description in record other than his formal written acts from 1185 was also *comes*, in two charters of King Richard I dated 15 and 16 September 1189, one being an original, David is named as a witness without comital rank,[9] although he does appear as an earl in another of this king's acts issued on 13 September in the same year.[10] A similar inconsistency can be found in Scottish sources: in the texts of three *acta* in which he is mentioned about the 1190s, his title is that of *dominus*.[11] There is no certain evidence of the omission of *comes* from David's style in the charters he issued from 1185. For his career as a whole, the conclusion is quite plain nonetheless. David was not always given, nor did he necessarily use, the comital style to which he was, or appears to have been, entitled. This poses some difficulty as regards the dating of the *acta*. In the few cases where the subject-matter or the names of witnesses provide not even an approximate guide to dating, it is generally supposed that those charters passed in David's name as *comes* belong no earlier than 1185 and the converse when the style is lacking. It will be clear, however, that the absence of this title does not constitute sure proof that an act antedates his succession to the Huntingdon honour as Henry II's liegeman – nor, given his status in England and Scotland prior to 1185, does its presence provide incontrovertible evidence of a later date.

The superscription continues, discounting minor variants, *frater regis Scocie* (or *Scott*). There is no information to indicate that the charter style was altered upon the death of William the Lion and the accession of David's nephew Alexander II in December 1214. While it is possible that none of the earl's surviving charters in fact belongs to King Alexander's reign, it may seem equally possible, in light of the irregular and flexible conventions of styling in this period, that his customary style was retained.[12]

Handwriting. In royal and episcopal chanceries a cursive or semi-cursive business hand had generally prevailed over book hand before the end of the twelfth century.[13] The originals in the present collection can be associated with this movement, though it is still possible to distinguish the odd example of solid, upright handwriting with the characteristics of, or actually identifiable as, book hand.[14] As a rule they are accomplished productions, written with economy and expertise, although there are instances of scrappy work. In particular, No.68 was written in a wild and slovenly hand, with a badly cut pen.

Analysis of the originals, including one text extant in facsimile form, suggests that a multiplicity of scribes were active. The calligraphy of Nos.36 and 38 is, however, barely distinguishable, while in a group of four charters (Nos.33, 53, 56, 79) the hands are so alike as to be possibly identical. The hands of three scribes have been positively identified.

Scribe A. Nos.27–8, 34. Active in Scotland, 1172 × c.1185. An expert charter hand, clear but angular, using a broad, well-cut pen and achieving good differentiation of thick and fine strokes. Distinctive letters include h, long s, C, S and a compressed O, narrowing into a point at the top. The use of the *punctus versus* is noteworthy; Nos.27 and 34 end with this sign. This scribe was possibly trained in the Scottish royal chancery since two of his charters bear dates of place, unusual for David's *acta*, but essential in royal charters. He wrote for different beneficiaries on different occasions and was presumably in the earl's employ. The likely candidate is David's clerk Robert, a known associate of the Scots king's *clerici*,[15] who is a witness in each act.

Scribe B. Nos. (?18), 19, 20. Active in England, 1194 × 1208. A large, crudely ornamental charter hand. Among its distinctive forms are S and R. Note also the prevalent form of tironian et and the regular use of a vertical wavy line as a general mark of abbreviation. All the charters for which this scribe was, or is presumed to have been, responsible were issued for Clerkenwell priory, Nos.19 and 20 probably on the same occasion. He may have been a Clerkenwell scribe.

Scribe C. Nos.3, 4. Active in England, 1206 × 1219. A good, regular charter hand characterised especially by elaborate forms for H, N and S. Other distinctive features include the marked backward-sloping ascender in d; the use of the 'tittle' or 'papal knot' abbreviation; ascenders in b, h and l distinguished by a slight splaying almost at the top; and, finally, the loops in long s and f. Both acts executed by this scribe, done on different occasions, were in favour of Aldgate priory. He was presumably an Aldgate scribe.

Seals. Magnates of Earl David's standing often employed more than one seal in the course of their lives. The earl himself used at least three different seals during his career.[16]

First Seal. Circular, diameter about 2.7 in (6.8 cm); equestrian, knight to sinister; wearing hauberk of mail, surcoat with flowing tasselled fringe, round-topped helmet with nasal; broadsword in right hand and shield on left arm bearing central spike; horse trotting.

Legend: SIGILLVM DAVID [FRATRIS] REG[IS] SCOT[IE]

Illustrated: H. Laing, *Supplemental Descriptive Catalogue of Ancient Scottish Seals* (Edinburgh, 1866), pl.4, no.2 (from No.23); *Bibliotheca Phillippica: Catalogue of the celebrated collection of MSS formed by Sir Thomas Phillipps, Bt. (1792–1872)*, new ser., part iii (Sotheby and Co., London, 1967), facing p.23 (from No.28); *Art at Auction, 1966–7* (London, 1967), p.353 (from No.28).

Second Seal. Circular, diameter about 2.8 in (7.1 cm); equestrian, knight to sinister; wearing hauberk of mail, long surcoat with tasselled fringe, flat-topped helmet; broadsword in right hand and shield on left arm bearing arms (? three piles in point); horse trotting.

Legend: +SIGILL' DAVID COMITIS FRATRIS REGIS SCOCIE

Illustrated: *Selectus Diplomatum et Numismatum Scotiae Thesaurus*, etc., ed. J. Anderson (Edinburgh, 1739), pl.39 (from No.76); *Cambridge Borough Documents*, ed. W. M. Palmer (Cambridge, 1931), pl.5 (from No.69).

Third Seal. Circular, diameter about 2.8 in (7.2 cm); equestrian, knight to sinister; wearing hauberk of mail, surcoat with tasselled fringe, flat-topped helmet; broadsword in right hand and shield on left arm bearing arms (three piles in point); horse at full speed.

Legend: +SIGILL' DAVID COMITIS FRATRIS REGIS SCOCIE

Illustrated: See plate 1 (p.x, from No.3); Laing, *Lindores*, p.44 (from No.3); *Lind. Cart.*, following p.331 (from No.3); R. H. Ellis, *Catalogue of Seals in the PRO, Personal Seals*, i (London, 1978), pl.7 (from No.3).

There are thirteen originals in this collection which retain their seals, although only the merest fragments survive of the seals attached to Nos.56 and 66.[17] In addition, there exist what appear to be competent drawings of the seals formerly carried by Nos.19 and 76. Among these seals or depictions of seals, there are three identifiable specimens of the first seal, all appended to charters certainly or probably datable to the early 1170s (Nos.23, 27–8). The second seal is extant in eight examples (Nos.18–20, 36, 53, 68–9, 76). Of the five charters bearing this seal that can be dated by their witnesses and subject-matter within reasonably narrow limits, none is earlier than 1190 or later than November 1208. The third seal is attached to two charters which probably passed about 1209 (Nos.3, 4).

The usage of the three different seals falls accordingly into a recognisable pattern. The first seal was appropriate to the period before David became earl of Huntingdon in 1185, the word *comes*, a rare feature of his style during that time, being omitted from its legend. The second seal, describing David as *comes*, was apparently the principal means of authenticating documents for some twenty-five years from 1185. Then, arguably no later than *c*.1209, the second seal was for some reason discarded, to be replaced by a new but virtually identical seal, the third seal.

As is to be expected of this collection, in which title-deeds to perpetuities predominate, the normal way of sealing the originals was by a parchment tag (*sur double queue*). One example is irregular: No.34 has a strip for a tie, but the seal hangs *sur double queue*. There is a single instance of sealing with a leather tag (No.28). 'From about the end of the twelfth century silk and wool cords of various colours were used by the higher ranks for their more important charters.'[18] Plaited cords twice replace the parchment *double queue* (Nos.23, 27), whereas No.69 is embellished with an elaborate seal-tag in the form of tablet-woven braid patterned in gold yarn on a green background.[19] Yet the subject-matter of none of these charters is especially imposing. They concern, respectively, a judicial settlement in Earl David's court, an enfeoffment and the grant of an annuity of £5.

There are two examples of sealing *sur simple queue* (Nos.17, 56). In each case the tongue has been made by cutting about three-quarters of the way across the foot of the parchment from the right-hand side. A narrow tie has also been cut in the same fashion from the top edge of the tongue. This method of *simple-queue* sealing is abnormal. Usually the tie was cut below the tongue. In contemporary royal and episcopal chanceries the use of the *simple queue* came to be restricted, by and large, to documents of ephemeral significance.[20] No.56, a quitclaim of neyfs, can perhaps be associated with that class of instrument (as can one or two *acta* sealed *sur double queue*); but No.17, a charter of enfeoffment, was intended to have lasting validity.

The seals are in green or red or white wax. It may be concluded from the surviving examples that green wax was normally reserved for those acts which had permanent value, and white, or natural, wax for those of temporary import. This principle is one that is clearly observable in English royal *acta* from *c*.1200,[21] but not in their Scottish counterparts, where – as in certain other contexts – there is little to indicate that the choice of seal colour bore any relation to the type of business being expedited.[22]

Methods of Editing

Full, or almost full, texts have been printed together with 'lost acts' in a single run arranged in alphabetical order by principal beneficiaries. A chronological presentation throughout proved to be quite impracticable, for the dates of a great many of the charters cannot be narrowed to single years, or even to periods of two or three years. Only when a group of *acta* survives in favour of the same beneficiary is an approximate chronological framework attempted, and the edition then proceeds, as far as possible, according to the sequence suggested by the date or date-limits assigned to each act.

A charter that survives as an original or as a copy is introduced by a short English summary of its main contents. The summary is followed by the place of issue, if recorded, and by the date or date-limits of the act. Where the sign × is used in dating, this means 'not earlier than the preceding date', and 'not later than the succeeding date'. Two dates which recur, 1185 and 1219, stand for the date of Earl David's succession to the earldom of Huntingdon, mid-March 1185,[23] and that of his death, 17 June 1219. The text itself is edited according to the following conventions.

Original charters are transcribed with a minimum of editorial rational-isation. Thus they are followed in their spelling of words and proper names and an attempt has been made to reproduce capital letters. Where, how-ever, a scribe employed 'small capitals', intermediate forms which he gave less emphasis than his genuine capitals, these are printed in lower case. Tironian symbols are retained. With the exception of place-names and some surnames and Christian names, other abbreviated forms are usually extend-ed, though this is done without italics only when the extension is minor and conventional. As regards punctuation, an effort has again been made to adhere as closely as possible to scribal usage. But a point or full-stop, etc., is placed immediately after a word whether or not this represents its actual position in the source. Scribal insertions are indicated by oblique strokes. Words or parts of words supplied editorially are contained within square brackets to emphasise that an editorial addition has been made.

The majority of these rules also apply to copies of originals now lost. But the usage of the source in respect of capital letters and punctuation has been standardised to conform with modern practice, as far as seems helpful and necessary, and *et* is given in full irrespective of the form in which it appears. There is some cautious emendation of the orthography, notably in texts whose sources are late and corrupt (Nos.75, 78).

The text of an original is followed immediately by the medieval en-dorsements, if any, and by a description of the principal physical features of the document. This includes measurements across the top of the sheet of parchment (given first) and down the left-hand side, and information on the method of sealing. A note is added on the handwriting, which is either attributed to an identified hand or classed as 'unidentified'. For MS copies, a note of the rubric and marginalia replaces notes of endorsement, physical features and handwriting.

The source or sources of the act is the next entry for both originals and copies, and the edited text is that of the original wherever possible. Where the original is no longer extant but more than one copy is known, what appears to be the best text has been selected as the basis for the printed edition, and major variants in the remainder are noted. In almost every case, the MS concerned will be the earliest in date. In order to avoid tiresome repetition of the dates and provenance of the MS sources from which *acta* have been edited, full details are set out forthwith.

CAPRINGTON CASTLE, KILMARNOCK, AYRSHIRE
> Muniments of Capt. R. Fergusson-Cuninghame. Cartulary of Lindores abbey. xiii cent. Nos.37–47, 49, 50.

EDINBURGH, NATIONAL LIBRARY OF SCOTLAND
> Advocates MSS
> 34.4.2 (Cartulary of Arbroath abbey. xiv cent.). Nos.5, 24.
> 34.5.1 (Cartulary of Kelso abbey. xiv cent.). No.35.
> 34.7.1 (Cartulary of Lindores abbey. xvi cent.). Nos.43, 45.

EDINBURGH, SCOTTISH RECORD OFFICE
GD 45/27/8 (Cartulary of St Andrews cathedral priory. xiii cent.).
Nos.71–4.

LONDON, BRITISH LIBRARY
Additional MS 33245 (Cartulary of Arbroath abbey. xvi cent.). No.5.
Cotton MSS
Faustina B. ii (Cartulary of Clerkenwell priory. xiii cent.). No.19.
Nero C. xii (Cartulary of Burton Lazars hospital. xv cent.). No.15.
Vespasian E. xvii (Cartulary of St Andrew's priory, Northampton. xv cent.). Nos.58–61, 65.
Lansdowne MS 391 (Cartulary of Harrold priory. xv cent.). No.31.
Royal MS 11 B. ix (Cartulary of St Andrew's priory, Northampton. xiii cent.). Nos.58–61, 65.
Sloane MS 986 (Cartulary of the family of Braybrooke of Braybrooke, Northants. xiii cent.). Nos.11–13.

LONDON, PUBLIC RECORD OFFICE
C 66/167 (Patent Roll, 1 Edward III, A.D. 1327–8). No.54.

NORTHAMPTON, NORTHAMPTONSHIRE RECORD OFFICE,
DELAPRE ABBEY
Finch-Hatton MS 170 (Sir Christopher Hatton's Book of Seals. xvii cent.). No.19.

OXFORD, BODLEIAN LIBRARY
Rawlinson MS B. 142 (Transcript by Sir Richard St George of a cartulary of Sawtry abbey. xvi/xvii cent.). Nos.75, 78.

Where a charter has been previously published, the note on sources is followed by a record of the printed versions. No attempt has been made to comment on the accuracy of these versions. It perhaps suffices to say that the decision to print in full not only the unpublished *acta* but also those already printed elsewhere was prompted by the fact that the latter have rarely appeared in satisfactory – or easily accessible – editions. Finally, there are normally two sections under the headings *Note(s)* and *Comment*. Variant readings and other textual matters are dealt with in the former. The section *Comment* is reserved for entries of a more general significance and includes notes on dating.

With respect to 'lost acts', details are given, usually in English, of all that the act is known to have involved. The sources of Nos.8–10, being Latin abstracts of lost originals, are reproduced verbatim. Elsewhere, an asterisk is used to denote the explicit reference to a charter in the source. The act is normally assigned a date, its source is noted, and further information is provided as far as seems desirable.

Additional Note. The abbreviations used in the Appendix conform wherever possible to the list printed below, pp.271–4.

1. Cathedral church of Aberdeen. Grants to Bishop Matthew and the church of Aberdeen two measured ploughgates in Kennethmont (Aberdeenshire), for a quittance of all the teinds and customs which the bishops of Aberdeen used to have from the time of King David I in Garioch, Durno, Rothkes (Polnar Chapel in Inverurie), Monkeigie (Keithhall), Fintray and Bourtie. (× 1190, possibly × March 1189).

SOURCE: *RRS*, ii, no.295.

COMMENT: The source, King William I's confirmation of this agreement (March 1189 × 1190), was witnessed by Rayner, abbot of Melrose, and his predecessor Arnold, then abbot of Rievaulx. Both men may have been together in the king's court in March 1189, in which month Arnold was translated to Rievaulx and Rayner became abbot of Melrose (*Chron. Melrose*, p.47). The land granted was later described as the land of Ardlair (Nat. Grid Ref. NJ 557283), as was that ploughgate in Kennethmont given by Earl David to Arbroath abbey: *Aberdeen Reg.*, i, p.218; No.5. See also *RRS*, ii, no.348.

2. Men of Alconbury and Alconbury Weston (Hunts). Grants to the men of Alconbury and Alconbury Weston the assart of Alconbury. (1202 × 1209).

SOURCE: BL MS Harl. 4748, fo.24v; cf. PRO E 32/37, m.2.

COMMENT: On the dating see above, pp.116, 121.

3. Aldgate priory. Grants in alms to the priory of Holy Trinity, London, the rent of 2s. 6d. which the canons used to pay him for six acres of arable, two small groves and a half-acre of pasture in Tottenham (Middlesex). The canons have received the earl, Maud his wife, John his son and heir, and Ada his daughter into their fraternity, to share in all the benefits of their church for the living and the dead. (1206 × 1219, probably *c*.1209).

Comes Dauid Frater Regis Scocie Vniuersis Sancte matris Ecclesie Filiis presentibus 7 futuris Salutem. Noueritis*ᵃ* me caritatis intuitu Dedisse 7 concessisse 7 presenti carta confirmasse. Deo 7 Ecclesie Sancte Trinitatis London'. 7 Canonicis ibidem deo seruientibus pro salute anime méé 7 anime. M. vxoris mee 7 pro salute animarum Patris 7 matris mee 7 heredum meorum Duos solidat*os* 7 sex den*a*ratas redditus quas ipsi Canonici mihi reddere consueuerunt de sex acris terre arabilis. 7 de duabus grauettis. 7 de dimidia acra pasture In Villa de Toteham. Scilicet quicquid in hoc tenemento 7 eius pertinenciis habui sine aliquo retinemento. Habend*umᵃ* eisdem Canonicis integre in puram 7 perpetuam elemosinam liberam 7 quietam ab omni seculari seruitio 7 exactione. Ipsi uero Canonici receperunt me 7. M. Vxorem meam 7. J. filium meum 7 heredem. 7. A. filiam meam in Fraternitatem domus sue concedentes nos participes fieri omnium bonorum que fient in Ecclesia sua tam pro viuis quam pro defunctis in perpetuum. Et quia Volui hanc donationem ratam ⁊ stabilem haberi in perpetuum. eam presenti carta ⁊ sigilli mei munimine coroboraui. Hiis testibus. Willelmo Daco. Bartholom*eo* de mortem*er*. Dauid de Essebẏ. Gileb*erto* de Nuers. Hug*one* de Harington'. Rob*erto* fili*o* Rob*er*ti. Philippo monaco. Willelmo de Folevill'. Hug*one* Ridel. Ric*ardo* fili*o* Willelmj Senescall*o*. Henric*o* de Nuers. Gileb*erto* de Toteha*m*. Galfr*ido* de Sandon'. Johan*ne* de Lẏesne. Ric*ardo* maẏ. Gileb*erto* de Cel'. Nicola*o* de Gatesbur*y*. Hug*one* de sartrino. Rob*erto* probo. Turgis*io*. ⁊ multis aliis.

ENDORSED: Comes Dauid de Terris .xxx. d'. in Thoteh'. in elemosinam (xiii cent.); Thoteham (same hand).

DESCRIPTION: 6.7 × 6.6 in (17 × 16.7 cm). Ruled in drypoint. Foot folded to depth of 0.5 in (1.3 cm); single slits with tag. Third seal, in dark-green wax; good impression.

HAND: Scribe C.

SOURCE: Original, PRO E 42/44.

PRINTED: *CDS*, i, no.603 (summary). See also plate 1, p.x.

NOTE: *a* Exceptionally prominent initial.

COMMENT: Earl David's son John was born in 1206. A witness, Richard son of William *senescallus*, is known to have been the earl's steward in England in 1209: *PBKJ*, iv, no.3914. On the first witness William Dacus, a landowner in Somerset and Northamptonshire, see Barrow, *Era*, p.105; *Past and Present*, xlvii (1970), p.42 with n.79. Further details at No.4, comment.

4. Aldgate priory. Grants in alms to the priory of Holy Trinity, London, all the tithes of the hay from his whole demesne in Tottenham, and grants further that the canons may take without hindrance their tithes of his sown crops whenever those crops are carried. (1206 × 1219, probably *c*.1209).

C A R T A*a*

Comes Dauid Frater Regis Scotie Vniuersis sancte matris Ecclesie Filiis presentibus ⁊ futuris Salutem. Noueritis*b* me caritatis intuitu Dedisse ⁊ concessisse ⁊ presenti carta confirmasse. Deo ⁊ Ecclesie Sancte Trinitatis London' ⁊ Canonicis ibidem deo seruientibus pro salute anime mee ⁊. m. vxoris méé ⁊ pro salute animarum Patris mei ⁊ matris méé ⁊ heredum meorum. Omnes decimas omnium fenorum tocius dominii mei In Villa de Toteha*m*. Habendas eisdem Canonicis integre in liberam ⁊ puram ⁊ perpetuam elemosinam ⁊ eas per muilones recipiendas ⁊ cariendas licite ⁊ sine omni impedimento quandocumque uoluerent. Concessi etiam eisdem Canonicis ut cariari faciant libere ⁊ sine alicuius impedimento suas decima/s/ segetum mearum ⁊ heredum meorum in eadem villa quandocumque segetes nostras cariari fecerimus. Et quia volui hanc meam donationem ⁊ Concessionem ratam ⁊ stabilem haberi. eam presenti carta ⁊ sigilli mei munimine Roboraui. Hiis testibus. Gileberto de Nuers.*b* Willelmo de Wẏcheton'. Johan*ne* Bocuinte. Arnulfo capellano. Johan*ne* capellano de Toteha*m*.

Henr*ico* de Nuers. Henr*ico* de Sancto Albano. Rad*ulfo* Aswẏ. Adriano de Winton'. Thoma de Warderoba. Gileberto de Toteh*am*. Willelmo fil*io* Alani. Gileberto fil*io* Odon*is*. D*aui*D. fil*io* J*os*c*elini*. Galfr*ido* de Sandon'. Johanne de Lesn'. Stonhardo. Roberto probo. [Nicolao]*c* de Gatesb*uri*. Turgisio.

ENDORSED: Comes dauid de decimis feni sui de Thoteham. 7 de decimis bladi sui kariandis quandocumque. [volu]erimus (xiii cent.); Thotham (same hand).

DESCRIPTION: 7.3 × 5.3 in (18.5 × 13.5 cm). The lower half of a bipartite charter. Indented at top; ruled in drypoint. Foot folded to depth of 0.9 in (2.3 cm); single slits with tag. Third seal, in green wax; good impression.

HAND: Scribe C.

SOURCE: Original, BL Campbell Chart. xxx 3. (Copies in BL MS Addit. 11545, fo.13r (with drawing of seal at fo.14r), MS Stowe 551, fos.12v–13v.)

PRINTED: W. Robinson, *The History and Antiquities of . . . Tottenham*, 2nd edn (London, 1840), ii, p.1, n.1 (translation); not in 1st edn (Tottenham, 1818).

NOTES: *a* Letters cut through. *b* Exceptionally prominent initial.
c Obscured owing to smudging of source; name supplied from No.3.

COMMENT: Since eight of the twenty witnesses also attest No.3, both acts (each in the hand of Scribe C) were issued at about the same time. They were probably given in Tottenham or at Aldgate itself. Besides Gilbert of Tottenham (Nos.3, 4) and John, chaplain of Tottenham (No.4), the witnesses include Ralph Aswy, Richard May, Henry of St Albans and other local men. On Aswy, later sheriff and then mayor of London, see J. Stow, *A Survey of London*, ed. C. L. Kingsford (Oxford, 1971 reprint), ii, p.155. In 1254 nine out of the ninety-two acres of demesne meadow-land in Tottenham were earmarked in respect of the hay-tithes granted by Earl David: Robinson, *Tottenham*, i, pp.163–4. The tithes of sown crops were probably claimed by Aldgate as corporate rector of the church of Tottenham, with which the priory had been endowed by King David I: Lawrie, *Charters*, no.98.

5. Arbroath abbey. Grants in alms to Arbroath abbey one measured ploughgate of arable (in Ardlair) in Kennethmont, with common pasture, as perambulated for the monks by Reginald of Liston, Richard *marescallus*, Waltheof the clerk and Simon the Fleming. (19 Aug. 1190 × 21 April 1200).

Comes*a* Dauid frater regis Scottorum,*b* omnibus sancte matris ecclesie filjjs presentibus et futuris, salutem. Sciatis me dedisse et concessisse et hac presenti carta mea confirmasse Deo et ecclesie sancti Thome de Abirbr' et monachis ibidem Deo seruientibus pro animabus patris et matris mee et predecessorum et successorum meorum et pro*c* anima /mea/ et pro anima Matildis sponse mee vnam carrucatam terre in Kinalchmund*d* mensuratam et arabilem cum communi pastura, eamdem*e* scilicet quam Reginal*dus* de

Listerona*f* et Ric*ardus* marescallus*g* et Wald*evus* clericus*h* et Symon Flan-
drens*is* eis perambulauerunt, in puram et perpetuam elemosinam, liberam
et quietam ab omni seculari seruicio et exaccione eis tenendam, sicut aliqua
abbacia liberius et quietius et honorificencius aliquam elemosinam in regno
Scoc' tenet et possidet. Hijs test*ibus* Willelmo rege Scott'*i* fratre meo, H.
filio meo, Ricardo capellano meo, Bartholomeo Monacho, Malc*olmo* fili*o*
Bertolf*i*, Hug*one*^j de Kalledouer,*k* Will*elmo* Vacel*in*, Walkel*ino*^l filio*c*
Stephani, Gilb*erto* Dolepene et Philippo clerico meo.

RUBRIC: Carta com*itis* D*auid* de terra in Garuioch' (red, xiv cent., *A*).
Ardlath (right-hand margin, xv cent., *A*). Kynalthmund alias Ardlach'
terre carta comitis Dauid cum commun*j* pastura et pertinen*ciis* (red, xvi
cent., *B*).

SOURCE: NLS MS Adv. 34.4.2, fo.63r = *A*. BL MS Addit. 33245,
fo.89r = *B*. Text above from *A*, noting major variants in *B*.

PRINTED: *Arbroath Liber*, i, no.83 (from *A*). *Registrum de Panmure*, ed.
J. Stuart (Edinburgh, 1874), ii, p.202 (from *A*). *Aberdeen-Banff Coll.*,
pp.624–5 (abstract of *A*).

NOTES: *a* Large red initial and prominent 'o', both MSS. *b* Scotorum, *B*.
c Word omitted, *B*. *d* Kynalthmund, *B*. *e* eandem, *B*. *f* Sic; Listrona, *B*.
g de precedes marescallus, *B*. *h* meus follows clericus, *B*. *i* Sott', *A*; Scocie,
B. *j* fil' precedes Hugone, *B*. *k* Kaledouer, *B*. *l* Wallzel', *B*.

COMMENT: Although not confirmed by royal charter until 1213 (*RRS*, ii,
nos.512–13), the subject of this grant is presumed to be that ploughgate in
Garioch included among the possessions of Arbroath in Innocent III's bull
of 21 April 1200: *Arbroath Liber*, i, no.221. Earl David's marriage supplies
the *terminus post quem*.

6. David de Audri. Grants to David de Audri and his heirs the whole davoch
of Resthivet (in Chapel of Garioch, Aberdeenshire), with common pasture
on both sides of the river Urie as far as their beasts can reach by day and
return at nightfall, by specified marches; to be held for the tenth part of one
knight's service. Grants in addition that they may grind their corn at the
mill of Durno, quit of multure, whenever there is room in the hopper.
(1185 × 1219).

Sciant omnes tam presentes quam futuri quod Ego Comes Dauid frater
Regis Scocie dedi concessi 7 hac presenti Carta mea confirmaui Dauid de
Audree 7 heredibus suis totam dauatam terre de rossuthet pro homagio 7
seruicio suo cum Comuni*a* Pastura. ex vtraque parte aque de hur*y* in
quantum animalia sua possunt per diem attingere 7 ad noctem reuerti.
scilicet per has diuisas. Incipiend*o* ad vallem que est propinquior Le harlav.
ex parte occidentali. 7 sic de illa valle vsque ad aquam de hur*y* 7 sic de illa
valle descendendo in Maximo marassio 7 sic de illo Marassio vsque ad
terram roberti de Billyngam 7 sic de terra predicti roberti. ad terram
Episcopi que vocatur Crag' 7 sic de illa Crag' ad Maximam vadam de
Petscurri 7 sic de illa vada descendendo in aquam de huri Uolo autem 7

concedo quod predictus Dauid de Audree 7 heredes sui Molent bladum ad Molendinum de Durnach sine Multura. 7 quod erunt. rumfre. in dicto Molendino adeo^b libere quiete pacifice plenarie integre 7 honorifice. In bosco. 7 plano. in stangnis 7 aquis in Molendinis 7 multuris in viuariis 7 piscariis in pratis 7 pascuis. in viis 7 semitis. in Moris 7 Marisiis 7 in omnibus aliis aẏsiamentis ad dictam terram spectantibus vel de Iure spectare valentibus reddendo inde predictus Dauid de Audree 7 heredes sui Michi 7 heredibus meis decimam partem seruicij vnius Militis. pro omnj seculari Seruicio consuetudine exaccione 7 demanda. Ego predictus Dauid 7 heredes mei. totam predictam terram de rossuthet cum omnibus suis Iustis pertinenciis libertatibus 7 aẏsiamentis comoditatibus^a 7 exitibus 7 rectis diuisis suis aliquo tempore habitis seu de Iure habendis predicto Dauid de Audree 7 heredibus suis contra omnes homines 7 feminas Warantizabimus 7 in perpetuum defendemus In Cuius rei Testimonium presenti scripto sigillum meum apposui [Hii]^cs testibus Domino Roberto Basset Milite. domino Willelmo capellano domini regis domino Bartholomeo Moyne Milite domino Willelmo Walkelneo^a Milite Gilberto clerico 7 Multis aliis

ENDORSED: Only modern endorsements are legible.

DESCRIPTION: 9.9×5.6 in (25.1×14.3 cm). Foot folded to depth of about 1.4 in (3.6 cm). Double slits; tag and seal lost.

HAND: Unidentified.

SOURCE: Original, BL Cott. Chart. xviii 23.

NOTES: a Sic. b Sic. The text continues without the benefit of tenendam et habendam. c Tear in source. It should also be noted that the scribe is not consistent in his use of the cross-stroked tironian et.

COMMENT: The style and handwriting indicate a date nearer 1219 than 1185. Audri's earliest known appearance in other Scottish record is datable 1199 × 1215 (*Lind. Cart.*, no.37). On the identification of Resthivet (NJ 744261) see *Aberdeenshire Place-Names*, p.360. *Le Harlav* is now represented by West Mains of Harlaw, East Harlaw and Harlaw Ho. For the Billingham estate see Nos.8, 9. *Crag*' is probably Oldcraig in Daviot (NJ 736296). *Petscurri* is now Pitscurry. On the meaning of the Middle English word *rumfre* see Barrow, *Era*, p.202, and cf. *Calendar of the Laing Charters*, ed. J. Anderson (Edinburgh, 1899), nos.11, 21; *Hist. MSS Comm.*, *Reports*, vi, p.713; *Melrose Liber*, ii, p.680.

7. Robert of Bassingham. *Grants land to Robert of Bassingham for half of one knight's service. (1185 × 2 April 1212).

SOURCE: *CRR*, vi, p.280.

COMMENT: Dating derived from *CRR*, vi, pp.242, 273–4. The location of this fee is uncertain. The source indicates either Whissendine (Rutland) or Bozeat (Northants). By summer 1212 Helen de Moreville had established her greater right to both properties against Earl David (above, p.114), and in Nov. of that year Robert, among several men whom David had installed in these places, asked for an exchange (*PBKJ*, iv, no.4743). This may have been provided in Little Paxton, where Robert's son John held lordship in the 1230s: *HKF*, ii, p.409; *Calendar of the Feet of Fines relating to the County of Huntingdon*, ed. G. J. Turner (Cambridge Antiquarian Soc., 1913), p.15.

See also Nos.25, 64, 70.

8. Robert of Billingham. Grants to Robert of Billingham and his heirs one ploughgate in the district of *Durnachehell* (? Durno in Chapel of Garioch) and a toft in David's burgh of Inverurie. (? × 1185).

David frater regis Scotie dedit Roberto de Billighin et heredibus suis unam carrucam [terre in]*ᵃ* territorio de Durnachehell et unum toftum in burgo suo de Inuerowry. Testibus Roberto et Willelmo filio*ᵇ* Stephani, Normanno filio Malcolmi, cum diversis aliis.

SOURCE: SRO GD 124/12/141a, fo.4r (xvi-/xvii-cent. abstract of the original full text, which is lost).

PRINTED: *Hist. MSS Comm., Mar and Kellie*, p.3 (translation).

NOTES: *a* Words in square brackets omitted in source. *b* Sic.

COMMENT: The source is late and corrupt, but for the suggested identification with Durno (or possibly with Durnoshiels, now lost) cf. No.6; *The Exchequer Rolls of Scotland*, ed. J. Stuart *et al.* (Edinburgh, 1878–1908), vii, pp.89, 161 (Dornochschelis, 1461; Dornoschelis, 1463).

9. Simon of Billingham. Grants to Simon of Billingham and his heirs one ploughgate in the district of *Durnachehell Lethim* (? Durno and Lethenty in Chapel of Garioch) and a toft in David's burgh of Inverurie. (? × 1185).

David frater regis Scotie dedit Symoni de Billighin et heredibus suis unam carrucam terre in territorio de Durnachehell Lethim et unum toftum in burgo suo de Inuerowry. Testibus Willelmo de Lindsey, Hugone Gyffert, magistro Laurentio de P[e]ramsol,*ᵃ* cum diversis aliis.

SOURCE: SRO GD 124/12/141a, fo.4r (xvi-/xvii-cent. abstract of the original full text, which is lost).

PRINTED: *Hist. MSS Comm., Mar and Kellie*, p.3 (translation).

NOTE: *a* 'e' uncertain owing to smudging of source.

COMMENT: For the probable identification of *Lethim* with Lethenty (NJ 765254) see *Aberdeenshire Place-Names*, p.320. The name Mr Laurence de P[e]ramsol, otherwise unknown, is possibly a corruption of that of Earl David's clerk Mr Thomas de Paraviso.

10. Henry de Boiville. Grants to [Henry de] Boiville and his heirs all the land of Ardoyne (in Oyne, Aberdeenshire). (? 1185 × 1219).

Comes David frater regis Scotie concessit et dedit [   ] Boiuill et heredibus suis totam terram Ardowin coram his testibus, Henrico filio meo, Roberto de Adles, Willelmo [   ] et multis aliis.

SOURCE: SRO GD 124/12/141a, fo.4r (xvi-/xvii-cent. abstract of the original full text, which is lost).

PRINTED: *Hist. MSS Comm., Mar and Kellie*, p.4 (translation).

NOTE: Square brackets indicate blanks in MS.

COMMENT: The identification with Henry de Boiville is most probable, since this man was a follower of Earl David and his son Earl John in Scotland: Nos.49, 51, 56; *Lind. Cart.*, nos.15–17; SRO GD 204/23/2.

11. Henry of Braybrooke. Grants to Henry of Braybrooke for a consideration of 100 marks all his land in Potton (Beds), reserving the tenements of Robert Fitz Roger, William Burdet, Robert son of Martin and Hugh Richespaud, to be held for the fourth part of one knight's service. (1214, *c*.April).

Comes*ª* Dauid frater regis Scocie, omnibus hominibus tam presentibus quam futuris, salutem. Sciatis me dedisse et presenti carta mea confirmasse Henr*ico* de Braibroc, pro homagio et seruicio suo et pro centum marcis argenti quas mihi dedit, totam terram quam tenui in Potton' cum omnibus pertin*enciis* suis, in dominicis et vilenagiis, in bosco et plano, in pratis et pascuis et in omnibus aliis locis, scilicet quicquid ibidem habui uel habere potui, exceptis tenementis que Robert*us* fil*ius* Rog*eri* et Willelmus Burdet et Robert*us* fil*ius* Martini et Hugo Riskepaud de me tenuerunt in eadem villa et exceptis seruiciis illorum tenementorum que mihi et heredibus meis remanent, habendam et tenendam predicto Henr*ico* et heredibus suis de me et heredibus meis bene et in pace, libere et quiete, integre et hereditarie, per seruicium quarte partis vnius militis pro omni seruicio. Et ego predictus comes Dauid et heredes mei*ᵇ* warantizabimus predicto Henr*ico* et heredibus suis totam predictam terram cum omnibus pertin*enciis* suis, sicut predictam est, contra omnes gentes. Hiis t*e*stibus.*ᶜ*

RUBRIC: Carta comitis Dauid (red, contemporary with text).

SOURCE: BL MS Sloane 986, fo.42r–v.

NOTES: *a* Initial omitted for rubrication. *b* MS me. *c* Hiis t*e*stibus struck through in red; witness-list omitted by copyist.

COMMENT: This text is supplemented by a fine of 14 April 1214, by which Wiscard Leidet and Margery Foliot, his wife, quitclaimed their rights at Potton, Tottenham (Middlesex), Toseland and Abbotsley (Hunts) to Earl David, who in turn conveyed Potton to Henry of Braybrooke, reserving the four tenements as specified above: *Fines sive Pedes Finium*, etc., ed. J.Hunter (Rec. Comm., 1835–44), i, p.88. The consideration is mentioned only in the charter, and Braybrooke was liable for 100 marks of David's debts to the English crown by Michaelmas 1214 (*PR 16 John*, p.22).

The identification with Robert Fitz Roger, lord of Warkworth (d.1214), is proved in *HKF*, ii, p.337.

12. Robert of Braybrooke. Confirms to Robert of Braybrooke the grant made by Alan de Audri of two virgates in Braybrooke (Northants), as Alan's charter bears witness. (1185 × 29 Sept. 1211).

Comes Dauid frater regis Scocie,^a omnibus amicis suis et hominibus suis presentibus et futuris, salutem. Sciatis me concessisse et hac presenti carta mea confirmasse donacionem quam Alanus de Auldree fecit Roberto de Braibroc de duabus virgatis terre in Braibroc pro homagio et seruicio suo, scilicet virgatam quam Andre*as* Wakeman tenuit et virgatam quam Walterus tegulator tenuit, tenend*as* ei et heredibus suis de predicto Alano et heredibus suis sicut carta prenominati Alani testatur, saluo seruicio meo. Hiis te*stibus.*^b

RUBRIC: Confirmacio comitis Dauid de terra Alani de Auldri (red, contemporary with text).

SOURCE: BL MS Sloane 986, fo.9v.

NOTES: *a* MS Scocile. *b* Hiis te*stibus* struck through in red; witness-list omitted by copyist.

COMMENT: Audri's grant, made for a consideration of six marks, survives in BL MS Sloane 986, fo.9r–v. It is datable before 25 July 1208 (*Rot. Chart.*, p.181a). The *terminus ante quem* of Earl David's confirmation is supplied by Braybrooke's death (Richardson, *English Jewry*, p.271).

13. Robert of Braybrooke. Confirms to Robert of Braybrooke the grant made b^v Richard son of Simon of Foxton of the land of Gumley (Leics), as Richard's charter bears witness. (Oct. 1197 × 29 Sept. 1211).

Comes^a Dauid frater regis Scocie, omnibus amicis et hominibus suis Francis et Anglicis tam presentibus quam futuris, salutem. Sciatis me concessisse et hac presenti carta mea confirmasse donacionem quam Ric*ardus* fili*us* Sim*onis* de Foxton' fecit Roberto de Braibroc de terra de Gudum*un*del' cum omnibus eiusdem terre pertin*enciis,* tenendam^b sibi et heredibus suis de prenominato Ric*ardo* et heredibus suis sicut carta eiusdem Ric*ardi* testatur, saluo seruicio meo. Hiis te*stibus.*^c

RUBRIC: Confirmacio comitis Dauit de eadem terra (red, contemporary with text).

SOURCE: BL MS Sloane 986, fo.32r.

NOTES: *a* Initial omitted for rubrication. *b* MS tenenda. *c* Hiis te*stibus* struck through in red; witness-list omitted by copyist.

COMMENT: Richard's charter, given for a consideration of 60 marks, was issued on or about 24 Oct. 1197: BL MS Sloane 986, fo.31r–v; *Feet of Fines of the Ninth Year of . . . Richard I* (PRS, 1898), no.67.

14. Hugh le Bret. Grants to Hugh le Bret the land of Gillandres Buch in Garioch, a half-ploughgate in Flinder (in Kennethmont), seven acres, and the land which Abraham the mair and Eyncus held, in exchange for a quittance of the rights and claims of Hugh and his heirs in Conington (Hunts). Hugh has sworn to observe the agreement, in the presence of King William I, in the hand of David of Lindsey, justiciar of the king of Scots, and undertakes that whenever Earl David, on the advice of his men, demands surety from him, he will give surety to the earl in England. (*c.* 1208 × 4 Dec. 1214).

SOURCE: *Lind. Cart.*, no.129.

COMMENT: David of Lindsey became justiciar of Lothian *c*.1208 (Barrow, *Kingdom*, p.137). The land of Gillandres Buch is evidently represented by Glanderston (NJ 586292), near Flinder (now Little, New and Old Flinder), in the eastern part of Kennethmont parish.

15. Hospital of Burton Lazars. Grants in alms to the infirm of St Lazarus of Jerusalem 20*s*. worth of meadow-grass annually in his meadow of Whissendine (Rutland) at the time of mowing. (1185 × summer 1212).

Comes[a] Dauid frater regis[b] Scott', omnibus hanc cartam uisuris et audituris presentibus et futuris, salutem. Noueritis me dedisse et concessisse et presenti carta mea confirmasse infirmis de sancto Lazaro de Iherolimis[c] pro salute anime mee et antecessorum et successorum meorum viginti solidatas prati in prato meo de Wissenden' annuatim, recipiendas in tempore falcacionis, in liberam et puram et perpetuam elemosinam et quiet*as* ab omni exaccione seculari. Hijs testibus Ric*ardo* de Lindes', Henr*ico* et Henr*ico* filijs meis, Hug*one* de Lisures, Willelmo Burdet, Rob*erto* Basset, Ric*ardo* capell*ano* meo, Ric*ardo* fili*o* Willelmi, Henr*ico* de Nuers, Rob*erto* fili*o* Martini, Rob*erto* de Olepen', Dauide[c] de Audr', Petro de Herdwic et pluribus alijs.

RUBRIC: Comes Dauid (left-hand margin; contemporary with text). Wissenden' (left-hand margin; same hand).

SOURCE: BL MS Cott. Nero C. xii, fo.4v.

PRINTED: J. Nichols, *History and Antiquities of the County of Leicester* (London, 1795–1815), II, i, Appendix, p.128.

NOTES: *a* MS Comit'. *b* MS Rogeri. *c* Sic.

COMMENT: No earlier than 1185 (cf. *CRR*, vi, pp.273–4). By summer 1212 Whissendine had been restored to Helen de Moreville.

It has been stated for no good reason that Hugh de Lisures, a witness, was dead by *c*.1207 (e.g., *VCH Northants*, iii, p.77). He was still presumed alive some years later (PRO E 32/249, m.13; *Red Book of the Exchequer*, ed. H. Hall (RS, 1896), ii, p.618), although he had died by 1215: *Henry of Pytchley's Book of Fees*, ed. W. T. Mellows (Northants Rec. Soc., 1927), p.77n.

16. Ralph de Camoys. Grants to Ralph de Camoys 100*s*. worth of land in Great Stukeley (Hunts), for the fourth part of one knight's service. (29 Sept. 1197 × 1209, probably × 1202).

SOURCE: *Liber Memorandorum Ecclesie de Bernewelle*, ed. J. W. Clark (Cambridge, 1907), p.272.

COMMENT: Earl David offered 200 marks for Ralph's custody in the Exchequer year 1197–8: *PR 10 Richard I*, pp.107, 165. Presumably earlier than No.17. In 1265 this Camoys fee was valued at £9: *Calendar of Inquisitions Miscellaneous*, i, no.715.

17. Robert de la Carneille. Grants to Robert de la Carneille, in fee and heritage, his *manerium* and lands in Great Stukeley, with infangenthief and utfangenthief, with pit and gallows, for one knight's service. (29 Sept. 1197 × 1209, probably × 1202).

Comes d*aui*d frater Regis scocie omnibus baronibus militibus et probis hominibus suis de Honore Huntigdo' francis et Anglis presentibus et futuris sal*utem*. Sciatis me dedisse concessisse et hac carta mea confirmasse Roberto de Kernelio manerium meum et terras per suas rectas diuisas in Magna steuecle. tenend*um* sibi et hered*ibus* suis de me et hered*ibus* meis in feodo et hereditat*e* in bosco et plano in pratis pascuis in terris pasturis et Molendinis et cum omnibus iustis suis pertinenciis. libere. quiete. plenarie. et honorifice cum infangenthef et outfangenthef cum fossa et furcis et cum omnibus suis libertatibus quascumque habui in eadem villa. Faciend*o* inde mihi et hered*ibus* meis inperpetuum seruicium vnius militis. et tenebit sicud aliquis Militum meorum adeo liberius quiecius plenarius honorificencius tenet feodum suum de honore antedicto. Hiis testibus. Roberto de bid*un*. H' du lac. Willelmo du lac. Roberto filio lanceles. H' burd*et*. Eimer*o*. de Acle senescallo. Willelmo de basingham Mar*escallo*. Willelmo de Essebi. Alano fili*o* Allan*i*. Roberto. Alb*o*. Johan*ne* de dag'. Elmaing' de Auib'. Willelmo de laceles. Gerard*o* fili*o* bellan'. ale dapifero. ad*am* de Trembl'. Hosmundo. piuad'.*ᵃ* Baldewino Geiner'. hug*one*. de terl' Reiner*o*. fratre Gilmer*i* alac de kel'.

ENDORSED: Steuecle (xiii cent.).
DESCRIPTION: 7.9 × 5.4 in (20.1 × 13.7 cm). Tongue for sealing *sur simple queue*, and tie above; seal missing.
HAND: Unidentified.
SOURCE: Original, BL Addit. Chart. 22612.
NOTE: *a* The reading of this name is doubtful.
COMMENT: Robert was certainly a proprietor at Great Stukeley by 1209 (PRO E 32/37, m.1), and probably by 1202 (BL MS Cott. Faust. C. i, fo.16v, with *VCH Hunts*, iii, pp.13–14). If H. Burdet, a witness, is the same man as Hugh Burdet of Lowesby (Leics), a tenant of the Huntingdon honour, the later date-limit should be 1202 (*HKF*, ii, p.330). Presumably subsequent to No.16.

18. Clerkenwell priory. Grants in alms to Clerkenwell priory three acres of meadow-land in his manor of Tottenham, in Wild Marsh, beside that acre of meadow-land which King David gave to the nuns, so that these three acres will flank that acre towards the south. (1194 × 1196).

Comes d*aui*d frater Regis Scott' Omnibus hominibus suis francis 7 Anglis presentibus 7 futuris salutem. Sciatis me pro salute anime mee 7 antecessorum meorum 7 heredum meorum dedisse 7 concessisse 7 presenti carta mea confirmasse in puram 7 perpetuam elemosinam deo 7 sancte marie de Clerkenwelle 7 Monialibus ibidem deo seruientibus tres acras prati in manerio meo de toteha*m* in Wildemers. iuxta illam acram prati quam d*au*id Rex scott' dedit predictis Monialibus. ꝫ ita quod hee tres acre erunt a latere predicte acre uersus meridiem. Unde uolo ꝫ precipio. quod eas liberas solutas ꝫ quietas ab omni seculari seruicio ꝫ Exaccione*ᵃ* ꝫ opere seruili teneant. Et libere ꝫ quiete ꝫ honorifice possideant.*ᵇ* his testibus. Ric*ardo* de pec. hugone de lisures. Willelmo reuel. Johanne Mauduit. Nicol*ao* de adles. Willelmo b*ur*det. Magistro petro de Paxt*on*. Ric*ardo*. anfredo. Radulfo. hernaldo. capellanis. benedicto. Mattheo. Ric*ardo*. Galfrido. clericis. ꝫ multis aliis.

ENDORSED: In manerio de Toteham in Wildemersh (late xiii/early xiv cent.).

DESCRIPTION: 4.9 × 8.1 in (12.4 × 20.5 cm). Ruled in ink. Foot folded to depth of 1.4 in (3.5 cm); double slits with tag. Second seal, in light-green wax.

HAND: ? Scribe B.   SOURCE: Original, BL Harl. Chart. 83.C.23.

NOTES: *a* Apparently corrected from xaccione. *b* Corrected from possident.

COMMENT: Dating supplied by Earl David's acquisition of Tottenham in 1194 (*PR 6 Richard I*, p.6) and the death of Richard del Peak by 1196 (*HKF*, i, p.37). Wild Marsh was in the north-eastern part of Tottenham, beside the river Lea. The text of King David I's grant does not survive. At least three of the four chaplains who attested this charter, and two of the four clerks, were Clerkenwell personnel: cf. *Cartulary of St Mary Clerkenwell*, ed. W. O. Hassall (Camden Soc., 1949), nos. 19, 47, 53. Tottenham or the priory itself was apparently the place of issue.

19. Clerkenwell priory. Confirms in alms to Clerkenwell priory 140 acres in the Hanger of Tottenham granted by Robert son of Sewin of Northampton, and the moiety of an island which Ingram had held, four tree trunks for the priory's fire from the earl's wood of Tottenham, and ten swine quit of pannage, as the charter of King William bears witness and confirms. (1194 × 29 Nov. 1208).

Comes Dauid frater Regis Scocc'*ᵃ* Omnibus hominibus suis de Honore de Hunted'*ᵇ* presentibus ꝫ futuri/s/ Salutem Noueritis vniuersi me concessisse. ꝫ presenti carta mea confirmasse. Deo ꝫ Ecclesie Sancte MaRIE de Clerkenewell'*ᶜ* illas septies viginti Acras terre. in Hangre de Toteham. qua/s/ Robertus filius Sewini. de Norhamton' eis ded*it* ꝫ medietatem vnius Insule. quam Engelrammus*ᵈ* tenuerat. ꝫ Quatuor truncos ad ignem suum de Bosco meo de Toteham. ꝫ Decem Porcos quieto/s/ a Pannagio tenenda ꝫ habenda sibi in perpetuam elemosinam. Ita libere ꝫ quiete plenarie ꝫ honorifice. sicut carta Regis Willelmi fratris mei eis testatur ꝫ confirmat. Saluo in omnibus seruitio meo. quod Ego ꝫ Antecessores mei Inde*ᵉ* habuimus. His*ᵉ* testibus Roberto de Basingha*m* tunc Senescallo*ᶠ* meo. Radulfo basset. Roberto basset. Roberto de mortuomari. Regin*aldo* de Acle. Sẏmone de Sancto Licio Willelmo burdet Galfrido de Waltervill'. Magistro Petro de Paxton'. Ricardo filio Will*c*lmi.

ENDORSED: It is not known whether this charter was endorsed. *B*'s rubric reads: De confirmatione comitis Dauid fratris regis Scot'.

DESCRIPTION: 8.2 × 4.3 in (20.7 × 10.8 cm). Foot folded to depth of 0.7 in (1.8 cm); double slits with tag. Second seal, in greenish wax.

HAND: Scribe B.

SOURCE: NRO MS Finch-Hatton 170, fo.62r (drawn facs. of untraced original, formerly *penes* Sir William Le Neve) = *A*. BL MS Cott. Faust. B. ii, fo.12r = *B*. Text above from *A*, which for editorial purposes is treated as an original act, noting major variants in *B*.

PRINTED: *Book of Seals*, no.294 (from *A*). *Cart. of St Mary Clerkenwell*, ed. Hassall, no.17 (from *B*). W. Robinson, *The History and Antiquities of . . . Tottenham*, 2nd edn (London, 1840), i, p.259 (from *B*); not in 1st edn (Tottenham, 1818).

NOTES: *a* Sic; Scott', *B*. *b* Huntedon', *B*. *c* Clerek', *B*. *d* Engelramus, *B*. *e* Word omitted, *B*. *f B* ends here.

COMMENT: The earliest possible date is fixed by Earl David's acquisition of Tottenham. A witness, Reginald of Oakley, had died by 29 Nov. 1208: *Fines sive Pedes Finium*, etc., ed. J. Hunter (Rec. Comm., 1835–44), i, pp.325–6. The name Hanger is preserved in Hanger Lane, in the southern part of Tottenham, towards Hackney. For Robert's grant and the confirmation by King William I see *Cart. of St Mary Clerkenwell*, no.18; *RRS*, ii, no.146.

20. Clerkenwell priory. Confirms to Clerkenwell priory the grant made by Alice, daughter of Roger son of Folbert, and confirmed by her charter, of her part of the inheritance which she had in Tottenham and of that part which she bought from her sister Letia. (1194 × 29 Nov. 1208).

Comes Dauid frater Regis Scocc' Omnibus hominibus suis de Honore de Hunted'. presentibus 7 futuris Salutem. Noueritis. vniuersi quod Ego pro salute mea. 7 Antecessorum meorum concessi. 7 presenti carta mea confirmaui. Ecclesie Sancte MARIE de Clerkenewell'. 7 Monialibus jbidem deo seruientibus. Donationem quam Alicia filia Rogeri. filij Folberti eis fecit. 7 carta sua confirmauit de parte sua hereditatis quam habuit in Toteham 7 de parte illa quam emit a sorore sua Letia. Volo itaque quod Ipse predictas terras teneant. 7 possideant bene 7 in pace. libere 7 quiete. 7 honorifice cum omnibus ad predictas terras pertinentibus. saluo seruitio meo quod Ego 7 Antecessores mei de prefatis terris habuimus. His testibus. Roberto de Basingham tunc senescallo meo. Radulfo basset. Roberto basset. Roberto de mortuomari. Reginaldo de Acle. Symone de Sancto Litio. Willelmo burdet. Galfrido de Wateruill'. Magistro Petro de Paxton. Ricardo filio Willelmi

ENDORSED: In Tothenham (late xiii/early xiv cent.).

DESCRIPTION: 8.7 × 3.6 in (22.2 × 9.2 cm). Ruled; traces of ink. Foot folded to depth of 0.8 in (2 cm); double slits with tag. Second seal, in greenish wax.

HAND: Scribe B.
SOURCE: Original, BL Addit. Chart. 19909. (Copy in BL MS Addit. 5937, fo.160r, with rough drawing of seal.)
COMMENT: Since the witness-lists are identical, it is probable that this charter was issued simultaneously with No. 19.

21. Delapré abbey. *Confirms to Delapré abbey half an acre in Fotheringhay (Northants). (? 1185 × Aug. 1212).
SOURCE: *Mon. Angl.*, v, p.210a.
COMMENT: Earl David was deprived of Fotheringhay castle and probably the manor as well from Aug. 1212, save apparently for a short period from June 1215.

22. Delapré abbey. *Confirms in alms to Delapré abbey one cart roving (? daily) in his wood of Yardley Hastings (Northants), to collect fuel for the needs of the abbey. (? 1185 × 1219).
SOURCE: *Mon. Angl.*, v, p.211b.

23. Stephen of Ecton and his son Stephen. Confirms to Stephen of Ecton and his son Stephen the grant of land in Draughton (Northants) made by William de Audri and confirmed by his charter. King Malcolm had previously given that land to the elder Stephen; and Audri has received the Ectons' homage in David's presence and in his court. (Early summer 1174).

Dauid frater Regis Scoc' Omnibus hominibus suis 7 amicis francis 7 Angl*is*. tam presentibus quam futuris.' Salutem. Sciatis me concessisse 7 hac carta mea presenti confirmasse Stephano de heketon' 7 Stephano filio suo donationem 7 concessionem. quam Willelmus de Audre eis fecit 7 carta sua confirmauit de terra de Drachton' que est de Feudo Regis Scoc' fratris mei 7 meo. 7 quam Rex malcolmus eidem Stephano de Eketon' prius dederat. 7 vnde idem Willelmus homagium eorum cepit coram me 7 incuria*a* mea 7 vnde ab eis cepit. v. Marcas argentj 7 ad opus Matild*is* vxoris sue vnam marcam argentj. Quare uolo 7 firmiter precipio quod hec donatio 7 concessio coram me. in curia mea facta stabil*is* 7 inconcussa 7 firma permaneat. sine omni diminutione uel uexatione quam ipse Willelmus uel aliquis de Successoribus suis eis uel heredibus suis.' inde faciat. Testi*bus*. hug*one* Ridel Dapi*fero*. 7 Willelmo Burdet. 7 hug*one* Giffard'. 7 Willelmo de Rikespaud. 7 Willelmo fil*io* Emme. 7 Waltero de Lindesia. 7 Roberto de Wilebi. 7 Roberto de Monasteriis. 7 Thom*a* clerico de Barton' 7 Roberto fratre suo.

ENDORSED: Donacio Dauid fratris regis Scot'. Stephano de Eketon 7 Stephano filio suo (late xiii cent.).
DESCRIPTION: 6.5 × 5.2 in (16.5 × 13.1 cm). Foot folded to depth of 0.6 in (1.6 cm); plaited cords threaded through four holes in foot and fold. First seal, in light-green wax.
HAND: Unidentified.

SOURCE: Original, BL Harl. Chart. 43.B.6. (See NRO MS Finch-Hatton 170, fo.43v, for drawn facs. of original. A xiv-cent. transcript of original is in NRO Finch-Hatton Muniments, no.2665.)

PRINTED: *Book of Seals*, no.200.

NOTE: *a* Run together in source.

COMMENT: In *Book of Seals*, no.200, notes, the elder Stephen of Ecton is shown to have died *c.*1188. The same source gives 1185 as the *terminus post quem*. But the second witness is probably the William Burdet of Lowesby who may have been deceased by 1184 (*PR 31 Henry II*, p.104); and William de Richespaud, another witness, is without doubt to be identified with the Bedfordshire man of that name who was evidently dead by 1178 (*Harrold Recs.*, p.207). This Huntingdon charter must therefore belong to 1173 × 1174, and the date can be narrowed to Earl David's English campaign in the early summer of 1174. Two charters given by William de Audri for the Ectons survive: *Book of Seals*, no.220; NRO Finch-Hatton Muniments, no.2665 (4th charter). The Draughton fee had been a disputed tenancy, Audri having claimed it as his wife's *maritagium*. For King Malcolm IV's grant to Stephen of Ecton *senior* see *RRS*, i, no.150.

Fitz Roger, Robert, *see* No.70.

24. Robert Furmage. Grants to Robert Furmage and his heirs the toft in Dundee which belonged to Philip the clerk, for an annual rent of 1*d.* payable at Michaelmas. (? 1185 × 4 Dec. 1214).

Comes*a* Dauid frater regis Scoc', omnibus has lit*ter*as visuris vel audituris, salutem. Sciatis me dedisse et concessisse et hac presenti carta mea confirmasse Rob*erto* Furmage toftum quod fuit Philippi clerici in Dunde, tenend*um* et habend*um* et illi et heredibus suis de me et heredibus meis libere et quiete, reddendo annuatim vnum denarium ad festum sancti Mich*aeli*s pro omnibus seruicijs. Hijs test*ibus* Henrico fili*o* comitis, Bartholomeo [de]*b* Mortim*er*, Rob*erto* Basseth', Will*elmo* de Folevill', Constantino de Mortim*er*, Rob*erto* fili*o* Rob*er*ti, Ricard*o* fili*o* Willelmi, Adam fili*o* Alani, Malcolmo de Garuiach', Ricardo clerico et multis alijs.

RUBRIC: Carta comiti/s/ Dauid de tofto de Dunde (red, contemporary with text).

SOURCE: NLS MS Adv. 34.4.2, fo.82r.

PRINTED: *Arbroath Liber*, i, no.135.

NOTES: *a* Large red initial and prominent 'o'. *b* Omitted in source.

COMMENT: Philip was Earl David's clerk and his estate steward in Scotland. Furmage later sold this toft to his kinsman Robert, who was Philip's nephew: *Arbroath Liber*, i, no.136 (apparently 1209 × 4 Dec. 1214; cf. D. E. R. Watt, *A Biographical Dictionary of Scottish Graduates to A.D. 1410* (Oxford, 1977), p.483).

25. Alan of Galloway, Constable of Scotland. *Grants to Alan son of Roland, Constable (of Scotland), the whole of Whissendine, with the exception of certain lands, for one knight's service. (1185 × 2 April 1212, apparently 19 Dec. 1200 ×).

SOURCE: *CRR*, vi, p.280.

COMMENT: Alan had a prior claim to this fee and other interests in the Huntingdon honour through his mother Helen de Moreville. When Helen established her right to the entire property by process of law in 1212, Alan was entitled to demand an exchange (*PBKJ*, iv, nos.4668, 4743; *CRR*, vii, p.213), which he may have received in Harringworth, Northants (cf. *HKF*, ii, p.337). The earliest possible date of Earl David's charter is fixed by *CRR*, vi, pp.273–4. But if the source is correct in saying that Alan was already Constable of Scotland, then the act belongs no earlier than 19 Dec. 1200 (*RRS*, ii, p.37). See further *CRR*, vi, p.242.

26. Hugh Giffard. Grants a feu to Hugh Giffard. (Probably × 1174).

SOURCE: No.27.

COMMENT: The whereabouts of this feu are uncertain. It can possibly be identified with either *Hadgillin* or *Roskelin* in Dundee-*scira*, or both: see for these interests of Hugh Giffard *RRS*, ii, no.149; *St Andrews Liber*, p.59. Later, Giffard acquired Fintry, another appurtenance of Dundeeshire, from Earl David (No.27).

27. Hugh Giffard. Grants to Hugh Giffard, in feu and heritage, Fintry (Angus), with soke and sake, toll, team and infangenthief, with pit and gallows, in augmentation of the other feu which the earl had given him, to be held together for half of one knight's service. (1173 × 1174, possibly 1185, March ×).

Dau*i*D Comes huntend' frater Regis scott'. Omnibus hominibus 7 amicis suis francis 7 anglis scotis 7 GalWalensibus clericis 7 laicis salutem. Sciant presentes 7 futuri me dedisse 7 concessisse 7 hac Carta mea Confirmasse hug*oni* giffard fintre per suas Rectas diuisas. cum omnibus Natiuis eiusdem terre. in aumento alterius feodi sui quod ei antea dederam. Tenend*am* sibi 7 heredibus suis de me 7 heredibus meis in feodo 7 hereditate. libere 7 quiete plenarie 7 honorifice. in bosco 7 plano in pratis 7 pascuis in Moris 7 Caciis in aquis 7 stangnis 7 Molendinis. Cum socke 7 sacke 7 tol 7 tem 7 infangenthef cum fossa 7 furcis. 7 cum omnibus aliis Rectitudinibus 7 consuetudinibus ad eam iuste pertinentibus. Quare volo ut ipse hug*o* 7 heredes sui teneant 7 possideant hanc prenominatam terram fintre cum alio feodo suo quod de me tenet. ita libere 7 quiete plenarie 7 honorifice. sicut ille militum meorum qui melius liberius quietius plenarius aut honorificentius feodum suum tenet 7 possidet; faciendo mihi 7 heredibus meis de hoc feodo. 7 de alio feodo quod ei antea dederam. seruicium dimid*ii* militis. Test*ibus* Seier*o* de tenes constab*ulario* meo. hug*one* burdet. Willelmo fil*io* emme. alano filio hug*onis*. Jordan*o* Ridel. Willelmo de sancto mich*ae*le. Roberto clerico meo;

ENDORSED: ffÿntre. (xv cent.).

DESCRIPTION: 6.9 × 4.9 in (17.6 × 12.4 cm). Foot folded to depth of about

0.9 in (2.3 cm); four green cords threaded through double holes in foot and fold. First seal, in green wax.

HAND: Scribe A.

SOURCE: Original, SRO GD 28/4.

PRINTED: *Calendar of Writs preserved at Yester House, 1166–1503*, ed. C.C.H. Harvey and J. Macleod (Scottish Rec. Soc., 1930), no.4, dated 1178 × *c*.1190.

COMMENT: David's title points to a date in or after 1185. On the other hand, the charter is sealed with his first seal, and this indicates that it was issued earlier, viz. in 1173 or 1174, when he claimed rights over the Huntingdon earldom and may have adopted the comital style. Further, the scribe penned two other originals in this collection, and these can be dated 1172, 1174 (Nos.28, 34). A date within the period 1173–4 would also be consistent with the evidence that at least five of the seven witnesses were then in the earl's following. The possibility remains, however, that the first seal continued to be attached to charters for a short time after David's accession as earl of Huntingdon in March 1185, until the matrix for the new seal he required had been struck.

28. Gilbert, 'nepos' of Bishop Andrew of Caithness. Grants to Gilbert, *nepos* of the bishop of Caithness, in feu and heritage, Monorgan (in Longforgan, Perthshire), for a reddendo of a goshawk still in its first year. Markinch. (1172 × 2 April).

*Daui*D fRater Regis Scott'. Omnibus hominibus 7 amicis suis clericis 7 laicis salutem. Sciant presentes 7 futuri me dedisse 7 Concessisse 7 hac Carta mea Confirmasse Gileberto Nepoti episcopi katenessis Monorgrun per suas Rectas diuisas tenend*am* sibi 7 heredibus suis de me 7 heredibus meis in feudo 7 hereditate in bosco 7 plano in terris 7 pratis in pascuis 7 aquis 7 in Omnibus Justis pertinenciis suis libere 7 quiete ab omnibus seruciis*ᵃ* 7 Consuetud[in]*ᵇ*ibus Reddendo inde mihi singulis annis unum hosturum Sorum. Test*ibus* Dunec*ano* Com*ite*. matheo*ᶜ* electo de abredon. Roberto de quinci. hug*one* Giff*ard*. Willelmo fil*io* Emme. Roberto de kernell'. Gilleb*erto* fil*io* Rich*eri* Willelmo de [   ].*ᵈ* Rogero de [Valonii]s.*ᵉ* Roberto clerico meo. Willelmo de Sancto mich*ael*e. apud Marking.

ENDORSED: No medieval endorsement visible; parchment obscured by repair work.

DESCRIPTION: 6.4 × 4.4 in (16.2 × 11.2 cm). Foot folded to depth of about 0.8 in (2 cm); single slits with leather tag. First seal, in dark-green wax.

HAND: Scribe A.

SOURCE: Original, NLS Chart. 7710 (acquired at sale of Phillipps MSS, Sotheby and Co., 26 June 1967). (Copy in NLS MS Adv. 31.2.4, p.11, by Alexander Brown from original, then *penes* Henry Crawfurd of Monorgan, Collector of Customs in Dundee, 1785.)

PRINTED: *Art at Auction, 1966–7* (London, 1967), p.353 (facs. of original; size reduced). *Bibliotheca Phillippica: Catalogue of the celebrated collection of*

MSS formed by Sir Thomas Phillipps, Bt. (1792–1872), new ser., part iii (Sotheby and Co., London, 1967), p.23 (description of original, with facs., size reduced, on facing page).

NOTES: *a* Sic. *b* Letters obliterated by tear. *c* Corrected from andr (Andr*ea* = Andrew, bishop of Caithness). *d* Name illegible; Haya in MS copy. *e* About seven letters badly damaged; Valoniis is the probable reading. Grem, given in MS copy, is unacceptable.

COMMENT: Matthew was consecrated bishop of Aberdeen on 2 April 1172. The village of Markinch, where the act was presumably issued, belonged to the first witness, Earl Duncan of Fife. The seal was once preserved in a fine leather case, perhaps made for it *c.*1400, which is now deposited separately in the National Museum of Antiquities of Scotland, Edinburgh. The decoration comprises leaf-ornament in relief on a ground patterned with impressions of a small punch.

For King William I's confirmation of this charter see *RRS*, ii, no.133.

29. William de Harcourt. Grants to William de Harcourt custody of the land and heir of John of Sproxton. (1212 × 1219).

SOURCE: *CRR*, xii, no.459; also in *Bracton's Note Book,* ed. F.W. Maitland (London, 1887), ii, no.708.

COMMENT: John of Sproxton, a tenant of the Huntingdon honour, was still alive in 1212 (cf. *HKF*, ii, p.318). Harcourt served as a steward of King John's household: S. Painter, *The Reign of King John* (Baltimore, 1949), p.87.

30. Robert Hardy. *Grants to Robert Hardy one virgate in Godmanchester (Hunts). (1190 × May 1212).

SOURCE: *Rot. de Ob.*, p.542.

COMMENT: Earl David was lord of Godmanchester from 1190 to May 1212. On Robert Hardy of Sudbury (now lost) in Eaton Socon, Beds, see *Cartulary of Bushmead Priory*, ed. G.H. Fowler and J. Godber (BHRS, 1945), nos.202–3. The manor of Sudbury pertained to the Huntingdon honour: *HKF*, ii, pp.310–12; *VCH Beds*, iii, pp.195–6. BL MS Cott. Faust. C. i, fos.6v, 7r, 11r, give details of a Robert Hardy of Huntingdon.

31. Harrold priory. Confirms in alms to Harrold priory the grants made by Sampson Fortis and Robert, son of Pain de Briouze, as the charters of Malcolm and William, kings of Scotland, bear witness. (? 1185 × 1219).

Carta Dauid comitis Huntingdon' facta monialibus huius loci qua confirmat omnes donaciones quas fecit*a* Sampson Fortis et Robertus filius Pagani de Brausea*b* in ecclesijs, in decimis, in terris, in aquis, in pratis, in pascuis, in piscacione, in bosco, in pasnagio, et in omnibus alijs rebus, ut eas habeant in perpetuam elemosinam liberas et quietas, ab omni seculari seruicio absolutas, sicut carte eorum testantur et sicut carte Malcolmi*c* et Willelmi regum*d* Scocie testantur.

SOURCE: BL MS Lansdowne 391, fo.5r–v (abstract of the original full text, which is lost).

PRINTED: *Harrold Recs.*, no.6 (translation).

NOTES: *a* Sic. *b* Reading uncertain. *c* MS adds filij sui (sic). *d* MS Willm̄ regē.

COMMENT: See *RRS*, i, nos.139, 149, 180; ii, no.56.

32. Hinchingbrooke priory. *Grants to Hinchingbrooke priory 'Tower Meadow' ('pratum turris') and two virgates in (Great) Stukeley. (1185 × *c*.1194).

SOURCE: BL Addit. Chart. 33595.

COMMENT: The source, a confirmation charter by Hugh of Avalon, bishop of Lincoln, is witnessed by Mr Robert of Bedford, who had died by *c*.1194: John Le Neve, *Fasti Ecclesiae Anglicanae, 1066–1300*, iii: *Lincoln*, ed. D. E. Greenway (London, 1977), pp.13, 116. Earl David's grant is also referred to in a charter by Archbishop Hubert Walter: BL Addit. Chart. 33596 (1195 × 1198). The land conveyed is apparently the same as that claimed by Hinchingbrooke in Great Stukeley *c*.1303 'par le donn et le graunt le comite Davy frere le Roy de Escoce' (BL Addit. Chart. 34093).

33. Hinchingbrooke priory. Confirms to Hinchingbrooke priory the annual rent of 30*d*. owed by Andrew of Ketton to William de Camera in Little Hambleton (Rutland), which William gave to the nuns in alms, as is contained in his charter. (1185 × 1215).

Omnibus sancte matris ecclesie fil*iis* presentibus ⁊ futuris. Comes d*au*id frater Regis scot' Salutem. Noueritis me caritatis intuitu concessisse ⁊ presenti carta mea confirmasse deo ⁊ sancto Jacobo de hunted' ⁊ monial*ibus* Ibidem deo seruientibus redditum triginta denari*orum* quos Andr*eas* de keten' annuatim debuit Willelmo de camera de molend*ino* de parua hameld' ⁊ de duobus pratis quos ipse Willelmus in elemosinam dedit predictis monialibus sicut in carta ipsius Willelmj quam ipse habent continetur. Hiis testibus. Hug*one* de lisor'. Walkel*ino* fil*io* stephani. Roberto basset. Sim*one* de seinliz. Rob*erto* de la Kerneill'. phil*ippo* monacho. ⁊ multis aliis

ENDORSED: hamelton'. (xv cent.).

DESCRIPTION: 6.1 × 3 in (15.5 × 7.6 cm). Foot folded to depth of about 0.7 in (1.9 cm); single slits with long tag. Seal missing.

HAND: Unidentified.

SOURCE: Original, BL Addit. Chart. 34255.

COMMENT: Simon de Senlis did not join Earl David's following until 1185. The first witness, Hugh de Lisures, was dead by 1215 (No.15, comment).

34. Holyrood abbey. Confirms to Holyrood abbey the church of (Great) Paxton (Hunts) granted by King Malcolm, as Malcolm's charter and the charter of King William bear witness and confirm. Haddington. (1174 × May).

D*au*iD fRater Regis Scott' Episcopo lincolniensi ⁊ vniuersis Sancte Matris ecclesie filiis clericis ⁊ laicis tam futuris quam presentibus tocius comitatus de huntend' salutem Sciatis me Concessisse 7 hac Carta mea Confirmasse ecclesie Sancte Crucis que est iusta edenesburc 7 fratribus ibidem deo seruientibus Ecclesiam de pacstonia quam Malc*olmus* Rex frater meus eis dedit inperpetuam*ᵃ* elemosinam. cum Omnibus iustis pertinenciis suis 7 libertatibus sicut Carta sua 7 Carta. W'. Regis fratris mei eis Testantur 7 Confirmant; Test*ibus* hug*one* Giff*ard*. alexand*ro* de Sancto Martin*o* Rob*erto* clerico meo. Willelmo de Sancto Mich*aele*. apvD hadintu*n*;

ENDORSED: dauit de paxtun. (xiii cent.); Tercia. (xiv cent.).

DESCRIPTION: 6.6 × 4.1 in (16.7 × 10.4 cm). Foot folded to depth of about 0.7 in (1.9 cm); single slits, with a narrow tie cut from right-hand corner of top of fold. Seal and tag torn away and lost.

HAND: Scribe A.

SOURCE: Original, Lincoln, Lincolnshire Archives Office, Dean and Chapter records, Dij/91/1/80. (Copied in MS 'Registrum', no.282.)

PRINTED: *RAL*, iii, no.813, with facs., size reduced, facing p.158, and dated *c*.1185 × 1190.

NOTE: *a* Run together in source.

COMMENT: The lack of comital style suggests that this charter in Earl David's Huntingdon series passed before 1185. Further, the scribe also wrote No.28, which can be assigned to 1172. These two *acta* have other similarities. Both were issued in Scotland and witnessed by Hugh Giffard, Robert the clerk and William de St Michael. They seemingly belong to the same period of David's career, and the most likely date of the Holyrood confirmation is the eve of his campaign in England in 1174, when the canons would have been particularly anxious to secure ratification of their rights in Great Paxton from their new lord. The burgh of Haddington, where the act passed, was held in dower by Countess Ada de Warenne until her death in 1178.

The royal charters mentioned in the text are printed in *RRS*, i, no.197; ii, no.41.

Huntingdon, priory of St James, *see* Nos.32–3.

35. Kelso abbey. Grants in alms to Kelso abbéy, after the death of the son of Ralph *de camera*, the churches of Campsie and Antermony (in Campsie, Stirlingshire) in Lennox. Roxburgh. (1174 × May).

Vniuersis*ᵃ* sancte matris ecclesie filiis, D*au*id frater regis Scott', salutem. Sciant presentes et futuri me, post dicessum filii Radulphi de camera, in liberam et perpetuam elemosinam pro animabus omnium antecessorum meorum et pro salute Willelmi regis fratris mei et mea dedisse et concessisse et hac mea carta confirmasse ecclesie sancte Marie de Kelch' et monachis ibidem Deo seruientibus ecclesiam de Camsy et ecclesiam de Altermunin in Leuenas cum terris et decimis et omnibus aliis rectitudinibus ad easdem ecclesias iuste pertinentibus. Quare uolo ut ipsi prenominatas ecclesias ita libere et quiete, plenar*ie* et honorifice tene/a/nt et posside/a/nt sicut ipsi alias ecclesias suas in regno regis fratris mei liberius, quietius et honorificencius tenent et possident. Test*ibus* Hug*one* Giff*ard*, Willelmo fil*io* Emme, Roberto de Kernell', Will*elmo* de sancto Mich*aele*, Willelmo de Mortem*er*, Bernard*o* fil*io* Brieni, Waltero Giff*ard*. Apud Rokesburg'.

RUBRIC: Carta super ecclesias de Camsy et de Altermunyn' cum terris et decimis in Lewenas (red, contemporary with text).

SOURCE: NLS MS Adv. 34.5.1, fo.91r.

PRINTED: *Kelso Liber*, i, no.226.

NOTE: *a* Initial interlined in red.

COMMENT: See above, pp.14–15, 22. Both benefices passed to the bishopric of Glasgow following a later grant (1208 × 1214) by Alwyn II, earl of Lennox, and Antermony subsequently became a chapel of Campsie: I. B. Cowan, *The Parishes of Medieval Scotland* (Scottish Rec. Soc., 1967), pp.6, 26. The son of Ralph *de camera* was presumably the incumbent in 1174. On Ralph, an important chamber official of the Scottish crown, see *RRS*, ii, p.33.

36. Priory of La Chaise-Dieu-du-Theil (dép. Eure). Grants in alms to the priory of La Chaise-Dieu an annual rent of one silver mark at Michaelmas from the profits of his mill of Fotheringhay. (19 Aug. 1190 × 1194).

Omnibus sancte matris ecclesie filijs. presentibus. 7 futuris. Comes dauid frater regis scocie salutem. SciatiS me dedisse. 7 concessisse. 7 hac carta mea confirmasse deo 7 ecclesie sancte Marie de casa dei. 7 monialibus ibidem deo seruientibus inpuram.*a* 7 liberam. 7 perpetuam elemosinam tenendam de me. 7 heredibus meis unam Marcam argenti. ad festum sancti Michael*is*. annuatim recipiendam de exitu molendini mei. de frodRigéé pro anima patris mei. 7 pro anima Matris Mee. 7 pro salute anime méé. 7 anime comitisse. Matil'. Sponse Méé. 7 pro anima. Regis. d*au*id. avi mei. 7 pro anima. Malcolmi regis fratris Mei. 7 pro anima. Thome bigot. 7 pro animabus antecessorum meorum. 7 successorum. T*estibus*. W. de Warennja. Rog*ero* conestab*ulario*. Cestrie. Eustacio de uesci. Rob*erto*. de Mortuo Mari. HenR*ico* filio Meo. Simon*e* de sancto litio. Ric*ardo*. de lindesia. Rob*erto* de basingham. Will*elmo*. de essebi. Will*elmo*. de foleuill'. Regin*aldo*. de acle. Will*elmo*. daco. Rob*erto* de lakerneill' cum multis aliis.*b*

ENDORSED: ffrodrige De j marc*a* redd*itus* concess*a* Priorisse de Casa Dei (late xiii cent.); Non irrotulatur quia domus de Eton' nichil inde h*abet* ut intelligitur (late xiii cent.); Carta Comit*is* Dauid fratris Regis Scotie (xvi/xvii cent.).

DESCRIPTION: 5.7 × 4.7 in (14.4 × 11.9 cm). Foot folded to depth of about 1.4 in (3.6 cm); double slits with tag. Second seal, in natural wax.

HAND: Unidentified.

SOURCE: Original, BL Addit. Chart. 47386.

NOTES: *a* Run together in source. *b* Final 's' extended sideways in order to finish last line of text.

COMMENT: Dated by Earl David's marriage and by the appearance of

Roger, constable of Chester, in the witness-list without the style 'de Lacy', indicating a date before he inherited the honours of Clitheroe and Ponte-fract in 1194 (*VCH Lancs,* i, p.300). W. de Warenne, the first witness, is probably one and the same man as David's cousin William de Warenne of Wormegay (d.1209). Eustace de Vesci, lord of Alnwick, also attests. The presence of these important men in the witness-clause suggests an especially weighty occasion. It is possible that Thomas Bigod, for the good of whose soul, among others, the gift was made, can be identified with a probable son of Roger, second earl of Norfolk, on whom see *Cambridge Law Journal,* x (1950), pp.96–7 with n.86. This Thomas was apparently still alive in 1196, but the use of 'pro anima' in the text is not conclusive proof that Thomas Bigod was already dead (cf. *EYC,* iv, pp.xxvii–xxx). Alternatively, it may be that the *terminus ante quem* should be set later than 1194, at 29 Nov. 1208 when Reginald of Oakley was deceased. David's relationship with Thomas remains mysterious, but provides some evidence for a connection between the Scottish royal house and the senior Bigod line a generation before William the Lion's daughter Isabel was married to Roger Bigod, future fourth earl of Norfolk, in 1225.

37. Lindores abbey. Grants to his abbey of Lindores all the churches in his gift in *Scotia,* with their chapels and teinds and lands, by those marches which they had when the boundaries of Garioch were ascertained, together with the men bound to the lands and their issue. (*c.*1190 × 8 March 1195).

Omnibus*a* hoc scriptum visuris uel audituris, comes Dauid frater regis Scott', salutem. Sciatis me dedisse, concessisse et hac carta mea confirmasse Deo et abbacie mee de Lundors omnes ecclesias que fuerunt in donacione mea in Scocia cum capellis et decimis et terris ad ipsas pertinentibus per illas diuisas quas habuerunt quando feci mensurare terram de Garuiach et cum hominibus manentibus in ipsis terris et eorum sequela, et ut habeant omnes libertates in terris meis quas alii habent in regno Scocie manentes in terris aliarum ecclesiarum. Quare uolo et firmiter precipio ut nullus successorum meorum aliquod grauamen uel molestiam faciat predicte abbacie contra hanc meam concessionem. Hiis test*ibus* Dauid de Lindes', Walkelino filio Stephani, Willelmo Wascelyn, Roberto Basset, Roberto filio Roberti, Wil-lelmo et D*aui*d capellanis, Walkelino de Nuers, Gilberto Dolepain, Roberto filio Martini et multis aliis.

RUBRIC: Carta com*itis* D*aui*d de terris ecclesiarum de Garuiach (red, contemporary with text).

SOURCE: Caprington Castle, Kilmarnock, MS Lindores Cartulary, fo.32r–v.

PRINTED: *Lind. Cart.,* no.4.

NOTE: *a* Large red initial.

COMMENT: Arguably the earliest of Earl David's surviving Lindores *acta.* It apparently belongs before Pope Celestine III's letter of 8 March 1195, which solemnly confirms the churches granted here (*Lind. Cart.,* no.93),

and may well predate the first known charter of foundation (No.37A).
We shall not be far from the mark if we accept *c.*1190 as the *terminus
post quem*: cf. above, pp.93–4.

37A. Lindores abbey. *A foundation charter of Lindores abbey. (*c.*1190
× 8 March 1195).
SOURCE: *RRS*, ii, no.363; also mentioned in *Lind. Cart.*, no.93.
COMMENT: See the discussion above, pp.93–4.

38. Lindores abbey. Grants in alms to Lindores abbey the church of
Conington (Hunts), for its own uses. (*c.*1190 × 8 March 1195, probably late
1194 or early 1195).

Uniuersis sancte [matris ecclesie filiis ꝛ fidelibus Comes] D*aui*D. frater
Regis. Scot'. salutem. Nouerint omnes tam presentes quam futuri me
dedisse. ꝛ concessisse. [ꝛ hac mea carta confirmasse deo ꝛ] ecclesie sancte
marie ꝛ Sancti andree de lundores ꝛ monachis ibidem deo seruientibus in
[liberam]. ꝛ pur[am ꝛ perpetuam ele]mosinam ecclesiam de Cunigton'.
cum omnibus ad eam iuste [perti]nentibus. Quare uolo ut predicti m[onachi
habeant ꝛ] possideant prenominatam ecclesiam ad proprios usus ꝛ ad
sustentationem eorundem monachorum ita quiete libere ꝛ ho[nor]ifice
sicut aliqua abbacia in episcopatu lincolniensi [aliquam] ecclesiam quietius
liberius ꝛ honorificentius tenet. ꝛ possidet. His. T*estibus*. H*en*rico. Abbate
de Sancto thoma. Will*el*mo ꝛ Ric*ar*do. capellanis. Com*itis*. d*au*id. Galfr*id*o
clerico. S*y*mon*e*. de Saintliz. Walkel*in*o. fil*io*. Stephan*i*. Rob*er*to. de Betun'.
Malcolm*o*. fil*io*. Bertoldi. Nichol*a*o. de adles. Bartholom*e*o. monacho. Rob-
*er*to. Basset. Will*el*mo. Burdet. Will*el*mo. fil*io*. Walt*er*i. [cum multis aliis.]
ENDORSED: Medieval endorsements possibly obliterated by damage.
B's rubric reads: Carta com*itis* D*au*id de ecclesia de Cunington' (red,
contemporary with text).
DESCRIPTION: 7 × 2.6 in (17.7 × 6.5 cm). Foot folded to depth of 0.6 in
(1.5 cm); double slits with tag. Seal missing.
HAND: Unidentified.
SOURCE: Original, Lincoln, Lincolnshire Archives Office, Dean and
Chapter records, Dij/61/4/1 (badly mutilated) = *A*. Caprington Castle,
Kilmarnock, MS Lindores Cartulary, fo.35r = *B*. Text above from *A*, with
matter lost through injury supplied from *B* and placed within square
brackets. For this purpose, *B* is transcribed according to the rules followed
for originals.
PRINTED: *RAL*, iii, no.796 (from *A*, supplemented by *B*). *Lind. Cart.*,
no.13 (from *B*).
COMMENT: Confirmed by Celestine III on 8 March 1195. The witness-lists
in Nos.39–41 are similar to that above and all four *acta* must have been
issued within the same short space of time. The text of No.40 repeats the
terms of the present charter, but the former was doubtless given on the same
occasion as No.41 – each act is attested by the same persons – and No.41,

Earl David's grant of Whissendine church to Lindores abbey, is not referred to in Celestine's letter of 1195. No.41 is a duplicate of No.39. On the basis of this information, it appears that the earliest in the series is the text edited above. Nos. 39 and 41 (and No.40) were given only slightly later, but too late for their subject-matter to be known at Rome in March 1195. They had to wait for papal ratification until 20 March 1199 (*Lind. Cart.*, no.94).

39. Lindores abbey. Grants in alms to Lindores abbey the church of Whissendine (Rutland). (1195 × 20 March 1199, probably *c*.March 1195).

Uniuersis*a* sancte matris ecclesie filiis et fidelibus tam presentibus quam futuris, comes Dauid frater regis Scott', salutem. Sciatis me dedisse et concessisse et hac carta mea confirmasse Deo et ecclesie sancte Marie et sancti Andree de Lundors et monachis ibidem Deo seruientibus in liberam et puram et perpetuam elemosinam ecclesiam de Wyssindene cum omnibus ad eam iuste pertinentibus. Quare uolo ut predicti monachi habeant et possideant prenominatam ecclesiam ita libere, quiete et honorifice sicut aliqua abbacia in episcopatu Lincolniensi aliquam ecclesiam quietius, liberius et honorificencius tenet et possidet. Hiis testibus Henrico abbate de sancto Thoma, Willelmo et Ricardo capellanis comitis Dauid, Gaufrido clerico eius, Philippo clerico eius, Henrico filio comitis, Roberto Basset, Willelmo Burdet, Gaufredo [de]*b* Wateruile, Waltero Olifard, Radulfo [de]*b* Cames, Gilleberto [de]*b* Olepain, Walchelino [de]*b* Nuerres.

RUBRIC: Carta comitis Dauid de ecclesia de Wissinden' (red, contemporary with text). Nota de ecclesiis nobis donatis in Anglia (top of fo.34v; ? xvi cent.).
SOURCE: Caprington Castle, Kilmarnock, MS Lindores Cartulary, fo.34r–v.
PRINTED: *Lind. Cart.*, no.11.
NOTES: *a* Red initial. *b* Supplied editorially.

40. Lindores abbey. Grants in alms to Lindores abbey the church of Conington. (1195 × 20 March 1199, probably *c*.March 1195).

Comes*a* Dauid frater regis Scott', omnibus sancte matris ecclesie filiis presentibus et futuris, salutem. Noueritis me caritatis intuitu et pro salute anime mee et antecessorum et successorum meorum dedisse et concessisse et hac carta mea confirmasse Deo et ecclesie sancte Marie et sancti Andree de Lundors et monachis ibidem Deo seruientibus in puram et perpetuam elemosinam ecclesiam de Cunigton' cum omnibus ad eam iuste pertinentibus. Quare uolo quod predicti monachi habeant et possideant prenominatam ecclesiam ita quiete, libere et honorifice sicut aliqua abbacia in episcopatu Lincolniensi aliquam ecclesiam quiecius, liberius et honorificencius tenet et possidet. Hiis testibus Henrico abbate de sancto Thoma, Willelmo et Ricardo capellanis, magistro Petro de Paxton', Ricardo filio Willelmi, Philippo clerico, Petro de Hach, Henrico de Scott', Roberto

Basset, Simone de Seynliz, Roberto de Basingham,[b] Ricardo de Lindes',
Willelmo Burdet, Galfrido de Wateruile, Waltero Olifard, Radulfo de
Camais, Gilberto de Holepen', Walkelino de Nuers, Henrico de Nuers.
RUBRIC: Duplicacio carte de Cunigton' (red, contemporary with text).
SOURCE: Caprington Castle, Kilmarnock, MS Lindores Cartulary,
fo.35r–v.
PRINTED: *Lind. Cart.*, no.14.
NOTES: *a* Turquoise initial. *b* MS Basingh.
COMMENT: This charter is similar to, but not identical with, No.38. The
passing of two charters for the same grant evokes the contemporary practice
of issuing duplicates in the Scottish royal chancery, the precise reasons for
this remaining unclear: *RRS*, ii, p.83. Perhaps we can accept that the
monks' need of a second proof of title was prompted by anxiety over their
ability to control this remote church – its twin, Whissendine, was certainly a
disputed benefice (above, pp.146, 148). The originals of both *acta* were
apparently still available in the abbey's archives c.1260 for copying into its
cartulary. The one original now extant, No.38, was later exhibited to the
diocesan, was then retained by his clerks, and remains today at Lincoln.

41. Lindores abbey. Grants in alms to Lindores abbey the church of
Whissendine. (1195 × 20 March 1199, probably c.March 1195).

Comes[a] Dauid frater regis Scott', omnibus sancte matris ecclesie filiis
presentibus et futuris, salutem. Noueritis me caritatis intuitu et pro salute
anime mee et antecessorum et successorum meorum dedisse et concessisse
et hac carta mea confirmasse Deo et ecclesie sancte Marie et sancti Andree de
Lundors et monachis ibidem Deo seruientibus in puram et perpetuam
elemosinam ecclesiam de Wissinden' cum omnibus ad eam iuste pertinentibus. Quare uolo quod predicti monachi habeant et possideant prenominatam ecclesiam ita libere, quiete et honorifice sicut aliqua abbacia in
episcopatu Lincolniensi aliquam ecclesiam quietius, liberius et honorifi-
centius tenet et possidet. Hiis testibus Henrico abbate de sancto Thoma,
Willelmo et Ricardo capellanis, magistro Petro de Paxton', Ricardo filio
Willelmi, Philippo clerico, Petro de Hach, Henrico de Scott', Roberto
Basset, Simone de Seynliz, Roberto de Basingham,[b] Ricardo de Lindes',
Willelmo Burdet, Galfrido de Wateruile, Waltero Olifard,[c] Radulfo de
Kamais, Gilberto de Holep', Walkelino de Nuers, Henrico de Nuers.
RUBRIC: Duplicacio carte de Wissinden' (red, contemporary with text).
SOURCE: Caprington Castle, Kilmarnock, MS Lindores Cartulary,
fos.34v–5r.
PRINTED: *Lind. Cart.*, no.12.
NOTES: *a* Turquoise initial. *b* MS Basingh. *c* MS Olifrard, with first 'r'
underlined for deletion.
COMMENT: This charter is similar to, but not identical with, No.39; on the
duplication see No.40, comment.

42. Lindores abbey. Confirms to Lindores abbey that ploughgate (in *Balemawe* in Newtyle, Angus) granted in alms by his daughter Ada, wife of Malise son of Earl Ferteth (of Strathearn), as her charter bears witness. (1195 × 17 March 1199).

Omnibus*a* sancte matris ecclesie filiis et fidelibus, comes Dauid frater regis Scott', salutem. Sciant presentes et futuri me concessisse et hac carta mea confirmasse Deo et ecclesie sancte Marie et sancti Andree de Lundors et monachis ibidem Deo seruientibus illam carucatam terre quam Ada filia mea, uxor Malisii filij comitis Fertheth, eis dedit, tenendam in liberam et puram et perpetuam elemosinam ita libere, quiete, plenarie et honorifice sicut carta predicte Ade testatur. Hiis testibus Henrico abbate de Aberbrothoc, Malisio filio Fertheth, Henrico filio comitis Dauid, Willelmo Reuel, Nicholao de Anes, Willelmo Burdeth, Roberto Basset, Galfrido de Wateruile.

RUBRIC: Confirmacio comitis Dauid de carucata terre de Balemawe (red, contemporary with text). Confirmacio comitis David de carucata (foot of fo.33v, with other words apparently cut away; ? xvi cent.).
SOURCE: Caprington Castle, Kilmarnock, MS Lindores Cartulary, fos.33v–4r.
PRINTED: *Lind. Cart.*, no.9.   NOTE: *a* Turquoise initial.
COMMENT: Not ratified by Celestine III on 8 March 1195, but confirmed in No.44, which shows that Balemawe (now lost) lay in Newtyle. Ada's charter survives: *Lind. Cart.*, no.36 ('in uilla de Balemagh').

43. Lindores abbey. Grants in alms to Lindores abbey the whole island of Mugdrum, and all the fisheries beside it in the river Tay, reserving a tidal fish-trap at *Colcrike*. (29 Sept. 1197 × 1198).

Uniuersis*a* sancte matris ecclesie filiis et fidelibus, comes Dauid frater regis Scoc',*b* salutem. Sciant tam presentes quam futuri me dedisse et concessisse et hac carta mea confirmasse Deo et ecclesie sancte Marie et sancti Andree de Lundors et monachis ibidem Deo seruientibus et seruituris totam insulam que uocatur Redinche et omnes piscarias in They iuxta prenominatam insulam, preter vnam piscariam meam, scilicet vnam iharam ad Colcrike.*c* Tenebunt autem predictam insulam in puram et perpetuam elemosinam ita libere, quiete, plenarie et honorifice sicut alias terras suas ex dono meo liberius, quiecius, plenius et honorificencius tenent et possident. Hiis testibus domino A. abbate de Dunfermelyn,*d* comite·Duncano, Malisio filio*e* comitis Ferteht,*f* Malcolmo filio comitis Duncani, Walkelino filio Stephani, Nicholao de Anas, Roberto Basset, Johanne de Wiltun, W. Olifard,*g* Radulfo de Cameys.*h*

RUBRIC: Carta comitis Dauid de Redinch (red, contemporary with text). De Redinche (foot of fo. ; ? xvi cent.).*i*
SOURCE: Caprington Castle, Kilmarnock, MS Lindores Cartulary, fo.33r =*A*. NLS MS Adv. 34.7.1, fo.6v =*B*. Text above from *A*, noting major variants in *B*.

PRINTED: *Lind. Cart.*, no.6 (from *A*). *Lindores Liber*, no.4 (from *B*). Laing, *Lindores*, p.469 (abstract of *B*).

NOTES: *a* Red initial, *A*. *b* Soc', *A*; Scocie, *B*. *c* Colcrik, *B*. *d* Dunfermlin, *B*. *e* Word omitted, *B*. *f* Fertheth, *B*. *g* Oliphant, *B*. *h* *B* breaks off here with etc. *i* *A* only.

COMMENT: Archibald, abbot of Dunfermline, died in 1198, after 15 Feb. (*The Bibliotheck*, ii (1959), p.13); while another witness, Ralph de Camoys, entered Earl David's circle shortly after Michaelmas 1197. The gift was first ratified by papal bull on 20 March 1199 (*Lind. Cart.*, no.94).

Presumed to be earlier than No.44, which recites the grant sanctioned here.

44. Lindores abbey. Announces his foundation of Lindores abbey and grants and confirms the liberties and possessions given to the abbey by himself and by his daughter Ada. (15 Feb. 1198 × 17 March 1199).

Uniuersis*a* sancte matris ecclesie filiis et fidelibus tam presentibus quam futuris, comes Dauid frater regis Scott', salutem. Sciatis me fundasse quandam abbaciam apud Lundors de ordine Kelkoensi ad honorem Dei et sancte Marie et sancti Andree et omnium sanctorum pro salute anime Dauid regis aui mei et pro salute anime comitis Henr*ici* patris mei et comitisse Ade matris mee et Malcolmi regis fratris mei et pro salute anime regis Willelmi fratris mei et regine Ermegard et omnium antecessorum meorum et pro salute anime mee et Matilde comitisse sponse mee et pro salute anime Dauid filij mei et omnium successorum meorum et pro salute animarum fratrum et sororum mearum. Dedi eciam et concessi et hac presenti carta mea confirmaui predicte abbacie de Lundors et monachis ibidem Deo seruientibus in liberam et puram et perpetuam elemosinam ecclesiam de Lundors cum omnibus iustis pertinenciis suis et terram ad predictam ecclesiam pertinentem per rectas diuisas suas in bosco et plano, sicut magister Thom*as* eandem terram tenuit et habuit. Preterea dedi eis omnem terram ab occidentali parte riuuli descendentis de magno lacu usque in They et totam insulam que uocatur Redinche, preter vnam piscariam meam, scilicet vnam jharam. Boues autem mei et vacce mee proprie de Lundors utentur pastura dicte insule. Dedi eciam eis molendinum predicte uille de Lundors cum omni secta sua et multtura, ita ut homines mei faciant omnia que pertinent ad molendinum sicut solent facere tempore quo habui illud in manu mea. Si autem molendinum meum non potuerit molere, molam proprium bladum meum ad molendinum eorum sine mulctura, et si molendinum monachorum non potuerit molere, ipsi molent proprium bladum suum ad molendinum meum sine multtura. Concedo eciam eis ecclesiam de Dunde cum omnibus iustis pertinenciis suis et vnum toftum in burgo meo de Dunde liberum et quietum ab omni seruicio et auxilio et consuetudine et exaccione, et ultra Muneth Fintr*ith* per rectas diuisas suas cum omnibus pertinenciis suis et ecclesiam eiusdem uille cum pertinenciis suis omnibus, et in Garuiach Lethgauel et Malind cum omnibus pertinentiis suis et per rectas diuisas suas. Concedo eciam eis ecclesiam de Inueruri cum capella de Munkegin et cum omnibus aliis pertinenciis suis et ecclesiam de Durnach et ecclesiam de Pramet et ecclesiam de Rathmuriel et ecclesiam de Inchemabanin et ecclesiam de Culsamuel et ecclesiam de Kelalcmond, cum capellis earundem ecclesiarum et terris et decimis et omnibus earum pertinenciis, ad proprios vsus et sustentaciones eorundem monachorum. Concedo eciam eis totam[b] terram meam de Perth que uocatur Insula cum omni plenitudine sua et libertatibus suis, sicut eam plenius et melius tenui et habui, et vnum plenum toftum infra uillam de Perth quod Euerardus Flandren*sis* de me tenuit, tenendum sibi in libero burgagio liberum et quietum, sicut illud liberius et quietius tenui et habui. Concedo eciam eis vnam carrucatam terre in uilla de Neutile quam Ada filia mea, uxor Malisij filij com*itis* Fertheth, eis dedit, tenendam sibi in liberam et puram et perpetuam elemosinam ita libere, quiete, plenarie et honorifice sicut carta predicte filie mee Ade testatur. Concedo eciam eis vnum plenarium toftum in burgo meo de Inuerurin liberum et quietum ab omni seruicio et auxilio et consuetudine et exaccione. Concedo eciam eis decimam omnium lucrorum et placitorum meorum infra terram meam et extra ultra Moneth quam habui tempore quo feci donacionem istam, et decimam omnium lucrorum meorum que michi proueniunt de lucris domini regis fratris mei in toto regno suo, et decimam omnium rerum mearum et heredum meorum ultra Moneth, scilicet decimacionem bladi et farine, butiri et casei, carnis et venacionis, cibi et potus, coriorum ferarum cum mota canum captarum, cere et salis, vncci et sepi, et omnium aliarum rerum que decimari possunt et que dabuntur uel uendentur uel ad firmam ponentur de maneriis meis ultra Moneth uel eciam que in eis expendentur, scilicet in maneriis meis et terris quas habui tempore quo feci donacionem istam. Quare uolo et concedo ut predicta ecclesia de Lundors et monachi ibidem Deo seruientes habeant et teneant in liberam et puram et perpetuam elemosinam de me et heredibus meis prenominatas terras ita libere, quiete, plenarie et honorifice sicut ego eas unquam liberius, quietius, plenius et honorificencius tenui et habui. Concedo eciam eis curiam suam omnino liberam et dignitatem pacis et omnes alias libertates quas abbacia habere debetur. Volo eciam et concedo ut predicti monachi habeant et teneant predictas terras et ecclesias cum capellis et terris et decimis et omnibus aliis pertinenciis suis in bosco et plano, in pratis et pascuis, in aquis et molendinis, in stangnis et uiuariis et piscariis, in uiis et semitis, cum omnibus libertatibus et liberis consuetudinibus sine omni seruicio et consuetudine et auxilio seculari et exaccione, in liberam et puram et perpetuam elemosinam, bene et in pace, libere, quiete, plenarie, integre et honorifice, sicut aliqua abbacia uel domus religionis in toto regno Scocie melius, liberius, quiecius, plenius et honorificencius aliquam elemosinam habet et possidet. Hec autem omnia prenominato monasterio de Lundors et monachis ibidem Deo seruientibus ita libere et pacifice iure perpetuo possidenda confirmaui ut michi succedencium nullus aliquid ab eis nisi solas oraciones ad anime salutem exigere presumat. Hiis test*ibus* Willelmo rege Scottorum, Rogero episcopo sancti Andr*ee*, Jocelino episcopo Glasg', Johanne episcopo Dunkeld', Matheo episcopo Aberdon', Hugone cancell*ario* regis, Dunecano com*ite* de Fyf', com*ite* Patricio, Gilberto com*ite* de Strathern', Roberto de Lund', Malcolmo filio com*itis* Duncani, Seier de Quinci, Philippo de Valuniis, Willelmo de Lindes', Willelmo Cumyn, Dauid de Lindeseie, Waltero Olif*ard*, Walkelino filio Stephani, Willelmo Wacel*in*, Roberto Basset, Henr*ico* filio com*itis*, Ricardo capellano comitis.

RUBRIC: Magna carta com*itis* D*au*id de fundacione monasterij (red, contemporary with text). Nota de secundis decimis (left-hand margin, fo.30v; ? xvi cent.).

SOURCE: Caprington Castle, Kilmarnock, MS Lindores Cartulary, fos.29v–31r.

PRINTED: *Lind. Cart.*, no.2.

NOTES: *a* Turquoise initial. *b* Written twice.

COMMENT: See the discussion above, pp.93–4. Most of the places mentioned are identified in *Lind. Cart.*, pp.xxxix–xli. The suggestion that the parish church of Lindores can be identified with that of Abdie is proved in *Dunfermline Reg.*, p.208; see also NLS MS Adv. 33.2.23, p.19. *Malind* is now represented by Mellenside in Culsalmond, where Lindores disputed 'debatable land' with the bishop of Aberdeen in 1521 (*Aberdeen Reg.*, i, p.386). *Lethgauel* possibly survives in the names Little Ledikin and South Ledikin, near Mellenside (cf. Simpson, *Mar Earldom*, p.13).

45. Lindores abbey. Grants in perpetuity to his monks of Lindores the right to take as much stone as they wish from his quarry in *Hyrneside*, both for their church and for all other necessary buildings. (*c.*1190 × 1219).

Omnibus*a* hoc scriptum visuris uel audituris, comes D*au*id frater regis Scott', salutem. Sciatis me dedisse,*b* concessisse et hac carta mea confirmasse monachis meis de Lundors ut capiant lapidem in quarrario meo in Hyrneside quantum uoluerint in perpetuum, vbi melius eis uisum fuerit, tam ad ecclesiam suam quam ad omnia alia edificia que sibi fuerint necessaria construend*a*. Hiis test*ibus* Willelmo Wascelin, Walkelino filio Stephani, Roberto Basset, Nich*olao* de Anes, Waltero Olifart, Philippo clerico, Henrico de Nueris et aliis.

RUBRIC: Carta com*itis* D*au*id de quarrario (red, contemporary with text). De quarrario (foot of fo.; ? xvi cent.).*c*

SOURCE: Caprington Castle, Kilmarnock, MS Lindores Cartulary, fo.33r = *A*. NLS MS Adv. 34.7.1, fo.22r = *B*. Text above from *A*, noting the one major variant in *B*.

PRINTED: *Lind. Cart.*, no.7 (from *A*). *Lindores Liber*, no.21 (from *B*). Laing, *Lindores*, p.469 (abstract of *B*).

NOTES: *a* Large red initial. *b* *B* adds et. *c* *A* only.

COMMENT: This cannot be closely dated. The grant is not mentioned in any of the confirmations issued for the abbey in the 1190s or later. It should possibly be assigned to *c.* 1190, and ought perhaps to have been placed at the beginning of the Lindores series. Hyrneside (now lost) was located near Parkhill in Abdie (NO 246186): Laing, *Lindores,* p.53, n.2.

46. Lindores abbey. Grants in alms to Lindores abbey all the land of *Pethergus* and the land between the torrent of Mathers and the torrent of Ecclesgreig (St Cyrus, Kincardineshire), as they fall into the sea, with two oxgangs in *Pethannot.* (1199 × 23 Jan. 1215).

Uniuersis[a] sancte matris ecclesie filiis et fidelibus tam futuris quam presentibus, comes Dauid frater regis Scott', salutem. Sciatis me dedisse et concessisse et hac presenti carta mea confirmasse Deo et ecclesie sancte Marie et sancti Andree de Lundors et monachis ibidem [Deo][b] seruientibus pro salute anime mee et animarum antecessorum et successorum meorum totam terram de Pethergus per rectas diuisas suas, et terram que iacet inter torrentem de Matheres et torrentem de Eglesgirg' sicut cadunt in mari, et duas bouatas terre in Pethannot pro centum solidatis terre in liberam et puram et perpetuam elemosinam, in bosco et plano, in pratis et pascuis et pasturis, in moris et mariciis, in stagnis et uiuariis, in aquis et molendinis et in piscariis et in omnibus aliis libertatibus predictis terris iuste pertinentibus. Quare uolo et concedo ut predicti monachi de Lundors habeant et possideant predictas terras cum omnibus iustis pertinenciis suis ita libere, quiete, plenarie et honorifice sicut aliqua abbacia uel domus religionis in toto regno Scocie aliquam elemosinam liberius, quiecius, plenius et honorificencius tenet et possidet. Hiis testibus Waltero Olifard, Henrico filio comitis Dauid, Walkelino filio Stephani, Willelmo Wascelyn, Roberto filio Roberti, Johanne de Wiltun, Gilberto Scoto, Willelmo filio Orm, Roberto de Inuerkileder, Alano clerico de Munros, Simone Albo, cum multis aliis.
RUBRIC: Carta comitis Dauid de Witheston' etc. (red, contemporary with text). De Wicheston' (foot of fo.; ? xvi cent.).
SOURCE: Caprington Castle, Kilmarnock, MS Lindores Cartulary, fo.33v.
PRINTED: *Lind. Cart.,* no.8.
NOTES: *a* MS Unniuersis; turquoise initial. *b* Supplied editorially.
COMMENT: These lands are neither mentioned in No.44 nor included in the detailed lists of properties confirmed to Lindores by papal bulls dated 1195 and 1199. They no doubt represent the property in Mearns ratified by Innocent III on 23 Jan. 1215 (*Lind. Cart.,* no.95). The names Pethergus and Pethannot seem to be obsolete. The former is Pittargus, 1600; Pethannot appears variously Pettenhous (xv cent.), Pittannous, 1600. The *Witheston'* of the rubric, now Mains of Woodstone (NO 750663) and Nether Woodston (NO 754651), stands for the land between Milton of Mathers and Ecclesgreig.

47. Lindores abbey. Confirms to Lindores abbey that grant made by William Wascelin of one oxgang beside the glebe of Newtyle, with common pasture with William's men in Newtyle for ten work animals, thirty sheep and one horse, as William's charter bears witness. (1199 × 1219, probably × 23 Jan. 1215).

Omnibus*ᵃ* ad quos presens scriptum peruenerit, comes Dau*i*d frater regis Scocie, salutem. Sciatis me concessisse et hac presenti carta mea confirmasse Deo et ecclesie sancte Mar*i*e et sancti Andr*ee* de Lundors et monachis ibidem Deo seruientibus et seruituris donacionem illam quam Willelmus Wascelin illis fecit de vna bouata terre in uilla de Neutile que iacet proxima terre ecclesie illius uille inter superiorem uiam et collem, cum communi pastura cum hominibus eius in eadem uilla ad decem aueria et triginta oues et vnum equum. Quare uolo et concedo ut predicti monachi teneant et habeant prenominatam terram cum predicta pastura ita libere, quiete, plenar*i*e et honorifice sicut carta predicti Willelmi testatur. Hiis test*ibus* Ernaldo capellano meo, Philippo clerico de Dunde, Henr*i*co filio meo, Bartholomeo de Mortemer, Roberto filio Roberti, Constantino de Mortemer, Adam filio Alani, Willelmo Gubiun, Henrico filio Walkelini.

RUBRIC: Confirmacio com*itis* Dau*i*d de terra de Neutyl (red, contemporary with text). Confirmacio com*itis* de vna bouat*a* terre in Neutile de dono W. Wascelyn (foot of fo. ; ? xvi cent.).

SOURCE: Caprington Castle, Kilmarnock, MS Lindores Cartulary, fo.34r.

PRINTED: *Lind. Cart.*, no.10.

NOTE: *a* Red initial.

COMMENT: Dated 1199 × for same reason as No.46; the property concerned is probably included in the lands at Newtyle confirmed by Innocent III on 23 Jan. 1215. Wascelin's charter is *Lind. Cart.*, no.37.

48. Lindores abbey. Grants to Lindores abbey one toft in Inverbervie (Kincardineshire). (1199 × 1219).
SOURCE: *Lind. Cart.*, no.18.

49. Lindores abbey. Grants in alms to Lindores abbey all his property in Culsalmond and Monkeigie (Aberdeenshire), reserving the cain that belongs to the bishop of St Andrews. Grants also a court for the men bound to the lands of the monks' churches; quits the monks' own men of all toll and secular custom; and forbids the monks to receive any of his *firmarii* or men in their lands. (26 Dec. 1199 × 13 Oct. 1207).

Sciant*ᵃ* presentes et futuri quod ego comes Dauid frater regis Scoc' dedi et concessi et hac presenti carta mea confirmaui Deo et ecclesie sancte Mar*i*e et sancti Andr*ee* de Lundors et monachis ibidem Deo seruientibus pro salute anime mee et uxoris mee et antecessorum et successorum meorum omne ius quod habui in Culsamuel et in Munkegyn, saluo cano quod pertinet ad episcopum sancti Andr*ee*, scilicet vj sol*idos* et vj denar*ios* de Culsamuel et iiij sol*idos* et iiij d*e*nar*ios* de Munkegyn, in liberam et puram et perpetuam elemosinam. Concedo eciam eis curiam suam liberam et quietam de hominibus suis qui manent in terris ecclesiarum suarum. Preterea concedo eis ut homines sui proprij quieti sint ab omni tolneio et consuetudine seculari.

249

Nolo autem quod predicti monachi aliquem firmariorum meorum uel hominum super terras suas recipiant. Quare uolo ut prefati monachi predicta teneant et possideant ita libere et quiete, plenarie et honorifice sicut aliqua abbacia in regno domini regis fratris mei elemosinam liberius et quietius, plenarius et honorificencius tenet et possidet. Hiis test*ibus* domino J. episcopo de Aberdon', Roberto decano de Aberdon', Malisio filio com*itis* Fertheth, W. Olifart, duobus Henricis filiis comitis, Roberto de Parco, J. de Wiltune, W. Wascelyn, R. capellano, Kineth iudice, H. de Bouilla, N. filio Malcolmi, Waldeuo clerico, H. de Noiers clerico com*itis*, Gilberto clerico com*itis*.

RUBRIC: Carta com*itis* Dauid de Culsamuel et Munkegin (red, contemporary with text). De Culsamuel et de Munkegyn (foot of fo.32v; ? xvi cent.).

SOURCE: Caprington Castle, Kilmarnock, MS Lindores Cartulary, fos.32v–3r.

PRINTED: *Lind. Cart.*, no.5.

NOTE: *a* Turquoise initial, extended into a long tail.

COMMENT: The date-limits are set by Bishop John of Aberdeen. Land at Culsalmond and presumably at Monkeigie (Keithhall), granted to Earl David as lord of Garioch, had formed part of the ancient patrimony of the bishops of St Andrews. This charter confirms that the bishopric was deprived of this property as a result of David's infeftment, save for certain rights of cain: see *SHR*, lv (1976), p.108 with n.3.

50. Lindores abbey. Confirms to Lindores abbey the grant made by Norman son of Malcolm of the church of Leslie (Aberdeenshire), for its own uses, as Norman's charter bears witness. (26 Dec. 1199 × 13 Oct. 1207).

Vniuersis*a* sancte matris ecclesie filiis et fidelibus tam presentibus quam futuris, comes D*aui*d frater regis Scott', salutem. Sciatis me concessisse et hac presenti carta mea confirmasse Deo et ecclesie sancte Mar*i*e et sancti Andr*ee* de Lundors et monach*is* ibidem Deo seruientibus donacionem quam Normannus filius Malcolmi predictis monachis dedit, scilicet ecclesiam de Lescelin cum terris et decimis et omnibus aliis prouentibus et iustis pertinenciis suis, in perpetuam et puram elemosinam, in proprios usus et sustentaciones ipsorum monachorum, libere, quiete, plenarie et honorifice, sicut carta predicti Normanni testatur. Quare uolo et concedo ut prefati monachi predictam ecclesiam habeant et possideant ita libere, quiete, plenarie et honorifice sicut aliqua alia abbacia uel domus religionis aliquam elemosinam uel aliquam ecclesiam in toto regno domini regis fratris mei liberius, quiecius, plenius et honorificencius tenet et possidet. Hiis test*ibus* Johanne episcopo Aberdonen*si*, Simone archidiac*ono*, Roberto decano, Ricardo capellano com*itis*, duobus Henricis filiis domini com*itis*, Willelmo Wascelyn, Henr*ico* et Ricardo clericis domini com*itis*, cum multis aliis.

RUBRIC: Confirmacio comitis Dauid super donacione patronatus ecclesie de Lesselyn (? late xiv cent.).
SOURCE: Caprington Castle, Kilmarnock, MS Lindores Cartulary, fos.6ov–ir.
PRINTED: *Lind. Cart.*, no.82.
NOTE: *a* Red initial.
COMMENT: Issued at about the same time as No.49. Norman's charter is *Lind. Cart.*, no.81.

51. Lindores abbey. Confirms in alms to the abbey he has founded at Lindores the churches of Lindores (Abdie) and Dundee, and (in Aberdeenshire) the churches of Fintray and Inverurie, with the chapel of Monkeigie, and of Durno, Premnay, Radmuriel (Christ's Kirk on the Green in Kennethmont), Insch, Culsalmond and Kennethmont, with their chapels, lands and teinds, for its own uses. (1202 × 1203, probably 1202 × 7 July).

Uniuersis sancte matris ecclesie filiis et fidelibus tam presentibus quam futuris Comes DauiD frater regis scocie salutem. Sciatis me fundasse quandam abbaciam apud londors de ordine kelchoensi ad honorem dei et sancte marie uirginis et sancti andree apostoli omniumque sanctorum. pro salute anime DauiD regis aui mei. et pro salute anime comitis henrici patris mei et comitisse ade matris mee. et malcolmi regis fratris mei. et pro salute anime regis willelmi fratris mei et regine armegard. et omnium antecessorum meorum. et pro salute anime mee et matildis comitisse sponse mee. et pro salute anime DauiD filii mei. et omnium successorum meorum. et pro salute animarum fratrum et sororum mearum. Concessi etiam et hac carta mea confirmaui predicte abbacie de londors et monachis ibidem deo seruientibus in liberam et puram et perpetuam elemosinam ecclesiam de londors cum omnibus pertinenciis suis et terram ad predictam ecclesiam pertinentem in bosco et plano sicut eam magister thomas tenuit et habuit. et Ecclesiam de dunde cum omnibus pertinenciis suis. et Ecclesiam de fintrith cum omnibus pertinenciis suis. et Ecclesiam de inuerurin cum capella de munkegin et cum omnibus aliis pertinenciis suis. et Ecclesiam de durnach. et Ecclesiam de prame. et Ecclesiam de radmuriel. et Ecclesiam de inchemabanin. et Ecclesiam de culsamuel. et Ecclesiam de kelalcmund. cum capellis earumdem ecclesiarum et terris et decimis et omnibus aliis pertinenciis earum ad proprios usus et sustentationes eorumdem monachorum. Quare uolo et concedo ut predicti monachi habeant et teneant in perpetuam et puram elemosinam predictas ecclesias cum capellis et terris et decimis et omnibus aliis pertinenciis suis. sine omni seruicio et consuetudine et auxilio seculari et exactione. bene et in pace. libere. quiete. plenarie. integre. et honorifice: sicut aliqua abbacia uel domus relligionis in toto rengno scotie. melius. liberius. quietius. plenius. et honorificentius. aliquas ecclesias uel aliquas alias elemosinas habet et possidet. Has autem ecclesias prenominato monasterio de londors et monachis ibidem deo seruientibus ita libere et pacifice iure perpetuo possidenda*ᵃ* concessi et confirmaui: ut mihi succedentium nullus aliquid ab eis nisi solas orationes ad anime salutem exigere presumat. Hiis testibus. Willelmo rege scotie. Johanne episcopo aberdonensi. Radulfo episcopo brehinensi. Osberto abbate kelchoensi. henrico abbate de aberbrudoc. simone archidiacono de aberdoen. Roberto decano de aberdoen. Waltero officiali. Matheo de aberdoen clerico domini regis. Dauid de lindeseia. Waltero olifard. Roberto basset. Walkelino filio stephani. Willelmo wascelin. Galfrido de watervile. Normano filio malcomi^a constabulario de inuerurin. henrico de beuile. Matheo falconario. simone flamang cum aliis multis.

ENDORSED: No medieval endorsements visible. *B*'s rubric reads: Carta com*itis* Dauid de ecclesiis de Lundors de Dunde et de Garuiach (red, contemporary with text).

DESCRIPTION: 8.6 × 11.5 in (21.8 × 29.1 cm). Ruled in drypoint. Foot folded to depth of about 0.9 in (2.3 cm); double slits. Seal and tag torn away and lost.

HAND: Unidentified.

SOURCE: Original, NLS MS Adv. 15.1.18, no.40 = *A*. Caprington Castle, Kilmarnock, MS Lindores Cartulary, fos. 31v–2r = *B*. The text given above is that of the original.

PRINTED: *Aberdeen-Banff Coll.*, pp.246–7 (from *A*). C. Leslie, *Historical Records of the Family of Leslie* (Edinburgh, 1869), i, pp.150–2 (from *A*). *Lindores Liber*, pp.37–8 (from *A*). *Mon. Angl.*, vi, p.1150 (from *A*). Laing, *Lindores*, pp.467–8 (abstract of *A*). *Lind. Cart.*, no.3 (from *B*).

NOTE: *a* Sic.

COMMENT: Extreme date-limits supplied by Ralph, bishop of Brechin, and Osbert, abbot of Kelso. Probably issued simultaneously with the charter by which Bishop Roger of St Andrews, at Earl David's request, confirmed the church of Abdie to Lindores *in proprios usus*: *Lind. Cart.*, no.107, with note on date at p.267. In acquiring the earl's ratification of dispositions already given his written approval, the abbey was taking a precaution entirely consistent with the care of monasteries to safeguard rights by charter, especially in the case of spiritualities, which could be both a valuable source of income and the cause of much dispute. But this act can hardly be regarded as another foundation charter of Lindores abbey, as V. H. Galbraith believed: *Cambridge Historical Journal*, iv (1932–4), p.221. The scribe had the *magna carta* (No.44) before him as he wrote: he copied the address and, with minor variants, the long preamble beginning 'Sciatis me fundasse'. But unlike No.44, the text is in the form of a confirmation rather than that of a grant and does not deal with the whole foundation endowment.

52. Lindores abbey. Grants to Lindores abbey all the teinds of Kinnaird in Abdie.

SOURCE: Laing, *Lindores*, p.440 (citing an untraced MS of Sir James Balfour of Denmilne (1600–57), former owner of Kinnaird).

COMMENT: Possibly not the subject of separate written record. Earl David's grant of Abdie church to Lindores (No.44) may have implicitly embraced the teinds of Kinnaird, which were certainly attached to the rectorial estate in the xv cent. (Laing, *Lindores*, p.416). In 1281 the monks assumed that the mill of Lindores, as granted by the earl, included suit and multure from Kinnaird: *Lind. Cart.*, no.125.

53. Richard of Lindsey. Grants to Richard of Lindsey, in fee and heritage, twelve and a half virgates in (Earls) Barton (Northants), one toft and 8*s*. rent, for the sixth part of one knight's service. (29 Sept. 1197 × *c*.1209).

Sciant presentes ⁊ futuri quod Ego Comes Dau*i*D frater Regis Scot'. dedi ⁊ concessi. ⁊ presenti carta mea confirmaui Ricard*o* de Lindes'. pro homag*io* ⁊ Seruicio suo duodecim virgat*as* terre ⁊ dimid*iam* in bart'. scilicet septem virgat*as* ⁊ dimid*iam* quas habui in dominico meo. ⁊ vnam virgat*am* quam Rober*tus* prepositus tenuit. ⁊ vnam virgat*am* quam Gilber*tus* tenuit. ⁊ vnam virgatam quam Ric*ardus* fili*us* Godwini tenuit. ⁊ vnam virgat*am*. quam Rand*ulfus*. ⁊ alanus tenuerunt. ⁊ vnam virgat*am*. quam Ric*ardus* harding' ⁊ achardus ⁊ Willelmus child. ⁊ Willelmus fili*us* Gunwar' tenuerunt. ⁊ toft*um* quod Ingenulfus faber tenuit. ⁊ octo solidatas redditus. de ill*is* duabus virgat*is* terre. quas Walt*erus* fili*us* arkill*i* tenuit. tenend*as* Sibi ⁊ hered*ibus* suis in feod*o* ⁊ hereditate de me ⁊ hered*ibus* meis. libere. honorifice. ⁊ quiete. cum omnibus pertin*enciis* suis. in pratis ⁊ pascuis. in viis ⁊ semitis. in aquis ⁊ molend*inis*. ⁊ in omnibus locis infra uillam ⁊ extra. saluis boscis meis quos mihi ⁊ hered*ibus* meis retinui: faciendo inde Seruicium sexte partis vnius militis pro omnibus Seruic*iis*. Et ego ⁊ hered*es* mei terras predictas warantizabimus predicto Ric*ardo* ⁊ hered*ibus* suis contra omnes homines. vel excambias ad equiualenciam eis inde faciemus de terris nostris in anglia: si ipsas eis warantizare non poterimus. Hiis testibus. Rober*to* de Basingha*m*. Sim*one* de seinliz. hug*one* de lisuris. Rober*to* Lupo. magistro Petro de paxt*un*. Ric*ardo* filio Willelmi. henr*ico*. ⁊ henrico filiis meis. Dauid' de Eÿsebi. Galfr*ido* de Walteruill'. Galfr*ido* de Waldegraue. Rober*to* filio Rober*ti*. Johanne de Willeghebi. Rad*ulfo* de Kamais. Petro de hach. ⁊ pluribus aliis.

ENDORSED: barton (? xv cent.).
DESCRIPTION: 6.5 × 3.5 in (16.5 × 8.8 cm). Foot folded to depth of about 0.5 in (1.2 cm); single slits with tag. Second seal, in light-green wax.
HAND: Unidentified.
SOURCE: Original, BL Loans 29/242, file 2.
PRINTED: *Hist. MSS Comm., Portland*, ii, p.1 (summary).
COMMENT: Ralph de Camoys entered Earl David's connection in 1197/8; and this charter is authenticated by the earl's second seal, which is not known to have been used after *c*.1209. Also, the first witness, Robert of Bassingham, occurs as David's estate steward in England in 1194 × 1208 (Nos. 19, 20). Though not styled *senescallus* above, he appears in the position where the steward's name might be expected.

The statement in *HKF*, ii, p.378, that Richard of Lindsey was probably dead before 1201, can be discounted: see *CRR*, ii, p.168; vi, p.27.

London, Clerkenwell priory, *see* Nos.18–20.

London, priory of Holy Trinity, Aldgate, *see* Nos.3, 4.

54. Robert Luvet. Grants to Robert Luvet, in fee and heritage, two and a half virgates and six acres in Exton (Rutland) which Swain *hostiarius* held, for the twentieth part of one knight's service. (? 1185 × Nov. 1215).

D*aui*d comes frater regis Scott', senescallo*ᵃ* suo et omnibus baronibus et probis hominibus suis de honore Hunted', clericis et laicis, Francis et Angl*is*, presentibus et futuris, salutem. Sciatis me dedisse et concessisse et hac carta mea confirmasse Rob*erto* Luuet et heredibus / suis / ii uirgatas terre et dimid*iam* et vj acras in Extune que fuerunt Swain hostiarii cum omnibus pertinenciis et libertatibus suis in pratis et pascuis et aliis aisiamentis, tam non nominatis quam nominatis, tenendas sibi et heredibus suis de me et heredibus meis in feodum et hereditatem, libere et quiete et honorifice, faciendo michi inde xx*ᵐᵃᵐ* partem [servitii]*ᵇ* vnius mil*itis*. Hiis testibus Ric*ardo* de Petwill de Basigh*am*, Willelmo de Esseby, Reginal*do* Monacho, Waltero de Basigh*am*, Nicol*ao* de Adles, Bartholom*eo* Monacho, m*agistro* Thom*a* de Paruiso.
SOURCE: PRO C 66/167, m.27.
PRINTED: *Calendar of Pat. Rolls, 1327–30*, p.95 (summary).
NOTES: *a* MS senescalli. *b* Added editorially.
COMMENT: Earl David does not seem to have regained control of Exton after his rebellion in Nov. 1215 (above, p.124). This grant enabled Robert Luvet to augment his patrimonial lands in the manor, on which see BL MS Cott. Vesp. E. xvii, fo.196r; PRO CP 25(1) 192/2/2.

55. Malcolm son of Bertolf. Grants to Malcolm son of Bertolf, in feu and heritage, Malcolm's land in Leslie, and *Hachennegort* and *Mache*, with sake and soke, toll, team and infangenthief, with gallows but not ordeal-pit, for one knight's service. (2 April 1172 × 20 Aug. 1199, probably × 1185).

. Daui*D*. frater Regis Scott' Omnibus probis hominibus tocius terre sue. clericis 7 laicis. francis 7 anglis. flaminggis*ᵃ* 7 Scott*is*. tam presentibus quam futuris Salutem. Sciatis me dedisse 7 concessisse 7 hac carta mea confirmasse. Malcolmo fil*io* Bertolf 7 heredibus suis terram suam in lessel'. sicut perambulata fuit ei coram. m*atheo*. episcopo de ab*er*den 7 per probos homines meos. 7 hachennegort per rectas diuisas suas 7. mache per rectas diuisas suas. cum omnibus iustis pertinentiis suis. 7 libertatibus. in bosco. in plano. in terris 7 aquis. in pratis 7 pascuis. in moris. 7 mosis. 7 maresiis. in ecclesiis. 7 capell*is*. in molendinis. 7 stagnis. in uiuariis 7 piscator*iis*. 7 omnibus aliis aisiamentis. tam non nominatis quam nominatis. tenendas Sibi 7 heredibus suis. de me 7 heredibus meis. in feudum 7 hereditatem libere. 7 quiete. 7 honorifice. Scilicet Cum Saca 7 Soco. cum thol. 7 tem. 7

infaggen thef. cum furca. 7 omnibus aliis libertatibus. preter fossam. per seruitium unius militis. test*ibus*. m*atheo*. episcopo de aberden. mal*isio* fili*o* com*itis*. Anegus fili*o* Dvnec*ani*. BRocchin judice. Roberto de kernel. herberto de arch'. Alano fili*o* hug*onis*. Waltero de basigh*am*. Gileberto de lacu. Nicholao de adles. Willelmo Waccel*in*.

ENDORSED: Carta de lessely ha[ ]chen[n]e[ ] Mache (? xiii cent.).

DESCRIPTION: 5.9 × 6.1 in (15 × 15.4 cm). Foot folded to depth of about 0.7 in (1.8 cm); double slits with single slit in crease. Seal and tag torn away and lost.

HAND: Unidentified.

SOURCE: Original, SRO GD 204/23/1 = *A*. NLS MS Adv. 34.3.25, p.385 (xviii-cent. copy of original by Walter Macfarlane of Macfarlane) = *B*. The text edited above is that of the original.

PRINTED: Leslie, *Hist. Recs. of the Family of Leslie*, i, p.147 (from *A*). *Hist. MSS Comm.*, *Reports*, iv, part one, p.493 (summary of *A*). Walter Macfarlane, *Genealogical Collections concerning Families in Scotland* (SHS, 1900), ii, p.453 (from *B*). *Aberdeen-Banff Coll.*, pp.546–7 (from *B*).

NOTE: *a* Sic; the word is hyphenated after the first 'g' at the end of a line, and the scribe has continued with 'gis'.

COMMENT: Dated by Matthew, bishop of Aberdeen. David's style suggests that the charter passed no later than 1185. *Hachennegort* and *Mache* are unidentified. They are rendered as Achÿnegort' and Mawe in a charter by Earl John referring to this grant: SRO GD 204/23/2.

56. Gillecrist, earl of Mar. Grants and quitclaims for himself and his heirs to G(illecrist), earl of Mar, and his heirs, Gillecrist son of Gillekungal and the four named sons of Set. (26 Dec. 1199 × 13 Oct. 1207).

Comes Dauid frater Regis Scocie omnibus Has Literas uidentibus. et*a* audientibus Salutem. Noueritis me 7 heredes meos dedisse. remisisse. 7 quietos clamasse. G. Comiti de MaR 7 heredibus suiS Gillecrist' fili*um* Gillekungal. 7 duos Gillecristos. 7 Gillenem. 7 Gillemartin. iiij*or*. filios Set eos quietos 7 heredes eorum ab omnibus mihi uel heredibus pertinentibus; Hiis Testibus. Malisio filio Comit*is* fertet. .W. olifard. Duobus Henr*icis* fil*iis* Comit*is*. Johanne de Wilton'. kinet iudice. H. de Boiuill'. Normanno constab*ulario*. Dunecano maro. 7 aliis Multis*b*

ENDORSED: No medieval endorsement.

DESCRIPTION: 7.1 × 2.7 in (18 × 6.8 cm). Tongue for sealing *sur simple queue*, with tie above; fragment of seal survives, in natural wax.

HAND: Unidentified.

SOURCE: Original, BL Harl. Chart. 83.C.24. (Copies in BL MS Stowe 552, fo.100v; SRO RH 1/2/29.)

PRINTED: *Illustrations of Scottish History from the Twelfth to the Sixteenth Century*, ed. J. Stevenson (Maitland Club, 1834), pp.23–4. *Illustrations of the Topography and Antiquities of the Shires of Aberdeen and Banff* (Spalding Club, 1847–69), iii, p.402; iv, pp.693–4.

NOTES: *a* Elsewhere, the scribe is consistent in his use of a tironian et. *b* Final 's' prolonged into an immense tail in order to complete last line of text.
COMMENT: Since all but one of the witnesses also appear among the sixteen witnesses to No.49, these two *acta* were probably issued at about the same time.

57. Robert de Mortimer. *Grants to Robert de Mortimer and his heirs £10 worth of land in Godmanchester (Hunts), with appurtenances inside and outside the vill, for half of one knight's service. (1190 × 16 Sept. 1199).
SOURCE: *Rot. Chart.*, p.23.
COMMENT: Earl David was lord of Godmanchester from 1190. The source is King John's confirmation of 16 Sept. 1199.

58. Northampton, priory of St Andrew. Grants in alms to St Andrew's priory at Northampton 20*s.* from the rent of his mills at Paxton in four annual instalments, and three horse-loads of wheat from his barn at (Earls) Barton at Michaelmas, the money to procure wine and the wheat to make wafers for the consecration of the body and blood of Our Lord in the church of St Andrew. (Early summer 1174).

Dauid[a] frater[b] regis Scocie,[c] senescallo suo et omnibus baronibus[d] et probis hominibus suis de honore de[e] Huntend',[f] clericis et laicis, Francis et Anglis, tam presentibus quam posteris, salutem. Sciatis me concessisse et dedisse et hac carta mea confirmasse ecclesie sancti Andree de Norh't[g] et monachis ibidem Deo seruientibus in puram et liberam[h] et perpetuam elemosinam xx sol*idos* de redditu molendinorum meorum de Paxton' ad iiii[or] terminos annuatim, scilicet ad festum sancti Mich*aelis* v s*olidos*, ad natal*e* Domini v s*olidos*, ad Pascha v s*olidos*, ad festum sancti Iohannis Baptiste[i] v s*olidos*, et iii summas frumenti de horreo meo de Barton' ad festum sancti Mich*aelis*, denarios scilicet ad uinum conparandum et frument*um* ad oblatas faciendas in consecracionem corporis et sanguinis Domini Nostri Iesu Christi in predicta ecclesia sancti Andree. Et ut hec elemosina mea rata habeatur diebus meis et heredum meorum et[e] firma, sigilli mei attestacione corroboraui. Hiis testibus Hug*one* Ridel,[j] Willelmo de[k] Basingham, Waltero fratre eius,[l] Willelmo de Esseby,[m] Alano fil*io* Hug*onis*, Gilberto[n] de Lacu,[o] Nicholao de Adles, Radulfo Ridel,[j] Iohanne de Cantoc,[p] Petro Petitgr*a*unt, Waltero de Quent*on*,[q] magistro Thoma de Parauiso.
RUBRIC: Confirmacio Dauid fratris regis Scocie de viginti solidis de molendinis de Paxton annuatim percipiendis per equales porciones ad quatuor terminos vsuales (red, contemporary with text).[r]
SOURCE: BL MS Royal 11 B. ix, fo.12v = *A*. BL MS Cott. Vesp. E. xvii, fo.12r–v = *B*. BL MS Cott. Vesp. E. xvii, fo.236r = *C*. Text above from *A*, save for four readings from *B*.
NOTES: *a* Large red initial, *A*. *b* ffrater, *A*. *c* Scott', *C*. *d* boronibus, *A*. *e* Word omitted, *C*. *f* Huntyndon', *B*; Huntyngd', *C*. *g* North', *B*, *C*.

h in liberam et puram, *B*. *i* Word omitted, *A*, *C*. *j* Rydell', *C*. *k* Obliterated in *A*. *l* suo, *C*. *m* Asscheby, *C*. *n* Gilleberto, *C*. *o* Lacit', *B*. *p* Cantok, *C*. *q* Quinton, *B*. *r B* only.

COMMENT: David's style suggests an early date; and Hugh Ridel was his steward for the Huntingdon honour in 1174 (No.23). Although he is not called steward in the text, Ridel's position as first witness would have been appropriate for this official. Several other witnesses are also known to have joined David's camp against the English crown in 1174, and the charter presumably belongs to the series of Huntingdon *acta* issued during his campaign in the Midlands.

This act, albeit written in the form of an original grant, acknowledges an earlier disposition by Earl Simon de Senlis I: *Mon. Angl.*, v, p.191a.

59. Northampton, priory of St Andrew. Confirms in alms to St Andrew's priory at Northampton all the property it held, by grant of his predecessors, in the honour of Huntingdon on the day that he was seised of the earldom of Huntingdon, and whatever it has fairly acquired there since. The monks and their men of the honour are to be quit of his hundred courts, and when the view of frankpledge is exercised by his bailiffs in their lands of the honour, the monks are to receive any amercement for their own use. (1185 × 4 April 1218).

Uniuersis^a sancte matris ecclesie filiis presentibus et futuris, comes^b Dauid frater regis Scot', salutem in Domino. Nouerit vniuersitas uestra me caritatis intuitu et pro salute anime mee et pro animabus omnium antecessorum^c et successorum meorum concessisse et hac carta mea confirmasse^d Deo et ecclesie sancti Andree de Norh't^e et monachis ibidem Deo seruientibus terras, possessiones et redditus quos antecessores mei eisdem rationabiliter dederunt et quos habuerunt^f in honore de Huntendon'^{g} die qua seisitus^h fui de comitatu de Huntend', et quicquid postea rationabiliter adepti sunt in eodem honore de Huntendon'. Quare uolo et firmiter precipio quod dicti monachi teneant omnia predicta bene et in pace, quiete et honorifice, in liberam et puram et perpetuam elemosinam, et ipsi et homines /sui/ de dicto honore de Huntendon' quieti sint de secta hundredorum meorum et de placitis et querelis et exaccionibus et de omnibus seruiciis secularibus ad me uel ad heredes meos pertinentibus. Et cum francplegium in terris eorum de honore de Huntendon' per balliuos meos uisitabitur, si admerciamentum in visitacione illa acciderit, ipsum admerciamentum sit ipsorum monachorum. Hiis testibus Roberto^i de Basingham, Ricardo de Lindes', Willelmo de Foleuile, Dauid^j de Esseby, Roberto Basset, Willelmo Reuell, Roberto filio Roberti, Willelmo Quarrell, Constantino de Mortim*er*, Ricardo de Boseuile,^{k} Sahero de Wolauston' et multis aliis.

RUBRIC: Confirmacio comitis Dauid fratris regis Scocie de possessionibus in honore de Huntyngdon' (red, contemporary with text).^{l}

SOURCE: BL MS Royal 11 B. ix, fo. 10r–v = *A*. BL MS Cott. Vesp. E. xvii, fo. 10r–v = *B*. *A* and *B* collated for this edition, with *A*'s readings generally preferred.

NOTES: *a* Prominent red initial, both MSS. *b* Last four words illegible, *A*. *c* pro animabus antecessorum meorum omnium, *B*. *d* confirmauisse, *B*. *e* Northampton', *B*. *f* habuerunt follows honore, *B*. *g* Huntyndon' here and throughout, *B*. *h* seisatus, *B*. *i* Robertus, *A*; the Christian names of the second, third, fifth and seventh witnesses are also rendered in the nominative case, *A*. *j* ? Rauid', *B*. *k* Bosuile, *B*. *l B* only.

COMMENT: Robert of Bassingham, the first witness, was dead by 4 April 1218 (No.67, comment); probably issued not long after 1185, when Robert served as steward of the Huntingdon honour.

60. Northampton, priory of St Andrew. Grants in alms to the monks of St Andrew at Northampton two-thirds of the tithes of his demesne in Yardley (Hastings, Northants), both of assarts and of land anciently cultivated, and two-thirds of the small tithes of his *curia*. (1185 × 1196).

Comes*a* Dauid frater*b* regis Scocie, omnibus sancte matris ecclesie filiis ad quos presens scriptum peruenerit, salutem. Nouerit vniuersitas uestra me pro salute anime mee et antecessorum meorum dedisse et concessisse et presenti carta mea confirmasse in puram et perpetuam elemosinam Deo et monachis sancti Andree de Norh't*c* duas partes dominii mei decimarum in Ierdele, tam de essartis*d* meis presentibus et futuris quam de ueteri dominio meo in eadem uilla, et preterea duas partes minutarum decimarum de curia mea proueniencium. Volo itaque et firmiter precipio quod predicti monachi prenominatas duas partes decimacionum, tam in garbis quam in minutis decimis, libere, quiete et plenarie et sine contradiccione percipiant et in pace possideant. Hiis testibus Ricardo de Peco,*e* Symone de sancto Licio, Reg*inaldo* de Acle*f* tunc senescallo meo, Willelmo de Esseby, Simone*g* de Houton', magistro Petro de Paxton', magistro Alex*andro* de Norh't,*c* Reg*inaldo**h* de Carnayll', Simone de Dauentre, Thom*a* portario, Roberto clerico, Laurencio de Aula et pluribus aliis.

RUBRIC: Confirmacio eiusdem Dauid comitis de decimis et de assartis de Yerdele (red, contemporary with text).*i*

SOURCE: BL MS Royal 11 B. ix, fo.11r = *A*. BL MS Cott. Vesp. E. xvii, fo.11r = *B*. Text above from *A*, save for two readings from *B*.

NOTES: *a* Large red initial, *A*. *b* ffrater, *A*. *c* North', *B*. *d* escarcis, *B*. *e* Petto, *B*. *f* Ade, *B*. *g* Illegible, *A*. *h* Rog', *B*. *i B* only.

COMMENT: Simon de Senlis supported Earl David from 1185, and Richard del Peak was dead by 1196. The demesne tithes of Yardley Hastings were originally given to St Andrew's by Earl Simon de Senlis I (*Mon. Angl.*, v, pp.190a, 191a), but the small tithes – later, 'de curia seu manso comitis' (e.g., BL MS Cott. Vesp. E. xvii, fo.95v) – may represent a new grant.

61. Northampton, priory of St Andrew. Confirms in alms to St Andrew's priory at Northampton the church of Potton (Beds), with the chapel of St Swithin, saving the life-interest of Mr T(homas de Paraviso), his clerk, in the same church. (1185 × 1196).

Uniuersis*ᵃ* sancte matris ecclesie filiis presentibus et futuris,*ᵇ* Dauid comes Huntendon'*ᶜ* frater*ᵈ* regis Scocie, salutem. Sciatis me pro Deo et pro*ᵉ* animabus predecessorum meorum et mea*ᶠ* concessisse et hac presenti*ᵉ* carta mea confirmasse ecclesie sancti Andree de Norhmt'*ᵍ* et monach*i*s ibidem Deo seruientibus in liberam et puram et perpetuam elemosinam ecclesiam de Pottona et capellam eiusdem uille, beati scilicet Swithini, et /cum/ omnibus earum pertinenciis in terris et decimis, in pratis et pascuis et mariscis et omnibus aliis aysiamentis, in liberam elemosinam tenendam et quietam ab omni exaccione seculari de me et heredibus meis in perpetuum, saluo iure*ʰ* magistri T. clerici mei quod habet in eadem ecclesia in uita sua. Hiis testibus magistro Willelmo persona de Ierdeleya, Willelmo capellano meo, Waltero capellano meo, Willelmo de Bassingham, Roberto de Kernelia, Waltero de Bassingham, Alano fil*i*o Hug*o*nis, Nicholao de Adles, Roberto de Betona, magistro Thom*a* de Kirkebi, magistro Radulpho de sancto Neoto, Ricardo de Pek, Galfrid*o* fil*i*o Galfrid*i*, Roberto de Gildinge-ham,*ⁱ* Willelmo Waufre, Roberto de Boneire, Willelmo de Stottona, Ricardo de Pottona et multis aliis.

RUBRIC: Confirmacio Dauid fratris regis Scocie de ecclesia de Potton et capella eiusdem (red, contemporary with text).*ʲ*

SOURCE: BL MS Royal 11 B. ix, fo. 10v = *A*. BL MS Cott. Vesp. E. xvii, fo. 10v = *B*. Text above from *A*, save for five readings.

NOTES: *a* Large red initial, both MSS. *b* ffuturis, *A*. *c* Initials of last three words interlined in red, *A*; Huntyndon', *B*. *d* ffrater, both MSS. *e* Word omitted, *A*. *f* meo, *A*. *g* North', *B*. *h* vite, *B*. *i* Gyloingeham, *B*. *j B* only.

COMMENT: Richard del Peak was dead by 1196. See also above, p. 145.

62. Northampton, hospital of St John. Confirms to the brethren of St John's hospital at Northampton 30 cartloads of wood every year from the wood of Yardley Hastings, as granted by King Malcolm IV and King William I. (1173 × 1174, or 1185 × 1219).

SOURCE: Castle Ashby, Northants, Marquess of Northampton's Muniments, FD 247.

COMMENT: Neither royal charter is extant. £10 is still paid annually by the Marquess of Northampton to St John's hospital in lieu of firewood from Yardley Hastings.

Northampton, abbey of St Mary de la Pré, *see* Nos. 21–2.

63. Nuneaton priory. Confirms to Nuneaton priory an annual rent of 20s. from the mill of Harringworth (Northants). (1173 × 1174, or 1185 × 1219).

SOURCE: BL Addit. Chart. 47742.

COMMENT: Originally a grant by Countess Ada de Warenne, who held Harringworth in dower: W. Dugdale, *The Antiquities of Warwickshire*, 2nd edn (London, 1730), ii, p. 1066. Her gift stood despite the Senlis conveyance of Harringworth mill to Crowland abbey. See further S. Raban, *The Estates of Thorney and Crowland* (Cambridge University, Dep. of Land Economy, 1977), pp. 34, 37.

64. Philip of Orby. *Grants to Philip of Orby 40 acres of meadow-land. (1185 × 3 June 1212).

SOURCE: *CRR*, vi, p.280.

COMMENT: Dates supplied by source and *CRR*, vi, pp.273–4. The precise location of this property is uncertain, but source indicates either Whissendine (Rutland) or Bozeat (Northants). By Nov. 1212 Philip was asking for an exchange: *PBKJ*, iv, no.4743. On the background cf. No.7, comment.

Philip, founder of the line of Orby of Dalby (Lincs), was justiciar of Chester for Earl Ranulf de Blundeville: *HKF*, ii, p.100. He also controlled interests at Sawtry (Hunts), and his family did not lack connections with Scotland: see *VCH Hunts*, iii, p.211; Barrow, *Era*, p.28.

65. Master Thomas de Paraviso. Confirms to Mr·T(homas de Paraviso), his clerk, the church of Potton, to be held for life of the monks of St Andrew at Northampton. (1185 × 1196).

Vniuersis*a* sancte matris ecclesie filiis presentibus et futuris,*b* Dauid comes Huntend'*c* frater regis Scocie, salutem. Noueritis me diuine caritatis intuitu concessisse et presenti carta mea confirmasse magistro T. clerico meo ecclesiam de Pottona cum omnibus pertinenciis suis, tenendam tota uita sua de monachis sancti Andree de Norh't*d* soluendo*e* inde eis annuatim debitam pensionem. Testibus Willelmo et Waltero capellanis meis, Ricardo de Pek, Willelmo de Assebi senescallo meo, Willelmo et Waltero de Basingham, Roberto de Kernelia, Roberto de Bartona*f* clerico meo, Galfrido filio Galfridi.

RUBRIC: Quomodo idem Dauid comes concessit magistro [Thome] clerico suo ecclesiam de Pottona ad terminum vite sue redd*endo* inde monach*is* annuam pensionem (red, contemporary with text).*g*

SOURCE: BL MS Royal 11 B. ix, fo.11r = *A*. BL MS Cott. Vesp. E. xvii, fo.11r = *B*. Text above based on *A*, noting major variants in *B*.

NOTES: *a* Large red initial, both MSS. *b* ffuturis, *A*. *c* Huntyndon', *B*. *d* North', *B*. *e* solum̃, *A*; solumo̊, *B*. *f* Bertona, *B*. *g* *B* only.

COMMENT: Probably issued at the same time as No.61, with which it is closely related. Both *acta* belong with the grant by Henry, prior of St Andrew's, to Thomas de Paraviso of the church and chapel of Potton, for an annual pension of seven marks: BL MS Cott. Vesp. E. xvii, fo.267v (witnessed by Earl David).

66. Master Peter of Paxton. Grants to Mr Peter of Paxton, his clerk, the church of Potton, as freely as any of Peter's predecessors held it. (1185 × 22 May 1201, possibly *c*.1194).

Omnibus*a* sancte matris Ecclesie filiis Comes Dauid frater Regis Scocie Salutem. Nouerit uniuersitas uestra me intuitu karitatis. 7 pro salute mea. 7 omnium antecessorum meorum dedisse 7 concessisse. 7 presenti carta confirmasse Magistro Petro de Paxtun clerico meo Ecclesiam de Pottun' cum omnibus pertinenciis suis. 7 libertatibus ad eam*b* pertinentibus. ten-

endam sibi ita libere 7 quiete sicut umquam aliquis antecessorum suorum
eam melius 7 liberius tenuit. Hiis Testibus Simone de Sainzliz. Philippo
monacho. Bartholomeo monacho. Roberto filio Roberti. Dauid de Essebi.
Ricardo 7 Willelmo capellanis. Galfrido 7 magistro Thoma clericis comitis.
Walkelino de Nuiers. Michaele pincerna. 7 Dauid daudre. 7 multis aliis.
ENDORSED: Quedam scripta conting*ens* presentaciones factas ad ecclesiam
de Paxton' cum quadam finali concordia leuata in Curia Regis de Aduoca-
cione (xiv cent.).
DESCRIPTION: 5.7 × 2.6 in (14.5 × 6.5 cm). Foot folded to depth of about
0.7 in (1.8 cm); single slits with tag. Fragment of seal, in white wax.
HAND: Unidentified.
SOURCE: Original, Lincoln, Lincolnshire Archives Office, Dean and
Chapter records, Dij/90/3/22. (Copied in MS 'Registrum', no.287.)
PRINTED: *RAL*, iii, no.655, with facs., size reduced, facing p.16.
NOTES: *a* Large initial. *b* Second letter of word altered from 'u'.
COMMENT: The endorsement confuses the church of Potton with that of
Great Paxton. The latter was the subject of a final concord between Earl
John and Holyrood abbey in 1232 (*RAL*, iii, no.823). For Mr Peter's
interest in the Potton benefice and for the extreme date-limits see above,
p.145 with n.121. If Simon de Senlis was named as chief witness because he
was then steward of the Huntingdon honour, the date can be narrowed to
*c.*1194: *Rolls of the King's Court in . . . 1194–5*, ed. F. W. Maitland (PRS,
1891), p.28.

67. William Marshal, earl of Pembroke. Grants to William Marshal, earl of
Pembroke and *rector* of England, custody of the land and heir of Robert of
Bassingham. (1218, 13 March × 9 May).
SOURCE: *RLC*, i, p.316a.
COMMENT: Bassingham, a Huntingdon tenant, was dead shortly before 4
April 1218 (*HKF*, ii, p.409). Earl David was restored in the honour on 13
March; the source is a royal mandate dated 9 May in the same year.

68. Repton priory. Confirms in alms to Repton priory the church of (Great)
Baddow (Essex), as the charter of Countess Maud bears witness. *Wanntona.*
(19 Aug. 1190 × *c.*1209, probably 1200 ×).

Comes D*aui*D frater Regis Scocie. Omnibus hominibus suis tam presenti-
bus quam futuris Salutem. Sciatis me concessisse 7 carta mea confirmasse
deo 7 Sancte Marie 7 Sancto Wistano de Rap*an*dona 7 canonic*is* ibidem
deo seruientibus Ecclesiam de BdeWen in elemosinam sicut carta Matill'
Comitisse testatur. his Testibus Rob*er*to de Basigham. Bertolomeo Monaco.
Will*elmo* Reuel. Will*elmo* Burdet Nicolao de hanes. 7 Multis aliis apud
Wanntona*m.* Valete
ENDORSED: Confirmatio comitis d*aui*d de ecclesia de badwe (? xiii cent.);
carta prima (? xiii cent.).
DESCRIPTION: 5.7 × 2.2 in (14.5 × 5.7 cm). Foot folded to depth of about

0.5 in (1.2 cm); single slits with tag. Second seal, in red wax; good impression.

HAND: Unidentified.

SOURCE: Original, BL Campbell Chart. xxx 4. (Drawn facs. of original in BL MS Stowe 666, fo.82v; for other copies see BL MS Addit. 5844, fo.64v, MS Addit. 11545, fo.15r, MS Stowe 551, fo.14r–v.)

PRINTED: J. Ayloffe, *Calendars of the Ancient Charters*, etc. (London, 1774), p.350. *Descriptive Catalogue of Derbyshire Charters*, ed. I.H. Jeayes (London, 1906), no.1946.

COMMENT: Great Baddow formed part of the dowry brought to Earl David by Countess Maud. This confirmation may have followed the legal action begun by Repton against David over the advowson in 1200 (*CRR*, i, p.294). Apparently no later than *c.*1209 because the act was issued under the earl's second seal. Further, although Robert of Bassingham, the first witness, is given no descriptive style, his senior position possibly indicates that he was serving as steward, as when he attested Nos.19, 20 (1194 × 1208). The lady mentioned in the text may be not Earl David's wife but her namesake, the wife of Ranulf de Gernons, earl of Chester: cf. *Derbyshire Chrs.*, no.1945. The place-date remains unidentified.

69. Richard son of William. Grants to Richard son of William, in fee and heritage, 100s. annually in his third penny in the town of Cambridge, payable in equal instalments at Michaelmas and on Hock Tuesday, for one pound of pepper or 6d. at Christmas. (29 Sept. 1197 × 25 Nov. 1202).

Comes Dauid frater Regis Scott' Omnibus Hominibus suis 7 amicis tam presentibus quam futuris Salutem. Sciatis me dedisse 7 Concessisse 7 hac Presenti Carta mea Confirmasse Ricardo filio Willelmi Pro Homagio 7 seruicio suo Centum solidos in tercio denario meo IN villa Cantebrigie. annuatim recipiendos ad duos terminos. Scilicet ad festum sancti Micahel*is* Quinquaginta solidos Et ad Hockestiwesday Quinquaginta solidos. Hunc uero prenominatum redditum dedi predicto Ric*ardo* 7 Heredibus suis tenendum de me 7 Heredibus meis in feodo 7 Hereditate libere 7 quiete. Plenarie integre 7 Honorifice reddendo inde annuatim unam libram Piperis vel sex denarios ad Natale Domini pro omni seruicio 7 exactione seculari. Et si forte Ego vel Heredes mei prenominatum redditum prefato Ric*ardo* fili*o* Willelmi vel Heredibus suis warantizare non poterimus. faciemus eis Excambium Ad Equiualenciam IN terris nostris IN Anglia. Hiis Testibus. Rob*erto* de Mortemer. Ric*ardo* de Lindes'. Sim*one* de Senliz. Henrico fili*o* meo. PHilippo monaco. Rob*erto* Basset. Rob*erto* fili*o* Rob*er*ti. Dauid de Essebi. Galfr*ido* de Wauteruill'. Roberto tallebois. Constant*ino* de Mortem*er* Waltero Olifard. Rad*ulfo* de Kameis Petro flettari*o*. Gileb*erto* Clerico de Totenham Micahele Pincerna. Rob*erto* fili*o* Mart*ini*. Walkel*ino* de Nuers. Henr*ico* de Nuers. et Pluribus Aliis*a*

ENDORSED: heredes com*itis* Dauid Huntind'
            Domina Isabella de Brus

Dominus Henricus de hastinges
Dominus Joh*annes* de Baylol 7 Dereuergoil uxor eius.
(xiii cent.).
Prima carta donacionis (xiii cent.).

DESCRIPTION: 7.3 × 4 in (18.5 × 10.3 cm). Foot folded to depth of about
1 in (2.7 cm); double slits, and slit in fold, with tag of tablet-woven braid
patterned in gold on a green background. Second seal, in green wax; good
impression.

HAND: Unidentified.

SOURCE: Original, B L Addit. Chart. 15509. (Copy in B L MS Addit. 5842,
fos. 109v–10r, with drawing of seal.)

PRINTED: *Cambridge Borough Documents*, ed. W. M. Palmer (Cambridge,
1931), pp. 11–12, with facs., size reduced, facing p. 10.

NOTE: *a* Final 's' extended sideways in a long flourish to finish last line of
text.

COMMENT: Ralph de Camoys entered Earl David's affinity in 1197/8; and
Robert Taillebois, another witness, was dead by 25 Nov. 1202 (*CRR*, ii,
pp. 135, 163). For the provisions made by Richard son of William out of his
annuity see *Cambridge Borough Docts.*, pp. xx–xxii, 12–14, 26–7.

70. Robert son of Roger. *Grants to Robert son of Roger £15 worth of land
in Whissendine. (1185 × 2 April 1212).

SOURCE: *CRR*, vi, p. 280.

COMMENT: Dates supplied by *CRR*, vi, pp. 242, 273–4. Robert had asked
for an exchange by Oct. 1212 (*PBKJ*, iv, nos. 4668, 4743). Cf. No. 7,
comment. He can probably be identified with Robert Fitz Roger, lord of
Warkworth, who in 1214 occurs as a tenant of the Huntingdon honour in
Potton and whose son, John Fitz Robert, held in addition a half-fee of the
honour at Harringworth: No. 11; *HKF*, ii, p. 337.

71. St Andrews cathedral priory. Grants in alms to St Andrews priory
(Fife) two ploughgates (Seggieden) in Kennethmont, until he may give the
canons a rent in a church in exchange. (2 April 1172 × 8 March 1195,
probably 1185 ×).

Comes*a* Dauid frater regis Scocie, omnibus sancte matris ecclesie filiis,
salutem. Sciant*b* tam presentes quam futuri me dedisse et concessisse et hac
mea carta confirmasse Deo et ecclesie beati apostoli Andree et canonicis
ibidem Deo seruientibus et seruituris duas carucatas terre in Kinalchmund
in perpetuam elemosinam, per easdem diuisas sicut Malcolmus et Walke-
linus et Waldeuus clericus et alii probi homines perambulauerunt. Quare
uolo ut predicti canonici terram illam ita libere et quiete, et sine omni
exaccione et seruicio seculari, teneant et possideant sicut aliqua elemosina
liberius [et]*c* quiecius tenetur et possidetur in regno fratris mei, quousque
eis donem redditum in ecclesia ad ualenciam predictarum duarum
carucarum terre, eis in perpetuam elemosinam et cum eadem libertate

tenendum. Testibus Matheo episcopo Aberdenensi, Simone archidiacono, Malcolmo senescaldo, Walkelino,[d] Willelmo capellano, Philippo clerico, Winemero, magistro Waltero cementario et pluribus aliis.

RUBRIC: De duabus caru*catis* terre (red, contemporary with text). Kynalcmund que vocatur Segyden (left-hand margin, ? xiv cent.). SOURCE: SRO GD 45/27/8, fo.110v. PRINTED: *St Andrews Liber*, p.239. *Aberdeen-Banff Coll.*, p.624 (abstract). NOTES: *a* Large blue initial. *b* Initial flourished in red. *c* Supplied editorially. *d* Sic; ? read Walkelino filio Stephani.

COMMENT: Bishop Matthew of Aberdeen was consecrated 2 April 1172 and died 20 Aug. 1199; but presumably issued before Earl David endowed Lindores abbey with all the churches in his gift in Scotland (No.37; *Lind. Cart.*, no.93). The identification with Seggieden (NJ 547278) is supplied under RUBRIC. An exchange was not made, and Earl John confirmed his father's grant: *St Andrews Liber*, p.240.

72. St Andrews cathedral priory. Grants in alms to St Andrews priory (Fife) all the cain and conveth owed by the canons for the land of Ecclesgreig (St Cyrus), and grants and quitclaims the service owed by their men of *Egleskirch'*. (1189 × 1219).

Comes[a] Dauid frater regis Scotorum, omnibus Christi fidelibus hanc cartam uisuris uel audituris, salutem. Sciatis me pro salute anime mee et pro animabus antecessorum et successorum meorum dedisse et concessisse et presenti carta confirmasse Deo et ecclesie sancti Andree et canonicis ibidem Deo seruientibus in puram et perpetuam elemosinam totum kanum et kuneveth' quod canonici ipsi michi debebant de terra de Eglesgirg. Et seruic*ium* quod homines sui de Egleskirch' michi debebant eis dedi in puram et perpetuam elemosinam et quiet*um* clamaui a me et hered*ibus* meis in perpetuum. Hiis testibus Walkelino filio Stephani, Willelmo Wacelin', Henrico et Henrico fil*iis* meis, Roberto Basset, Bartholo*meo* de Mortem*er*, Roberto filio Roberti, Cons*antino* de Mortem*er*, Ricardo fil*io* Willelmi, Roberto de Brus, Johanne Giffard, Adam filio Alani, Henrico de Nuers, Philippho et Petro clericis et aliis multis.

RUBRIC: De Eglisgirg (red, contemporary with text). SOURCE: SRO GD 45/27/8, fo.110r. PRINTED: *St Andrews Liber*, p.238. NOTE: *a* Large red initial. COMMENT: Ecclesgreig was still regarded as royal domain in 1189 × 1195 (*RRS*, ii, no.352).

73. St Andrews cathedral priory. Grants in alms to St Andrews priory (Fife) one full toft in his burgh of Dundee and, to make oblations, one silver mark payable at Easter out of his burgh ferme by the grieve. (*c.*1190 × 1204).

Comes[a] Dauid frater regis Scotorum, vniuersis sancte matris ecclesie filiis, salutem. Sciant tam presentes quam futuri me dedisse et concessisse et hac carta mea confirmasse Deo et ecclesie beati Andree apostoli et canonicis ibidem Deo seruientibus et seruituris in perpetuam elemosinam vnum plenarium toftum in burgo meo de Dundeo, tenendum de me et de heredibus meis liberum et quiet*um* ab omni seruicio et consuetudine et exaccione seculari, sicuti aliqua elemosina liberius et quietius tenetur et possidetur in toto regno regis fratris mei.*b* Dedi*c* eciam illis et concessi cum predicto tofto unam marcham argenti in perpetuam elemosinam, habendam de me et de heredibus meis ad oblatas faciendas, annuatim eis reddendam ad Pasca de firma burgi mei de Dundeo ita ut quicumque prepositus ibi fuerit reddat eis marcam illam ad prefatum terminum Pasche prompte et absque ulla disturbacione. Testibus hiis Dunecano comite, Malcolmo filio eius, Widone abbate de Lundors, Alano dapifero regis, Malisio fratre com*itis* de Strathernth, Willelmo capellano meo, Dauid de Lindeseia, Roberto Basset, Nicholao de Alles, Willelmo Reuel, Willelmo Burdet, Gaufrido de Watervilla. Val*ete*.

RUBRIC: De marcha de Dunde (red, contemporary with text).

SOURCE: SRO GD 45/27/8, fo. 110r–v.

PRINTED: *St Andrews Liber*, pp. 238–9.

NOTES: *a* Large blue initial. *b* MS ? meii. *c* Initial interlined in red.

COMMENT: Earliest possible date set by Guy, first abbot of Lindores. Earl Duncan of Fife and Alan son of Walter, steward of King William I, both died in 1204.

74. St Andrews cathedral priory. Grants in alms to St Andrews priory (Fife) all the land of Longforgan (Perthshire) which was disputed between him and the canons, with the half-ploughgate given to the church of Longforgan by his predecessors. (18 Sept. 1202 × ? *c.* 1208).

Omnibus*a* sancte matris ecclesie fil*iis* futuris et presentibus, comes Dauid frater regis Scocie, salutem. Nouerit uniuersitas uestra me dedisse, concessisse et hac mea carta confirmasse Deo et ecclesie sancti Andree de Kinrimoned et canonicis ibidem Deo seruientibus et seruituris totam terram de Forgrunt vnde controuersia uertebatur inter me et eosdem canonicos, cum dimidia carucata terre quam antecessores mei dederunt ecclesie de Forgrunt in dotem, per easdem diuisas per quas Alexander persona ecclesie de Forgrunt easdem terras in uita sua tenuit. Hoc autem eis dedi et concessi in puram et perpetuam elemosynam pro salute anime regis Willelmi fratris mei et pro salute anime mee et anime sponse mee Matildis comitisse et antecessorum et successorum meorum, ita libere et quiete et honorifice sicut aliqua terra uel elemosina in regno Scotorum liberius, quiecius et honorificencius tenetur et possidetur. Testibus domino Willelmo episcopo sancti Andree, Waltero Olifard, Dauit de Lindesey, Walkelino filio Stephani, Willelmo Wacelin, Roberto Basset, Constantino de Mortem*er*, Galfrido de Walteruile, Ricardo capellano, Ph*ilippo* et Ricardo clericis meis*b* et multis aliis.

RUBRIC: Comes D*auid* de terra de Forgrund (red, contemporary with text).

SOURCE: SRO GD 45/27/8, fos. 109v–10r.

PRINTED: *St Andrews Liber*, p.237.

NOTES: *a* Large blue initial. *b* Word underlined for deletion.

COMMENT: Earliest date set by Bishop William of St Andrews; another witness, David of Lindsey, is not called justiciar, which may suggest a date before *c*.1208.

75. Sawtry abbey. Confirms in alms to the abbot and monks of Sawtry one virgate in Great Paxton and the meadow-land perambulated by Hugh Ridel and Oger of Sproxton, as confirmed by King Malcolm's charter; confirms also, as King William's charter confirms, his mills of Paxton in fee-farm, for 50*s*. 8*d*. a year. (Early summer 1174).

Dauid frater regis Scotie, omnibus filiis*a* sancte matris ecclesie,*b* salutem. Sciatis me concessisse*c* et presenti carta*d* confirmasse abbati et monachis de Saltreia vnam virgatam terr*e* in Magna Paxton et illam partem prati de prato meo, quam partem perambulauerunt Hugo Ridell et Ogerus de Sproximer,*e* in perpetuam elemosinam,*f* sicut carta Malcolmi*g* regis fratris mei predict*is* monachis confirmauit. Concedo et eis confirmo molendina mea de Paxton, sicut carta Willelmi regis fratris mei eisdem monachis confirmat, in feodali firma tenenda cum omnibus iustis pertinent*iis* suis reddendo mihi annuatim*h* plenariam firmam quam predicta molendina reddiderunt*i* anno quo rex Malcolmus*j* frater meus fuit viuus et mortuus, scilicet l *solidos* viij *denarios.*k*

SOURCE: Bodl. MS Rawlinson B. 142, fo. 19v.

NOTES: *a* MS filliis. *b* MS eclesiæ. *c* MS concesisse. *d* MS charta, here and throughout. *e* Sic; for Sproxton (cf. *RRS*, i, p.273, n.2). *f* MS elimosinam. *g* MS Malcolini. *h* MS anuatim. *i* MS rediderunt. *j* MS Malcolnus. *k* Copyist ends here.

COMMENT: Henry II recognised Earl David as lord of the Huntingdon honour from mid-March 1185, but this charter was issued before 15 March 1185 when Pope Lucius III confirmed it: *Papsturkunden in England*, ed. W. Holtzmann (Berlin and Göttingen, 1930–52), i, no.231. It therefore belongs to David's midland campaign of 1174. For the royal charters referred to in the text see *RRS*, i, no.259; ii, no.58.

76. Sawtry abbey. Confirms in alms to the Cistercians of Sawtry the whole of Sawtry, as granted by King Malcolm and confirmed by his charter. (1185 × *c*.1205).

Comes. Daui*D*. fRater Regis Scottorum senescaldo suo. ⁊ Omnibus probis hominibus suis tam clericis quam laicis honoris de Huntendun' salutem. Sciant tam posteri quam presentes me concessisse. ⁊ hac carta mea confirmasse deo ⁊ sancte marie. ⁊ monachis de Sautereia ordinis cistercii in perpetuam elemosinam pro salute anime mee ⁊ antecessorum ⁊ successorum meorum totam Sauteriam cum omnibus pertinentijs suis in bosco ⁊ in plano. In pratis ⁊[a] in aquis ⁊ pasturis ⁊ marescis. ⁊ in omnibus alijs rebus. sicut Rex Scotie Malcolmus bone memorie frater meus eis eam dedit ⁊ carta sua confirmauit. Quare uolo ⁊ firmiter precipio ut predicti monachi eam habeant ⁊ teneant de me ⁊ de heredibus meis in perpetuam elemosinam bene ⁊ in pace honorifice. ⁊ quiete libere. ab omni exaccione temporali ⁊ seruicio. sicut carta Malcolmi Regis Scotie bone memorie eis testatur. His testibus. Willelmo de Lindesi. Willelmo de Basing'. Willelmo de essebi. DauiD. filio suo. Ricardo. de Freinei. Alano filio Hugonis. Nicholao de Asinis. Willelmo capellano. Waltero capellano. Magistro Thoma. Johanne de crossebi. helẏa tailebis. Walkelino filio Sephani.[b]

ENDORSED: Carta dauid. fratris Regis scott' (xiii cent.); De tota saltr' (xiv cent.).

DESCRIPTION: 9.1 × 5.4 in (23 × 13.5 cm). The coloured decoration at the edges of this charter is presumably a later addition. Foot folded, but depth unknown owing to mutilation. Second seal formerly attached on tag; seal and tag now lost.

HAND: Unidentified.

SOURCE: Original, BL Cott. Chart. xii 78 (damaged by fire in 1731 and partly restored) = *A. Selectus Diplomatum et Numismatum Scotiae Thesaurus*, etc., ed. J. Anderson (Edinburgh, 1739), plates 39, 40 (drawn facs. of original, executed before 1731, with transcript) = *B*. Text above is that of *A*; details of sealing from *B*.

PRINTED: See *B* above.

NOTES: *a* The scribe has not invariably written the tironian et with a cross-stroke. *b* Sic.

COMMENT: Issued under the second seal, probably in or shortly after 1185; certainly no later than *c*.1205 when William of Lindsey was dead (*RRS*, ii, p.513). This confirmation, passed in identical terms to that of William I (*RRS*, ii, no.263), perpetuates the fiction of Malcolm IV's charter (*RRS*, i, no.128), which gives the impression that Malcolm, and not Earl Simon de Senlis II, had founded Sawtry abbey: see *Journal of the Soc. of Archivists*, vi, no.6 (1980), pp.325–34.

77. Sawtry abbey. Confirms to Sawtry abbey, and augments, the grant by King William I of the hermitage of *Stanwell* in the wood of Fotheringhay. (1185 × Aug. 1212).

SOURCE: Bodl. MS Rawlinson B. 142, fo.20v.

COMMENT: Cf. No.21, comment, for date. Pope Alexander III confirmed the hermitage to Sawtry on 3 June 1176, while a later papal bull (15 March 1185) specifies the hermitage 'apud Stanguelle . . . sicut illustris rex Scotie Willelmus et comes Simon vobis dederunt et cartis suis confirmarunt': *Papsturkunden in England*, ed. Holtzmann, i, nos.139, 231. These charters are now lost. In 1340 Sawtry held a messuage in Fotheringhay called *Ermytage*, and land to provide a chaplain for performing divine service at the hermitage on Mondays, Wednesdays and Fridays, for the souls of John de Balliol and his predecessors, the kings of Scotland: J. Bridges, *The History and Antiquities of Northamptonshire* (London, 1791), ii, p.451.

78. Sawtry abbey. Grants in alms to Sawtry abbey five acres in Little Paxton, which the monks claimed as appurtenances of the mill, with Alexander who held them, and a croft which Edward held in front of their mill; and land beside the river-bank in Great Paxton to rebuild their mill-pond, and two oaks yearly in his wood to repair their mills. (1185 × Nov. 1215).

Omnibus sancte matris ecclesie*ᵃ* filiis*ᵇ* presentibus et futuris, comes Dauid Huntingtonie, salutem. Sciatis me dedisse et concessisse*ᶜ* et presenti carta*ᵈ* confirmasse Deo et sancte Marie de Saltreia et monachis ibidem Deo seruientibus quinque acras terr*e* in Parua Paxton, quas clamabant pro pertinentibus ad molendinum, simul*ᵉ* cum Alexandro qui eas tenuit, et croftam unam quam Edward*us* tenuit ante molendinum suum, que solebat reddere iiij d*enarios*, et terram iuxta ripam in Magna Paxton rationabiliter sumptam ad stagnum suum reficiend*um*, et duas quercus in bosco meo ad molendina sua reparanda annuatim,*ᶠ* in puram et perpetuam elemosinam,*ᵍ* libere et quiete [et]*ʰ* ab omni exactione seculari solutas. Test*ibus*.*ⁱ*

SOURCE: Bodl. MS Rawlinson B. 142, fo.19v.

NOTES: *a* MS eclesiæ. *b* MS filliis. *c* MS concesisse. *d* MS charta. *e* MS simull. *f* MS anuatim. *g* MS elimosinam. *h* Supplied editorially. *i* Witness-list omitted by copyist.

COMMENT: This charter, as is partly obvious from its tenor, in fact largely confirms earlier dispositions: *RRS*, i, no.234; Bodl. MS Rawlinson B. 142, fo.19v. Earl David's control of the Paxtons apparently terminated in Nov. 1215 (cf. above, p.124).

79. Sawtry abbey. Grants in alms to the monks of Sawtry five acres in the Hanger (of Tottenham), to buy wine for the celebration of divine service in their house. (29 Sept. 1197 × 1215).

Comes dauid frater Regis Scot'. Omnibus Hominibus 7 Amicis Suis Salutem. Quam sibi. Noueritis me intuitu caritatis. 7 pro Salute anime mee. concessisse*ᵃ* dedisse 7 presenti carta mea confirmasse in puram 7 perpetuam elemosinam Monachis*ᵇ* de Sauter'. quinque acras terre In Hangres. ad emendum vinum. vnde celebrentur*ᵃ* in domo Sua. Hiis Test*ibus*. Domino Rogero de Thorpel. Hugone de Lysur'. Rad*ulfo*. de Kameis Rob*erto*. Basset. Rad*ulfo* de Mortem*er*.*ᵇ* Rob*erto*. fil*io*. Rob*er*ti. Ric*ardo*. fil*io* Willelmi. 7 multi/s/ Aliis

ENDORSED: No medieval endorsements.

DESCRIPTION: 6.1 × 2.6 in (15.4 × 6.6 cm). Foot folded to depth of about 0.7 in (1.7 cm); double slits with tag. Seal torn away and lost.

HAND: Unidentified.

SOURCE: Original, BL Addit. Chart. 34032.

NOTES: *a* Word uncertain owing to smudging in source. *b* Especially prominent initial.
COMMENT: Date-limits supplied by Ralph de Camoys and Hugh de Lisures.

80. Sawtry abbey. *Bequeaths to Sawtry abbey with his body eight virgates in Conington. Witnesses: abbots of Sawtry and Warden (unnamed), Henry, the earl's son, David of Ashby and many others. Sealed with the earl's seal.
SOURCE: PRO JUST 1/341, m. 2d.
COMMENT: The source shows that in 1228 Earl John challenged the validity of this bequest, arguing that his father had not made the gift in *liege poustie* and, more significantly, that he was still seised of the property when he died. This lawsuit, although it cannot be followed throughout its course, provides an excellent illustration of the way in which the ruling that a grant of real estate was valid only upon an actual transfer of seisin undermined the successful conveying of land by death-bed gift.

81. Simon de Senlis. Grants to Simon de Senlis £10 worth of land in Great Stukeley, for half of one knight's service. (1185 × 1209, probably × 1202).
SOURCE: *Liber Memorandorum Ecclesie de Bernewelle*, ed. J.W.Clark (Cambridge, 1907), p.272.
COMMENT: Senlis joined Earl David's following in 1185. Earlier than No.17.

82. Simon de Senlis. Grants to Simon de Senlis 100s. yearly out of his third penny of Cambridge, for the fourth part of one knight's service. (1185 × 1219).
SOURCE: *Rotuli Hundredorum temp. Hen. III et Edw. I*, etc., ed. W.Illingworth (Rec. Comm., 1812–18), ii, p.360a.
COMMENT: On the service due cf. *Cambridge Borough Documents*, ed. W.M.Palmer (Cambridge, 1931), pp.24–5.

83. Simon de Senlis. Grants to Simon de Senlis six and a half marks out of his third penny of the county of Huntingdon, for the fourth part of one knight's service. (1185 × 1219).
SOURCE: *Calendar of Close Rolls, 1288–96*, pp.176–7, with *Close Rolls 1247–51*, p.79.

84. Simon de Senlis. *Grants to Simon de Senlis land in Godmanchester. (1190 × 6 Oct. 1207).
SOURCE: *PBKJ*, iv, no.4749, with *RLC*, i, p.217a.
COMMENT: Earl David acquired Godmanchester in 1190. Simon de Senlis cast an essoin *de malo lecti* from this manor on 6 Oct. 1207: *PBKJ*, iv, no. 2702.

85. Gilbert, earl of Strathearn. Grants to Earl Gilbert of Strathearn, his cousin, Kinnaird in Abdie (Fife).

SOURCE: Laing, *Lindores*, p.440 (citing an untraced MS of Sir James Balfour of Denmilne (1600–57), former owner of Kinnaird). R. Sibbald, *The History, Ancient and Modern, of the Sheriffdoms of Fife and Kinross* (Edinburgh, 1710), p.159 (? from same source).

COMMENT: Possibly spurious. But the source further states that Earl Gilbert's son gave Kinnaird to Elcho priory *temp.* King Alexander II, and Elcho was certainly in possession of the property by *c.*1247: *Lind. Cart.*, no.125. Also, the reference to Gilbert as Earl David's 'cousin' fits well with the fact that Gilbert had married Maud, the daughter of William d'Aubigny *Brito* (d.1168), lord of Belvoir. Her mother Maud de Senlis was David's first cousin: *PSAS*, lxxxvii (1952–3), pp.56–7; Barrow, *Era*, p.89. Another tie was forged when Gilbert's brother Malise allied himself with David's illegitimate daughter Ada.

86. Jocelin of Stukeley. Grants to Jocelin of Stukeley a meadow outside Little Stukeley, for his homage and service. (1185 × 1219).
SOURCE: BL Addit. Chart. 34091.
COMMENT: Jocelin served as the steward of Ramsey abbey and a royal justice in the early thirteenth century: D. M. Stenton, *English Justice between the Norman Conquest and the Great Charter, 1066–1215* (London, 1965), p.113.

87. Order of the Knights Templars. Grants to the Knights Templars in England four perches of land in the Inch of Perth. (1178 × 17 March 1199).
SOURCE: SRO GD 160/112/4.
COMMENT: Earl David acquired the Inch of Perth later than *RRS*, ii, no.205 (1178 × 1182), and this grant must have passed before 17 March 1199, by which date he had transferred his whole interest there to Lindores abbey (No.44).

88. Unknown beneficiary. Grants three and a half virgates of his demesne in Great Stukeley. (1173 × 1174, or 1185 × 1209, probably × 1202).
SOURCE: *Rot. Hundredorum*, ii, pp.598–9.
COMMENT: Beneficiary unknown owing to defacement. Possibly an act of King David I before his succession, though the grant is not listed in *RRS*, i. On the dating cf. No.17. These remarks also apply to No.89.

89. Unknown beneficiary. Grants one messuage with a croft of two acres in *Baldewinho* (in Great Stukeley). (1173 × 1174, or 1185 × 1209, probably × 1202).
SOURCE: *Rot. Hundredorum*, ii, p.599b.
COMMENT: For the location of Baldewinho (obsolete) see *RRS*, i, no.208.

90. Unknown beneficiary. *Grants nine acres in Brampton (Hunts), for an annual rent of one pound of cumin. (1202 × 1219).
SOURCE: *Rot. Hundredorum*, ii, p.607b.
COMMENT: Datable by the period of Earl David's lordship over Brampton.

ABBREVIATIONS

The abbreviation of Scottish works has been facilitated by the guidelines set out in *List of Abbreviated Titles of the Printed Sources of Scottish History to 1560*, published as a supplement to the *Scottish Historical Review*, October 1963. Minor conventional abbreviations are not noted.

Aberdeen-Banff Coll.	*Collections for a History of the Shires of Aberdeen and Banff* (Spalding Club, 1843)
Aberdeen Reg.	*Registrum Episcopatus Aberdonensis*, 2 vols (Spalding and Maitland Clubs, 1845)
Aberdeenshire Place-Names	W. M. Alexander, *The Place-Names of Aberdeenshire* (Third Spalding Club, 1952)
Acts Parl. Scot.	*The Acts of the Parliaments of Scotland*, ed. T. Thomson and C. Innes, 12 vols in 13 (Record Commission, 1814-75)
Arbroath Liber	*Liber S. Thome de Aberbrothoc*, 2 vols (Bannatyne Club, 1848-56)
Barrow, *Era*	G. W. S. Barrow, *The Anglo-Norman Era in Scottish History* (Oxford, 1980)
Barrow, *Kingdom*	G. W. S. Barrow, *The Kingdom of the Scots* (London, 1973)
BF	*The Book of Fees commonly called Testa de Nevill*, 2 vols in 3 (London, 1920-31)
BHRS	Bedfordshire Historical Record Society
BIHR	*Bulletin of the Institute of Historical Research*
BL	British Library, London
Bodl.	Bodleian Library, Oxford
Book of Seals	*Sir Christopher Hatton's Book of Seals*, ed. L. C. Loyd and D. M. Stenton (Oxford, 1950)
Brechin Reg.	*Registrum Episcopatus Brechinensis*, 2 vols (Bannatyne Club, 1856)
CChR	*Calendar of the Charter Rolls preserved in the PRO*, 6 vols (London, 1903-27)
CDS	*Calendar of Documents relating to Scotland*, ed. J. Bain, 4 vols (Edinburgh, 1881-8)
Chron. Bower	Walter Bower, *Joannis de Fordun Scotichronicon cum Supplementis et Continuatione*, ed. W. Goodall, 2 vols (Edinburgh, 1759)
Chron. Fantosme	*Jordan Fantosme's Chronicle*, ed. R. C. Johnston (Oxford, 1981)

Chron. Fordun John of Fordun, *Chronica Gentis Scotorum*, ed.
W. F. Skene, 2 vols (Edinburgh, 1871-2)

Chron. Howden Roger of Howden, *Chronica*, ed. W. Stubbs, 4 vols
(RS, 1868-71)

Chron. Melrose *The Chronicle of Melrose*, ed. A. O. Anderson *et al.*
(London, 1936)

Chron. Stephen *Chronicles of the Reigns of Stephen, Henry II, and
Richard I*, ed. R. Howlett, 4 vols (RS, 1884-9)

Comp. Pge. *The Complete Peerage* by G. E. C[okayne], revised by
V. Gibbs *et al.*, 13 vols in 14 (London, 1910-59)

CRR *Curia Regis Rolls . . . preserved in the PRO*, 16 vols
(London, 1922-79)

Danelaw Docts. *Documents Illustrative of the Social and Economic
History of the Danelaw*, ed. F. M. Stenton
(London, 1920)

Dryburgh Liber *Liber S. Marie de Dryburgh* (Bannatyne Club, 1847)

Duncan, Scotland A. A. M. Duncan, *Scotland: The Making of the
Kingdom* (Edinburgh, 1975)

Dunfermline Reg. *Registrum de Dunfermelyn* (Bannatyne Club, 1842)

EHR *English Historical Review*

EYC *Early Yorkshire Charters*, vols i-iii (1914-16), ed.
W. Farrer; vols iv-xii, ed. C. T. Clay (Yorks
Archaeol. Soc., Record Ser., Extra Ser., 1935-65)

Foedera *Foedera, Conventiones, Litterae*, etc., ed. T. Rymer,
4 vols in 7 (Record Commission, 1816-69)

Gesta Henrici *Gesta Regis Henrici Secundi Benedicti Abbatis*, ed.
W. Stubbs, 2 vols (RS, 1867)

Harrold Recs. *Records of Harrold Priory*, ed. G. H. Fowler
(BHRS, 1935)

Hist. MSS Comm. Royal Commission on Historical Manuscripts.
1st to 9th Reports cited by number; others normally
by name of owner or collection

HKF W. Farrer, *Honors and Knights' Fees*, 3 vols
(London and Manchester, 1923-5)

Holt, *Northerners* J. C. Holt, *The Northerners: A Study in the Reign of
King John* (Oxford, 1961)

Holyrood Liber *Liber Cartarum Sancte Crucis* (Bannatyne Club,
1840)

Kelso Liber *Liber S. Marie de Calchou*, 2 vols (Bannatyne Club,
1846)

Laing, *Lindores* A. Laing, *Lindores Abbey and its Burgh of Newburgh*
(Edinburgh, 1876)

Landon, *Itinerary* L. Landon, *The Itinerary of King Richard I*
(PRS, 1935)

Lawrie, *Annals* *Annals of the Reigns of Malcolm and William, Kings
of Scotland*, ed. A. C. Lawrie (Glasgow, 1910)

Lawrie, *Charters* *Early Scottish Charters prior to 1153*, ed. A. C. Lawrie
(Glasgow, 1905)

Le Patourel, *Norman Empire* J. Le Patourel, *The Norman Empire* (Oxford, 1976)

Lind. Cart.	*Chartulary of the Abbey of Lindores*, ed. J. Dowden (SHS, 1903)
Lindores Liber	*Liber Sancte Marie de Lundoris* (Abbotsford Club, 1841)
Melrose Liber	*Liber Sancte Marie de Melros*, 2 vols (Bannatyne Club, 1837)
Mem. Roll 1 John	*The Memoranda Roll for the Michaelmas Term of the First Year of the Reign of King John, 1199-1200*, ed. H. G. Richardson (PRS, 1943)
Mem. Roll 10 John	*The Memoranda Roll for the Tenth Year of the Reign of King John (1207-8)*, ed. R. A. Brown (PRS, 1957)
Mon. Angl.	W. Dugdale, *Monasticon Anglicanum*, ed. J. Caley *et al.*, 6 vols in 8 (London, 1817-30)
Moray Reg.	*Registrum Episcopatus Moraviensis* (Bannatyne Club, 1837)
Mowbray Chrs.	*Charters of the Honour of Mowbray, 1107-1191*, ed. D. E. Greenway (London, 1972)
NLS	National Library of Scotland, Edinburgh
Northants Assize Rolls	*The Earliest Northamptonshire Assize Rolls, A.D. 1202 and 1203*, ed. D. M. Stenton (Northants Record Soc., 1930)
Northants Chrs.	*Facsimiles of Early Charters from Northamptonshire Collections*, ed. F. M. Stenton (Northants Record Soc., 1930)
Northumberland Hist.	*A History of Northumberland*. Issued under the direction of the Northumberland County History Committee, 15 vols (Newcastle upon Tyne, 1893-1940)
NRO	Northamptonshire Record Office, Delapre Abbey, Northampton
Pat. Rolls	*Patent Rolls of the Reign of Henry III preserved in the PRO*, i (1216-25), 1901; ii (1225-32), 1903
PBKJ	*Pleas before the King or his Justices, 1198-1212*, ed. D. M. Stenton, 4 vols (Selden Soc., 1953-67)
PR	*Pipe Roll*, as published by the Pipe Roll Society, 1884-
PRO	Public Record Office, London
PRS	Pipe Roll Society
PSAS	*Proceedings of the Society of Antiquaries of Scotland*
Raine, *North Durham*	Appendix to J. Raine, *The History and Antiquities of North Durham* (London, 1852)
RAL	*The Registrum Antiquissimum of the Cathedral Church of Lincoln*, ed. C. W. Foster and K. Major, 12 vols (Lincoln Record Soc., 1931-73)
RCAHMS	Royal Commission on the Ancient and Historical Monuments of Scotland
RCHME	Royal Commission on Historical Monuments, England
RCR	*Rotuli Curiae Regis*, ed. F. Palgrave, 2 vols (Record Commission, 1835)

Reg. Mag. Sig.   *Registrum Magni Sigilli Regum Scotorum*, ed. J. M. Thomson *et al.*, 9 vols (Edinburgh, 1882-1912)

Richardson, *English Jewry*   H. G. Richardson, *The English Jewry under Angevin Kings* (London, 1960)

Ritchie, *Normans*   R. L. G. Ritchie, *The Normans in Scotland* (Edinburgh, 1954)

RLC   *Rotuli Litterarum Clausarum in Turri Londinensi asservati*, ed. T. D. Hardy, 2 vols (Record Commission, 1833-4)

RLP   *Rotuli Litterarum Patentium in Turri Londinensi asservati*, ed. T. D. Hardy (Record Commission, 1835)

Rot. Chart.   *Rotuli Chartarum in Turri Londinensi asservati*, ed. T. D. Hardy (Record Commission, 1837)

Rot. de Ob.   *Rotuli de Oblatis et Finibus in Turri Londinensi asservati*, ed. T. D. Hardy (Record Commission, 1835)

RRS   *Regesta Regum Scottorum*, ed. G. W. S. Barrow *et al.*, i (1153-65), 1960; ii (1165-1214), 1971; vi (1329-71), 1982

RS   Rolls Series

St Andrews Liber   *Liber Cartarum Prioratus Sancti Andree in Scotia* (Bannatyne Club, 1841)

Scots Pge.   *The Scots Peerage*, ed. J. Balfour Paul, 9 vols (Edinburgh, 1904-14)

SHR   *Scottish Historical Review*

SHS   Scottish History Society

Simpson, *Mar Earldom*   W. D. Simpson, *The Earldom of Mar* (Aberdeen, 1949)

Simpson, *Mar Province*   W. D. Simpson, *The Province of Mar* (Aberdeen, 1943)

SRO   Scottish Record Office, Edinburgh

Stenton, *First Century*   F. M. Stenton, *The First Century of English Feudalism, 1066-1166*, 2nd edn (Oxford, 1961)

TCWAAS   *Transactions of the Cumberland and Westmorland Antiquarian and Archaeological Society*

TDGAS   *Transactions of the Dumfriesshire and Galloway Natural History and Antiquarian Society*

TRHS   *Transactions of the Royal Historical Society*

VCH   *Victoria History of the Counties of England*

Wardon Cart.   *Cartulary of the Abbey of Old Wardon*, ed. G. H. Fowler (BHRS, 1930)

NOTES

CHAPTER ONE
The Setting

1. *RRS*, i, no.131.
2. *RRS*, i, no.128.
3. *RRS*, i, p.11.
4. A Fécamp abbey source quoted in R. W. Southern, *Medieval Humanism and Other Studies* (Oxford, 1970), p.229.
5. Barrow, *Kingdom*, pp.7-68.
6. Most recently, Le Patourel, *Norman Empire*, pp.67-9, 207-9.
7. Ailred of Rievaulx, *Relatio de Standardo*, ed. R. Howlett in *Chron. Stephen*, iii, p.193.
8. Orderic Vitalis, *Historia Ecclesiastica*, iv, ed. M. Chibnall (Oxford, 1973), p.274.
9. C. W. Hollister and T. K. Keefe, 'The making of the Angevin Empire', *Journal of British Studies*, xii (1973), p.3; a different emphasis in Le Patourel, *Norman Empire*, esp. pp.68-73, 207-10.
10. I follow here C. W. Hollister, 'Normandy, France and the Anglo-Norman *regnum*', *Speculum*, li (1976), p.214; *RRS*, i, p.102. Professor Le Patourel was the first to admit that there is no positive evidence for his suggestion in *Norman Empire*, p.209, n.5, that after David became king he renewed his homage to Beauclerk for the Huntingdon honour.
11. Barrow, *Kingdom*, pp.321-8.
12. Ailred of Rievaulx, *Relatio de Standardo*, pp.192-5.
13. D. Bethell, 'English monks and Irish reform in the eleventh and twelfth centuries', *Historical Studies*, viii (1971), p.134.
14. The French mother houses were Arrouaise (dioc. Arras), St Quentin of Beauvais (not in Normandy as stated in Duncan, *Scotland*, p.150), and Tiron (dioc. Chartres).
15. E.g., *RRS*, i, no.8; G. W. S. Barrow, 'A Scottish collection at Canterbury', *SHR*, xxxi (1952), pp.18-26. Relatedly, see Duncan, *Scotland*, p.147.
16. J. C. Dickinson, *The Origins of the Austin Canons and their Introduction into England* (London, 1950), pp.134, 141; R. H. C. Davis, *King Stephen, 1135-1154* (London, 1977 reprint), pp. 98-106.
17. Cf. Barrow, *Kingdom*, p.187; similarly, Duncan, *Scotland*, pp.143-4. I note here for its valuable perspective C. N. L. Brooke, 'Princes and kings as patrons of monasteries: Normandy and England', *Il monachesimo e la riforma ecclesiastica (1049-1122)* (Milan, 1971), pp.125-44.
18. L. Halphen, 'La place de la royauté dans le système féodal', *Revue Historique*, clxxii (1933), p.250. Cf. Le Patourel, *Norman Empire*, pp.96-8, 102.
19. D. Hay, 'Geographical abstractions and the historian', *Historical Studies*, ii (1959), p.12.
20. *RRS*, i, p.47.
21. M. Bloch, *Feudal Society* (London, 1961), p.400.
22. G. W. S. Barrow, 'Das mittelalterliche englische und schottische Königtum: ein Vergleich', *Historisches Jahrbuch*, cii (1982), p.365, adding on Galloway Walter Daniel, *Vita Ailredi Abbatis Rievall'*, ed. F. M. Powicke (London, 1950), p.45.
23. R. L. G. Ritchie, *Chrétien de Troyes and Scotland* (Oxford, 1952); R. S. Loomis, 'Scotland and the Arthurian legend', *PSAS*, lxxxix (1955-6), pp.1-21.
24. Respectively, K. J. Stringer, 'Galloway and the abbeys of Rievaulx and Dundrennan', *TDGAS*, 3rd ser., lv (1980), pp.174-7; G. W. S. Barrow, 'The reign of William the Lion,

king of Scotland', *Historical Studies*, vii (1969), p.33; B. E. Crawford, 'The earldom of Caithness and the kingdom of Scotland, 1150-1266', *Northern Scotland*, ii (1974-7), pp.99-104.

25. J.-F. Lemarignier, *Recherches sur l'Hommage en Marche et les Frontières Féodales* (Lille, 1945), pp.92ff.; Le Patourel, *Norman Empire*, pp.207-21.

26. I. A. Milne in *An Introduction to Scottish Legal History* (Stair Soc., 1958), p.148. Cf. the ill-considered comments in H. A. Cronne, *The Reign of Stephen, 1135-1154* (London, 1970), pp.35, 181; followed, albeit cautiously, in Duncan, *Scotland*, p.220.

27. A. Morey and C. N. L. Brooke, *Gilbert Foliot and his Letters* (Cambridge, 1965), p.1.

28. Barrow, *Kingdom*, chs.10-12; idem, *Era*. See also the invaluable contributions in Duncan, *Scotland*, esp. chs.15, 16.

29. S. Painter, *William Marshal* (Baltimore, 1933); C. Ellis, *Hubert de Burgh* (London, 1952); C. Bémont, *Simon de Montfort, Earl of Leicester, 1208-1265*, new edn (Oxford, 1930); N. Denholm-Young, *Richard of Cornwall* (Oxford, 1947).

30. Reference to Earl David's charters in the notes is made simply by citing the Arabic serial numbers assigned to them in the Appendix: thus, as in the first citation, No.44.

CHAPTER TWO
Early Life

1. Following William of Newburgh, *Historia Rerum Anglicarum*, ed. R. Howlett in *Chron. Stephen*, i, p.71; cf. *RRS*, i, p.22, for Newburgh's excellent knowledge of the Scottish royal house. The conventional date, 1144, must be discarded for lack of authority.

2. Reginald of Durham, *Libellus de Admirandis Beati Cuthberti Virtutibus*, ed. J. Raine (Surtees Soc., 1835), p.219.

3. E.g., *Chron. Fantosme*, lines 254-5, 325, 339, 348; cf. also Walter Daniel, *Vita Ailredi*, pp.xli-iii, xlvi-vii.

4. Barrow, 'Reign of William', p.26.

5. Idem, *Kingdom*, p.328; R. C. Reid, *TDGAS*, 3rd ser., xx (1935-6), pp.133-9; *RRS*, ii, nos.131, 170.

6. W. Dugdale, *The Antiquities of Warwickshire*, 2nd edn (London, 1730), ii, p.1066; *Wardon Cart.*, no.340b; J. Hodgson, *History of Northumberland*, ii, iii (Newcastle upon Tyne, 1840), p.17.

7. *RRS*, i, pp.6-7. Queen Maud, wife of David I, had died in 1130/1; see further V. Chandler, 'Ada de Warenne, Queen Mother of Scotland', *SHR*, lx (1981), pp.119-39.

8. *RRS*, i, nos.131, 184, 195, 198, 236; *Calendar of the Laing Charters*, ed. J. Anderson (Edinburgh, 1899), no.2; *Registrum S. Marie de Neubotle* (Bannatyne Club, 1849), no.69.

9. On Earl Henry see Richard of Hexham, *De Gestis Regis Stephani*, ed. R. Howlett in *Chron. Stephen*, iii, p.178; Henry of Huntingdon, *Historia Anglorum*, ed. T. Arnold (RS, 1879), p.265.

10. Robert of Torigni, *Chronica*, ed. R. Howlett in *Chron. Stephen*, iv, p.218; cf. *A Scottish Chronicle known as the Chronicle of Holyrood*, ed. M. O. Anderson (SHS, 1938), p.141.

11. W. L. Warren, *Henry II* (London, 1973), pp.141-2; more generally, C. L. H. Coulson, *Château Gaillard*, vi (1973), pp.59-67.

12. Duncan, *Scotland*, pp.224-7. For further comment, inevitably reflecting the vagueness or ambiguity of the chronicle evidence, see *RRS*, i, p.19; Warren, *Henry II*, pp.177-80, 183.

13. R. A. Brown, 'A list of castles, 1154-1216', *EHR*, lxxiv (1959), p.251; idem, 'Royal castle-building in England, 1154-1216', *EHR*, lxx (1955), esp. p.379.

14. D. C. Douglas, *The Norman Achievement* (London, 1969), p.49.

15. *RRS*, ii, nos.30, 79.

16. *Chron. Melrose*, p.38.

17. *RRS*, ii, nos.8-10, 30, 45, 51, 72, 79, 84, 86, 91, 100, 107, 109, 116, 140. Here, as elsewhere, David's itinerary has to be reconstructed from his appearances as a witness to charters. In accepting that charter witness-lists provide a reasonably

reliable guide to a person's movements, I follow the views expressed in *RRS*, i, p.79; ii, p.80. See also below, p.307, n.6.

18. E.g., *Arbroath Liber*, i, nos.56, 91; *Kelso Liber*, ii, no.321; *Melrose Liber*, i, nos.116, 127.
19. G. W. S. Barrow, 'A twelfth-century Newbattle document', *SHR*, xxx (1951), p.44. David witnessed SRO GD 241/254: unpublished charter, *c*.1170, by Robert de Quincy to Pain de Hedleia, granting the lands later known as Penston (East Lothian).
20. *RRS*, ii, nos.106, 192, 204.
21. Other examples in *Arbroath Liber*, i, no.85; *Melrose Liber*, i, no.97; *St Andrews Liber*, p.319.
22. No.44.
23. Ritchie, *Normans*, pp.164-9.
24. Duncan, *Scotland*, pp.126, 164-5; *RRS*, i, p.97.
25. William also received some provision in Lothian: *RRS*, ii, no.5.
26. *RRS*, ii, no.205.
27. *Origines Parochiales Scotiae* (Bannatyne Club, 1851-5), i, pp.20-48; W. Fraser, *The Lennox* (Edinburgh, 1874), ii, no.25. For map see J. Irving, *History of Dumbartonshire*, revised edn (Dumbarton, 1917-24), ii, frontispiece.
28. SRO GD 220/2/202; printed from later transcripts as *Cartularium Comitatus de Levenax* (Maitland Club, 1833).
29. E.g., W. F. Skene, *Celtic Scotland*, 2nd edn (Edinburgh, 1886-90), iii, pp.69-70; *Lind. Cart.*, p.229; *Scots Pge.*, v, pp.326-7. The most recent account of the descent of the medieval earldom is given in *Comp. Pge.*, vii, pp.585ff.
30. *Chron. Fantosme*, lines 1100-4; noted but not discussed in *Comp. Pge.*, vii, p.588n.
31. No.35; *RRS*, ii, no.120. There would be little reason to question Fantosme if we could fully accept Professor Legge's date of '1175 or even the end of 1174' for the composition of his chronicle, but positive proof is lacking: M. D. Legge, *Anglo-Norman Literature and its Background* (Oxford, 1971 reprint), p.75; followed in *Chron. Fantosme*,

p.xxiii.
32. Below, p.94.
33. *Origines Parochiales*, i, p.35; cf. Barrow, *Kingdom*, pp.274-5.
34. Skene, *Celtic Scotland*, iii, pp.117-19, 454-5; W. J. Watson, *The History of the Celtic Place-Names of Scotland* (Edinburgh, 1926), pp.220-1.
35. Barrow, *Kingdom*, pp.288-91, 339-47; C. Tabraham, *TDGAS*, 3rd ser., liii (1977-8), pp.114-28.
36. Norwegian marauders crossed the Arrochar-Tarbet isthmus, dividing Loch Long from Loch Lomond, when they raided Lennox in 1263.
37. Barrow, *Kingdom*, p.339.
38. Idem, *Era*, p.68; also W. D. Simpson, *Trans. of the Glasgow Archaeol. Soc.*, new ser., ix (1937-40), pp.152-83.
39. A. A. M. Duncan and A. L. Brown, 'Argyll and the Isles in the earlier Middle Ages', *PSAS*, xc (1956-7), p.199.
40. *Scots Pge.*, v, p.328.
41. This paragraph owes much to Duncan, *Scotland*, pp.164-7, 178-9, 187-8, 192-6, 199-200. See also Crawford, 'Earldom of Caithness', pp.106-15.
42. Though it is a common view: e.g., *Lind. Cart.*, p.xxix; *Scots Pge.*, v, pp.327-8; Ritchie, *Normans*, p.166, n.3.
43. *RRS*, ii, no.205. For Fife see Barrow, *Kingdom*, pp.283, 304.
44. No.35; below, pp.213-14. According to Fantosme, David was to hold Lennox 'tuz les jorz de sa vie': *Chron. Fantosme*, line 1103.
45. This possibility, originally mooted in Skene, *Celtic Scotland*, iii, p.70, finds some support in the fact that Lennox did not figure in David's arrangements for the endowment of his abbey of Lindores, begun *c*.1190.
46. Adequate surveys exist only for the mottes in western Stirlingshire: RCAHMS, *Inventory of Stirlingshire* (1963), i, pp.173-5. Balloch castle (Nat. Grid Ref. NS 388826) and Catter Law (NS 472871), Dunbartonshire, were favoured residences of the thirteenth-century earls of Lennox: *Origines Parochiales*, i, p.35.
47. E.g., *Cart. . . . de Levenax*, pp.37-

40, 49-51; Fraser, *Lennox*, ii, nos.3, 6-10, 12-15. See further *Scottish Genealogist*, xxii, no.2 (1975), pp.34-5.

48. *Registrum Monasterii de Passelet* (Maitland Club, 1832; New Club, 1877), p.167; *Acts Parl. Scot.*, i, p.96.

49. Respectively, *RRS*, ii, no.374; N. F. Shead, 'The administration of the diocese of Glasgow in the twelfth and thirteenth centuries', *SHR*, lv (1976), pp.128, 144-5; J. D. Marwick, *Early Glasgow*, ed. R. Renwick (Glasgow, 1911), pp.13-14.

50. The castle and burgh of Dumbarton existed by 1222; the first known sheriff held office by June 1237: Irving, *Dumbartonshire*, ii, p.287; *Reg. . . . de Passelet*, p.218. See further Barrow, *Kingdom*, pp.97, 121, 309.

51. *Cart. . . . de Levenax*, p.1.

52. J. G. Dunbar and A. A. M. Duncan, 'Tarbert castle: a contribution to the history of Argyll', *SHR*, l (1971), pp.1-17.

53. *RRS*, ii, nos.51, 79.

54. Cf. Lawrie, *Annals*, pp.112, 114-15. There is no evidence to support the assumption made in Barrow, 'Reign of William', p.27, that David accompanied William to France in 1166.

55. Le Patourel, *Norman Empire*, esp. pp.162, 329-30.

56. That Earl Simon III gained seisin of the Huntingdon honour in 1153 has usually been denied on the grounds that he was then a minor and custody devolved upon the crown; but see now K. J. Stringer, *Journal of the Soc. of Archivists*, vi, no.6 (1980), p.329, n.23.

57. The precise conditions under which King Malcolm III (Canmore) had been allocated land in England remain unclear: Ritchie, *Normans*, pp.386-8; Le Patourel, *Norman Empire*, p.208. See also above, p.3 with n.10.

58. Henry II was similarly compromised in his relations with the French crown: most recently, Hollister, 'Normandy, France', pp.235-42. But the fact remains that Malcolm IV and William I were King Henry's acknowledged vassals, whereas the Angevin was not a vassal of the king of Scots.

59. *RRS*, ii, p.4; Warren, *Henry II*, p.184.

60. M. F. Moore, *The Lands of the Scottish Kings in England* (London, 1915), pp.57-9.

61. The chief strongpoint, Huntingdon castle, commanded Ermine Street between Hertford and Stamford. The English crown was careful to ensure that the Scottish lords of the honour did not control Northampton, however: J. Tait, *The Medieval English Borough* (Manchester, 1936), pp.155, 175.

62. Lawrie, *Annals*, pp.117, 119.

63. Cf. W. Kienast, *Untertaneneid und Treuvorbehalt in Frankreich und England* (Weimar, 1952), p.194; J. Boussard, *Le Gouvernement d'Henri II Plantegenêt* (Paris, 1956), p.391. Quotation from *Gesta Henrici*, i, p.6.

64. Lawrie, *Annals*, p.118.

65. Warren, *Henry II*, p.184.

66. *Chron. Fantosme*, lines 348-51.

67. *Chron. Melrose*, p.40; dissension among the king's counsellors reported in *Chron. Fantosme*, lines 383-406.

68. Correcting F. Barlow, *The Feudal Kingdom of England, 1042-1216*, 3rd edn (London, 1972), p.340.

69. Lawrie, *Annals*, pp.131-2; cf. *RRS*, i, no.207; *VCH Cambs*, ii, pp.388-9.

70. *Chron. Fantosme*, lines 1102-6.

71. Ibid., line 1100: 'el meis daueril' (Lincoln MS); 'en mai enprés avril' (Durham MS). The former reading seems preferable, though for May see *RRS*, ii, no.205, comment.

72. G. V. Scammell, *Hugh du Puiset, Bishop of Durham* (Cambridge, 1956), pp.38ff.

73. William of Newburgh, *Historia*, p.180; see also n.88 below.

74. *VCH Leics*, ii, pp.81-2.

75. *Chron. Fantosme*, lines 947-9.

76. William of Newburgh, *Historia*, p.180.

77. *Chron. Fantosme*, line 1116; Ralph Niger, *Chronica*, ed. R. Anstruther (Caxton Soc., 1851), p.176.

78. Warren, *Henry II*, p.125.

79. Ralph Niger, *Chronica*, p.176; cf. *VCH Leics*, ii, p.83.

80. *PR 19 Henry II*, pp.33, 173.
81. Ralph de Diceto, *Opera Historica*, ed. W. Stubbs (RS, 1876), i, p.384. *Gesta Henrici*, i, p.70, describes how close investment began no earlier than late June, however.
82. *Chron. Fantosme*, lines 1109-14; also Lawrie, *Annals*, p.148.
83. *Chron. Fantosme*, lines 1119-30; *Gesta Henrici*, i, p.68.
84. Reginald of Durham, *Libellus*, p.273.
85. *Chron. Fantosme*, line 1121; *Gesta Henrici*, i, p.64.
86. J. H. Beeler, *Warfare in England, 1066-1189* (Ithaca, 1966), p.186.
87. *Gesta Henrici*, i, p.69.
88. Ibid., p.68. David attested charters by Roger and Nigel de Mowbray datable *c.*1166 × 86: *Mowbray Chrs.*, nos.29-31. Had he paused on his march through England for discussions with the Mowbrays?
89. *RRS*, i, p.108.
90. Nos.23, 34, 58, 75.
91. A witness, William de St Michael, was one of King William's emissaries at the French royal court in 1173 (*Chron. Fantosme*, line 421), and may have brought back the young King Henry's charter confirming the Huntingdon honour to David.
92. *Cartulary of the Monastery of St Frideswide at Oxford*, ed. S. R. Wigram (Oxford Historical Soc., 1895-6), ii, no.791: bull of Pope Alexander III, dating-clause abridged but issued at Ferentino and therefore datable Oct. 1174 × Oct. 1175. The original act of disseisin was attributed to King William; see also *VCH Oxon*, v, p.251.
93. *Book of Seals*, no.220; NRO Finch-Hatton Muniments, no.2665.
94. The basic thirteenth-century investigations are Holt, *Northerners*, ch.4; E. F. Jacob, *Studies in the Period of Baronial Reform and Rebellion, 1258-1267* (Oxford, 1925), pp.276ff.
95. *PR 22 Henry II*, p.184; *Gesta Henrici*, i, pp.72-3; below, p.111.
96. *VCH Leics*, ii, pp.82-3; *PR 22 Henry II*, p.184. See also *Gesta Henrici*, i, p.64; amplified in *Chron. Howden*, ii, p.57.
97. *PR 21 Henry II*, pp.47, 150, 157; *Gesta Henrici*, i, p.106. On Ralph's

main estates see *VCH Northants*, ii, pp.483, 499-500.
98. *PR 20 Henry II*, p.104; *RRS*, ii, no.382, comment. For David's association with the Hownam line see *Melrose Liber*, i, nos.116, 127.
99. Since no *carta* was returned for the honour of Huntingdon in 1166, information on their standing in the estate has to be pieced together from a range of sources, valuable details being found in *HKF*, ii. Many of these men, or their kinsfolk, figure in subsequent chapters.
100. *RRS*, i, no.150.
101. *RRS*, i, pp.100-2; No.23. Walter of Lindsey is not identical with the Huntingdon steward of that name, but with the latter's son: see below, p.309, n.64.
102. Holt, *Northerners*, p.44.
103. Possibly also relating to this period is NRO MS Finch-Hatton 123, p.284: copy of a charter by William of Knightley of Fawsley (Northants). Hugh Ridel *dapifer*, William Burdet, Walter of Lindsey and Alcmund of Oxendon, another of David's supporters in 1174, are among the witnesses, the first name being that of Simon de Tosny, bishop of Moray (1172-84): for 'Wigon'' in the source, read 'Morau''. For caution's sake, however, the date ascribed to this charter must be 1172 × 4.
104. On Henry II's policy as regards allegiance to the crown see Kienast, *Untertaneneid und Treuvorbehalt*, pp.194-7; Boussard, *Henri II*, pp.387-92.
105. *PR 22 Henry II*, pp.74-5, 85, 113; *PR 23 Henry II*, p.92; *PR 24 Henry II*, p.52.
106. *Anglo-Scottish Relations, 1174-1328: Some Selected Documents*, ed. E. L. G. Stones (Oxford, 1970 reprint), no.1.
107. Nos.34-5; quoting *Chron. Fantosme*, line 1101.
108. *PR 11 Henry II*, p.96; *PR 16 Henry II*, p.23; *PR 23 Henry II*, p.78.
109. *PR 21 Henry II*, p.47; cf. *Northants Assize Rolls*, no.685.
110. C. T. Clay, *Early Yorkshire Families* (Yorks Archaeol. Soc., rec. ser., 1973), pp.64-5; *VCH Cambs*, v,

p.49. David witnessed for Robert's son concerning Eltisley, 1189 × 98 (Cambridge, Emmanuel College Muniments, Box 12.A, no.4). The Musters were also associated with the Mowbrays: *Mowbray Chrs.*, no.301; *VCH Cambs*, v, p.48.

111. *PR 20 Henry II*, pp.135-6.

112. *HKF*, i, pp.94-5; *Annales Monastici*, ed. H. R. Luard (RS, 1864-9), iii, p.21. The Richespauds can be shown to have had a Huntingdon interest, but no earlier than 1200: *PBKJ*, i, no.3085; *HKF*, ii, p.384. See further *Harrold Recs.*, pp.206-7.

113. On Henry of Oxendon (*alias* of Glendon), a knight of good substance in Great Oxendon and neighbouring villages, see *The Cartulary of Cirencester Abbey*, ii, ed. C. D. Ross (London, 1964), nos.704-5, 707, 709; BL MS Cott. Calig. A. xii, fos.92v-3v, 99v, MS Cott. Claud. D. xii, fo.84r.

114. Below, pp.76, 145, 152.

115. Fined under the accounts of Northampton for communing with the rebels (*PR 21 Henry II*, p.46), Simon Vitor is elsewhere styled 'of Northampton' and was one of those responsible for recording the laws of the town in *c.*1189: BL MS Cott. Tib. E. v, fo.75v; *Luffield Priory Charters*, ed. G. R. Elvey (Northants Rec. Soc., 1968-75), i, no. 103; F. Lee, *Leges Ville Norht* (Northampton, 1951), p.8. On his Huntingdon fee see BL MS Sloane 986, fos.31r-2r; also *HKF*, ii, pp.366, 386-7.

116. Philip de Colville, William of Lindsey, Richard de Moreville, Thomas de Muscamp, Walter Olifard: *RRS*, ii, nos.126, 135, 144; *Gesta Henrici*, i, p.66; *HKF*, ii, pp.325, 355.

117. M. Powicke, *Military Obligation in Medieval England* (Oxford, 1962), p.51. Cf. J. E. A. Jolliffe, *The Constitutional History of Medieval England*, 4th edn (London, 1961), p.161: 'Leicester, Mowbray, and Norfolk fought with armies of hired Flemings.'

118. *Gesta Henrici*, i, p.106.

119. On Saer de Quincy II and his family connections – his mother was a stepdaughter of King David I – see S.

Painter, *Feudalism and Liberty* (Baltimore, 1961), pp.232-7; G. G. Simpson, 'An Anglo-Scottish Baron of the thirteenth century: The Acts of Roger de Quincy, earl of Winchester and Constable of Scotland' (unpublished Edinburgh University Ph.D. thesis, 1965), pp.9-12.

120. Below, esp. ch.8, passim.

121. *Gesta Henrici*, i, p.71; also Gerald of Wales, *Opera*, ed. J. S. Brewer *et al.* (RS, 1861-91), iv, p.368; *PR 20 Henry II*, pp.10, 63. See further *Medieval Archaeology*, xii (1968), p.175.

122. Lawrie, *Annals*, pp.186-7.

123. Ibid.

124. *Anglo-Scottish Relations*, ed. Stones, no.1.

125. Robert of Torigni, *Chronica*, p.268, refers to Angevin rights of control over the exercise of Scots royal patronage.

126. *Gesta Henrici*, i, p.71. An independent account is given in *De Comitissa*, ed. F. Michel in *Chroniques Anglo-Normandes* (Rouen, 1836-40), ii, p.129.

127. *Wardon Cart.*, no.207f: abstract of a charter by Earl Simon III confirming property as it was held 'in die qua venit ad obsidionem de Huntyngdon'; *Rufford Charters*, ed. C. J. Holdsworth (Thoroton Soc., 1972-81), ii, no.745 (where the date in the printed text should be corrected to read M.C.lxxiiii).

128. *Tractatus de Legibus et Consuetudinibus Regni Angliae*, etc., ed. G. D. G. Hall (London, 1965), p.106.

129. *Chron. Fantosme*, lines 954, 1096-9, 1131, 1135-8, 2034-5.

CHAPTER THREE

Lord of Garioch and Earl of Huntingdon

1. Lawrie, *Annals*, pp.201-3.

2. Duncan, *Scotland*, pp.231-5.

3. *RRS*, ii, nos.158-9, 166, 178, 182, 186, 190-2, 195-6, 200-4, 206, 214-16, 220-1, 237, 251, 264-5.

4. *RRS*, ii, nos.236, 253; Lawrie, *Annals*, pp.236, 251-2; *St Andrews Liber*, p.334; *Arbroath Liber*, i, no.3; *Dryburgh Liber*, no.63.

5. *RRS*, ii, no.205.

6. No.28.

7. *Chron. Bower*, ii, p.33.
8. Nos.44, 46, 72 (the Inch, Eccles-greig). John of Fordun correctly describes David as lord of Inverbervie: *Chron. Fordun*, i, p.281; cf. No.48. For Brechin see below, p.58.
9. Ibid., p.64.
10. For my argument, ibid., pp.64-8.
11. *Moray Reg.*, no.30; *Scots Pge.*, iv, p.8; vi, p.127.
12. Cf. ibid., viii, pp.318-22; B. E. Crawford, *Northern Scotland*, ii (1974-7), pp.108-9; Duncan, *Scotland*, pp.188, 191, 197; Barrow, *Era*, p.86.
13. Duncan, *Scotland*, p.164.
14. *Scots Pge.*, v, pp.572-4; Simpson, *Mar Province*, pp.115-16; W. D. Simpson, 'The excavation of Coull castle, Aberdeenshire', *PSAS*, lviii (1923-4), pp.47-8. Note, however, that this Durward lordship was already in the making by *c.*1205: *RRS*, ii, no.452.
15. Lawrie, *Annals*, p.227. Earlier visits by David to Moray indicated in *RRS*, ii, nos.116, 159.
16. *RRS*, ii, pp.12, 64.
17. C. R. Cheney, *From Becket to Langton* (Manchester, 1956), p.121; *RRS*, ii, p.32.
18. *RRS*, ii, no.520; W. Fraser, *The Sutherland Book* (Edinburgh, 1892), iii, no.3.
19. *RRS*, ii, p.40; Duncan, *Scotland*, p.205. The earliest known sheriffs of Aberdeen and Banff occur by 1222 and 1242 respectively: *Illustrations of the Topography and Antiquities of the Shires of Aberdeen and Banff* (Spalding Club, 1847-69), ii, pp.18-19, 109.
20. G. S. Pryde, *The Burghs of Scotland: A Critical List* (Oxford, 1965), p.14; W. D. Simpson, 'Fyvie castle', *PSAS*, lxxiii (1938-9), p.34.
21. Barrow, *Kingdom*, pp.287-8, 291-4, 311-12.
22. Cf. *RRS*, i, pp.12, 43, 51-2.
23. Duncan, *Scotland*, p.188; quotation from W. D. Simpson, 'The early castles of Mar', *PSAS*, lxiii (1928-9), p.105.
24. Cf. G. G. Simpson and B. Webster, 'Charter evidence and the distribution of mottes in Scotland', *Château Gaillard*, v (1972), pp.177-8, 181-2;

K. J. Stringer, *TDGAS*, 3rd ser., lv (1980), pp.176-7.
25. Simpson, *Mar Province*, pp.108-9; *PSAS*, cii (1969-70), pp.142-3; and *Moray Reg.*, no.31: concerning Moy, between Tomatin and Daviot, but also lower-lying Culdoich in Croy and Dalcross (on these identifications cf. *RRS*, ii, no.142, comment). One reason alleged for the transfer of the see of Moray to Elgin in 1224 was that Spynie, although in the heart of the Laich, was too exposed to the dangers of war: *Moray Reg.*, no.57.
26. *Chronicle of Holyrood*, ed. Anderson, pp.170-1.
27. G. Duby, *La Société aux XIe et XIIe siècles dans la Région Mâconnaise* (Paris, 1953), p.347.
28. It is just possible that David's acquisition of Garioch coincided with the banishment of Bishop Matthew of Aberdeen from the kingdom. Since Matthew witnessed King William's charter for David (1178 × 82), it must have passed by June 1180 or after his return to Scotland in summer 1181. If the later date is preferred, the actual grant could have been made during the bishop's exile, when the king's position in the northeast Lowlands was weaker than before.
29. *Lind. Cart.*, no.18; *Brechin Reg.*, i, no.4.
30. Below, pp.65-6.
31. Lawrie, *Annals*, pp.238, 263-4.
32. *L'Histoire de Guillaume le Maréchal*, ed. P. Meyer (Paris, 1891-1901), i, p.167. S. Painter, *William Marshal* (Baltimore, 1933), pp.44-6, suggests the date 1179; but David is not known to have been in France during that year, whereas he is recorded there in 1181 and 1182.
33. *Recueil des Actes de Henri II concernant les Provinces Françaises*, ed. L. Delisle and E. Berger (Paris, 1909-27), ii, no.617; *Gesta Henrici*, i, p.333. See further *EYC*, iv, no.80: charter by Duke Geoffrey of Brittany, issued at Winchester and attested by David – 'Dauid de Scoce' (*sic*) – as first witness (1171 × 84).
34. Duncan, *Scotland*, p.231. On her father's standing see J. Boussard, *Le*

Comté d'Anjou sous Henri Plantegenêt et ses Fils (Paris, 1938), p.55 with n.7.

35. Lawrie, *Annals*, pp.265-6.
36. *Gesta Henrici*, i, p.351.
37. Ibid., ii, p.3; *Transcripts of Charters relating to the Gilbertine Houses*, etc., ed. F. M. Stenton (Lincoln Rec. Soc., 1922), p.38.
38. *Gesta Henrici*, i, p.337; further, *Chron. Howden*, ii, p.285. Henry II's charter 'de reddicione', now lost, was removed from the Scottish treasury on Edward I's instructions: *Acts Parl. Scot.*, i, p.108.
39. *Gesta Henrici*, i, p.317; *PR 30 Henry II*, pp.50, 108-9, 119.
40. G. H. Fowler in BHRS, ix (1925), p.181.
41. *Gesta Henrici*, i, p.337; on the Mauduit claim see *The Beauchamp Cartulary Charters, 1100-1268*, ed. E. Mason (PRS, 1980), pp.xxviii-ix.
42. *RRS*, i, p.102. Compare the policy of Henry I and Stephen with respect to Normandy: Hollister, 'Normandy, France', pp.224-7.
43. BL MS Sloane 986, fo.3r; Spalding Gentlemen's Soc., Crowland Cartulary, fo.241r; Richardson, *English Jewry*, p.274; *CRR*, vi, pp.274, 362; cf. *CRR*, viii, p.105; ix, p.153.
44. *Anglo-Scottish Relations*, ed. Stones, no.2; *Chron. Howden*, iv, p.141; below, p.53.
45. Ibid., pp.49-50.
46. Ibid., pp.48, 115-16.
47. Le Patourel, *Norman Empire*, pp.68, 97.
48. Orderic Vitalis, *Historia Ecclesiastica*, vi, ed. M. Chibnall (Oxford, 1978), p.525.
49. *Gesta Henrici*, ii, p.81.
50. Landon, *Itinerary*, pp.6, 8.
51. Ibid., pp.19, 21.
52. See H. A. Cronne, 'Ranulf de Gernons, earl of Chester, 1129-53', *TRHS*, 4th ser., xx (1937), pp.103-34.
53. This marriage was later annulled, though no earlier than 1199: *Comp. Pge.*, iii, p.168.
54. *Mon. Angl.*, v, p.456; also below, pp.40, 44, 155. On Ranulf see now B. E. Harris, 'Ranulph III, earl of Chester', *Journal of the Chester Archaeol. Soc.*, lviii (1975),

pp.99-114.
55. Below, p.115.
56. *Chron. Melrose*, p.47; misdated 26 Aug. in *Comp. Pge.*, vi, p.647, and Lawrie, *Annals*, p.286. The venue of the wedding is not recorded.
57. Ibid., pp.254-5; R. W. Eyton, *Court, Household and Itinerary of King Henry II* (London, 1878), pp.261, 285. Earl David's visit to Geddington was possibly connected with Angevin hopes for a Scottish contribution to the crusading tithe: cf. Lawrie, *Annals*, pp.271-3.
58. Notably Robert de Quincy, lord of Leuchars: *Comp. Pge.*, xii, 11, p.747. Since this chapter was completed, an account of Scottish participation in the Third Crusade has been given in A. D. Macquarrie, 'The Impact of the Crusading Movement in Scotland, 1095-c.1560' (unpublished Edinburgh University Ph.D. thesis, 1982), pp.86-94. The possibility of Earl David's involvement is briefly discussed – and dismissed – at pp.91-3.
59. Below, pp.93-4.
60. *Chron. Fordun*, i, pp.257, n.11, 315, n.7.
61. *The Original Chronicle of Andrew of Wyntoun*, ed. F. J. Amours (Scottish Text Soc., 1903-14), v, pp.242-3.
62. Suggestions that David Aubert was the actual author have generally found little favour (e.g., P. Meyer, *Bibliothèque de l'École des Chartes*, 6th sér., iii (1867), p.304, n.3; G. Doutrepont, *La Littérature Française à la Cour des Ducs de Bourgogne* (Paris, 1909), p.52); but cf. now B. Woledge, *Bibliographie des Romans et Nouvelles en Prose Française antérieurs à 1500: Supplément, 1954-73* (Geneva, 1975), p.27. See also R. Vaughan, *Philip the Good* (London, 1970), pp.110-12 (Scoto-Burgundian relations). The *Histoire*, also known as the *Histoire Royale* or the *Chronique de Naples*, lacks detailed critical attention.
63. *Recueil des Historiens des Gaules et de la France*, ed. M. Bouquet *et al.* (1738-1904), xviii, p.800. See C. R. Cheney, *Pope Innocent III and England* (Stuttgart, 1976), pp.258-9.

64. Cf. *Original Chron.*, i, pp.xxxix, 98.
65. John Major, *A History of Greater Britain*, trans. A. Constable (SHS, 1892), p.165. For an English translation of *c.*1500 (BL MS Harl. 326) see *The Three Kings' Sons*, ed. F. J. Furnivall (Early English Text Soc., extra ser., 1895).
66. John Barbour, *The Buik of Alexander*, i, ed. R. L. G. Ritchie (Scottish Text Soc., 1925), p.xliv.
67. Earl David's territorial style in his charters is invariably 'of Huntingdon'. Elsewhere, he is sometimes 'of Scotland' but never 'of Northampton', that designation having been reserved for the Senlis lords of the Huntingdon honour. Moreover, his itinerary places him in Scotland, Normandy and Maine at dates evenly spread throughout the period *c.*July 1202-Jan. 1204.
68. J. B. Black in *Quatercentenary of the Death of Hector Boece* (Aberdeen, 1937), p.31; *Lind. Cart.*, p.xxxiv. See also A. A. M. Duncan, 'Hector Boece and the medieval tradition', in *Scots Antiquaries and Historians* (Abertay Historical Soc., 1972), pp.1-11.
69. Another version corrects this slip and also reads, again correctly, 'David . . . in Angliae partibus existens': *Chron. Fordun*, i, p.257.
70. See, e.g., W. W. Scott, 'Fordun's description of the inauguration of Alexander II', *SHR*, l (1971), pp.198-200. Further, *Chron. Fordun*, i, pp.xxxv-xl. I have been struck by the accuracy of Fordun's comments on other aspects of David's career.
71. Raine, *North Durham*, no.462 (the dating of this source assumes that the scribe began the year on 25 March). For the earl's possible presence in Scotland during 1193 see *RRS*, ii, nos.365, 367; *Melrose Liber*, i, no.121, with *Chron. Melrose*, p.48. He attested a charter given at Derby by Count John of Mortain between 20 July 1189 and 10 Feb. 1194: *The Sherwood Forest Book*, ed. H. E. Boulton (Thoroton Soc., 1965), p.50.
72. *Chron. Howden*, iii, pp.237, 241.
73. Landon, *Itinerary*, pp.88-9.
74. *Oeuvres de Rigord et de Guillaume le Breton*, ed. H. F. Delaborde (Paris, 1882-5), i, p.197; further, F. M. Powicke, *The Loss of Normandy, 1189-1204*, 2nd edn (Manchester, 1961), pp.97-106.
75. *PR 9 Richard I*, p.166; Landon, *Itinerary*, p.121.
76. Raine, *North Durham*, nos.462, 466. On the details of this settlement see F. Barlow, *Durham Jurisdictional Peculiars* (London, 1950), pp.131ff.
77. *St Andrews Liber*, pp.318-19 (1198 × 9); discussed in Barrow, *Kingdom*, pp.224-5.
78. *RRS*, ii, nos.257-8, 266-9, 294, 298, 325, 335, 350-1, 360-2, 364-7, 385, 388, 420. For other court appearances in this period see Nos.5, 44; *Arbroath Liber*, i, nos.85, 147-8; *Dunfermline Reg.*, no.154; *Lind. Cart.*, p.284; *Melrose Liber*, i, nos.97, 121-2.
79. E.g., ibid., nos.29-31; ii, p.668. Earlier instances in *Holyrood Liber*, p.210; Raine, *North Durham*, no.116.
80. A marriage certainly contracted by 1199 (Nos.42, 44).
81. *RRS*, ii, no.388. Earl David is also recorded at Elgin and Forres in *RRS*, ii, nos.360-2 (1189 × 95).
82. Landon, *Itinerary*, p.21; *Anglo-Scottish Relations*, ed. Stones, no.2.
83. For David's attendance see ibid., no.3; *The Cartae Antiquae Rolls 11-20*, ed. J. Conway Davies (PRS, 1960), no.550; Landon, *Itinerary*, pp.88-91.
84. *Chron. Howden*, iii, pp.298-9, 308.
85. G. G. Simpson, 'The claim of Florence, count of Holland, to the Scottish throne, 1291-2', *SHR*, xxxvi (1957), pp.111-24; G. W. S. Barrow, *Robert Bruce*, 2nd edn (Edinburgh, 1976), pp.52ff.; *Edward I and the Throne of Scotland, 1290-1296: An Edition of the Record Sources for the Great Cause*, ed. E. L. G. Stones and G. G. Simpson (Oxford, 1978), i, pp.19, 122-4; ii, pp.311-13, 323-5.
86. Printed most recently ibid., ii, pp.150-1. On its anachronistic features see Simpson, 'Claim of Florence', pp.120-1; more emphatically, Barrow, *Bruce*, pp.63-4.
87. *Chron. Howden*, iii, p.299; cf.

Barrow, *Bruce*, p.54.

88. In a subsequent passage, however, Howden says that it was news of Queen Ermengarde's pregnancy that persuaded the king to withdraw his proposals: *Chron. Howden*, iii, p.308.

89. *Melrose Liber*, i, nos.121-2. These *acta*, issued at the Scottish court, were attested by Howden and Earl David. The former can be dated 1193 or a little later (cf. *Chron. Melrose*, p.48); the date-limits of the latter are supplied by Bishop Reginald of Ross, consecrated in Sept. 1195, and Bishop Jocelin of Glasgow, d. March 1199. Howden's visits to Scotland in the 1190s are not mentioned by F. Barlow and Lady Stenton in their notes on his career, respectively, *EHR*, lxv (1950), pp. 352-60; lxviii (1953), pp.574-82.

90. Lawrie, *Annals*, p.313. David may have attended King William at the time: *Arbroath Liber*, i, nos. 147-8.

91. Lawrie, *Annals*, pp.287-8. Compare the argument of Robert de Brus the Competitor in 1291-2 that, by Scottish custom, the king's brother was preferred to his son on account of proximity: Stones and Simpson, ii, pp.175, 201. See further Duncan, *Scotland*, p.611.

92. Lawrie, *Annals*, pp.330, 348. I owe to a paper by W. D. H. Sellar (Conference of Scottish Medieval Historical Research, 1980) the suggestion that the memory of some such resignation may have formed the basis for Count Florence's claim.

93. *RRS*, ii, no.467. Private and episcopal charters, for example, show that the drop in his attendance at the royal court was scarcely as dramatic as analysis of the king's *acta* alone would indicate: e.g., No.51; *Arbroath Liber*, i, nos.47, 52; *Holyrood Liber*, no.37; *Lind. Cart.*, no. 107; *Melrose Liber*, i, nos.101-2, 104; *Calendar of Writs preserved at Yester House, 1166-1503*, ed. C. C. H. Harvey and J. Macleod (Scottish Rec. Soc., 1930), no.7.

94. Holt, *Northerners*, pp.208-9, a brief commentary on the landholding ties, is marred by inaccuracies. See further below, ch.9, passim.

95. *Chron. Howden*, iv, p.88.

96. Ibid., pp.88-9; cf. *RCR*, i, p.411.

97. *CRR*, i, p.135. On this proposed meeting at York, where John waited in vain for King William to appear from 25-28 March 1200, see Lawrie, *Annals*, p.321.

98. Ibid., pp.322, 324-5; cf. *CRR*, i, pp.275, 294.

99. Lawrie, *Annals*, pp.315-17, 320-1.

100. Ibid., pp.315, 322, 324. Ros and Vesci also acted in negotiations between the crowns in 1208-9 (ibid., p.361; *CRR*, v, p.189); Ros was last used in 1217 (*Pat. Rolls 1216-25*, p.122).

101. Lawrie, *Annals*, pp.323-4. Ignoring Saer's Scottish lands, S. Painter, *The Reign of King John* (Baltimore, 1949), pp.289-90, states that his 'ancestral possessions were insignificant and lay in Northamptonshire and Cambridge'. See now Simpson, 'Roger de Quincy', pp.14-24, 64-6.

102. Lawrie, *Annals*, pp.317-18, 323-4. Bishop Roger, who seems to have been more at home in Angevin than in Scottish circles, regularly attested for King John in England and Normandy from Aug. 1199 to late 1201.

103. Robert of Swaffham in *Historiae Anglicanae Scriptores Varii*, ed. J. Sparke (London, 1723), ii, p.106; Painter, *King John*, p.155. For John's grant to Saer de Quincy of two manors at Chinnor and Sydenham (Oxon), dated 1 March 1203, see *Bodleian Library Record*, iii (1950-1), pp.166-7.

104. *RCR*, i, p.444; ii, p.35; *Rot. Chart.*, pp.15-16, 17b, 21a, 22b, 23a, 24; *The Cartae Antiquae Rolls 1-10*, ed. L. Landon (PRS, 1939), nos.57, 61; *Foedera*, I, i, p.78b; T. Madox, *The History and Antiquities of the Exchequer*, 2nd edn (London, 1769), i, p.57n.; London, Lambeth Palace Library, Cart. Misc., xi.18.

105. *Rot. Chart.*, p.57a.

106. *CRR*, i, p.210; *CChR*, i, p.44; *Northants Assize Rolls*, no.561.

107. *Rot. Chart.*, p.113.

108. Painter, *William Marshal*, pp.136-44.

109. *Rot. Chart.*, pp.147b, 150b, 153, 155a; *The Charters of Norwich Cathedral Priory*, i, ed. B. Dodwell (PRS,

1974), no.38; BL Addit. Chart. 34040.

110. *RLC*, i, pp.41b, 94-5; *PR 7 John*, p.265.

111. *Rot. Chart.*, pp.157b, 158b, 159.

112. Holt, *Northerners*, pp.205-7.

113. Lawrie, *Annals*, pp.341, 351.

114. E.g., *Rot. Chart.*, p.118.

115. *CRR*, iv, p.15.

116. *RLP*, p.56a. Earl David's most recent recorded visit to the Scottish royal court was in 1202 (*Lind. Cart.*, no.107), shortly before he left England to spend the summer in France. He was apparently also in Scotland in early 1204 (*CRR*, iii, p.99).

117. *RRS*, ii, p.103.

118. *Melrose Liber*, i, nos.101-2, 104; *Rot. Chart.*, pp.180a, 181b; *Northants Chrs.*, no.17.

119. *PBKJ*, iv, no.3914.

120. Duncan, *Scotland*, pp.243-4; further, Painter, *King John*, pp.253-5.

121. Matthew Paris, *Historia Anglorum*, ed. F. Madden (RS, 1866-9), ii, p.118. The authority for David's presence at Stirling is *Chron. Bower*, i, p.525, evidently using a contemporary source now lost.

122. Duncan, *Scotland*, p.249.

123. Ibid., p.241.

124. E.g., *RCR*, ii, p.35; *CRR*, i, pp.275, 294.

125. E.g., *Mem. Roll 1 John*, p.47; *RLP*, pp.15b, 22b; *PR 3 John*, p.178.

126. *Rot. Chart.*, p.28b.

127. Below, p.116 with n.75.

128. *RLC*, i, p.36a. Contrary to *Scots Pge.*, ii, p.216, this marriage, if indeed one was planned, did not take place: see *PR 9 John*, p.52. In 1203 Earl David had proffered 1,000 marks for the marriage of Maud de Cauz, lady of Shelford, on behalf of the same or another son; but Maud was allowed to remain a widow and the money was never paid into the Exchequer: *PR 5 John*, p.6; *PR 6 John*, p.116; *RAL*, vii, pp.216-17.

129. After David joined the king at King's Cliffe on 23 and 25 July 1208, his next known occurrence *in curia regis* was at Lambeth on 4 May 1212, when he attested the important treaty between John and Renaud de Dammartin. He is not found with the king again until 23 Aug. 1213,

and this was apparently his last visit to the Angevin royal court. See *Rot. Chart.*, pp.186a, 194b. But since the charter rolls are missing from April 1209 until May 1212, David may have attended King John from 1205 more frequently than the surviving evidence suggests.

130. Below, p.155; *PR 13 John*, p.100.

131. *CRR*, iv, p.102.

132. *Mem. Roll 10 John*, p.34; *PR 3 & 4 Richard I*, p.159. Cf. *RLP*, pp.15b, 22b.

133. *PR 11 John*, p.189; PRO E 32/249, mm.6, 11d, 12d, 17, 18. Further, below, pp.120-1; also *PR 6 John*, p.141; *Rot. Chart.*, pp.154-5; *PR 9 John*, p.109 (concerning the immunities of St Andrew's priory, Northampton, and Sawtry abbey).

134. *PR 13 John*, p.263.

135. Below, p.124.

136. *RLP*, p.94b; *RLC*, i, p.122. John, by 1212 the earl's heir designate, had presumably been yielded up as one of the hostages for the treaty of Norham in 1209: cf. *PR 13 John*, p.98.

137. Holt, *Northerners*, p.81.

138. *BF*, i, pp.183, 185, 188, 196.

139. *PR 13 John*, p.263.

140. *Foedera*, I, i, p.48. Exemption from scutage was omitted from Henry III's confirmation charter for Earl John of 7 Nov. 1233: *Cartae Antiquae Rolls 11-20*, ed. Davies, no. 333; cf. *HKF*, ii, p.300.

141. R. Fox, *The History of Godmanchester* (London, 1831), plate 1; *Rot. Chart.*, p.186b; *PR 14 John*, pp.76-7, 82; *RLC*, i, pp.216-17; *Rot. de Ob.*, p.542; *PR 16 John*, p.74. Further, Nos.30, 57, 84. A royal grant to Earl David of land apparently worth £15 in the hundred of Godalming, Surrey, was made at about this time (*PR 14 John*, p.99); but since King John put Godmanchester at farm to the men of the manor for £120, this was scarcely an adequate exchange.

142. Below, p.114.

143. *RLC*, i, p.131b; below, p.184.

144. Lawrie, *Annals*, pp.384-5.

145. *Mem. Roll 10 John*, p.65; also *PR 13 John*, p.263.

146. Lawrie, *Annals*, pp.250, 359-60.

147. *Chron. Bower*, i, pp.528-9; *RRS*, ii, no.467. On the credibility of Bower's account and the dating of these events see A. A. M. Duncan, 'Perth: the first century of the burgh', *Trans. of the Perthshire Soc. of Natural Science*, Special Issue (1974), pp.39-41, 50; idem (with J. G. Dunbar), *SHR*, l (1971), pp.11-12.

148. Holt, *Northerners*, pp.82, 94-5.

149. *PBKJ*, iv, no.4668. The following April Earl David was in receipt of royal letters now lost: *Documents Illustrative of English History in the Thirteenth and Fourteenth Centuries*, ed. H. Cole (Rec. Comm., 1844), p.258.

150. *Rot. Chart.*, p.194b. Painter, *King John*, p.214, seemingly accepts the earl's opposition to the campaign; but, amongst other grounds for caution, the evidence for knight-service and payment is incomplete: S. K. Mitchell, *Studies in Taxation under John and Henry III* (New Haven, 1914), pp.109-16; *PR 16 John*, pp.xiv-xvi. See, however, ibid., p.75; *PR 3 Henry III*, p.65.

151. *RLC*, i, p.213a (the dorse of the roll).

152. *RLC*, i, p.189b. For difficulties over its collection earlier in the reign see *RLC*, i, p.33b.

153. *RLC*, i, pp.196a, 213a; *RLP*, pp.132b, 143-4.

154. *RLP*, p.144a. J. C. Holt, *Magna Carta* (Cambridge, 1965), pp.163-4, holds the former view; but it was not always clear to John who had remained loyal between 5 May and 19 June, and who had not: cf. C. R. Cheney, 'The eve of Magna Carta', *Bulletin of the John Rylands Library*, xxxviii (1955-6), p.322.

155. He witnessed with all three a charter by Robert Fitz Roger, lord of Warkworth, 1200 × 8 (Raine, *North Durham*, no.786).

156. *HKF*, ii, pp.337, 357, 370, 384, 396; *Dunfermline Reg.*, no.154; *Holyrood Liber*, no.37; below, p.155.

157. *Chron. Fordun*, i, p.281; *RLP*, p.144a. If Earl David were to die before he could do homage, the castle was to remain with the crown.

158. *RLC*, i, pp.235a, 242a, 244a, 264b.

159. *RLP*, p.170; *RLC*, i, pp.250b, 253a, 266b, 299b, 305b; *Pat. Rolls 1216-25*, pp.55, 75-6.

160. *Foedera*, I, i, p.144; 'Walter of Coventry', *Memoriale*, ed. W. Stubbs (RS, 1872-3), ii, p.225.

161. *RLC*, i, pp.246a, 249b; *RLP*, pp.167-8.

162. BL MS Royal 11 B. ix, fo.84v; *Rot. de Ob.*, p.589; *PR 3 Henry III*, p.126; *RLP*, p.162a; *HKF*, ii, p.331.

163. Gervase of Canterbury, *Historical Works*, ed. W. Stubbs (RS, 1879-80), ii, p.111.

164. *Pat. Rolls 1216-25*, pp.93-5.

165. *RLC*, i, p.348a; here freely translated.

166. *RLC*, i, p.397a; *Royal . . . Letters Illustrative of the Reign of Henry III*, ed. W. W. Shirley (RS, 1862-8), i, p.4 (preferring the date June 1219; cf. ibid., pp.47-8).

167. *RLC*, i, p.354b.

168. *Chron. Fordun*, i, pp.281-2. Fordun's statement that David was buried at Sawtry is confirmed by the terms of the earl's death-bed gift to the abbey: No.80.

169. A. Nisbet, *A System of Heraldry* (Edinburgh, 1722-42), i, p.426.

170. *Excerpta e Rotulis Finium in Turri Londinensi asservatis, 1216-72*, ed. C. Roberts (Rec. Comm., 1835-6), i, p.33; *RLC*, i, p.397a.

171. *RLC*, i, p.395b.

172. *RLC*, i, p.406b; *PR 14 Henry III*, p.262. For William Marshal see *Royal . . . Letters*, i, pp.4, 47-8; *Pat. Rolls 1216-25*, pp. 236, 257, 272; *RLC*, i, pp.429b, 442a; W. Prynne, *The History of King John, King Henry III*, etc. (London, 1670), p.49.

173. *Pat. Rolls 1216-25*, p.285; *RLC*, i, p.455a. Cf. *RLC*, i, p.443b.

174. Holt, *Northerners*, p.63.

175. *Chronicon de Lanercost* (Maitland Club, 1839), p.27.

CHAPTER FOUR
The Estates in Scotland (1)

1. E.g., C. T. Clay, *Antiquaries Journal*, liv (1974), p.349.

2. Below, pp.76, 82-3, 98, 101, 152.

3. Ibid., p.213.

4. See further ibid., pp.104-7, 126-7.
5. Principal acquisitions listed in *RRS*, ii, no.205; see also above, p.31.
6. *Lind. Cart.*, no.60; cf. *Brechin Reg.*, i, nos.3, 4. Earl David's interest here is assumed in A. Jervise, *Memorials of Angus and the Mearns*, new edn (Edinburgh, 1885), i, p.185, and *Registrum de Panmure*, ed. J. Stuart (Edinburgh, 1874), i, p.cl.
7. *RRS*, i, p.28.
8. Barrow, *Kingdom*, pp.292-3.
9. Lawrie, *Charters*, nos.221, 225; *RRS*, i, p.42, nos.122-3, 248; No.28.
10. No.46.
11. W. F. H. Nicolaisen in *Dundee and District*, ed. S. J. Jones (British Association, 1968), pp.149-50. More generally, see Barrow, *Kingdom*, pp.59-60; G. Whittington, 'Placenames and the settlement pattern of dark-age Scotland', *PSAS*, cvi (1974-5), pp.99-110. The names North, South and Little Ballo (Northbelah, Suthbelah, Belache, etc.) in Longforgan derive from Gaelic *bealach*, 'pass'; but note the *baile*-names Ballindean and Balgay beside the earl's property at Inchmartine (in Errol) – in later records described as 'in baronia de Langforgrund': *Chron. Bower*, ii, p.42; W. Fraser, *The Melvilles Earls of Melville and the Leslies Earls of Leven* (Edinburgh, 1890), iii, nos.18, 45; SRO GD 103/2/11, p.197.
12. W. J. Watson, *The History of the Celtic Place-Names of Scotland* (Edinburgh, 1926), p.381.
13. Most recently, Barrow, *Kingdom*, pp.7-68; G. R. J. Jones, 'Multiple estates and early settlement', in *Medieval Settlement: Continuity and Change*, ed. P. H. Sawyer (London, 1976), pp.15-40.
14. *RRS*, i, nos.243, 248; ii, no.16.
15. *RRS*, ii, no.352; cf. *PSAS*, cii (1969-70), p.143; I. B. Cowan and D. E. Easson, *Medieval Religious Houses: Scotland*, 2nd edn (London, 1976), p.48.
16. W. F. H. Nicolaisen, *Scottish Place-Names* (London, 1976), p.164.
17. *RRS*, ii, no.149. See further No.27 (Fintry); *Lind. Cart.*, nos.40-1

(Craigie, *Abrahe*); *Reg. Mag. Sig.*, i, nos.655, 687 (Craigie 'in baronia de Dunde').
18. Lindores, possibly once appurtenant to the large thanage of Abernethy, is described in thirteenth-century sources as a 'scyra', apparently in the sense of 'shire' rather than simply 'parish' (Gaelic, *sgir*): *Lind. Cart.*, nos.114, 125; cf. Barrow, *Kingdom*, p.51. For the 'schira' of Brechin see *Brechin Reg.*, i, no.3.
19. *RRS*, i, no.123; ii, nos.110, 134, 352.
20. *RRS*, ii, nos.149, 197. Hugh Gifford's interest included Roskelin (unidentified) 'in sira de Dunde' (*St Andrews Liber*, p.59); for the property of the bishop of St Andrews at Lochee in Dundee see *RRS*, ii, no. 276; *Liber Ecclesie de Scon* (Bannatyne and Maitland Clubs, 1843), nos.40-1.
21. *RRS*, ii, nos.135, 205.
22. M. M. Postan in *The Cambridge Economic History of Europe*, i, 2nd edn (Cambridge, 1966), p.585.
23. *VCH Northants*, i, pp.351, 354; Barrow, *Kingdom*, pp.9-10.
24. *Danelaw Docts.*, pp.cvii-viii.
25. Walter Daniel, *Vita Ailredi*, ed. Powicke, p.xiii. The seminal study is J. E. A. Jolliffe, 'Northumbrian institutions', *EHR*, xli (1926), pp. 1-42.
26. Cf. Barrow, *Kingdom*, p.39; also *Medieval Settlement*, ed. Sawyer, pp.40, 80-1.
27. J. Romilly Allen and J. Anderson, *The Early Christian Monuments of Scotland* (Edinburgh, 1903), iii, pp. 157ff.; I. M. Henderson, 'The origin centre of the Pictish symbol stones', *PSAS*, xci (1957-8), pp.44-60. For the possibility of renaming see Whittington, 'Placenames', pp.108-9; differently, Nicolaisen, *Scottish Place-Names*, pp.154, 156.
28. K. Walton, 'The distribution of population in Aberdeenshire, 1696', *Scottish Geographical Magazine*, lxvi (1950), p.23.
29. No.44.
30. No.55.
31. *RRS*, ii, no.205.

287

32. For the royal charters see *Reg. Mag. Sig.*, i, p.461a; *RRS*, vi, no.167; for regality status, *Reg. Mag. Sig.*, i, pp.562b, 563b; *RRS*, vi, no.224; *Hist. MSS Comm.*, *Mar and Kellie*, pp.2-4; for the Lindores abbey claim, *Lind. Cart.*, no.149.

33. Below, p.102. Though this conclusion is my own, I have read with profit the discussion of regalities in A. Grant, 'The Higher Nobility in Scotland and their Estates, *c.*1371-1424' (unpublished Oxford University D.Phil. thesis, 1975), pp. 109-31; cf. pp.125-6 for Garioch, there regarded as 'one "ancient regality" among the lay estates'.

34. No.27; also Nos.37, 56; *Lind. Cart.*, no.84.

35. *RRS*, ii, no.205; also Nos.27, 55.

36. *RRS*, ii, no.363; Nos.44, 49, 72.

37. *RRS*, ii, no.363; No.44.

38. Below, pp.88, 98; Nos.6, 44. On mills see also *Lind. Cart.*, nos.19, 37, 90, 114, 125-6; *Brechin Reg.*, i, no.3.

39. *RRS*, ii, no.205; No.49.

40. For the *exercitus* or *servitium regis* due from Garioch and the Tayside lands see *Lind. Cart.*, nos.116-21.

41. R. R. Davies, *Lordship and Society in the March of Wales, 1282-1400* (Oxford, 1978), p.390. This paragraph has benefited from the essential discussions in Duncan, *Scotland*, chs.13, 14.

42. Le Patourel, *Norman Empire*, pp. 307-12.

43. G. W. S. Barrow, 'The pattern of lordship and feudal settlement in Cumbria', *Journal of Medieval History*, i (1975), pp.117-38 (quotations from pp.132, 136).

44. W. F. Skene, *Celtic Scotland*, 2nd edn (Edinburgh, 1886-90), iii, pp. 252-4; W. Temple, *The Thanage of Fermartyn* (Aberdeen, 1894). For William thane of Kintore, fl. 1253, see *Lind. Cart.*, no.84.

45. *Aberdeen Reg.*, i, pp.6, 85; *RRS*, i, p.43.

46. *Arbroath Liber*, i, pp.244-5; *St Andrews Liber*, pp.357-8. On the dating see below, p.295, n.116.

47. 'Bagimond's Roll', ed. A. I. Dunlop in *Miscellany of the SHS*, vi (1939), p.42.

48. Cowan and Easson, *Med. Relig. Houses: Scotland*, pp.52-3; cf. *Arbroath Liber*, i, p.244.

49. *Aberdeen Reg.*, i, pp.5-6, 84-5; *RRS*, ii, no.344; *St Andrews Liber*, pp.266-7.

50. *RRS*, ii, no.205; cf. also Nos.1, 44. *Aberdeenshire Place-Names*, p.285, doubting the traditional derivation of Garioch on the grounds that 'if the predominant feature of the Garioch is looked for, then its fertility is more notable than its roughness', ignores the original usage.

51. No.37; also *Lind. Cart.*, nos.20-1.

52. No.37.

53. Below, p.81.

54. Ibid., p.92.

55. E.g., *Mowbray Chrs.*, pp.xxi-iv; R. V. Lennard, *Rural England, 1086-1135* (Oxford, 1959), p.32; J. F. A. Mason, *William the First and the Sussex Rapes*, revised edn (Historical Association, 1972); *VCH Yorks*, ii, pp.165-7; W. E. Wightman, *The Lacy Family in England and Normandy, 1066-1194* (Oxford, 1966), esp. pp.28-31.

56. E.g., P. H. Sawyer, 'The charters of Burton abbey and the unification of England', *Northern History*, x (1975), pp.28-39.

57. R. R. Davies, 'Kings, lords and liberties in the March of Wales, 1066-1272', *TRHS*, 5th ser., xxix (1979), p.52.

58. Barrow, *Era*, p.63, describes Earl David's eastern Scottish fief as a 'socially-motivated lordship'.

59. Above, pp.33-4. The political background was wholly different when Garioch was partitioned among the coheirs of David's son Earl John in 1237 (Simpson, *Mar Earldom*, p.15) – by that time the pacification of the north had been achieved.

60. Cf. *RRS*, ii, p.5: 'for William, Gowrie, Angus and Mearns seem almost to have formed a miniature kingdom within a kingdom'.

61. The fragmentation of lower Nithsdale into knights' feus is associated with the rise of Dumfries in R. C. Reid, 'The feudalisation of lower Nithsdale', *TDGAS*, 3rd ser., xxxiv (1955-6), pp.102-5.

62. Holt, *Northerners*, p.199.
63. E. Miller, 'La société rurale en Angleterre, xe-xiie siècles', *Agricoltura e mondo rurale in occidente nell'alto medioevo* (Spoleto, 1966), p.116.
64. No.49. For the quasi-servile status of thanes, at least in Aberdeenshire, see *RRS*, ii, no.251, with Barrow, *Kingdom*, p.50. A charter of King Alexander II, dated 1232, refers to the king's 'firmarii vel thayni' of Kinmylies, Inverness-shire: *Moray Reg.*, no.34.
65. *Lind. Cart.*, p.xxiv.
66. Above, p.34.
67. M. W. Beresford, *New Towns of the Middle Ages* (London, 1967), p.335.
68. Cf. G. S. Pryde, *The Burghs of Scotland* (Oxford, 1965), pp.37ff.
69. *The Early Records of the Burgh of Aberdeen*, ed. W. C. Dickinson (SHS, 1957), pp.xxv-vi, xxxi; most recently, B. Dicks, 'The Scottish medieval town: a search for origins', in *Scottish Urban History*, ed. G. Gordon and B. Dicks (Aberdeen, 1983), pp.23-51.
70. Pryde, *Burghs*, pp.16, 39; *Aberdeen Reg.*, i, p.11.
71. I. B. Cowan, *The Parishes of Medieval Scotland* (Scottish Rec. Soc., 1967), pp.90, 174. Further, W. D. Simpson, 'The Bass of Inverurie and its embedded history', *Scottish Notes and Queries*, 3rd ser., ii (1924), pp.39-42.
72. This comment may assume too much. I accept the conclusion in Simpson, *Mar Province*, p.127, that Earl David's burgh was located in the low-lying area now known as the Stanners, but draw attention to the view in R. Gourlay and A. Turner, *Historic Inverurie: The Archaeological Implications of Development* (Scottish Burgh Survey, 1977), p.2, that its location has yet to be positively identified.
73. A. J. Otway-Ruthven, *A History of Medieval Ireland*, 2nd edn (London, 1980), p.116; L. Musset, 'Peuplement en bourgage et bourgs ruraux en Normandie du xe au xiiie siècle', *Cahiers de Civilisation Médiévale*, ix (1966), pp.177-208.
74. E. Miller, *Northern History*, iii (1968), p.196. Inverurie is, however, associated with a deliberate policy of urbanism in *Early Records . . . of Aberdeen*, ed. Dickinson, p.xxiii.
75. Nos.1, 5, 6, 8, 9, 14, 71. Note also the place-names Davah in Inverurie, Dais in Kennethmont, and Daies (formerly Davax) in Premnay; and cf. *The Exchequer Rolls of Scotland*, ed. J. Stuart *et al.* (Edinburgh, 1878-1908), vii, p.89.
76. No.44.
77. Cf. SRO GD 204/23/2; *Lind. Cart.*, nos.17, 57, 116, 123, 126.
78. Formerly Bondes 'in parochia de Inverury': see ibid., no.116; Barrow, *Kingdom*, p.271.
79. *Lind. Cart.*, no.17.
80. R. Glentworth in *The North-East of Scotland* (British Association, 1963), p.44; idem, 'Studies on the soils developed on basic igneous rocks in central Aberdeenshire', *Trans. of the Royal Soc. of Edinburgh*, lxi (1942-9), pp.149-70.
81. Cf. *Lind. Cart.*, nos.55-7, 116, 118, 123, 126.
82. See Plate 2, p.72. The disproportionately small bailey, now shrouded in trees, may lend some support to the argument that Inverurie was not an important centre of demesne farming: cf. T. E. McNeill, *Anglo-Norman Ulster: The History and Archaeology of an Irish Barony, 1177-1400* (Edinburgh, 1980), pp.65, 84-9.
83. Pryde, *Burghs*, pp.15, 39. Dundee was not designated as a *burgus* in King William's charter of *c.*1179, and thus unlike Renfrew (Stewart) was apparently not a royal burgh alienated to a feudatory. On the castle, note a Norman de Castello, burgess of Dundee, who witnesses by 1248 (*Lind. Cart.*, no.40); and for a late but fascinating reference (1496) to a house in Dundee known as 'Erle David Huntlintoune Haw' see *Reg. Mag. Sig.*, ii, no.2317; also A. C. Lamb, *Dundee: Its Quaint and Historic Buildings* (Dundee, 1895), p.4.
84. Archibald of Forgan, once responsible for the king's wheat rents of Longforgan, was married to the

heiress of William Maule of Fowlis Easter in Angus. This may provide a rare example of a thane being transferred from his shire to hold as a tenant of the crown by knight-service: *RRS*, ii, nos. 16, 302, 338.

85. Nos. 43-5.
86. *Lind. Cart.*, no. 62.
87. A. Maxwell, *The History of Old Dundee* (Edinburgh, 1884), pp. 19, 117, 121.
88. Cf. G. R. J. Jones, 'Early territorial organization in England and Wales', *Geografiska Annaler*, xliii (1961), p. 181, for the transition from an ancient focal settlement to a borough, 'whose subsequent prospects were enhanced by . . . a ready-made sphere of influence'.
89. Nos. 44, 73; *Arbroath Liber*, i, no. 136; *Liber Sancte Marie de Balmorinach* (Abbotsford Club, 1841), no. 31; *Lind. Cart.*, no. 19.
90. *PR 14 John*, p. 25; *Arbroath Liber*, i, no. 136 (probably 1209 × 14); also *Liber . . . de Balmorinach*, no. 32.
91. J. B. Mitchell, 'The Matthew Paris maps', *Geographical Journal*, lxxxi (1933), pp. 27-34.
92. *PR 14 John*, p. 25.
93. *Mem. Roll 10 John*, p. 111.
94. *Rot. Chart.*, p. 28b.
95. No. 24. The surname Furmage (Old French, *fourmage*, 'cheese') occurs in Lincolnshire by 1160 (*PR 7 Henry II*, p. 17); but a relationship between Robert and that family cannot be traced.
96. *RRS*, ii, no. 467. For later disputes between Dundee and Perth over the control of shipping in the Tay see Maxwell, *Old Dundee*, pp. 114-16, 119-22; on Perth's earlier predominance, A. A. M. Duncan, *Trans. of the Perthshire Soc. of Natural Science*, Special Issue (1974), pp. 30-50.
97. No. 58; BL MS Stowe 941, fo. 51r, MS Cott. Faust. A. iv, fo. 69v. Alan's nephew and successor in the Paxtons, the knight Robert son of Robert, was a prominent member of Earl David's following: ibid.; *RAL*, iii, nos. 829, 857-8; below, p. 156. On Alan as *senescallus* see *RRS*, ii, no. 265; *Melrose Liber*, i, no. 39.
98. *Lind. Cart.*, nos. 37-8; No. 24 with comment.

99. *Aberdeen Reg.*, i, p. 11; also Nos. 50-1, 55; below, p. 84.
100. *HKF*, ii, p. 343.
101. *Calendar of the Laing Charters*, ed. J. Anderson (Edinburgh, 1899), no. 2; C. W. Hollister, *History*, lviii (1973), p. 25, n. 33; L. R. Buttle, 'The de Tanys of Stapleford Tawney', *Trans. of the Essex Archaeol. Soc.*, new ser., xx (1930-3), pp. 153-72.
102. BL MS Royal 11 B. ix, fo. 63v; also BL Addit. Chart. 28479; *BHRS*, i (1913), p. 106. Perhaps rightly, a connection between Tenes and the Tanys is not explored in Barrow, *Era*, p. 97, where it is suggested that Saer took his name from Thennes near Amiens, dép. Somme. Note also, however, that the Richard de Tany attorned by Earl David in England in 1205 (*CRR*, iii, p. 274) may be identical with Richard de Tany of Eastwick, Peter's probable father.
103. No. 27.
104. No. 73.
105. Below, pp. 122-3.
106. Nos. 49, 55-6; *Lind. Cart.*, no. 81. See generally Barrow, *Kingdom*, pp. 67-82.
107. *Lind. Cart.*, nos. 20-1.
108. Nos. 44, 49.
109. Davies, *Lordship and Society*, p. 458. Cf. McNeill, *Anglo-Norman Ulster*, p. 122, for the view that the Norman settlers in Ulster were supported by 'a basically Irish agricultural organisation'.
110. Below, p. 123.
111. W. W. Scott, 'The use of money in Scotland, 1124-1230', *SHR*, lviii (1979), pp. 105-31; more specifically, N. J. Mayhew, 'Money in Scotland in the thirteenth century', in *Coinage in Medieval Scotland (1100-1600)*, ed. D. M. Metcalf, British Archaeol. Reports, xlv (1977), pp. 85-102.
112. J. M. W. Bean, *The Estates of the Percy Family, 1416-1537* (Oxford, 1958), p. 12; J. Hatcher, *Rural Economy and Society in the Duchy of Cornwall, 1300-1500* (Cambridge, 1970), esp. pp. 10, 52, 80-1; Davies, *Lordship and Society*, esp. ch. 5.
113. B. Harvey, *Westminster Abbey and its Estates in the Middle Ages* (Oxford,

1977), p.3; for a general review, E. Miller and J. Hatcher, *Medieval England: Rural Society and Economic Change, 1086-1348* (London, 1978), pp.201-3, 234-9.

114. Communal renders may not have remained immune from adjustment, however: cf. Davies, *Lordship and Society*, pp.140, 192.

115. *RRS*, ii, pp.51-2.

116. Implied by No.49, concerned to prevent the earl's *firmarii* and men from securing better terms on the estates of Lindores abbey. Cf. also *Moray Reg.*, no.40 (1238), for the distinction it draws between royal *firmarii* and *feodifirmarii* in Moray.

117. Cf. Scott, 'Use of money', p.123: 'Before about 1200 most of the evidence of the use of coin comes from Scotland south of the Tay. In the north, payments in kind were probably more strongly entrenched.'

118. Duncan, *Scotland*, p.427.

119. Ibid., pp.426-7. Professor Duncan's view is advanced with due acknowledgement of the paucity of the available evidence.

120. For Liddesdale (Sules) cf. I. D. Whyte, *Agriculture and Society in Seventeenth-Century Scotland* (Edinburgh, 1979), p.37.

CHAPTER FIVE
The Estates in Scotland (II)

1. See, however, the trail-blazing studies in Barrow, *Kingdom*, ch.11; idem, *Era*, chs.2-5; Duncan, *Scotland*, ch.15.

2. Below, pp.113-14, 126ff.

3. *RRS*, ii, p.18. A distinction between a *theynus* and a *dominus* is specifically made concerning Moray in *RRS*, ii, no.281 (1185 × 9).

4. Barrow, *Kingdom*, p.238, n.12; *RRS*, ii, no.564.

5. *RRS*, ii, no.344.

6. *Edward I and the Throne of Scotland, 1290-1296*, ed. Stones and Simpson, ii, pp.140, 208; No.44. Henry and David were dead before *c.*1209 when John, the youngest, was described as Earl David's heir (No.3); Fordun's reference to a son Robert who died in infancy in unconfirmed: *Chron. Fordun*, i, p.281.

7. Philip, another bastard son, occurs only in Gervase of Canterbury, *Historical Works*, ed. W. Stubbs (RS, 1879-80), ii, p.111.

8. Nos.42, 44.

9. *Lind. Cart.*, nos.60, 65; also *Brechin Reg.*, i, nos.3, 4. For Henry of Brechin's estate outside the fief at Inverquiech, Perthshire, see *Rental Book of the Cistercian Abbey of Cupar Angus* (Grampian Club, 1879-80), i, p.343.

10. *RLC*, i, p.216b. It is difficult to distinguish between the two Henrys before they adopted toponymics, which they did only on the eve of Earl David's death: *Lind. Cart.*, no.86.

11. W. Fraser, *The Melvilles Earls of Melville*, etc. (Edinburgh, 1890), iii, no.11; SRO GD 1/346/1. For Stirling see further *Select Scottish Cases of the Thirteenth Century*, ed. Lord Cooper (Edinburgh and London, 1944), no.39; W. Fraser, *The Stirlings of Keir* (Edinburgh, 1858), pp.1-2.

12. No.85.

13. No.28.

14. M. O. Anderson, *Kings and Kingship in Early Scotland*, revised edn (Edinburgh, 1980), p.242; *St Andrews Liber*, pp.269-70. Gilbert Scot witnessed No.46; his father was apparently sheriff of Scone for Malcolm IV: *RRS*, i, p.47.

15. Gilbert's property was evidently divided between his son Magnus and Henry of Stirling: *St Andrews Liber*, pp.270-1; *Lind. Cart.*, no.65.

16. The pattern of subinfeudation where discussed below depends, without further reference, upon the following *acta*: Nos.6, 8-10, 14, 26-7, 47, 55; *Lind. Cart.*, no.37.

17. Barrow, *Kingdom*, p.328; *Reg. Mag. Sig.*, ii, no.610; *Registrum S. Marie de Neubotle* (Bannatyne Club, 1849), nos.81, 86; *Dunfermline Reg.*, no.151; J. Hodgson, *History of Northumberland*, II, iii (Newcastle upon Tyne, 1840), p.17. On Hugh's relationship with Walter and William Giffard see NRO Finch-Hatton Muniments, no.2665; *Northumberland and Durham Deeds* (Newcastle upon Tyne Records Committee, 1929), p.121.

18. *RRS*, ii, no.48.
19. *RRS*, ii, nos.202, 358. See further above, pp.25-6; below, p.129.
20. L. C. Loyd, *The Origins of Some Anglo-Norman Families* (Harleian Soc., 1951), p.3; cf. A. Renoux, *Archéologie Médiévale*, ii (1972), pp.5-67.
21. *RRS*, i, nos.213-14; ii, no.39; *Holyrood Liber*, no.17; *Melrose Liber*, i, no.39.
22. Above, p.24; *HKF*, ii, p.386; *PR 2 Richard I*, p.29. Hervey de Audri of Cowton attested a charter by William's son Alan copied into BL MS Royal 11 B. ix, fo.124r. No direct connection can be established between the Huntingdon Audris and their namesakes in Northumberland and County Durham; but see Raine, *North Durham*, no.738 (witnessed by Geoffrey of Northampton).
23. No.12; BL MS Royal 11 B. ix, fos.123v-4v, MS Cott. Calig. A. xiii, fos.102v-3r; NRO Finch-Hatton Muniments, no.2665.
24. BL MS Cott. Vesp. E. xvii, fo.49v, attested by Earl David as 'dominus feodi'.
25. Above, p.24.
26. No.55; *Aberdeen-Banff Coll.*, p.548. Further, No.5 (Simon Flandrensis); n.41 below (*Flandres* in Kennethmont). Bonds between the Flemish settlers of Garioch and those of Clydesdale are in fact indicated by Nicholas of Biggar's otherwise obscure claim to lands in Garioch in 1290, noted in G. W. S. Barrow, *Robert Bruce*, 2nd edn (Edinburgh, 1976), pp.59-60.
27. G. F. Black, *The Surnames of Scotland* (New York, 1979 reprint), pp.90-1; cf. *EYC*, viii, pp.147-8.
28. *EYC*, vii, p.11; Lawrie, *Charters*, no.187. Generally, W. S. Sykes, 'The de Boyvils of Millum and Kirksanton', *TCWAAS*, new ser., xli (1941), pp.15-40.
29. *RRS*, i, p.13, n.2; *Wigtownshire Charters*, ed. R. C. Reid (SHS, 1960), pp.xx with n.3, xxiii, xxv-vii; Barrow, *Era*, pp.80-3.
30. *EYC*, vii, pp.277-8; *Coucher Book of Furness Abbey*, 11, ii, ed. J. Brownbill (Chetham Soc., new ser., 1916),

pp.301-5. For Boyle of Kelburne see Barrow, *Era*, pp.81, 176.
31. In the sometime Moreville manor of Bozeat, where the interest of William and that of his great-grandson, John de Mowbray, are recorded in 1212 and 1313 respectively (*HKF*, ii, pp.357, 359). This Mowbray concern may have stemmed from Earl David's patronage: cf. below, p.114.
32. Nos.49, 51, 55-6; *EYC*, vii, pp.183-4; *CRR*, xi, no.1092. For Herbert de Arches' connection with David's circle see also *Melrose Liber*, i, no.39.
33. *Coucher Book of Furness*, 11, ii, pp.313-14; *Register of the Priory of St Bees*, ed. J. Wilson (Surtees Soc., 1915), no.439. But since no positive proof exists, note the occurrence of another Henry de Boiville, of Gunthorpe by Oakham (*VCH Rutland*, ii, p.17), who is found in association with Helen de Moreville in 1212 (*CRR*, vi, p.274).
34. *Cartularium Prioratus de Gyseburne*, etc., ed. W. Brown (Surtees Soc., 1889-94), ii, no.1150. Robert of Billingham witnessed a charter by Hugh du Puiset, bishop of Durham: *EYC*, ii, no.937 (1153 × c.1160).
35. *RLC*, i, p.375a. On Birdsall cf. *Pedes Finium Ebor. regnante Johanne*, ed. W. Brown (Surtees Soc., 1897), p.144.
36. E.g., *Coucher Book of Selby*, ed. J. T. Fowler (Yorks Archaeol. and Topographical Association, rec. ser., 1891-3), ii, nos.1108-9; *Danelaw Docts.*, nos.5, 14, 51, 93-4, 98; *RAL*, ii, no.564; iv, no.1137.
37. *BF*, i, p.188; *Danelaw Docts.*, no.97. On William Wascelin of Redbourne see further *PR 21 Henry II*, p.154; BL Addit. Chart. 22570.
38. *Lind. Cart.*, no.39; *RAL*, viii, no.2297; ix, nos.2611-12; *BF*, i, p.193; ii, pp.1096, 1461-2.
39. *RRS*, i, p.30; *EYC*, xi, pp.213ff.
40. Barrow, *Era*, pp.24-6, 185-6.
41. The following names derive from otherwise unrecorded Anglo-continental settlement in Garioch by c.1250: Flinder in Kennethmont, Johnston in Leslie, and Williamston in Culsalmond. Their respective

thirteenth-century forms are 'Flandres', 'villa Henrici filii Johannis', and 'villa Willelmi': *Aberdeenshire Place-Names*, pp.278, 305, 410.

42. G. W. S. Barrow, 'The reign of William the Lion', *Historical Studies*, vii (1969), p.34; cf. W. Fraser, *Memoirs of the Maxwells of Pollok* (Edinburgh, 1863), i, pp.122-3.

43. Barrow, *Kingdom*, ch.11; idem, *Era*, esp. chs.2-4.

44. Below, pp.127ff.

45. *Dundee and District*, ed. Jones, p.104.

46. E. J. King, 'Large and small land-owners in thirteenth-century England', *Past and Present*, xlvii (1970), p.29. The low social position of the 'professional knights' of Domesday England has been clearly established by Dr Harvey: S. Harvey, 'The knight and the knight's fee in England', reprinted in *Peasants, Knights and Heretics*, ed. R. H. Hilton (Cambridge, 1976), pp.133-73.

47. Above, p.83.

48. *Lind. Cart.*, nos.21, 39, 56-9; *HKF*, ii, p.316; Barrow, *Kingdom*, pp.335-6.

49. G. Duby, *The Chivalrous Society* (London, 1977), p.122.

50. Ritchie, *Normans*, p.378.

51. SRO GD 204/23/2.

52. Cf. Barrow, *Era*, p.134.

53. Cf. Duncan, *Scotland*, pp.386-7.

54. P. Thomas, *Le Droit de Propriété des Laïques sur les Églises et le Patronage Laïque au Moyen Âge* (Paris, 1906), p.28.

55. *RRS*, ii, p.50; Barrow, *Kingdom*, p.41. Hugh Giffard's enjoyment of this jurisdiction at Fintry, with ordeal-pit and gallows, was presumably justified by his high social position: cf. Stenton, *First Century*, pp.101-11; Barrow, *Era*, pp.135-6.

56. Idem, 'Northern English society in the twelfth and thirteenth centuries', *Northern History*, iv (1969), p.11.

57. *Miscellany of the Spalding Club* (1841-52), v, pp.210-11.

58. Cf. below, pp.158-9, 162, 169-70 (Mortimer, Olifard, Revel).

59. *CDS*, i, no.564.

60. No.14.

61. *Lind. Cart.*, nos.37, 39; *RLC*, i, p.375a.

62. Nos.5, 6, 8, 9, 28, 34-5, 37-8, 45-6, 49-51, 55-6, 72, 74.

63. E.g., *Lind. Cart.*, nos.81, 107, p.284.

64. E.g., ibid., nos. 36-7, 75; *Arbroath Liber*, i, no.211; *St Andrews Liber*, pp.42, 270.

65. Nos.5, 44, 46, 49, 50, 56, 72; *Arbroath Liber*, i, no.211; *Lind. Cart.*, nos.29, 36-7, 81; below, p.175.

66. Duncan, *Scotland*, esp. pp.407-8. In fairness to Professor Duncan, it should be said that Earl David's estate could be classed as a twelfth-century lordship and that, in the main, his comments are probably intended for the older established fiefs of southern Scotland.

67. Cf. J. B. Freed, 'The origins of the European nobility: the problem of the ministerials', *Viator*, vii (1976), pp.216, 222-8.

68. Simpson, *Mar Earldom*, p.136.

69. W. D. Simpson, 'The castles of Dunnideer and Wardhouse', *PSAS*, lxix (1934-5), pp.460-70.

70. Nos.47, 50; *Lind. Cart.*, no.81.

71. For a recent discussion of castle-guard in Scotland, documented solely in royal records, which provide only one instance north of the Forth, see Duncan, *Scotland*, pp.383-5.

72. Le Patourel, *Norman Empire*, pp.308-12; Harvey in *Peasants, Knights and Heretics*, ed. Hilton, esp. pp.154-5. On the early Scottish sheriffdom, 'the counterpart rather of the continental *châtellany* than of the Anglo-Saxon shire', see *The Sheriff Court Book of Fife, 1515-22*, ed. W. C. Dickinson (SHS, 1928), esp. pp.370ff.

73. Albeit involving the older Scottish Church: e.g., N. F. Shead, 'Benefactions to the medieval cathedral and see of Glasgow', *Innes Review*, xxi (1970), pp.3-4.

74. Nos.49, 72, 74.

75. No.1. For Scottish examples of detention or non-payment see *RRS*, i, pp.65-6; ii, p.73; B. E. Crawford, *Northern Scotland*, ii (1974-7), pp.101-3.

76. No. 87; SRO GD 160/112/4.
77. No. 5.
78. Nos. 71, 73; also No. 72 for remission of, *inter alia*, cain and conveth owed from Ecclesgreig.
79. No. 35.
80. *Chron. Bower*, i, p.475; ii, p.34.
81. *RRS*, ii, no.363, comment. The quitclaim survives as BL Campbell Chart. xxx 16; printed in *Lind. Cart.*, p.284. The *magna carta* is edited below, No. 44.
82. *RRS*, ii, no.363; *Lind. Cart.*, no.93. Lindores shared the costs of sending to Rome for a confirmation of its rights and possessions with Kelso and Melrose: cf. *Hist. MSS Comm., Reports*, xiv, Appendix iii, p.36; *Melrose Liber*, i, no.124.
83. *Lind. Cart.*, no.94.
84. No. 43.
85. Even though corroborated by witnesses who would not have been physically present when the revised charter passed. By the late twelfth century it appears to have become normal for attestors to attend upon the execution of charters and be fully informed of their provisions (below, p.307, n.6). But there were no absolute rules in this matter, and it was not yet a legal requirement for a witness to be present in person when grants were made, augmented or confirmed by charter. For a clearcut example of 'constructive presence' in Scottish record see *SHR*, xxxii (1953), p.48, adding *Melrose Liber*, i, nos.305-6 (1216 × 22).
86. No. 1.
87. V. H. Galbraith, 'Monastic foundation charters of the eleventh and twelfth centuries', *Cambridge Historical Journal*, iv (1932-4), pp.205-22. Galbraith knew of the Lindores material, though he did not analyse it closely. The *magna carta* is certainly or probably predated by seven of Earl David's surviving *acta* for the abbey and by a charter of his daughter Ada: Nos. 37-43; *Lind. Cart.*, no.36.
88. Barrow, *Kingdom*, p.203.
89. *Arbroath Liber*, i, nos.2, 3. King William and Earl David attested the later of these, and set their seals to it.

90. *Cartulaire de l'Abbaye de la Sainte-Trinité de Tiron*, ed. L. Merlet (Chartres, 1883), i, no.31.
91. Barrow, *Kingdom*, pp.175, 208-9.
92. *Chron. Melrose*, p.41; *Kelso Liber*, ii, no.398.
93. Nos. 44, 51.
94. *Lind. Cart.*, p.lxxvii.
95. Ibid., no.93, rubricated 'Magnum priuilegium Celestini de exempcione'. See further on census and exemption W. E. Lunt, *Financial Relations of the Papacy with England to 1327* (Cambridge, Mass., 1939), ch.2.
96. *Lind. Cart.*, no.94.
97. *Le Liber Censuum de l'Église Romaine*, ed. P. Fabre and L. Duchesne (Paris, 1889-1910), deuxième fasc., p.231. Lindores was also listed in papal records as a payer of census in 1282: *Calendar of Entries in the Papal Registers relating to Great Britain and Ireland. Papal Letters*, i (1893), p.476.
98. *Vetera Monumenta Hibernorum et Scotorum Historiam Illustrantia*, ed. A. Theiner (Rome, 1864), no.335.
99. *Calendar of . . . Papal Letters*, i, p.476; *Le Liber Censuum*, deuxième fasc., pp.230-2.
100. For Kelso see F. Barlow, *Durham Jurisdictional Peculiars* (London, 1950), pp.123-4. Recently, Celestine's letter has been re-edited in *Scotia Pontificia: Papal Letters to Scotland before the Pontificate of Innocent III*, ed. R. Somerville (Oxford, 1982), no.158, where the difficulties it poses have also received attention.
101. *Calendar of Papal Letters to Scotland of Benedict XIII of Avignon, 1394-1419*, ed. F. McGurk (SHS, 1976), p.293.
102. Statement based on figures supplied in Cowan and Easson, *Medieval Religious Houses: Scotland*.
103. The following paragraphs are founded without further reference upon Earl David's series of Lindores charters: Nos.37-52.
104. *Lindores Liber*, no.3.
105. Above, p.59.
106. Ibid.
107. Ibid., p.74.
108. J. Davidson, *Inverurie and the Earl-*

dom of the Garioch (Edinburgh, 1878), p.19. The churches granted in Garioch were at Culsalmond, Durno, Fintray, Insch, Inverurie, Kennethmont, Premnay and Rathmuriel (now Christ's Kirk on the Green in Kennethmont).

109. G. Constable, *Monastic Tithes from their Origins to the Twelfth Century* (Cambridge, 1964), p.99.

110. *Lind. Cart.*, p.lxvii.

111. No.1. The cartularies of Aberdeen cathedral see provide frequent references to the bishop's second teinds of all royal returns and escheats in the sheriffdoms of Aberdeen and Banff. The earliest royal charters in which these references occur are manifestly spurious, though authentic *acta* may lie behind them. But the phrase 'decima eorum que sunt inter duas aquas que De et Spe dicuntur' is found in a genuine bull of Adrian IV confirming the possessions of the bishopric in 1157: *Aberdeen Reg.*, i, pp.6, 85. See also *The Exchequer Rolls of Scotland*, ed. J. Stuart *et al.* (Edinburgh, 1878-1908), i, pp. clxxv-lxxxii.

112. *Danelaw Docts.*, p.lxxiv.

113. D. Knowles, *The Monastic Order in England, 940-1216*, 2nd edn (Cambridge, 1963), p.597. Further, B. R. Kemp, 'Monastic possession of parish churches in England in the twelfth century', *Journal of Ecclesiastical History*, xxxi (1980), pp.133-60.

114. For Scotland, the seminal work is I. B. Cowan, *The Parishes of Medieval Scotland* (Scottish Rec. Soc., 1967).

115. Laing, *Lindores*, p.431.

116. 'Bagimond's Roll', ed. A. I. Dunlop, *Miscellany of the SHS*, vi (1939), pp.39, 40, 53, 64, 67, 70-1. Since the abbey had added few new reserves after Earl David's gifts, Bagimond's assessment provides a useful commentary on the original distribution of wealth. Also valuable are the less full returns copied into *Arbroath Liber*, i, pp.244-6, and *St Andrews Liber*, pp.357-9, for which a date in the 1240s is indicated by internal evidence: cf. D. E. R. Watt, *A Biographical Dictionary of Scottish Graduates to A.D. 1410* (Oxford,

1977)), pp.1, 475.

117. Simpson, *Mar Earldom*, p.16. For the possible site of the abbey's buildings at Fintray see W. Temple, *The Thanage of Fermartyn* (Aberdeen, 1894), p.656.

118. The abbey had a toft in Inverurie from Earl David, and another in Aberdeen from King William (*RRS*, ii, no.366).

119. *Lind. Cart.*, nos.20-1, 57. These records show that teind-arrears where due in an uncommuted form were calculated in money terms, and that subinfeudation was a major threat to the abbey's rights.

120. Ibid., no.57.

121. PRO DL 25/120; *Lind. Cart.*, nos.116-19, 123.

122. Ibid., nos.93-4.

123. Below, pp.147, 307, n.140.

124. The first abbots received all the revenues of these churches, appointing a chaplain at Abdie and a stipendiary vicar at Dundee: *Lind. Cart.*, nos.29, 63-4, 107; *Lindores Liber*, no.15.

125. In *c.*1240 the rectorial cash income from the eight Garioch churches of Earl David's gift was assessed at £74 14s. 4d., probably a conservative estimate; there were also teind-renders not commuted into money payments (*Arbroath Liber*, i, pp.244-5; *St Andrews Liber*, p.358). Insch and Culsalmond were rated at £15 4s. 4d. and £17 6s. 8d. respectively. The figures presented in *Lind. Cart.*, p.xlvii, derive from a later source: *Aberdeen Reg.*, ii, pp.53-4.

126. *Lind. Cart.*, nos.103-6; *Aberdeen Reg.*, i, pp.20-1. The final vicarage settlements were ratified by the pope in 1257: ibid., pp.23-6. For the general background see I. B. Cowan, 'Vicarages and the cure of souls in medieval Scotland', *Records of the Scottish Church History Soc.*, xvi (1966-8), pp.111-27.

127. *Lind. Cart.*, no.92 (correcting the date 1375 in the printed text to 1275).

128. *RRS*, vi, no.205; *Lind. Cart.*, no.149.

129. Ibid., nos.24, 29, 60, 127.

130. Ibid., nos.37, 81. Quotation from C.

Harper-Bill, 'The piety of the Anglo-Norman knightly class', *Proceedings of the Battle Conference on Anglo-Norman Studies*, ii (1979), p.67.

131. *Lind. Cart.*, no.86.
132. Simpson, *Mar Earldom*, p.15; *Lind. Cart.*, nos. 87-8. An exchange of 1260 shows the monks surrendering the Leicestershire interest for three marks a year from Borgue in Galloway: ibid., no.113.
133. The best guide to the abbey's remains is RCAHMS, *Inventory of Fife, Kinross and Clackmannan* (1933), pp.215-19.
134. J. O. Prestwich, 'Anglo-Norman feudalism and the problem of continuity', *Past and Present*, xxvi (1963), p.52.
135. Cf. Davies, *Lordship and Society*, esp. ch.14.
136. Duncan, *Scotland*, p.413.
137. Nos.44, 49.
138. L. Genicot, *Études sur les Principautés Lotharingiennes* (Louvain, 1975), p.89.
139. Simpson, *Mar Earldom*, p.15.
140. The regality, described as an earldom from the late fourteenth century, was also considered, quite incorrectly, to have been held by David as earl of Garioch: *RRS*, vi, no.167; *Hist. MSS Comm.*, *Mar and Kellie, Supplementary Report*, p.6; *Arbroath Liber*, ii, no.48. This has misled, amongst others, Ritchie, *Normans*, p.307, and Simpson, *Mar Earldom*, p.11.
141. Cf. H. M. Cam, *Law-Finders and Law-Makers in Medieval England* (London, 1962), pp.22-43; R. R. Davies, *TRHS*, 5th ser., xxix (1979), pp.41-61.
142. Above, p.33 with n.19.
143. Ibid., p.77.
144. Nos.55, 71, disregarding No.44, issued in the Scots king's court. Though the perambulation of marches may suggest that Bishop Matthew had entered Garioch for an official purpose (cf. Barrow, *Kingdom*, pp.73, 116-18), we do not know for certain that he was acting as a justiciar on either of these occasions. He was, of course, a powerful local lord, whose lands marched cheek by jowl with Earl David's.

145. S. F. C. Milsom, Introduction to F. Pollock and F. W. Maitland, *The History of English Law*, 2nd edn (Cambridge, 1968 reprint), i, p.xlvii.
146. *Sheriff Court Book of Fife*, ed. Dickinson, pp.370-88.

CHAPTER SIX
The Estates in England (1)

1. A. Grant, 'Earls and earldoms in late medieval Scotland', *Essays presented to Michael Roberts*, ed. J. Bossy and P. Jupp (Belfast, 1976), pp.35-6.
2. E.g., Stenton, *First Century*, p.230, n.2; similarly, *Eynsham Cartulary*, ed. H. E. Salter (Oxford Historical Soc., 1907-8), i, nos.78, 98; BL Addit. Chart. 11233, MS Royal 11 B. ix, fos.7v, 9r, 82r.
3. Nos.69, 82-3; above, p.51.
4. *Foedera*, I, i, p.48. Other texts in BL MS Stowe 937, fos.152v-3r, Addit. Chart. 33441.
5. Above, pp.49-50; below, p.120.
6. W. L. Warren, *Henry II* (London, 1973), p.368.
7. The *valor* and extents commissioned for the Huntingdon honour upon Earl John's death in 1237 do not survive: *Calendar of Pat. Rolls, 1232-47*, p.189; *Close Rolls 1237-42*, p.24.
8. Most recently, C. Dyer, *Lords and Peasants in a Changing Society: The Estates of the Bishopric of Worcester, 680-1540* (Cambridge, 1980); B. Harvey, *Westminster Abbey and its Estates in the Middle Ages* (Oxford, 1977); E. Searle, *Lordship and Community: Battle Abbey and its Banlieu, 1066-1538* (Toronto, 1974).
9. Studies of lay honours include M. Altschul, *A Baronial Family in Medieval England: The Clares, 1217-1314* (Baltimore, 1965); W. E. Wightman, *The Lacy Family in England and Normandy, 1066-1194* (Oxford, 1966).
10. *HKF*, ii, pp.294-416; more generally, reference can also be made to M. F. Moore, *The Lands of the Scottish Kings in England* (London, 1915).
11. *HKF*, ii, p.296.
12. Cf. C. R. Hart, *The Early Charters of Eastern England* (Leicester, 1966),

p.238, n.1.

13. Ibid., pp.237-8; R. A. Welldon Finn, *Proceedings of the Cambridge Antiquarian Soc.*, liii (1960), p.31. See also F. S. Scott, 'Earl Waltheof of Northumbria', *Archaeologia Aeliana*, 4th ser., xxx (1952), pp.185-9, with map following p.208.

14. *VCH Northants*, i, pp.365ff. For gains in the 1140s see, e.g., *The Chronicle of Hugh Candidus*, ed. W. T. Mellows (Oxford, 1949), p.128; *RAL*, ii, no.310; BL MS Royal 11 B. ix, fos.8v-9r.

15. Northampton may never have been regarded as an integral part of the honour. Late references to King Malcolm IV as 'dominus ville Bedfordie' (BL MS Cott. Vesp. E. xvii, fos.228v-30v; *Mon. Angl.*, iii, p.414) appear to be erroneous.

16. *HKF*, ii, pp.393, 399-400, 403, 405-6, 410-11; *The Leicestershire Survey*, ed. C. F. Slade (Leicester, 1956), pp.86-9, 91; *VCH Cambs*, vi, p.265; *VCH Essex*, vi, p.253.

17. Cam, *Law-Finders and Law-Makers*, p.69; F. M. Page, *The Estates of Crowland Abbey* (Cambridge, 1934), p.163.

18. R. V. Lennard, *Rural England, 1086-1135* (Oxford, 1959), p.30.

19. Cf. W. J. Corbett in *Cambridge Medieval History*, v (Cambridge, 1968 reprint), pp.510-11.

20. The standard account is Lennard, *Rural England*, ch.4.

21. Cf. ibid., p.33, n.1.

22. S. Painter, *Studies in the History of the English Feudal Barony* (Baltimore, 1943), p.30.

23. Barrow, *Kingdom*, p.321.

24. A. C. Chibnall, *Beyond Sherington* (London and Chichester, 1979), p.28; *HKF*, ii, pp.308, 310, 390; *VCH Northants*, i, p.366; Stenton, *First Century*, p.35; *Leics Survey*, pp.29, 32-3, 91; *RRS*, i, nos.5, 54-5, 74. Much of the Basset fee pertained by c.1130 to the earldom of Leicester.

25. Spalding Gentlemen's Soc., Crowland Cartulary, fo.223r; Lawrie, *Charters*, no.53; *RRS*, i, nos.34, 102, 305; *VCH Rutland*, ii, p.141.

26. *PR 13 John*, p.263.

27. *RRS*, i, nos.7, 21, 58, 62, 148, 204, 208; Barrow, *Kingdom*, p.179; C. A. R. Radford, *Archaeol. Journal*, cxxx (1974), p.133.

28. *Mon. Angl.*, v, pp.190-2.

29. *The Sandford Cartulary*, ed. A. M. Leys (Oxfordshire Rec. Soc., 1938-41), ii, no.424; *Cartulary of the Monastery of St Frideswide at Oxford*, ed. S. R. Wigram (Oxford Historical Soc., 1895-6), ii, nos.790, 793; *VCH Oxon*, v, pp.223-4, 229-30, 251-2.

30. K. J. Stringer, 'A Cistercian archive: the earliest charters of Sawtry abbey', *Journal of the Soc. of Archivists*, vi, no.6 (1980), pp.325-34.

31. *VCH Cambs*, vi, p.265; *VCH Essex*, vi, p.253.

32. Daventry, Eynesbury and, in the next generation, Great Paxton: *HKF*, ii, pp.370-1, 395-6; *BF*, ii, p.1288; Bodl. MS Rawlinson B. 142, fo.19v; BL MS Royal 11 B. ix, fo.12v.

33. Respectively, *The Beauchamp Cartulary Charters, 1100-1268*, ed. E. Mason (PRS, 1980), no.177; *Book of Seals*, no.438; *PR 30 Henry II*, p.108. Alice's dower manor of Harringworth reverted, of course, on her death, shortly after 1185.

34. William I's grant to Countess Margaret of land worth £100 and twenty enfeoffed knights, surviving only as a 'lost act', has been assumed to relate exclusively to Scotland (most recently, Barrow, *Era*, pp.62-3). Property in West Lothian passed into Bohun hands (*RRS*, ii, no.486); but in essence this gift belongs to the Scottish series of Huntingdon *acta*. See below, p.115.

35. Ibid. with n.67.

36. *Pipe Roll 31 Henry I*, ed. J. Hunter (Rec. Comm., 1833), pp.46, 49, 85, 104, 134, 152. See, for comparison, C. W. Hollister, *Speculum*, xlviii (1973), p.649, n.67; idem, *Proceedings of the Battle Conference on Anglo-Norman Studies*, ii (1979), pp.98ff.

37. BL MS Royal 11 B. ix, fos.7v-8v; *Northants Chrs.*, no.55; *Harrold Recs.*, no.7.

38. Harvey, *Westminster Abbey*, p.63; E. King, *Peterborough Abbey, 1086-1310: A Study in the Land Market* (Cambridge, 1973), pp.143-5; E. Miller, *The Abbey and Bishopric of Ely* (Cambridge, 1951), p.94.
39. C. G. Crump, *History*, viii (1924), p.295, quoted by G. Barraclough, *Trans. of the Historic Soc. of Lancashire and Cheshire*, ciii (1952), p.35.
40. Quite apart from the effects of unimpeded subinfeudation upon the profits of wardship, note *CRR*, ii, p.163; *RLC*, i, p.407a.
41. *PR 31 Henry II*, p.60; *PR 30 Henry II*, p.108.
42. These figures, rounded to the nearest £10, are for escheated honours and show their value to the crown as set out in *PR 31 Henry II*. Since the majority were at farm rather than in custody, the sums given generally underestimate actual incomes. Local manorial costs have been deducted, but not centrally authorised expenses relating to the king's special needs, e.g., allowances *in terris datis*.
43. Similarly, E. Mason, 'The resources of the earldom of Warwick in the thirteenth century', *Midland History*, iii (1975-6), pp.67-75.
44. *Comp. Pge.*, vi, p.645.
45. Exton and Great Paxton: *PR 3 & 4 Richard I*, pp.159, 263. Aaron died in April 1186, when his debts escheated to the crown. £300 was still owed to the Exchequer on these manors in 1211; but Earl David remained in seisin and possibly kept the profits: *PR 13 John*, p.263; Nos.54, 78.
46. Most recently in E. Miller and J. Hatcher, *Medieval England: Rural Society and Economic Change, 1086-1348* (London, 1978); J. L. Bolton, *The Medieval English Economy, 1150-1500* (London, 1980).
47. The Viatores, *Roman Roads in the South-East Midlands* (London, 1964), pp.232-8.
48. On Fotheringhay see RCHME, *Inventory of Northants*, i (1975), pp.43-6. At Earls Barton, the earthwork remains once identified as a motte are now believed to be of Anglo-Saxon, or even prehistoric,

origin: ibid., ii (1979), pp.40, 42; B. K. Davison, *Archaeol. Journal*, cxxiv (1968), pp.209-10.
49. *PR 31 Henry II*, p.54; *HKF*, ii, p.384; *CRR*, vii, p.189.
50. *RRS*, i, pp.80, 108; ii, no.55; also No.60 (Harringworth, Kempston, Yardley Hastings).
51. *CDS*, ii, nos. 736, 1024; cf. also *Calendar of Inquisitions Miscellaneous*, i, no.846. Other sources are given at n.84 below.
52. R. A. Brown, 'A list of castles, 1154-1216', *EHR*, lxxiv (1959), p.252.
53. Above, p.49. King John's mandates for the seizure of the castle supply the earliest references to it. It seems, however, to have existed by 1174, in which year Earl Simon III held a session of the honour court at Fotheringhay (ibid., p.28); and had possibly been built by *c*.1163 when, in a charter dated at Fotheringhay, Walter son of Alan announced his intention to found a Cluniac monastery at Paisley: *Registrum Monasterii de Passelet* (Maitland Club, 1832), pp.1-2.
54. *RLC*, i, p.395b.
55. *RRS*, i, pp.80, 108; *VCH Northants*, iv, p.296. Earl David accounted 'pro torneamentis' in 1201: *PR 3 John*, p.178; see also *Calendar of Pat. Rolls, 1232-47*, pp.62, 133; *Calendar of Inquisitions Post Mortem*, v, no.412.
56. Above, p.53. For the possible site of his demesne manor-house, mentioned in No.60, see RCHME, *Inventory of Northants*, ii, p.185.
57. Discussed below, pp.142-3.
58. Nos.7, 16, 17, 25, 29, 53-4, 64, 67, 69, 70, 81-3, 86.
59. Below, p.124.
60. L. Genicot, *L'Économie Rurale Namuroise au Bas Moyen Âge*, ii: *Les Hommes-La Noblesse* (Louvain, 1960), p.4.
61. Above, pp.82, 97-101.
62. *PR 14 John*, p.81; *PBKJ*, iv, no.4749; *HKF*, ii, pp.374-5. In *c*.1208 × 14 the earl bought out the (unexplained) claims of Hugh le Bret in Conington with lands in Scotland: No.14.
63. *PR 3 & 4 Richard I*, p.159; No.78. On Walter's interest see Bodl. MS

298

Rawlinson B. 142, fo.19v; BL MS Royal 11 B. ix, fo.12v. Potton can conceivably be added to the list of recovered manors. Philip of Kyme's rights there before 1185 may have been confined to the church (*RAL*, iii, no.654); but cf. also No.11, comment.

64. S. F. C. Milsom, *Historical Foundations of the Common Law*, 2nd edn (London, 1981), chs.5, 6; elaborated in idem, *The Legal Framework of English Feudalism* (Cambridge, 1976).

65. *HKF*, ii, p.357.

66. *HKF*, ii, pp.357-8, adding *CRR*, i, p.375; vi, pp.272-4, 280, 362; vii, pp.189, 213; Nos.7, 25, 64, 70.

67. *PR 6 John*, p.254; *PR 7 Richard I*, pp.106-7. In 1195 seisin of Ryhall was adjudged to Margaret in the king's court, apparently against the Dammartins, on whose claims to the manor see *Boarstall Cartulary*, ed. H. E. Salter (Oxford Historical Soc., 1930), p.69.

68. *PBKJ*, iii, no.1020; *CRR*, iii, pp.99-100. However, the counterclaims of the Dammartins continued to embarrass the Bohuns, whose tenure of Ryhall terminated in 1218: *VCH Rutland*, ii, p.269.

69. BL Cott. Chart. xxiv 15, *HKF*, ii, pp.82-4; *BF*, i, pp.163, 166, 168-9.

70. *Danelaw Docts.*, pp.cvii-viii.

71. On the Humber crossings, certainly used by William the Lion, see *RRS*, i, p.9, n.2; *EYC*, ii, no.764; Wightman, *Lacy Family*, p.78; BL MS Cott. Vesp. E. xx, fo.43r.

72. *PR 1 John*, p.9; *PR 14 John*, p.99. But see *Red Book of the Exchequer*, ed. H. Hall (RS, 1896), ii, pp.502, 592; *PR 5 John*, p.244, for the service of nine knights' fees allocated from the honour of Hatfield Peverel.

73. Painter, *Feudal Barony*, pp.189-90.

74. BL MS Cott. Nero C. iii, fo.191r; *PR 2 Richard I*, p.112; *PR 3 & 4 Richard I*, pp.112, 153.

75. *Rot. Chart.*, p.29a. Earl David's seisin of Tottenham from the mid-1190s is shown by, *inter alia*, Nos.18-20. Note, however, the crown's control over the manorial resources in 1194, 1196-7; also King John's quittance of the claims of

Jews in 1199: *PR 6 Richard I*, p.6; *Chancellor's Roll 8 Richard I*, p.208; *PR 9 Richard I*, p.165; *Rot. Chart.*, p.29a. The suggestion in Richardson, *English Jewry*, pp.100, 255, that David acquired Tottenham by liquidating the tenant's debt, is not followed here. But possibly at some date in Richard's reign 'the earl, in turn, mortgaged the manor'.

76. *Rot. Chart.*, p.29a; *Mem. Roll 1 John*, p.44; *PR 2 John*, p.52.

77. *PR 5 John*, pp.1, 2; *CRR*, xv, no.1363; *Close Rolls 1242-7*, p.544.

78. BL MS Harl. 4748, fo.24v; *Rotuli Hundredorum temp. Hen. III et Edw. I*, etc., ed. W. Illingworth (Rec. Comm., 1812-18), ii, pp.607b, 610b.

79. H. J. M. Green, 'Early medieval Godmanchester', *Proceedings of the Cambridge Antiquarian Soc.*, liv (1961), pp.90-8.

80. Lawrie, *Charters*, no.53. Moated enclosures have been identified at the Alconburies, but their date and function are unclear: RCHME, *Inventory of Hunts* (1926), pp.10, 12. The royal hunting-lodge at Brampton remained at the king's disposal.

81. A list of Earl David's feoffees at Godmanchester seems to be preserved in *RLC*, i, pp.216-17. See also Nos.30, 57, 84.

82. R. H. Hilton, *A Medieval Society: The West Midlands at the End of the Thirteenth Century* (London, 1967 reprint), p.68.

83. Moore, *Lands of the Scottish Kings*, esp. pp.67-83.

84. Notably, PRO C 132/16/7 (Tottenham), C 132/36/6 (Conington), C 133/57/1 (Fotheringhay, Nassington, Yarwell, Kempston), C 133/73/11 (Alconbury); adding PRO SC 12/5/7 (Kempston). For printed versions see most usefully W. Robinson, *The History and Antiquities of . . . Tottenham*, 2nd edn (London, 1840), i, pp.163-4; *CDS*, i, nos. 1945, 2543; ii, no.410; *Documents Illustrative of the History of Scotland, 1286-1306*, ed. J. Stevenson (Edinburgh, 1870), i, pp.123-4.

85. *The Domesday Geography of Midland England*, ed. H. C. Darby and I. B. Terrett, 2nd edn (Cambridge,

1971), pp.396-9, 404.

86. *Land Utilisation Survey*, ed. L. D. Stamp, part 58 (Northants), by S. H. Beaver (1943), p.379.

87. *Wellingborough Manorial Accounts, 1258-1323*, ed. F. M. Page (Northants Rec. Soc., 1936).

88. *RRS*, i, no.208.

89. No.75; *RRS*, i, no.210.

90. BL MS Cott. Faust. A. iv, fo.38r-v. Cf. E. M. Carus-Wilson and R. V. Lennard in *Economic History Review*, xi (1941), pp.39-60, and ibid., 2nd ser., iii (1951), pp.342-3, respectively.

91. Nos.4, 15.

92. *The Domesday Geography of Eastern England*, ed. H. C. Darby, 3rd edn (Cambridge, 1971), p.339.

93. *RRS*, i, no.54; *Papsturkunden in England*, i, ed. W. Holtzmann (Berlin, 1930), no.102; also *RAL*, iii, no.835, comment.

94. *RRS*, i, no.234; *Cartulary of Bushmead Priory*, ed. G. H. Fowler and J. Godber (BHRS, 1945), no.42.

95. E.g., BL MS Cott. Faust. A. iv, fo.95r-v.

96. No.78; *RAL*, iii, no.858.

97. BL MS Cott. Nero C. iii, fo.196r, printed in T. Hearne, *Guilielmi Neubrigensis Historia* (Oxford, 1719), iii, pp.785-9. For contemporary notices of David of Hackleton see BL Addit. Chart. 22474; *Book of Seals*, no.131; *PR 10 John*, p.179.

98. It is known that the 'thirteenth' and the 'fifteenth' were spring assessments, the latter with grain for domestic consumption exempted: S. K. Mitchell, *Studies in Taxation under John and Henry III* (New Haven, 1914), pp.84-92, 159-69.

99. On this, and for the principles of interpretation adopted here, see the seminal discussion in M. M. Postan, *Essays on Medieval Agriculture and General Problems of the Medieval Economy* (Cambridge, 1973), ch.11.

100. Cf. *Land Utilisation Survey* (Northants), p.382.

101. *Foedera*, I, i, p.48.

102. PRO CP 25(1) 192/2/18; J. Hatcher, *Rural Economy and Society in the Duchy of Cornwall, 1300-1500* (Cambridge, 1970), p.180.

103. *RRS*, ii, no.49; Nos.22, 62; J. E. B. Gover *et al.*, *The Place-Names of Northamptonshire* (English Place-Name Soc., 1933), pp.108, 153.

104. *RRS*, i, no.208; Nos.19, 78; D. Moss and I. Murray, *Trans. of the London and Middlesex Archaeol. Soc.*, xxiv (1973), pp.207, 209.

105. *Foedera*, I, i, p.48.

106. M. L. Bazeley, 'The extent of the English forest in the thirteenth century', *TRHS*, 4th ser., iv (1921), maps following pp.140, 160.

107. Cf. *Dialogus de Scaccario*, ed. C. Johnson (London, 1950), pp.56-61. On John's forest policy see Holt, *Northerners*, pp.157-63.

108. Above, p.49.

109. See now J. A. Raftis, *Assart Data and Land Values: Two Studies in the East Midlands, 1200-1350* (Toronto, 1974).

110. PRO E 32/248, m.1, E 32/249, mm.6, 17, 18.

111. No.60.

112. *PR 11 John*, p.186; PRO E 32/62, m.2, E 32/249, mm.11d, 13, 15d.

113. *Select Pleas of the Forest*, ed. G. J. Turner (Selden Soc., 1901), p.lxxix.

114. *PR 31 Henry II*, p.59.

115. *Chronicon Abbatiae Rameseiensis*, ed. W. D. Macray (RS, 1886), p.290; *The Letters of Pope Innocent III (1198-1216) concerning England and Wales*, ed. C. R. and M. G. Cheney (Oxford, 1967), no.131.

116. A. Mawer and F. M. Stenton, *The Place-Names of Bedfordshire and Huntingdonshire* (English Place-Name Soc., 1926), p.224.

117. Largely noted in Raftis, *Assart Data*, pp.151-2; but here supplemented by PRO E 32/37, mm.1, 2, an independent record ignored by that study.

118. The statement by the reeve of Alconbury receives corroboration in BL MS Harl. 4748, fo.24v. On Alconbury Weston see further PRO E 32/38, m.3.

119. King, *Peterborough Abbey*, ch.4; Miller, *Abbey and Bishopric of Ely*, pp.95-100, 108, 119-20; J. A. Raftis, *The Estates of Ramsey Abbey* (Toronto, 1957), pp.73-5.

120. P. D. A. Harvey, 'The pipe rolls and the adoption of demesne farming in

England', *Economic History Review*, 2nd ser., xxvii (1974), p.352.

121. David of Ashby, William of Ashby, Robert of Bassingham, Philip le Moyne, Gilbert de Nuers, Aymer of Oakley, Reginald of Oakley, Richard son of William and Simon de Senlis. Sources: Nos.3, 17, 19, 20, 60, 65; PRO E 159/2, m.1d, E 368/3, m.8d; *CRR*, ii, p.135; *Mem. Roll 1 John*, p.46; *Rolls of the King's Court in . . . 1194-5*, ed. F. W. Maitland (PRS, 1891), p.28; *PBKJ*, iii, no.572; iv, no.3914.

122. *RRS*, i, p.100. More generally, Painter, *Feudal Barony*, pp.139-40.

123. No.17; John Le Neve, *Fasti Ecclesiae Anglicanae, 1066-1300*, iii: *Lincoln*, ed. D. E. Greenway (London, 1977), p.142; *Book of Seals*, no.375; *Acta Stephani Langton, Cantuariensis Archiepiscopi, 1207-28*, ed. K. Major (Canterbury and York Soc., 1950), nos.10, 34; *EYC*, xii, no.113; *PBKJ*, iii, p.xcviii. On the known family relationships see E. M. Poynton, *Genealogist*, new ser., xvi (1899-1900), p.31; *RAL*, vii, nos.2005-6; *Rotuli Hugonis de Welles, Episcopi Lincolniensis, 1209-35*, ed. W. P. W. Phillimore *et al.* (Canterbury and York Soc., 1907-9), i, p.13.

124. Nos.82-3 (Simon de Senlis). On Ashby see No.76; *HKF*, ii, p.334.

125. *CRR*, ii, pp.135, 163; *Mem. Roll 1 John*, p.46; PRO E 159/2, m.1d.

126. *CRR*, i, pp.89-90, 93; *PBKJ*, iii, pp.ccxcvi-vii; *HKF*, ii, pp.238-9.

127. E.g., *CRR*, i, pp.210, 453; ii, p.66; *PBKJ*, iii, no.572; *Northants Assize Rolls*, no.546; *RCR*, ii, p.63.

128. *Walter of Henley and other Treatises on Estate Management and Accounting*, ed. D. Oschinsky (Oxford, 1971), p.265.

129. PRO E 32/37, m.2; Nos.53, 59.

130. *PR 30 Henry II*, p.108. For some evidence of direct farming at Alconbury and Brampton before Earl David acquired the manors in 1202 see R. S. Hoyt, *The Royal Demesne in English Constitutional History, 1066-1272* (Ithaca, 1950), pp.213, 223-4; *CRR*, xv, no.1981. Additionally, *CRR*, ii, p.66; *Northants Assize Rolls*, no.546 (attempted

recovery of an alleged leasehold in Fotheringhay, 1201-2).

131. Harvey, 'Pipe rolls', pp.355-8.

132. King, *Peterborough Abbey*, p.145; Raftis, *Ramsey Abbey*, pp.105, 120, 127; Searle, *Battle Abbey*, pp.135-8; Hilton, *A Medieval Society*, pp.78-9.

133. *Close Rolls 1234-7*, pp.452-3, 507-8.

134. *PR 5 John*, pp.1-2, 175-6. When Godmanchester was reassigned in 1212, its annual value to the Exchequer was revised from £50 to £120: *Rot. Chart.*, p.186b; *PR 14 John*, p.82.

135. Cf. K. B. McFarlane, *The Nobility of Later Medieval England* (Oxford, 1973), p.10: 'the improving landlord was only too often one whose assets were in danger of shrinking and whose other traditional outlets were barred'.

136. R. W. Southern, *Medieval Humanism and Other Studies* (Oxford, 1970), p.211.

137. Holt, *Northerners*, ch.12. On the patronage system of Henry II see J. E. Lally, 'Secular patronage at the court of King Henry II', *BIHR*, xlix (1976), pp.159-84.

138. *PR 13 John*, p.263. The residue was owed as a pledge 'de debitis Aaron' of Countess Ada de Warenne and King William.

139. *PR 14 John*, p.131; *PR 16 John*, pp.22-3; No.11. £326 was still owed 'de pluribus debitis' at the earl's death: *PR 3 Henry III*, p.81.

140. Above, pp.49-50, 114.

141. *RLC*, i, pp.235a, 429b; above, pp.53, 113. See further on Exton and Paxton *CDS*, i, no.733; *VCH Hunts*, ii, p.328.

142. Painter, *Feudal Barony*, pp.187-8; Holt, *Northerners*, esp. pp.167-74, 176ff.; idem, *Magna Carta* (Cambridge, 1965), pp.107-12.

CHAPTER SEVEN
The Estates in England (II)

1. William Farrer's notes in *HKF*, ii, pp.294-416, provide an invaluable framework of reference and are cited sparingly. The documentation of the text is thus essentially supplementary to his material.

2. *De Comitissa*, ed. F. Michel in *Chroniques Anglo-Normandes*

(Rouen, 1836-40), ii, p.130. On this short account of the Senlis earls see now B. J. Levy, *Cahiers de Civilisation Médiévale*, xviii (1975), pp.193-5.

3. E. Miller, 'The state and landed interests in thirteenth century France and England', *TRHS*, 5th ser., ii (1952), p.111.

4. Nos.17, 19, 20, 34, 54, 58, 76.

5. On the continuing Mauduit connection see *Beauchamp Cartulary Chrs.*, ed. Mason, no.230; NRO MS Finch-Hatton 123, p.339.

6. H. Malo, *Un Grand Feudataire: Renaud de Dammartin et la Coalition de Bouvines* (Paris, 1898), p.27.

7. *VCH Northants*, ii, pp.110-12; Richardson, *English Jewry*, pp.250-1.

8. Extended, too, to tenants of escheated baronies. The revenues of Hallamshire were directed to the Exchequer for some two decades from 1181 because the Luvetots also held of the Tickhill honour: see *EYC*, iii, pp.2-6. A similar instance in *HKF*, i, p.96.

9. *Beauchamp Cartulary Chrs.*, no.231; *HKF*, ii, pp.324-6; *RRS*, i, no.155; *Book of Seals*, no.204; *Northants Assize Rolls*, no.490.

10. *PR 6 Richard I*, pp.16, 22, 26; *HKF*, ii, pp.338-40. Also BL Harl. Chart. 83. A. 6., showing that the chief messuage at Mears Ashby had already been alienated.

11. *RRS*, i, pp.101-2; *VCH Northants*, ii, p.539.

12. The relationship between the Anglo-Scottish Vieuxponts and their namesakes in central Normandy has yet to be fully worked out. For the present, see R. C. Reid, 'De Veteripont', *TDGAS*, 3rd ser., xxxiii (1954-5), pp.91-105, which may be supplemented by F. M. Powicke, *The Loss of Normandy, 1189-1204*, 2nd edn (Manchester, 1961), p.357. Cf. Barrow, *Era*, p.73, n.73, for William de Vieuxpont II as the husband of both Maud de Moreville and Emma de St Hilaire.

13. *Scots Pge.*, iii, pp.3-4.

14. *RRS*, i, no.139; ii, no.48. Both men stood with the aforementioned in the Scottish camp during the young King Henry's war: see above, pp.25-6 with n.116.

15. *RRS*, i, p.96; Spalding Gentlemen's Soc., Crowland Cartulary, fo.223r. The Sules fee, which had reverted to the demesne in the 1140s, was possibly recovered by the family for a time from 1157; certainly, Scottish ties had been reconstituted by the mid-thirteenth century, when Great Doddington was controlled by the Campanias of Borgue in Kirkcudbrightshire: ibid.; *HKF*, ii, pp.345-6; *Wigtownshire Charters*, ed. R. C. Reid (SHS, 1960), p.xvii and n.2.

16. *VCH Rutland*, ii, p.150. The Brus family was conceivably still associated with the honour in the 1170s: cf. *Harrold Recs.*, no.70.

17. Stringer, 'A Cistercian archive', pp.325-34; *Book of Seals*, no.439.

18. Above, p.114; below, p.193. Hugh Giffard apparently received compensation from Earl David in Scotland: above, p.83.

19. *HKF*, ii, pp.342, 355, 358, 378.

20. Barrow, *Kingdom*, pp.322-6; adding Raine, *North Durham*, nos. 155-6, for Vieuxpont as a family represented in Scotland by 1153.

21. Barrow, *Era*, pp.97ff.

22. Ibid., pp.22-3; G. G. Simpson, 'An Anglo-Scottish Baron of the thirteenth century: The Acts of Roger de Quincy, earl of Winchester and Constable of Scotland' (unpublished Edinburgh University Ph.D. thesis, 1965), pp.10-12.

23. *Archaeologia Aeliana*, 4th ser., xiv (1937), pp.256-7; *RRS*, ii, no.486.

24. *Registrum Monasterii S. Marie de Cambuskenneth* (Grampian Club, 1872), nos.80, 86; *RRS*, ii, no.292; *Kelso Liber*, i, no.92 (Umfraville; similarly, above, pp.84, 86: Mowbray); above, p.114 (Galloway).

25. Below, p.170; Barrow, *Era*, pp.99, 124, n.44.

26. Note also the instructive case concerning the Vieuxponts of Horndean and Hardingstone discussed below, pp.144-5. On the Lindseys, *HKF*, ii, p.378; D. E. R. Watt, *A Biographical Dictionary of Scottish Graduates to A.D. 1410* (Oxford, 1977), p.46 – see further ibid.,

pp.248, 269-70, 353-4, for probable representatives of the Huntingdon family of Houghton of Great Houghton (Northants) in the *familia* of Bishop Andrew of Moray (1222-42). The other chief branch of the Lindsey house, Lindsey of Crawford (Lanarkshire), held land at Earls Barton in the Huntingdon honour by 1241 (*HKF*, ii, pp.343-4).

27. *HKF*, ii, pp.378-9.

28. F. M. Page, *The Estates of Crowland Abbey* (Cambridge, 1934), p.162.

29. *The Earliest Lincolnshire Assize Rolls, 1202-1209*, ed. D. M. Stenton (Lincoln Rec. Soc., 1926), p.xvii.

30. *Danelaw Docts.*, no.460; B H R S, vii (1923), p.230; B L M S Sloane 986, fos.7v-8r.

31. N R O Finch-Hatton Muniments, no.2665; *Book of Seals*, no.238.

32. B L M S Cott. Faust. C. i, fos.2r, 12r.

33. *Preparatory to Anglo-Saxon England*, ed. D. M. Stenton (Oxford, 1970), p.212.

34. Cambridge University Library, M S 3021, fo.221r. Morin was under-sheriff to Thomas in Northampton-shire in 1184 and his tenant outside the honour in Kent. He gave the advowson of Eythorne, near Dover, to Harrold priory for the souls of Thomas and two other royal func-tionaries, Ralph and William Picot: N R O Stopford-Sackville Muni-ments, no.3974. See also on Morin below, p.139.

35. *RLC*, i, p.122b.

36. *Foedera*, I, i, p.48; cf. *RLC*, i, p.596b.

37. For the role of Huntingdon tenants in Earl David's following see below, ch.8, and cf. above, p.122.

38. Stenton, *First Century*, p.51.

39. É. Perroy, 'Social mobility among the French *noblesse* in the later Middle Ages', *Past and Present*, xxi (1962), p.25.

40. M. M. Postan, *The Medieval Economy and Society* (Harmonds-worth, 1975), p.180. Postan's thesis received renewed emphasis in P. R. Coss, 'Sir Geoffrey de Langley and the crisis of the knightly class in thirteenth-century England', *Past*

and Present, lxviii (1975), pp.3-37, which also provides a summary of the literature then available.

41. Miller and Hatcher, *Medieval Eng-land*, pp.170-3; Bolton, *Medieval English Economy*, pp.105-9; D. A. Carpenter, 'Was there a crisis of the knightly class in the thirteenth cen-tury? The Oxfordshire evidence', *EHR*, xcv (1980), pp.721-52.

42. P. D. A. Harvey, 'The English infla-tion of 1180-1220', reprinted in *Peasants, Knights and Heretics*, ed. R. H. Hilton (Cambridge, 1976), pp.57-84.

43. B L M S Sloane 986 (xiii cent.) = G. R. C. Davis, *Medieval Cartularies of Great Britain* (London, 1958), no.1206. For printed extracts see Richardson, *English Jewry*, pp.271-80; *Wardon Cart.*, pp.361-2. A Braybrooke cartulary, not listed by Dr Davis, appeared as lot 874 in one of the series of Phillipps sales, held at Sotheby's on 30 Nov. 1976, and was then bought by a private collector. See C. R. Cheney, *Traditio*, xxiii (1967), p.515; *Biblio-theca Phillippica: Medieval Manu-scripts*, new ser., part xi (Sotheby and Co., London, 1976), pp.51-2. I have been unable to examine this M S, which is of fifteenth-century date, but I am grateful to A. R. A. Hobson of Sotheby's for his letter of 10 Dec. 1976 expressing the opinion that it is an exact duplicate of the earlier M S Sloane 986.

44. Paragraph based on *HKF*, ii, pp.346-7, with additions from B L M S Cott. Calig. A. xii, fos.32r-7v, 42r-3r, M S Sloane 986, fos.2r-3r; P R O E 32/249, m.12; *CRR*, iii, p.35; *Northants Assize Rolls*, nos.455, 457, 539, 764.

45. Stenton, *First Century*, p.90, n.6. See further *HKF*, ii, pp.365-8; *VCH Leics*, v, pp.91-4, 117, 222-3.

46. *HKF*, ii, pp.365-7, adding *Mon. Angl.*, v, p.180; B L Addit. Chart. 21204, M S Royal 11 B. ix, fos.111v-13v.

47. *HKF*, ii, pp.365-6; *Beauchamp Cartulary Chrs.*, nos.230-1; *CRR*, i, p.366; *Mon. Angl.*, v, p.437; B L M S Sloane 986, fos.9v-10r.

48. B L M S Cott. Claud. D. xii,

fo.146r, MS Royal 11 B. ix, fos.112v-13r, Addit. Chart. 21205, MS Cott. Tib. E. v, fo.75v; *Mon. Angl.*, v, p.180.

49. Richardson, *English Jewry*, pp.138, 248-9; *PR 10 Richard I*, p.125.

50. *Feet of Fines of the Ninth Year of ... Richard I* (PRS, 1898), no.67; BL MS Sloane 986, fos.31r, 32r-v.

51. *Northants Assize Rolls*, nos.541, 541A.

52. BL MS Sloane 986, fos. 32v-3v; *Rot. Chart.*, p.180b; also Richardson, *English Jewry*, pp.271-2.

53. *Foedera*, I, i, p.144.

54. *HKF*, ii, p.366; *CRR*, ix, p.319; x, p.132.

55. Basic details on the Foliot-Leidet line are set out in *HKF*, ii, pp.383-5; *Wardon Cart.*, pp.325-8; A. Morey and C. N. L. Brooke, *Gilbert Foliot and his Letters* (Cambridge, 1965), pp.38-41.

56. *HKF*, ii, pp.314, 383-4; *RRS*, i, no.12; BL MS Addit. 46701, fos.68v, 92r.

57. On these last see A. Saltman, *Theobald Archbishop of Canterbury* (London, 1956), nos.206-8, 277; J. A. Robinson, *Gilbert Crispin, Abbot of Westminster* (Cambridge, 1911), pp.48-9.

58. *Red Book of the Exchequer*, ed. Hall, i, pp.331-2. On the date of Robert Foliot's marriage see Saltman, *Theobald*, no.277 (there dated 1148 × 54, but more likely 1148 × 50), with *VCH Northants*, i, p.384 and n.3.

59. Respectively, Morey and Brooke, *Gilbert Foliot*, p.41; *Wardon Cart.*, p.325.

60. Extract from BL MS Sloane 986, fos. 72v-3r (copy of an inquest dated *temp*. King John), also translated, with different wording, in *Wardon Cart.*, p.325.

61. BL MS Sloane 986, fo.73r; *Red Book of the Exchequer*, i, p.332; *VCH Northants*, iii, p.181. For corroboration of the account in the Braybrooke cartulary see further *CRR*, viii, p.6.

62. *VCH Cambs*, viii, pp.70-2, 86; *VCH Oxon*, ix, p.175.

63. Richardson, *English Jewry*, pp.272-5; *PR 6 John*, p.139.

64. *Wardon Cart.*, nos.113, 118, 209a;

Gover, *Place-Names of Northants*, pp.36-7.

65. BL MS Sloane 986, fos.36v, 41r.

66. Richardson, *English Jewry*, pp.272-5.

67. *PR 14 John*, p.131; *PR 17 John*, p.51; *PR 3 Henry III*, pp.80-1; BL MS Sloane 986, fos.20v-1r; No.11, comment.

68. For brief accounts of Braybrooke's career see *Wardon Cart.*, pp.323-4; Richardson, *English Jewry*, pp.100-2.

69. On the latter see *CRR*, vi, pp.151, 361; *PR 12 John*, pp.214-16; *PR 13 John*, pp.269-72.

70. The original of King John's confirmation of 25 July 1208 survives as BL Addit. Chart. 6014; for the chancery enrolment see *Rot. Chart.*, pp.180-1. That of 24 March 1211 is known only from BL MS Sloane 986, fos.67v-71r. See also *Northants Chrs.*, no.17.

71. Based on the 'prices' of property recorded in BL MS Sloane 986, which no doubt seriously underestimate his true expenses.

72. Ibid., fos.37r-9v; *HKF*, iii, pp.251, 264.

73. *Feet of Fines of the Seventh and Eighth Years of ... Richard I* (PRS, 1896), no.91; *Feet of Fines of the Tenth Year of ... Richard I* (PRS, 1900), no.209; *PR 10 Richard I*, p.105; BL MS Sloane 986, fos.1r-2r, 3r-6r, 7r-13r, 20v; PRO CP 25(1) 171/12/201, 210.

74. RCHME, *Inventory of Northants*, ii, pp.11-13; BL MS Sloane 986, fo.10r, MS Cott. Claud. D. xii, fo.157r.

75. W. P. Baildon, *Braybrooke: Its Castle, Manor and Lords* (privately printed, 1923), attempted to unravel the tenurial pattern, but without reference to the Braybrooke cartulary.

76. BL MS Sloane 986, fos.8r-9r, MS Cott. Claud. D. xii, fo.157r-v; *EHR*, xcii (1977), p.814.

77. See most conveniently *CChR*, i, pp.206-7; *Mon. Angl.*, v, pp.432, 437.

78. BL MS Cott. Otho B. xiv, fo.173r. For Braybrooke's wrangles with Pipewell see, e.g., BL MS Cott.

Calig. A. xii, fos.83r, 100v-11r, 103r-4r; *Book of Seals*, no.238.

79. Above, p.83 (Audri); *Descriptive Catalogue of Ancient Deeds in the PRO*, i (1890), pp.525, 554-5; ii (1894), pp.454, 458-9, 471-2, 477, 488, 556; BL MS Cott. Vesp. E. xvii, fos.40r-2r (Boughton; but see also *VCH Northants*, iv, pp.77-8); *Rot. de Ob.*, p.370; *RLP*, pp.79b, 97b (Lisures).

80. Below, p.171; and for his land investments see Holt, *Northerners*, pp.238-9.

81. *Register of the Hospital of S. John the Baptist . . . Dublin*, ed. E. St. J. Brooks (Irish MSS Comm., 1936), nos.75-6; *Harrold Recs.*, pp.185-6.

82. E. Mason, 'The Mauduits and their chamberlainship of the Exchequer', *BIHR*, xlix (1976), pp.10-11.

83. Below, p.143.

84. Examples as follows: *HKF*, ii, pp.316, 388, 409; *RAL*, viii, no.2341 (marriage); *HKF*, ii, p.381 (litigation); *HKF*, ii, pp.352-3 (farming); PRO E 32/249, mm.6, 11d, 12d, 17, 18 (assarting); BL MS Cott. Calig. A. xii, fos.52r-3v (purchase).

85. E.g., *HKF*, i, pp.36, 50, 95-9, 254; ii, pp.321-2 (Preston); *VCH Northants*, iv, pp.140, 182, 236-7; *HKF*, ii, pp.388-9 (Cogenhoe).

86. D. Herlihy, 'Three patterns of social mobility in medieval history', *Journal of Interdisciplinary History*, iii (1972-3), p.640.

87. *Harrold Recs.*, no.183, p.187.

88. Ibid., no.13, p.188; *VCH Bucks*, iv, pp.324-5.

89. Cf. Coss, 'Sir Geoffrey de Langley', p.28: 'the height of the crisis was not the period of heaviest inflation but the reign of Henry III'.

90. For the random instances of genuine decay note, in addition to Morin, *HKF*, ii, pp.335-6 (Ashby), 379 (Lindsey of Molesworth); BHRS, xix (1937), pp.145-6, 149 (Houghton-Aubigny).

91. E. J. King, 'Large and small land-owners in thirteenth-century England', *Past and Present*, xlvii (1970), p.48.

92. Above, p.138; BL MS Sloane 986, fos.1r-v, 12v-13r, 36r-v, 40r-v;

No.11.

93. Farrer's notes need to be supplemented by *CRR*, i, p.340; *Harrold Recs.*, pp.207-8; *VCH Hunts*, ii, pp.323, 374; *VCH Leics*, v, p.277. Thus, Bassingham, Foliot, Foxton, Houghton, Lindsey of Molesworth, Malesoures, Oakley, Offord, Richespaud, Rushton, Sproxton and Taillebois.

94. E. Miller, *Northern History*, xi (1976), p.239; also a useful résumé in T. Evergates, *Feudal Society in the Bailliage of Troyes under the Counts of Champagne, 1152-1284* (Baltimore and London, 1975), p.150.

95. King, 'Large and small land-owners', p.48.

96. *Mon. Angl.*, vi, p.763; *VCH Hunts*, i, p.397.

97. *RRS*, ii, no.539. The translation is wrongly assigned to the Conqueror's reign in *VCH Hunts*, i, pp.389-90, and D. Knowles and R. N. Hadcock, *Medieval Religious Houses: England and Wales*, 3rd edn (London, 1971), pp.258-9. Dervorguilla de Balliol was received as patron in 1275: *Mon. Angl.*, iv, pp.388-9.

98. No.80 with comment. For the contemporary inadequacy of testamentary dispositions as a means of transferring freeholds see M. M. Sheehan, *The Will in Medieval England* (Toronto, 1963), esp. pp.269-74.

99. Nos.58, 60.

100. The relevant *acta* are Nos.3, 4, 15, 18-20, 31, 34, 36, 38-41, 62-3.

101. *EHR*, xxxii (1917), pp.246, 248; *Inventaire Sommaire des Archives Départementales: Eure, Archives Ecclésiastiques, Sér. H* (Évreux, 1893), p.274; Évreux, Arch. Dép. de l'Eure, H 1437, p.59, H 1438, p.5.

102. No.32.

103. Cf. J. W. Alexander, 'A pinchpenny patron: Ranulf III earl of Chester', *Cîteaux*, xii (1971), pp.23-39; E. Mason, 'Timeo barones et donas ferentes', *Studies in Church History*, xv (1978), pp.61-75.

104. R. W. Southern, *Western Society and the Church in the Middle Ages* (Harmondsworth, 1970), p.233.

105. For Meppershall and Oakley see *HKF*, ii, pp.351-2, 381-2; also BHRS, i(1913), p.115; *BF*, ii, p.1154; *Wardon Cart.*, nos.251, 348.
106. *Cartulary of Bushmead Priory*, ed. Fowler and Godber, pp.xvi-xvii, nos.48, 207, 295, 301; *Mon. Angl.*, v, pp.212-13 (Braybrooke); *HKF*, ii, p.328; *Harrold Recs.*, p.187; above, p.132 with n.34 (Morin).
107. E.g., *HKF*, ii, p.341; *VCH Northants*, iv, pp.129, 279; *Wardon Cart.*, no.205g.
108. E.g., *HKF*, ii, p.352; BL MS Cott. Calig. A. xii, fo.44r (burial); *HKF*, ii, p.311 (chantry); Spalding Gentlemen's Soc., Crowland Cartulary, fo.241r (martyrology). Otherwise see *HKF*, ii, p.418; *CRR*, vi, pp.276, 343; BL MS Cott. Calig. A. xii, fo.54r-v, MS Royal 11 B. ix, fo.84v.
109. E.g., *CRR*, xi, no.2533; xii, no.176.
110. Harvey, *Westminster Abbey*, p.41; S. Raban, *The Estates of Thorney and Crowland* (Cambridge University, Dep. of Land Economy, 1977), ch.4; *The Cartulary of Cirencester Abbey*, i, ed. C. D. Ross (London, 1964), pp.xxii-v.
111. *Roll of the Justices in Eyre at Bedford, 1202*, ed. G. H. Fowler (BHRS, 1913), pp.162-5; *PR 6 John*, p.141; *PR 9 John*, p.109; *Rot. Chart.*, pp.154-5; *Wardon Cart.*, nos.205d-g, 344f, 347.
112. R. A. Donkin, *The Cistercians: Studies in the Geography of Medieval England and Wales* (Toronto, 1978), pp.129-30, 132. For 'active reclamation and improvement' by the Knights Templars at Merton see *VCH Oxon*, v, p.225.
113. *Cartulary of Holy Trinity Aldgate*, ed. G. A. J. Hodgett (London Rec. Soc., 1971), pp.xvi-xix; PRO E 40/2446; above, p.134; BL MS Cott. Faust. A. iv, fos.62v-4v, 76v.
114. *Mon. Angl.*, v, p.192; BL MS Royal 11 B. ix, fos.42v, 124v, MS Cott. Vesp. E. xvii, fo.44r.
115. Richardson, *English Jewry*, p.99.
116. N. Denholm-Young, 'An early thirteenth-century Anglo-Norman MS', *Bodleian Quarterly Record*, vi

(1929-31), pp.229-30. For corroborative detail see *RRS*, ii, no.84; *VCH Northants*, iv, p.255.
117. Ibid.
118. J. D. Mansi, *Sacrorum Conciliorum Nova . . . Collectio* (Florence, 1759-98), xxii, p.413. What follows can claim to be only a plausible interpretation of the sources, for the precise sequence of events is sometimes hard to establish.
119. M. G. Cheney, *Roger, Bishop of Worcester, 1164-1179* (Oxford, 1980), p.322; *RAL*, iii, no.654 with notes.
120. BL MS Royal 11 B. ix, fos.22r, 35v-6r. On Ralph Foliot, a valued Angevin royal servant, see *Cambridge Historical Journal*, viii (1944), pp.15-16.
121. BL MS Cott. Vesp. E. xvii, fo.267v; Nos.61, 65-6. Mr Peter's occupation of the church had terminated by 22 May 1201, when the priory had reasserted its rights: BL MS Royal 11 B. ix, fos.36v-7r.
122. Raban, *Estates of Thorney and Crowland*, p.89.
123. Nos.38-41; *Lind. Cart.*, no.86; *VCH Rutland*, ii, p.69.
124. Barrow, *Kingdom*, pp.180-1.
125. *HKF*, ii, pp.356-7.
126. Barrow, *Era*, pp.170-1; *TDGAS*, 3rd ser., xxvi (1947-8), pp.153-4.
127. No.34; *RRS*, i, nos.197, 277.
128. For Jedburgh abbey's churches of Arthuret, Bassenthwaite and Kirkandrews-on-Esk, Cumberland, see *VCH Cumberland*, ii, pp.14-15; *TCWAAS*, new ser., xxviii (1928), pp.42-5; *RRS*, ii, no.62.
129. I provide a fuller account in the forthcoming *Essays on the Nobility of Medieval Scotland*, ed. K. J. Stringer, ch.3. See for now Stringer, *History of the Berwickshire Naturalists' Club*, xl, part one (1974), pp.34-49.
130. *HKF*, ii, p.343; *VCH Northants*, iv, pp.116, 122. Further, *CRR*, i, p.22; *RCR*, i, p.411; ii, pp.14, 35, which show that in 1196-9 Sempringham priory claimed the advowson of Great Doddington against Earl David.
131. *HKF*, ii, pp.357-8; *VCH Rutland*, ii, p.164.

132. I also deal with this case in more detail, and supply the supporting documentation, in the book cited at n.129 above. See for now Stringer, *Innes Review*, xxiv (1973), pp.133-47.
133. *RAL*, iii, nos.825-6. For earlier evidence of the difficulties of proprietorship and the canons' attempt in 1217 to assume parochial responsibilities without recourse to a rector or a vicar, which apparently came to nothing, see ibid., nos.812, 820-1, 823.
134. *Lind. Cart.*, no.102.
135. *RAL*, iii, no.838.
136. *VCH Rutland*, ii, p.164.
137. Regrettably, we do not know the fate of the Northampton priory's annual rents in Scotland, which are not mentioned in the agreement with Dryburgh.
138. *RAL*, iii, nos.837-45.
139. *VCH Northants*, iv, p.252; *VCH Hunts*, ii, pp.259-60; *CRR*, xii, no.176; Oxford, Balliol College, Abbotsley Deeds, E 7/1, 4-8, 17.
140. *VCH Rutland*, ii, p.164. There appears to be no evidence of proprietorship by Lindores at Conington.

CHAPTER EIGHT
Household and Following
1. J. F. Baldwin, *EHR*, xlii (1927), p.180.
2. Harvey, *Westminster Abbey*, p.132.
3. On the contemporary use of administrative mandates in estate management see *Documents . . . of Walter de Wenlok, Abbot of Westminster, 1283-1307*, ed. B. F. Harvey (Camden Soc., 1965), p.11 with n.2.
4. For an up-to-date review see G. L. Harriss, Introduction to K. B. McFarlane, *England in the Fifteenth Century: Collected Essays* (London, 1981). The basic point of departure for late medieval Scotland is the excellent study by J. M. Brown (now Wormald), 'Bonds of Manrent in Scotland before 1603' (unpublished Glasgow University Ph.D. thesis, 1974), with a brief discussion in *Scottish Society in the Fifteenth Century*, ed. idem (London, 1977), pp.54-8.

5. To save space, details drawn from these witness-lists are not given references. It may be added here that Dr G. D. Simpson is preparing his study of the *familia* of Roger de Quincy, earl of Winchester (d. 1264), for publication in *Nobility of Medieval Scotland*, ed. Stringer.
6. For a recent consideration of the problems posed by charter-witnessing see D. E. Greenway in *Studies in Church History*, xi (1975), pp.57-60; also S. Bond, *Journal of the Soc. of Archivists*, iv (1970-3), pp.276-84. Dr Greenway concludes (at p.60): 'Witness-clauses of the late twelfth and early thirteenth century bear their own peculiar brand of verisimilitude.' But for the difficulties raised by No.44 in this collection see above, pp.93-4.
7. Cf. *Recueil des Actes des Comtes de Pontieu (1026-1279)*, ed. C. Brunel (Paris, 1930), no.37: charter of Count Guy II of Ponthieu, attested by certain knights 'qui forte ad curiam convenerant' (1126 × 47).
8. C. R. Cheney, *Hubert Walter* (London, 1967), ch.8; K. Major, 'The *familia* of Archbishop Stephen Langton', *EHR*, xlviii (1933), pp.529-53. For twelfth-century lay households see most usefully Stenton, *First Century*, pp.66-83; *Mowbray Chrs.*, pp.lix-lxix. N. Denholm-Young, *Seignorial Administration in England* (London, 1937), remains indispensable for the thirteenth century.
9. *RRS*, i, pp.28-35; ii, pp.29-39.
10. Denholm-Young, *Seignorial Administration*, p.67; cf. *EYC*, viii, p.253.
11. Below, pp.166-7.
12. Stenton, *First Century*, p.80. But contrast the chief constable and his importance in the Chester and Mowbray households, also his prominence at the Scots royal court: *Mowbray Chrs.*, pp.lix-lxii; *RRS*, ii, pp.37-8.
13. *HKF*, ii, p.409.
14. No.33; *Danelaw Docts.*, no.473 (erroneously ascribed to Earl Simon II); *Lind. Cart.*, no.86.
15. *Materials for the History of Thomas Becket*, etc., ed. J. C. Robertson and

J. B. Sheppard (RS, 1875-85), i, pp.326-7.

16. *Northants Assize Rolls*, no.98; *CRR*, iv, pp.282-3; v, pp.42-3, 67.

17. *RRS*, ii, p.32; C. R. Cheney, *English Bishops' Chanceries, 1100-1250* (Manchester, 1950), p.9.

18. *Charters of the Abbey of Inchcolm*, ed. D. E. Easson and A. Macdonald (SHS, 1938), no.5.

19. Above, p.76; *Arbroath Liber*, i, no.136; *Lind. Cart.*, nos.37-8, 75; *St Andrews Liber*, p.42.

20. BL Addit. Chart. 11233, MS Royal 11 B. ix, fo.9v; *Book of Seals*, no.349; *RRS*, ii, no.56.

21. Not identifiable as Henry de Nuers of Churchill (Oxon) and Norton (Northants), who was apparently dead by July 1192 (BHRS, xiv (1931), pp.52-3, 74, n.23); but a probable kinsman of Earl David's steward Gilbert de Nuers, who held at Santon in Harrold parish (Beds), in the Huntingdon honour: *Harrold Recs.*, no.15; *CRR*, x, p.293.

22. Above, p.145.

23. *RAL*, iii, no.812; *Danelaw Docts.*, nos.337-8.

24. *RAL*, iii, nos.821-2; Cheney, *Bishops' Chanceries*, p.144. See also S. Kuttner and E. Rathbone, 'Anglo-Norman canonists of the twelfth century', *Traditio*, vii (1949-51), p.322.

25. Above, p.145. For Thomas' apparent translation to Abdie see No.44.

26. *RAL*, iii, nos.812, 814-16.

27. BL MS Royal 11 B. ix, fo.111r; No.60. Both charters were issued on the same occasion.

28. *CRR*, i, pp.73, 93; iii, p.274.

29. Cf. Nos. 37A, 48, 52.

30. Although Nos.54, 58 and 76 include the steward of the Huntingdon honour among the addressees, they cannot be classed as administrative mandates.

31. Below, p.215 with n.14.

32. T. A. M. Bishop, *Scriptores Regis* (Oxford, 1961), pp.9-10; *RRS*, ii, p.70; F. Gasparri, *L'Écriture des Actes de Louis VI, Louis VII et Philippe Auguste* (Geneva, 1973), pp.43-6, 73-4.

33. M. Jones, 'A Collection of the *Acta*

of John, lord of Ireland and count of Mortain' (unpublished Manchester University M.A. thesis, 1949), i, pp.31ff.

34. G. Barraclough, 'The earldom and county palatine of Chester', *Trans. of the Historic Soc. of Lancashire and Cheshire*, ciii (1952), pp.35-6.

35. H. A. Cronne, *The Reign of Stephen, 1135-54* (London, 1970), p.212.

36. *RRS*, i, p.107. Stephen's *nepos* Richard was a clerk of Bishop Robert of Lincoln and apparently served the Senlis earls also: see *Danelaw Docts.*, nos.337-40. An interesting minor administrative family, the Ectons later supplied a chancellor for Stephen Langton: Major, 'The *familia* of . . . Langton', pp.550-3.

37. Morey and Brooke, *Gilbert Foliot and his Letters*, p.212; W. Prevenier, 'La chancellerie des comtes de Flandre . . . à la fin du xiie siècle', *Bibliothèque de l'École des Chartes*, cxxv (1967), p.63.

38. *Mowbray Chrs.*, pp.lxvi-vii; Cheney, *Bishops' Chanceries*, pp.22-3, 26, n.12, 29.

39. *RRS*, ii, esp. pp.57-9.

40. A. Young, 'The political role of the Comyns in Scotland and England in the thirteenth century' (unpublished Newcastle upon Tyne University Ph.D. thesis, 1974), pp.106-12, 139, 147-8, 287-93.

41. G. Duby, *Medieval Marriage: Two Models from Twelfth-Century France* (Baltimore and London, 1978), p.3.

42. PRO E 159/2, m.1d; *PR 8 John*, p.179; *RLP*, p.143b; *Rotuli de Liberate ac de Misis et Praestitis, regnante Johanne*, ed. T. D. Hardy (Rec. Comm., 1844), pp.178, 189, 205, 212, 223.

43. PRO DL 25/42; Bodl. MS Rawlinson B. 103, fo.95v.

44. Compare the approach in C. W. Hollister's two articles: 'Magnates and *curiales* in early Norman England', *Viator*, viii (1977), pp.63-81, and (with J. W. Baldwin) 'The rise of administrative kingship: Henry I and Philip Augustus', *American Historical Review*, lxxxiii (1978), pp.887-90.

45. Above, pp.89-91.

46. *VCH Hunts*, ii, p.374; *CRR*, iii, p.99; *HKF*, ii, pp.310-11.
47. *VCH Warwicks*, vi, p.282.
48. *Wardon Cart.*, no.103.
49. *VCH Beds*, iii, p.145; *Mon. Angl.*, v, pp.212, 435; I. H. Jeayes, *Descriptive Catalogue of the Charters and Muniments . . . at Berkeley Castle* (Bristol, 1892), nos.72, 76, 116, 149, 177, 274.
50. Morey and Brooke, *Gilbert Foliot*, p.46.
51. Assuming that the three attestations by 'W. Olifard' stand for Walter rather than William Olifard, a knight of the earldom of Atholl: *Scots Pge.*, vi, pp.530-1; *Charters of the Abbey of Coupar Angus*, ed. D. E. Easson (SHS, 1947), i, pp.49-50.
52. The family histories in *Scots Pge.*, vi, pp.521ff., and J. Anderson, *The Oliphants in Scotland* (Edinburgh, 1879), retain much value but require revision. The view that Walter I was still alive in the 1210s or '20s is certainly erroneous: he witnessed Scots royal *acta* no later than *c.*1190, with some fifteen years elapsing before Walter II appeared at court.
53. *Scots Pge.*, vi, p.527.
54. *HKF*, ii, p.355.
55. *SHR*, ii (1905), pp.174-5; *RRS*, ii, no.484; *Miscellany of the Spalding Club* (1841-52), v, p.211.
56. *HKF*, ii, pp.329ff.; *EHR*, xxxii (1917), pp.246, 248.
57. *HKF*, ii, pp.330-1.
58. *Earliest Lincs Assize Rolls*, ed. Stenton, nos.346, 360; *Feet of Fines for the County of Lincoln for the Reign of King John*, ed. M. S. Walker (PRS, 1954), nos. 142, 252; *BF*, i, p.185. This William, who claimed his interest at Allington by grant of William Burdet I, was apparently dead by 1218: *Rolls of the Justices in Eyre . . . for Lincolnshire, 1218-9, and Worcestershire, 1221*, ed. D. M. Stenton (Selden Soc., 1934), no.109.
59. No.11. In 1291 a William Burdet of Allington resigned his capital messuage in Potton: *HKF*, ii, p.332.
60. *RRS*, i, nos.190-1.
61. *Danelaw Docts.*, no.139; *The Cartulary of Blyth Priory*, ed. R. T. Timson (Thoroton Soc., 1973), i,

no.170.
62. Though requiring careful use, the best family histories are provided by *Scots Pge.*, iii, pp.1ff., and Lord Lindsay, *Lives of the Lindsays* (London, 1849).
63. *HKF*, ii, pp.83, 145, 377-8; No.53 with comment.
64. Spalding Gentlemen's Soc., Crowland Cartulary, fo.192r. Lindsey genealogists regard Walter II as Walter I's grandson, but note especially the charter by Walter of Lindsey, son of Walter 'dapifer Malcolmi regis Scocie', granting to Crowland abbey the churches of Fordington and Ulceby, upon the retirement of his father as a monk of the house (1162 × 5); and cf. *HKF*, ii, pp.376-7. Walter II was thus a brother rather than a son of William of Lindsey of Crawford, justiciar of Lothian (d. *c.*1205).
65. J. C. Holt in *Album Helen Maud Cam* (Louvain, 1960-1), i, p.67.
66. Above, p.83.
67. Ibid., p.128. It seems safe to identify William son of Emma as William de Vieuxpont's eldest son by Emma de St Hilaire, although he was one of three offspring called William: *Holyrood Liber*, nos.33, 41, 44. He inherited most, though not all, of the family patrimony upon his father's death in England by 1203 (*Kelso Liber*, i, no.143).
68. *HKF*, i, pp.36-8; ii, pp.302-4; *Henry of Pytchley's Book of Fees*, ed. W. T. Mellows (Northants Rec. Soc., 1927), p.139n.
69. *HKF*, iii, pp.385-7; *Comp. Pge.*, ix, pp.244-5.
70. *VCH Northants*, iii, p.77; *Henry of Pytchley*, p.77n.
71. For the continued use of the term *miles* as a military rather than a social designation cf. Barrow, *Era*, pp.121-6; also G. Duby, *The Chivalrous Society* (London, 1977), pp.161-2.
72. Above, pp.128-9, 144.
73. *St Andrews Liber*, p.209. The Christian name Constantine was popular with the Attleborough line, at least in the later thirteenth century. *Comp. Pge.*, ix, p.244, makes the unlikely suggestion that William

de Mortimer of Aberdour was identical with Robert de Mortimer's father William, lord of Attleborough to *c.*1180.

74. *VCH Somerset*, iii, p.51; cf. Barrow, *Era*, pp.104-5, 191-2. The appearance of William Dacus as a witness to two of Earl David's *acta* provides a further link between the earl and William son of Richard Revel *senior*. See also *Calendar of Documents preserved in France*, ed. J. H. Round (London, 1899), no.436; *CRR*, iii, pp.62, 129-30.

75. Hugh de Lisures can be connected with Berengar Engaine of Crailing (Roxburghshire), who was also associated with Sawtry (Hunts) and was therefore a cadet of the Engaines of Pytchley and Benefield, Hugh's ancestors: *RRS*, ii, no.62; *Mon. Angl.*, v, p.524; *Wardon Cart.*, pp.309ff. For Gilbert Dolepene (de Olepenno, etc.) cf. Barrow, *Era*, pp.103-4, 184, but suggesting Owlpen (Olepenne; *BF*, i, p.310), Gloucestershire, as an alternative derivation to Lopen, Somerset. On Robert Basset as a possible kinsman of the Scottish Ridels cf. Barrow, *Era*, p.171.

76. *PR 16 John*, p.74; *Rot. de Ob.*, p.542; *RLC*, i, p.217a. Geoffrey de Waterville stood pledge for Robert in 1206: *CRR*, iv, p.183.

77. Above, pp.25-6.

78. Uncle of Robert of Bassingham and brother of William of Bassingham, *marescallus comitis*.

79. On the Revels of Northamptonshire, whose Huntingdon interest at Puxley dates from Robert Revel, a tenant of King David I, see *VCH Northants*, i, p.374; Bodl. MS Top. Northants c.5, p.409; *CRR*, xiii, no.1335; *BF*, ii, pp.932, 944.

80. See my forthcoming edition of Senlis *acta* for the Northamptonshire Record Society.

81. Stenton, *First Century*, pp.95-6.

82. Basic details in *HKF*, ii, pp.320-1, 334, 351-3, 409.

83. *BHRS*, ix (1925), pp.181-2; N. Moore, *History of St Bartholomew's Hospital* (London, 1918), i, p.137; *The Cartae Antiquae Rolls 11-20*, ed. J. C. Davies (PRS, 1960), no.508;

CRR, v, p.205. Other former Senlis followers include William of Ashby, Robert and William of Bassingham, and Richard del Peak: BL MS Royal 11 B. ix, fo.9v; *Book of Seals*, no.349; *Genealogist*, new ser., xvi (1899-1900), pp.31-2; *Rufford Charters*, ed. C. J. Holdsworth (Thoroton Soc., 1972-81), ii, nos.721, 745; iii, no.825.

84. On liege homage as a solution to the dilemma of divided loyalties see F. Pollock and F. W. Maitland, *The History of English Law*, 2nd edn (Cambridge, 1968 reissue), i, pp.298ff.; Stenton, *First Century*, pp.30-2.

85. Simpson, 'Roger de Quincy', pp.129-53; cf. Miller, *Abbey and Bishopric of Ely*, pp.192-8; also J. R. L. Maddicott, *Thomas of Lancaster, 1307-1322: A Study in the Reign of Edward II* (Oxford, 1970), p.58.

86. *Lind. Cart.*, no.86; *Foedera*, I, i, p.144; No.6.

87. Landon, *Itinerary*, p.68; *Rotuli de Liberate*, etc., ed. Hardy, pp.190, 203, 228.

88. Duby, *Chivalrous Society*, ch.7.

89. Above, pp.87, 91.

90. No.69.

91. B. D. Lyon, *From Fief to Indenture: The Transition from Feudal to Non-Feudal Contract in Western Europe* (Cambridge, Mass., 1957), pp.32, 83, 187. Cf. P. S. Lewis, *BIHR*, xxxvii (1964), p.158: 'The money fee . . . was known to the English royal chancery, though not to that of any magnate.'

92. That Richard endowed Caldwell priory, Bedford, out of his Cambridge annuity suggests his identity with the Richard son of William who received a writ for reseisin in Bedfordshire in 1217: *Cambridge Borough Documents*, ed. W. M. Palmer (Cambridge, 1931), pp.xx-i, 12-14; *RLC*, i, p.374b.

93. *L'Histoire de Guillaume le Maréchal*, ed. P. Meyer (Paris, 1891-1901), i, p.168.

94. *Somerset Pleas . . . from the Rolls of the Itinerant Justices, close of 12th century-41 Henry III*, ed. C. E. H. Chadwyck-Healey (Somerset Rec. Soc., 1897), nos.23, 36-7; *A Cartu-*

lary of Buckland Priory, ed. F. W.
Weaver (Somerset Rec. Soc., 1909),
no.116; CRR, i, p.113; iii, p.62;
RLC, i, pp.49a, 51a, 296b. References to William son of Richard
Revel I of Langport, on whose tour-
neying in England see CRR, i, p.50.
For another William Revel, a proprietor at Folksworth (Hunts) by
1212 and in Hertfordshire: Cambridge University Library, MS 3020,
fos.77v-8r; CRR, vi, pp.234, 262,
377; VCH Herts, iii, p.426.

95. Royal . . . Letters Illustrative of the
Reign of Henry III, ed. W. W.
Shirley (RS, 1862-6), i, p.5. In 1219
Marshal influence brought Bartholomew the king's commission as a
bailiff of Stamford fair: Pat. Rolls
1216-25, p.189; Danelaw Docts.,
no.441.

96. The relevant acta are Nos.7, 16, 17,
26-7, 47, 53, 57, 81, 84.

97. Nos.81-4.

98. No.57; The West Fields of Cambridge, ed. C. P. Hall and J. R.
Ravensdale (Cambridge Antiquarian Records Soc., 1976), p.144;
HKF, ii, p.362.

99. Above, pp.76, 158-9 (Alan son of
Hugh, Basset, Burdet); Bodl. MS
Rawlinson B. 142, fo.20r; Northants
Assize Rolls, no.462 (Lisures); BL
MS Cott. Faust. A. iv, fos.64r,
69v, 109v; Wardon Cart., no.75
(Moyne). This last, Philip le Moyne
of Little Paxton (and Grafham,
Hunts: CRR, iv, p.233, with BL
Addit. Chart. 34036), is not to be
confused with his contemporary and
namesake Philip le Moyne of
Offord: see BL Addit. Chart.
33633.

100. I exclude Hugh Giffard, whose Scottish endowment apparently compensated him for the loss of his
Huntingdon fee in 1173-4: above,
p.83.

101. BL MS Sloane 986, fo.37r: charter
by Hugh de Beauchamp of Eaton
Socon (d. 1217) referring to his
landed knight Reginald de Ba, alias
de Bathonia.

102. Rotuli de Dominabus et Pueris et
Puellis, ed. J. H. Round (PRS,
1913), p.24.

103. RLP, pp.79b, 97b; PR 10 John,

p.176; HKF, iii, p.385.

104. E. Türk, Nugae Curialium: Le
Règne d'Henri II Plantegenêt et
l'Éthique Politique (Geneva, 1977),
p.40; but more informatively, J. E.
Lally, BIHR, xlix (1976),
pp.159-84.

105. Cf. below, pp.179ff.

106. Registrum S. Marie de Neubotle
(Bannatyne Club, 1849), nos.35-6,
pp.301-5; Melrose Liber, i, nos.88,
261-3; SRO RH 1/2/35; BL Loans
29/355, no.30. See further, on
Lisures, Dunfermline Reg., no.200;
St Andrews Liber, pp.44, 282; also
n.136 below.

107. RRS, ii, nos.302, 338, 375.

108. B. J. Levy, Cahiers de Civilisation
Médiévale, xviii (1975), p.196.

109. And perhaps his tenant, unless the
reference to Earl David as 'dominus
meus' in Charters of . . . Inchcolm,
ed. Easson and Macdonald, no.5, is
a mere courtesy.

110. Possibly, though by no means certainly, Roger de Mortimer of Fowlis
can be identified with Roger, the son
of Earl David's follower Constantine
de Mortimer: Arbroath Liber, i,
no.136.

111. Cf. St Andrews Liber, p.313. For the
Lincolnshire lands see Records of the
Templars in England in the Twelfth
Century, ed. B. A. Lees (London,
1935), p.113; Rot. de Ob., p.576;
PR 3 Henry III, p.125.

112. RRS, ii, nos.408, 473; No.17. The
earl may also have endowed Robert
at Earls Barton: see Northants Assize
Rolls, no.758 (though Barton is
there identified as Barton Seagrave),
with VCH Northants, iv, p.117; BL
Addit. Chart. 20293.

113. Arbroath Liber, i, no.189.

114. EYC, vii, pp.113-14; Scots Pge., vi,
p.528; and now Barrow, Era, pp.35
with n.23, 178-9. It is tempting to
link Peter son of William of Ashby
(Asseby) of Lilliesleaf (Roxburghshire) with the Castle Ashby line. In
1200 he relinquished Grangehall in
Pettinain (Lanarkshire) to the
canons of Dryburgh abbey, from
whom his father (Earl David's
follower?) had bought that land:
Dryburgh Liber, nos.221-3; also Miscellany of the SHS, iv (1926), p.310.

115. Following I. J. Sanders, *English Baronies: A Study of their Origin and Descent, 1086-1327* (Oxford, 1963 reprint), p.30; but cf. *HKF*, ii, p.344; *Scots Pge.*, iii, p.3.
116. *TDGAS*, 3rd ser., xxxiii (1954-5), pp.91-3; Holt, *Northerners*, pp.220-1, 233-4, 238-9. Robert had a hereditary claim to Westmorland through his mother Maud de Moreville, but on its weakness cf. ibid., p.226, amplified below, p.197 with n.80. Ivo de Vieuxpont of Alston in Tynedale, Robert's brother, was denounced with him by Roger of Wendover as one of King John's 'evil counsellors'.
117. *PR 10 Richard I*, pp.107, 165.
118. Sanders, *English Baronies*, pp.19, 45; *CRR*, v, pp.153, 229-30; vi, p.141; vii, p.65; ix, p.127; *RLC*, i, p.256a; *Henry of Pytchley*, p.34n.; *Calendar of Inquisitions Post Mortem*, i, no.443. See more fully the biographical note in *The 1235 Surrey Eyre*, ed. C. A. F. Meekings and D. Crook, i (Surrey Rec. Soc., 1979), pp.176-7, which lacks some of the information set out in text, however.
119. *HKF*, i, p.64; ii, p.409; *The Kalendar of Abbot Samson of Bury St Edmunds*, ed. R. H. C. Davis (Camden Soc., 1954), p.28; No.7; *EYC*, ix, pp.29, 34.
120. *RLC*, i, pp.328b, 332b; *HKF*, ii, pp.409-10.
121. In relation to Bassingham's marriage, note that in 1196 Hubert Walter – on whose connection with the Bassinghams see above, p.122 – had acquired the Wahull barony in full wardship: *HKF*, i, p.63.
122. N. B. Lewis in *Essays in Medieval History selected from the TRHS*, ed. R. W. Southern (London, 1968), p.200.
123. G. Duby, *The Early Growth of the European Economy* (London, 1974), p.270.
124. E.g., M. Altschul, *A Baronial Family in Medieval England: The Clares, 1217-1314* (Baltimore, 1965), p.236; R. H. Hilton, *A Medieval Society: The West Midlands at the End of the Thirteenth Century* (London, 1967 reprint), pp.24, 57-8.

125. *Harrold Recs.*, no.7: charter by Earl Simon de Senlis II (d. 1153).
126. E. Miller, 'The background of Magna Carta', *Past and Present*, xxiii (1962), p.78.
127. For private indentures of retainer prior to 1327 see M. Jones, *Journal of the Soc. of Archivists*, iv (1970-3), pp.384-94. Cf. also J. R. L. Maddicott, *Law and Lordship: Royal Justices as Retainers in Thirteenth- and Fourteenth-Century England*, Past and Present Supplement, no.4 (1978).
128. Respectively, J. M. W. Bean, 'Bachelor and retainer', *Medievalia et Humanistica*, new ser., iii (1972), pp.117-31; Lyon, *From Fief to Indenture*, pp.262-5.
129. Cf. C. Carpenter, 'The Beauchamp affinity: a study of bastard feudalism at work', *EHR*, xcv (1980), pp.514-32. It may be noted that apart from Richard del Peak – on whose offices and influence 'in provincia mea' see *HKF*, i, p.37; *Rufford Chrs.*, ed. Holdsworth, i, no.99 – those of Earl David's followers who acquired a record of important public service in England did so after his death: *HKF*, ii, p.334 (David of Ashby); *Trans. of the Leicestershire Archaeol. Soc.*, xi (1913-20), pp.455-6; *HKF*, ii, p.320 (William de Folville).
130. Above, pp.49-50, 104, 114.
131. The evidence of Earl David's original charters is the most significant with regard to the numbers in attendance upon him at different times. The majority have between seven and fifteen recorded witnesses, including household servants and others not defined as 'followers'. Four originals have less than seven witnesses, two have nineteen, and three have twenty or more. But scribes rarely provided a comprehensive list of persons present, as phrases such as *et multis aliis* make plain, the number of named witnesses being determined, in the first instance, by the size of the sheet of parchment selected for use.
132. Barrow, *Era*, pp.192-3.
133. Above, p.83; *Reg. Mag. Sig.*, ii, no.610.

134. Cf. above, pp.25-6.

135. *The Scottish Tradition*, ed. G. W. S. Barrow (Edinburgh, 1974), pp.29-30. But if David's follower was John *senior*, rather than John *junior*, of Wilton, then he was not certainly lord of Tarvit in Ceres.

136. Although Lisures does not appear with David in Scotland, it should be noted that he was a witness to a charter for Kelso abbey of William de Vieuxpont II, concerning shielings on Lammermuir pertaining to Horndean in Berwickshire: *Kelso Liber*, ii, no.319.

137. The evidence of David's *acta* apart, see *Lind. Cart.*, no.107, p.284.

138. It cannot be gainsaid that 'record of early baronial courts in Scotland is pitifully meagre' (Barrow, *Era*, p.136). Note, however, *CDS*, i, no.704; *Charters, Bulls and other Documents relating to the Abbey of Inchaffray*, ed. W. A. Lindsay *et al.* (SHS, 1908), no.43; *Registrum Monasterii S. Marie de Cambuskenneth* (Grampian Club, 1872), no.73.

139. R. C. van Caenegem, *The Birth of the English Common Law* (Cambridge, 1973), p.80.

140. *Rufford Chrs.*, ii, no.745.

141. No.23; *PBKJ*, i, no.3085; *RCR*, ii, p.55.

142. Cf. Stenton, *First Century*, pp.42-57, 176-7.

143. E.g., *PR 10 Richard I*, p.107; *Lind. Cart.*, nos.81, 85-6, 107, p.284; BL MS Cott. Vesp. E. xvii, fo.49v; Bodl. MS Rawlinson B. 103, fo.95v; PRO DL 25/42. See also BL Cott. Chart. xxiv 15.

144. David of Ashby, Basset, Bassingham, Camoys, Carneille, Mortimer, Olifard, Richard son of William, Wascelin: *RLC*, i, pp.256a, 286b, 318a, 328b, 374-5; *RLP*, p.161a; *Rot. de Ob.*, pp.576, 589; *Foedera*, I, i, p.144.

145. See now C. Rawcliffe, 'Baronial councils in the later Middle Ages', in *Patronage, Pedigree and Power in Later Medieval England*, ed. C. D. Ross (Gloucester, 1979), pp.87-108. For conciliar administration in Scotland: *Scottish Society in the Fifteenth Century*, ed. Brown, pp.61, 221-8.

146. A. W. B. Simpson, *An Introduction to the History of the Land Law* (Oxford, 1961), p.51.

CHAPTER NINE
Anglo-Scottish Proprietorship:
A Wider View

1. G. W. S. Barrow, *PSAS*, lxxxvii (1952-3), p.51.

2. To describe these magnates as 'Anglo-Scottish' is convenient but, of course, anachronistic. On the Anglo-Norman baronage see notably J. Le Patourel, *Norman Barons* (Historical Association, 1971 reprint); idem, *Norman Empire*, esp. pp.190-201. On the Anglo-Welsh and Anglo-Irish dimensions, R. R. Davies, *Lordship and Society in the March of Wales, 1282-1400* (Oxford, 1978); R. Frame, *English Lordship in Ireland, 1318-1361* (Oxford, 1982).

3. Thus, most recently, Barrow, *Era*, pp.12-19. This important reservation aside, Professor Barrow's Ford Lectures form an indispensable starting-point.

4. M. F. Moore, *The Lands of the Scottish Kings in England* (London, 1915), includes commentaries on Tynedale and Penrith (held from 1242).

5. E.g., *Chartulary of the Cistercian Priory of Coldstream* (Grampian Club, 1879), no.46.

6. Anglo-Scottish magnates are here defined as earls or greater lay barons, proprietors of course in both countries, but not necessarily of equal weight in each. Any dividing-line set between these men and the lesser cross-Border nobility is by nature arbitrary. The need to give the dominant élite in Scotland a wider definition in terms of personal wealth and landed influence than its counterpart in England has also to be stressed: cf. Barrow, *Kingdom*, p.295. Wherever possible, details of property and of family relationships are drawn, without further reference, from *Comp. Pge.*; *Scots Pge.*; Sanders, *English Baronies*.

7. J. H. Round, *Studies in Peerage and Family History* (London, 1901), p.128; Barrow, *Era*, p.19.

313

8. The following references are essential: *Dryburgh Liber*, no.150 (Bertram); *Kelso Liber*, i, nos.207-10, 294 (Courtenay, Vesci); *St Andrews Liber*, p.283 (Merlay); *Melrose Liber*, i, nos.168, 232-3, 256 (Muscamp, Vere, Vesci); *EYC*, xii, no.53 (Fife).

9. Barrow, *Era*, pp.12-19.

10. Earl David's daughter Maud, wife of John of Monmouth II, died childless earlier than Earl John. For her marriage, hitherto unknown to the family historians, see PRO DL 42/2, fos.196v-7r.

11. Barraclough, 'Earldom and county palatine of Chester', pp.33-4. The marriage agreement is printed from a late copy in G. Ormerod, *History of the County Palatine and City of Chester*, 2nd edn (London, 1882), i, p.43. The original survives as BL Cott. Chart. xxiv 17.

12. E.g., *Close Rolls 1227-31*, pp.273, 289; ibid. *1231-4*, pp.8, 219; ibid. *1234-7*, p.208; *Calendar of Pat. Rolls, 1232-47*, p.81.

13. *Pat. Rolls 1225-32*, p.360; *Close Rolls 1227-31*, p.252; *Diplomatic Documents preserved in the PRO*, i, ed. P. Chaplais (London, 1964), nos.218-19; *Annales Monastici*, ed. H. R. Luard (RS, 1864-9), i, p.88; Matthew Paris, *Chronica Majora*, ed. idem (RS, 1872-83), iii, pp.247-8.

14. R. H. Morris, *Chester in the Plantagenet and Tudor Reigns* (Chester, 1894), p.15.

15. *CChR*, i, p.156; *CRR*, xv, no.1363; BL MS Harl. 4748, fos.24v, 25v.

16. B. M. C. Husain, *Cheshire under the Norman Earls, 1066-1237* (Chester, 1973), p.80.

17. *Chron. Melrose*, p.79; *RRS*, vi, nos.244, 246; *Reg. Mag. Sig.*, ii, no.1791 (c); iii, no.2308; *Lind. Cart.*, nos.16, 19.

18. Ibid., nos.15-21.

19. Duncan, *Scotland*, p.187.

20. K. J. Stringer, 'A new wife for Alan of Galloway', *TDGAS*, 3rd ser., xlix (1972), pp.49-55.

21. R. Greeves, 'The Galloway lands in Ulster', *TDGAS*, 3rd ser., xxxvi (1957-8), pp.115-21, describes Alan's Irish acquisitions and those of Earl Thomas of Atholl, who like Alan was also an Anglo-Scottish landowner. See on Dryburgh and Ulster A. Gwynn and R. N. Hadcock, *Medieval Religious Houses: Ireland* (London, 1970), pp.203-4.

22. Burton, in the Mowbray honour, had descended from Richard de Moreville to Roland of Galloway: *Coucher Book of Furness Abbey*, II, ii, ed. J. Brownbill (Chetham Soc., new ser., 1916), pp.301-2, 334-7; *EYC*, ix, no.43. For the earlier Galloway interest at Torpenhow see *Register of the Priory of St Bees*, ed. J. Wilson (Surtees Soc., 1915), p.ix, n.1; *PR 9 Henry II*, p.10. This had passed in unrecorded circumstances to Philip de Valognes, Chamberlain of Scotland, by 1178: *PR 24 Henry II*, p.126; *BF*, i, p.198; *EYC*, ix, p.16, no.54.

23. Above, p.114.

24. Stringer, 'A new wife', pp.50-4.

25. C. T. Clay, *EHR*, lxv (1950), pp.89-91; *EYC*, ix, pp.20-1; *CChR*, i, p.156.

26. I hope to give fuller details of this episode elsewhere. The main evidence is: (1) charter by Alan concerning Newbiggin, Kirkby Thore and Hillbeck, 1215 × 17, printed by F. W. Ragg – who missed its true significance – in *TCWAAS*, new ser., xvii (1917), pp.228-9; (2) letter of the regency government ordering Alan to relinquish his conquests, 23 Sept. 1217 (*Pat. Rolls 1216-25*, p.94).

27. *RLC*, i, pp.415a, 420.

28. *HKF*, ii, passim; R. Stewart-Brown, 'The end of the Norman earldom of Chester', *EHR*, xxxv (1920), pp.26-54.

29. *Excerpta e Rotulis Finium in Turri Londinensi asservatis, 1216-72*, ed. C. Roberts (Rec. Comm., 1835-6), i, p.137; *VCH Beds*, iii, p.229; *Wardon Cart.*, no.239. See also L. J. Redstone, 'The Liberty of St Edmund', *Proc. of the Suffolk Institute of Archaeology and Natural History*, xv (1915), pp.207-9; J. H. Round, *The King's Serjeants and Officers of State* (London, 1911), pp.223-4.

30. *RLC*, i, p.36b; cf. also *CRR*, vi,

p.361.

31. BL MS Sloane 986, fo.46r; G. F. Black, *The Surnames of Scotland* (New York, 1979 reprint), p.347.

32. Henry de Hastings' brother-in-law was Stephen of Seagrave, Earl John's intimate associate and beneficiary. Their respective marriages cannot be closely dated. But Hastings may in fact have owed his union with Ada more to Seagrave than to his family's connection with Earl David.

33. *EYC*, ii, pp.11, 16-19. For an account of the Annandale line see also G. W. S. Barrow, *Robert Bruce*, 2nd edn (Edinburgh, 1976), pp.28-38.

34. *Cartularium Prioratus de Gyseburne*, etc., ed. W. Brown (Surtees Soc., 1889-94), ii, no.1156.

35. William of Newburgh, *Historia Rerum Anglicarum*, ed. R. Howlett in *Chron. Stephen*, i, p.70.

36. C. Sharp, *History of Hartlepool* (Hartlepool, 1851), pp.22ff.; *VCH Durham*, iii, pp.270-1; F. W. Ragg, 'The earlier owners of Edenhall', *TCWAAS*, new ser., xiii (1913), pp.199ff.

37. *Gesta Henrici*, i, pp.48, 51, n.4.

38. Mr G. Stell has in hand an account of the Balliols for the forthcoming *Essays on the Nobility of Medieval Scotland*, ed. Stringer. The most useful of the works on the family that I have hitherto been able to consult is probably G. A. Moriarty, 'The Baliols in Picardy, England and Scotland', *New England Historical and Genealogical Register*, cvi (1952), pp.273-90.

39. *Recueil des Actes des Comtes de Pontieu (1026-1279)*, ed. C. Brunel (Paris, 1930), nos.38, 153; *Mon. Angl.*, vi, p.819. See also *Le Cartulaire de l'Abbaye de Selincourt*, ed. M. G. Beaurain (Soc. des Antiquaires de Picardie, 1925), no.113.

40. R. L. Hine, *The History of Hitchin* (London, 1927-9), i, pp.29-33; *VCH Herts*, iii, pp.8, 10; *Wardon Cart.*, nos.316-17; BL MS Cott. Vesp. E. xvii, fo.236v.

41. E.g., *Northumberland Hist.*, vi, p.22; Ritchie, *Normans*, p.231; Holt, *Northerners*, p.208.

42. Full details available in Moriarty, 'Baliols', pp.285-90; R. C. Reid, *TDGAS*, 3rd ser., xxi (1936-8), pp.17ff.

43. *Wigtownshire Charters*, ed. idem (SHS, 1960), pp.xxxix-xl; *CDS*, i, nos.1686, 1697.

44. *Rôles Gascons*, i, ed. F. Michel (Paris, 1885), nos.2111, 2154, 2248; *Calendar of Pat. Rolls, 1258-66*, pp.107, 121.

45. *Liber Sancte Marie de Balmorinach* (Abbotsford Club, 1841), no.32: possibly, but not certainly, an act of Henry de Hastings II. His English possessions are partly described in PRO C 132/37/12, the Scottish in *Lind. Cart.*, no.118; *Reg. Mag. Sig.*, i, pp.510b, 553b; SRO GD 103/2/11, pp.194-5.

46. J. Nichols, *History and Antiquities of the County of Leicester* (London, 1795-1815), II, i, pp.322-3; *CChR*, iv, p.476; *Wardon Cart.*, no.349; *BHRS*, i (1913), p.106; BL MS Royal 11 B. ix, fo.63v; Bodl. MS Rawlinson B. 142, fo.22v. For aspects of Brus lordship in Essex see K. C. Newton, *The Manor of Writtle* (London and Chichester, 1970), pp.41-2, 53-4; *Book of Seals*, no.336; BL Addit. Chart. 28479; Chelmsford, Essex Record Office, D/D Ba Q1/1, 11, D/D Ba T2/9.

47. *Chronicon de Lanercost* (Maitland Club, 1839), p.134. See further W. Huyshe, *Dervorgilla, Lady of Galloway* (Edinburgh, 1913).

48. *Chron. Lanercost*, p.159.

49. Barrow, *Bruce*, pp.34-5; G. O. Sayles, *SHR*, xxv (1928), p.388.

50. *Chron. Lanercost*, pp.159-60.

51. Chamberlains: Philip de Valognes, Walter de Berkeley, William de Valognes, Henry de Balliol, Earl William of Mar, David of Lindsey (Barnweill), John of Lindsey, Alexander de Balliol. Justiciars of Lothian: Richard Comyn, Robert de Quincy (not when in office), Walter Olifard I, William of Lindsey, Earl Patrick of Dunbar, David of Lindsey (Crawford), Walter Olifard II, David of Lindsey (Barnweill), Walter de Moravia, Hugh de Berkeley, William de Sules, Geoffrey de Mowbray.

Justiciars of *Scotia*: Earl Duncan of Fife, Earl William of Buchan, Alan Durward (not when in office), Earl Alexander of Buchan, Andrew de Moravia. Lists of chamberlains and justiciars set out in *Handbook of British Chronology*, ed. F. M. Powicke and E. B. Fryde, 2nd edn (London, 1961), pp.177-8; Barrow, *Kingdom*, pp.137-8.

52. Sanders, *English Baronies*. Thus, barony of Miles of Gloucester (Bohun, Hastings), Alnwick (Vesci), Appleby (Galloway), Beanley (Dunbar), Bennington (Balliol of Cavers, Maule, Comyn of Kilbride), Bourn (St Andrews), Bulwick (Courtenay), Burstwick (Forz), Bywell (Balliol), Castle Cary (Lovel), Cavendish (Lindsey of Crawford, Pinkney), Chester, Chilham (Atholl, Balliol of Cavers), Eaton Bray (Hastings), Eton (Windsor, Lascelles), Fotheringhay, Headington (Siward), Hedingham (Vere), Helmsley (Ros), Hunsingore (Ros), Kendal (Lindsey of Lamberton, Guines), Kington (Bohun), Kirklinton (see below, p.200), Leicester (Quincy, Comyn, Ferrers, Zouche), Long Crendon (Marshal, Vesci, Quincy), Mitford (Bertram), Morpeth (Merlay), Papcastle (Forz), Pevensey (Marshal), Pleshey (Bohun), Prudhoe (Umfraville), Skelton (Ros), Skipton (Forz), Stansted Mountfitchet (Forz, Corbet), Styford (Corbet), Trowbridge (Bohun), Wark (Ros), Warter (Ros), Weedon (Pinkney), Whitchurch (Vere), Wooler (Muscamp, Strathearn, Mar, Graham), Writtle (Brus).

53. An early example concerning the earl of Fife and the barony of Morpeth in *PR 34 Henry II*, p.100.

54. The interesting case of the English Fitz Alans and the Scottish Stewarts is noted in F. M. Powicke, *The Thirteenth Century, 1216-1307*, 2nd edn (Oxford, 1962), p.580, n.1.

55. *CDS*, ii, no.1108; iii, no.492; *Henry of Pytchley*, ed. Mellows, pp.76-7, 93.

56. T. M'Michael, 'The feudal family of de Soulis', *TDGAS*, 3rd ser., xxvi (1947-8), p.168.

57. Quotation from *Scots Pge.*, i, p.168; similarly, Barrow, *Bruce*, p.386; Duncan, *Scotland*, p.585. For Earl Gilbert II's lordship in Scotland see, e.g., W. Fraser, *The Douglas Book* (Edinburgh, 1885), iii, nos.4, 6, 286. He married Elizabeth, daughter of Alexander Comyn, earl of Buchan.

58. *Northumberland Hist.*, vi, p.46 with n.3; *The Oxford Deeds of Balliol College*, ed. H. E. Salter (Oxford Historical Soc., 1913), pp.324ff.; *Hist. MSS Comm.*, *Reports*, iv, part one, pp.442-4. Balliol's money-lending provides a striking contrast to the record of family indebtedness in the late twelfth century: see most of all G. V. Scammell, *Hugh du Puiset, Bishop of Durham* (Cambridge, 1956), pp.208-9.

59. G. Stell, *TDGAS*, 3rd ser., lv (1980), p.185; *CDS*, ii, no.670. See further *Journal of the British Archaeol. Association*, cxxxiii (1980), esp. p.84, for the extensive improvements to John de Balliol's principal English seat at Barnard Castle evidently made possible by his new-found wealth.

60. Simpson, 'Roger de Quincy', pp.76-81, 214-16.

61. *CDS*, i, nos.2463, 2541; *Three Early Assize Rolls for . . . Northumberland, saec. XIII*, ed. W. Page (Surtees Soc., 1891), p.75; *EYC*, x, p.66; Young, 'The political role of the Comyns', pp.297-8, 304-8.

62. PRO C 133/73/3 (= *CDS*, ii, no.824). For the partition of Earl Roger's English lands in 1277, the Zouche share of which was then set at £146, see *Hist. MSS Comm., Hastings*, i, pp.323-31.

63. I deal with this more fully in *Nobility of Medieval Scotland*, ed. Stringer, ch.3.

64. Robert of London, Robert de Brus v, John Comyn of Badenoch and Alan Durward were among the pensioners of John or Henry III; Brus, Comyn and Durward also received land from the English crown: see, most conveniently, *CDS*, i, nos.746, 1984-5, 2099, 2105, 2285, 2431, 2462, 2489-91.

65. See chiefly *RLC*, i, p.131b (Alan of

Galloway), but note also G. W. S. Barrow, 'Wales and Scotland in the Middle Ages', *Welsh History Review*, x (1980-1), p.309.

66. Examples of the former, all dating after the abrogation of English suzerainty in 1189 but before 1291, in Barrow, *Kingdom*, p.114; *Rot. Chart.*, pp.118, 180b; *CRR*, v, pp.40-1; *Pat. Rolls 1225-32*, p.382; *Close Rolls 1227-31*, p.508; *CDS*, i, no.2302; ii, no.133; *TCWAAS*, new ser., xi (1911), p.321 with n.; xvii (1917), p.233. See also n.88 below. On the latter, note the interesting case *Comyn v. Zouche* (1277) in *CDS*, ii, nos.91-2, although proceedings in the Scottish courts were halted when Edward I complained of the damage to his dignity and crown.

67. Cf. above, p.44; D. E. R. Watt, 'The minority of Alexander III of Scotland', *TRHS*, 5th ser., xxi (1971), pp.1-23. Scottish awareness of the value of such connections is made plain in the terms of the settlement for the marriage of Alexander II's youngest sister (*CDS*, i, no.1113), to be interpreted in conjunction with Matthew Paris, *Chron. Majora*, iii, pp.372-3. For Scots royal military intervention serving the rise of cross-Border landholding: Duncan, *Scotland*, pp.530-2 (partition of Galloway, 1234-5).

68. Ibid., pp.587, 589-91.

69. For the latter's respect of this principle see *Foedera*, I, i, p.231.

70. J. C. Holt, 'Politics and property in early medieval England', *Past and Present*, lvii (1972), pp.3-52, quotations at pp.22, 44.

71. For light on the procedure adopted, and the conflicts sometimes arising, see, e.g., *Excerpta e Rot. Fin.*, ed. Roberts, i, p.81; *CDS*, ii, no.23; Barrow, *Era*, p.143. These and the ensuing comments on the exercise of royal marriage rights necessarily draw heavily on the English evidence.

72. J. C. Holt, *The Making of Magna Carta* (Charlottesville, 1965), p.14.

73. For fines see, e.g., *Cartularium Abbathiae de Rievalle*, etc., ed. J. C.

Atkinson (Surtees Soc., 1889), no.306; *CDS*, i, no.1983; ii, no.602. On Douglas, and for the eventual transfer of seisin: Fraser, *Douglas*, i, pp.75-9; *CDS*, ii, nos.468, 736. Other instances of unauthorised marriages in *CDS*, i, no.1909 (Quincy-Ferrers); *Genealogist*, new ser., xxii (1906), p.110 (Balliol-Chilham).

74. F. M. Powicke, *King Henry III and the Lord Edward* (Oxford, 1966 reprint), pp.157-8; *Annales Monastici*, ed. Luard, iii, p.143. The marriage portion included Haddington, East Lothian: Barrow, *Era*, p.134. See further J. C. Holt, *Magna Carta* (Cambridge, 1965), pp.45-7, 113-15, 210-11, for the general limiting of English royal control over marriage, adding now S. S. Walker, 'Free consent and the marriage of feudal wards in medieval England', *Journal of Medieval History*, viii (1982), pp.123-34.

75. For Scotland, albeit sparse in informed commentary, see Barrow, *Era*, ch.5; Duncan, *Scotland*, pp.369-75 with p.652 (bibliographical note). C. F. Kolbert and N. A. M. Mackay, *History of Scots and English Land Law* (Cambridge, 1977), has little value for the medieval period.

76. Barrow, *Era*, p.19.

77. K. J. Stringer, *History of the Berwickshire Naturalists' Club*, xl, part one (1974), p.37; Barrow, *Era*, p.73.

78. It has usually been assumed that the younger Hugh de Moreville's estates escheated for his support of the Scots in 1173-4 (most recently, ibid., p.75); but see *Chron. Howden*, ii, p.17; *PR 19 Henry II*, pp.1, 2. More generally, Holt, *Northerners*, pp.199-201.

79. *PR 16 Henry II*, p.53; *Coucher Book of Furness*, II, ii, ed. Brownbill, pp.301-2, 334-5. Cf. *EYC*, ix, no.43.

80. In 1203, King John's grant of Westmorland in inheritance to Robert de Vieuxpont, younger son of Maud de Moreville, excluded the direct Lauderdale line in preference for a collateral male descended from a non-inheriting female. But for the

persistent claims against Robert and his progeny, involving among others Alan of Galloway, Dervorguilla de Balliol and Alexander Comyn, earl of Buchan, see chiefly above, p.184; PRO JUST 1/983, m.13 (= *CDS*, ii, no.169).

81. On the Lovels see L. C. Loyd, *Notes and Queries for Somerset and Devon*, xviii (1924-6), pp.173-6; C. A. R. Radford and R. C. Reid, *TDGAS*, 3rd ser., xxxvii (1958-9), pp.26-35; Barrow, *Era*, pp.184-5.

82. J. Bain, 'Some notes on William de Courtenay', *Genealogist*, new ser., iii (1886), pp.193-7.

83. On a junior Graham branch ensconced in Eskdale and Tynedale see idem, *Archaeol. Journal*, xliii (1886), pp.121-2; *Scots Pge.*, vi, p.197.

84. The impartibility of Scottish earldoms, however, was normally secure.

85. K. B. McFarlane, *The Nobility of Later Medieval England* (Oxford, 1973), p.59. The depth of feeling on this issue is well illustrated by the case of John Russell, an obscure English knight. He married Isabel, *suo jure* countess of Menteith, with the Scots king's permission, but was forced to surrender the earldom in 1260 due to aristocratic antagonism towards a low-born adventurer.

86. Ibid., p.72.

87. In an extreme case, Robert de Ros (d. 1226), lord of Wark on Tweed and Helmsley, settled Wark and his Scottish barony, based on Sanquhar in Nithsdale, upon his younger son. This was clearly the creation of a large mesne fee rather than a partition: *CChR*, i, p.56; *Cart. Abbathiae de Rievalle*, p.360. An early instance of a younger son endowed in both realms in *Scots Pge.*, iii, p.248; *Northumberland Hist.*, vii, p.94.

88. E.g., *Kelso Liber*, i, no.129; *RLC*, i, pp.309a, 327a; *Excerpta e Rot. Fin.*, i, p.6; *CRR*, viii, pp.152, 240-1 (Ada de Courtenay); *CDS*, ii, no.1108 (Joanna, countess of Fife); *SHR*, xxv, pp.386-9; *CDS*, ii, no.826 (Christiana de Brus: dower alone). In 1249 a Lovel widow,

dowered chiefly in Somerset but jealous of her Scottish interest, recovered the advowson of Cavers in Roxburghshire from her brother-in-law in the English royal courts: *Pedes Finium, commonly called Feet of Fines, for . . . Somerset, 1196-1307*, ed. E. Green (Somerset Rec. Soc., 1892), pp.371-2; cf. *Somerset Pleas*, ed. Chadwyck-Healey, nos. 1371, 1417.

89. Notably Maud, *suo jure* countess of Angus (Umfraville, Chilham), and Isabel of Chilham (Atholl, Balliol). Dervorguilla de Balliol, a long-lived dowager and heiress, was exceptional in that she did not remarry.

90. T. F. T. Plucknett, *Legislation of Edward I* (Oxford, 1949), p.131; cf. Stringer, 'A new wife', pp.53-4, and (for Scotland) Kolbert and Mackay, *Hist. of . . . Land Law*, pp.172-3.

91. First reference must be made to Barrow, *Era*, esp. pp.172-98: a basic source from which to piece together some of the non-magnate cross-Border tenures.

92. Simpson, 'Roger de Quincy', p.220.

93. Barrow, *Era*, pp.79-83; idem, *Scottish Genealogist*, xxv, no.4 (1978), pp.101-3; above, pp.145-3.

94. Barrow, *Kingdom*, pp.33-4 (Corbet); *Northumberland Hist.*, xv, pp.422-3; *Melrose Liber*, i, nos.234, 301; *CDS*, ii, p.199 (Burradon); Barrow, *Era*, p.178; *Melrose Liber*, i, no.205 (Derman).

95. *RRS*, i, p.13, n.2; *Wigtownshire Chrs.*, ed. Reid, pp.xxff.; F. W. Ragg, 'De Culwen', *TCWAAS*, new ser., xiv (1914), pp.343-432; G. S. H. L. Washington, *Early Westmorland M.P.s, 1258-1327* (CWAAS, tract ser., 1959), pp.24-6.

96. The colonisation of 'Scots by nation' at Bennington, Hertfordshire (Balliol of Cavers), was reported in 1296: *CDS*, ii, no.736, cited in Barrow, *Bruce*, p.97.

97. *EYC*, ix, no.54. But Philip enjoyed rights or claims to other English lands: *CRR*, v, pp.156-8, 171, 179, 317.

98. W. Fraser, *The Annandale Family Book* (Edinburgh, 1894), i, no.2; SRO GD 103/2/11, pp.299-300; *PR 13 John*, p.156. Adam's family

was rich in cross-Border interests: T. H. B. Graham, 'The sons of Truite', *TCWAAS*, new ser., xxiv (1924), pp.43-9; *Wigtownshire Chrs.*, p.xx with n.3.

99. *Selected Letters of Pope Innocent III*, ed. C. R. Cheney and W. H. Semple (London, 1953), no.11; G. W. S. Barrow, *TDGAS*, 3rd ser., xxxiii (1954-5), pp.84-90. For collateral succession see, e.g., idem, *Era*, pp.10, 101-2, 104-5, 110 (Clere, London, Revel, Stawell). For purchase see, e.g., Raine, *North Durham*, no.365; G. Tate, *History of the Borough, Castle, and Barony of Alnwick* (Alnwick, 1866-9), ii, Appendix, pp.xiv-xv.

100. Early instances in *RRS*, i, p.111; ii, nos.143, 320; J. H. Round, 'The Cumins of Snitterfield', *The Ancestor*, ix (1904), pp.146-9.

101. *EYC*, xi, p.216 (Chamberlain); C. T. Clay, *Early Yorkshire Families* (Yorks Archaeol. Soc., rec. ser., 1973), p.40 (Ryedale); *TCWAAS*, new ser., lx (1960), pp.46-51 (Ketel son of Dolfin). Of these cases, however, it now appears possible that the Chamberlain fee may not in fact have been divided on the line of the Border: A. C. Chibnall, *Beyond Sherington* (London and Chichester, 1979), p.156 with n.27.

102. *CDS*, ii, no.736; *Documents Illustrative of the History of Scotland, 1286-1306*, ed. J. Stevenson (Edinburgh, 1870), ii, pp.41-9 (English sheriffs' returns of 1296 identifying Balliol supporters and their confiscated holdings).

103. D. Hay, 'England, Scotland and Europe: the problem of the frontier', *TRHS*, 5th ser., xxv (1975), pp.77-91.

104. Lascelles: Barrow, *Era*, pp.115-16, but also *TCWAAS*, new ser., xxi (1921), pp.51ff.; *VCH Bucks*, iii, pp.172, 266. Montfiquet: *VCH Northants*, iii, p.228. Mowbray: Barrow, *Era*, pp.24-6, 185-6; *CDS*, ii, no.736. Ridel: J. Bain, *Genealogist*, new ser., vi (1890), pp.1-3; *HKF*, ii, p.316. Siward: *CDS*, ii, nos.723, 736, 930, 963, 1005; *VCH Worcs*, iii, p.331. Wishart: *CDS*, ii, nos.736, 832. Richard Siward

(d. 1248), a follower of Earl Gilbert Marshal and the founder of the Anglo-Scottish line, was a lord whose substance pushed him for a time into the magnate class: *Foedera*, I, i, p.231; N. Denholm-Young, *Richard of Cornwall* (Oxford, 1947), pp.28-9; Altschul, *The Clares*, pp.65, 68, 70-3; Sanders, *English Baronies*, p.52.

105. To Dr R. C. Reid's notes in *TDGAS*, 3rd ser., xxxiii (1954-5), pp.94-5, 97-100, must be added F. M. Powicke, *The Loss of Normandy, 1189-1204*, 2nd edn (Manchester, 1961), p.357; *Dryburgh Liber*, no.186; *CRR*, viii, pp.104-5. The commentary in Barrow, *Era*, p.76, ignores the possessions that Ivo and William held across the Border line.

106. *TDGAS*, 3rd ser., xxxiii, pp.95-7; *The Pipe Rolls of Cumberland and Westmorland, 1222-60*, ed. F. H. M. Parker (CWAAS, extra ser., 1905), pp.80-1, 85-6; *TCWAAS*, new ser., xii (1912), pp.347-8; *CDS*, i, no.1808. These references are to Ivo's son Robert, whose brother Nicholas, lord of Alston, was also a Scottish landowner, at Swanston in Midlothian: *Registrum Domus de Soltre* (Bannatyne Club, 1861), no.33.

107. J. Greenstreet, *Notes and Queries*, 6th ser., v (1882), p.143. See also J. H. Round, 'Comyn and Valoignes', *The Ancestor*, xi (1904), pp.129-35; *CRR*, xv, no.1432.

108. *The English Church and the Papacy in the Middle Ages*, ed. C. H. Lawrence (London, 1965), p.86.

109. H. M. Colvin, *The White Canons in England* (Oxford, 1951), p.198.

110. Cf. G. W. S. Barrow, 'A Scottish collection at Canterbury', *SHR*, xxxi (1952), pp.26-8.

111. G. G. Coulton, *Scottish Abbeys and Social Life* (Cambridge, 1933), p.36.

112. D. E. R. Watt, *A Biographical Dictionary of Scottish Graduates to A.D. 1410* (Oxford, 1977), pp.306-8. This splendid book is a mine of information on the making of such careers.

113. D. J. A. Matthew, *The Norman Monasteries and their English Possessions* (Oxford, 1962).

114. *Northumberland Hist.*, xi, pp.117, 159, 182-3, 189-90, 281-2; xii, p.97; xv, p.239; *Chartulary of . . . Coldstream*, nos.27-8, 53-5; *VCH Cumberland*, ii, pp.14-15; *EYC*, ix, p.196; *TCWAAS*, new ser., xxviii (1928), pp.42-5; *Ancient Petitions relating to Northumberland*, ed. C. M. Fraser (Surtees Soc., 1966), no.25; *Kelso Liber*, i, no.54; ii, nos.325-31.

115. *Chartulary of Brinkburn Priory*, ed. W. Page (Surtees Soc., 1893), nos.155-8; *Northumberland Hist.*, xv, pp.459-60; Raine, *North Durham*, no.712.

116. *VCH Cumberland*, ii, p.15; *Register of . . . St Bees*, ed. Wilson, pp.viii-xi.

117. I. B. Cowan, 'The early ecclesiastical history of Edinburgh', *Innes Review*, xxiii (1972), pp.18-19; *Melrose Liber*, ii, p.673; *The Register and Records of Holm Cultram*, ed. F. Grainger and W. G. Collingwood (CWAAS, rec. ser., 1929), nos.256, 256a; *RRS*, ii, p.22, n.19a.

118. Above, pp.145-8.

119. *CChR*, iii, pp.90-2.

120. Respectively, Bodl. MS Fairfax 7, fo.83r; *RRS*, i, no.156; G. Neilson and G. Donaldson, 'Guisborough and the Annandale churches', *TDGAS*, 3rd ser., xxxii (1953-4), pp.142-54. For further evidence of the Annandale lords' devotion to Guisborough cf. F. Wormald, *Yorkshire Archaeol. Journal*, xxxi (1934), pp.14-17, 19-20.

121. Below, p.205; *Registrum Monasterii de Passelet* (Maitland Club, 1832), pp.19, 401-2; *RRS*, ii, no.105; W. Fraser, *The Scotts of Buccleuch* (Edinburgh, 1878), ii, no.372; *Melrose Liber*, i, nos.192-4; *Holyrood Liber*, no.78; *Wardon Cart.*, no.311.

122. Barrow, *Era*, p.10; idem, *The Stewarts*, ix, no.3 (1953), pp.230-3.

123. Respectively, *Dunfermline Reg.*, no.164; *Reg. Domus de Soltre*, no.6; *CDS*, iii, no.976; Barrow, *Era*, p.10.

124. Simpson, 'Roger de Quincy', pp.91-4. Note, too, that elsewhere Anglo-Scottish links were not necessarily as tenuous as may perhaps seem at first sight. Earl David's con-temporary Robert de Vere, earl of Oxford, who was not a significant proprietor in Scotland, could easily be classed as one who never visited his Scottish lands were it not for the survival of Robert's charter (1214 × 21) recording his gift to Melrose abbey of four acres at Old Roxburgh, as perambulated by him in person and as granted at the abbey 'in the presence of the convent and many of my men' (*Melrose Liber*, i, no.256).

125. *Coucher Book of Furness*, II, ii, ed. Brownbill, p.307.

126. *Cart. . . . de Gyseburne*, ed. Brown, ii, nos.1180-1, 1184-5, 1187-8.

127. *Reg. . . . of Holm Cultram*, ed. Grainger and Collingwood, no.95g and pp.47ff.; R. C. Reid, *TDGAS*, 3rd ser., xiv (1926-8), pp.201-15; *Melrose Liber*, ii, pp.671-3.

128. Barrow, *Kingdom*, pp.168-9; R. B. Dobson, *Durham Priory, 1400-1450* (Cambridge, 1973), p.317.

129. Above, pp.128-30, 144-8.

130. Respectively, *Registrum de Panmure*, ed. J. Stuart (Edinburgh, 1874), ii, p.147; *Chartulary of . . . Coldstream*, no.55; *RLC*, i, p.126a.

131. A common Comyn (Buchan) procedure: see chiefly *CDS*, ii, nos.216, 369, 421.

132. *Holyrood Liber*, no.54; *Melrose Liber*, ii, p.675; *Reg. . . . of Holm Cultram*, no.40d; Fraser, *Annandale*, i, no.5.

133. For a lease evidently inspired by the preparations for war in 1295 see *CDS*, ii, no.1596.

134. *Charters, Bulls and other Documents relating to the Abbey of Inchaffray*, ed. W. A. Lindsay et al. (SHS, 1908), pp.155-7.

135. G. W. S. Barrow, 'The Gilbertine house at Dalmilling', *Collections of the Ayrshire Archaeol. and Natural History Soc.*, 2nd ser., iv (1958), pp.50-67.

136. J. Edwards, 'The order of Sempringham and its connexion with the west of Scotland', *Trans. of the Glasgow Archaeol. Soc.*, new ser., v, part one (1905), p.82.

137. A good instance concerning the Muscamp fee in the Merse in *Melrose Liber*, i, nos.232-7, 330-1; *Acts*

Parl. Scot., i, pp.408-9; *Close Rolls 1227-31*, p.508. However, although the earls of Dunbar held little or no land in Northumberland *in proprio dominio*, they were nevertheless notably active in defence of their residual rights and claims: *BF*, ii, p.1122; *Northumberland Hist.*, vii, pp.30-86.

138. Above, pp.129, 145; *Lind. Cart.*, nos.87-8, 113; Raine, *North Durham*, no.642; M. Walcott, 'A breviate of the cartulary of . . . Lanercost', *Trans. of the Royal Soc. of Literature*, 2nd ser., viii (1866), pp.441, 499.

139. Respectively, above, pp.147-8; Barrow, *Kingdom*, p.338; *Melrose Liber*, i, no.195. For Vaudey's short-lived grange at Carsphairn see *CDS*, i, no.795.

140. Lay records are largely silent on this point, though not on the exchange of lands within one kingdom: e.g., *Genealogist*, old ser., vi (1882), p.4; *Book of Seals*, no.418; BL Addit. Chart. 75848. Cf., however, Duncan, *Scotland*, p.587; also the sales in Barrow, *Era*, p.105; Raine, *North Durham*, no.366.

141. Above, pp.191-2; below, p.209. Notable examples of estates carefully maintained in England by lay lords much more extensively endowed in Scotland include those of Comyn of Badenoch, Lindsey of Lamberton, Moreville and Sules, whose success in ultimately adding new English lands would not have been lost on magnates with possessions across the Border that remained small, or the gentry living in their shadow. No doubt there was also some element of sentimental attachment to the original patrimony, however humble: cf. Le Patourel, *Norman Empire*, p.331 with n.2.

142. E.g., *CDS*, i, no.2656.

143. An interesting case in *RLC*, ii, pp.161b, 172b; PRO SC 1/6/7, involving Bishop Ralph of Chichester, chancellor of Henry III, as the custodian of the entire Lascelles estate in England and Scotland. I am indebted to Professor E. L. G. Stones for the last reference.

144. *Cart. . . . de Gyseburne*, ii, no.1188, p.357.

145. Edwards, 'Order of Sempringham', pp.84-8.

146. *TDGAS*, 3rd ser., xiv (1926-8), pp.212-13; I. B. Cowan, *The Parishes of Medieval Scotland* (Scottish Rec. Soc., 1967), pp.47, 120.

147. Respectively, *CDS*, iii, no.1561; *Northumberland Hist.*, xi, p.190; R. B. Dobson, 'The last English monks on Scottish soil', *SHR*, xlvi (1967), pp.1-25.

148. Respectively, *Northumberland Hist.*, vii, pp.85-6; *VCH Northants*, ii, p.540; *Comp. Pge.*, viii, p.206.

149. Simpson, *Mar Earldom*, p.12, n.27.

150. Le Patourel, *Norman Barons*, p.27.

151. Idem, *Norman Empire*, pp.190-201.

152. Restated in Barrow, *Era*, pp.147-56.

153. The subject has a large literature: a recent review in K. F. Werner, 'Les nations et le sentiment national dans l'Europe médiévale', *Revue Historique*, ccxliv (1970), pp.285-304. For Scottish historians, two works just published have, in their different ways, particular interest: M. T. Clanchy, *England and its Rulers, 1066-1272: Foreign Lordship and National Identity* (London, 1983); A. Kalckhoff, *Nacio Scottorum: schottischer Regionalismus im Spätmittelalter* (Frankfurt, 1983).

154. Revealing examples in Young, 'The political role of the Comyns', pp.310, 312. Similarly, *Documents . . . of Scotland*, ed. Stevenson, i, pp.26-7, 49-50, 52-3, 115-16. In the last resort, possessions in another realm also provided a refuge from political misfortune: see above, p.53; Holt, *Northerners*, p.209.

155. Duncan, *Scotland*, p.587.

156. Respectively, Robert de Muscamp and John de Vesci: see *Archaeologia Aeliana*, 4th ser., xiv (1937), pp.256-7 (giving quotation in text, from Matthew Paris); *Chron. Stephen*, ii, p.570; *Melrose Liber*, i, nos. 345-7; ii, pp.683-5; *Rotuli Scotiae in Turri Londinensi . . . asservati*, ed. D. Macpherson *et al.* (Rec. Comm., 1814-19), i, pp.45-6.

157. Ailred of Rievaulx, *Relatio de Standardo*, ed. R. Howlett in *Chron.*

Stephen, iii, pp. 192-5; *Chron. Fantosme*, lines 385-406.

158. Note the prominent part of Anglo-Scottish magnates in reinforcing the treaties of York (1237) and Newcastle (1244): *Anglo-Scottish Relations, 1174-1328: Some Selected Documents*, ed. E. L. G. Stones (Oxford, 1970 reprint), no. 7; Matthew Paris, *Chron. Majora*, iv, p. 383; *Foedera*, I, i, p. 257.

APPENDIX
Notes to Introduction

1. *RRS*, ii, nos. 106, 192, 204. For *acta* not issued in the earl's name, but to which his seal was attached, see, e.g., *Dryburgh Liber*, no. 63 (agreement between the abbeys of Dryburgh and Jedburgh over Lessudden, *alias* St Boswells, and Longnewton, in Ancrum, Roxburghshire, 1177); *Arbroath Liber*, i, no. 3 (quitclaim by Abbot John of Kelso, 1179); *RRS*, ii, no. 236 (agreement between Melrose abbey and Richard de Moreville over the forest between the Gala and Leader Waters, 1180); *Melrose Liber*, i, no. 97 (quitclaim by Alan son of Walter, 1189 × 93).

2. Above, pp. 93-4.

3. *Essays on the Nobility of Medieval Scotland*, ed. Stringer, ch. 4.

4. E.g., *EYC*, viii, pp. 46-7; J. F. A. Mason, 'Roger de Montgomery and his sons (1067-1102)', *TRHS*, 5th ser., xiii (1963), p. 4; *RRS*, i, p. 110. See also J.-F. Lemarignier, *Le Gouvernement Royal aux premiers temps Capétiens, 987-1108* (Paris, 1965), p. 130.

5. *RRS*, ii, no. 190.

6. *Melrose Liber*, i, nos. 39, 40.

7. Cf. *RRS*, ii, no. 264 and comment; also Watt, *Scottish Graduates*, pp. 428-9, s.v. 'Neuport, Roger de'. *Melrose Liber*, i, no. 40, concerns the distribution of pittances to mark four anniversaries, including that of Avenel's death.

8. Cf. *Past and Present*, lvii (1972), p. 29. The witness-clause of *Melrose Liber*, i, no. 39, includes the name of William de Audri, a tenant of the Huntingdon honour (above, pp. 24, 83).

9. *Memorials of the Abbey of St Mary of Fountains*, ed. J. R. Walbran *et al.* (Surtees Soc., 1863-1918), ii, I, p. 10 (for the alteration in date followed here see Landon, *Itinerary*, p. 6); *Cartulaire Général de l'Ordre des Hospitaliers de S. Jean de Jérusalem*, ed. J. M. A. Delaville Le Roulx (Paris, 1894-1906), i, no. 877 (= BL Harl. Chart. 43.C.28).

10. E. M. Poynton, 'Charters relating to the priory of Sempringham', *Genealogist*, new ser., xvi (1899-1900), p. 228.

11. *Arbroath Liber*, i, no. 85; *Melrose Liber*, i, no. 97; *St Andrews Liber*, p. 319.

12. It may be observed that Count John of Mortain did not abandon, upon the death of Henry II, the seal describing him as 'son of the king of England', and continued to use it until as late as Oct. 1197: M. Jones, 'A Collection of the *Acta* of John, lord of Ireland and count of Mortain' (unpublished Manchester University M.A. thesis, 1949), i, p. 35. Cf. also *Earldom of Gloucester Charters: The Charters and Scribes of the Earls and Countesses of Gloucester to A.D. 1217*, ed. R. B. Patterson (Oxford, 1973), pp. 24-5.

13. C. R. Cheney, *English Bishops' Chanceries, 1100-1250* (Manchester, 1950), pp. 51-4; *RRS*, ii, pp. 84-91.

14. No. 51, which was more than likely produced in Lindores abbey, is a fine example of pure book hand.

15. Above, p. 151.

16. Descriptions, not noted for their accuracy, are given in H. Laing, *Descriptive Catalogue of . . . Ancient Scottish Seals* (Bannatyne and Maitland Clubs, 1850), pp. 78, 225; W. de G. Birch, *Catalogue of Seals in the . . . British Museum* (London, 1887-1900), iv, pp. 252-3; J. H. Stevenson and M. Wood, *Scottish Heraldic Seals* (Glasgow, 1940), i, p. 40. None distinguishes more than two different seals.

17. Unfortunately, the *acta* other than Earl David's own to which his seal was appended offer no further examples.

18. C. H. Hunter Blair, 'A note upon mediaeval seals with special reference to those in Durham treasury',

Archaeologia Aeliana, 3rd ser., xvii (1920), p.261.

19. For other examples of this type of seal-tag see A. Henshall, 'Five tablet-woven seal-tags', *Archaeol. Journal*, cxxi (1965), pp.154-62.

20. P. Chaplais, *English Royal Documents: King John-Henry VI, 1199-1461* (Oxford, 1971), p.12; *RRS*, ii, p.93; Cheney, *Bishops' Chanceries*, p.49.

21. Chaplais, *Royal Documents*, p.15.

22. *RRS*, ii, p.92; similarly, Hunter Blair, 'Mediaeval seals', pp.257-8.

23. The exact date of Earl David's acquisition of the earldom of Huntingdon in 1185 remains uncertain due to the conflicting chronicle accounts of the date of the council of Clerkenwell, in which King William was restored in the earldom and then immediately endowed David: R. W. Eyton, *Court, Household and Itinerary of King Henry II* (London, 1878), pp.261-2. *Chron. Melrose*, p.45, which says that William did not regain the earldom until Henry II had moved to Windsor, i.e. by 31 March, must be in error.

INDEX

Place-names are indexed under modern forms as far as possible. Cross-references from medieval forms are given only for place-names found in these forms in the printed texts of the Appendix and not identified in the adjacent editorial apparatus. Places in England and Scotland of less than parochial status are located by parish (in square brackets) and by pre-1975 county; places of parochial status, save for county towns and other well-known centres, by pre-1975 county. Counties are noted for baronies or honours only when the barony or honour indexed lay largely or exclusively in that county.

The letters [AS] following a name mean that the person, family or religious house concerned is shown to have been engaged in Anglo-Scottish proprietorship. Wherever possible, individuals are indicated rather than families; females are excluded.